LEADERSHIP TRAINING IN ADAPTED PHYSICAL EDUCATION

LEADERSHIP TRAINING IN ADAPTED PHYSICAL EDUCATION

Editor

Claudine Sherrill, EdD
Texas Woman's University

Human Kinetics Books
Champaign, Illinois

Library of Congress Cataloging-in-Publication Data

Leadership training in adapted physical education.

  Bibliography: p.
  Includes index.
  1. Physical education for handicapped children.
2. Physical education teachers—Training of.
I. Sherrill, Claudine.
GV445.L42 1988   371.9'044   86-27696
ISBN 0-87322-101-X

Senior Editor: Gwen Steigelman, PhD
Production Director: Ernie Noa
Projects Manager: Lezli Harris
Copy Editor: Ann Bruehler
Assistant Editors: Julie Anderson and Phaedra Hise
Proofreader: Judy Weidman
Text Design: Keith Blomberg
Typesetter: Brad Colson
Text Layout: Gordon Cohen and Ronit Klemens
Cover Design: Jack Davis
Printed By: Versa Press and R & R Bindery Service, Inc.

ISBN: 0-87322-101-X

Printed in the United States of America

10 9 8 7 6 5 4 3 2 1

Human Kinetics Books
A Division of Human Kinetics Publishers, Inc.
Box 5076, Champaign, IL 61820

1-800-DIAL-HKP
1-800-334-3665 (in Illinois)

This book is dedicated to the growing community of scholars in adapted physical education. We invite you to join us, as teacher-scholars, seeking to extend the knowledge base of physical education so that we can better serve all persons, regardless of ability level, health, and fitness.

Contents

Contributors   xi

Preface   xiii

PART I: Foundations of Adapted Physical Education Teacher Training

Chapter 1   *Adapted Physical Education as a Specialization*—Claudine Sherrill   1

Chapter 2   *Personnel Preparation in Adapted Physical Education: Early History*—Claudine Sherrill   23

Chapter 3   *Contemporary Adapted Physical Education Teacher Training: A History Beginning With 1967*—Claudine Sherrill   43

Chapter 4   *Evolution of a Profession: History and Contributions of Organizations*—Claudine Sherrill   63

Chapter 5   *Legislation, Funding, and Adapted Physical Education Teacher Training*—Claudine Sherrill and William Hillman   85

Chapter 6   *Grant Writing to Fund Adapted Physical Education Teacher Training*—Claudine Sherrill   105

Chapter 7   *Adapted Physical Educator Research Responsibilities*—Geoffrey D. Broadhead   117

Chapter 8   *Evaluation and Curriculum Processes in Adapted Physical Education: Understanding and Creating Theory*—Claudine Sherrill and Thomas Oakley   123

Chapter 9   *Professional Preparation and Public School Service Delivery*—Claudine Sherrill, Janet Wessel, and Julian U. Stein   139

PART II: Service Delivery in the Public Schools: Functions of the Adapted Physical Education Specialist

Chapter 10   *Competencies Needed to Function in the Interdisciplinary Arena*—Janet A. Seaman and Lynne Heilbuth   161

Chapter 11   *Assessment: A Foundation*—Janet A. Seaman   169

Chapter 12   *Individualized Educational Programming*—Claudine Sherrill   177

Chapter 13   *Program Models in Adapted Physical Education: Implications For Teacher Training*—Walter F. Ersing   191

Chapter 14   *A Service Delivery Model in Adapted Physical Education: An Ecological Approach*—Michael Churton and James R. Tompkins   199

Chapter 15   *Perceptual-Motor Programming*   207
              in the School: Application—Jean
              L. Pyfer

Chapter 16   *Advocacy: Perspectives on Theory*   217
              and Practice—Wanda Rainbolt
              and Claudine Sherrill

Chapter 17   *Opinion and Attitude Assessment:*   227
              The First Step in Changing Public
              School Service Delivery—Jo E.
              Cowden and Nancy Megginson

Chapter 18   *Counseling in Adapted Physical*   257
              Education—Glenda Adams and
              Trudy Younger

Chapter 19   *Instructional Accountability in*   265
              Adapted Physical Education: A
              Review of Research—Claudine
              Sherrill

PART III: Adapted Physical Education Teacher
Training Approaches, Programs, and
Pedagogies

Chapter 20   *Vintage Years: Competency,*   289
              Certification, and Licensure in
              Adapted Physical Education—
              Karen P. DePauw and Ernest
              Bundschuh

Chapter 21   *Teaching the Introductory Adapted*   301
              Physical Education Course—Paul
              Jansma

Chapter 22   *Practicum Experiences for*   311
              Reinforcing Theory and Changing
              Attitudes—Glenn M. Roswal

Chapter 23   *Motor Behavior and Learning: A*   329
              Multidisciplinary Practicum for
              Undergraduate Students—Robert
              Strauss

Chapter 24   *Leadership Training in Adapted*   333
              Physical Education—Claudine
              Sherrill

Chapter 25   *Teacher Training To Enhance*   349
              Motor Learning by Mentally
              Retarded Individuals—Gail M.
              Dummer

Chapter 26   *Personnel Preparation in Physical*   361
              Education and Litigation—David
              Auxter and Charles Jelley

Chapter 27   *CAFIAS: A Systematic Observa-*   373
              tion Tool to Improve Teaching
              Behaviors—Sarah M. Rich,
              Deborah A. Wuest, and Victor
              H. Mancini

Chapter 28   *Of Bits, Bytes, and Boxes: Using*   379
              Simulations and Games in
              Professional Preparation of
              Adapted Physical Educators—Sue
              Gavron

Chapter 29   *The Computer in Adapted Physical*
              Education Professional Preparation   385
              —Tom Montelione and Ronald
              Davis

Chapter 30   *Personnel Preparation for Adapted*   395
              Physical Education Administrative
              Roles—Kenneth W. Duke

Chapter 31   *In-Service Teacher Education: A*   401
              Review of General Practices and
              Suggested Guidelines for Adapted
              Physical Education Teacher
              Trainers—Garth Tymeson

Chapter 32   *Personnel Training for Leader-*   411
              ship in Sport for Athletes With
              Handicapping Conditions—Julian
              U. Stein

Chapter 33   *Teacher Training in Adapted*   423
              Physical Education for Severely
              and Profoundly Handicapped
              Students—Paul Jansma

Chapter 34   *The Use of Efficiency Systems in*   439
              Adapted Physical Education
              Professional Preparation at the
              College Level—Ronald French
              and Paul Jansma

Appendix A   *National Awards and Recipients*   443

Appendix B   *Adapted Physical Education*—   451
              Functions and Competencies

Appendix C   *Glossary of Contemporary*   457
              Adapted Physical Education
              Leaders in the United States

Appendix D   *Outline for Writing a Résumé*   465

Appendix E   *Adapted Physical Education Books*   467
              (published since 1975)

Appendix F   *AAHPERD Publications in*   471
              Adapted Physical Education
              (1968-1981)

Appendix G   *Voluntary and Professional*   475
              Organizations

Appendix H   *Federal Legislation Impacting*   479
              on Education, Training, and
              Research in Adapted Physical
              Education

Appendix I   *Example of a Written Committee*   483
              Report

Appendix J   *Sample of Letter to Congress-*   489
             person

Appendix K   *The Golden Rule and Eleven*   493
             Cardinal Principles of Grant
             Application Writing—John
             Nesbitt

Author Index   499
Subject Index   507

Contributors

Glenda Adams, PhD
School Counselor
Jefferson County Public Schools
Green Mountain High School
13175 W. Green Mountain Drive
Lakewood, CO 80228

David Auxter, PhD
Physical Education Department
Slippery Rock State College
Slippery Rock, PA 16057

Geoffrey D. Broadhead, PhD
School of Physical Education, Recreation,
  and Dance
Kent State University
Kent, OH 44242-0001

Ernest Bundschuh, PhD
Georgia Retardation Center
850 College Station Road
University of Georgia
Athens, GA 30602

Michael Churton, PhD
Department of Language, Reading, and Exceptionalities
Appalachian State University
Boone, NC 28606

Jo E. Cowden, PhD
Department of Health and Physical Education
University of New Orleans
New Orleans, LA 70148

Ronald Davis, PhD
Physical Education Department
Ball State University
Muncie, IN 47306

Karen P. DePauw, PhD
Women's Physical Education Department
Washington State University
Pullman, WA 99164

Kenneth W. Duke, PhD
Adapted Physical Education
Dallas I.S.D.
3700 Ross Avenue
Dallas, TX 75204

Gail M. Dummer, PhD
Physical Education Department
132 IM Sports Circle Building
Michigan State University
East Lansing, MI 48824

Walter F. Ersing, PhD
Physical Education Department
The Ohio State University
Columbus, OH 43210

Ronald French, PhD
Physical Education Department
Texas Woman's University
Denton, TX 76204

Sue Gavron, DPE
Physical Education and Recreation Department
Bowling Green State University
Bowling Green, OH 43403

Lynne Heilbuth, PhD
Physical Education Department
San Diego State University
San Diego, CA 92182

William Hillman, MA
Vice President
Ability, Inc. Publishers
700 7th St. SW
T.S.T., Suite 134
Washington, DC 20024

Paul Jansma, PhD
Physical Education Department
The Ohio State University
Columbus, OH 43210

Charles Jelley, MA
Research Institute for Independent Living
Slippery Rock State College
Slippery Rock, PA 16057

Victor H. Mancini, PhD
School of Health, Physical Education, and Recreation
Ithaca College
Ithaca, NY 14850

Nancy Megginson, PhD
Consultant
10646 W. Evan's Creek Rd.
Rogue River, OR 97537

Thomas Montelione, PhD
Health and Physical Education Department
Queens College, City University of New York
Flushing, NY 11367-0904

John Nesbitt, PhD
Recreation Department
University of Iowa
Iowa City, IA 52242

Thomas Oakley, PhD
Adapted Physical Education
Dallas I.S.D.
3700 Ross Avenue
Dallas, TX 75204

Jean L. Pyfer, DPE
Physical Education Department
Texas Woman's University
Denton, TX 76204

Wanda Rainbolt, MA
Department of Health, Physical Education, & Recreation
Northern Michigan University
Marquette, MI 49855

Sarah M. Rich, PhD
School of Health, Physical Education, and Recreation
Ithaca College
Ithaca, NY 14850

Glenn M. Roswal, PhD
Department of Health, Physical Education, and Recreation
Jacksonville State University
Jacksonville, AL 36265

Janet A. Seaman, DPE
Department of Physical Education and Athletics
California State University
Los Angeles, CA 90032

Claudine Sherrill, EdD
Physical Education Department
Texas Woman's University
Denton, TX 76204

Julian U. Stein, PhD
Physical Education Department
George Mason University
Fairfax, VA 22030

Robert Strauss, PhD
Motor Behavior & Learning Laboratory
Trinity University
San Antonio, TX 78284

James R. Tompkins, PhD
Department of Language, Reading, & Exceptionalities
Appalachian State University
Boone, NC 28606

Garth Tymeson, PhD
Physical Education Department
Northern Illinois University
DeKalb, IL 60115

Janet Wessel, PhD
1040 Village Circle Drive S.
Phoenix, AZ 85022

Deborah A. Wuest, PhD
School of Health, Physical Education, & Recreation
Ithaca College
Ithaca, NY 14850

Trudy Younger, MA
School Counselor
Jefferson County Public Schools
Manning Junior High
13200 W. 32nd Ave.
Golden, CO 80401

Preface

*A*dapted physical education has undergone many changes during the last quarter of a century. It has been influenced by legislation and research, the advocacy of professional organizations, and the leadership of bold, innovative thinkers throughout the world. Its future is strong, and its history is increasingly rich.

This book is designed for persons who are or will be shaping the future of adapted physical education: administrators and university-based teacher trainers, graduate students preparing to become teacher trainers, researchers, and others wishing information on trends, issues, history, and current practices. The content will be especially helpful to professionals advocating employment of adapted physical education specialists in each of the nation's 16,000 school districts as well as in nonschool settings that provide fitness, sport, dance, and aquatics for America's 35 million disabled citizens. Research documenting the values of adapted physical education is presented, and grant writing skills to help fund services are highlighted.

Adapted physical education has many faces, numerous names, and seemingly conflicting definitions. It has been called corrective, remedial, rehabilitative, therapeutic, developmental, and special. It has been conceptualized as

- a segregated program of activities conducted for students who cannot safely or successfully engage in mainstream physical education;

- a comprehensive service delivery system designed in compliance with the Public Law 94-142 mandate of physical education as a *direct* service for all handicapped children; services within the psychomotor domain

include assessment, individualized educational programming, diagnostic and/or prescriptive teaching; counseling; and coordination of related resources and services; and

- an attitude, a way of teaching in both mainstream and segregated environments, and a set of beliefs and practices demonstrated by teachers who routinely adapt learning experiences to meet developmental and other needs of their students.

Adapted physical education is all of these things and more. It is the implementation of the dream of quality physical education for all children and youths. It is not only for disabled individuals who are eligible for special services under Public Law 94-142, but also for the clumsy, overweight, and asthmatic students—students with psychomotor and/or health problems that cause them to perform below average in physical education activities and tests.

The idea for this book was conceived in an experimental summer school workshop at the Texas Woman's University (coeducational at the graduate level), currently the largest adapted physical education training program in the country. Designated as a doctoral/postdoctoral seminar, the workshop facilitated collaborative thinking of established leaders in physical education (Lane Goodwin, Jean Pyfer, Janet Seaman, Claudine Sherrill, Julian Stein, and Joseph Winnick) and emerging young leaders. Karen DePauw served as the student coordinator of the seminar and provided much of the initial impetus for analyzing the new directions of adapted physical education and formulating teacher training guidelines. As others throughout the country heard about the project, they, too, wanted to be involved. This book evolved as a reflection of what can happen when professionals of varying ages and backgrounds share the joy of learning and becoming. Our commitment, as a group, to excellence in adapted physical education teacher training is expressed in the following credo:

> The graduate school is more than an area inhabited by graduate faculty. It is an expression of faith, a manifestation of knowledge, an accumulation of understanding, and a dedication to serve by persons of intellectual accomplishment and of scholarly ability. . . . If a graduate education is for excellence, the graduate teachers must lead the students in an expression of human excellence in human appearance, in human manner, and in human accomplishment. (Leona Holbrook)

Thirty-five leaders in adapted physical education, representing all parts of the country, varied philosophies, and widely different professional preparation programs, have joined together to produce this textbook. Most of the contributors are grant writers, textbook authors, and past officers of national and state organizations that help to shape adapted physical education policies and directions. All believe that adapted physical education is a viable academic specialization with an increasingly strong knowledge base. Many of the contributors are actively seeking recognition of adapted physical education as a separate discipline and/or profession. This book represents a first attempt by leaders in the field to create a body of knowledge cooperatively in order to stimulate the scholarly inquiry necessary to sustain a discipline.

The book is organized into three major parts: Part I, Foundations of Adapted Physical Education Teacher Training: History, Trends, and Issues; Part II, Service Delivery in the Public Schools: Functions of the Adapted Physical Education Specialist; and Part III, Teacher Training Approaches, Programs, and Pedagogies. Each part is comprised of eight or more chapters that have sufficient substance to serve as the basis for professional conferences and workshops, in-service training, and graduate level seminars. Each part is directed toward broad knowledge areas in which professionals must stay abreast and graduate students must gain competency.

The content has been field tested with graduate students at the Texas Woman's University. Information presented is appropriate for use in the orientation and/or socialization of students into adapted physical education as a profession. The book can also be used as a text for administration or grant writing courses or units. In general, the text is a comprehensive treatment of the content that university professors want their students to know about adapted physical education and that is not covered in current textbooks.

Part I

Foundations of Adapted Physical Education Teacher Training

Chapter 1
Adapted Physical Education as a Specialization

Claudine Sherrill

*L*eadership comes from the Anglo-Saxon word *laedan*, meaning to go, and is defined by Webster as guiding, conducting, preceding, or being foremost among. Essential elements in becoming a leader are commitment to one or more causes, ideas, or dreams, a willingness to dedicate one's self to their achievement, and sufficient physical and mental health to persevere. Leaders live, teach, research, speak, and write in ways that draw others to the same commitment. Leaders are action oriented and typically exemplify the best in service, research, teaching, and administration. They "guide, conduct, precede, or are foremost among" because followers respect them and seek their help. Leadership should not be confused with administration. Administrators are appointed, usually salaried, and may or may not be leaders. In contrast, individuals lead because potential followers elect or choose them. Leaders may serve in a nonsalaried capacity (e.g., as an officer or committee member of a professional organization) or in a salaried position such as teaching, research, or administration. Generally, the more outstanding individuals are, the more persons will seek them out, thereby investing them with leadership.

Some professionals are natural leaders. Others who aspire to leadership must be helped to acquire the essential qualities through personnel preparation programs. In the early 1980s, the Office of Special Education Programs (OSEP) of the U.S. Department of Education (the government agency that funds adapted physical education personnel preparation) designated the term *leadership training* as specifically denoting doctoral study or work beyond the master's degree. Implicit in this act was the belief that universities and other agencies responsible for advanced or continuing education should place greater emphasis on the development of leaders. Little is known, however, about pedagogy in relation to leadership development (Heller, 1974; Kroll, 1978; McIntyre, 1981; Snyder & Scott, 1954). This book is an attempt to initiate scholarly inquiry concerning leadership training in adapted physical education. Dialogue with readers is invited, and hopefully together we can, as the years pass, strengthen professional preparation in adapted physical education and produce increasing numbers of individuals who "guide, conduct, precede, and are foremost among."

Leadership Qualities

How is leadership determined? Examination of the criteria for awards established by the American Alliance for Health, Physical Education, Recreation and Dance (AAHPERD) lends insight into characteristics valued by our profession. The Luther Halsey Gulick Medal, the highest award that the Alliance bestows, requires that the recipient shall

- be clearly outstanding in his or her profession;

- exemplify the best in service, research, teaching, and administration;

- be recognized by the membership of the Alliance as a noteworthy leader;

- be the type of person whose life and contributions could inspire youth to live vigorously, courageously, and freely as citizens in a free society;

- currently be a member of the Alliance and shall have held such membership for at least 10 years; and

- have been formally recognized by his or her peers by some form of national award for outstanding professional contributions, for example, a National Honor Award.

Individuals who meet such criteria are likely to be respected, admired, and modeled by others. Their lives are worthy of study. Criteria for several other awards and names of selected recipients appear in Appendix A. Of these, the Mabel Lee Award is designed especially for professionals less than 36 years of age. Three adapted physical educators have received this recognition: Sue Grosse, Karen DePauw, and Dean Gorman. Awards are also given at the district, state, and local level by many organizations. Criteria are worthy of study because they indicate the broad areas in which professional colleagues evaluate one another. Such criteria can also be used for self-evaluation and goal setting.

Leaders are typically outstanding in one of three areas: service, research, and teaching. These areas are the same ones used by university administrators in evaluating faculty and making decisions about merit raises, tenure, and promotion. Illustrated in Figure 1.1 are criteria for judging faculty performance as either commendable, excellent, or outstanding.

Graduate students need to be acquainted early in their careers with the criteria by which their performance will be judged. Hopefully they will aspire to exemplify the best in service, research, and teaching and will set professional preparation goals accordingly. A good way to begin is to write out a résumé, using service, research, and teaching as center headings. This procedure facilitates self-evaluation in regard to the quantity and quality of entries under each heading. An outline for writing a résumé appears in Appendix D. Professors should develop a pool of faculty and alumnae résumés that beginning graduate students can study, thus reinforcing their understanding of leadership qualities and the role of balanced contributions in service, research, and teaching to professional success.

Criteria for Evaluating Faculty Performance

COMMENDABLE PERFORMANCE	EXCELLENT PERFORMANCE	OUTSTANDING PERFORMANCE
Teaching: Characterized by punctual and professional discharge of responsibilities; competence and currency in subject matter for teaching; consistent updating of courses taught to reflect current trends in the field; faculty development related to instruction.	Teaching: Characterized by enthusiastic and effective discharge of responsibilities; leadership in developing subject matter areas for teaching; participation in the development of clinical practice.	Teaching: Characterized by exemplary discharge of responsibilities; clear and documented record of innovation in teaching or exceptional effectiveness in teaching; frequent and significant contributions to clinical practice.
Research and Creative Activity: Submission of research grant proposal or manuscript for publication; service as a panelist or moderator for a professional meeting; local presentation of exhibitions; concerts, recitals, or programs; faculty development related to research.	Research and Creative Activity: Contributions to research in the field by publication of findings in professional journals or by presentations of regional or national conferences; creative, artistic activity before state or regional audiences; attainment of institutional grant or application for external grant.	Research and Creative Activity: Significant contributions to knowledge in the field as demonstrated through authorship of major articles, chapters of books, or books; artistic participation in invitational, juried exhibitions, concerts, or shows for regional or national audiences; attainment of an externally-funded grant; significant contributions to theory development.
Service: Active membership on departmental and university committees; willingness and competence in student advising; membership in professional organizations; attendance at campus events; participation in community service.	Service: Service on graduate students' committees; service as chairman of a departmental, college, school, or university committee; effective student advising; leadership in professional organization; sponsorship of a student organization; attendance and participation in campus events; leadership in community service.	Service: Service as chairman or research director on several graduate students' committees; outstanding student advising; service as chairman of a college or university committee; executive officer of a major professional organization or learned society; officer in a community service organization; sponsorship of a student organization; participation in and support of campus events.

Figure 1.1 Criteria for judging faculty performance—commendable, excellent, or outstanding.

Support of Professional Organizations

Leaders support professional organizations through membership, service, research, and conference presentations. Adapted physical educators typically affiliate with several organizations: the Adapted Physical Activity Council within AAHPERD's Association for Research, Administration, Professional Councils and Societies (ARAPCS), the National Consortium on Physical Education and Recreation for the Handicapped (NCPERH), the Council for Exceptional Children (CEC), and various sport organizations for individuals with disabilities. These organizations are described in chapter 4.

Organizations help shape the nature of the professions they serve. For example, the adapted physical education competencies that universities seek to develop in their students were written by AAHPERD leaders and published in 1973 and 1981 respectively (see Appendix B). Chapter 20 by Karen DePauw and Ernie Bundschuh

describes in detail how these competencies were developed. The physical education passages in Public Law (PL) 94-142, the Education for All Handicapped Children Act, which mandates that all handicapped children shall receive physical education, can be traced directly to NCPERH. Likewise, the grant monies generated by federal legislation to support teacher training in adapted physical education can be attributed, in large part, to the work of NCPERH leaders. Physical educators who are members of the CEC (the professional organization to which most special educators belong) have contributed to the growing understanding and cooperation between physical education and special education and thus to improved interdisciplinary service delivery to handicapped children and youth. CEC members have also applied special education research to physical education settings, thereby enriching our knowledge base. Affiliation with sport organizations for individuals with disabilities has led to greater understanding of the needs, interests, and capabilities of the students we serve and to innovative adaptation of sport rules, strategy, and equipment. This understanding, in turn, has changed the pedagogy of adapted physical education in the school setting.

Leaders not only attend professional conferences; they plan the meetings, make presentations, serve on committees, and devote whatever time and effort are needed to promote optimum functioning of the organization. Volunteers are always welcome, and students should be encouraged to introduce themselves to officers and chairs of meetings and to offer their services. Through working together, ideas are shared and collegiality is promoted. Leaders are concerned not with the benefits of membership, but with how they can serve their profession through organizational activities.

Philosophy of Adapted Physical Education

Leaders are continuously inquiring into the nature of their beliefs and practices and the meaning of their profession and discipline. Leaders are guided by a personal and professional philosophy and can trace the evolution of their beliefs.

The word *philosophy*, which literally means love of wisdom or love of truth, is variously defined in most dictionaries as

- the body of principles underlying a given branch of learning or discipline;

- the science that investigates the facts and principles of reality and of human nature and conduct; and

- the science that comprises logic, ethics, aesthetics, metaphysics, epistemology (the theory of knowledge), and politics.

Examples of philosophical inquiry are often found in *Quest*, the biannual journal of the National Association for Physical Education in Higher Education (Henry, 1978; Lawson & Morford, 1979; Rose, 1986; Sage, 1984; Zeigler, 1979). Few examples exist in adapted physical education literature. Sherrill (1985) analyzed integration practices in relation to pragmatism, idealism, and realism in an effort to find reasons other than compliance with federal law for combining handicapped and nonhandicapped children in physical education. She developed this article as an exercise in personal values clarification, hoping that other professionals would share the process of their own search for meaning by writing similar articles.

Development of a philosophy of adapted physical education and of teacher training begins with identification of basic questions. Often these questions are issues on which leaders take a definite stand, and they devote much time and energy to developing followers. Some of the basic questions, with possible answers, that each leader must resolve as he or she shapes a personal philosophy of adapted physical education follow.

1. *What is adapted physical education?*

   - A service delivery system that includes assessment, placement, prescriptive and developmental teaching, and fitness and leisure counseling

   - A program of medically prescribed therapeutic exercise, education, and adapted physical activities

   - A diversified program of developmental activities, games, sports, and rhythms suited to the interests, capabilities, and limitations of students with disabilities who may not safely or successfully engage in unrestricted participation in the vigorous activities of the general physical education program

2. *Whom should adapted physical education serve?*

   - Students with handicapping conditions defined in PL 94-142 or similar legislation

   - Students who meet special education eligibility requirements under PL 94-142

   - Students who consistently perform below the 50th percentile in tests and observations of physical and motor fitness, motor skills and patterns, and aquatics, dance, and sport

3. *Where do adapted physical education specialists deliver services?*

   - A separate setting

   - A mainstreamed setting

   - A continuum of placements: separate, combined, and mainstreamed

4. *What are the goals and objectives of adapted physical education?*

   - Same as regular physical education

   - Goal same, but objectives prioritized differently from those of regular physical education

   - Both goal and objectives different from regular physical education

5. *What is the best name for our service delivery system?*

   - Adapted physical education

- Developmental physical education
- Special physical education

6. *How should adapted physical education be mandated and governed?*

   - Federal law
   - State law and/or educational policy
   - Local school systems

7. *How should adapted physical education be funded?*

   - Same as regular physical education
   - Federal monies
   - All available sources

In contrast, illustrative questions that must be answered in shaping a philosophy of adapted physical education teacher training are as follows.

1. *Which best describes adapted physical education as a course of study?*

   - Specialization area within physical education
   - Combination of knowledge and skills from both special education and physical education
   - Multidisciplinary area (i.e., an emerging discipline) encompassing knowledge and skills from physical education, special education, recreation, occupational and physical therapy, counseling, and the like

2. *How should undergraduates be taught adapted physical education?*

   - Separate course taught by adapted physical education specialist
   - Informal infusion of content into regular physical education courses
   - Inclusion of specific units on adapted physical education in several required major courses
   - Some combination of the above

3. *Should undergraduate students be allowed to specialize in adapted physical education?*

   - Yes
   - No
   - Depends on certain factors

4. *Who is qualified as an adapted physical education specialist prepared to teach and direct university training in this area?*

   - Individual who can pass national competency test
   - Individual who has completed at least 18 credits in adapted physical education
   - Individual who has engaged in noncredit in-service training
   - Other (describe)

5. *Which university students, other than physical education majors, should be required to complete learning experiences (i.e., course, infusion, or inclusion) in adapted physical education?*

   - Special education majors
   - Elementary education majors
   - Prospective principals
   - Other (describe)

6. *For graduate students specializing in adapted physical education, what proportion of their course work should be theory and practice, respectively?*

   - 50/50
   - 60/40
   - 70/30
   - 80/20

7. *Should graduate students specializing in adapted physical education be required to join professional organizations, attend conferences, and demonstrate other leadership attitudes and habits?*

   - Yes
   - No
   - Depends

Chapters in this book, written by authors with various philosophical stances, address these and many more questions. Of special concern to adapted physical education leaders in university teaching is *epistemology*, the theory of knowledge. Foremost among the epistemological questions to be answered are

- What is the knowledge base of adapted physical education? How does it differ from that of regular physical education?
- Is adapted physical education an emerging discipline, subdiscipline, or specialization area?

Knowledge Base of Adapted Physical Education

Prerequisite to scholarly inquiry concerning the epistemology of adapted physical education is the need to examine its different meanings. Sherrill (1986a) indicates that three definitions are needed to fully explain the believing, doing, and knowing components of adapted physical education. These correspond to the affective, psychomotor, and cognitive domains; all are interrelated, yet require separate attention. First, adapted physical education is an *attitude*, a way of teaching in both mainstream and segregated environments, that is reflected in the beliefs and practices of teachers who *adapt* learning experiences to meet individual needs and assure optimal success in physical and motor functioning. Undergraduate physical education training should focus primarily on attitudes and the development of a strong commitment to serve all children (Santomier, 1985). Likewise, inservice training seeks to instill positive attitudes about individual differences and to provide the ego strength and competencies necessary for coping with a broad spectrum of individual differences. Both the doing and knowing components of adapted physical education are shaped by opinions, attitudes, beliefs, and values. Teacher trainers must have a thorough understanding of the affective domain.

The doing component of adapted physical education is what makes it a profession. Adapted physical educators deliver services in order to achieve the goal of helping individuals resolve the problems that prevent their optimal physical, motor, and leisure functioning. As a doing component, adapted physical education is also a *comprehensive service delivery system* designed to identify and ameliorate problems within the psychomotor domain. Services include individualized educational planning, psychomotor assessment, developmental and prescriptive teaching, fitness and leisure counseling, coordinating related services and resources, and advocacy for high quality physical education experiences for all human beings. This definition of adapted physical education as a profession seems most appropriate for adapted physical education specialists. Strong feelings exist that each of our nation's 16,000 school districts, as well as residential private and state-supported facilities for special populations, should employ one or more adapted physical education specialists to design and implement such service delivery systems.

The knowing component of adapted physical education is its theory. For teacher training and the shaping of university curricula, adapted physical education can be defined as the *body of knowledge* that focuses on identification and remediation of problems within the psychomotor domain in individuals who need assistance in the mainstream and/or in specially designed physical educa-

tion services. Adapted physical education is concerned primarily with individual differences, particularly with persons who perform below the 50th percentile (i.e., those who fail or consistently score below average on tests and observations of fitness, motor skill, and participatory abilities in sport, dance, and aquatics).

Adapted physical education theory encompasses all knowledge that enables us to understand variability within the psychomotor domain and to advocate for the rights of persons who are different. This delineation of our knowledge base negates the popular but inaccurate idea that adapted physical education pertains exclusively to the "handicapped, the disabled, and the ill." This misconception, which seems to have evolved with special education funding in the 1960s and 1970s, has caused much confusion about the nature and structure of our theory. Adapted physical education does not categorize human beings as "handicapped" or "nonhandicapped" as do the eligibility procedures for special education funding. Instead it analyzes individual differences within the lower ranges of performance in both groups, seeks to find psychomotor strengths to build upon, and strives to help persons help themselves and others within the psychomotor domain.

The theory of individual differences in the psychomotor domain, and thus of adapted physical education, encompasses the following areas of knowledge:

- Problems within the psychomotor domain— particularly in relation to motor development, learning, and control and the neurological bases for normal and abnormal motor functioning. Biomechanics and exercise physiology, taught from a developmental perspective, are crucial also to problem solution. In infants and young children, psychomotor problems may be interwoven with social and cognitive delays and/or deficits. Thus "learning to play" is often as significant a psychomotor problem as sensory-motor input or integration.

- Solution of problems in the psychomotor domain (i.e., changing and improving behaviors) with particular emphasis on preserving ego strength and facilitating a good self-concept. This problem solving entails using assessment, curriculum, and instruction theory as well as educational accountability for success in applying such theory to practice. Especially important are self-concept, perceived competence, motivation, achievement, and self-actualization theory in relation to both learning and teaching.

- Social psychology, attitude theory, and techniques for fighting prejudice, promoting integration, and helping persons understand, appreciate, and accept themselves and others.

• Advocacy, human relations, and communication theory with particular emphasis upon legislation, litigation, and rules, regulations, and procedures that affect the rights of the "different" person.

In summary, adapted physical education has a definite knowledge base. It not only demands understanding and appreciation of "normal" but also of "abnormal" motor development, learning, and functioning that were once believed to be the property of the therapies. Cratty states in this regard,

> As the background of the adapted specialist broadens, the knowledge of strategies and interventions seems at times to be similar to, if not identical to, many techniques and approaches traditionally employed by other professionals, notably the physical therapist, recreational therapist, and occupational therapist. (Cratty, 1980, p.9)

Adapted physical education utilizes knowledge from all the professions concerned with the psychomotor domain—physical education, special education, leisure and recreational services, physical therapy, and occupational therapy. Moreover, adapted physical education is a helping profession like counseling and guidance, psychology, and health education. Professionals are meeting the challenge of borrowing knowledge from various sources and combining it in new and different ways to establish a conceptual framework for adapted physical education.

Rarick's conclusion to his treatise on physical education as a discipline in 1967 might well be applied to adapted physical education today. Rarick stated,

> We have a considerable body of knowledge to draw upon. However, it is widely scattered and at the moment not well structured. An immediate need is to bring order out of chaos. If, in fact, we are serious in our belief that there is an identifiable body of knowledge which belongs to what we call physical education, we need to begin at once to build the general framework for structuring this body of knowledge. With this accomplished, we can perhaps more clearly pinpoint scholarly efforts. (Rarick, 1967, p. 52)

Sherrill (1986a) suggests that whereas adapted and regular physical education share the same long-range goals, the ranking of these goals is different for low-skilled and developmentally delayed students than for the average performer. Attention to self-concept and preservation of ego strength are more important in teaching movement to low-skilled than to normal students. In a pilot study of 152 physical educators (adapted and regular) from two states, Sherrill and Montelione (1983) found that positive self-concept was ranked first out of nine long-range goals for adapted physical education (see Table 1.1) in a paired comparison ranking procedure. Social competency, motor skills and patterns, and physical and motor fitness ranked second, third, and fourth, respectively. More research needs to be directed toward this issue to determine if long-range goals vary with different populations of students.

Attention needs to be focused also on similarities and differences between adapted and regular physical education in terms of content (activities) and methods, materials, and instructional strategies. It is hypothesized that these variables do differ in effective adapted versus regular physical education programming. Task analysis and behavior management techniques, for instance, are used far more often in adapted than in regular physical education.

Goals and Objectives of Adapted Physical Education

A clear understanding of goals and objectives is important in the development of philosophy. A general consensus seems to be that the major purpose or goal of adapted physical education is the same as that of regular physical education. Sherrill emphasizes that both should be changing "psychomotor behaviors, thereby facilitating self-actualization, particularly as it relates to understanding and appreciation of the body (and the self) in motion and rest" (1986a, p. 6). Seaman and DePauw write: "The goal of any adapted or general physical education program is for the children to achieve their maximum potential in the motor domain through physical education experiences" (1982, p. 18). To alleviate persons' fears about teaching handicapped students, we have all too often emphasized that they are more like their nonhandicapped peers than unlike them, that they have the same needs, and that the same instructional approaches will work. This is true of some handicapped students, the ones with appropriate mainstream placement. Sameness is relative. The words may be reassuring but they lack truth, integrity, and perhaps common sense when applied to students who cannot successfully participate in mainstream physical education (i.e., youth who repeatedly function below the 50th percentile).

Pedagogy that works with different skill and fitness levels, interacting in combination with varying health, ego, and other psychological and social problems warrants serious research. Illustrative of authors whose

Table 1.1 Goals of Adapted Physical Education Classified According to Domains

Domain	Goals
Affective	
• *Positive self-concept.*	To strengthen self-concept and body image through activity involvement; to increase understanding and appreciation of the body and its capacity for movement; to accept limitations that cannot be changed and to learn to adapt environment so as to make the most of strengths (i.e., to work toward self-actualization).
• *Social competency.*	To reduce social isolation, to learn how to develop and maintain friendships, to demonstrate good sportsmanship and self-discipline in winning and losing, and to develop other skills necessary for success in the mainstream, including appropriate social behaviors (i.e., how to interact with others—sharing, taking turns, following, and leading).
• *Fun/tension release.*	To improve attitude toward exercise, physical activity, and sports, dance, and aquatics so that involvement represents fun, recreation, and happiness; to improve mental health through activity involvement; to learn to release tensions in a healthy, socially acceptable manner; to reduce hyperactivity and learn to relax.
Psychomotor	
• *Motor skills and patterns.*	To learn fundamental motor skills and patterns; to master the motor skills indigenous to games, sports, dance, and aquatics participation; to improve fine and gross motor coordination for self-care, school, work, and play activities.
• *Physical and motor fitness.*	To develop the cardiovascular system, promote ideal weight, increase muscular strength, endurance, and flexibility, and improve posture.
• *Leisure time skills.*	To learn to transfer physical education learnings into habits of lifetime sports, dance, and aquatics; to become acquainted with community resources for recreation; to expand repertoire of and/or to refine skills in individual and group games and sports and dance and aquatic activities.
Cognitive	
• *Play and game behaviors.*	To learn to play spontaneously; to progress through developmental play stages from solitary and parallel play behaviors up through appropriate cooperative and competitive game behaviors. To promote contact and interaction behaviors with toys, play apparatus, and persons; to learn basic game formations and mental operations needed for play; to master rules and strategies of simple games.
• *Perceptual motor function and sensory integration.*	To enhance visual, auditory, tactile, vestibular, and kinesthetic functioning; to reinforce academic learnings through games and perceptual-motor activities; to improve cognitive, language, and motor function through increased sensory integration.
• *Creative expression.*	To increase creativity in movement and thought. When posed a movement problem, to generate *many* responses, *different* responses, *original* responses. To learn to imagine, to embellish and add on, to risk experimentation, to devise appropriate game strategy, and to create new games, dances, and movement sequences.

Note. From *Adapted Physical Education And Recreation: A Multidisciplinary Approach*, 3rd ed. (p. 13) by C. Sherrill, 1986, Dubuque, IA: Wm. C. Brown. Copyright 1986 by Wm. C. Brown. Reprinted by permission.

works should be studied and extended in this regard are Mosston (1981) and Morris (1980a,b). Mosston has developed a spectrum of teaching styles that permits adaptation to individual differences. Morris has shown how changing assessment practices and modifying games enables teachers to meet the different objectives of adapted physical education.

Philosophic positions about population to be served, goals, content, and pedagogy can have considerable impact on teaching effectiveness. Philosophies of adapted physical education leaders need not agree, but they should be set down in writing and periodically analyzed, challenged, and changed. Adapted physical educators, like other professionals, should be involved in a continuous process of redefining beliefs and evolving a sound philosophy to guide their actions.

Terminology as a Philosophical Issue

Terminology reflects philosophy. Some textbook authors persist in using such terms as adapted, developmental, special, corrective, remedial, and therapeutic to describe different aspects of their discipline (Fait & Dunn, 1984; French & Jansma, 1982; Winnick, 1979). Others believe that multiple terms are confusing to the many groups with which adapted physical education interacts and thus self-defeating in terms of growth and development of their discipline (Cratty, 1980; Masters, Mori, & Lange, 1983; Seaman & DePauw, 1982; Sherrill, 1986a). The latter group uses the term *adapted physical education* in their textbooks and does not discuss adapted, special, and developmental aspects as different subparts, whereas the former group seems to prefer the term *special physical education* and does differentiate between adapted, special, and developmental aspects in their writings. Broadhead (1981) summarizes the problem as follows:

> It is likely that the rather sluggish development and low level sophistication of adapted physical education, and how seriously it is being studied, is due in large measure to the complexity of the terminology used to describe those who receive adapted physical education. There is perhaps additional confusion when one considers the vastly differing backgrounds presented by professionals and academicians, researchers, teachers, community workers, physicians and the like who use terms and concepts with little reference to each other. (p. 234)

The problem of terminology is indeed magnified by the confusion of ownership of adapted physical education, questions concerning funding, and the dilemma, in some minds, as to whom should be served. It seems ill-advised to split a discipline or academic specialization into subparts with different definitions until the whole of the discipline is well understood and accepted. This writer prefers the term *adapted* because its use is more widespread internationally than other terms. The first scholarly journal to be initiated for the discipline, which began publication in 1984, has been named *Adapted Physical Activity Quarterly*. The AAHPERD structure to which we belong is called the Adapted Physical Activity Council, and the major international organization in this area is the International Federation of Adapted Physical Activity. Additionally, more textbooks (see Appendix G) use *adapted* in their title than any other term.

Adapt means to make suitable; to adjust, accommodate, or modify in accordance with needs. These needs may be developmental or environmental. Educators *adapt* curriculum content, instructional pedagogy, assessment and evaluation methodology, and physical environment, but they also help students to adapt. Thus physical education is continuously being adapted; the broadest of all possible concepts is adapting. Perhaps that is why Piagetian theory continues to emphasize *adaptation* as the process of continuous interaction between existing schemata and environmental stimulation and as the broad concept that encompasses assimilation and accommodation. Adapting is a process that relates to all persons and thus negates any bias that may be associated with "special" needs or "special" students. To adapt is to be creative, innovative, and flexible —certainly desirable behaviors to be promoted through the discipline of adapted physical education.

Adapted Physical Education as an Academic Discipline

The knowledge explosion of the past 2 decades has affected adapted physical education just as it has influenced biomechanics, exercise physiology, sport psychology and sociology, and athletic training. In the 1980s adapted physical education is a clearly recognizable graduate level academic specialization. Two or three institutions of higher education offer this specialization in every state, and many receive federal funding for innovative and effective teacher training curricula. Little attention, however, has been given to the body of knowledge that is unique to adapted physical education. Seaman and DePauw (1982) state in this regard:

> The emergence of adapted physical education as a viable entity is a new direction of the 1980s. The extent to which it will affect the whole of education depends upon the leadership and common goals of adapted physical education professionals. Just as leaders in general physical education have attempted to identify the body of knowledge unique to that discipline, so must leaders in adapted physical education clarify the content of the subdiscipline. (p. 6)

An important issue to be resolved is whether adapted physical education is a subdiscipline of physical education or a discipline within its own right. Much confusion exists about the ownership and funding of adapted physical education because of its inclusion in PL 94-142 as a part of special education. The August 23, 1977, *Federal Register* (p. 42480) states,

> (a) (1) As used in this part, the term "special education" means specially designed instruction at no cost to the parent, to meet the unique needs of a handicapped child, including classroom instruction, *instruction in physical education*, home instruction, and instruction in hospitals and institutions.

Legally, this definition makes specially designed physical education for handicapped students a component of special education. Auxter and Pyfer (1985) describe adapted physical education as a *discipline* in their discussion of the blending of adapted physical education and special education.

> The inclusion of physical education as an integral part of special education, as a matter of public policy, has made adapted physical education a unique discipline.
>
> * It has enabled an identifiable body of content that is the physical education curriculum (defined by federal law), developed out of a substantial history and tradition.
>
> * It now has unique integrity with the recognized procedure and products associated with special education (specially designed instruction to meet unique needs as set forth in the individualized education program).
>
> * The integrated disciplines of special and physical education rely on accurate language to meet public policy demands. (p. 9)

Sherrill (1982) also believes that adapted physical education is an academic discipline. Since the late 1970s she has assigned classes of graduate students to critique the articles in *Quest* by Nixon (1967) and Rarick (1967) entitled respectively "The Criteria of a Discipline" and "The Domain of Physical Education as a Discipline." More than 100 graduate students at the Texas Woman's University have written personal essays on whether or not adapted physical education meets the criteria of Nixon. (p. 47)

* A discipline has an identifiable domain; it asks vital questions; it deals with immensely significant themes, a specifiable scope of inquiry, a central core of interest; it has a definite beginning point; and it has stated goals.

* A discipline is characterized by a substantial history and a publicly recognized tradition exemplified by time-tested works.

* A discipline is rooted in an appropriate structure; it has its unique conceptual structure, and it employs a syntactical structure; the structure organizes a body of imposed conceptions (basic concepts); and it consists of conceptual relationships as well as appropriate relations between fact.

* A discipline possesses a unique integrity and an arbitrary quality.

* A discipline is recognized by the procedures and methods it employs; it utilizes intellectual and conceptual tools as well as technical and mechanical tools; it follows a relevant set of rules; it is recognized by its basic set of procedures, all of which lead to ways of learning and knowing in the domain of the discipline.

* A discipline is recognized as a process as well as noted for its products (knowledge, principles, generalizations).

* Finally, a discipline relies on accurate language, a participants' language, to provide precise, careful communication both within its ranks and to outsiders.

The consensus of opinion among the professionals at Texas Woman's University is that adapted physical education does indeed meet Nixon's criteria for a discipline or is in the process of doing so. Sherrill's emphasis on the *multidisciplinary approach* in her textbook pertains primarily to the knowledge base of adapted physical education, not to cooperative service delivery that might more properly be called interdisciplinary or crossdisciplinary.

> Adapted physical education thus does not draw its knowledge exclusively from physical education. Adapted physical education, as a discipline, merges information from physical education, physical therapy, occupational therapy, counseling and guidance, leisure/recreation services, special education, and other professions as well as from the pure sciences. The beliefs, practices, and knowledge base of adapted physical education are, therefore, *multidisciplinary*. (Sherrill, 1986a, p. 12)

Some leaders, like Julian Stein, are uncomfortable with conceptualizing adapted physical education as a discipline but agree readily that it is a viable academic specialization (Stein, personal communication, 1983). The definition one accepts for the word *discipline* no doubt influences one's philosophical position. The definition of Henry (1964), for instance, might negate adapted physical education. Henry states,

An academic discipline is an organized body of knowledge collectively embraced in a formal course of learning. The acquisition of such knowledge is assumed to be an adequate and worthy objective as such, *without any demonstration or requirement of practical application* (italics mine). The content is theoretical and scholarly as distinguished from technical and professional. (p. 332)

It is difficult to conceptualize a body of knowledge for adapted physical education that has no practical application. Yet, when the pressing need for applied knowledge is assuaged, it is possible that adapted physical education specialists may become intrigued with pure or basic research. History seems to repeat itself in the evolution of disciplines. Henry's opening paragraph on regular physical education as an academic discipline in the 1960s seems to apply to adapted physical education today.

College physical education in America owes much of its genesis to the concept that exercise and sports are therapeutic and prophylactic. . . . It is understandable that our professional concern has tended to center on what physical education can do for people rather than the development of a field of knowledge. (Henry, 1964, p. 331).

To promote cooperation and cohesiveness among adapted physical education leaders, it seems sagacious at this time to operationally define a discipline as a specialization and vice versa. I am reminded of Browning's words as we search for our identity: "Man's reach should escape his grasp . . . or what's a heaven for." Aspirations, hopes, and dreams can shape the future. As Nixon (1967) concluded, "In the final analysis, the collective behavior, the quality of endeavors, of the scholars of a field must command a sufficient respect by observers for the label 'discipline' to be truly deserved and thus bestowed on the field in academic circles" (p. 48).

Graduate Training

If adapted physical education is to fulfill its potential as a scholarly discipline, graduate training must encompass all of the behaviors that comprise the cognitive and affective domains (see Figures 1.2 and 1.3 and their accompanying explanations, pp. 12–14). These behaviors were identified, analyzed, and classified by members of the American Psychological Association in the 1950s. The resulting taxonomies (Bloom, 1956; Krathwohl, 1964) still serve as the primary sources for organizing the content and sequence of learning experiences at all levels of education. *Taxonomy*, as defined by Webster's dictionary, means "classification, especially of animals and plants according to their natural relationships." Benjamin Bloom, David Krathwohl, and colleagues extended this definition to include a classification system for describing, in hierarchial order from simple to complex, the cognitive and affective processes involved in learning. Following is a brief synopsis of each domain, with descriptions of behaviors written to apply directly to adapted physical education leadership training.

Affective Domain

Affective refers to feelings, opinions, attitudes, beliefs, values, interests, and desires. The taxonomy for the affective domain includes five levels, beginning with the least complex and moving toward the most complex.

Cognitive Domain

This domain is subdivided into two major categories: (a) knowledge and (b) intellectual abilities. Knowledge includes "those behaviors and test situations which emphasize the remembering, either by recognition or recall, of ideas, material, or phenomena" (Bloom, 1956, p. 62). The hierarchy of knowledge shows the progression from simple (specifics) to most difficult (universals and abstractions). Intellectual abilities refer to "organized modes of operation and generalized techniques for dealing with materials and problems" (Bloom, 1956, p. 204). Comprehension is the least complex ability, and evaluation is the most complex.

Graduate students who are learning to develop courses, construct tests, shape curricula, and evaluate programs should be taught to refer again and again to these taxonomies. Every effort should be exerted to ascertain that graduate study goes beyond recall and sparks the desire to utilize fully one's higher resources. Several chapters in this text focus upon teacher training, but none integrate the work of Bloom (1956) and Krathwohl (1964); this task remains a challenge for the 1980s.

Creative Behaviors

Another area much neglected in adapted physical education teacher training is the development of creativity (Sherrill, 1986a,b). The ability to adapt instruction to the individual needs, interests, and abilities of all students is largely dependent upon such teacher behaviors as originality, fluency, flexibility, elaboration, courage, and willingness to take risks. Brief definitions of these behaviors lend insight into the kind of teacher training that will facilitate their development. Originality is the ability to think in unique or novel ways, to evolve an idea or an approach that no one else has thought of. Fluency is skill

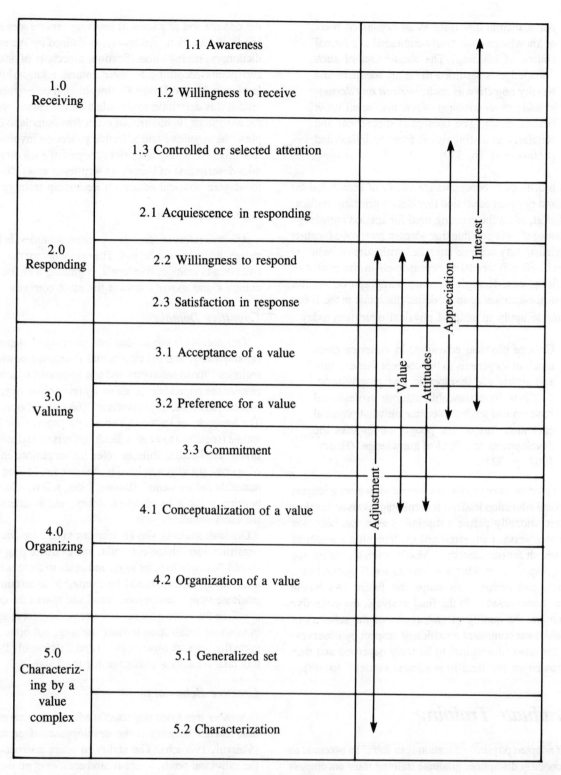

Figure 1.2   Taxonomy for the affective domain. From *Taxonomy of Educational Objectives: The Classification of Educational Objectives. Handbook II: Affective Domain* (p. 37) by D. Krathwohl, B. Bloom, & B. Masia, 1964, New York: David McKay Co., Inc. Copyright by David McKay Co., Inc. Adapted by permission.

Explanation of Taxonomy for the Affective Domain

1.0 Receiving (learning)

1.1 *Awareness*—neutral consciousness of something; can be measured by an information test (e.g., can pass multiple choice test over PL 94-142 as it relates to physical education; can discuss values of PE for handicapped and document research substantiating these values; can explain adapted physical education services).

1.2 *Willingness to receive*—tolerance and/or neutral acceptance of idea or concept. Often measured by interest inventory. Willingness encompasses such observable behaviors as listens to others with respect, attends carefully, observes well, appears interested but does not initiate conversation, interaction, or action.

1.3 *Controlled or selected attention*—alertness to problems of handicapped persons against a diverse figure-background of ideas; sensitive to the need to become informed; leafs through TV Guide hunting programs on handicapped persons; notes newspaper articles, movies, and other learning opportunities. Pays attention to handicapped persons within the mainstream. Interest is increasingly overt and enthusiastic.

2.0 Responding (believing, acting)

2.1 *Acquiescence*—obedience or compliance behavior, a passiveness so far as initiation of the activity is concerned. Makes correct response (implements PL 94-142 or asks that PE be included in IEP) but has not fully accepted the necessity for doing so.

2.2 *Willingness*—voluntary initiation and/or implementation of an activity; voluntarily attends training session without being required/encouraged to do so; asks questions, shares anecdotes, reinforces points made by speaker; voluntarily seeks new information; actively participates in PE for handicapped projects and advocacy activities; accepts responsibility of PE for own handicapped children.

2.3 *Satisfaction in response*—involvement accompanied by a "feeling of satisfaction, an emotional response, generally of pleasure, zest, or enjoyment." Attending ARC and ACLD meetings becomes a habit; talking about PE for the handicapped becomes a habit; overt behaviors begin to show persons want to share satisfaction with others, "come with me," "you'd really like it," "did you know that?", "let's help."

3.0 Valuing

3.1 *Acceptance of a value*—neutral, expressed mostly in readiness to know more, to evaluate one's position on an issue or to study priorities. Shows sense of responsibility for listening to and participating in training concerning PE for handicapped persons; believes but not yet ready to become really involved.

3.2 *Preference for a value*—willingness to be identified with a cause or a belief, to pay membership dues but not necessarily to attend, to list name on a petition but not necessarily work actively for cause; partial commitment kept in perspective so it does not interfere with other work or leisure; writes to press or congresspersons; participates actively in advocacy activities as long as there is no major problem (i.e., no threat to job, family, or personal happiness).

3.3 *Commitment*—conviction, certainty beyond a shadow of doubt. Loyalty to a position, group, or cause. Faith; firm emotional acceptance of a belief upon admittedly nonrational grounds. Loyal to . . . Faith in . . . Devotion to . . . Active involvement in . . . Commitment is characterized by consistency and stability.

4.0 Organization of a value system

4.1 *Conceptualization*—higher level cognitive behaviors such as analysis, synthesis, and evaluation. Preliminary stages in developing a philosophy; abstract reasoning to see how a belief relates to those already held or under consideration; prioritizing. Demonstrated by (a) comparative evaluations of values, (b) evolution of concepts through abstract or symbolic thinking, and (c) generalization of beliefs to action and to other belief-systems.

4.2 *Organization*—the placing of concepts in order into a harmonious and internally consistent philosophy of life with a clearly identifiable central theme. Develops techniques for coping with indifference, hostility, and aggression of others with different values. Develops strategies for finding and cooperating and/or competing with persons having similar values.

5.0 Characterization by a value system

5.1 *Generalized set*—in a sense person loses his/her identity, becomes known as the PE for handicapped advocate/leader. Predisposition to act in a certain way, always to advocate and lead. Consistency.

5.2 *Characterization*—peak of the internalization process—beliefs incorporated into one's morality or character. Commitment to PE for handicapped pervades all aspects of behavior; a consistent philosophy and pattern of action. Great humanitarians like Socrates, Lincoln, and Einstein are cited as reaching the characterization level.

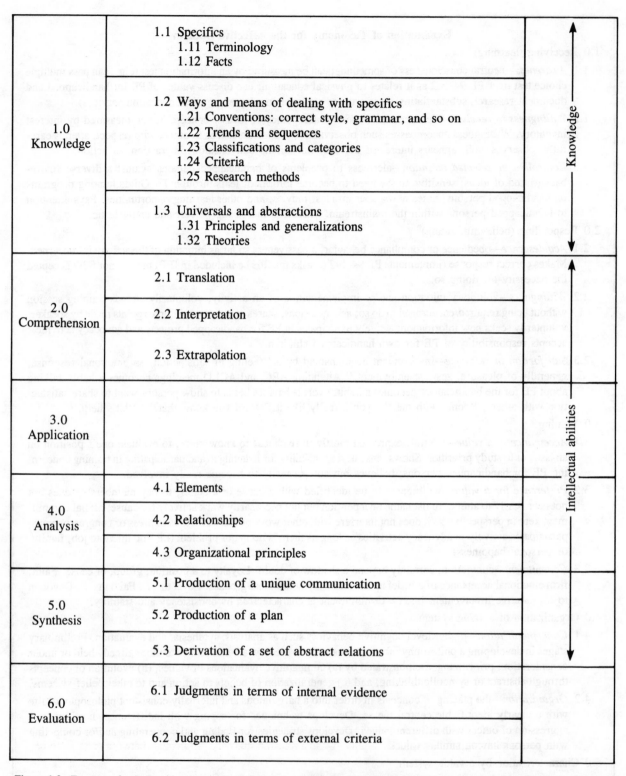

Figure 1.3 Taxonomy for the cognitive domain. From *Taxonomy of Educational Objectives: The Classification of Educational Goals. Handbook I: Cognitive Domain* by B. Bloom, M. Engelhart, E. Furst, W. Hill, & D. Krathwohl, 1956, New York: David McKay Co., Inc. Copyright by David McKay Co., Inc. Adapted by permission.

Explanation of Taxonomy for the Cognitive Domain

1.0 Knowledge (recall of information)

1.1 *Knowledge of specific terms and facts*—can be measured by various kinds of information tests. Includes mastery of vocabulary/terminology of one's profession and ability to recall major facts about specific handicapping conditions and/or such topics as behavior management, assessment instruments, or sports organizations for disabled individuals.

1.2 *Knowledge of ways and means*—category pertaining to ways of organizing, studying, judging, and criticizing is divided in five subparts.

1.21 *Conventions*—refers to library and computer skills, the ability to speak and write correctly, to act in accordance with parliamentary or etiquette rules.

1.22 *Trends and sequences*—pertains to history and philosophy, the ability to grasp relationships, understand causality, significance, and direction.

1.23 *Classifications and categories*—ability to use observations to classify handicapped children in PL 94-142 categories; to know which educational practices are governed by which law or litigation; to group like facts together in proper category and know why they go together.

1.24 *Criteria*—rules or standards by which facts, principles, opinions, and conduct are tested or judged; ability to use criteria when asked to evaluate.

1.25 *Research methods*—knowledge and use of scientific method of problem solving.

1.3 *Knowledge of universals and abstractions*—encompasses the ability to cite the principles of biomechanics, exercise physiology, motor development/learning/control, curriculum/instruction, and the like. It also includes recall of major theories underlying the profession and facts concerning their evolution.

2.0 Comprehension

2.1 *Translation*—the ability to paraphrase into one's own words. This includes the ability to synthesize ideas or facts in a lengthy document into a brief summary and to make sense of abstractions (like principles) by giving concrete examples.

2.2 *Interpretation*—the ability to go beyond rephrasing and to draw meaning for self and/or profession. It involves relating ideas/theories to one's own experiences and finding ways to use the information.

2.3 *Extrapolation*—the ability to draw conclusions and generalize to other situations, to grasp possible consequences or implications. To use knowledge of the past to predict the future; to conceptualize the consequences of something new (theory, discovery, legislation, litigation, method, or procedure).

3.0 Application

This involves the use of knowledge (facts, principles, theories) in everyday teaching and/or problem solving. Bloom et al. do not break application down into 3.1, 3.2, 3.3 subparts as they do other components of the cognitive domain.

Application is the combined *process of knowing and doing*; it is typically measured through observation by experts who use rating forms to objectify the evaluation process. Self-ratings also lend insight into application. *Why do you teach as you do?* Are you consciously applying facts, principles, and theories in active problem solving or are you modeling the behavior of your former teachers?

Application is *transfer of knowledge into practice*. When it is not possible to observe and rate persons in making applications, paper-pencil tests describing new situations can be used. Given a concrete situation, the student is asked to select the one best response, behavior, technique, or decision.

4.0 Analysis

4.1 *Task, idea, or activity analysis*—breaking a task down into its separate parts. Analyzing a movement like the overarm throw into its parts. The ability to read a research study and differentiate between parts: purpose, problem, hypotheses, conclusions, implications, recommendations, and the like. Skill in dissecting a problem and identifying the questions to be resolved.

4.2 *Relationships analysis*—this involves placing elements in order according to difficulty (simple or hard), time (to be done first, second, or third), or development (characteristics of sensorimotor or preoperational stage). It also encompasses the ability to distinguish relevant from irrelevant statements, ideas, or parts; to arrange parts in order of their value or significance; and to differentiate between cause-and-effect relationships and chance happenings.

Continued

Continued

4.3 *Systems or organization analysis*—the ability to break down a system or organization into the principles that make it work and to identify and explain the underlying philosophy. The ability to infer purpose, point of view, or political stance of decision-makers by studying their actions (i.e., breaking actions down into subparts and asking why in relation to each). Skill in taking apart a speech or paper and recognizing the philosophy and/or particular biases or beliefs of the writer. Analysis of group dynamics principles; recognition of what holds a group together or tears it apart. Analysis of legislation like PL 94-142; recognition of the human being as a composite of systems; analysis of principles or processes underlying optimal biological, physiological, or biomechanical function; identifying the cause of a problem.

5.0 Synthesis

5.1 *Development of a product* (term paper, speech, case study, educational diagnosis)—the putting together of parts so as to form a whole. The emphasis is on uniqueness and originality, taking elements from many sources, and putting them together in a different way which offers new insights or understanding. Studying assessment data from different sources and arriving at a new diagnosis. Drawing upon existing research literature to advance theory; tracing the development of theory in order to expand and refine theoretical concepts.

5.2 *Development of a plan or set of operations*—this might be an individualized education program (IEP), a course outline, specifications for restructuring a department or business, or a protocol to be followed in a self-study or evaluation.

5.3 *Derivation of hypotheses, concepts, constructs, or theories*—this involves examining observations and/or facts and developing a logically consistent schema for classifying or organizing them (i.e., the use of the scientific method in structuring and carrying through a research study). The ability to examine individual facts and put them together in new relationships that describe, explain, or predict.

6.0 Evaluation

6.1 *Judgements in terms of internal evidence* (i.e., logical consistency)—usually pertains to accuracy and includes such questions as "Has the writer (or speaker) been consistent in use of terms, does one idea follow from another, do conclusions follow logically from the material presented?"

6.2 *Judgments in terms of external evidence*—refers to evaluating a work against known standards or comparing it with other works of recognized excellence. This includes weighing values of alternative courses of action in relation to a particular goal.

in brainstorming, the ability to generate many relevant solutions to a problem or ideas for implementation. Flexibility is the ability to shift categories of thought, to avoid dead ends, and to conceptualize widely different (even opposite) approaches. Elaboration is the ability to stretch or expand upon ideas, to imagine, and to fantasize in ways that make learning and problem solving more interesting. Courage and willingness to take risks are the personal traits that give individuals the confidence to be different, take guesses, pose solutions, and expose oneself to possible failure or criticism.

Leadership, particularly the trait of "being foremost among," is in some ways synonymous with creativity. The following definition of creativity, for instance, describes leadership behaviors.

It [creativity] involves a response or an idea that is novel or at the very least, statistically infrequent. But novelty or originality, while a necessary aspect of creativity, is not sufficient if a response is to lay claim to being part of the creative process; it must also to some extent be adaptive to reality. It must serve to solve a problem, fit a situation, or accomplish some recognizable goal. And thirdly, creativeness involves a sustaining of the original insight, an evaluation and elaboration of it, a developing of it to the full. (MacKinnon, 1975, pp. 68-69)

MacKinnon (1975) summarizes creativity as "a process that is extended in time and characterized by originality, adaptiveness, and realization" (p. 68). Certainly this definition also describes leadership.

Personnel Roles

Adapted physical education specialists are employed in an increasing number of personnel roles (i.e., jobs or positions). Broadly speaking, personnel roles include (a) direct service delivery to students with psychomotor problems, their families, and significant others; (b) admini-

Adapted physical education classes. A game of Sockley played by children in Prince George's County, Maryland (top) (from M. Marsallo & D. Vacante, *Adapted Games and Developmental Motor Activities for Children*). Swimming instruction for USPCAA class/cerebral palsied adolescent (bottom).

stration, supervision, and consultation; and (c) preservice and in-service training. Personnel preparation for each of these roles is different. Grant writers must, for instance, delineate specific tasks and services for each role and then indicate the competencies necessary to perform these tasks and services. This exercise is helpful for university teachers who are designing courses to meet the needs of prospective teachers.

Direct service delivery is a term that is new to many physical educators. It is widely used, however, in special education and other helping professions in which workers perform multiple job functions rather than one main role like teaching. Adapted physical educators are expected to deliver many nonteaching direct services such as assessment, educational diagnosis, multidisciplinary planning, parent conferences, home visitations, one-on-one counseling and problem solving, and writing individualized education programs (IEPs) in compliance with federal law. Often these services require more time and energy than the traditional role of teaching. Service delivery is therefore a better description of role than teacher.

Administration is a broad role that encompasses all forms of management, supervision, and consulting. Large school systems employ an administrator of adapted physical education to direct, guide, and integrate the work of others. Illustrative of persons who have been employed in this personnel role are Robert Roice of the Los Angeles county public schools, Kenneth Duke of the Dallas public schools, Gwen Bruton of the Baton Rouge (Louisiana) public schools, and Curly Bollesen of the Rochester (Minnesota) public schools.

State education agencies, regional education service centers, and private organizations like Special Olympics, Inc. and United Cerebral Palsy, Inc. also employ administrators. Sport administration for the disabled appears to be a new career option that will flourish with the growth of such organizations as the United States Cerebral Palsy Athletic Association, the United States Association for Blind Athletes, Special Olympics, Inc., and the National Wheelchair Athletic Association. Some colleges and universities employ adapted physical educators as directors of intramurals and recreation for disabled students.

Preservice, in-service, and parent training refers to the role of teaching others how to deliver services to handicapped children and youth. Preservice training is conducted by college and university teachers for undergraduate and graduate students. In-service training is conducted by any qualified person and generally is directed toward teachers and teacher aides who are already employed. Public school adapted physical educators are generally expected to provide in-service training for mainstream and special educators. Heilbuth (1983) reported, for instance, that 74% of the adapted physical educators in Texas taught ''other professionals outside your profession to deliver direct programming'' and 44.2% taught parents ''to deliver direct programming.''

Employment Settings—School and Nonschool

Employment settings in which school adapted physical education services are delivered include the mainstream, a resource room, a separate or self-contained class, and separate school and residential facilities. Many adapted physical education specialists work in two or more settings and are designated as itinerant teachers.

Most handicapped and ''normal'' students who function motorically in the upper 50th percentile receive mainstream physical education in accordance with PL 94-142, which mandates that children must be educated in the ''least restrictive environment'' possible. Adapted physical educators who have baccalaureate degrees in regular physical education are well qualified to teach part or full time in the mainstream. In large schools many principals schedule a regular physical educator and an adapted physical education specialist to team teach in the mainstream, thereby assuring that the special needs of low-skilled and health-impaired students will be met.

The adapted physical education resource room features combined placement in the mainstream and in adapted physical education as a means of providing low-skilled students with support services that enable them to succeed. Students may be assigned part time (2 days a week) to the mainstream and part time (3 days a week) to a resource room where they can receive individual or small group help. Other students may be assigned to the resource room for set periods of intensive *supplementary* instruction to enable them to keep up with peers in the mainstream. The resource room parallels the concept of a nurse's station or athletic injuries room. Either teachers or students can receive help in the resource room. The most commonly used resource room appears to be the perceptual-motor learning laboratory, but the special room may include exercise bicycles and equipment to assist with weight management, fitness, relaxation training, or the improvement of general appearance. The adapted physical education resource room is modeled after the concept of Jenkins and Mayhall (1976) and Wiederholt, Hammill, and Brown (1978).

The separate or self-contained physical education class most often is the placement for students whose educational goals include lifetime sport skills specific to their disability like beep baseball and goalball for blind individuals, wheelchair sport for cerebral palsied and spinal cord injured individuals, and relaxation activities and cooperative (as opposed to competitive) games for emotionally disturbed and learning disabled individuals. Severely and profoundly mentally retarded students are also assigned to separate classes. Students with health problems like obesity, which may require special kinds of exercise and fitness counseling, also seem to profit from placement in separate settings with small, homogeneous groups.

Separate schools and residential facilities that employ adapted physical education specialists include state-supported institutions for blind, deaf, mentally retarded, and mentally ill individuals. Additionally, many private schools for special populations like learning disabled or emotionally disturbed students prefer adapted physical educators over mainstream teachers. Some public school systems still maintain separate schools for special populations like, for instance, orthopedically impaired individuals who need physical and occupational therapy and other related services with costly equipment that is centralized in one location.

Early childhood adapted physical education, a specialized area in which increasing numbers of persons are being employed, is generally conducted in separate classes or schools because public education is not provided for nondisabled children younger than age 5. PL 94-142 provides for special education for handicapped children aged 3 years and above. Additionally, some state laws provide educational programs for handicapped children from birth on.

Nonschool employment options include sport organizations for the disabled, year-round and seasonal camps for special populations, privately run health spas and fitness centers, businesses and industries that employ individuals with health or fitness problems, and sport and fitness programs conducted for special populations by agencies like YMCAs, Scouts, the American Lung Association, and the American Heart Association. By the year 2000, senior citizens aged 65 and over will number at least 31 million; these persons, too, need special exercise programs as do the millions of adults with such chronic conditions as heart disease, cancer, asthma, and obesity. With effective information dissemination, plans for acquainting potential employers with the values of adapted physical education training will succeed. Specialists with strong backgrounds in working with individual differences thus will stand a better chance in the job market than traditionally trained regular physical educators.

Services and Job Functions

The nature and scope of adapted physical education have changed dramatically over the past two decades. No longer is adapted physical education simply a program of activities suited to the interests, capabilities, and limitations of students with disabilities who cannot engage safely or successfully in the regular programs. Today's adapted physical education specialists are employed to perform a wide variety of job functions, only one of which is teaching.

Adapted physical education services (job functions) include some tasks in each personnel role: direct service delivery, administration, and preservice, in-service, and parent training. The most important job functions within the direct service delivery role include assessment, individualized educational programming, developmental and prescriptive teaching, counseling, advocacy for lowskilled and disabled persons, and coordination of related services in the psychomotor domain.

Assessment

Assessment is the combined process of testing, measuring, and evaluating. It includes screening of all school children to identify those functioning in the lower 50th percentile of the psychomotor domain as well as comprehensive testing of individual students. Assessment also entails the continuous evaluation of program, personnel, and resources.

Individualized Educational Programming

The IEP process used in adapted physical education is based on the sequence of procedures prescribed by PL 94-142 that are directed toward finding unserved handicapped students, admitting them to the school district's special education program, referring them for special services, and subsequently dismissing them from special education. The adapted physical education IEP process includes screening all children to find those with psychomotor problems (not just the handicapped); multidisciplinary decision making about physical education placement; developing written IEPs specifying present level of psychomotor functioning, goals and objectives, services, dates, and evaluation protocol; designing adapted physical education programs to implement the written IEPs; and monitoring the conduct of such programs.

Developmental and Prescriptive Teaching

This teaching is the process in adapted physical education whereby psychomotor behaviors are changed and optimal growth and development are promoted. The teaching is *prescriptive* in that the long-range goals and short-term objectives are agreed upon by a multidisciplinary committee, including one or both parents and (where appropriate) the student. The agreement constitutes an educational prescription. Adapted physical education is *developmental* because the teacher adapts the learning activities or interventions to the developmental motor, fitness, or play level of the student.

Movement, Fitness, and Leisure Counseling

Counseling is the process (either verbal or movementoriented) through which students are helped to understand and accept themselves and others in various dimensions of the psychomotor domain. It entails one-to-one and small group problem solving directed toward specific areas where change is needed: attitudes, feelings, and motivations about the body, physical activity, movement strengths and weaknesses, fitness, leisure, and acceptance or nonacceptance in integrated physical education and recreation.

Advocacy for Low-Skilled and Disabled Persons

This service includes all actions directed toward promoting, maintaining, and defending the legal and humanistic rights of persons who differ from the norm in physical appearance, movement, fitness, and other parameters of the psychomotor domain. Advocacy generally focuses upon integration barriers that impede successful physical education mainstreaming. For lack of a better term, advocacy refers mainly to the time and efforts devoted to nondisabled persons (children, parents, teachers) in heightening their understanding and appreciation of handicapped individuals.

Coordination of Related Services in the Psychomotor Domain

Because physical education is required as a *direct service* within special education under PL 94-142, adapted physical education specialists are the logical personnel to request, coordinate, and support related services such as physical and occupational therapy, corrective therapy, and therapeutic recreation. This job function reinforces the multidisciplinary basis of adapted physical education and the importance of broad professional training.

The job functions of school-based adapted physical educators depend in large part on the professional preparation, hopes, dreams, and aspirations of the persons employed in direct service delivery roles. They can be as wide as the imagination, as broad as the energy level, and as effective as the amount of work the teacher is willing to perform. Although no exact statistics exist to document the number of adapted physical education specialists in this country, a good estimate is somewhere around 15,000. An important research goal of the 1980s is to identify and describe these persons, survey their needs, analyze their job functions, and determine future directions for service delivery as well as personnel preparation.

Concerns About Teacher Training

The quality of teacher training received by adapted physical education specialists is a matter of grave concern. No area of specialization within physical education has changed over the past 10 years as drastically as has adapted and developmental physical education. Whereas several states have created a special teacher certification or licensure to assure quality control, most state education agencies have not yet coped with the problem (Cowden & Tymeson, 1983). In several states

persons with no physical education training can be employed full time to teach adapted and developmental physical education; the only criterion for such employment is teacher certification in special education.

Goals for the Future

Regular physical educators, adapted physical educators, and special educators need to unite in working toward achievement of the following goals:

- Every state should pass legislation that parallels PL 94-142 in regard to physical education for the handicapped. Ideally, state law should be more stringent than federal legislation and require physical education for all children, including those with handicapping conditions.

- Adapted physical education teacher certification, licensure, or endorsement should be required for specialists. Possibly national level registration by a professional organization is needed to monitor state efforts.

- At least one adapted physical education theory course with practicum experiences should be required of all physical education generalists, of all special educators, and of all elementary education majors.

- Adapted physical education theory should be infused into all aspects of the undergraduate physical education curriculum.

The phenomenal growth of adapted physical education specialists in the public schools has made identification and study of its work force difficult. Whereas some research has been reported on mainstream physical educators who teach handicapped students, almost nothing is known about the full-time adapted physical education specialist. In perhaps the first research to be completed in this area, Heilbuth (1983) reported that only 20.55% of the full-time adapted physical educators in Texas had earned a degree specific to their job functions (i.e., either in adapted physical education or a combination of physical education and adapted physical education). More than 43% of Heilbuth's sample reported that their educational training did not prepare them adequately to perform job functions.

The need to evaluate teacher training in adapted and developmental physical education is clear. What is the dream? What is the reality? What are we, and where are we going? To whom does adapted physical education belong—special education or physical education? Now is the time to assess our goals, develop a philosophy, and clarify our values.

References

Auxter, D., & Pyfer, J. (1985). *Principles and methods of adapted physical education and recreation* (5th ed.). St. Louis: The C.V. Mosby Co.

Bloom, B. (Ed.). (1956). *Taxonomy of educational objectives, Handbook I: Cognitive domain.* New York: David McKay.

Broadhead, G.D. (1981). Time passages in adapted physical education. In G. Brooks (Ed.), *Perspectives on the Academic Discipline of Physical Education* (pp. 234-212). Champaign, IL: Human Kinetics.

Cowden, J., & Tymeson, G. (1983). Certification in adapted/special physical education: National status. *NCPERH Newsletter, 2*(3), 8-10.

Cratty, B.J. (1980). *Adapted physical education for handicapped children and youth.* Denver: Love.

Fait, H., & Dunn, J. (1984). *Special physical education: Adapted, individualized, developmental* (5th ed.). Philadelphia: W.B. Saunders.

Federal Register (p. 42480). (1977, August 23).

French, R., & Jansma, P. (1982). *Special physical education.* Columbus: Charles E. Merrill.

Heilbuth, L. (1983). *Psychomotor job functions of Texas public school adapted physical education teachers, occupational therapists, and physical therapists.* Unpublished doctoral dissertation, Texas Woman's University, Denton.

Heller, M. (1974). *Preparing educational leaders: New challenges and new perspectives.* Bloomington, IN: Phi Delta Kappa Educational Foundation.

Henry, F.M. (1978). The academic discipline of physical education. *Quest, 29,* 13-29.

Henry, F. (1978). The academic discipline of physical education. *Quest, 29,* 13-29.

Jenkins, J.R., & Mayhall, W.F. (1976). Development and evaluation of a resource teacher program. *Exceptional Children, 43,* 21-29.

Krathwohl, D. (Ed.). (1964). *Taxonomy of educational objectives. Handbook II: Affective domain.* New York: David McKay.

Kroll, W. (1978). *Graduate study and research in physical education.* Champaign, IL: Human Kinetics.

Lawson, H., & Morford, W. (1979). The crossdisciplinary structure of kinesiology and sports studies: Distinctions, implications, and advantages. *Quest, 31*(2), 222-230.

MacKinnon, D.W. (1975). IPAR's contribution to the conceptualization and study of creativity. In I. Taylor & J. Getzels (Eds.), *Perspectives in creativity* (pp. 60-89). Chicago: Aldine.

Masters, L., Mori, A., & Lange, E. (1983). *Adapted physical education: A practitioners guide.* Rockville, MD: Aspen Systems Corporation.

McIntyre, M. (1981). Leadership development. *Quest, 33*(1), 33-41.

Morris, G.S.D. (1980a). *Elementary physical education: Toward inclusion.* Salt Lake City, UT: Brighton.

Morris, G.S.D. (1980b). *How to change the games chilren play* (2nd ed.). Minneapolis: Burgess.

Mosston, M. (1981). *Teaching physical education* (2nd ed.). Columbus, OH: Charles E. Merrill.

Nixon, J. (1967). The criteria of a discipline. *Quest, 9,* 42-48.

Rarick, G.L. (1967). The domain of physical education as a discipline. *Quest, 9,* 49-52.

Rose, D. (1986). Is there a discipline of physical education? *Quest, 38*(1), 1-2.

Sage, G. (1984). The quest for identity in college physical education. *Quest, 36*(2), 115-121.

Santomier, J. (1985). Physical educators, attitudes, and the mainstream: Suggestions for teacher trainers. *Adapted Physical Activity Quarterly, 2*(4), 328-337.

Seaman, J., & DePauw, K. (1982). *The new adapted physical education: A developmental appproach.* Palo Alto: Mayfield.

Sherrill, C. (1982). Adapted physical education: Its role, meaning, and future. *Exceptional Education Quarterly, 3*(1), 1-9.

Sherrill, C. (1985). Integration of handicapped students: Philosophical roots in pragmatism, idealism, and realism. *Adapted Physical Activity Quarterly, 2*(4), 264-272.

Sherrill, C. (1986a). *Adapted physical education and recreation: A multidisciplinary approach* (3rd ed.). Dubuque: Wm. C. Brown.

Sherrill, C. (1986b). Fostering creativity in handicapped children. *Adapted Physical Activity Quarterly, 3*(3), 236-249.

Sherrill, C., & Montelione, T. (1983). *A ranking of the goals of adapted physical education.* Unpublished manuscript, Texas Woman's University, Denton.

Snyder, R., & Scott, H. (1954). *Professional preparation in health, physical education, and recreation.* New York: McGraw Hill.

Wiederholt, J.L., Hammill, D.D., & Brown, V. (1978). *The resource teacher.* Boston: Allyn & Bacon.

Winnick, J. (1979). *Early movement experiences and development: Habilitation and remediation.* Philadelphia: W.B. Saunders.

Ziegler, E. (1979). Sport and developmental physical activity in worldwide perspective: A philosophical analysis. *Quest, 31,* 6-11.

Chapter 2

Personnel Preparation in Adapted Physical Education: Early History

Claudine Sherrill

A discipline is characterized by a substantial history and a publicly recognized tradition exemplified by time-tested works. (Nixon, 1967, p. 47)

Adapted physical education leaders know the history of their discipline and understand its role in shaping contemporary service delivery and personnel preparation. It has been said that history is a prophet with its face turned backward. A study of the past provides insights into today's problems and enhances our appreciation of the role of leaders in effecting change. In chapter 1 it was established that leadership evolves from outstanding teaching, research, and service. In this and subsequent chapters, it will be shown that upward mobility within the profession also relates to the prestige of the graduate department in which one receives the doctorate, the extent that one is supported by mentors, and one's ability to relate to leaders of the past and present. Who one knows is often as important as individual achievement factors (Massengale & Sage, 1982). To become leaders, graduate students must be closely associated with leaders. Academic mentors must assume responsibility for helping students get acquainted with leaders, both through reading and personal introductions. Through studying this and subsequent chapters, readers will learn about many of the leaders in adapted physical education.

In this chapter and the next the development of personnel preparation in adapted physical education is traced to determine the major influences in the evolution of both our knowledge base and service delivery system. It is impossible to separate the history of personnel preparation from that of service delivery. Problems and needs in serving handicapped and clumsy children influence teacher training and vice versa. Likewise, trends and issues in the physical education of able-bodied (AB) students have affected adapted physical education personnel preparation. Because adapted physical education is multidisciplinary, its roots are found in medicine, physical and occupational therapy, special education, counseling, physical education, recreation, teacher education, and the like (see Appendix G for a chronology of organizations). Although all major adapted physical education textbooks include a brief section on history, no work provides in-depth coverage. The most comprehensive sources, to date, are Clarke and Clarke (1963), Daniels and Davies (1965), Wheeler and Hooley (1969), and Sherrill (1986). The April 1986 issue of the *Adapted Physical Activity Quarterly* includes several articles that chronicle recent history, including the role of the federal government (Hillman, 1986), AAHPERD (DePauw, 1986; Goodwin, 1986; Stein, 1986), and NCPERH (Bundschuh, 1986; Johnson, 1986). The bicentennial issue of *Able Bodies* (Fall, 1985) also serves as a source of adapted physical education history. The historical chapters in this book are based on these and various primary sources such as correspondence, interviews, and minutes of meetings. For organizational purposes, the same stages are described as those identified earlier by Sherrill (1986): (a) Stage 1—Medically Oriented Gymnastics and Drill, Prior to 1900s; Stage 2—Conceptualization of the Whole Child: Education Through the Physical, 1900–1929; (c) Stage 3—Corrective Physical Education, 1930–1951; (d) Stage 4—Adapted Physical Education, 1952–1966; (e) Stage 5—Multidisciplinary/Interdisciplinary Adapted Physical Education, 1967 to Present.

Leaders in adapted physical education who have served as mentors from left to right are Lane Goodwin, Claudine Sherrill, Larry Rarick, and John Hall.

Overview of Teacher Training

The early leaders of physical education were physicians. Their training can be described as follows:

> The practicing physician in the second half of the nineteenth century continued to derive his training from a variety of sources. The old apprenticeship system still hung on, although the ease of obtaining diplomas guaranteed that most doctors had some type of medical degree. . . . The better physician obtained a bachelor's degree from a reputable school, took an M.D. in an equally good institution, and then spent one to three years studying abroad. The average physician, however, had no more than a high-school education—and frequently less—and had acquired his medical degree by attending the same four- or five-month course of medical lectures for two years in a row. (Duffy, 1976, p. 260)

Just as the early medical schools were proprietary in nature, teacher training was not associated with colleges and universities. Training was done in normal schools that varied widely in quality. The average teacher, like the average physician, had no more than a high school degree and acquired specialized training by attending courses of short duration. Early leaders in physical education came either from medical school or normal school backgrounds. To this was added special training in gymnastics (i.e., exercise). Although women had been earning medical degrees since 1849, they still found admission to medical school exceedingly difficult. Thus the early training of physical education leaders differed according to gender.

The historical roots of regular and adapted physical education in America were the same. Both were dominated by European systems of gymnastics until the early 1900s, when the American system of sport, dance, and aquatics evolved. The struggle for dominance between the European and American systems is known as the Battle of the Systems; its official beginning is documented as around 1885, the year that the Association for the Advancement of Physical Education, the forerunner of AAHPERD, was established. Until the end of this Battle, sometime after World War I, physical education was typically called *gymnastics* and defined as *systematic bodily exercises* (Nissen, 1892). Gymnastics was divided into various branches and was described by Nissen (1892) as follows:

- *How many kinds of gymnastics are there?* Four kinds, viz.: Medical, Educational, Military, and Esthetical gymnastics.

- *What are Medical gymnastics?* Exercises—either passive, assistive, active, or resistive—prescribed by a physician or medical gymnast, with a view of restoring health to diseased parts, or developing certain parts of the body.

- *What are Educational gymnastics?* Active or resistive exercises performed in classes, at the command of a teacher, with a view of educating the mind and body.

- *What are Military gymnastics?* Exercises which have a strictly military purpose.

- *What are Esthetical gymnastics?* Active exercises performed either after music or command, with a special view of producing graceful postures and an easy and graceful body. (pp. 1-2)

Often the educational, military, and esthetical branches were grouped together as *hygienic* gymnastics (Posse, 1901). These branches were apparently of little concern at the time of the Battle of the Systems; instead individuals were agonizing over the similarities and differences between the Swedish and German systems. Gour (1916) explains,

> In comparing the Swedish and the German systems, it is well to remember what their founders had in mind. Guts-Muth, the real father of modern gymnastics, in his writings at the latter part of the 18th century, had Jahn, the father of German, and Ling, the father of Swedish gymnastics, as pupils. Among his writings, Guts-Muth states that he has two aims in his work: "(a) Work in the garb of youthful play, and (b) a system of exercise having bodily perfection as the aim." The first appealed to Jahn and the second to Ling. Jahn founded the modern German system which is particularly noted for its variety of stunts and amusing features, but having nothing about it that is aimed primarily to correct the defects and promote the health of its adherents. Ling developed his system with the primary object of promoting bodily perfection in all who practiced it. So that, while amusement and skill are the aims of the German system, health, control and bodily perfection are the aims of the Swedish. The German system contains more of the rhythmic type of gymnastics. Drills with wands, clubs and dumb-bells and free-standing drills set to music, are among its characteristic features. In the Swedish system, no music is employed except to encourage athletes in performing difficult feats. The characteristic features of this system are that all gymnastic movements are practiced without music and each movement is performed at the instructor's command. (p. iv)

The first three teacher training programs in physical education each reflected a different system or knowledge base. The first program founded in Boston in 1861 by Dio Lewis emphasized the Swedish system of medical gymnastics. The second program, established in New York City in 1866 by the North American Turnerbund, stressed the German system. The third program, founded by Dudley A. Sargent in conjunction with Radcliffe College (Harvard annex) for women in 1881, was eclectic in nature and soon became known as the American system. Later it became the Sargent School of Physical Education and moved to Boston. Detailed descriptions of these three systems appear in Weston (1962).

Teacher training in physical education thus began about the time of the Civil War. Three factors were especially important in the evolution of teacher training: (a) the creation of public schools, (b) the enactment of a physical education requirement in these schools, and (c) the development and acceptance of an American system of physical education. The first compulsory school attendance law was passed in 1852; between 1870 and 1890 the number of high schools in the United States increased 500%. The first states to require physical education to be taught in public schools were California (1866), Ohio (1892), Wisconsin (1897), and North Dakota (1899). Although early public school physical education emphasized gymnastics, exercise, and military drill, the American love of sport gradually led to a broadening of the curriculum. Most sports played in schools and colleges today were not created until the 1800s: fencing in 1814; baseball in 1839; intercollegiate track around 1868; intercollegiate football in 1869; competitive swimming in 1875; tennis in 1881; basketball in 1891; golf in 1894; and volleyball in 1895. These sports were accepted very slowly as a part of the physical education curriculum as pointed out by Weston (1962).

> The new physical education posed a serious challenge to German, Swedish, and other types of formal gymnastics, which tended to ignore overall education in their preoccupation with corrective or postural exercises that concentrated only on developing the human body. Its effects were felt only gradually, however, for the time lag between the formulation of a sound program and the placing of it in operation meant that the new physical education was slow in finding its way, on a large scale, into schools and colleges until after World War I. (p. 52)

The changing philosophy and content of physical education naturally affected professional preparation. In the next section the history of adapted physical education personnel preparation is summarized in five stages.

Stage 1--Professional Preparation Prior to 1900

The early leaders of American physical education were physicians. The first college programs and subsequently the public schools stressed exercise for maintaining good health and preventing physical deformities. Particular emphasis was accorded correction of postural defects through exercise. Foremost among early physician-physical educators were Edward Hitchcock of Amherst College, Dudley Allen Sargent of Harvard University, William G. Anderson of Yale University, Delphine Hanna of Oberlin College, Thomas D. Wood of Stanford and Columbia, Luther Halsey Gulick of the YMCA in Springfield, Massachusetts, and Clark W. Hetherington of the University of Missouri. Virtually all physical education in the 19th century was medically oriented and corrective or adapted in nature.

Of the Swedish, German, and American systems of physical education taught in the newly created teacher training programs, the Swedish system had a lasting effect on adapted physical education. Daniels and Davies (1965) cite Wide (1899) as stating that the beginning of adapted physical education had its real foundation in Sweden in the work of Per Henrik Ling (1776-1839). Wheeler and Hooley (1969) describe Ling as follows:

> Ling's physical education experience started with fencing in Copenhagen, where he taught poetry, mythology, and history. The improvement of his afflicted arm through fencing exercises inspired him to study the effect of exercise on the body. With much vigor, he developed a system of gymnastics as the fencing master at the University of Lund. In 1813, the Central Institute of Gymnastics of Stockholm was created to train teachers. Here, Ling developed a system of medical gymnastics which attracted physicians. His system introduced dosage, counting, and detailed directions with classified starting positions and degrees of activity. . . . Ling authored many books on fencing and gymnastics, including *Manual for Gymnastics*, 1836; *Manual for Bayonet-Fencing*, 1836; *Soldiers Manual of Bayonet Fencing*, 1838. After his death, his pupils published a book, *General Principles of Gymnastics* in 1839, which Ling started in 1831. Reaction to his work was virtual worship by most of his students and followers and mixed emotions and abhorrence by a few. (pp. 12-13)

George H. Taylor, Medical Director of the Remedial Hygienic Institute of New York City, introduced the

Ling system of medical gymnastics into the United States before the Civil War (Posse, 1891). Clarke and Clarke (1963) state in this regard:

> While Swedish gymnastics were first utilized by physicians in America around 1850, little was known of the aim, content and method of the Ling system until much later. Not until 1889 were the claims for this system brought forward with sufficient clearness and cogency to attract general attention. (p. 4)

Several persons are accredited for heightening interest in Swedish gymnastics in the 1880s. Hartwig Nissen, Vice Consul for Norway and Sweden in Washington, DC, introduced Swedish gymnastics to the nation's capitol in 1883. Mary Hemenway, Amy Morris Homans, Baron Nils Posse, and Edward Hartwell brought Swedish gymnastics to the Boston public schools and also worked together in the creation of the Boston Normal School of Gymnastics in 1888, which later became the Department of Hygiene and Physical Education at Wellesley College in 1909. Primary sources by Posse and Hartwell, describing Swedish gymnastics, appear in Weston (1962).

Books cited as influencing training of physician-educators in the 19th century are *Medical Gymnastics* (1821) by French physician Charles Londe and *Handbook of Medical Gymnastics* (1899) by British physician Anders Wide (Daniels & Davies, 1965; Wheeler & Hooley, 1969). A book on orthopedic gymnastics, published in Spain in 1864, was the first to use the term *rehabilitation* (Licht, 1961).

As early as 1890, references to the division of gymnastics into educational and curative branches exist, with comments concerning the training of teachers of each.

> This profession, then, differs from any that now exists. It is readily seen that it is not merely a department of medicine, which relates primarily to the prevention and cure of disease. The mere fact that a man is an excellent medical practitioner will not qualify him to take hold of educative gymnastics, although it would qualify him to understand curative gymnastics. On the other hand, the study of psychology and pedagogy will not qualify a man to take hold of curative gymnastics, although it might qualify him to understand educative exercises (Gulick, 1890, cited by Weston, 1962, p. 149)

Little else is known about personnel preparation. Training, for the most part, clearly followed the medical model.

Stage 2—Professional Preparation From 1900 to 1930

By 1900 physical education was increasingly conceptualized as a profession separate from medicine. Work was already underway to create a course of study specific to the training of physical educators and to assure that all practitioners had at least 2 years of this training. The emergence of teacher training as a viable academic major and the establishment of departments of education in major universities contributed largely to this change. Scholars such as William James, G. Stanley Hall, Edward Thorndike, John Dewey, and William H. Kilpatrick created the knowledge base on which courses in teacher education were founded and subsequently influenced the nature of physical education teacher training. The social and psychological aspects of children began to receive equal attention with the physical aspect as the "whole child" was conceptualized. As the goal of physical education changed from education *of the physical* to development of the whole child *through the physical*, so also teacher training changed.

Affiliation With Universities

After universities opened departments of education, they began to establish departments of physical education teacher training (Snyder & Scott, 1954). Among the first state institutions to do this were Illinois in 1905, Oregon in 1907, Wisconsin in 1911, Missouri in 1917, and Iowa in 1918 (Weston, 1962). The first private college to offer professional preparation in physical education was Oberlin College in Ohio in 1900; this program was directed by a woman, Delphine Hanna, whose training consisted of the 1-year course at the Sargent School followed by a medical degree from the University of Michigan (Snyder & Scott, 1954). Wellesley College in Boston and Teachers College at Columbia University in New York were the next private schools to initiate such training. Oberlin, Teachers College, and Wellesley were known as leaders in the training of physical educators throughout the 1900 to 1930 era.

Most of the early proprietary normal schools merged with colleges and lost their identity (e.g., the Boston Normal School of Gymnastics became the Department of Hygiene and Physical Education at Wellesley College; the Posse School of Physical Education affiliated with Tufts College). Two of the most famous proprietary schools, however, remained independent until 1929 and 1941, respectively. These were the Sargent School of Physical Education in Boston and the traveling Normal School of the North American Gymnastic Union. Up to 1920, one out of every three graduates of a physical education teacher training program came from Sargent (Snyder & Scott, 1954).

Physical Education Teacher Training

Leaders helped to assure the quality of early physical education teacher training programs through the Association for the Advancement of Physical Education. The work of its Committee on Teacher Training is described as follows:

> The Committee on Teacher Training which had been at work for two years offered preliminary recommendations in 1901 for qualifications to be considered for admission to normal training courses, as follows: 18 years of age or older; high school graduation or the equivalent; courses completed in physics, chemistry, mathematics, biology, and gymnastics; good health; endorsement as to character and fitness; and acceptance only on probation. The Committee also outlined recommended requirements for a two-year training course, with a preference for three years, which covered physics, chemistry, anatomy, physiology, kinesiology, hygiene, first aid, anthropometry, history of physical education, pedagogy, psychology, theory of gymnastics, voice training, medical gymnastics, pathology, physiology of exercise, and school government. To these were added marching, calisthenics, heavy gymnastics, exercises, athletics, and games. The Committee further recommended the granting of certificates and recognition of a rating to be known as "Master of Physical Training" conferred either by the AAAPE Council or a Board of Examiners to be appointed by the Council. (Lee & Bennett, 1985, p. 34)

In 1908, Dudley Allen Sargent addressed the question, "Should the teacher of physical education in public schools have the training of a physical director and instructor of hygiene or that of a physician?" He concluded that the teacher should have "all the vigor, energy, and technical ability of the physical director, most of the book knowledge of the hygienist, and some of the scientific attainments of the physician" (Weston, 1962, p. 186).

Creation of Graduate Degrees

Several patterns were emerging for the achievement of this kind of preparation, which clearly demanded advanced study. Some individuals continued to combine medical and physical education training, but a growing number began work toward the newly created graduate degrees in physical education. In 1901, Teachers College, Columbia, became the first university to establish a master's degree in physical education (Snyder & Scott, 1954). Lillian Curtis Drew, author of *Individual Gymnastics: A Handbook of Corrective and Remedial Gymnastics*, was direc-

tor of the department of corrective gymnastics there in the early 1900s and thus contributed to the development of strong training in this area. By 1929, 14 universities were granting master's degrees in physical education.

The first doctoral degrees with an emphasis in physical education were granted by Teachers College, Columbia, and New York University in 1924. This initiation of doctoral study specifically in physical education helped to strengthen the trend away from medical education of leaders in our profession. Doctoral study also contributed to a split in the nature of professional preparation deemed appropriate for regular versus corrective teachers.

Corrective and Remedial Gymnastics

The Battle of the Systems was coming to a close in the 1920s. The evolution of the American system of physical education intensified the existing division between branches, regular (i.e., hygienic) and corrective. Louisa Lippitt, Director of Corrective Gymnastics for Women at the University of Wisconsin, described the status quo in one of the first textbooks published concerning the new specialization. In discussing the changes in physical education in recent years, Lippitt noted,

> The addition to courses in physical education of a branch termed *corrective*, or *therapeutic*, *gymnastics* is of rather recent date, and in many schools corrective work has not yet become a required subject. It may be considered a new science, which has developed as the field of physical education has broadened. It results from the realization on the part of instructors in physical education of the benefit to be derived from properly directed individual exercises. (1923, p. 3)

In describing the scope of corrective gymnastics, Lippitt explained that some schools divided it into two departments, termed the "Corrective or Orthopedic Department" and the "Medical or Remedial Department," respectively. The purpose of correctives was to correct such problems as postural defects, pronated or flat feet, weak joints, paralysis, and conditions caused by rickets and malnutrition. In contrast, the purpose of remedial gymnastics was to relieve such conditions as "ptosis, constipation, menstrual disorders, cardiac weakness, neurasthenia, digestive disorders, and general debility and excessive fatigue" (Lippitt, 1923, p. 21). Emphasis was placed on every student receiving a medical and orthopedic examination as the basis for assignment to regular, corrective, or remedial physical education. The medical examination was administered by a physician, but the orthopedic examination was the responsibility of the instructor.

Assignment to gymnasium classes was made by the

instructor in charge of the orthopedic department. In this regard, Lippitt stated,

> In making this assignment, the student's health, her posture, and the presence of any orthopedic deformity should be the determining factors. Both gymnastics and sports should be so planned as to give each student work which is adapted to her strength and condition. The gymnasium work may be divided into *regular* work for those able to take apparatus work and heavy gymnastics, *light* gymnastics for those not able to take strenuous exercises but not needing special or corrective work, and *special* gymnastics for those whose condition can be improved by pre-scribed and directed exercises. In sports, the same division into heavy, light, and medium sports may be made. (p. 25)

It is evident in this passage, and in other parts of Lippitt's book, that such terms as adapted and special were already in use in the 1920s and that already the terminology was becoming confusing. In describing the nature of class instruction, Lippitt (1923) emphasized that *corrective exercise* and *individual exercise* should be considered synonymous terms. *Individual* did not mean one-to-one instruction; the ideal class size was described as one to eight, but every student had her own individually prescribed exercises. The term *gymnastics* was used synonymously with *exercises*, and clearly Lippitt's textbook was designed to teach undergraduates specific exercises for every part of the body. Although the importance of adapting sport to individual needs was mentioned, no information was included on the pedagogy for doing so.

Services to Handicapped Children

Although medical gymnastics and correctives in the early 1900s were used primarily with individuals we would consider to be nonhandicapped today, there is some indication that physical educators were beginning to serve handicapped children and youth. The history of residential facilities dates back to 1817, when the American School for the Deaf in Hartford, Connecticut, was founded. Residential institutions were opened for blind students in 1830, for mentally retarded persons in 1848, and for orthopedically handicapped individuals (called *crippled* until the 1960s or 70s) in 1863. Little has been recorded about the physical education provided in these facilities except for the excellent descriptions of Charles Buell (1966), who chronicles the historical development of physical education for the blind from 1840 onward.

Public schooling for handicapped students began in 1899, with the opening of a school specifically for crippled children in Chicago (Mackie, 1945). Shortly thereafter most large cities created classes and schools for public education of handicapped children. Many of these students were physically disabled, with polio and cerebral palsy most often the cause. Separate classes for mentally retarded children were established also as described by R. Tait McKenzie (1923), author of the classic *Exercise in Education and Medicine*.

> Unless retardation is sufficient to require treatment and protection in an institution, cases of backwardness may be taught in classes composed of children who show about the same degree of mental deficiency. They should, however, be put in a special room or, where possible, in special schools. In this way the low-grade children are prevented from interfering with the regular work of the class. . . . Their physical education would vary with the degree of defect. In a school system special classes should be provided for them, and teachers should be specially prepared to take charge of the atypical individuals. (pp. 311–312)

McKenzie devotes an entire chapter to the physical education of "mental and moral defectives." He cites Barr (no date), stating that "the best results are obtained from military drill, games and gymnastics, with manual training varying in difficulty with the grade of backwardness" (p. 314). No information about teacher training is offered, but obviously individuals who studied from McKenzie's textbook were given considerable background. This text also included a strong chapter entitled "The Physical Education of the Blind and the Deaf-Mute."

In the inclusion of these two chapters, McKenzie's book was different from all others of the era. His humanism, as reflected in this book, is perhaps one reason why AAHPERD created the R. Tait McKenzie Award (see Appendix A) given annually in his honor. Of the many corrective and adapted physical education specialists in American history, McKenzie has achieved the most recognition. A Canadian, he was director of the Physical Education Department at McGill University in Montreal until moving to the University of Pennsylvania in 1904. He served as president of the Association in 1912. McKenzie's biography was the topic of a dissertation by Hunter (1950). R. Tait McKenzie was one of the first physical educators to be influenced by special education; he was almost 50 years ahead of the times.

Emergence of Special Education

By 1922 special education was sufficiently established in the public schools, and the first professional organization was formed (Aiello, 1976). Called the International

Council for the Education of Exceptional Children, it held its first meeting at Teachers College, Columbia, and was essentially American in membership. In 1958, the name was changed to the Council for Exceptional Children (CEC). No evidence can be found in the literature of formal communication between physical and special education from 1900 to 1930.

Relationship With Physical Therapy

From about 1920 on, many leaders in correctives were also physiotherapists. A brief history of physical therapy lends insight into the relationship between the two disciplines. Frank Granger, of Boston City Hospital, is documented as practicing physical therapy at the time World War I started (Hazenhyer, 1946). He was given responsibility for all physical therapy in the army, both at home and abroad. These services were provided during World War I by Reconstruction Aides, members of an all-female corps, within the Reconstruction Department of the United States, which was organized in 1917 by surgeons Joel Goldthwait and E.G. Brackett. This corps consisted of physiotherapy aides who were "to give massage and exercise and other remedial treatment to the returned soldiers" and occupational therapy aides who were "to furnish forms of occupation to convalescents in long illnesses and to give patients the therapeutic benefits of activity" (Hopkins & Smith, 1978, p. 11). One of the earliest descriptions of the physiotherapy (cited by Hazenhyer, 1946) shows the commonalities of early physical education and physiotherapy training.

> There is a splendid group of young women—designated as Reconstruction Aides in Physiotherapy, scattered throughout the 47 hospitals. These women, thoroughly trained in *physical education*, have supplemented that knowledge in special courses in military massage and muscle re-education. (p. 3)

At the outbreak of World War I, no training courses in physical therapy existed. Most physiotherapy reconstruction aides were physical educators. Fourteen institutions established courses during the war to offer the additional training needed to provide "reconstruction" exercises for the rehabilitation of the wounded. The largest of the training programs, at Reed College in Portland, Oregon, was administered by Mary (Molly) McMillan, a physical educator, who later became the first president of the American Physiotherapy Association, which was founded in 1921. During the height of the war, over 2,000 Reconstruction Aides were in service.

At the close of the war it was only natural that many of these individuals, known as physiotherapists after 1921, were employed by universities and schools to conduct corrective and remedial gymnastics programs. Illustrative of these was Louisa Lippitt, whose credentials indicate she was formerly a Chief Head Aide in Physiotherapy, Medical Department, U.S. Army.

Gradually, from 1920 to 1930, the training of specialists in correctives switched from that of medicine to physical therapy. Training in physical therapy began with graduation from recognized schools of physical education or nursing (Hazenhyer, 1946, p. 71). Onto this was added a minimum of 1,200 hours of theory and practice (approximately 9 months) in massage, therapeutic exercise, hydrotherapy, and electrotherapy. The early leaders in correctives thus had dual identities, physical education and physical therapy.

Textbooks

Individuals from 1900 to 1930 who provided leadership through the authoring of books included Hartwig Nissen (1892, 1903, 1916); Nils Posse (1894, 1901); Jesse Bancroft (1913); Lillian Curtis Drew (1922); Louisa Lippitt (1923); R. Tait McKenzie (1923); Andrew Gour (1916); George Stafford (1928); and Charles Lowman (Lowman, Colestock, & Cooper, 1928). The latter two individuals are discussed as part of the 1930–1952 stage because their work largely influenced professionals during these years. The knowledge base of 1900 to 1930, as evidenced by the textbooks used in teacher training, was primarily in the areas of medical gymnastics (the Swedish system), posture, physical examination, and corrective exercises.

Summary

In summary, the nature of teacher training changed drastically from 1900 to 1930. The major change in teacher training during this stage was the shift from the medical to the educational model. Physical education generalists were, however, required to take a course in medical gymnastics or correctives as part of their training. Also characteristic of this period was the emergence of the correctives specialist. Illustrative of these individuals were Claire Colestock and Hazel Cooper of the Pasadena Public Schools in California (Lowman, Coleman, & Cooper, 1928). No information can be located on the training of the correctives specialist, but it can be inferred from the textbooks that created their knowledge base. The credentials of the persons who wrote these books also lend insight into the type of training that promoted leadership. About half of the authors were either physicians or physical therapists who also had special training in physical education.

Stage 3—Professional Preparation From 1930 to 1952

During this era the primary organization of the profession changed its name to the Association for Health, Physical Education, and Recreation, affiliated further with the National Education Association by establishing a headquarters within its building, and sought to improve teacher education standards and competencies through numerous professional conferences. Regular physical education was identified closely with education, although most individuals believed that physical education was a profession and/or a discipline with its own unique body of knowledge. Publication of the *Research Quarterly* began in 1930, and the field became increasingly scholarly.

Influence of Wars

Physical education, both regular and corrective, was strengthened by the increased demands for fitness accompanying the two world wars. The appalling number of rejections for military service in World War I resulted in widespread legislation requiring physical education in public schools. In 1919, only 18 states required physical education. The number increased to 27 in 1921; 32 in 1923, and 38 in 1935. Regular physical education utilized sport, dance, and aquatics as the means for developing the "whole child," whereas corrective or remedial physical education emphasized change or improvement in function or structure by means of selected exercises. Early professional preparation courses in correctives were concerned primarily with the evaluation of postures and fitness and the use of specific exercises to correct or ameliorate defects. The advent of World War II sparked renewal of interest in physical fitness and provided impetus for more physical education legislation so that by 1949, 44 states (embracing more than 90% of the population of the United States) had enacted laws requiring public school physical education.

Requiring more students to take physical education, of course, resulted in the identification of increasing numbers of unfit and handicapped children who needed special services. The knowledge base of correctives changed little during this period; what previously had been called medical gymnastics was now referred to as corrective or remedial exercise and posture training.

First Use of Term "Corrective Physical Education"

Although references to *corrective exercise* can be found in several sources (Nissen, 1916; Williams, 1922), it was not until 1928 that the term *corrective physical education* appeared in the title of a book. Two such books were published in 1928:

- *Corrective Physical Education for Groups* by Charles Lowman, Claire Colestock, and Hazel Cooper

- *Preventive and Corrective Physical Education* by George Stafford

Charles Lowman began his professional career as a physician but became interested in physical education through involvement in track and basketball at the Los Angeles YMCA (Fornas, 1968). While doing advanced study in orthopedic surgery in Boston, he devoted 10 to 12 hours a day to observing and learning about medical gymnastics. He was especially influenced by Joel Goldthwait and other orthopedists in the Boston area, crediting them with helping him to understand the relationship between medicine and corrective physical education.

Upon his return to Los Angeles, Lowman became director of the orthopedic clinic at the University of Southern California (USC) Medical School, where he worked closely throughout his career with physical therapists. Appointed orthopedic consultant to the Los Angeles School System, he used his influence to create a model corrective physical education program. As a lecturer in kinesiology and corrective physical education, Lowman influenced innumerable students, among whom were Claire Colestock and Hazel Cooper, who served as coauthors of his 1928 book.

Among Lowman's many books are *Balance Skills in Physical Education* (1935), *Technique of Underwater Gymnastics* (1937), *Therapeutic Use of Pools and Tanks* (1952), *Underwater Therapy* (1961), and *Postural Fitness* (1960). As is evident from these titles, Lowman was a pioneer in the development of hydrotherapy. Lowman's biography is preserved in a dissertation by Fornas (1968).

George Stafford earned the BPE degree at Springfield YMCA College in 1917, served in the Reconstruction Department of the U.S. Army, and then established a physiotherapy practice in Boston from 1919 to 1923. From there he went to the University of Illinois as Supervisor of Corrective Physical Education. In 1937 he completed a doctoral degree in physical education at New York University. Besides *Preventive and Corrective Physical Education* (1928), in which he acknowledges the influence of Lowman at various professional meetings, Stafford's best known book is *Sports for the Handicapped* (1939, 2nd ed. in 1947). His combined interest in sport and medicine helped to make the University of Illinois a leader in disabled sport.

In 1934, Josephine Rathbone of Teachers College,

Josephine Rathbone, author of *Corrective Physical Education*, the text most frequently used in teacher training from the 1930s to the late 1950s. Rathbone taught at Teachers College, Columbia University, from 1930 to 1957 and was instrumental in shaping the early history of both adapted physical education and physical therapy.

Columbia University, published her classic textbook *Corrective Physical Education*, which has endured through at least seven editions. Rathbone became interested in corrective physical education through involvement in physical therapy. A student at Wellesley College, she was influenced by Mary McMillan, the first president of the American Physiotherapy Association (1921–1923), and by physician Frank B. Granger, at the Boston City Hospital, who was both her teacher and coworker. Granger has been recognized as the "father and friend and promoter of the new profession" of physiotherapy (Hazenhyer, 1946). Rathbone taught at the Normal School in New Britain, Connecticut, and at Wellesley College before accepting a position at Teachers College, Columbia University, in the late 1920s. There she was to influence more teachers in the areas of corrective education, massage, and relaxation than perhaps anyone else in this country. Two of Rathbone's students, Evelyn Davies and Claudine Sherrill, subsequently authored textbooks and became leaders in adapted physical education.

The term *corrective physical education* endured from the 1920s through the 1950s. Rathbone's textbook underwent a number of revisions. Ellen Kelly, then chairman of the physical education department of the University of Oklahoma, wrote *Preventive and Corrective Physical Education*, published in 1950 and revised in 1958. *Correc-*

tive Therapy for the Handicapped Child, coauthored by Eleanor B. Stone and John W. Deyton, appeared in 1951.

Training of Correctives Specialists

Academia during this period was profoundly affected by the wars and the Great Depression. Leaders had typically served in either World War I or II or had been influenced by the rehabilitation movement and a new awareness that reconditioning techniques developed for war veterans could be applied to handicapped children as well. The training of specialists was primarily physical education in combination with physical or corrective therapy. The latter had arisen with the founding, in 1946, of the Association for Physical and Mental Rehabilitation, the forerunner of the American Corrective Therapy Association. Just as physical therapy developed with the reconstruction aides of World War I, corrective therapy was founded by the reconditioning specialists and physiotherapy aides of World War II. The need for separate organizations, looking back, is not exactly clear but may pertain to conflicts regarding minimal standards for training and certification. To meet war needs, numerous individuals were recruited into intensive, accelerated physical therapy training courses and assigned the U.S. Civil Service rating of Apprentice Physiotherapy Aide (Hazenhyer, 1946). The resulting workers were considered to be "in a subprofessional category" (Hazenhyer, 1946, p. 181). At the end of the war these individuals (and no doubt others) seem to be the ones who created the new corrective therapy organization. The employment setting for most corrective therapists was Veterans Hospitals, whereas physical therapists accepted positions in a variety of settings, including schools (Beard, 1961).

In the early 1940s physical therapists began a discussion of a "4-year course leading toward a degree so that physical therapy might stand alone, independent of physical education or nursing" (Hazenhyer, 1946, p. 178). By 1946 this was a reality, with 15 of 21 approved schools planning to offer such degrees. As physical therapy training gained independence from physical education, it gradually became a competitor for public school jobs. One factor operative in the employment of PTs in the public schools was the 1944 poliomyelitis epidemic, considered the worst in history. As children recovered from polio and returned to school with special health and exercise problems, individuals were needed who had experience with this disease. Physical therapy training concentrated on orthopedics and met this need. The evolution of physical therapy into a profession with a national headquarters and its own executive director is closely tied to polio; in 1944 the National Foundation for Infantile Paralysis awarded the grant that created its national office.

The era from 1930 to 1952 thus was a time of separation for physical educators and physical therapists. In 1952 the American Physical Therapy Association ceased to co-sponsor the joint annual meetings with the Therapeutics Section of the American Association for Health, Physical Education, and Recreation. Fewer and fewer physical educators had dual training. It appears also, perhaps because of the wars and the Depression, that fewer corrective physical educators were being employed in public schools (Clarke & Clarke, 1963).

Training of Regular Physical Educators

During the years from 1930 to 1952, it appears that the training of regular physical educators began to neglect the therapeutics and correctives aspects. Clarke (1948) reported a survey of 192 physical education training programs in which only 53% required a course in corrective physical education. The two national conferences on physical education professional preparation in 1948 (the Jackson's Mill Conference) and in 1950 (the Pere Marquette Conference) did not mention training in therapeutics and correctives in their reports. The Jackson's Mill Conference did, however, capture the intent of contemporary adapted physical education in the statement of some of its competencies to be developed through teacher training.

> Understand individual differences in children and youth which are especially significant to the learning of physical education activities and be able to adjust the teaching to meet these differences.

> Be able to adapt methods of instruction to different teaching situations as may be determined by available facilities and resources (National Conference, 1948, p. 21).

Harry A. Scott, Teachers College, Columbia University, as chairman of the physical education area at the Jackson's Mill Conference, was one of the first teacher trainers to emphasize *infusion* and *integration* of adapted physical education competency training into the professional preparation of regular physical educators. Ten years later (the mid-1950s) Scott served as the graduate advisor of Claudine Sherrill and was a tremendous influence in the shaping of her ideas about teacher education. Daniels and Davies (1965) lists Harry A. Scott, along with Charles Lowman, George Stafford, and Josephine Rathbone, as individuals who made major contributions to the adapted program.

Transition From Correctives to Adapted Physical Education

Legislative provisions for special education began to appear in the 1940s. The total enrollment of handicapped children and youth in day schools and classes, as well as residential facilities, was 441,820 during 1947–1948. The total number of handicapped individuals of school age was estimated as 4 million, with only about 11% receiving special education services (Daniels & Davies, 1965). With the growing awareness of these numbers came concern about the nature of teacher training required to serve such children. In 1946, the Therapeutics Section of the American Association for Health, Physical Education, and Recreation created a number of committees to study the problem and make recommendations (see chapter 4). This movement was led by H. Harrison Clarke, Syracuse University in New York, and Arthur Daniels, Ohio State University, who had served together in the Physical Reconditioning Branch of the Army Air Force in World War II. The Therapeutics Section study led to the changing of terminology from correctives to adapted physical education and to the development and publication of adapted physical education guidelines (Bishop, 1963). These changes began in 1952 and are discussed in the next section of this chapter.

Sport for the Handicapped

The inevitable use of sport, dance, and aquatics in hospitals as part of the total rehabilitation of veterans led to a whole new concept of public school physical education for students with handicapping conditions. George T. Stafford's classic book *Sports for the Handicapped*, published in 1939 and again in 1947, attracted attention to the innovative use of sport and other recreational activities in the total rehabilitation of handicapped students at the University of Illinois, which even today is well known for its leadership in the education of the handicapped.

Also at the University of Illinois was Tim Nugent, Director of Student Rehabilitation and coach of its wheelchair basketball team, the Gizz Kids. Nugent conducted the first wheelchair basketball tournament in the United States in 1949 and was instrumental in the organization of the National Wheelchair Basketball Association (Labanowich, 1975).

This early sport for the handicapped movement seemed to interest recreators more than physical educators, perhaps because the activities focused on adults, mainly war veterans, rather than school-aged youth. Thus coaching and sport administration for handicapped individuals were not assimilated into adapted physical education professional preparation until much later.

Influence of Parents

In 1950 the National Association for Retarded Citizens (NARC) was founded. Its early membership was comprised primarily of parents of retarded children and youth who wanted to keep their offspring at home rather than conforming to the widespread practice of institutionalization. The research of psychoanalyst Rene Spitz (1945) was influential in this beginning advocacy movement by parents. Spitz's research showed high mortality rates and greater retardation among normal infants placed in foundling homes compared to those reared by their own mothers in prison nurseries.

In ensuing years NARC initiated litigation and influenced legislation that affected professional preparation in adapted physical education. As increasing numbers of retarded youth remained with their parents in the community, special education gained status as a profession and sought to improve public school education for retarded students (Aiello, 1976).

First Research on Professional Preparation

The first nationwide survey of professional preparation in corrective physical education appears to have been completed by Evelyn Davies (1950), a doctoral candidate

Evelyn Davies, of the Daniels and Davies textbook, *Adapted Physical Education*, who directed the adapted physical education training program at Indiana University from 1958 to 1982. A graduate student of Josephine Rathbone, Davies was both a physical therapist and a physical educator.

under Rathbone at Teachers College, Columbia University. Entitled *An Analysis of Corrective Physical Education in Schools With Implications for Teacher Education*, the dissertation included findings on curricula of 23 institutions that offered specializations in corrective physical education. Evelyn Davies, who was a physical therapist as well as a correctives specialist, in later years achieved considerable recognition as director of the teacher training program in adapted physical education at Indiana University. She became author of *The Elementary School Child and His Posture Patterns* and coauthor, with Daniels, of *Adapted Physical Education*.

Research

The period from 1930 to 1951 marks the beginning of research as we know it today. Studies in adapted physical education conducted during these years are identified by Pyfer (1986). The earliest research, reflecting the knowledge base of the era, was primarily on posture, dysmenorrhea, and fitness. The first special population to be investigated in relation to motor abilities was the deaf (Long, 1932; Morsh, 1936). In 1948 David Brace of the University of Texas at Austin published a paper on motor learning of feeble-minded girls. In 1950 Charles Buell published the findings of his dissertation on the motor performance of visually handicapped children. These early studies, however, seemed not to contribute much to the content of courses being taught in colleges and universities. Research was not yet a vital part of teacher training.

Summary

In summary, teacher training in therapeutics and correctives during the 1930 to 1951 era was sluggish except for the last 4 to 5 years, during which the Therapeutics Section initiated study that effected profound change in the 1950s. The textbooks that dominated these years were primarily written in the 1920s and 1930s, heralding the transition from medical gymnastics to corrective exercise and posture education. Leaders were mainly Charles Lowman, George Stafford, Josephine Rathbone, Ellen Kelly, and Harry A. Scott, with H. Harrison Clarke, Arthur Daniels, and Evelyn Davies beginning to gain visibility. During this period physical therapy matured as a profession and separated itself from physical education.

Stage 4—Professional Preparation From 1952 to 1966

During this stage emphasis in corrective and adapted physical education professional preparation gradually broadened from normal children with health, postural, or fitness problems to those with handicapping conditions. This paralleled the strengthening of special education as a profession and the trend toward educating handicapped children and youth in public schools rather than in residential facilities. The year 1952 marked the first major study of personnel preparation in special education in the United States (Connor, 1976). In conjunction with this research by the U.S. Department of Education, 122 colleges and universities were identified as offering special education specialization sequences. Most frequently offered were programs in speech and hearing (67), mental retardation (40), deaf (22), and crippled (13) specializations.

Changing Terms and Definitions

The year 1952 also marked the official adoption of the term *adapted physical education* in place of *corrective physical education*. This change can be traced back to the appointment of a national committee in 1946 to consider alternative ways of serving handicapped students in the public schools. The committee, led by H. Harrison Clarke, Springfield College (1946–53), was appointed by the chairman of the Therapeutics Section of the American Association for Health, Physical Education, and Recreation (see chapter 4 for details). The efforts of this ad hoc committee resulted in the publication of a document written by Arthur Daniels, Ohio State University, entitled *Guiding Principles for Adapted Physical Education in Elementary and Secondary Schools and Colleges*, which was approved by the Board of Directors of AAHPER and endorsed by the Joint Committee on Health Problems in Education of the American Medical Association and the National Education Association.

The following definition of adapted physical education was part of this document:

> Adapted physical education is a diversified program of developmental activities, games, sports, and rhythms suited to the interests, capacities, and limitations of students with disabilities who may not safely or successfully engage in unrestricted participation in the vigorous activities of the general physical education program. (Committee on Adapted Physical Education, 1952)

Textbooks Using Adapted Physical Education in Their Titles

Textbooks are a major influence on professional preparation, and several new books highlighted work with handicapped students. In 1954, Arthur S. Daniels published the first textbook to incorporate the term *adapted physical education* into its title: *Adapted Physical Education: Principles and Practices of Physical Education for Exceptional Students*. Radically different from previous publications in the profession, the book included chapters on body mechanics problems, amputations, rheumatic fever, cardiac conditions, cerebral palsy, epilepsy, poliomyelitis, visual and auditory handicaps, and other conditions requiring special services. Daniels, whose approach was shaped partly by World War II experience and partly by his work with the Therapeutics Section, had earned the doctoral degree at Teachers College, Columbia. There he was influenced both by Harry A. Scott and Josephine Rathbone. As president of AAHPER in 1961–1962, Art Daniels is the only adapted physical education/therapeutics/correctives textbook writer to have this honor other than R. Tait McKenzie in 1912–1915. During his major leadership years, Daniels taught at Ohio State University and Indiana University.

Numerous other authors followed his example. In 1960 Hollis Fait of the University of Connecticut published his first edition of *Adapted Physical Education*, which has now undergone a name change and several revisions. This was the first text since R. Tait McKenzie's *Exercise in Education and Medicine* to include a chapter on mental retardation. As such, it was a tremendous influence in broadening the scope of adapted physical education. Fait's doctoral degree was earned under Charles H. McCloy at

H. Harrison Clarke, a pioneer who emphasized the developmental aspects of adapted physical education, and who taught at Syracuse University (1930-1946), Springfield College (1946-1953), and University of Oregon (1953-1972).

the University of Iowa; there he rounded out a strong liberal arts background that enabled him to author or co-author 23 books on numerous topics. Most of Fait's professional life was spent at the University of Connecticut, from 1954 until his untimely death in 1984. Fait was one of the first university professors to offer courses and practica in conjunction with a state school for mentally retarded individuals; his writing, teaching, and other contributions reflected a rich association with the Mansfield State Training School.

H. Harrison Clarke, who had moved to Oregon, and his son David Clarke, then at the University of California at Berkeley, published *Developmental and Adapted Physical Education* in 1963. This textbook emphasized the role of measurement and evaluation in adapted physical education and introduced the reader to the case study approach. H. Harrison Clarke earned his doctoral degree from Syracuse University in New York and attributes much of his interest in underdeveloped and muscularly weak children to Frederick Rand Rogers, who was state director of physical education in New York. After completing his doctoral study, Clarke taught at Syracuse University, Springfield College, and University of Oregon, respectively.

Textbooks by Other Titles

The explosion of knowledge from 1952 to 1967 resulted in the publication of several other textbooks with various titles. In 1965 Ellen Kelly's third edition of her 1950 textbook bore the title *Adapted and Corrective Physical Education*. Among the new books were the following:

- 1962—*The Science of Physical Education for Handicapped Children*, by Donald K. Matthews, Ohio State University; Robert Kruse, School of Physical Therapy, Cleveland Clinic; and Virginia Shaw, Washington State University.

- 1964—*Adaptations of Muscular Activity*, by Gene Logan, then at Southwest Missouri State College.

- 1966—*A Practical Program of Remedial Physical Education*, by Grover Mueller, executive director of the American College of Sports Medicine and former director of the Division of Physical and Health Education of the Philadelphia Public Schools, and Josephine Cristaldi, Supervisor of Remedial Physical Education of the Philadelphia Public Schools.

In 1966, on the second edition of his textbook, Hollis Fait changed the title to *Special Physical Education*. This action reflects the growing emphasis in the 1960s on special populations and coordination of efforts with special education. It also indicates a trend toward conceptualizing our specialization as pertaining to individuals with handicapped conditions rather than encompassing the psychomotor problems of the entire population. The pendulum had begun to swing to the opposite extreme, from "normal" students with problems that prevented safe and successful participation in regular physical education to handicapped or special education students. Only Josephine Rathbone, then retired and residing in Springfield, Massachusetts, with her husband Peter Karpovich, a well-known authority in exercise physiology and sports

Hollis Fait, University of Connecticut, discussing the future of adapted physical education with Janet Wessel, Michigan State University. Fait coined the term *Special Physical Education*. Wessel developed the I CAN model.

medicine, remained steadfast in her retention of the term *Corrective Physical Education* as the title of revisions of her textbook first published in 1934. In this book Rathbone states,

> Correctives is not a narrow field. The scope of the work is much greater than most people envision. It is not just a few exercises for strengthening specific muscles, or a method of training a person to stand in perfect balance. It includes consideration of the athlete, to protect him from injury and strain, and bring him back to normal functioning again if he is hurt. It even includes helping the ill-formed and otherwise physically handicapped person to get as much joy out of living as possible. The scope of "correctives" involves consideration of the individual at different stages in development, and includes every known physiological and psychological aid to bring a person to a high level of accomplishment. (Rathbone & Hunt, 1965, pp. 2–3)

Status of Adapted Physical Education Personnel Preparation

In 1964 Agnes M. Hooley of Bowling Green State University of Ohio reported certification and course work practices in adapted physical education teacher preparation (Hooley, 1964). The findings were reported also in her textbook (Wheeler & Hooley, 1969). In this study, questionnaires were addressed to the Education Director of each state and to the Physical Education Director in every National Council for Accreditation of Teacher Education (NCATE)-or American Association of Colleges for Teacher Education (AACTE)-accredited institution offering degrees in health, physical education, and recreation ($n = 260$).

Of the 47 state Education Directors (94%) who responded, 34 indicated that their states neither required nor strongly recommended an adapted physical education course for their undergraduate physical education majors. Adapted physical education was required in 10 states, while 3 states strongly recommended the course. In states where the course was not required, some institutions nevertheless required it for graduation.

Of the 260 universities surveyed, 245 administrators (94%) responded. Approximately 40% did not require an adapted physical education course, 39% required an adapted physical education or adapted and corrective physical education course, 17% required corrective physical education, and 4% combined correctives and adapted physical education with kinesiology. Hooley reported that field experiences in adapted physical education were required by 121 departments (49%). These included work with handicapped students in the following settings: area organizations or hospitals (43); regular or remedial college courses (40); area schools (35); and camps (3). From her findings, Hooley indicated that professional educators needed to take immediate action in determining acceptable adapted physical education professional preparation. A need also existed to establish criteria to be met by personnel who teach adapted physical education theory courses in teacher training institutions.

Early Practica in Personnel Preparation

Warren Johnson, University of Maryland, College Park, is generally accredited with beginning the first organized practicum training for undergraduates in working with handicapped children and youth. Johnson began the Children's Physical Development Clinic in 1957 with 26 handicapped children and 12 student-clinicians (Johnson, 1971). The purpose of this clinic originally was community service rather than teacher training. Throughout the 1950s and 1960s university professors in all parts of the country initiated physical education, recreation, and camping programs for mentally retarded children. Often as a result of this community service, interest on campus led to the creation of course work and programs of study in adapted physical education. Whenever the word *clinic* was used to describe practica, the influence more than likely could be traced to Warren Johnson. Among the graduates of the University of Maryland who started similar programs were Louis Bowers, University of South Florida; Ernie Bundschuh, University of Georgia; Ricardo Chavez, Colorado State University; and Glenn Roswal, Jacksonville State University in Alabama.

Influence of Research on Personnel Preparation

Several leaders in contemporary adapted physical education first became known through their research on mental retardation. Their studies had a direct influence on the shaping of university courses on physical education and recreation for the mentally retarded.

G. Lawrence Rarick, then at the University of Wisconsin in Madison, was largely responsible for the research (Francis & Rarick, 1959) that revealed mentally retarded children to be 2 to 4 years behind their normal peers in motor performance. An expert in motor development, Rarick conducted numerous studies from 1959 on that enriched our knowledge base. Consequently he was present, usually as a speaker or a consultant, at most of the meetings and conferences pertaining to adapted physical education teacher training for almost a quarter of a century.

Julian Stein's first national visibility came from the publication of the related literature (1963) for his doc-

Warren Johnson, University of Maryland, whose Children's Physical Development Clinic is considered the first organized practica training in adapted physical education (top). Johnson's first and last doctoral advisees (bottom). Left, Ernest Bundschuh, University of Georgia; right, Glenn Roswal, Jacksonville State University in Alabama.

toral dissertation (1966b). In this first publication Stein focused attention on the motor function and physical fitness of mentally retarded individuals by reviewing 70 books and articles on the topic. Stein's interest in adapted physical education was sparked initially by Cecil (Cy) Morgan, a career army man stationed at the Pentagon who was a contemporary of H. Harrison Clarke and Arthur Daniels. Morgan had worked closely with these leaders on the AAHPER Therapeutics Section in the late 1940s

in shaping the direction of the new adapted physical education. Now he was moonlighting by teaching a course entitled Kinesiology of Sport for the Atypical at George Washington University. The young Julian Stein found this course fascinating and applied its content to instructing mentally retarded students in his high school in Fairfax, Virginia. These students subsequently served as Stein's subjects for a 442-page dissertation entitled *Physical Fitness in Relation to Intelligence Quotient, Social Distance, and Physique of Intermediate School Mentally Retarded Boys*. This dissertation was completed in 1966 at George Peabody College for Teachers in Tennessee, an institution well known in the 1960s for its excellence in special education. Stein, in the meantime, had been employed by the University of Rhode Island; from there he became Director of the AAHPER Project on Programs for the Mentally Retarded.

The research of James Oliver (1958), of the University of Birmingham, England, was located by Julian Stein in his review of literature for the dissertation. Oliver's study was the first to document that mentally retarded students could profit from physical education instruction. Correspondence between Stein and Oliver led to Oliver's traveling to the United States and conducting a number of teacher training workshops. Oliver's work influenced W. Owen Corder of George Peabody College to undertake a similar study using a Hawthorne group (Corder, 1966).

Other early researchers included Hollis Fait and Harriet Kupferer (1956), Clifford Howe (1959), Wayne Sengstock (1966), Frank Hayden (1966), David Auxter (1966), and David Brace (1968). Research during these years not only revealed the need for better physical education service delivery to handicapped students but also constituted the beginning of a knowledge base specifically in adapted physical education. In writing textbooks, adapted physical education leaders increasingly could rely upon research in their own discipline rather than that of special education or the therapies.

Influence of the Kennedy Family

An important force in personnel preparation in adapted physical education in the 1960s was the Joseph P. Kennedy, Jr. Foundation (Laprioloa, 1972, 1973; Sherrill, 1986). This foundation provided the impetus for the establishment of the Unit on Programs for the Handicapped, first designated as the Task Force on Programs for the Mentally Retarded, as an integral part of AAHPER in 1965. This unit, directed by Robert L. Holland in 1965, and by Julian U. Stein from 1966 until 1981, has cooperated in and/or conducted most of the professional preparation conferences and needs assessment studies over the years. Funded heavily in the 1960s by the Kennedy Foundation, the work of the Unit on the Handicapped in the early years is difficult to separate from that of the Kennedy Foundation.

Among the earliest references to personnel training in physical education for the handicapped are the speeches that appeared in the *Proceedings of the Seminars on Physical Education and Recreation for the Mentally Retarded* held May 1 through May 10, 1967, in Dallas, Texas;

Atlanta, Georgia; and Greensboro, North Carolina. The objectives of these seminars were as follows:

- To provide information, "take home materials," and practical workshop experience for college faculty preparing teachers for physical education and special education and state level consultants who advise public schools on physical or special education programs.

- To introduce physical education and recreation content into teacher education programs for the mentally retarded and mental retardation content into physical education and recreation teacher education programs.

- To introduce physical education and recreation activities into local school programs for the mentally retarded through state planned and implemented workshops conducted by seminar participants. (Joseph P. Kennedy, Jr. Foundation, 1967, p. iii)

Speakers on professional preparation at these seminars included G. Lawrence (Larry) Rarick, Julian U. Stein, James N. Oliver, and several special educators. Among the strongest proponents of special teacher training for persons working with handicapped children and youth was Rarick, who stated,

> With our knowledge of the motor characteristics of the mentally retarded, and our present understanding of how to deal with the retardate in the gymnasium, in the swimming pool, on the playground and in his general recreational activities, it is our conviction that we need to put this knowledge to work through teachers specially trained to work in programs of physical education for the retarded. This, we believe, can be accomplished with minor modifications in the curricula of our teacher training programs. (Joseph P. Kennedy, Jr. Foundation, 1967, p. 57)

Summary

In summary, the era from 1952 to 1966 was characterized by great diversity in professional preparation. AAHPER officially adopted the term *adapted physical education* to replace correctives, and new textbooks by Daniels (1954), Fait (1960), and Clarke and Clarke (1963) emphasized vastly different content from earlier books. Many university teachers were unfamiliar with the new textbooks and emerging trends and continued to teach as they had been taught. The national survey (Hooley, 1964) of administrators in 260 universities revealed that 56% required an adapted physical education or adapted and corrective physical education course. Public schools largely continued to call their programs by such terms as corrective, remedial, rehabilitative, and modified. As awareness of handicapped children in public schools heightened, physical education leaders began to initiate programs of physical education and recreation for them; these were largely conceptualized as community service projects rather than teacher training practica. Research began to influence the shaping of the knowledge base underlying adapted physical education. The AAHPER Project on Programs for the Mentally Retarded was begun in 1965. Among the leaders most influential from 1952 to 1966 were Arthur Daniels, Hollis Fait, H. Harrison Clarke, Evelyn Davies, Warren Johnson, Larry Rarick, Julian Stein, Robert Holland, James Oliver, and Frank Hayden. French and Jansma (1982) summarize this stage as follows:

> Before the 1960s, the role of the special physical educator was that of teaching segregated classes in regular schools, or in special schools and residential institutions. Trained as regular physical educators, these teachers might have taken one introductory course in the area of special physical education. They were, therefore, compelled to study independently; most were essentially self-taught. It was not until 1966 that a concerted effort to prepare special physical educators began. (p. 351)

References

Aiello, B. (1976). Especially for special educators: A sense of our own history. *Exceptional Children, 42*(5), 244–251.

Auxter, D. (1966). Strength and flexibility of differentially diagnosed educable mentally retarded boys. *Research Quarterly, 37,* 455–461.

Bancroft, J. (1913). *The posture of school children.* New York: Macmillan.

Barr, M.W. (no date). *Mental defectives.* New York: Blakiston & Sons.

Beard, G. (1961). A review of the first forty years in terms of education, practice, and research. *Physical Therapy Review, 41*(12), 843–861.

Bishop, R. (1963). *The origin and development of adapted physical education in the United States.* Unpublished doctoral dissertation, Indiana University, Bloomington.

Brace, D. (1948). Motor learning of feeble-minded girls. *Research Quarterly, 19,* 269–275.

Brace, D. (1968). Physical education and recreation of mentally retarded pupils in public schools. *Research Quarterly, 39,* 779–782.

Buell, C. (1966). *Physical education for blind children.* Springfield, IL: Charles C. Thomas.

Bundschuh, E. (1986). The national consortium on physical education and recreation: Addressing a need. *Adapted Physical Activity Quarterly, 3*(2), 147–151.

Clarke, H.H. (1948, April). Select your physical educator with care. *Education, 68*(8), 463.

Clarke, H.H., & Clarke, D. (1963). *Developmental and adapted physical education.* Englewood Cliffs, NJ: Prentice-Hall.

Committee on Adapted Physical Education. (1952). Guiding principles for adapted physical education. *Journal of Health, Physical Education, and Recreation, 23,* 15.

Connor, F. (1976). The past is prologue: Teacher preparation in special education. *Exceptional Children, 42*(7), 366–378.

Corder, W. (1966). Effects of physical education on the intellectual, physical and social development of educable mentally retarded boys. *Exceptional Children, 32,* 357–364.

Daniels, A. (1954). *Adapted physical education.* New York: Harper & Row.

Daniels, D., & Davies, E. (1965). *Adapted physical education.* New York: Harper & Row. (Originally published in 1954)

Davies, E. (1950). *An analysis of corrective physical education in schools with implications for teacher education.* Unpublished doctoral dissertation, Columbia University, New York.

DePauw, K. (1986). Merger of special populations programs within the American Alliance for Health, Physical Education, Recreation and Dance. *Adapted Physical Activity Quarterly, 3*(2), 139–141.

Drew, L.C. (1922). *Individual gymnastics: A handbook of corrective and remedial gymnastics.* Philadelphia: Lea & Febiger.

Duffy, J. (1976). *The healers: The rise of the medical establishment.* New York: McGraw-Hill.

Fait, H. (1960). *Adapted physical education.* Philadelphia: W.B. Saunders.

Fait, H., & Kupferer, H. (1956). A study of two motor achievement tests and its implications in planning physical education activities for the mentally retarded. *American Journal of Mental Deficiency, 60,* 729–732.

Fornas, V. (1968). *Charles L. Lowman: His role in physical education.* Unpublished doctoral dissertation, University of Southern California, Los Angeles.

Francis, R.J., & Rarick, G.L. (1959). Motor characteristics of the mentally retarded. *American Journal of Mental Deficiency, 63*, 792–811.

French, R., & Jansma, P. (1982). *Special physical education.* Columbus: Charles E. Merrill.

Goodwin, L. (1986). AAHPERD: Addressing the needs of the handicapped. *Adapted Physical Activity Quarterly, 3*(2), 127–132.

Gour, A. (1916). *The therapeutics of activity.* Chicago: Author.

Hayden, F. (1964). *Physical fitness for mentally retarded.* Toronto: Metropolitan Toronto Association for Mentally Retarded.

Hazenhyer, I.M. (1946). A history of the American Physiotherapy Association. *The Physiotherapy Review, 26*(1), 3–14.

Hillman, W. (1986). The role of the federal government in adapted physical education. *Adapted Physical Activity Quarterly, 3*(2), 124-126.

Hooley, A.M. (1964). *A study of certification and course work practices in the preparation of teachers for the area of adapted physical education.* Unpublished manuscript, Bowling Green State University, Bowling Green, OH.

Hopkins, H., & Smith, H. (1978). *Willard and Spackman's occupational therapy* (5th ed.). Philadelphia: J.B. Lippincott.

Howe, C. (1959). A comparison of motor skills of mentally retarded and normal children. *Exceptional Children, 25*, 352–355.

Hunter, A. (1950). *R. Tait McKenzie: Pioneer in physical education.* Unpublished doctoral study, Teachers College, Columbia University, New York.

Johnson, L. (1986). The need for a national consortium. *Adapted Physical Activity Quarterly, 3*(2), 143–146.

Johnson, W. (1971). Children's physical development clinic. In American Association for Health, Physical Education, and Recreation (Ed.), *The best of challenge* (Vol. 1, pp. 102–103). Washington, DC: AAHPERD.

Joseph P. Kennedy, Jr. Foundation. (1967). *Proceedings of the seminars on physical education and recreation for the mentally retarded.* Washington, DC: Author.

Labanowich, S. (1975). *Wheelchair basketball: A history of the national association and an analysis of the structure.* Unpublished doctoral dissertation, University of Illinois, Urbana.

Lapriola, E.M. (1972). *The Joseph P. Kennedy, Jr. Foundation and its role in physical education and recreation for the mentally retarded.* Unpublished master's thesis, University of Maryland, College Park.

Lapriola, E. (1973). The Joseph P. Kennedy, Jr. Foundation and its role in physical education and recreation for the mentally retarded. *Therapeutic Recreation Journal, 7*(2), 13.

Lee, M., & Bennett, B. (1985). Alliance centennial— 100 years of health, physical education, recreation, and dance. *Journal of Physical Education, Recreation, and Dance, 56*(4), 17–67.

Licht, S. (1961). *Therapeutic exercise.* New Haven: Elizabeth Licht.

Lippitt, L. (1923). *A manual of corrective gymnastics.* New York: Macmillan.

Long, J. (1932). *Motor abilities of deaf children.* New York: Teachers College, Columbia University.

Lowman, C., Colestock, C., & Cooper, H. (1928). *Corrective physical education for groups.* New York: A.S. Barnes.

Mackie, R. (1945). *Crippled children in American education.* New York: Bureau of Publications, Teachers College, Columbia University.

Massengale, J., & Sage, G. (1982). Departmental prestige and career mobility patterns of college physical educators. *Research Quarterly for Exercise and Sport, 53*(4), 305–312.

McKenzie, R.T. (1923). *Exercise in education and medicine* (3rd ed.). Philadelphia: W.B. Saunders. (Originally published in 1909)

Morsh, J.E. (1936). Motor performance of the deaf. *Comparative Psychological Monographs, 13*, 1–51.

National Conference on Undergraduate Professional Preparation in Health Education, Physical Education, and Recreation. (1948, May 16–27). Report of Conference held at Jackson's Mill, Weston, West Virginia.

Nissen, H. (1892). *ABC of Swedish educational gymnastics.* New York: Educational Publishing.

Nissen, H. (1903). *Rational home gymnastics.* Boston: E.H. Bacon.

Nissen, H. (1916). *Practical massage and corrective exercise.* Philadelphia: F.A. Davis.

Nixon, J. (1967). The criteria of a discipline. *Quest, 9*, 42–48.

Oliver, J. (1958). The effect of physical conditioning exercises and activities on the mental characteristics of educationally subnormal boys. *British Journal of Educational Psychology, 28*, 155–165.

Posse, N. (1891). *Handbook of school gymnastics of the Swedish system.* Boston: Lothrop, Lee, & Shepard.

Posse, N. (1894). *The Swedish system of educational gymnastics* (2nd ed.). Boston: Lea & Febiger. (Originally published in 1890)

Posse, N. (1901). *The special kinesiology of educational gymnastics*. Boston: Lea & Febiger.

Pyfer, J. (1986). Early research concerns in adapted physical education, 1930–1969. *Adapted Physical Activity Quarterly, 3*(2), 95–103.

Rathbone, J., & Hunt, V. (1965). *Corrective physical education* (7th ed.). Philadelphia: W.B. Saunders.

Sengstock, W. (1966). Fitness of mentally retarded boys. *Research Quarterly, 37*, 113–120.

Sherrill, C. (1986). *Adapted physical education and recreation: A multidisciplinary approach* (3rd ed.). Dubuque, IA: Wm. C. Brown.

Snyder, R., & Scott, H.A. (1954). *Professional preparation in health, physical education, and recreation*. New York: McGraw Hill.

Spitz, R.Z. (1945). Hospitalism: An inquiry into the genesis of psychiatric conditions in early childhood. *Psychoanalytic studies of the child* (Vol. 1). New York: International Universities Press.

Stafford, G. (1928). *Preventive and corrective physical education*. New York: A.S. Barnes.

Stafford, G. (1939). *Sports for the handicapped*. New York: Prentice-Hall.

Stein, J. (1963). Motor function and physical fitness of the mentally retarded. *Rehabilitation Literature, 24*, 230–263.

Stein, J. (1966). *Physical fitness in relation to intelligence quotient, social distance, and physique of intermediate school mentally retarded boys*. Unpublished doctoral dissertation, George Peabody College for Teachers.

Stein, J. (1986). AAHPER(D) unit on programs for the handicapped. *Adapted Physical Activity Quarterly, 3*(2), 133-138.

Weston, A. (1962). *The making of American physical education*. New York: Appleton-Century-Crofts.

Wheeler, R., & Hooley, A.M. (1969). *Physical education for the handicapped*. Philadelphia: Lea & Febiger.

Wide, A. (1899). *Handbook of medical gymnastics*. London: Sampson Low, Marston & Co.

Williams, J.F. (1922). *The organization and administration of physical education*. New York: Macmillan.

Chapter 3

Contemporary Adapted Physical Education Teacher Training: A History Beginning With 1967

Claudine Sherrill

*T*he year 1967 was selected to begin the contemporary era of adapted physical education because it marks the enactment of PL 90-170, Title V, the first legislation to mandate funding specifically in professional preparation in physical education and recreation for handicapped persons. According to Hillman (1986), PL 90-170 has had a greater influence on adapted physical educators than PL 94-142 (see appendix for chronology of laws). To understand the impact of PL 90-170 and subsequent legislation, it is important to review the status quo in the mid-1960s.

Status of Adapted Physical Education in the Mid-1960s

Approximately 50% of the colleges and universities that prepared physical education teachers required a course in adapted physical education (Flint, 1967). These courses pertained primarily to posture problems, physical disabilities, and medical conditions. Only 12% of the institutions surveyed ($N = 170$) offered graduate work in adapted physical education with the course offerings ranging from 1 to 20 semester units (Flint, 1967). Clearly, adapted physical education was well established as a course but was not considered a possible preservice specialization in the mid-1960s.

In-service training, however, had been conceptualized as a means of exposing experienced college teachers to physical education for the handicapped. Two innovative college programs received federal funding for specialization training in physical education for handicapped students in the early 1960s. The first (Buttonwood Farms) brought together such future adapted physical education leaders as Leon Johnson, Lane Goodwin, John Dunn, and Steve Klesius, and the second (Colorado State College) influenced leaders such as Dolores Geddes (see glossary of leaders in the appendix).

The earliest federally funded teacher training program in physical education for handicapped students appears to be the Buttonwood Farms—Temple University Project, which was funded from 1964 through 1974 by the National Institute of Mental Health (NIMH). This 8-week summer training program for college and university personnel involved practica experience with emotionally disturbed and mentally retarded children and work on adapted physical education curriculum development.

The program was directed by Lester Mann and William Phillips of Buttonwood Farms, Inc., Philadelphia, and Harold Jack and Donald Hilsendager of the Department of Health, Physical Education, and Recreation at Temple University. Hilsendager, Jack, and Mann are remembered for their Basic Motor Fitness Test for Emotionally Disturbed and Mentally Handicapped Children, published in

1968, which now serves as the basis for PROJECT ACTIVE (Vodola, 1976) assessment. Temple University thus became an early leader in adapted physical education.

The other early federally funded program was the Experienced Teacher Fellowship Program in Physical Education and Recreation for the Handicapped at Colorado State College (now the University of Northern Colorado) in Greeley. During 1966–1967 13 graduate students, including Dolores Geddes, completed this training, which was funded by the U.S. Office of Education. The grant director was Vince Cyphers, who still teaches at the University of Northern Colorado, mainly in outdoor education.

Most universities, however, had no federal funding and no adapted physical education specialization training. Some, like George Peabody College in Nashville, Tennessee, permitted students to develop individualized doctoral programs by electing courses from both the special education and physical education departments. Among the first to do this was Julian Stein, who received his doctoral degree from George Peabody in 1966. This college was later recognized for its excellence by the creation of the Joseph P. Kennedy, Jr. Foundation Visiting Professors program. In the 1970s the new adapted physical education specialization was directed by Cy Morgan.

The status of public school physical education affects university teacher training and vice versa. In the 1960s several states had well-developed programs of adapted physical education service delivery. Pennsylvania, Michigan, Tennessee, Illinois, and Nebraska indicated they had a state physical education requirement for the handicapped (Flint, 1967). California and South Carolina, while reporting no requirement, emphasized that they strongly encouraged schools to provide such services. Nineteen of 29 states surveyed by Seaman (cited by Flint, 1967) indicated that their state physical education requirement would apply to physically handicapped individuals. Flanagan (1969), in describing the Pennsylvania service delivery program, indicated that 89% and 58% of the public secondary and elementary schools, respectively, had ongoing programs of adapted physical education. These services were in compliance with a 1963 state board of education regulation that required adapted physical education to be provided for physically handicapped and physically underdeveloped students.

Little attention was given to mentally retarded students; presumably many were integrated into regular physical education. Barney Anooshian (1961), perhaps the first physical educator to conduct research on such integration, reported that 66% of California high school physical education teachers ($N = 96$) believed that integration of mentally retarded and normal students was good and should continue. Some cities and states, however, provided no services. A national survey conducted in 1966 by Brace (1968) revealed that nearly one third of

Historical moments. Julian Stein, director of the AAHPER Unit on Programs for the Handicapped, illustrating tire activities at a teacher training workshop emphasizing inexpensive, homemade equipment in the early 1970s (top left); Ernie Lange, University of Mexico, and Lane Goodwin, University of Wisconsin at LaCrosse, at one of the many Midwest Conferences on Physical Education and Recreation for the Handicapped at LaCrosse (top right). Mrs. Eunice Shriver and Kyle Rote, Jr. encouraging Special Olympians (bottom).

the mentally retarded children in U.S. elementary schools received no physical education. Supported by a grant from the Joseph P. Kennedy, Jr. Foundation, Brace's research also solicited opinions about teacher training. Brace summarized these findings as follows:

> There is from 85–95 percent agreement that physical education teachers who have mentally retarded children in classes should have some professional preparation for work with the mentally retarded. There is an equally strong feeling that all teachers of the mentally retarded should have a basic understanding of physical education and recreation. There is an almost unanimous opinion that colleges and universities should have courses in physical education and recreation for workers with mentally retarded pupils in public schools. (Brace, 1968, p. 781)

This research and the growing national awareness of mental retardation led to authorization of the first federal funding specifically in physical education for the handicapped.

First Federal Legislation in Physical Education for the Handicapped

PL 90-170, the Mental Retardation Facilities and Community Mental Health Centers Construction Act, was passed in 1967. Title V of this act authorized the U.S. Department of Health, Education, and Welfare to make grants to colleges and universities for personnel preparation and research in physical education for the handicapped. This legislation was introduced by Senator Ted Kennedy of Massachusetts, whose sister Rose was mentally retarded. The Joseph P. Kennedy, Jr. Foundation was largely instrumental in gaining the Congressional support needed to pass this law (Hillman, 1986) and to sustain interest in physical education and recreation for the handicapped during the next 2 decades. Today's federal funding of teacher training programs can be traced directly to PL 90-170 via PL 91-230, as amended by PL 93-380, Part D, the Education of the Handicapped Act (EHA), and subsequent authorization and appropriation legislation. EHA should not be confused with the Education for All Handicapped Children Act, PL 94-142.

Although authorized, monies were not actually appropriated until 1969 (Burke, 1976). The influence of this legislation on teacher training in adapted physical education was summarized by Hillman (1981) as follows:

> In 1969 the total funding for both areas (physical education and recreation) was $300,000,

sixteen programs supported, emphasis was on planning and development. In 1980 total funding of approximately 3.89 million dollars, 91 programs funded . . . approximately 1.5 million dollars has been targeted for pre- and in-service activities in physical education. (p. 57)

The First Graduate Training Programs

Of the 16 programs supported in 1969, nine developed specialization training in physical education for the handicapped:

Institution	Program Director
Ohio State University	Walt Ersing
University of South Florida	Lou Bowers
University of Missouri	Leon Johnson
University of California at Berkeley	Lawrence Rarick
Indiana State University at Terre Haute	Dolores Geddes
University of Texas	Lynn McCraw
Southern Connecticut State College	Edith DeBonis
University of South Carolina	Walter Hambrick
George Washington University	Honey Nashman

Writers of these first grant proposals and shapers of the resulting graduate curricula became the leaders of the new adapted physical education. Ersing, Bowers, Johnson, Rarick, and Geddes (see glossary in appendix) particularly gained prominence through their service in professional organizations and influence of thousands of university students through teaching and research. Additionally, Rarick and Geddes authored a number of books.

In 1970 Hollis Fait of the University of Connecticut and David Auxter of Slippery Rock State College in Pennsylvania joined the ranks of the grant writers and program directors. Their leadership in professional preparation is well known. These individuals and the other pioneer grant writers all had doctoral degrees in physical education or education; none had medical backgrounds or extensive experience in working with handicapped children and youth.

Early Accomplishments

By 1970 several accomplishments in program development could be documented: (a) the beginning of university courses on physical education and recreation for the mentally retarded; (b) the beginning of graduate level specialization in adapted physical education; and (c) the evolution of perceptual motor training as an aspect of physical education. Two new textbooks published in 1969 helped to shape course content:

- *Principles and Methods of Adapted Physical Education* by David Auxter of Slippery Rock and Daniel Arnheim and Walter Crowe of California State College at Long Beach

- *Physical Education for the Handicapped* by Ruth Wheeler of Ohio State University and Agnes Hooley of Bowling Green University in Ohio

The knowledge base was broadening.

University Training in Physical Education for the Mentally Retarded

The Joseph P. Kennedy, Jr. Foundation played a large role in the early training of physical educators and recreators to work with mentally retarded individuals. Among

Daniel Arnheim, San Diego State University, who is senior author of *Principles and Methods of Adapted Physical Education*, first published in 1969. This book, now in its fifth edition, is currently authored by Dave Auxter and Jean Pyfer. In 1985 Arnheim published a new text, *Physical Education for Special Populations*, with William Sinclair.

their early contributions were (a) funding the AAHPER Task Force on Programs for the Mentally Retarded in 1965; (b) sponsoring seminars for college teachers on physical education and recreation for the mentally retarded in 1967; (c) lobbying for congressional support of PL 90-170, enacted in 1967; and (d) creating the Special Olympics in 1968. To carry out their goals the Kennedy Foundation relied heavily upon such persons as Robert Holland, Julian Stein, Frank Hayden, and Lawrence Rarick.

The leadership of these and other persons led to the addition of courses and units in courses on mentally handicapped individuals in university physical education and recreation departments throughout the country. Stein (1969) published an article on professional preparation in physical education and recreation for the mentally retarded that was based on a survey of 63 experienced teachers from 26 states, Washington, DC, and England. In it he set forth several concepts that still tend to prevail.

> Basically, activities, methods and philosophy of physical education and recreation programs for the retarded differ little from those designed to meet individual needs of nonretarded groups. (p. 103)

> Most physical education and recreation personnel possess the technical know how for working with the retarded. However, they have emphasized the differences between the retarded and nonretarded rather than the similarities. . . . The similarities . . . should be reflected in activities, programs, and approaches. (p. 105)

> While instructors need some knowledge of mental retardation (characteristics, causes, incidence, types, nature of impairment, the great variability among the retarded) as undergraduates, detailed . . . in depth treatment . . . should be reserved for those specializing. (p. 106)

Also explored in Stein's article was the relationship between special education and adapted physical education content. Stein recommended requiring a survey course of exceptional children as a prerequisite to an adapted physical education course that emphasized "diagnosis of motor problems and physical deficiencies along with prescription of activities for these anomalies" (p. 105). In conjunction with this, "practical experience, including observation, supervised field work, and some student teaching or practice with the handicapped, was felt to be obligatory for the undergraduate" (p. 105). The recommendations set forth in Stein's article (1969) were implemented by colleges and universities in ensuing years.

Beginning of Graduate Level Specialization

In the early 1970s leaders debated about whether specialization training in adapted physical education should be designed primarily for the graduate level or the junior and senior years. No federal monies, however, were available for the funding of undergraduate physical education programs, and the pattern of graduate specialization predominated "because BEH [the funding agency] decreed that it was limiting its program assistance money to graduate level programs" (Winnick, 1986, p. 113).

Another factor operative in the development of graduate rather than undergraduate specializations was the belief that adapted physical educators should have a strong liberal arts background and in-depth preparation in regular physical education before undertaking studies involving diagnosis, prescription, and remediation of motor problems. This approach was soon complicated by the desire of individuals with baccalaureate degrees in special education and related areas to enter graduate programs in adapted physical education. Entry requirements into the new graduate specialization varied by university, as did the courses comprising the program.

The grant writing world of the 1960s and 1970s, as today, was dominated by special education. In proposing graduate curricula to be funded, physical educators were therefore sensitive to special education trends and issues. Many master's and doctoral programs were designed as double majors in special education and physical education, with only two or three courses specifically in adapted physical education. In accordance with the prevailing special education practice in the 1960s, many of the new adapted physical education specializations embraced the *categorical* approach to professional preparation (i.e., separate courses on teaching each disability category). In response to research by Brace (1968) and Stein (1969), almost every university began to offer courses on physical education and recreation for the mentally retarded.

In addition to the original program directors, several new successful grant writers were developing graduate specializations by 1971. These included

Jack Keogh	UCLA
Ellen Kelly	Illinois State University at Normal
Evelyn Davies	Indiana University
Joseph Winnick	State University of New York (SUNY) at Brockport
Robert Carlson	University of Kansas
Leroy Walker	North Carolina Central University
Lane Goodwin	Wisconsin State University at LaCrosse
O.N. Hunter and Joan Moran	University of Utah

Of these individuals, five were or became authors of textbooks in adapted physical education or motor develop-ment (Keogh, Kelly, Davies, Winnick, Moran). One, Leroy Walker, became president of AAHPER (1977-78). Another, Robert Carlson, became editor of the *American Corrective Therapy Journal*. All were leaders in curriculum development.

Other leaders also were emerging in universities that developed graduate specializations in adapted physical education without the benefit of federal funding. Among these were Claudine Sherrill at Texas Woman's University, Janet Seaman at California State University at Los Angeles, and Cy Morgan at George Peabody College. A survey of adapted physical education professional preparation (Ersing & Wheeler, 1971) revealed that 24 (13%) of 178 institutions offered curricula to prepare specialists; the nature of these curricula was diverse, reflecting the educational backgrounds and philosophies of their directors.

Evolution of Perceptual Motor Training in Physical Education

Many adapted physical education professional preparation programs in the 1960s and 70s emphasized perceptual-motor training. Interest among physical educators was first evidenced on a large scale by national and regional AAHPER conferences in 1968 and 1971. Conference reports, available through AAHPERD Publications, were entitled *Motor Foundations: A Multidisciplinary Concern* and *Foundations and Practices in Perceptual Motor Learning*, respectively. Leaders in this movement were mostly elementary school and motor development specialists and motor learning theorists. Of the present day grant writers, authors, and leaders in adapted physical education, only a few participated in the 1968 conference: Louis Bowers, Dolores Geddes, Jack Keogh, Claudine Sherrill, and Julian Stein.

Adapted physical education teacher training appears to have been influenced mostly by special educators who put into practice the writings of Newell C. Kephart, an educational psychologist; Gerald Getman, an optometrist, Ray Barsch, a special educator; and Marianne Frostig, a developmental psychologist. These authors were all closely allied with the Association for Children with Learning Disabilities (ACLD), which formed in 1964. They advocated perceptual-motor training for children with brain injuries, minimal brain dysfunction, dyslexia, developmental aphasias, perceptual handicaps, learning disabilities, and mental retardation. Hallahan and Cruickshank (1973) point out that perceptual-motor training was the most popular method of educating learning disabled children from 1936 through 1970. For the most part this perceptual-motor training was directed toward improving cognitive abilities, academic achievement, and sensorimotor functioning.

Activities commonly used to achieve these goals were balance beam walking, stork stands and all kinds of balancing tasks, angels in the snow, trampoline bouncing, chalkboard exercises and games, tracking small suspended swinging balls, identification of body part games, and crossing the body's midline activities. Bryant Cratty, physical education professor at UCLA, wrote numerous books that assisted adapted physical education teacher trainers to present the content of perceptual-motor training. Among these were the following:

- *Developmental Sequences of Perceptual-Motor Tasks*, 1967

- *Perceptual-Motor Efficiency in Children*, with M.M. Martin, 1969

- *Motor Activity and the Education of Retardates*, 1969

- *Physical Expressions of Intelligence*, 1972

In these books Cratty extended the concepts underlying perceptual-motor training to include attention, memory, and central processing. He insisted that movement will improve a student's academic performance and cognitive functioning only if he or she is engaged in problem solving (reading, spelling, arithmetic, letter and number recognition) during the movement. To the traditional perceptual-motor activities Cratty added games on floor patterns or grids that promoted such problem solving.

Research in the 1970s designed to assess the effectiveness of perceptual-motor training in remediating academic learning problems concluded that such programs failed (Goodman & Hammill, 1973; Hallahan & Cruickshank, 1973). As a result, special education university training programs shifted their focus to other intervention modalities. For practitioners, the efficacy of perceptual-motor training became increasingly controversial. Some special educators and physical educators continue to use it (see chapter 15 by Pyfer). In 1983, Kavale and Mattson wrote, "The deep historical roots and strong clinical tradition will make it difficult to remove perceptual-motor training from its prominent position as a treatment technique for exceptional children" (p. 172). Based on a meta-analysis of data from 180 studies, Kavale and Mattson (1983) concluded that perceptual-motor training is not an effective intervention technique for improving academic, cognitive, or perceptual-motor variables.

The goal of adapted physical education in using perceptual-motor activities is different from that of special education. Physical educators believe that perceptual-motor activities help improve the balance, agility, and coordination of awkward children and thus achieve traditional physical education goals. Some leaders today consider activities to be sensory integration that were once conceptualized as perceptual-motor or sensorimotor activities. The focus on perceptual-motor remediation in the 1960s and 1970s, and in some contemporary programs, reflects a shift from the medical model of corrective exer-

cise to the educational model of activities and games as the basis for curriculum content.

In the 1980s perceptual-motor training is still controversial (Reid, 1981). Regardless of its future, it has been significant in the history of adapted physical education. A survey in 1979 requesting 111 adapted physical education teacher trainers to rank activity areas in terms of their special expertise with handicapped children and youth resulted in 54 (48.6%) persons marking perceptual-motor training or sensory integration as their strongest area (Sherrill & Tymeson, 1979). In contrast, the next most frequently indicated areas were individual-dual sports, 15; fitness, 13; aquatics, 12; and team sports, 8.

The Early 1970s

Ersing and Wheeler (1971), Ersing (1972), and Winnick (1972) give insight into trends and issues in the 1970s, many of which appear to be relevant today. At this time, approximately 300 colleges and universities offered professional preparation in adapted physical education. Already there was controversy about the best name for this area of study; 11 different course titles were identified (Ersing & Wheeler, 1971). Most of the universities offered only generalist training via one or two courses; 24 institutions had developed graduate specializations. Based on a survey of university faculty (57% return), Ersing and Wheeler identified 25 critical issues confronting adapted physical education. In rank order, the most important were

- the need for improved public relations and understanding with physicians and school administrators;

- improved coordination and integration of professional preparation in adapted physical education with other areas—namely, special education;

- the lack of adequately trained teachers in professional preparation programs; and

- developing professional curriculums to meet student needs; curriculums that are practical and realistic, rather than traditional in design. (Ersing & Wheeler, 1971, pp. 9-10)

Leaders, with the help of federal funding, had created specialization training (i.e., they had convinced their universities to approve the intent to develop a sequence of learning experiences that would lead to a degree). This first action was usually relatively easy; few universities turn down money. The implementation, as indicated by these critical issues, was complex and difficult. No one knew what this new specialization should be; the goal was to train teachers to work with handicapped children and youth, but university professors did not themselves possess knowledge and skill in this area. Improved public relations, coordination, and integration were obviously necessary for university professors to seek out individuals who could help them in designing courses and preparing lectures; awareness of the advantages of multi- and interdisciplinary experiences was at an all-time high. Many physical education teacher trainers enrolled in or audited special education courses. Although everyone strove toward the development of an educational model to guide curriculum innovation, the emphasis was on characteristics of handicapping conditions rather than the pedagogy of adaptation and individualization.

Creation of AAHPER Guidelines

Because no guidelines existed for professional preparation in physical education for handicapped students, AAHPERD and the Bureau of Education for the Handicapped (BEH) collaborated in the sponsorship of several regional institutes in 1971-1972 to bring adapted physical educators together (see chapter 5 for details). These institutes helped university professors to systematize their curriculum planning in terms of roles that adapted physical education specialists should train for as well as special functions. Institute participants were also taught the competency approach and helped to determine learning experiences that might develop specific competencies. The idea that adapted physical education teacher training should be noncategorical (generic) was also advanced; this implied that courses no longer should be offered specifically on mentally retarded children or any other category of handicapping conditions. Instead, training should be general, directed toward the competencies needed to perform such functions as assessment, program design and implementation, and interprofessional cooperation. These institutes provided the content for the excellent articles by Ersing (1972) and Winnick (1972).

New Directions and Issues

Among several new directions of the 1970s discussed by Ersing were (a) the inclusion of multi- and interdisciplinary experiences in adapted physical education professional preparation, (b) the inclusion of practicum and field experience with handicapped students as part of training, (c) the need for adapted physical education training opportunities for special education majors and others in related academic areas, (d) the education model versus the therapeutic or rehabilitative model with emphasis on role of corrective and recreation therapies, and (e) the need for improved communication and interaction with community agencies as well as other academic areas within the university.

Ersing believed that the foremost problem was "the need to clarify and identify kinds of professional preparation desired for the generalist versus the specialist in adapted physical education" (1972, p. 79). This need subsequently was addressed by the publication of competencies as guidelines for training adapted physical educators (American Association for Health, Physical Education, and Recreation, 1973; Hurley, 1981). The 1981 competencies were included in the appendices of several of the new adapted physical education textbooks in the 1980s (see Appendix B).

Issues analyzed by Winnick (1972) were (a) the medical versus the educational model as the main basis of adapted physical education content; (b) the generic, noncategorical versus the traditional medical, pathological, categorical approach; (c) specialist versus generalist training; (d) the level at which specialization training should be directed—graduate versus undergraduate; (e) whether or not disadvantaged (poor, low socioeconomic status) are eligible for adapted physical education services; and (f) planning for future financial support: subsidized versus self-supported training programs. Although he discussed both sides of each issue, Winnick clearly favored the educational model, the generic, noncategorical approach, specialization limited to the graduate level, and the inclusion of disadvantaged students with physiomotor needs in adapted physical education. With regard to specialist versus generalist training, he states,

> Few would argue the need for specialists to teach at the university level, to conduct research related to adapted physical education, or to teach children with severe deviances at the grassroots level. It is generally agreed that specialists are needed for professional leadership and for certain practitioner roles. However, there are dangers in overemphasizing the development of specialists. . . . It is apparent that the vast majority of pupils with special needs in physical education will be the responsibility of regular physical educators and/or special educators. (Winnick, 1972, p. 76)

To the problem of diminished or discontinued federal funding of training programs, Winnick suggested two solutions. One was to limit the number of universities that could offer specialization, thereby increasing enrollment in the approved and accredited programs. The other was to increase the spin-off from adapted physical educators and students in other disciplines to enroll. These suggestions deserve attention today when the actuality of reduced funding is occurring.

The Late 1970s

By 1975, most of the adapted physical education leaders were directing federally funded projects: Dan Arnheim, Dave Auxter, Pat Bird, Lou Bowers, Ernie Bundschuh, Bill Chasey, Walt Cooper, Evelyn Davies, Walt Ersing, Hollis Fait, Dolores Geddes, Lane Goodwin, Leon Johnson, Jack Keogh, Ernie Lange, Jim Little, Joan Moran, Cy Morgan, Jean Pyfer, Claudine Sherrill, Julian Stein, Larry Rarick, Leroy Walker, Ray Weiss, Janet Wessel, and Joe Winnick. Of these 26 individuals, 14 were or became textbook authors in adapted physical education and/or motor development. They were the shapers of knowledge as well as curricula; yet most of them were learning day by day as much as they taught. Just when they mastered the characteristics of major handicapping conditions, the trend changed, and they endeavored to become experts in generic functions of assessment, diagnosis, and prescription. Concurrently each had had to master the intricacies of grant writing and project management, become involved in the politics of legislation and funding, and learn state and local educational policy in regard to handicapped students. Moreover, they were establishing practicum sites, creating rapport with numerous new individuals and groups, and testing their newly acquired skills and knowledge in demonstration teaching of handicapped children. Every day was full, and often the demands seemed insurmountable. But the greatest challenge of all remained.

Enactment of PL 94-142

In 1975, Congress passed PL 94-142, the Education for All Handicapped Children Act. In-service training began immediately; the law had created an entire new body of knowledge: individualized education programs (IEPs), multidisciplinary assessment, parent rights, due process, eligibility criteria, least restrictive placement, state plans, and on and on. Now, for the first time in history, handicapped children were assured physical education instruction. Soon it was evident, however, that knowledge of the law was not enough. Advocacy techniques had to be acquired so as to convince state and local education agency personnel, as well as school administrators, to implement the PL 94-142 sections relative to physical education. Involvement in parent education became the new thrust, as physical educators met with and informed parents of their rights under the new law.

Founding of National Consortium

The grant directors looked to one another for help; in 1975, they founded (together with colleagues in therapeutic recreation) the National Consortium on Physical Education and Recreation for the Handicapped (see chapters 4 and 5 for details). This organization not only provided a means to learn and share together at annual conferences, but it also created the vehicle for input to the federal government concerning rules and regulations for implementation of PL 94-142, which were not finalized until 1977 (see *Federal Register*, August 23, 1977). The Consortium also served to sensitize adapted physical education leaders to the laws that reauthorize, approximately every 3 years, the funding of university teacher training (i.e., PL 91-230 and its amendments). Adapted physical education leaders learned that involvement in the legislative process is a never-ending responsibility, a habit to be acquired in oneself and instilled in others.

Influential Individuals

Especially outstanding during this period was William Hillman, the advocate for physical education and recreation within the Bureau of Education for the Handicapped (BEH) from 1968 onward. Hillman was the individual from whom grant writers and prospective grant writers sought advice and assistance; he also was largely responsible for keeping physical educators and recreators abreast of new funding and legislative developments. As the only advocate and consultant for our discipline within BEH, he frequently had to fight fiercely to maintain the status quo. Much of the progress in teacher training in physical education for the handicapped can be attributed to his masterful negotiations and his ability to facilitate the leadership of grant directors.

Throughout the 1970s the AAHPER(D) Unit on Programs for the Handicapped continued to provide assistance to university professors in shaping programs (see chapters 4 and 5). As director, Julian Stein influenced new directions and practices. Chief among these was the involvement of handicapped individuals as consumer advocates and leaders in the adapted physical education movement. Illustrative of this is Stein's role in bringing the work of Charles Buell and Harry Cordellos (both of whom are blind) to the attention of teacher trainers.

Other individuals particularly outstanding in the 1970s were Tom Vodola, director of PROJECT ACTIVE, and Janet Wessel, director of I CAN. Both of these individuals generated curriculum materials and assessment instruments for use in the public schools as well as textbooks for teacher training. Vodola's first book (1973) entitled *Individualized Physical Education for the Handicapped* presented many of the ideas embodied later in PL 94-142. This was the first textbook to explain the diagnostic-prescriptive teaching model and to illustrate how individualized, personalized learning can be implemented successfully in the

Leaders in adapted physical education. (Clockwise around the table:) Janet Wessel, William Hillman, and Hollis Fait at a meeting of grant directors in Washington, DC.

public school setting. Wessel (1977) was the first to develop a detailed text specifically on the IEP process in physical education; its title was *Planning Individualized Education Programs in Special Education.*

Textbooks

In addition to these books, several others were published between 1972 and 1979.

- *Developmental Activities for Children in Special Education* (1972) by Cynthia Hirst and Elaine Michaelis, both of Brigham Young University in Provo, Utah

- *Physical Education for Individuals With Handicapping Conditions* (1974) by Dolores Geddes, then a staff member at AAHPER headquarters

- *Adapted Physical Education and Recreation: A Multidisciplinary Approach* (1976) by Claudine Sherrill, Texas Woman's University

- *Physical Activities for the Handicapped* (1977) by Maryhelen Vannier of Southern Methodist University in Dallas

- *Early Movement Experiences and Development: Habilitation and Remediation* (1979) by Joseph Winnick, State University of New York at Brockport

Of these, only the book by Sherrill survived into a second edition. The textbook by Winnick, however, deserves special mention because it was the first to be written and publicized as an advanced text specifically for graduate students. Several excellent books like those of Drowatsky

(1971) and Moran and Kalakian (1974) were published on physical education for mentally retarded and other special populations; these were used in universities that followed the categorical approach to teacher training and thus offered courses specifically on mental retardation. The trend was toward comprehensive texts. One reason Sherrill's text endured was its division of contents into generic (Parts 1 and 2) and categorical sections (Part 3), thus appealing to advocates of both teacher training approaches.

Research

Little research was published by adapted physical education leaders in the 1970s. Broadhead (1986), in identifying

Little research was published by adapted physical education leaders in the 1970s. Broadhead (1986), in identifying research thrusts in this decade, notes primarily the scholarly achievements of Larry Rarick (Rarick & Dobbins, 1972; Rarick, Dobbins, & Broadhead, 1976; Rarick & McQuillan, 1977; Rarick, Widdop, & Broadhead, 1970). These works pertained to the motor abilities of mentally retarded children. Rarick was recognized for these and other contributions by his selection in 1979 as the AAHPERD Alliance Scholar. This annual award was begun in 1976, making Rarick the fourth individual to be so honored (Bennett, 1985).

Three research studies in 1979 offer insight into the status of professional preparation at the turn of the decade. DePauw (1979), in a survey of 500 colleges and universities (38.4% return), reported that 45% required a course in adapted physical education of all majors. Of the 292 institutions responding, 22% indicated a specialization in adapted physical education; 31, 29, and 8 institutions, respectively, offered undergraduate, master's, and doctoral specializations. Practicum experience, ranging from 50 to 370 hours of work with special populations, was required in only 46% of the institutions with adapted physical education course work. The total number of hours or units required in a specialization varied from 9 semester hours to 31 quarter units in undergraduate programs, from 11 to 20 units in master's work, and from 6 to 18 units in doctoral degrees.

Bird and Gansneder (1979) focused their research on one state (Virginia), assessing the level of preparedness of physical educators to meet PL 94-142 requirements. This study had national impact because it was published in *Exceptional Children*, the major journal of special educators; the resulting visibility has led the findings to be cited often. A random sample of 912 public school physical educators were surveyed with a 40% return. Of the respondents, 65% rated their training in adapted physical education as poor. When asked to assess their competencies in planning, implementing, and evaluating physical education programs for handicapped students, from 24 to 48% indicated little or no ability to perform each task. On self-ratings of knowledge about 26 common handicapping conditions, over 50% had little or no knowledge of nine conditions, and over 30% had little or no knowledge of 23 handicapping conditions. An excellent grant writer, Patrick Bird of the University of Virginia, used these findings in his grant proposal to document the need for federal funds to upgrade university training in adapted physical education.

Clelland (1979) reported an in-depth survey of directors of the 34 training programs in physical education for the handicapped, which were funded by the BEH Division of Personnel Preparation for fiscal year 1979. Data were collected by personal interviews. Of the 34 programs, 6 were preservice, 12 were in-service, and 16 were combination in-service/preservice. Information on project management related to adapted physical education teacher training was gathered through 20 questions. Among the findings were the following:

- Groups who collaborated most often in the planning and implementation of physical education training projects were (a) special and regular education teachers, (b) special and regular education administrators, and (c) college and university faculty. (p. 21)

- The average number of graduate credit hours was 39 for preservice training and 10 for inservice training. (p. 22)

- The three most frequently mentioned practica/intern sites were regular and special education facilities and hospitals. Eighteen of 21 projects required between 1 and 3 semesters/quarters whereas three projects required from 100 to 400 contact hours spread out over one or more semesters. All practica were reported to meet the nine criteria established by AAHPERD (1973). (pp. 23-26)

- All projects, but one (the University of California at Berkeley) indicated that their training encompassed all handicapping conditions. (p. 27)

- The projects reported having trained between 1 and 117 graduate students and between 10 and 6,000 in-service trainees. Only two projects reported training undergraduate students: Montana State University and the University of Wisconsin at LaCrosse. (p. 29)

- The average faculty/staff size for preservice projects was three, for inservice projects was one, and for combination projects was two. (p. 30)

Many of the interview questions focused upon competency-based training. Each project director was read the 78 competencies stated in the *AAHPER Guidelines for Professional Preparation Programs for Personnel Involved in Physical Education and Recreation for the Handicapped* (AAHPER, 1973) and asked to indicate whether or not these competencies were developed in their trainees. From 63 to 81% of the project directors reported "yes" to each competency. Other findings related to the development of competencies were as follows:

- Of the 34 physical education projects, 27 responded "yes" to the question, "Do you have a specific listing of trainee competencies?" (p. 31)

- Of the 34 projects, 26 responded "yes" to the question, "Does your evaluation of project activities involve comparing trainee performance data with stated competencies?" (p. 31)

Overall, the report of findings on BEH-funded graduate training projects on physical education for the handicapped was 24 pages long. The study was one of several conducted and published by a BEH special project at the University of New Mexico under project director Gary Adamson. It can be concluded from this research that federally funded training programs in adapted physical education are competency-based and adhere to the 1973 AAHPER professional preparation guidelines. Many important questions, however, remain unanswered. For example, what is the average number of master's and doctoral students graduated each year? What factors affect the number graduating? Where are these individuals employed? What are the credentials of the faculty? Are they on hard money or soft? Approximately how much federal money is spent per graduate student?

Hillman (1986) reported that the federal government has spent over $22 million in training programs in physical education for the handicapped. Yet the Clelland study is the only research to examine and describe the characteristics of these programs. No research has been undertaken to determine their efficacy, to follow up their graduates, or to investigate other aspects of graduate training.

In-Service Training

Another trend of the late 1970s was in-service training. PL 94-142 changed service delivery in both special education and adapted physical education so drastically that teachers and administrators in the public schools required assistance to gain the new knowledge and skills for implementation. Federal funding priorities therefore changed from preservice to in-service, beginning around 1977. In order to obtain stipends for master's and doctoral students, many grant writers were forced to develop in-service training projects to meet public school needs rather than continue producing preservice grants. This required mastery of still another body of knowledge (see chapter 31 by Garth Tymeson). While learning about in-service training (often by trial and error) and writing and directing grants in this area, most university teachers concurrently taught in preservice programs. There was little time or energy for curriculum innovation. It was clear, however, that master's and doctoral work should train the new generation of leaders for both preservice and in-service roles (see chapter 24). Instrumental in helping university teachers learn the theory of in-service training was John Dunn, Oregon State University, who conducted a national conference on this topic in 1979 (Dunn & Harris, 1979).

Of the many new leaders who emerged in the late 1970s, perhaps the most outstanding was John Dunn, who completed his doctoral work at Brigham Young University in Utah and accepted a teaching position with Hollis Fait of the University of Connecticut. In the mid-70s, he moved to Oregon State University. As editor of the National Consortium on Physical Education and Recreation for the Handicapped (NCPERH) Newsletter, Dunn gained recognition and subsequently became the first and only individual to be elected to the top leadership position in all three adapted physical education structures: Chair, AAHPERD Therapeutics Council, 1978-79; NCPERH President, 1981-82; Chair, AAHPERD Adapted Physical Education Council, 1984-85. Dunn was also coauthor of the fifth edition (1984) of Fait's *Special Physical Education*. Dunn also found time to publish research (1978) and to write a book on the application of behavior management to the instruction of severely mentally retarded individuals (*A Data-Based Gymnasium*, 1980). Today, John Dunn is acknowledged as the first of the new generation of grant writers and program directors to achieve in all three areas of leadership: teaching, service, and research/publications. His leadership extends into the 1980s and sets an example for the new adapted physical educators.

Summary of the 1970s

In summary, the focus in the 1970s was on initiating graduate specialization programs, creating a new competency-based, generic noncategorical body of knowledge, and implementing the mandates of PL 94-142. Most university teachers in adapted physical education were grossly overextended as they sought to learn and improve grant-writing techniques to obtain optimal funding for their training programs while memorizing the content of PL 94-142 and analyzing its implications for physical education programs and practices. Much of the energies of adapted physical education leaders were spent in disseminating information about PL 94-142 and advocating its implementation. These tasks were sometimes achieved through formal in-service training but often represented volunteer efforts. Almost without exception, each leader in adapted physical education was the director of one or more federal grants. Additionally, many wrote books and served as officers in professional organizations. Too numerous to summarize, the contributions of these leaders appear in a glossary in the appendix. Most graduate students during this period were partly or fully funded by government stipends and scholarships. The federal government thus played a major role in adapted physical education teacher training.

Teacher Training in the 1980s

In the 1980s the emphasis in teacher training has switched from in-service back to preservice. Federal funds are no longer available for in-service training; nevertheless, many university teachers continue to work with public schools and parent organizations to assure optimal understanding of PL 94-142. Such involvement is now typically considered community service, although a few individuals are reimbursed as consultants for their efforts through state and local monies.

Increased Emphasis on Research and Scholarly Activity

Whereas in earlier decades the priority in professional preparation was teaching (i.e., service delivery in accordance with PL 94-142), today's better university programs strive to develop competencies in all three of the areas in which leaders are evaluated: teaching, service, and research. Many of today's teacher trainers now have 10 or more years of experience specifically in adapted physical education curriculum and course development; less time is needed to develop their own knowledge and skills. This frees them to devote more time to both students and professional colleagues and to engage in research and scholarly inquiry. The new generation of leaders comes to their university teaching programs with a sound academic background, an understanding of the limited knowledge base of the discipline, and a commitment to extend theory through research and publication. Winnick (1986) states in this regard,

> Through our programs an impressive list of graduates is prepared for the next decade's development. Short, Tymeson, Kelly, DePape, Poretta, Chalmers, Curtis-Pierce, Knowles, McQuillan, Rimmer, Rich, Loovis, Craft, Horvat, Cowden, Ryan, Brunt, DePauw, Karper, McClenaghan, Gavron, Jackson, Webster, Beuter, Dummer, Aufsesser, Kaylor-Krebs, Rizzo, DiRocco, Hall, Davis, Ulrich, Huber, Lavay, and Surburg are some of the names associated with our doctoral programs and/or from whom we can expect leadership. These people are the keys to the future of adapted physical education. With a list like this we can be confident that we did many things right, and we can take pride in that. Our future is in good hands. (p. 116)

Availability of Many Textbooks

The 1980s are a time of transition with new leaders gradually replacing the pioneers. Warren Johnson and Hollis Fait have died. Evelyn Davies, Cy Morgan, Ray Weiss, Larry Rarick, Tom Vodola, Janet Wessel, and others have retired but remain active in various projects. Many new textbooks vie for attention.

- *Adapted Physical Education for Children and Youth* (1980) by Bryant Cratty, University of California at Los Angeles

- *Special Physical Education* (1982) by Ron French, Texas Woman's University, and Paul Jansma, Ohio State University

- *Developmental/Adapted Physical Education: Making Ability Count* (1982) by Leonard Kalakian, Mankato State University in Minnesota, and Carl Eichstaedt, Illinois State University at Normal

- *The New Adapted Physical Education* (1982) by Janet Seaman, California State University at Los Angeles, and Karen DePauw, Washington State University

- *Teaching Physical Activities to Impaired Youth: An Approach to Mainstreaming* (1982) by Arthur Miller, Boston University, and James Sullivan, University of Southern Maine

- *A Practical Approach to Adapted Physical Education* (1982) by Douglas Wiseman, Plymouth State College, New Hampshire

- *Adapted Physical Education: A Practitioners Guide* (1983) by Lowell Masters, Nevada Department of Education, Allen Mori, University of Nevada at Las Vegas, and Ernest Lange, University of New Mexico

- *Physical Education for Special Populations: A Developmental, Adapted, and Remedial Approach* (1985) by Daniel Arnheim, San Diego State University, and William Sinclair, California State University, Long Beach

- *Physical Education Programming for Exceptional Learners* (1985) by Rhonda Folio, Tennessee Technological University, Cookeville, Tennessee

Julian Stein and Joe Winnick are both preparing new textbooks that will be ready in the late 1980s.

Of the pioneer textbooks, three dominate the market with relatively new editions.

- *Special Physical Education* (1984) by Hollis Fait, deceased, and John Dunn, Oregon State University

- *Adapted Physical Education and Recreation* (1985) by Dave Auxter, Slippery Rock State University, and Jean Pyfer, Texas Woman's University

- *Adapted Physical Education and Recreation: A Multidisciplinary Approach* (1986) by Claudine Sherrill, Texas Woman's University

A list of all available textbooks in adapted physical education appears in Appendix E. Although most of these are general in nature and designed primarily for undergraduate classes, the 1980s can be remembered also for the emergence of specialized texts for use in such courses as early childhood adapted physical education (*They Have To Be Carefully Taught* by Jane Evans, Brock University, Canada), physical education for the severely handicapped (*A Data-Based Gymnasium* by John Dunn, Oregon State University), curriculum design in adapted physical education (*Achievement Based Curriculum Development in Physical Education* by Janet Wessel, Michigan State University, and Luke Kelly, University of Virginia at Charlottesville), and the legal foundations of adapted physical education (*The Right to Participate* by Herb Appenzeller, Guilford College, Greensboro, North Carolina).

Assessment Instruments

Adapted physical educators in the 1980s were also beginning to provide substantial leadership in the development and refinement of assessment instruments. Whereas the 1970s were dominated by assessment approaches of Wessel (criterion-referenced) and Vodola (norm-referenced) and the revision of the Lincoln-Oseretsky Motor Development

Scale by special educator Robert Bruininks, University of Minnesota, the new decade brought commercially published tests by Loovis and Ersing (1979), Evans (1980), Folio and Fewell (1983), and Ulrich (1985). These and other assessment instruments are described in detail by Sherrill (1986a).

Journals

In the 1980s, two new journals were established. *Adapted Physical Activity Quarterly* was first published in January, 1984. Its editor, Geoffrey Broadhead, whose doctoral work was under Larry Rarick, is an acknowledged researcher of excellence. *Palaestra*, also a quarterly, was first published in fall, 1984. Dave Beaver, who is best known for his leadership in sport for the disabled (particularly the blind), is both editor and publisher-owner of *Palaestra*.

Studies in adapted physical education are also published in the *Research Quarterly for Exercise and Sport*. Michael Wade of the University of Minnesota and Jack Keogh of UCLA have served as section editors in adapted physical education.

Graduate students in the 1980s increasingly understand the importance of undertaking publishable research studies early in their careers. Individuals who accept tenure-track positions know that, in most universities, success in grant writing and project management does not substitute for research.

Grantsmanship as an Area of Knowledge

Grantsmanship continues to be an area of study within graduate programs. Regardless of changes in the economy, university administrators expect adapted physical education faculty to know how to obtain external funding. As more and more individuals compete for existing money, the pressure for high-quality, well-written proposals will increase. Professors who teach grant writing will include strong units on state and federal law in their courses and stress the relationship between legislation and funding. Adapted physical educators will need to become more knowledgeable about fiscal resources at every level.

Computers in Academia

Computers are and will continue to be an important part of graduate study. Not only do they permit ease in statistical treatment of research data, but they allow access to sources of information and knowledge bases (see chapter 29 by Montelione and Davis). Project CSPD-PE (Bundschuh, 1985) is one of the first attempts in adapted physical education to use computers in state needs assessment; in the future there will be many more.

Changing Directions in Curriculum

The sport for the disabled movement has matured sufficiently in the 1980s to exert a strong influence on the content of adapted physical education courses. Such organizations as Special Olympics, the U.S. Association for Blind Athletes, the United States Cerebral Palsy Athletic Association, and the National Wheelchair Basketball Association have adapted sport to the special needs of their athletes and created new sports (Sherrill, 1986a, 1986c). The rule books and other publications of these organizations offer a new body of knowledge that adapted physical educators are just now beginning to incorporate into their courses. Sherrill, for instance, believes that her involvement in blind and cerebral palsy sport and her presence at the 1984 International Games for the Disabled and the 1983 International Special Olympics are the most important factors in her growth as a professional during the past 5 years and in the changing content of her adapted physical education textbook. At last, sport and aquatics pedagogy exists so that the medical model truly can be replaced by an educational model.

In the 1980s most adapted physical educators are just becoming aware of a federal law passed in 1978 that has implications for adapted physical education teacher training. It is PL 95-606, the Amateur Sports Act, which includes several passages on sport for disabled individuals. Among its mandates are the inclusion of national sport organizations for the disabled within the United States Olympic Committee (USOC) structure. The influence of this law is reflected in the inclusion of chapters on sport for disabled individuals in the adapted physical education texts of the 1980s. The influence is felt also as pressures are being exerted on public school physical educators to coach and to serve as resource persons for volunteer coaches of disabled athletes. Like normal children, disabled youth need early sport instruction as part of their physical education curriculum in order to enjoy athletics and acquire lifetime habits of physical activity. Teacher training is increasingly preparing physical educators to achieve this goal.

Content on dance, movement education, and rhythmics for handicapped individuals (Barton, 1982; Crain, 1981; Fitt & Riordan, 1980; Sherrill, 1979, 1986a) is also becoming a part of teacher training curricula. The numerous performances of Peter Wisher's deaf dance group and the workshops of Anne Riordan, University of Utah, have been largely responsible for this, as has the support of AAHPERD's National Dance Association, which has Dance for Special Populations as one of its permanent substructures. Several adapted physical education specialists have double majors in dance (or vice versa) and are seeking to strengthen the role of dance in the adapted physical education curriculum. Illustrative of these individuals are Boni Boswell at East Carolina University, Peggy Roswal at Jacksonville State University in Alabama, Danielle Jay at Northern Illinois University, and Ellen Kowalski and Georgia Bonatis, doctoral students at Texas Woman's University. Wendell Liemohn, University of Tennessee, and Jane Evans, Brock University, Canada, have also made important contributions to rhythmic training and movement education, respectively.

Although knowledge of PL 94-142 remains essential and continues to demand a sizable portion of course time, leaders are increasingly aware that knowledge is not enough. Courses and units in courses are being developed on the strategy of change, with particular emphasis on attitudes and beliefs. More attention is being given to philosophy (Churton, 1986; Sherrill, 1985). As the pedagogy of adaptation and individualization is evolved, more emphasis will be accorded the development of creative abilities in teacher trainers (Sherrill, 1986a, b) as well as service deliverers.

Undergraduate courses in adapted physical education are focusing more and more on handicapped and clumsy children in the mainstream. Such individuals are seen as the responsibility of regular physical educators. Adapted physical education leaders, however, continue their efforts to convince administrators that consultants and resource room teachers with graduate degrees in adapted physical education should be available in every school district. The 1980s are a time of advocacy.

One method of advocacy is *infusion*. As used in personnel preparation, infusion refers to the inclusion of knowledge and skills pertaining to handicapped students in all courses and learning experiences within the regular physical education curriculum. Julian Stein (1969) is acknowledged as the innovator of this concept and remains its strongest advocate (French & Jansma, 1982; Kalakian & Eichstaedt, 1982). Whereas Stein sees infusion as replacing separate courses in adapted physical education for the nonspecialist, Sherrill believes the combination of infusion with a separate course is the desired approach. Winnick (1986) addresses the issue as follows:

> Of course, units or modules can and should be integrated into regular undergraduate physical education courses in certain instances. For example, as students are learning about the functioning of the cardiovascular system, it is appropriate that they also learn about defects and their impact on participation in physical activity. However, if the concept of infusion is adopted, the pupil with unique needs is never of priority concern—and that may be what is needed.

> There is a danger that failure to specifically earmark courses in adapted physical education may severely hamper the field because too often unmotivated and unprepared teachers using inadequate textbooks will be teaching the courses. (p. 115)

The greatest need today is helping administrators and teacher trainers in regular physical education to understand and appreciate assessment and programming for handicapped and clumsy children. These are the individuals who determine requirements for graduation, and far too many universities have supported neither infusion or a course. Note that DePauw's 1979 study indicated that fewer than 50% of the colleges and universities that train physical education majors require an adapted physical education course. This may be because they have no faculty member who wants to teach it or because adapted physical education is perceived of as lower priority than competing areas of knowledge.

Several 3-year special projects have been funded by the federal government to change attitudes and upgrade competencies of university teachers. Illustrative of these are the following: Project INFUSE was "an attempt to improve the preservice training of *all* physical educators by introducing into physical education preparation course concepts related to the handicapped" (Hall & Stiehl, 1978). The project was based on the philosophy that infusion can best be facilitated by updating existing university faculties regarding education of handicapped students and subsequently infusing such information into the courses that faculty now teach. The project ended with a National Symposium on November 16-18, 1978, at the University of Colorado at Boulder, which yielded a proceedings (Hall & Stiehl, 1978), one of the few resources devoted entirely to methods and approaches to infusion for university teachers. Its influence, however, is only now being felt as more and more leaders understand and advocate infusion.

Project GRAPES at the Texas Woman's University, funded in 1981-1982 for a 3-year period, was conceived by Sherrill as an approach to upgrade training of university professors assigned to teach preservice adapted physical education courses even though they had no background in education of the handicapped. GRAPES stood for *Grass Roots Adapted Physical Education Ecological Systems* training. It was based on the philosophy that university teachers without formal training need to be taught to identify and use local and state resources (i.e., ecological systems and structures) to assist in instruction. Through a series of workshops and institutes each year, GRAPES trainees learned to interact with the state education agency (SEA), state and national congresspersons, parent-professional organizations like the Association for Retarded Citizens, sport organizations for disabled athletes, and other groups within their immediate ecology. A strong emphasis within GRAPES was the involvement of disabled persons in adapted physical education teacher training.

The I'M SPECIAL project and the I'M SPECIAL network directed by Louis Bowers and Steve Klesius of the University of South Florida in Tampa have resulted in the development and nationwide dissemination of 15 color-sound videotapes with accompanying print guides. I'M SPECIAL is the acronym for *I*nstructional *M*odules *S*equential *P*hysical *E*ducation for *C*hildren *I*ndividualized *A*ppropriate *L*earning. Each videotape, with one exception, is 15 minutes long and focuses on some aspect of physical education for handicapped students, with emphasis on implementation of PL 94-142. This videotape series is reviewed in *Adapted Physical Activity Quarterly* (Churton, 1984). The creation of the I'M SPECIAL network, with videotapes placed in state education agency offices for ease in dissemination, had resulted in over 25,000 viewings by 1985. The videotape series is a viable approach to changing attitudes and increasing knowledge of regular physical educators. Recently Bowers and Klesius have extended I'M SPECIAL to encompass interactive microcomputer videodisk instructional approaches.

These and other projects have helped university teachers without specialization training to teach adapted physical education courses on their campuses. The gap between specialists and nonspecialists is, however, ever-widening. Several issues need to be resolved.

Issues in the 1980s

In the 1980s every state has colleges and universities that offer courses in adapted physical education. Many institutions allow graduate students to elect courses from several departments and call the resulting specialization adapted physical education. The nature and scope of such specializations are varied, and many appear to be guided by faculty without sound up-to-date training themselves in adapted physical education. Quality control of specialization training is a grave problem.

Several approaches to quality control may be taken. The one used most often in the past has been the grant award process. To obtain federal funds, an applicant university must document qualified faculty and propose a detailed plan for competency-based teacher training as well as an evaluation model to assure accountability. Too often, however, grant proposals are assessed and rated by panelists who have little knowledge of adapted physical education. Inasmuch as the selection of panelists is controlled by the funding agency, this approach to quality assurance has serious flaws. Improvement of the grant award process

is an issue of the 1980s. Strong leaders working through such organizations as the National Consortium on Physical Education and Recreation for the Handicapped are needed to effect change in the grant award process within the Office of Special Education Programs of the U.S. Department of Education.

Another approach to quality control is the development and implementation of an accreditation process whereby nonfunded, as well as funded, programs, can demonstrate adequacy or excellence in adapted physical education professional preparation. Accreditation demands the availability of standards, guidelines, and evaluation instruments to determine whether training programs meet specific criteria. Johnson (1975) was the first to undertake research to meet this need. His self-appraisal instrument for use by graduate adapted physical education specialization programs, although little known, represents progress in this area. Oakley (1984), with the help of Sherrill and French, developed guidelines for evaluating undergraduate adapted physical education training. Most of these guidelines are applicable to graduate programs.

For such standards to gain widespread acceptance, one or more professional organizations must assume responsibility for evaluating programs and publishing a list of institutions that meet agreed-upon standards. Attempts by professional organizations to upgrade their training programs usually begin with institutions volunteering to undergo evaluation. Experts, who travel from university to university as members of evaluation or accreditation teams, must be funded in some manner. Many problems must be resolved as leaders seek to determine the best method of accreditation, the standards to be used, and the organization to assume this responsibility. Adapted physical educators must learn more about the National Council for Accreditation of Teacher Education (NCATE) and how it can help them, as well as study methods used by the National Therapeutic Recreation Society and similar organizations.

Another approach to quality control is voluntary registration of adapted physical educators with a national organization similar to the system used by the National Therapeutic Recreation Society. A registration committee of the organization studies credentials of individuals who voluntarily mail their résumés. This registration committee ascertains that individuals meet minimal training standards and recommends their inclusion in the national registry of qualified personnel, which is published periodically and disseminated widely. Concurrently, an effort is made to sensitize employers to the registry.

A national examination for new members of the profession is another method of quality control. This examination could, in the beginning, be voluntary or administered by program directors as part of graduation requirements. These and other approaches require leaders willing to prioritize quality assurance as the major issue of the 1980s.

State level certification, endorsement, and credentialing can also play a major role in quality control. At present, however, only eight states have accepted responsibility for this by approving some kind of adapted physical education certification, endorsement, or credential, and only 11 states report working toward this goal (Cowden & Tymeson, 1983). Table 3.1 summarizes findings by Cowden and Tymeson in this regard.

Related to the issues of accreditation and credentialing are problems concerning the recognition of adapted physical education as a specialization and/or a profession or discipline and whether or not physical education of handicapped and/or clumsy, unfit students will be best facilitated by teachers taught through an infusion approach, a separate specialization approach, or some kind of combination of infusion and specialization. Assuming the combination approach is most effective, when during undergraduate training should infusion occur? How often? Supervised or taught by whom? When should the undergraduate specialization course (3 credits) in adapted physical education occur—the freshman year as orientation before infusion or the senior year as a synthesizing experience?

Answers also are needed to questions pertaining to infusion and specialization in relation to in-service training and technical assistance for university teachers. How can teachers of skills, methods, and materials courses be convinced to infuse a unit on the handicapped or clumsy child into their body of content? What kind of in-service

training will best sensitize university teachers to task analysis, assessment, and individualization of instruction?

Specialization in adapted physical education at the graduate level is now well accepted. But what should be the prerequisites for such specialization? Do experienced special education teachers who wish a graduate degree in adapted physical education need a certain number of credits in activity courses? Should they be expected to pass competency tests in sport, dance, and aquatics skills, strategies, and rules? If so, which activities? Should specialization be permitted of persons without a teaching credential? What kinds of jobs, other than teaching, can adapted physical education specialists expect?

What is the future of adapted physical education? How will it be affected by reduced federal and state funding? How will implementation of the least restrictive placement concepts of PL 94-142 affect the availability of jobs for adapted physical education specialists? Many questions like these need to be answered. Not only must individuals address issues, but professional organizations must become active, viable shapers of the future. Adapted physical education, as an emerging discipline and profession, must become strong enough to survive, if need be, without funding. Individual leadership (through teaching, service, advocacy, and research and publications) will determine the future.

Teacher training today can be summarized by a passage from Kalakian and Eichstaedt (1982):

> Adapted physical education is experiencing a state of transition and change never witnessed before. This profession's major responsibility is one of active participation in the change process. Any dynamic, viable profession must accept responsibility for initiating trends, not merely following them. (p. 451)

Table 3.1   States Implementing Adapted Physical Education Certification Plans

Certification, endorsement credential, in-field endorsement	Actively involved	Courses and/or competency "recommendations" for in-field employment
Alabama (in-field endorsement)	Massachusetts	Colorado
California	Illinois	Washington, DC
Georgia	Missouri	Wisconsin (special skills license)
Louisiana	Nebraska	
Michigan	N. Carolina	
Minnesota	Ohio	
New Mexico	Texas	
	Nevada	
	Maryland	
	Kentucky	
	Virginia	

Note. From "Certification in Adapted/Special Physical Education: National Status" by J. Cowden and G. Tymeson, 1983, *NCPERH Newsletter*, **2**(3), p. 9. Reprinted by permission.

References

American Association for Health, Physical Education, and Recreation. (1973). *Guidelines for professional preparation programs for personnel involved in physical education and recreation for the handicapped.* Washington, DC: Author.

Anooshian, V.B. (1961). *A survey of problems arising from the integration of educable mentally retarded boys in the California high school regular physical education class.* Unpublished master's thesis, Claremont College, Claremont, CA.

Barton, B. (1982). Aerobic dance and the mentally retarded. *The Physical Educator*, **39**(1), 25-29.

Bennett, B. (1985). This is our heritage: 1960-1985. *Research Quarterly for Exercise and Sport* [Centennial Issue], 102-120.

Bird, P., & Gansneder, B. (1979). Preparation of physical education teachers as required under Public Law 94-142. *Exceptional Children, 45*, 464-466.

Brace, D. (1968). Physical education and recreation for the mentally retarded. *Research Quarterly, 39*, 779-782.

Broadhead, G. (1986). Adapted physical education research trends: 1970-1990. *Adapted Physical Activity Quarterly, 3*, 104-111.

Bundschuh, E. (1985). *Needs assessment in special education*. Athens: University of Georgia, CSPD-PE Project.

Burke, P. (1976). Personnel preparation: Historical perspective. *Exceptional Children, 43*(3), 144-147.

Churton, M. (1984). I'M SPECIAL: A review of the videotape series. *Adapted Physical Activity Quarterly, 1*(1), 89-94.

Churton, M. (1986). Addressing personnel preparation needs to meet the challenges of the future. *Adapted Physical Activity Quarterly, 3*(2), 118-123.

Clelland, R. (1979). *A survey of personnel preparation in physical education and recreation for the handicapped: The consumer's guide series* (Vol. VI). Teacher Education/Special Education BEH Special Project. University of New Mexico, Albuquerque.

Cowden, J., & Tymeson, G. (1983). Certification in adapted/special physical education: National status. *NCPERH Newsletter, 2*(3), 8-10.

Crain, C. (1981). *Movement and rhythmic activities for the mentally retarded*. Springfield, IL: Charles C. Thomas.

Cratty, B.J. (1967). *Developmental sequences of perceptual-motor tasks*. Freeport, NY: Educational Activities.

Cratty, B.J. (1969). *Motor activity and the education of retardates*. Philadelphia: Lea & Febiger.

Cratty, B.J. (1972). *Physical expressions of intelligence*. Englewood Cliffs, NJ: Prentice-Hall.

Cratty, B.J., & Martin, M.M. (1969). *Perceptual-motor efficiency in children*. Philadelphia: Lea & Febiger.

DePauw, K. (1979). Nationwide survey of professional preparation in adapted physical education. *California Association for Health, Physical Education, and Recreation Journal, 42*(2), 28.

Drowatzky, J. (1971). *Physical education for the mentally retarded*. Philadelphia: Lea & Febiger.

Dunn, J. (1978). Reliability of selected psychomotor measures with mentally retarded adult males. *Perceptual and Motor Skills, 46*, 295-301.

Dunn, J. (1980). *A data-based gymnasium*. Monmouth, OR: Instructional Development Corporation.

Dunn, J., & Harris, J. (Eds.). (1979, May). *Physical education for the handicapped: Meeting the need through inservice education* (Proceedings of a National Conference Held at Oregon State University). Corvallis, OR.

Ersing, W. (1972). Current directions of professional preparation in adapted physical education. *Journal of Health, Physical Education, and Recreation, 43*(8), 78-79.

Ersing, W., & Wheeler, R. (1971). The status of professional preparation in adapted physical education. *American Corrective Therapy Journal, 25*(4), 111-118.

Evans, J. (1980). *Motor patterns achievement profile: They have to be carefully taught*. Reston, VA: American Alliance for Health, Physical Education, Recreation and Dance.

Fait, H., & Dunn, J. (1984). *Special physical education* (5th ed.). Philadelphia: W.B. Saunders.

Federal Register. (1977, August 23).

Fitt, S., & Riordan, A. (Eds.). (1980). *Dance for the handicapped—Focus on dance IX*. Reston, VA: American Alliance for Health, Physical Education, Recreation and Dance.

Flanagan, M.E. (1969). Expanding adapted physical education programs on a statewide basis. *Journal of Health, Physical Education, and Recreation, 40*(5), 52-56.

Flint, M.M. (1967). Current trends in adapted physical education on college level. *Journal of Health, Physical Education, and Recreation, 38*(7), 63-66.

Folio, M.R., & Fewell, R. (1983). *Peabody developmental motor scales*. Allen, TX: DLM Teaching Resources.

French, R., & Jansma, P. (1982). *Special physical education*. Columbus: Charles E. Merrill.

Goodman, L., & Hammill, D. (1973). The effectiveness of the Kephart-Getman Activities in developing perceptual-motor and cognitive skills. *Focus on Exceptional Children, 4*, 1-10.

Hall, J., & Stiehl, J. (1978, November). *National Infuse Symposium: Proceedings* (Project No. 451AH90509, U.S. Office of Education DPP, BEH). Boulder: University of Colorado.

Hallahan, D., & Cruickshank, W. (1973). *Psycho-educational foundations of learning disabilities*. Englewood Cliffs, NJ: Prentice-Hall.

Hillman, W. (1981). Federal involvement in physical education and recreation for handicapped individuals: The third decade. In J. Taylor, D. Compton, & T. Johnson (Eds.), *1979-80 Proceedings: National Consortium on Physical Education and Recreation for the Handicapped* (pp. 57-61). Urbana-Champaign, IL: University of Illinois.

Hillman, W. (1986). The role of the federal government in adapted physical education. *Adapted Physical Activity Quarterly, 3*(2), 124-126.

Hurley, D. (1981). Guidelines for adapted physical education. *Journal of Physical Education, Recreation, and Dance, 52*, 43-45.

Johnson, R. (1975). *Card for self-appraisal of graduate professional programs for the preparation of specialists in adapted physical education*. Unpublished doctoral dissertation, The Ohio State University, Columbus.

Kalakian, L., & Eichstaedt, C. (1982). *Developmental/adapted physical education: Making ability count*. Minneapolis: Burgess.

Kavale, K., & Mattson, P.D. (1983). One jumped off the balance beam: Meta-analysis of perceptual motor training. *Journal of Learning Disabilities, 16*, 165-173.

Loovis, E.M., & Ersing, W. (1979). *Assessing and programming motor development for children*. Loudonville, OH: Mohican.

Moran, J., & Kalakian, L. (1974). *Movement experiences for the mentally retarded or emotionally disturbed child*. Minneapolis: Burgess.

Oakley, T. (1984). *Evaluation of direct service delivery and teacher training in physical education for handicapped students in Arkansas*. Unpublished doctoral dissertation, Texas Woman's University, Denton.

Rarick, G.L., & Dobbins, D.A. (1972). *Basic components in the motor performance of educable mentally retarded children: Implications of curriculum development* (Final project report to the U.S. Dept. of HEW, Office of Education). Berkeley: University of California, Dept. of Physical Education.

Rarick, G.L., Dobbins, D.A., & Broadhead, G.D. (1976). *The motor domain and its correlates in educationally handicapped children*. Englewood Cliffs, NJ: Prentice-Hall.

Rarick, G.L., & McQuillan, J.P. (1977). *The factor structure of motor abilities of trainable mentally retarded children: Implications for curriculum development* (Final project report to the U.S. Dept. of HEW, Office of Education). Berkeley: University of California, Dept. of Physical Education.

Rarick, G.L., Widdop, J.H., & Broadhead, G.D. (1970). The physical fitness and motor performance of educable mentally retarded children. *Exceptional Children, 37*, 509-519.

Reid, G. (1981). Perceptual-motor training: Has the term lost its utility? *Journal of Health, Physical Education, Recreation, and Dance, 52*(6), 38-39.

Sherrill, C. (Ed.). (1979). *Creative arts for the severely handicapped*. Springfield, IL: Charles C. Thomas.

Sherrill, C. (1985). Integration of handicapped students: Philosophical roots in pragmatism, idealism, and realism. *Adapted Physical Activity Quarterly, 2*(4), 264-272.

Sherrill, C. (1986a). *Adapted physical education and recreation: A multidisciplinary approach* (3rd ed.). Dubuque, IA: Wm. C. Brown.

Sherrill, C. (1986b). Fostering creativity in handicapped children. *Adapted Physical Activity Quarterly, 3*(3), 236-249.

Sherrill, C. (Ed.). (1986c). *Sports for disabled athletes*. Champaign, IL: Human Kinetics.

Sherrill, C., & Tymeson, G. (1979). *Directory of resources in physical education and recreation for the handicapped*. Denton, TX: Texas Woman's University.

Stein, J. (1969). Professional preparation in physical education and recreation for the mentally retarded. *Education and Training of the Mentally Retarded, 4*, 101-108.

Ulrich, D. (1985). *The test of gross motor development*. Austin: PRO-ED.

Vodola, T. (1973). *Individualized physical education for the handicapped child*. Englewood Cliffs, NJ: Prentice-Hall.

Vodola, T. (1976). *Developmental and adapted physical education: A competency-based teacher training manual*. Oakhurst, NJ: PROJECT ACTIVE.

Wessel, J. (Ed.). (1977). *Planning individualized education programs in special education*. Northbrook, IL: Hubbard.

Wessel, J., & Kelly, L. (1986). *Achievement-based curriculum in physical education*. Philadelphia: Lea & Febiger.

Winnick, J. (1972). Issues and trends in training adapted physical education personnel. *Journal of Health, Physical Education, and Recreation, 43*(8), 75-78.

Winnick, J. (1986). History of adapted physical education: Priorities in professional preparation. *Adapted Physical Activity Quarterly, 3*, 112-117.

Chapter 4
Evolution of a Profession: History and Contributions of Organizations

Claudine Sherrill

A profession is the practice of an art that utilizes many disciplines in serving mankind. (Steinhaus, 1967, p. 69)

Adapted physical education is a profession. It draws its theory and practice more or less equally from physical education and special education and to a lesser degree from physical therapy, occupational therapy, recreation, social psychology, and several other specializations. It is multidisciplinary in nature, utilizing many disciplines in ascertaining that all persons have opportunities for self-actualization through movement, sport, dance, and aquatics.

Several authorities have posited criteria for a profession (Boone, 1904; Flexner, 1915; Parsons, 1951). The most important of these appears to be altruism (i.e., regard for and devotion to the welfare of others). Kroll (1982) differentiates between labor, work, trade, craft, and profession, each located progressively higher on a continuum based on amount of service to society. In his comprehensive discussion of the dimensions of a profession, he states,

> A profession comes into existence owing to some specific need of society for a particular kind of service. . . . Modern society . . . demands many different kinds of services. Very often these services require extended periods of formal preparation before an individual can acquire the knowledge and skills to perform satisfactorily . . . in a specialty, the occupation claims fulfillment of all criteria necessary for designation as a profession. (Kroll, 1982, pp. 105-106)

Underlying the stance that adapted physical education is a profession is the belief that adapted physical education services should be provided by professionals with a graduate degree or an undergraduate specialization specifically in adapted physical education. Moreover, every state should offer a teacher certification, licensure, or endorsement specifically in adapted physical education.

The evolution of a profession cannot occur without dreams. Chapters 2 and 3 have described the individuals who dared to dream of physical education for all persons and who provided leadership in this effort.

Additionally, hundreds of individuals have contributed to the growth and development of professional preparation in adapted physical education since 1967. Every college and university teacher shapes the profession through the addition of courses to the curriculum, introduction of new units in existing courses, revision of course outlines, conducting preservice and in-service instruction, engaging in community service, and participating in advocacy activities for and with disabled individuals.

Appendix C is a glossary of the individuals who most influenced adapted physical education from 1967 to the present. For the most part these leaders served their profession primarily as officers of organizations and as authors or coauthors of textbooks. Through their service, (a) physical education has become a significant part of the lives of many persons who previously lacked exposure to sport, dance, and aquatics; (b) an area of specialization is evolving into an academic discipline; and (c) monies are being generated to upgrade teacher training and research.

Individuals striving to become leaders must learn as much as possible about professional organizations and the group dynamics through which change is effected and collegiality promoted. Leadership entails a knowledge of the past: pride in the achievements of one's organization and commitment to continued efforts in areas of success. Likewise, leadership demands knowledge of problems and the wisdom not to repeat the errors of earlier generations. Leaders are humanistic in that they care about and recognize the contributions of past leaders as well as those of the membership. The purpose of this chapter is to acquaint readers with the history and present status of professional organizations in hopes that this will stimulate increasingly strong adapted physical education leadership.

Several organizations have contributed to the growth and development of adapted physical education personnel preparation. Among these are the American Alliance For Health, Physical Education, Recreation and Dance (AAHPERD), the National Consortium on Physical Education and Recreation for the Handicapped, Special Olympics, Inc., and other organizations.

American Alliance for Health, Physical Education, Recreation and Dance

Physical educators take pride in the long, rich history of the Alliance. Recent controversy concerning the role of this organization in relation to adapted physical education heightens the importance of an examination of its past. Several structures, merged into one in 1985 and named the Adapted Physical Activity Council, have provided leadership over the years. These structures were Therapeutics Council/Section, beginning in 1905; Adapted Physical Education Academy/Section, beginning in 1958; and the Unit/Office on Programs for the Handicapped, which can be traced to 1965. The history of these structures is presented chronologically and organized under five stages. A brief history of AAHPERD, as a whole, opens the description of each stage.

Before 1900

In 1885, the Association for the Advancement of Physical Education (the forerunner of AAHPERD) was formed, with 49 charter members. Edward Hitchcock, a physician, of Amherst served as the first president. Among the other physicians who were active members during the first 15 years were Dudley Sargent of Harvard, William Anderson of Adelphi Academy in Brooklyn, Edward Hartwell of Johns Hopkins University, Dio Lewis, founder of Women's Christian Temperance Union as well as the first physical education teacher training program, Luther Halsey Gulick of Springfield, Massachusetts, Eliza Mosher of New York City, and Delphine Hanna of Oberlin College.

When special interest groups within the organization were formed, however, therapeutics was conspicuously absent. Although most of the organization's members were physicians, their concern was primarily school or educational gymnastics (also called hygienic) rather than medical gymnastics. It should be noted that the development of school gymnastics was the lifework of Hjalmar Ling (1820-1886), the son of Per Henrick Ling (1776-1839), who is credited with beginning medical gymnastics (McKenzie, 1923, p.112). Many textbooks fail to emphasize the early division of gymnastics into separate branches.

1900 to 1930

The Association changed its name in 1903 to the American Physical Education Association (APEA). A Committee on Teacher Education was operative, and work was under way to assure quality training through the granting of certificates. The recommended requirements for the 2-year training course included medical gymnastics and pathology, the equivalents of today's courses in adapted physical education. Thus all teachers were expected to have some training in this area.

In 1905 a special interest section open only to persons working in therapeutics was created. Twenty persons attended the first meeting, and Baroness Posse, wife of Nils Posse, was elected as first chairman (Lee & Bennett, 1985). The Posses were the recognized leaders of Swedish gymnastics at the time, having been the driving force in establishing this system in the Boston public schools and the Boston Normal School. The formation of the Therapeutics Section thus helped to bring together persons who supported the medical gymnastics of Ling. This may help to explain the lasting effect of Ling's work on the teacher training pedagogy of correctives.

Little is known about the early leadership and accomplishments of the Therapeutics Section. R. Tait McKenzie, as chairman in 1917, offered the services of its members to the U.S. Army to assist with medical treatment during World War I (Lee & Bennett, 1960), and many of the physician members of the Association were involved in the war effort. In 1921 the Therapeutics Section was revived under Harry E. Stewart of New Haven (Lee & Bennett, 1985), but no facts are recorded concerning its influence.

1930 to 1951

By 1930, the Association had 5,733 members. A new constitution and bylaws were approved that year, and the literature indicates that therapeutics was one of the 12 section meetings held at the annual conference (Goodwin, 1986). In 1931, the Association gave its first awards, and two of the recipients were recognized, among other things, as contributing to the therapeutics/correctives movement: Amy Morris Homans, an early supporter of Swedish gymnastics, retired from Wellesley College, formerly Boston Normal School of Gymnastics and Jesse Bancroft, author of *The Posture of School Children*.

In 1937, the Association changed its name to the American Association for Health and Physical Education and, in 1938, Recreation became a part of the Association's title. At this time also, AAHPE became a department of the National Education Association (NEA) and established a national headquarters in the NEA Building in Washington, DC. Thereafter, better records were maintained of the achievements and leadership of the sections. When the Association reorganized in 1937, three divisions were created: Health Education, Physical Education, and Recreation. Sections within the Physical Education Division were therapeutics, teacher training, administrative directors, administrative measurement, camping, college men's physical education, intramural athletics, men's athletics, private schools, public schools, research, safety, and women's athletics.

Some controversy ensued concerning the proper placement of therapeutics. From 1937 to 1942 it remained in the Physical Education Division; for the next 7 years it was a part of the Health Education Division; in 1949, when the General Division was created, therapeutics was one of the 12 sections assigned to it.

Leadership of the Therapeutics Section. A list of chairpersons of the Therapeutics Section from 1938 to 1952 reflects leaders in this area as well as institutions having particularly good training or service delivery programs.

1938-39   Claire Colestock, Assistant Director of Physical Education, Pasadena, California. Also coauthor with Lowman of *Corrective Physical Exercise for Groups*

1939-40   Catherine Worthington, Stanford University, later Director of Professional Education, The

National Foundation for Infantile Paralysis, and coauthor of *Therapeutic Exercise for Body Alignment and Function*

1941-42   Loraine Frost, University of Iowa

1942-43   Harlan Metcalf, Peabody College

1943-46   Caroline Sinclair, William and Mary College

1946-47   Virginia Shaw, Washington State College, coauthor of *The Science of Physical Education for Handicapped Children* (1962)

1947-48   Ellen Kelly, Pennsylvania State College, author of *Preventive and Corrective Physical Education* (1950)

1948-49   Cecil (Cy) Morgan, Department of the Army, Office of the Surgeon General

1949-50   Leah Gregg, University of California at Los Angeles

1950-51   King McCristal, Michigan State University

1951-52   Valerie Hunt, University of California at Los Angeles, coauthor with Rathbone of *Corrective Physical Education*, 7th edition.

In addition, some of the individuals who provided leadership to correctives by chairing committees and/or speaking at the annual meetings were

Charles L. Lowman	1939, 1950
George Stafford	1939, 1940, 1950
Josephine Rathbone	1939, 1942, 1944, 1947, 1950, 1952
Catherine Worthington	1939, 1942
H. Harrison Clarke	1947, 1948, 1950

Leaders of the Therapeutics Section strove to maintain its multi- or interdisciplinary nature. Many individuals who attended the section meetings were affiliated with physical therapy and/or corrective therapy as well as physical education. Preconvention meetings therefore were held jointly with the American Physiotherapy Association in 1942, 1944, 1947, 1948, and 1952. These meetings, as well as many of the regularly scheduled ones, focused on topics of mutual interest to physical educators and physical therapists (Therapeutics Section, circa 1965). The scope of the Therapeutics Section thus was perceived as encompassing school correctives but also including reconditioning or rehabilitation (postwar terms) in general.

Examination of the Role and Scope of Therapeutics/ Adapted Physical Education.   Throughout the 1940s and 1950s both standing and ad hoc committees examined

the role and scope of the Section. The height of this activity came before 1952, the official date that the term *adapted physical education* was defined and publicized by AAHPER (Committee on Adapted Physical Education, 1952).

Daniels (1954) credits the use of this new term and the acceptance of new directions to a committee appointed in 1946 by the Chairman of the Therapeutics Section (this would have been either Caroline Sinclair, 1945-46, or Virginia Shaw, 1946-47). Originally called the Committee on Implications of Reconditioning for Physical Education, this committee held four meetings during 1946. Mimeographed materials from the Therapeutics Section's officer files (1965) state,

This committee (in 1946) consisted of Ben Boynton, Authur S. Daniels, Charles D. Giauque, Earl C. Elkins, Josephine Rathbone, Catherine Worthington, and H. Harrison Clarke, chairman. The committee was concerned with (a) extent and nature of the reconditioning field, (b) place of therapeutic exercise, and (c) preliminary considerations of training standards for personnel desiring to enter this work. (p.7)

In 1947 two committee reports were presented at the annual section meeting: *Implications of Reconditioning for Physical Education* by H. Harrison Clarke and *A Preliminary Statement of Standards for the Training of Reconditioning Specialists* by Josephine Rathbone. In 1948 and 1949 the Committee on Physical Education and Recreation in Rehabilitation made reports, but no names are recorded. In 1950, H. Harrison Clarke made this committee's report, and George Stafford and Cy Morgan reported on future plans for the Therapeutics Section and the promotion of research and publications in therapeutics, respectively.

Creation of the Adapted Physical Education Standing Committee.   No information is available on committee work in 1951 other than the statement, "The Committee on Adapted Physical Education was given status as a Standing Committee for a period of three years" (Therapeutic Section, 1965, p. 9). In 1952 the report of the Standing Committee on Adapted Physical Education was given by H. Harrison Clarke.

Eight years of work were devoted to the creation of the *Guiding Principles for Adapted Physical Education in Elementary and Secondary Schools and Colleges* (Committee on Adapted Physical Education, 1952), which officially changed the conceptualization of therapeutics/ correctives work to the modern day adapted physical education. This work serves as a primary example of how leaders contribute to their profession through service on Association committees. The changing membership of this committee from 1946 to 1952 is not recorded, but Arthur S. Daniels was also involved in its accomplishment. He recalls history as follows:

> A committee was appointed in 1946 by the Chairman of the National Therapeutics Section of the American Association for Health, Physical Education and Recreation to study the implications of reconditioning for physical education. This committee, in 1951, made one of its first projects the drafting of a set of guiding principles for adapted physical education. Arthur S. Daniels was commissioned to prepare the first draft of this document, which subsequently was approved by the Board of Directors of the American Association for Health, Physical Education and Recreation and endorsed by the Joint Committee on Health Problems in Education of the American Medical Association and the National Education Association. (Daniels, 1954, p. 88)

Thus the era of adapted physical education began. This new movement, however, brought friction within AAHPER, which was manifested by separate leaderships in the old Therapeutics Section and a newly created Adapted Physical Education Section.

1952 to 1967

By the 1950s, the Association had grown to approximately 20,000 members. The national headquarters staff was becoming increasingly large and helpful; Carl Troester was executive director assisted by Myrtle Spande. Emphasis was on fitness, and AAHPER was instrumental in President Eisenhower's creation of the President's Council on Youth Fitness in 1956. The Russians shot Sputnik into space in 1957. James Conant, in 1963, published *The Education of American Teachers*, attacking teacher education in physical education: "If I wished to portray the education of teachers in the worst terms, I should quote from the description of some graduate courses in physical education" (p. 201). The knowledge explosion was forcing university teachers to spend more time in scholarly activity merely to stay abreast. The internal struggle within AAHPER for independent organizations by health, physical education, recreation, and dance was beginning; the problems and concerns within the therapeutics/adapted area were dwarfed by larger issues.

Two major professional preparation conferences were held, one on undergraduate study and one on graduate study. Both resulted in publications (American Association for Health, Physical Education, and Recreation, 1962, 1967) that stated recommendations for training. These conferences reaffirmed our profession's belief in a broad liberal arts background as the foundation of teacher training and stressed that the undergraduate degree was for the preparation of generalists. Five years of professional preparation were deemed necessary because of the enormous expansion of knowledge in all fields. Each broad curricular area was listed and recommended on a 4-point scale from strongly recommended to not recommended. Adapted physical education was strongly recommended for all physical education majors (AAHPER, 1962).

Other AAHPER contributions from 1952 to 1967 to the growth of adapted physical education as a profession apparently were few; little written history has been preserved. Two sections (Therapeutics and Adapted Physical Education) held meetings at national conferences and presumably pursued different, but complementary, goals. The Therapeutics Section and the Adapted Physical Education Sections were, respectively, located in the General and the Physical Education Divisions of AAHPERD and were no doubt influenced by the separate personalities and politics of each. By 1966, when Sherrill was elected chair of the Therapeutics Section, few persons could remember the reason for separate structures and several individuals believed the two sections should be combined. It is noteworthy that Eunice Kennedy Shriver, in 1965, took her historic plea for help for mentally retarded children to the Recreation Division rather than to either of these structures.

Beginning of the Adapted Physical Education Section. The precise beginning of the Adapted Physical Education Section remains unclear; no records seem to exist. The Archives of the American Alliance for Health, Physical Education, Recreation and Dance has on file copies of the fifth (1950-51), sixth (1951-52), and seventh (1952-53) annual reports of the Committee on Adapted Physical Education. Thereafter the archivist can find no information until 1956-57, when the Report of the Physical Education Division indicates that appointments of officers need to be made for the Adapted Physical Education Section.

For 1958-59, Janet Wessel of Michigan State University was named the first chairperson of the Adapted Physical Education Section (AAHPERD Archives, Records of the Physical Education Division). The permanent status for the Adapted Physical Education Section was approved by the new Board of Directors at the close of the 1958 Kansas City Convention and subsequently by a mail vote of the Representative Assembly.

The official beginning of the Adapted Physical Education Section thus can be designated as 1958. The first chairpersons of this section were as follows:

1958-59   Janet Wessel, Michigan State University

1959-60   Thomas Scott, University of Florida at Gainesville

1960-61   Evelyn Davies, Indiana University

1961-62   Wayne Van Huss, Michigan State University

1962-63   Louise Temerson, University of Alabama, Tuscaloosa

1963-64   George Grover, NY State Education Dept.

1964-65   Dorothy Gillanders, Arizona State University at Tempe

1965-66   Frank Sills, East Stroudsburg State University, PA

1966-67   Helen Belknap, Oak Park, IL

Therapeutics Section Role and Scope.   The Therapeutics Section continued to function much as it had previously, but in 1956, the American Physical Therapy Association (APTA) requested that it be removed from the list of organizations affiliated with AAHPER. The last joint meeting of the Therapeutics Section with the APTA was in 1952. The interdisciplinary aspect of the Section gradually changed from physical to corrective therapy. In 1946 the Association for Physical and Mental Rehabilitation, the forerunner of the American Corrective Therapy Association, had been established. This organization held joint meetings with the Therapeutics Section at the annual AAHPERD conferences from 1961 on (Therapeutics Section, 1965). Many adapted physical educators undertook certification in corrective physical therapy, which was achieved by adding several months of hospital clinical work (usually in Veterans Administration facilities) to a strong scientifically based undergraduate background in physical education. Through the joint AAHPER meetings, many young professionals first learned of the existence of corrective therapy and sought this advanced training, which primarily focused on orthopedics, an area not typically well covered in university training programs.

Officers in the Therapeutics Section were

1952-54   Robert Shelton, University of Illinois

1954-56   Katharine Wells, University of Colorado, author of *Kinesiology* (1950)

1956-58   Charles Kovacic, Ohio State University

1958-59   Margaret Poley, University of Oregon

1959-60   Edwin Blesh, Yale University

1960-61   Frances Bascom, University of Colorado

1961-62   David H. Clarke, University of California at Berkeley, coauthor of *Developmental and Adapted Physical Education* (1963)

1962-63   Karl Klein, University of Texas, coauthor of *The Knee in Sports* (1969)

1963-64   Mildred Ringo, University of Wyoming

1964-65   Homer H. Merrifield, Ithaca College, New York

1965-66   Barbara Ryan, Central State College, Oklahoma

1966-67   Claudine Sherrill, Texas Woman's University, author of *Adapted Physical Education and Recreation* (1976)

These individuals demonstrated leadership primarily by planning and conducting the annual section meetings and by encouraging colleagues and students to join AAHPER and become involved in activities pertaining to therapeutics, correctives, and adapted physical education.

Project and National Task Force.   The most significant event of the 1952 to 1967 era was the creation of the AAHPER Project on Recreation and Fitness for the Mentally Retarded in 1965. This project, which evolved into the Unit on Programs for the Handicapped, was funded primarily by the Joseph P. Kennedy, Jr. Foundation and the federal government rather than by AAHPER (Stein, 1986a). Jackson Anderson, AAHPER Consultant in Recreation at that time, was largely responsible for the initiation of the proposal funded by the Kennedy Foundation. Robert Holland, on leave from the Ohio State Department of Education, was project director from July 1, 1965, through July 30, 1966, after which Julian Stein of the University of Rhode Island became director. The project was guided also by a national task force. The chairman of the first task force (1965) was Julian Stein; the members were

Laura Mae Brown, Webster Groves Public Schools, Webster Groves, MD

Hollis Fait, University of Connecticut

Belle Mead Holm, Lamar State College of Technology, Beaumont, TX

John McGinn, Union Free School District No. 14, Hewlett, NY

James A. Mello, Mansfield State Training School and Hospital, Mansfield, CT

Cecil W. Morgan, Ithaca College, Ithaca, NY

Wayne Nichols, Elwyn School, Media, PA

Janet Pomeroy, Recreation Center for the Handicapped, San Francisco, CA

Lawrence Rarick, University of Wisconsin

Lola Sadlo, San Fernando Valley State College, Northridge, CA

Thomas A. Stein, University of North Carolina

George T. Wilson, Division of Municipal Recreation and Adult Education, Milwaukee, WI

In 1966, three physical education members were added to the Task Force:

Dolores Geddes, Indiana State University

M. Louise Moseley, State University of New York at Cortland

Ernie Davis, St. Paul Public Schools, St. Paul, MN

The membership of this steering committee changed little over the next 15 years; these individuals thus helped to shape the role and scope of AAHPER services in both adapted physical education and recreation.

1967 to the Present

AAHPER membership climbed to 50,000 in the 1960s; today it is around 37,000. In 1974 the name of the Association officially became the American Alliance for Health, Physical Education, and Recreation. In 1979, Dance was added to the name. The nature of the organization thus changed from one large structure to six independent associations. Thereafter four of these organizations regularly offered programs concerning handicapping conditions at the annual conference.

- Association for Research, Administration, Professional Councils, and Societies (ARAPCS), specifically the Therapeutics Council

- National Association of Sport and Physical Education (NASPE), specifically the Adapted Physical Education Council

- American Association for Leisure and Recreation (AALR), specifically the Leisure for Special Populations substructure

- National Dance Association (NDA), specifically the Dance for Special Populations substructure

Additionally, the Task Force on Programs for the Handicapped sponsored programs, and preconference meetings were sometimes held by the Therapeutics Council and/or the Adapted Physical Education Council. For individuals wishing in-service or a chance to share ideas and concerns, the national conference was a feast.

Julian Stein, Director of the AAHPERD Unit on the Handicapped from 1966 through 1981, unofficially and informally coordinated the efforts of leaders within the various AAHPERD structures; achievements are described in chapter 5. Several times during this era, leaders in

Julian Stein, Director of the AAHPERD Unit on the Handicapped from 1966 through 1981, with Sue Grosse, public school leader and recipient of the Mabel Lee Award.

therapeutics/adapted physical education petitioned AAHPERD to create an umbrella structure. This structure was conceptualized in numerous ways, but many members dreamed of a separate association similar to ARAPCS or NASPE, with all the substructures pertaining to handicapping conditions in one administrative unit, with an independent budget and AAHPERD staff.

In the 1970s the number of AAHPERD members who checked the handicapped as one of their two major interest areas was approximately 5,000 (10% of the total membership). This seemed a strong rationale for an autonomous umbrella structure. Nevertheless, the request was repeatedly denied, partly because the change would decrease the fiscal resources of each existing association. Because the budget of each association was based partly on the number of individuals who annually checked one of the substructures as their main interest on the membership form when dues were paid, it is perhaps understandable why the politics within AAHPERD would not yield to the desire of specialists in therapeutics/adapted physical education. Each substructure therefore continued to do its best to meet the needs of its members.

Officers From 1967 to 1986. The officers of the Therapeutics Council were

1967-68 Jay Fischer, Kent State University in Ohio

1968-69 Ellen Kelley, author of *Adapted and Corrective Physical Education*

1970-76   Norma Sue Griffin, University of Nebraska

1970-71   Robert Shelton, University of Illinois

1971-72   Frank Papscy, University of New Mexico

1972-73   Elizabeth Lane, Northern Illinois University

1973-74   Edna Wooten, University of Oregon

1974-75   B. Robert Carlson, San Diego State University, California, later to become editor of *American Corrective Therapy Journal*

1975-76   Peter Wisher, Gallaudet College, Washington, DC

1976-77   Helen Connor, University of Alabama

1977-78   Jean Pyfer, University of Kansas, coauthor of *Adapted Physical Education and Recreation*

1978-79   John Dunn, Oregon State University, coauthor of *Special Physical Education*

1979-80   Dianne Hurley, University of Northern Colorado

1980-81   Robert Strauss, Trinity University, San Antonio, Texas

1981-82   Reba Sims, Southwest Missouri State University

1982-83   Karen DePauw, Washington State University, coauthor of *The New Adapted Physical Education*

1983-84   Michael Churton, Appalachian State University, North Carolina

1984-85   E. Michael Loovis, Cleveland State University, Ohio

1985-86   Garth Tymeson, Northern Illinois University

The officers of the Adapted Physical Education Section from 1967 until 1975 were

1967-68   Michael Flanagan, Pennsylvania Department of Public Instruction

1968-69   Karl Stoedefalke, University of Wisconsin, Madison

1969-70   Walter Gart, Mt. Prospect, Illinois

1970-71   Karl Klein, University of Texas

1971-72   Agnes Hooley, Bowling Green State University, Ohio

1972-73   David Auxter, Slippery Rock State College, Pennsylvania

1973-74   William Chasey, George Peabody University, Nashville

1974-75   Wendell Liemohn, Indiana University

1975-76   Lorraine Shearer, Oregon State University

In 1975 the Physical Education Division changed the status of several of its sections, including adapted physical education, to academies. Ross Merrick, Executive Director of NASPE, appointed William Chasey, the director of the National Consortium on Physical Education and Recreation for the Handicapped federally funded project, to chair the new Academy in 1976-77. Thereafter the officers were

1977-78   Lane Goodwin, University of Wisconsin at Lacrosse

1978-79   Leon Johnson, University of Missouri

1979-80   Robert Roice, Los Angeles County Public Schools, California

1980-81   Ernie Bundschuh, University of Georgia

1981-82   Pete Aufsesser, San Diego State University, California

1982-83   Jean Pyfer, Texas Woman's University, coauthor of *Adapted Physical Education and Recreation*

1983-84   Julian Stein, George Mason University, Virginia

1984-85   John Dunn, Oregon State University

1985-86   Jo Ellen Cowden, University of New Orleans

Accomplishments Prior to Closing the Unit on the Handicapped.   The accomplishments of AAHPERD in regard to therapeutics/adapted physical education from 1967 to 1984 were phenomenal. Numerous conferences, institutes, workshops, and clinics were held throughout the country. Foremost among these were the gatherings that led to the publication of professional preparation guidelines and competencies in 1973 and 1981 (see Appendix B). Consultation was available at all levels, and AAHPERD staff frequently traveled to universities and state and local association meetings to provide technical assistance. A Clearinghouse similar to that of the Educational Resources Information Center (ERIC) was established and contributed immeasurably to the quantity and quality of research in our field. Instrumental in helping to create a substantial knowledge base for adapted physical education was the publication of numerous books, periodicals, and newsletters (see Appendix F). These accomplishments, described by Stein (1986a), were primarily the work of the AAHPER(D) Unit on Programs for the Handicapped, not that of the Therapeutics and Adapted Physical Education substructures as it had been prior to 1965.

The AAHPER(D) Unit on Programs for the Handicapped is described further in chapter 5 because its work was made possible primarily through federal funding. This support ceased with fiscal year 1979-80, and controversy ensued over whether the unit should be continued through allocation of Alliance monies. Hundreds of members repeatedly wrote AAHPERD officers requesting retention of the unit, but special populations were not a high enough priority for the Alliance to act favorably.

Closing the Unit on the Handicapped.   On May 31, 1984, after 19 years as a staff-represented unit at our national headquarters, the AAHPERD Unit on Programs for the Handicapped ceased to exist. In response, Stein (1984) wrote,

> Recent actions by the Alliance Board of Governors turn the clock back to pre-1965 days. Although structures devoted to these populations can be found in four Associations, their track records over recent years show them to be dominantly, if not exclusively, convention planning bodies. . . . Despite elation by some individuals over the few services which were salvaged, *disappointment* and genuine concerns are far more characteristic. (p. 2)

Concurrent with the closing of the unit office was the long-sought merger of the Therapeutics Council and Adapted Physical Education Academy (DePauw, 1986). The pleasure of achieving this goal of 20 to 30 years duration was clouded by the realization that most services to the membership had been lost. The politics of what was happening were not clear. The adapted physical education leader who knew the most about the functioning of the Alliance, Julian Stein, was not appointed to the AAHPERD committee structured to study special population services within the Alliance and to make recommendations for change. Two AAHPERD presidents, Wayne Osness and Bea Orr, determined the individuals who would be influential in the restructuring. Ross Merrick, NASPE consultant, and Ray Ciszek, ARAPCS consultant, were also believed to be involved in this decision making. A changing of the committee structure halfway into the study no doubt affected its effectiveness. Individuals comprising the Coordinating Committee for Programs on Special Populations, under the two presidents, respectively, were

	1983	1984
NASPE	John Dunn	Charles Hungerfield
ARAPCS	Karen DePauw	Karen DePauw
NDA	Anne Riordan	Connie Jo Hepworth
AALR	Larry Neal	Dave Austin
Member-at-large —		Muriel Sloan

The complete report of the 1983 committee (Dunn, 1984) appears in Appendix I. Included in this report, the product of a 3-day meeting, were two recommendations: (a) that a commission on special populations be established to oversee and coordinate the efforts of those throughout the Alliance providing services and programs related to individuals with disabilities and (b) that the Adapted Physical Education Academy and Therapeutics Council be merged into one structure (Dunn, 1984). Although written in 1983, this report was not published and/or disseminated to the general membership until the May, 1984 issue of *Able Bodies*. The process of change was nevertheless proceeding in full compliance with Alliance procedures. The committee report was presented to the AAHPERD president, the executive committee, and the board of governors. In April, 1984 at the AAHPERD Conference in Anaheim, the board of governors accepted the committee report and approved the two recommendations (DePauw, 1986). The second committee was appointed at this time by Bea Orr to study and make recommendations specifically concerning the merger. Subsequent steps in the change process were described by DePauw (1986).

The Adapted Physical Activity Council.   In the fall of 1985, the resulting merged structure was named the Adapted Physical Activity Council and the decision was made to house it in ARAPCS. Garth Tymeson and Jo Ellen Cowden, chairs of the now nonexistent Therapeutics Section and Adapted Physical Education Academy, were directed to serve cooperatively during the transition. Janet Seaman and Michael Horvat, chair-elects of these structures, were named the first and second chairs, respectively, of the new Adapted Physical Activity Council for 1986-87 and 1987-88.

The purpose and objectives of the new structure, as determined by the committee appointed by Bea Orr and chaired by Karen DePauw, are the following:

> The purpose of Adapted Physical Activity Council shall be to (a) further the body of knowledge in physical education, sport, and recreation for individuals with disabilities by promoting research, (b) promote, stimulate, and encourage

habilitative and rehabilitative programs of and through physical activity for individuals with disabilities through contributions to the professional literature and dissemination of information and (c) to provide a unified base for cooperative interdisciplinary action in providing services for individuals with special needs.

Specific objectives include:

A. Developing and disseminating pertinent professional materials that can be utilized by those working with and/or preparing for careers serving individuals with disabilities,

B. Initiating, sponsoring, and/or collaborating in conferences, workshops, and projects promoting the physical activity needs of individuals with disabilities,

C. Planning and conducting informative programs at national convention of AAHPERD,

D. Encouraging professionals throughout the AAHPERD affiliated structures to initiate projects and research studies which recognize concerns specific to individuals with disabilities,

E. Soliciting input concerning training, program, and research needs from individuals with disabilities and special advocacy groups,

F. Coordinating efforts with other structures to provide a unified endeavor in serving those with disabilities, and

G. Maintaining cooperative relations with other professional and advocate organizations serving individuals with disabilities. (DePauw, 1985, p. 3)

The implementation of these goals and objectives presents a challenge to the new generation of AAHPERD leaders. Can the objectives be achieved by volunteers (i.e, officers of AAHPERD structures), or did the history of such services end with the failure to salary a director for the Unit on Programs for the Handicapped? History remains to be made. Leaders are sorely needed to direct and serve on AAHPERD committees; work of this nature often requires individuals to commit personal money as well as time. This includes money for travel to conferences, for telephoning and correspondence, and for typing, duplicating, and disseminating committee reports. Leaders either use their own money or are skillful in generating it from their places of work or external sources.

National Consortium on Physical Education and Recreation for the Handicapped

The purpose of the National Consortium on Physical Education and Recreation for the Handicapped (NCPERH) is to promote, stimulate, encourage, and conduct professional preparation and research in physical education and recreation for individuals with handicapping conditions. As such, this organization has played a major role in shaping the future of adapted physical education, particularly as a graduate specialization and a profession/discipline. Its membership has been active in promoting legislation and funding favorable to physical education and recreation for handicapped individuals, in disseminating information about PL 94-142, and in generating a growing knowledge base for adapted physical education through research and demonstration (Bundschuh, 1986; Johnson, 1986).

Membership is currently open to anyone who is or has been involved in training, demonstration, or research activity related to physical education and recreation for handicapped individuals. The membership chairman, beginning in 1986 (for the next 5 years), is Glenn Roswal, Physical Education Department, Jacksonville State University, Jacksonville, AL 36265.

Early Roots in Government Funding

The Consortium was founded in 1975, the date of the decision to incorporate as a nonprofit organization. Its early beginnings, however, can be traced to federal legislation (PL 90-170) in 1967. John Nesbitt, an early NCPERH president, recalls the beginning as follows:

The National Consortium and its program were triggered by, first, the passage of legislation on physical education and recreation for the handicapped children introduced by Senator Ted Kennedy and, in turn, the initiation of a program in physical education and recreation by the Bureau of Education for the Handicapped. Those of us working for the goals of the National Consortium are indebted to Senator Kennedy and the Bureau. (Nesbitt, 1977b, p. 1)

Title V, Section 501 of PL 90-170, The Mental Retardation Facilities and Community Mental Health Centers Construction Act, was the first federal legislation to authorize personnel training specifically in physical education and recreation for the handicapped. Implementation of this new program was assigned to the Bureau of Education for the Handicapped (BEH) within HEW, which is now known as the Office of Special Education Programs (OSEP) within the U.S. Department of Education. A flurry of activity ensued; William Hillman, a therapeutic recreation specialist, was employed by BEH to direct this new initiative, and a search was begun for colleges and universities to submit grant proposals. A conference (June 26-28, 1968) was also held to determine funding priorities and provide technical assistance to individuals who might wish to write grants (Gallagher, Lucito, & Hillman, 1968).

In fiscal year 1969, when money for PL 90-170 was finally appropriated, the Division of Training Programs of BEH allocated $300,000 to physical education and recreation. This money subsequently was awarded to 15 colleges and universities in sums of about $20,000 each. Seven of the awards went to physical education programs, six to recreation, and two to combined physical education and recreation (Table 4.1). Most of the directors of these first programs became charter members of NCPERH. Additionally, monies were awarded to physical education and recreation by the Research Branch of BEH. Early recipients of research funds included such individuals as Julian Stein, AAHPER; Janet Wessel, Michigan State University; Doris Berryman, New York University; Larry Rarick, University of California at Berkeley; and Jack Keogh, University of California at Los Angeles.

Needs of Early Leaders

Of these early recipients of training and research grants, none had a background of formal study in adapted or corrective physical education because this graduate specialization, as known today, did not yet exist. Several of the physical educators, however, were acknowledged leaders in motor and/or perceptual-motor development. Barbara Godfrey, coauthor of *Movement Patterns and Motor Education* (1969), had worked extensively with Newell C. Kephart. Larry Rarick had published a monograph on motor development (1952), and Janet Wessel (1957, 1963) had authored two books on fitness and movement. Additionally, Wessel was trained as a physical therapist. Some individuals, like Julian Stein, had completed several courses in special education as part of their graduate studies.

Much needed to be learned and shared in the shaping of new graduate curricula to prepare physical educators and recreators to serve handicapped children and youth. The early grant directors, however, did not know one another, and no structure existed for sharing. Moreover, it was clear that physical education and recreation leaders would need to become increasingly knowledgeable about

Table 4.1 Recipients of First Training Grants in Physical Education and Recreation for the Handicapped

Physical Education	Recreation
1. Lou Bowers University of South Florida	1. John Nesbitt San Jose State College
2. Barbara Godfrey University of Missouri	2. Edith Ball New York University
3. Larry Rarick University of California, Berkeley	3. Peter Verhoven University of Kentucky
4. Walt Ersing Ohio State University	4. Larry Neal University of Oregon
5. Lynn McCraw University of Texas	5. H. Douglas Sessoms University of North Carolina
6. Honey Nashman George Washington University	6. Allen Sapora University of Illinois
7. Walter Hambrick University of South Carolina	

Combined Physical Education and Recreation

1. Dolores Musgraves (Geddes)
   Indiana State University

2. Edith DeBonis
   Southern Connecticut State College

Note. All individuals on this list were program directors except Lynn McCraw and Allen Sapora, who were department heads who employed directors. Barbara Godfrey died unexpectedly shortly after the University of Missouri program was begun, and Leon Johnson became the new director.

legislation, proposal writing, and grants management if handicapped children were to receive desired services. NCPERH was created primarily to meet these two needs.

Founding of Official Structure

Two individuals are recognized as the founding fathers of NCPERH, Lou Bowers and Bill Hillman. Bowers, with the encouragement of Hillman, called for an informal meeting of grant directors at the 1972 annual AAHPER Conference in Houston. These individuals were enthusiastic about sharing program management ideas, and Bowers agreed to organize and publicize a symposium for grant directors at the 1973 AAHPERD annual conference. Twenty-five persons representing 22 BEH projects participated in the resulting symposium in Minneapolis, and the National Ad Hoc Committee on Physical Education and Recreation for the Handi-

Founders of the National Consortium on Physical Education and Recreation for the Handicapped: Lou Bowers (left) and Bill Hillman (right).

capped was formed. This was the forerunner of NCPERH.

The first official conference of the National Ad Hoc Committee was held several months later, December 3-5, 1973, in Washington, DC. This date and location were chosen because Congress would be in session and BEH grant directors could call upon their respective senators, get acquainted with their aides, and thereby increase the support of Congress in regard to physical education and recreation for handicapped children and youth. After visiting his or her congressperson, each grant director developed and presented to the Ad Hoc Committee a brief statement concerning the physical education and recreation needs of his or her state. This conference thus served as a first lesson in advocacy for many of the project directors.

Another purpose of this first National Conference on Program Development and Evaluation in Physical Education and Recreation for Handicapped Children and Youth was to identify and discuss issues in personnel training (Johnson & Nesbitt, 1973). The two issues ranked as most important were (a) educating the general public to the physical education and recreation needs of the handicapped and (b) communicating the importance of physical education and recreation to administrators. The advocacy mission of the Ad Hoc Committee was clear.

The National Ad Hoc Committee functioned from 1973 to 1975. Three sets of cochairpersons representing adapted physical education and therapeutic recreation, respectively, provided leadership as follows:

1973 Leon Johnson and John Nesbitt
1974 John Nesbitt and Joan Moran
1975 Joan Moran and Joseph Winnick

John Dunn, in 1974, became editor of a quarterly newsletter for the group. Early meetings of this Ad Hoc Committee were held in conjunction with the annual conferences of American Alliance for Health, Physical Education, and Recreation (AAHPER) and National Therapeutic Recreation Society (NTRS). Additionally, annual winter conferences were planned for Washington, DC. At the December 12-13, 1974, meeting, the National Ad Hoc Committee presented National Leadership Awards to Edwin Martin, Acting Deputy Commissioner of BEH, and Senator Edward Kennedy of Massachusetts. At this meeting also the membership became aware of the legislative action that was to culminate in PL 94-142, the Education for All Handicapped Children Act. It was obvious that physical education and recreation leaders should be involved in this effort, and the Ad Hoc Committee realized that, through incorporation as a nonprofit organization, it could apply for federal funds.

Incorporation of NCPERH

Joseph Winnick and Don Hawkins thus were directed to draft a constitution for a formal organizational structure to be voted upon at the next annual meeting (Winnick, 1975). Winnick, a physical education professor at the State University of New York (SUNY) at Brockport, would be the senior cochair of the Ad Hoc Committee at its next meeting. Hawkins, owner-director of several business enterprises related to recreation for the handicapped in Washington, DC, was asked to help because of his experience and expertise with regard to incorporation. Edith DeBonis, State University of Connecticut, also worked on this constitution.

At what would have been the third annual conference of the Ad Hoc Committee (not counting its 1-day meetings in conjunction with AAHPER and NTRS), the members voted to accept this constitution (with some changes, of course) and become a nonprofit organization known as the National Consortium on Physical Education and Recreation for the Handicapped (NCPERH). The conference, held in Lexington, Kentucky, on August 18-19, 1975, was cochaired by Joseph Winnick and Dennis Vinton. The first officers elected for the new organization were

President	Leon Johnson, University of Missouri
President-Elect	John Nesbitt, University of Iowa
Secretary	Stan Labanowich, University of Kentucky
Treasurer	Joan Moran, Texas Woman's University
PE Representative	Mel Evans, Jackson State University
PE Representative	Lane Goodwin, University of Wisconsin at LaCrosse
Rec Representative	Carol Peterson, Michigan State University
Rec Representative	Dennis Vinton, University of Kentucky

John Dunn continued to serve as editor of the quarterly newsletter until 1981.

NCPERH Achievements

These individuals, along with BEH employees Bill Hillman (Training) and Mel Appell (Research), can be considered the pioneers in initiating the body of knowledge in physical education and recreation known today as advocacy. In the early 1970s college and university professors were largely naive about the authorization, appropriation, and awarding of grant monies to fund teacher training and research. It was these NCPERH leaders who taught colleagues to establish rapport with the individuals representing their states in Congress and to ascertain that physical education and recreation needs of handicapped children were understood and acted upon via PL 94-142. These NCPERH leaders also strove to emphasize the relationship between high quality personnel

preparation, research, and service delivery. Documentation of their success is the inclusion of physical education and recreation in PL 91-230 (1970), PL 93-380 (1974), PL 95-49 (1977), PL 98-199 (1983), and PL 99-457 (1986). These are the laws that among other things, authorize Congress to appropriate monies for BEH (now Office of Special Education [OSE]) to award to colleges, universities, and agencies. Today all responsible physical education and recreation for the handicapped personnel regularly communicate with congresspersons through correspondence, telephoning, and personal visits (see chapter 16 on advocacy). Illustrative letters to congresspersons to guide readers of this text in initiating advocacy activities appear in Appendix J.

After its incorporation as a consortium in 1975, NCPERH alternated the position of president between representatives of physical education and recreation. The persons who have served as NCPERH presidents are listed in Table 4.2. These persons, as well as other NCPERH members, have provided leadership over the years in monitoring BEH/OSE activities in relation to physical education and recreation, communicating the rationale for continued personnel preparation funding to government officials, assessing and prioritizing needs, and in-servicing colleagues with respect to quality grant writing and management. Other persons who have contributed to accomplishment of the NCPERH mission are William Hillman and Mel Appell, BEH/OSE staff members, who have generously given of their time and energies in promoting, stimulating, and encouraging professional preparation and research in physical education and recreation for handicapped individuals (Nesbitt, 1983).

One of the most outstanding achievements of NCPERH was the inclusion of physical education and recreation in PL 94-142. This work began in 1973 when David Auxter chaired a committee (Rarick, Keogh, Szymanski, Moran, and Stein) that developed a strong position paper entitled *A Model Legislative Statue in Physical Education for the Handicapped*. This paper established that a model legislative statute (i.e., PL 94-142) should aim for a goal that included

1. A definition of the scope of the program;

2. A definition of the nature of the process of implementation of the program;

3. A definition of the capability of personnel implementing the program;

4. An evaluation and monitoring of program implementation; and

First presidents of National Consortium on Physical Education and Recreation for the Handicapped. Leon Johnson, John Nesbitt, and Claudine Sherrill (top). Dennis Vinton and Max Forman (center). Joseph Winnick and John Dunn (bottom).

Table 4.2 Presidents of the National Consortium on Physical Education and Recreation for the Handicapped

Year	President	Professional Affiliation
1975	Leon Johnson	University of Missouri
1976	John Nesbitt	University of Iowa
1977	Claudine Sherrill	Texas Woman's University
1978	Dennis Vinton	University of Kentucky
1979	Joseph Winnick	SUNY at Brockport
1980	David Compton	University of Missouri
1981	John Dunn	Oregon State University
1982	Fred Humphrey	University of Maryland
1983	Ernie Bundschuh	University of Georgia
1984	Max Forman	Private Practice, San Francisco
1985	Louis Bowers	University of South Florida
1986	Charles Bullock	University of North Carolina at Chapel Hill
1987	Mike Churton	Appalachian State University, North Carolina

5. Provisions for contingencies for failing to meet mandated legislation on the part of all responsible personnel concerned (Auxter, 1973, p. 2).

Nesbitt chronicled the years of work on PL 94-142 as follows:

> Functionally, the steps have been: 1) passage of legislation, 2) convening of a writing team to draft the rules, 3) public hearings on the rules where the public, the professions and agencies gave opinion on the draft rules, 4) preparation of final rules by HEW and BEH staff, and 5) implementation of the rules and regulations.
>
> Regarding step one, the passage of legislation, over the last 10 years there has been increasing interest and support for physical education and recreation for the handicapped. First, it was Senator Kennedy who introduced legislation that provided physical education and recreation for handicapped children. Successive testimony by physical educators and recreators resulted in the Senate and House's overt recognition of physical education and recreation for the handicapped. Through the leadership of Mrs. Eunice Kennedy Shriver, and the Kennedy Foundation, Public Law 94-142 calls for the provision of physical education [as a direct service] and mandates recreation as a related service. . . . For step two, over 100 professionals working in

all aspects of special education were called into Washington, D.C. by the Bureau of Education for the Handicapped to advise on the draft formulation of the Rules for Public Law 94-142. Physical Education and Recreation were presented by Dr. David Auxter, Dr. William Chasey, and Dr. Fred Humphrey.

> Public hearings, step three, were held during February in Washington, D.C., Boston, Chicago, Denver, San Francisco, and Atlanta. These were open to the public and a number of representatives of physical education and recreation testified.
>
> We are now in phase four. The testimony is being studied by HEW lawyers, OMB accountants, special education agency administrators and teachers, and the Bureau of Education for Handicapped professional staff. (Nesbitt, 1977a, pp. 2-3)

Auxter, Chasey, and Humphrey thus are the three professionals who contributed directly to the writing of the PL 94-142 physical education and recreation rules and regulations for the August 23, 1977 *Federal Register*.

David Auxter, a physical education professor at Slippery Rock State College in Pennsylvania, and one of the authors of *Principles and Methods of Adapted Physical Education*, has remained adapted physical education's leading expert on legislation over the years (see chapter 26). William Chasey, who had directed the first training program in physical education for the handicapped at the University of Texas in Austin (under Department Chair Lynn McCraw), was Director of the NCPERH Special Project at the time of the writing of the PL 94-142 rules and regulations. He has since left physical education and works as a consultant in the Washington, DC area. Fred Humphrey, recreation professor at the University of Maryland, was the eighth NCPERH president and continues to provide leadership in and through many organizations. It is noteworthy that staff members of AAHPER (Julian Stein) and NTRS (David Park) were not invited to participate in the PL 94-142 rules and regulations writing; likewise staff members of CEC were not permitted to contribute directly, apparently the result of a BEH administrative decision. These individuals were, however, involved later in the final editing, as were Bill Hillman and Mel Appell.

Concurrent with the work on PL 94-142, NCPERH launched a massive advocacy venture aimed toward educating state directors of special education and of physical education in regard to physical education and recreation for the handicapped. This project, entitled ''A Training Program in Special Education for State Education Agency (SEA) Directors of Physical Education and Special Education,'' was funded by a 30-month BEH grant, originally awarded for 36 months, but cut short when management problems between the project staff and the NCPERH Board of Directors became insurmountable.

Directed by William Chasey, the NCPERH project extended from June 1, 1975, to November 30, 1978. During this period, NCPERH maintained an office within the suite of offices of the National Association of State Directors of Special Education (NASDSE) in the National Education Association (NEA) Building in Washington, DC, which also housed AAHPER's national headquarters. Because NASDSE is the organization to which the top special education administrators of every state belong, the close proximity of NASDSE and NCPERH staff resulted in enormous gains in awareness of each other's mission and mutual support of goals.

Among the major accomplishments of the NCPERH Project was a presentation on physical education and recreation for the handicapped at the National Conference of State Education Agency (SEA) Directors at Gull Lake, Michigan, and successful sharing by special education and physical education state directors at four regional conferences:

- June 23-25, 1977—Southeast Regional Conference in Orlando, Florida. Conference Coordinator—Ernie Bundschuh.

- November 6-8, 1977—Northwest Regional Conference at Salishan Lodge in Gleneden Beach, Oregon. Conference Coordinator—John Dunn.

- December 8-10, 1977—Southwest Regional Conference at Scottsdale, Arizona. Conference Coordinator—Claudine Sherrill.

- September 14-15, 1978—Northeast Regional Conference at Columbus, Ohio. Conference Coordinators—Walter Ersing and Thomas Stevens.

As a result of these conferences and other activities, the NCPERH staff indicated that the project in part was responsible for the following:

- The best possible language in the final regulations for physical education in PL 94-142

- Much of the physical education language contained in Section 504 of the Rehabilitation Act of 1973

- A section dealing with sports participation for the handicapped in the final report of the President's Commission on Olympic Sports and its inclusion in the Amateur Sports Act

- The development of various state adapted physical education guides

- The physical education language in most state plans

- The inclusion of physical education representatives on State Advisory Committees

- Changes in state laws to include physical education as a direct service for handicapped children

- The use of State Part D monies for in-service training of physical education personnel

- The increase in Part B monies going to physical education in many states

- The interpretation of physical education in PL 94-142 for most SEAs

- The monitoring of state plans

- Cooperation between special education and physical education in most states (Chasey, 1979, p. 4)

After the close of the NCPERH project office in November, 1978, the organization's work once again was conducted primarily by its officers. An annual conference each summer, as well as meetings in conjunction with both AAHPERD and NTRS, provided forums for addressing issues relative to personnel preparation, research, and service delivery in physical education and recreation for handicapped children and youth. No other organization met this need for physical educators, and NCPERH is considered the major contributor to the sense of community that now exists among adapted physical educators in college and university positions.

NCPERH also continued directing advocacy activities toward both the members of Congress and the administration and staff of the Office of Special Education and Rehabilitation Services (OSERS) of the U.S. Department of Education. NCPERH has sought stronger support of physical education and recreation for handicapped individuals within authorization and appropriation legislation from members of Congress. Substructures of OSERS monitor compliance with PL 94-142 at the state level and make decisions as to how much of the money appropriated for personnel preparation and research will be awarded to physical education and recreation each year. Therefore, advocacy directed toward OSERS is aimed at increasing understanding and appreciation of physical education and recreation for handicapped children and youth, obtaining an equitable share of the training and research monies appropriated by Congress, ascertaining that grant proposals are reviewed and evaluated by experts, and monitoring the fairness of the grants award process.

One viable approach to achieving these goals is formal meetings between NCPERH officers or designates and the highest administrator within OSERS who can be accessed. In some instances this has been at the highest level—the Assistant Secretary of OSERS (Edwin Martin on May 24, 1979; Madeleine Will on September 19, 1985)—and in others it has been the acting director of the Office of Special Education Programs (Ed Sontag on January 20, 1982, and July 13, 1982; Patricia Guard on September 17, 1985). The infrequency of these meetings offers insight into the difficulty of gaining access. Such meetings are productive, however, and typically lead to position papers that clarify problems and propose solutions, followed by further meetings with staff members assigned by the administrator to work toward implementation.

Another approach to meeting advocacy goals has been inviting high ranking OSEP/OSERS officials and legislative aides of congresspersons to speak at annual meetings. The awareness of such individuals is increased by having to prepare speeches concerning physical education and recreation and state their position in regard to meeting needs. Likewise, the NCPERH membership is sensitized to priorities and concerns at the decision-making levels of government. Among the individuals who have recently spoken at NCPERH meetings are Carol Inman, Acting Deputy Secretary for OSERS (same office as Madeleine Will), Alton HOdges, National Institute of Handicapped Research, and Max Mueller, Director of the Division of Personnel Preparation, OSEP.

The annual NCPERH meeting continues to be the best source of information available concerning agencies that award training and research monies, legislation that funds grants, proposal writing, and grants management. The meeting also serves to keep the membership informed concerning OSERS' annual report to Congress (see chapter 6, p. 113). OSERS is implementing Congress's intent that all handicapped children and youth shall have free, appropriate physical education services provided by qualified personnel. Many more volunteers are needed among the nation's adapted physical educators for NCPERH's advocacy and monitoring roles to be optimally effective.

Over the years the membership of NCPERH has become increasingly diversified. Although the early members were mostly associated with funded programs, legislation, and advocacy, the focus of the organization appears to be broadening. Since 1982, both applied and experimental research have been reported on and discussed at the annual meeting. A leader in organizing these research sessions has been Michael Horvat, University of Georgia.

Information dissemination among members has become increasingly important. The *NCPERH Newsletter* has changed from a mimeographed to a sophisticated printed format. In 1985 the name was changed from *NCPERH Newsletter* to *NCPERH Advocate*. Its several editors have been John Dunn, 1974-80; Ellen Curtis Pierce and Christine Howe, 1982; Mike Churton, 1981-1986; and Jeff McCubbin, 1987, on.

Increasingly, NCPERH members view themselves as a community of scholars dedicated to physical education and recreation for handicapped individuals and appreciative of the opportunities their structure provides for sharing. Doctoral candidates wishing to develop leadership abilities and willing to assume responsibility for the future will find participation in annual meetings rewarding.

Sport Organizations

Today sport is an integral part of adapted physical education. Many colleges and universities offer courses and/or workshops on sport for disabled individuals. These include units on participation in integrated sport with able-bodied students as well as the rules and strategies of sports specific to certain disabilities such as wheelchair soccer (cerebral palsy), wheelchair basketball (mostly spinally paralyzed), beep baseball and goal ball (blind), and sitting volleyball (amputees). As university professors seek to balance their energies among teaching, research, and service, many consider their involvement in Special Olympics and similar sport organizations as community service. Others view sport for disabled individuals as a rich area for research. In 1984 the Olympic Scientific Congress (held in Eugene, Oregon, prior to the Olympic Games) included for the first time research presentations and discussions on sport and disabled athletes. The resulting proceedings (Sherrill, 1986) serves as a textbook for professors initiating and/or teaching courses on sport and disabled individuals.

Following is basic information on sport organizations for disabled individuals that every adapted physical educator should know. Two magazines, *Palaestra* and *Sports 'n Spokes*, are excellent sources for supplementary information.

Special Olympics, Inc.

This international program of physical fitness, sport training, and competition for mentally retarded children and adults was begun by the Joseph P. Kennedy, Jr. Foundation in 1968. Although the formation of other sport organizations for disabled individuals (American Athletic Association for the Deaf, National Wheelchair Athletic Association, National Wheelchair Basketball Association) preceeded that of Special Olympics, their impact on professional preparation was minimal. In contrast, the history of the Special Olympics is inextricably linked with improved public school physical education programming for mentally retarded students. This, in turn, intensified the need for specialization training of adapted physical educators and in-service training of regular physical educators.

Today Special Olympics serves more than 1 million athletes in more than 20,000 year-round programs of

Pioneers in the Special Olympics Movement. Eunice Shriver (top); Frank Hayden and Tom Songster (bottom).

training and competition in many official sports. These include track and field, swimming, diving, soccer (six-a-side), basketball, softball, volleyball, bowling, floor and poly hockey, gymnastics, cross-country and alpine skiing, figure and speed skating, and wheelchair events.

In 1981 Special Olympics, Inc. began a sport instructional program for the training and certification of Special Olympics coaches. Attractive, easy-to-understand Sports Skills Instructional Guides were published for major sports to help standardize the training of coaches. Certification criteria varied somewhat from state to state,

but generally required 3 to 6 hours of training for each sport.

Although the Special Olympics concept embodies year-round training of athletes, the focus tends to be on state games or, once every 4 years, on the International Summer Games. These have occurred as follows:

1968   Soldier Field, Chicago

1970   Soldier Field, Chicago

1972   University of California at Los Angeles

1975   Central Michigan University

1979   SUNY at Brockport, New York

1983   Louisiana State University at Baton Rouge

1987   Notre Dame University at South Bend, Indiana

At the 6th International Summer Special Olympics Games in Baton Rouge, 4,393 Special Olympians from 53 countries competed (Songster, 1986). Additionally, more than 4,000 family members and 1,000 Special Olympics coaches were involved in the week's events. Full media coverage heightened the impact of the Games by increasing awareness of the talent of mentally retarded athletes and the need for well-trained coaches.

The founder and president of Special Olympics, Inc. is Eunice Kennedy Shriver. Many members of the Kennedy family, including Senator Ted Kennedy, attend the International Summer Games. The leadership and support of this powerful family, coupled with the huge numbers of persons involved in various aspects of Special Olympics throughout the United States, have made this organization a viable factor in changing attitudes toward handicapped individuals and in shaping adapted physical education as a career option.

Other Organizations of Disabled Athletes

From the 1960s onward the United States was increasingly impacted by the sport for the disabled movement in Europe. Our wheelchair athletes in the National Wheelchair Athletic Association (NWAA) entered their first international competition in Rome in 1960 and subsequently competed in Tokyo in 1964, in Israel in 1968, in Germany in 1972, in Canada in 1976, in Netherlands in 1980, and in Great Britain in 1984. Early international involvement was promoted by the International Stoke Mandeville Games Federation (ISMGF), which is based in Aylesbury, England, where the National Spinal Cord Injuries Centre of the Stoke Mandeville Hospital is located.

The International Sports Organization for the Disabled (ISOD) was founded in France in 1963 to extend sport opportunities to blind athletes, amputees, and others not eligible to compete in the Stoke Mandeville Games. It was not until 1976, however, that the United States entered blind and amputee athletes into the international games conducted every 4 years in the country of the regular Olympics under Olympic rules. Subsequently, the United States Association for Blind Athletes (USABA) was formed in 1976 and the United States Amputee Athletic Association was created in 1982.

The International Cerebral Palsy Society conducted the first international competition for cerebral palsied (CP) persons in France in 1968. These games continue to be held every 2 years in Europe but are now under the sponsorship of Cerebral Palsy-International Sports and Recreation Association (CP-ISRA), which was formed in 1978. During this same year (1978) the National Association of Sports for Cerebral Palsy (NASCP) was organized in the United States. In 1986, several international level coaches and athletes separated from NASCP. The United States Cerebral Palsy Athletic Association (USCPAA) replaced NASCP in 1987. The U.S. Cerebral palsy team first competed in the CP-ISRA games in Denmark in 1980 and 1982. Additionally, ambulatory CP athletes participated in the 1980 Holland Disabled Olympiad along with CP, blind, amputee, and paraplegic athletes from 35 countries.

In 1984 the International Games for the Disabled were held at two sites. Three international sport organizations cooperated in providing competition for more than 1,500 blind, cerebral palsied, amputee, and *les autres* from approximately 50 countries in Nassau County, New York. The International Stoke Mandeville Games Federation representing spinal cord injured persons, whose U.S. organization member is the NWAA, chose to hold the games for their 2,000 athletes in Great Britain.

In 1988, games for disabled athletes will be held in Seoul, Korea. International and national competition is bringing to the attention of adapted physical education teacher trainers the need to expand their university curricula to include coaching the disabled athlete, rules and strategies of sports for disabled individuals, classification systems, and other topics.

The enactment of PL 95-606, the Amateur Sports Act, in 1978 also contributed to expansion of professional preparation content in that it included among its 14 purposes to

> Encourage and provide assistance to amateur athletic programs and competition for handicapped individuals, including, where feasible, the expansion of opportunities for meaningful participation by handicapped individuals in programs of athletic competition for ablebodied individuals. (DePauw & Clarke, 1986, p. 42)

PL 95-606 outlined the powers and jurisdiction of the United States Olympics Committee (USOC) and classified national sports governing bodies into Groups A through E. It also established the Olympic Training Center in Colorado Springs, which is available to elite disabled athletes as well as ablebodied ones.

Seven organizations now meet the criteria for membership in Group E of the USOC:

• United States Cerebral Palsy Athletic Association

• National Wheelchair Athletic Association

- United States Association for Blind Athletes

- Special Olympics, Inc.

- American Athletic Association of the Deaf

- United States Amputee Athletic Association

- National Handicapped Sports and Recreation Association

Each of these conducts a national program in two or more sports included on the program of the Olympic Games or Pan American Games on a level of proficiency appropriate for selection of amateur athletes to represent the United States in international competition.

Additionally, PL 95-606 called for the formation of a Handicapped in Sports Committee (name now changed to Disabled in Sports Committee) to work with USOC in implementation of the law. The membership included two representatives of each of the Group E organizations and others appointed by the President of USOC. PL 95-606 mandates that one of the members from each sport organization and at least 20% of the total committee shall be disabled. This mandate reflects a new direction in professional preparation: the significance of disabled persons (often called consumers) in policy-making positions.

The original Handicapped in Sports Committee was created in 1979. *Sports 'n Spokes* (November-December 1979) reports its membership as follows:

Special Olympics	Brig. Gen. Robert Montague, Jr. and Donna de Varona
AAAD	Kathy Sallade and Richard Caswell
NWAA	Ben Lipton and Diana Richardson
USABA	Arthur Copeland and David Beaver
NASCP	Craig Huber and Janice Lamarre

Five representatives at large, including past AAHPERD president Leroy Walker, appointed by USOC President Robert Kane.

In 1987 the chairperson of the Disabled in Sports Committee (new name) is Brig. Gen. Robert Montague. The USOC staff liaison is Mary Margaret Newsom, whose professional address is that of the U.S. Olympic Training Center: 1750 East Boulder Street, Colorado Springs, Colorado 80909. The membership of the Disabled in Sports Committee changes each quadrennium: members are appointed by the President of USOC.

The major contributions to professional preparation of the Disabled in Sports Committee and the numerous organizations of disabled athletes that arose in the 1970s and 1980s were largely in the area of Sociological Foundations (see Hurley, 1981, *Guidelines for Adapted Physical Education* in Appendix B for specific competencies). These organizations created a new body of knowledge that documented the role and significance of sport in the lives of individuals with disabilities. They also promoted the recognition of disabled athletes as resource persons and salaried professionals in adapted physical education. Most important, perhaps, they showed that disabled youth and adults could become elite athletes and needed the same serious training and coaching as able-bodied peers. The rules, strategies, and classification systems of disabled sports increasingly comprised a new knowledge area to be mastered.

In recognition of these new knowledge areas, BEH funded a 3-year special project to the National Wheelchair Basketball Association (NWBA) from 1978 through 1981, thereby setting a precedent for sport organizations to conduct in-service training. The project director and coordinator, respectively, were Stan Labanowich and Ed Owen of the University of Kentucky. Three large regional training institutes were subsequently held at the University of Illinois, California State University of San Jose, and Texas Woman's University.

Universities also began planning cooperative courses, workshops, and institutes concerning sport and disability in conjunction with annual national meets. Among the first teacher training facilities to experiment in this area was Texas Woman's University, which held graduate level 3-credit summer school courses in collaboration with the U.S. Association for Blind Athletes in 1982 (national meet in Austin), with Special Olympics, Inc. (international meet in Baton Rouge), and with the National Association of Sports for Cerebral Palsy (national meet in Fort Worth) in 1983.

International Organizations

In addition to the international sport organizations that adapted physical educators may join and serve, many opportunities exist for exchanges among different countries. Chief among these is participation in the symposia held by the International Federation for Adapted Physical Activities.[1] This organization was formed in 1977. Symposia have been held every other year as follows:

1977	Quebec City, Canada
1979	Brussels, Belgium
1981	New Orleans, U.S.A.

---

[1]For further information about this organization, contact Julian Stein, Physical Education Department, George Mason University, Fairfax, VA 22030.

1983 London, England

1985 Toronto, Canada

1987 Brisbane, Australia

Illustrative of the proceedings published for each symposium are the widely read collections of papers by Eason, Smith, and Caron (1983) and Berridge and Ward (1987).

Increasing numbers of adapted physical educators are traveling to other countries. Stein (1986b) gives the best available account of international perspectives in physical education and sport for individuals with handicapping conditions.

The years from 1981 through 1992 have been designated the Decade for Disabled Persons by UNESCO. Opportunities for teaching, research, and service in adapted physical education exist throughout the world. Never has the need for sound professional preparation been greater. Professional organizations are a viable approach to assuring excellence in leadership training.

References

American Alliance for Health, Physical Education, Recreation and Dance. (1951-1986). *Annual reports of the National Association of Sport and Physical Education.* Archives, Physical Education Division, Reston, VA: Author.

American Association for Health, Physical Education, and Recreation. (1962). *Professional preparation in health education, physical education, recreation education: Report of a national conference.* Washington, DC: Author.

American Association for Health, Physical Education, and Recreation. (1967). *Graduate education in health education, physical education, recreation education, safety education, and dance: Report of a national conference.* Washington, DC: Author.

Auxter, D. (1973, December 5-7). *A model legislative statue in physical education for the handicapped.* Paper developed at The National Conference on Program Development Needs and Evaluation of Physical Education and Recreation for Handicapped Children and Youth, Washington, DC.

Berridge, M.E., & Ward, G.R. (Eds.). (1987). *International perspectives on adapted physical activity.* Champaign, IL: Human Kinetics.

Boone, R. (1904). *Science of education.* New York: Scribner.

Bundschuh, E. (1986). The National Consortium on Physical Education and Recreation for the Handicapped: Addressing a need. *Adapted Physical Activity Quarterly,* **3**(2), 143-146.

Chasey, W. (1979, July). *A training program in special physical education for SEA directors of physical education and recreation* (Final Report, Grant No. G007603204, BEH). Washington, DC: National Consortium on Physical Education and Recreation for the Handicapped.

Committee on Adapted Physical Education. (1952). Guiding principles for adapted physical education. *Journal of Health, Physical Education, and Recreation,* **23**, 15.

Conant, J.B. (1963). *The education of American teachers.* New York: McGraw-Hill.

Daniels, A. (1954). *Adapted physical education.* New York: Harper & Row.

DePauw, K. (1985, March). Merger petition goes to Alliance board of directors. *Able Bodies,* **4**(2), 1, 3.

DePauw, K. (1986). Merger of special populations programs within the American Alliance for Health, Physical Education, Recreation and Dance. *Adapted Physical Activity Quarterly,* **3**(2), 139-142.

DePauw, K., & Clarke, K. (1986). Sports for disabled U.S. citizens: Influence of Amateur Sports Act. In C. Sherrill (Ed.), *Sport and disabled athletes* (pp. 41-50). Champaign, IL: Human Kinetics.

Dunn, J. (1984, May). Merger—Adapted academy & therapeutics council. *Able Bodies,* **3**(2), 1, 7.

Eason, R., Smith, T., & Caron, F. (Eds.). (1983). *Adapted physical activity: From theory to application.* Champaign, IL: Human Kinetics.

Flexner, A. (1915). Is social work a profession? *School and Society,* **1**, 901-911.

Gallagher, J., Lucito, L., & Hillman, W. (1968, June). *Conference on physical education and recreation services for the mentally retarded and other handicapped children.* Mimeographed report. Washington, DC: Bureau of Education for the Handicapped.

Godfrey, B., & Kephart, N. (1969). *Movement patterns and motor education.* New York: Appleton-Century-Crofts.

Goodwin, L. (1986). AAHPERD: Addressing the needs of the handicapped. *Adapted Physical Activity Quarterly,* **3**(2), 127-132.

Hurley, D. (1981). Guidelines for adapted physical education. *Journal of Physical Education, Recreation and Dance,* **52**, 43-45.

Johnson, L. (1986). The need for a national consortium. *Adapted Physical Activity Quarterly,* **3**(2), 143-146.

Johnson, L., & Nesbitt, J. (1973). *A report on the national conference on program development and evaluation in physical education and recreation for handicapped children and youth in Washington, DC on December 5, 1973.* (Mimeographed). Washington, DC: Ad Hoc Committee on Physical Education and Recreation for the Handicapped.

Kroll, W. (1982). *Graduate study and research in physical education.* Champaign, IL: Human Kinetics.

Lee, M., & Bennett, B. (1960). This is our heritage. *Journal of Health, Physical Education, and Recreation, 31*(4), 25-86.

Lee, M., & Bennett, B. (1985). Alliance centennial—100 years of health, physical education, recreation, and dance. *Journal of Physical Education, Recreation, and Dance, 56*(4), 17-67.

Nesbitt, J. (1977a). The chronology of recommendations on the recreation aspects of PL 94-142. *NCPERH Newsletter, 4*(3), 1-4.

Nesbitt, J. (1977b). *Professional advocacy at the national level in physical education and recreation for handicapped children: 1976-77 report of the president of the National Consortium on Physical Education and Recreation for the Handicapped.* Iowa City: Recreation Education Program, The University of Iowa.

Nesbitt, J. (Ed.). (1983). *New horizons in professional training in recreation service for handicapped children and youth.* Iowa City: Special Recreation.

Parsons, T. (1951). *The social system.* New York: The Free Press.

Rarick, G.L. (1952). *Motor development during infancy and childhood.* Madison, WI: College Printing & Typing Co.

Sherrill, C. (Ed.) (1986). *Sport and disabled athletes.* Champaign, IL: Human Kinetics.

Songster, T. (1986). The Special Olympics sports program: An international sport program for mentally retarded athletes. In C. Sherrill (Ed.), *Sport and disabled athletes* (pp. 73-79). Champaign, IL: Human Kinetics.

Stein, J. (1984, May). A different point of view. *Able Bodies, 3*(2), 2.

Stein, J. (1986a). AAHPER(D) unit on programs for the handicapped. *Adapted Physical Activity Quarterly, 3*(2), 133-138.

Stein, J. (1986b). International perspectives: Physical education and sport for participants with handicapping conditions. In C. Sherrill (Ed.), *Sport and disabled athletes* (pp. 51-64). Champaign, IL: Human Kinetics.

Steinhaus, A. (1967). The disciplines underlying a profession. *Quest, 9*, 68-72.

Therapeutics Section. (circa 1965). *History of the therapeutics section, American Association for Health, Physical Education, and Recreation.* Mimeographed materials in officers' files.

Wessel, J. (1957). *Movement fundamentals: Figure, form, fun.* Englewood Cliffs, NJ: Prentice-Hall.

Wessel, J. (1963). *Fitness for the modern teenager.* New York: Ronald Press.

Winnick, J. (1975, March 4). *Memo to BEH project directors and individuals interested in the National Consortium on Physical Education and Recreation for the Handicapped.* (Mimeographed).

Chapter 5
Legislation, Funding, and Adapted Physical Education Teacher Training

Claudine Sherrill and William Hillman

*L*egislation and funding shape the development of teacher training more than most university professors know. It is essential that teacher trainers understand the role of legislation in funding programs as well as in changing course content.

Local school districts and states have always provided most of the financial aid for education. Illustrative of this are the percentage contributions to public school funding presented in Table 5.1.

Table 5.1   Federal, State, and Local Contributions to Public School Funding

Year	Total revenues (billions)	Percentage distribution			
		Federal	State	Local	Total
1946	$10.5	1.4	34.7	63.8	100
1950	14.4	2.9	39.8	57.3	100
1954	18.3	4.5	37.4	58.1	100
1958	26.7	4.0	39.4	56.6	100
1962	36.5	4.3	38.7	56.9	100
1966	49.7	7.9	39.1	53.0	100
1970	66.8	8.0	39.9	52.1	100
1974	78.2	8.5	41.7	49.8	100
1978[a]	80.9	8.1	44.1	47.8	100

Note. From *Encyclopedia of Educational Research*, 1982, p. 674.
[a]Estimated.

Education is not a power explicitly delegated to the federal government by the U.S. Constitution as are its other powers. Congress interprets the general welfare clause of Article I of the Constitution broadly as the legal basis for its participation in education. Federal funding until 1979 was administered by the U.S. Department of Health, Education, and Welfare (HEW). Public Law 96-

88, enacted in 1979, restructured HEW into two cabinet level structures, the Department of Education and the Department of Health and Human Services. The Secretary and Assistant Secretary of each are appointed by the U.S. President. Now funds are administered by the U.S. Department of Education. A goal of individuals committed to high quality education is to retain and strengthen the influence of this cabinet level position.

Federal grant monies are important as a catalyst to equity in assuring that teachers are trained to meet the needs of all children. Federal funds are not and never have been a major source of revenue in higher education as indicated in Table 5.2. Of the 15 to 19% of federal monies received by colleges and universities, very little is earmarked for the handicapped.

Physical educators, like parents and special educators, must therefore continuously monitor local and state appropriations for the handicapped because these structures (not the federal government) provide most of the funding. Each state is unique in its funding structure; hence this chapter does not attempt to facilitate knowledge in this area. Teacher trainers are urged, however, to obtain and pass on to their students information about state and local funding. The surest route to optimal adapted physical education is state level legislation and appropriation. Also important are local and state board of education policies.

The purpose of this chapter is to describe the interrelationship between federal legislation, funding, and adapted physical education training. Historically, physical education funding has been in three areas: (a) personnel preparation, most of which is for teacher training; (b) special projects; and (c) research and demonstration. The scope of this chapter is limited to teacher training. Although historically the funding of physical education and recreation for handicapped individuals has been linked, no attempt is made to discuss recreation, which is covered in a recent publication by Nesbitt (1983).

Table 5.2   Revenue Sources for U.S. Public and Independent Higher-Education Institutions: Percentage Contribution From Each Source (1979)

Source	Public[a]	Independent[b]
State and Local Appropriations	59%	2%
Tuition and Fees	15	50
Private Gifts and Grants	4	20
Government Grants and Contracts	15	19
Other	7	9
Total Educational and General	100	100

Note. From *Encyclopedia of Educational Research*, 1982, p. 692.
[a]Total appropriations for public higher-education = $28,281,000,000.
[b]Total appropriations for independent higher-education = $12,614,000,000.

Education of the Handicapped Legislation: An Overview

Federal funding comes from legislation. In teacher training, however, some laws are best known for their authorization of training monies, whereas others are remembered more for their impact on the course content and research of an academic discipline. Most adapted physical educators are well versed, for instance, in PL 94-142 because it changed the nature of service delivery in the schools and consequently the content of courses taught in universities. Broadhead (1981) states in this regard,

The importance of the Public Law [94-142], and the ways in which it is being implemented cannot be stressed too much. It has clearly over-taken many of the developments which were underway before it was passed and has gone beyond what many have even dreamed of. The demands of the law are such that it can confidently be forecasted that our whole profession will be affected in some way. For the researcher, the personal or ideosyncratic approach to research may have to be replaced, for the Public Law requires a vast range of researchable topics of immediate importance. (p. 245)

It is not the intent of this chapter to discuss PL 94-142 because numerous other sources do this. The entire text of PL 94-142 appears in the book by Weintraub, Abelson, Ballard, and LaVor (1976); it can also be found in the *United States Code* (U.S.C.), a series of reference books found in most libraries. Sherrill (1986) gives a detailed explanation of the parts of PL 94-142 that relate to physical education service delivery.

Basic Concepts

PL 94-142 is now often called Subchapter II of the Education of the Handicapped Act (EHA); this is to help individuals see it in perspective and understand what it does and does not do. PL 94-142, for instance, does not provide the federal monies that fund teacher training in adapted physical education.

PL 94-142 (the Education for All Handicapped Children Act) is only one component (Part B) of PL 91-230, the Education of the Handicapped Act (EHA) enacted in 1970. Essentially PL 94-142, enacted in 1975, was an amendment to Part B of the earlier legislation. Part B pertains to direct services to handicapped children and youth, with emphasis on local and state compliance and procedures for states to obtain federal monies to assist with this compliance.

The parts of EHA (called subchapters in the reauthorization legislation of 1986) address the following:

Subchapter or Part		Title
I	A	General Provisions, including definitions
II	B	Assistance for Education of All Handicapped Children
III	C	Centers and Services to Meet Special Needs (like deaf-blind and transitional services)
IV	D	Training Personnel
V	E	Research
VI	F	Instructional Media
VII	G	Technology. Educational Media, and Materials for the Handicapped
VIII	H	Handicapped Infants and Toddlers

Part B (or Subchapter II) of EHA is *statutory* or permanent, whereas programs under Parts C through H have expiration dates and thus must be extended periodically by reauthorization legislation (e.g., PL 93-380, PL 95-49, PL 98-199, PL 99-457). These laws specify the maximum amount that Congress can appropriate in the year-by-year implementation of EHA. Table 5.3 illustrates how PL 98-199 extended the fiscal authorizations of all EHA discretionary programs through fiscal year 1986. Note that PL 94-142 is statutory, not *discretionary*, and thus is not included in Table 5.3. Discretionary refers to the power given by Congress to the Secretary of the U.S. Department of Education to decide specifically how funds are to be spent, provided that the purposes of the authorizing legislation are upheld.

Of particular interest to teacher trainers is the EHA program called Personnel Development. The money for this program is to support Part D of EHA; this is the source of all federal training grants for colleges and universities. The Office of Special Education and Rehabilitation Services (OSERS) of the U.S. Department of Education administers these funds and decides how much money physical education and recreation training will receive. Physical educators must therefore work in dual advocacy roles to assure federal funding of their university programs, (a) with Congress to assure the largest sum possible under Personnel Development and (b) with administrators and staff persons within OSERS and its substructures to obtain a fair share for physical education. To learn such advocacy skills, physical educators can become members of the National Consortium on Physical Education and Recreation for the Handicapped (see chapter 4).

Tremendous time and energy must be devoted to such advocacy activities approximately every 3 years when reauthorization legislation is being enacted. The acronym EHA is generic in the sense that it has been used as the title for reauthorization legislation since 1970 (e.g., PL 93-380 (1974); PL 95-49 (1977); PL 98-199 (1983); and PL 99-457 (1986). It is helpful to understand the influence of EHA legislation and of the laws that preceded EHA (PL 89-10 and PL 89-750).

To completely understand a law, one must read its rules and regulations. These are printed in a daily periodical called the *Federal Register*, which is found in most university libraries. For overall background on federal legislation in relation to handicapped individuals, the reader is referred to *Public Policy and the Education of Exceptional Children* (Weintraub et al., 1976) and *Special*

Table 5.3   Authorization of Appropriations for the Various EHA Programs

EHA Program	Fiscal Year		
	1984	1985	1986
Evaluations/Special studies	$ 3,100,000	$ 3,270,000	$ 3,440,000
Regional resource centers	5,700,000	6,000,000	6,300,000
Deaf-blind programs	15,000,000	15,000,000	15,000,000
Early childhood education	26,000,000	27,100,000	28,300,000
Severely handicapped projects	5,000,000	5,300,000	5,600,000
Postsecondary education	5,000,000	5,300,000	5,500,000
Secondary education and transitional services	6,000,000	6,330,000	6,660,000
Personnel development	58,000,000	61,150,000	64,370,000
Recruitment and information	1,000,000	1,050,000	1,110,000
Innovation and development	20,000,000	21,100,000	22,200,000
Media services and captioned films	19,000,000	20,000,000	21,100,000

Note. Annual totals are specified in PL 98-199, the EHA Amendments of 1983, and Authorization of Appropriations. From *Progress in the Education of the Handicapped and Analysis of PL 98-199* (p. 38) by F.J. Weintraub and B. Ramirez, 1985, Reston, VA: Council for Exceptional Children.

Education in America: Its Legal and Governmental Foundations (Ballard, Ramirez, & Weintraub, 1982). Three federal laws, all enacted in the 1960s, set the stage for present funding of teacher training in physical education for the handicapped. These are PL 89-10, PL 89-750, and PL 90-170.

The Elementary and Secondary Education Act

The enactment of PL 89-10, the Elementary and Secondary Education Act (ESEA), represents the first *serious* commitment by the federal government to improve public school education (LaVor, 1976). The year of this landmark legislation was 1965, a time of heightened awareness of due process and equality of educational opportunity brought on, in part, by civil rights legislation (PL 88-352) in 1964.

ESEA originally was comprised of five titles, as follows:

- *Title I*—funds for education of the disadvantaged (i.e., children from low income families.) Later known as *compensatory education*. Grants are distributed to states and then to school districts on the basis of income level. Main component of ESEA.

- *Title II*—funds for school library materials and instructional services.

- *Title III*—funds for innovative and/or exemplary local school district programs.

- *Title IV*—funds for education research and development.

- *Title V*—funds to State Education Agencies (SEAs) for improving and expanding their services.

Amendments to Title III, in 1970, required that 15% of the total state allocation be expended on the handicapped. In 1974, under President Nixon, several small programs under ESEA were consolidated under a new Title IV.

Many innovative local school district physical education programs, now nationally known, were funded under Title III (now IV C) like Project ACTIVE in New Jersey and Project PEOPEL in Arizona. Vodola (1973) describes the evolution of Project ACTIVE funding in a chapter on local, state, and federal funding in his adapted physical education textbook. Ersing, in chapter 13 of this book, discusses several ESEA projects and the impact they have had on teacher training.

Recently ESEA has been impacted by the Reagan federalism, and Title I was renamed Chapter I by PL 97-35, the Education, Consolidation and Improvement ACT (ECIA) of 1981. By 1983, according to Vodola (Personal communication, 1983), funds for most of the Title IV C innovative program grants like Project ACTIVE had been drastically reduced.

PL 89-750 and the Creation of BEH

In 1966 the Bureau of Education for the Handicapped (BEH) was created by PL 89-750, often known as Title VI of the Elementary and Secondary Education Act. The origi-

Thomas Vodola, renowned Title IV C grant writer, demonstrating PROJECT ACTIVE assessment techniques.

nal BEH, a structure within the Office of Education of the U.S. Department of Health, Education, and Welfare, had three divisions: training, research, and services (i.e., aid to states). James J. Gallagher served as the first Associate Commissioner of BEH and was succeeded by Ed Martin, who later became the first Assistant Secretary of OSERS.

PL 89-750 authorized a program of grants to the states to initiate, expand, and improve educational programs for handicapped children and created BEH to administer this program. Of most importance to university physical educators was the Division of Training Programs, later called the Division of Personnel Preparation (DPP). This division was first headed by Richard Schofer, a firm advocate of physical education, who now chairs the Special Education Department at the University of Missouri. Schofer was followed by Leonard Lucito, Harold Heller (Acting), Bruce Balow, Richard Whelan, Herman Saettler (Acting), Jasper Harvey, and others (Burke, 1976).

In the administrative hierarchy of the federal government, the rungs of the ladder are section, branch, division,

bureau, office, and department. BEH was renamed Office of Special Education and together with the Rehabilitation Services Administration became OSERS when PL 96-88, enacted in 1979, changed the Office of Education to the Department of Education. Physical education grant directors tended to shorten OSERS to OSE until government stationery appeared with a new heading, Office of Special Education Programs (OSEP), around 1981. The first directors of OSE or OSEP, respectively, were Ed Sontag (Acting) and Garry McDaniels.

One year after the creation of BEH, a law was passed that provided funding for personnel training in physical education and recreation for the handicapped. It was PL 90-170.

PL 90-170: The Beginning of Funding in Physical Education for Handicapped

In 1967, PL 90-170, the Mental Retardation Facilities and Community Mental Health Centers Construction Act, was passed after many years of work by Senator Edward Kennedy of Massachusetts, the Joseph P. Kennedy, Jr. Foundation, AAHPER, and others. Robert Holland, on leave of absence from the Ohio State Department of Education to direct the AAHPER project on Recreation and Fitness for the Mentally Retarded (begun in 1965 with a 3-year grant from the Joseph P. Kennedy, Jr. Foundation), was the leader who drafted the legislation that Senator Kennedy subsequently introduced to Congress in 1966.

Title V of this Act was entitled *Training of Physical Educators and Recreation Personnel for Mentally Retarded and Other Handicapped Children*. Specifically, Title V authorized the Secretary of Health, Education, and Welfare

BEH administrators Ed Martin and Terrell H. Bell congratulate Robert Holland, first Director of the Project on Recreation and Fitness for the Mentally Retarded in 1965 (later named AAHPERD Unit on Programs for the Handicapped).

to make grants to public and other nonprofit institutions of higher learning to assist them in providing professional or advanced training for personnel engaged or preparing to engage in employment as physical educators or recreation personnel for mentally retarded and other handicapped children, or as supervisors of such personnel or engaged or preparing to engage in research or teaching in fields related to the physical education or recreation of such children. (*U.S. Statutes at Large,* **81**, p. 530)

An outcome of the enactment of PL 90-170 was enlargement of the staff of the Division of Training Programs (DTP), of the Bureau of Education for the Handicapped (BEH) to include a consultant/advocate in physical education and recreation for the handicapped. William Hillman was employed as coordinator of physical education/recreation in 1968.

Monies authorized to implement this law were not the same as those awarded. Table 5.4 explains what actually happened during the first 3 years after the enactment of Title V.

In fiscal year (FY) 1969-70 (the first year money was available), training grants were awarded to 15 colleges and universities. Seven of these were in physical education, six in recreation, one in combined physical education and recreation (Indiana State University at Terre Haute under Dolores Musgraves Geddes), and one for short courses in both physical education and recreation (Southern Connecticut State College in New Haven under Edith DeBonis). The seven universities that received these first training grants in physical education for the handicapped and thus began graduate level specializations were (a) George Washington University—Honey Nashman, (b) Ohio State University—Walt Ersing, (c) University of Missouri—Barbara Godfrey, (d) University of South Florida—Lou Bowers, (e) University of Texas—Lynn McCraw, (f) University of California at Berkeley—Lawrence Rarick, and (g) University of South Carolina—Walter Hambrick. These first training grants averaged $20,000 each and ranged from $10,000 to $24,500.

In the late 1960s several other universities also began developing graduate specializations in adapted physical

education. Illustrative of the nonfunded universities that established such training were University of Maryland, Texas Woman's University, George Peabody University, Michigan State University, and California State University at Los Angeles. Several of these universities later applied for and received federal funding for their excellent programs.

Funding History of Physical Education and Recreation for the Handicapped

Since fiscal year 1969, the federal government has allocated more than $22 million for training programs in physical education (Hillman, 1986). Approximately $18 million of this sum was spent to stimulate the growth and development of master's and doctoral programs as well as various in-service training programs administered by colleges and universities. The remaining $4 million was awarded to research and demonstration projects (Hillman, 1986). Table 5.5 presents the funding history of physical education and recreation combined and of physical education separately.

From 1969 to 1980 funding of personnel training in physical education and recreation increased steadily under the skillful advocacy of William Hillman, the staff member responsible for these areas within the Division of Personnel Preparation (DPP) of BEH/OSEP. For reasons unknown, however, the chief administrators of OSEP decided to decrease funding of physical education and recreation in 1981. Additionally they transferred William Hillman to the Division of Assistance to States (DAS), so that his job description no longer permitted work with university training programs. This left no advocate whose main concern was physical education and recreation for the handicapped in DPP, the division responsible for decision making with regard to the funding of teacher training in colleges and universities. The structure of the panels that review and evaluate grant proposals for DPP was changed also so that, for the first time since inception, panelists did not include experts with doctoral degrees specifically in adapted physical education. Thus the grant proposals in physical education were evaluated primarily by special education experts with no input from the physical education profession. This, along with budget cuts, was believed to be a major factor in only 43 colleges and universities receiving training grants in physical education in 1982 as opposed to the 54 in 1980 and the 50 in 1981.

The year 1981 was a very bad time also for all of personnel preparation in special education and for education in general because the new Reagan administration was openly hostile to federal support of education (Ballard,

Table 5.4 Federal Funds (Title V, PL 90-170) for Use in Physical Education and Recreation Teacher Training

Fiscal	Funds authorized	Funds awarded
1968	$1,000,000	$ 0
1969	$2,000,000	$300,000
1970	$3,000,000	$300,000

Note. These sums do *not* include research or special project monies.

Table 5.5 **Division of Personnel Preparation Awards to Physical Education and Recreation**

Fiscal year	Physical education and recreation	Physical education
1969-70	$ 300,000	$ 160,000
1970	300,000	160,000
PL 91-230		
1971	740,000	400,000
1972	1,000,000	500,000
1973	1,250,000	525,000
1974	1,500,000	600,000
PL 93-380		
1975	1,600,000	660,000
1976	2,000,000	995,000
1977	2,195,000	910,000
PL 95-49		
1978	2,446,000	1,028,000
1979	3,408,000	1,450,000
1980	3,890,000	1,450,000
1981	2,900,000	1,000,000
1982	1,540,000	2,083,000
1983	3,200,000	2,100,000
PL 98-199		
1984	3,400,000	2,100,000
1985	3,680,000	

Note. Figures from Bill Hillman. Research monies are not included. Sums listed may or may not include special projects.

Ramirez, & Weintraub, 1982). Specifically, President Reagan sought to change the U.S. Department of Education from its present position of importance to a substructure that did not have Cabinet representation; this attempt failed but helped Americans realize how tenuous the relationship between government and education can be. The Reagan administration also attempted to limit the provision of services related to handicapped children. These efforts continue in three directions: "(a) reduction in levels of funding, (b) reduction or elimination of federal or state mandates, and (c) elimination of categorical funding in favor of more open-ended support (block grants)" (Ballard, Ramirez, & Weintraub, 1982, p. 5).

Today there is satisfaction in knowing that most of the early President Reagan administration goals in relation to special education were defeated. For example, in 1982, all training grants awarded by OSEP received a 48.5% cut in accordance with President Reagan's budget policy. The United States Congress, however, failed to support this cut and others, continuing to increase funding of special education, although at a significantly reduced rate

(Weintraub & Ramirez, 1985). This, of course, was largely because of the strong advocacy of educators in working with congresspersons.

In comparison, the funding history of physical education and recreation has not fared as well. Although a slight increase has occurred in funding year by year, the rate of increase is not the same as that of special education. Hillman (1983) wrote to colleagues,

> During the last funding year approximately a 40 percent reduction in funding occurred in physical education and recreation in *personnel preparation* due to a total lack of qualified readers and other circumstances. In research and demonstration only one project was supported at $27,000—this compares with an average of over $400,000 per year in physical education and recreation since 1969. (p. 1)

Bowers and Churton (1986), in a prepared statement for the National Consortium on Physical Education and Recreation for the Handicapped to the Subcommittee on the Handicapped of the U.S. Senate, stated,

> Since 1975, DE:OSERS has awarded on a nationwide basis financial assistance slightly in excess of 12 million dollars (less than $24,000/state) to research and personnel preparation programs in adapted physical education. . . . This amount has accounted for less than 8% of the total amount awarded to all special education funded programs. For 1985, federal assistance has been reduced to less than 6% of the total amount funded in special education. The issue, here, is not the total dollar amount, but whether the amount awarded to physical education programs has been sufficient to place qualified adapted physical education personnel throughout the nation's schools. Evidence, previously presented, suggests that there currently exists in this country a vast need to prepare specialists in the area of physical education for the handicapped. (p. 19)

In order to ameliorate these funding problems, physical educators must increase their understanding of categorical funding and improve existing strategies in relation to both Congressional and OSERS support of physical education and recreation for the handicapped. The following sections are designed to assist in these efforts.

Block Versus Categorical Grants

Reduced funding at the federal level as well as failure to specify categorical monies for physical education training are part of the Reagan administration's "New Federalism." These events reflect one of the main issues on which Republican and Democratic political parties differ—the role of the federal government in education. Peterson and Rabe (1983) summarize the role of partisan political relationships and overall economic trends on federal funding as follows:

> In general, one can expect higher levels of support for education if economic growth rates increase in the 1980s over what they were in the 1970s. If the economy continues to weaken and decline, then support for education can be expected to decline precipitously. Politically, the more power remains in the hands of the Republican party, the more responsibility for educational finance will shift to state and local governments. Should the Democratic party capitalize on its new congressional strength, and win a presidential race in 1984, one can expect greater political support for a significant federal role in education. (p. 725)

The issue of block versus categorical grants is part of the power play between political parties concerning who should control monies. Categorical federal funding began in the Great Depression under Roosevelt but was not extended to education until the 1960s. *Categorical grants* are "grants that are intended for specific program purposes and usually are limited to narrowly defined activities" (Kutner & Sherman, 1982, p. 68). Historically, categorical grants have been most common and have been used to equalize educational opportunity—to facilitate education for the blacks, the poor, and the handicapped because states were not doing so. Categorical grants may be *discretionary* (competitive with money directly to a college or university, organization or agency, or state or local government) or *formula* (noncompetitive with funds flowing only to state and local governments with amounts determined by a formula). PL 94-142 flow-through monies to SEAs and LEAs, for instance, are formula, whereas PL 91-230, PL 93-380, PL 95-49, PL 98-199, and PL 99-457 authorizations to teacher training programs are discretionary.

Block grants, on the other hand, are monies awarded directly to state and local governments to fund as they please formerly separately funded programs. Barrett (1983) elaborates upon "as they please" as follows: "States are generally given a wide range of latitude in dividing up this block grant money among the various programs. However, some guidelines do exist" (p. 8). Block grants, although occasionally awarded in the past, did not become a politically viable strategy of federal aid until the Reagan Administration. They represent a method whereby decision making on use of funds can be transferred from federal to state political entities. Opponents of block

funding believe that most state governments cannot be trusted to use monies fairly in equalizing educational opportunity; they point out that federal categorical funding would never have evolved in the 1960s had state governments been providing equal education opportunities for black and/or disadvantaged students. Some of the more important consequences of block grants are as follows:

> Block grants changed the influence of groups in the decision-making process, resulting in less influence for the poor and minorities than under categorical programs. . . . The shift from categorical to block grants produced a "spreading" effect. Activities targeted on small groups of people suffered reductions at the expense of activities affecting a much broader, diverse clientele. In jurisdictions that received large amounts of categorical funding, the shift to block grants resulted in less benefits to the poor. (Wolman cited by Kutner & Sherman, 1982, pp. 74-75)

Special educators, including adapted physical educators, believed that these findings concerning the relationship between block grants and "the poor and minorities" would hold true for handicapped students should block grants replace current categorical funding. Therefore, special educators fought and won against the Reagan administration's proposal in March, 1981 to consolidate approximately 80 categorical programs into six human service block grants: (a) health services, (b) preventive health services, (c) social services, (d) energy assistance, (e) local education services, and (f) state education services. As a result of the mass letter writing campaign by the American public, Congress refused to approve the local and state education block grant concept. A budget process known as reconciliation ensued with the eventual passage of PL 97-35, the Education Consolidation and Improvement Act of 1981, which became effective on July 1, 1982. This law affected ESEA rather than programs for handicapped individuals (i.e., PL 94-142 flow-through funds as well as training monies remained categorical).

Physical educators need to monitor the implementation of PL 97-35 carefully as they weigh the pros and cons of block funding. Vodola's Project ACTIVE (see chapter 13) is one physical education project for handicapped children that was eliminated (but revived in 1986 under Jo Karp) in the transition from categorical to block ESEA funding with its current shift from federal to state determination of priorities. Specifically, PL 97-35.

> gives state and local education agencies authority in administering federal funds for education programs. Chapter I of the Act, which supercedes Title I of ESEA, extends to state and local educa-

tion agencies prime responsibility for conducting the nation's largest federal education program, providing financial assistance to meet the needs of disadvantaged children. . . . Chapter II consolidates 42 other elementary and secondary education activities into block grants for three broad purposes: basic skills improvement, improvement of support services, and special projects. (McNutt & Wexler, 1983, p. 1)

Teacher training programs need to intensify efforts to prepare educators who understand public school funding and who can communicate effectively with SEA and LEA administrators concerning the appropriateness and need for physical education for handicapped students. It is highly probable that additional education block grants will be proposed in years to come. Physical educators must understand that block funding will decrease teacher training monies in their area of specialization; this should be incentive to advocate strongly against block grants.

Changing Funding Priorities at the Federal Level

Throughout the 1970s both physical education and recreation were specified in federal laws (PL 90-170, PL 91-230, and PL 93-380) as categorical funding priorities with set appropriations reserved. Professional preparation in physical education for the handicapped was therefore not in competition with any other area for monies. Table 5.6 is illustrative of how physical education ranked in comparison with other areas. Physical education grant

writers learned how to obtain projects, not only out of their own categorical pot of money, but also out of other categories like Regular Education and Severely Handicapped. The *Dean's Grants* of the 1970s, for instance, were funded out of regular education monies to enhance the power of deans of colleges to facilitate infusion of special education content into regular education courses. The ultimate goal was to promote mainstreaming in public schools by graduating education majors. Joan Moran at the Texas Woman's University was one of the few leaders in the country who obtained a Dean's Grant specifically for a college of health, physical education, and recreation rather than a college of education. Illustrative of physical education grants funded out of the severely handicapped monies was a project conceived and implemented by John Dunn at Oregon State University.

The 1983 application packet for new grants under Training Personnel for the Education of the Handicapped (disseminated in 1982) no longer specified physical education as a categorical funding priority with an established appropriation. The passage indicating this and other major changes in funding priorities read as follows:

The proposed regulations provide that the Secretary, in any fiscal year, may establish one or more of the following priorities:

(a) Preparation of special educators;

(b) Preparation of leadership personnel;

(c) Preparation of related services personnel;

(d) State educational agency programming;

(e) Special projects;

Table 5.6 Division of Personnel Preparation (DPP) Training Priorities. Amounts Expressed in Hundreds of Thousands of Dollars

	Fiscal Year 1977			Fiscal Year 1978	
Rank		Amount	Rank		Amount
1	General special education	$10,470	1	Regular education (inservice)	$9,920
2	Regular education (inservice)	9,465	2	Severely handicapped	9,431
3	Severely handicapped	8,075	3	General special education	8,220
4	Early childhood	5,655	4	Early childhood	6,220
5	Model development	4,530	5	Model development	4,487
6	Volunteer	1,510	6	Vocational/career	1,700
7	Vocational/career	1,142	7	Paraprofessional	1,414
8	Paraprofessional	1,415	8	Physical education	1,028
9	Physical education	910	9	Recreation	918
10	Recreation	810	10	Interdisciplinary	772
11	Interdisciplinary	610	11	Volunteer	665
12	Developmental assistance	500	12	Developmental assistance	600

Note. From grant application package disseminated by BEH.

(f) Specialized training of regular educators; and

(g) Preparation of trainers of volunteers, including parents. (U.S. Department of Education, 1982, p. 3)

Under this new funding plan *Preparation of Special Educators* included preservice training for adapted physical education specialists as well as special educators, early childhood specialists for the handicapped, speech and language pathologists and audiologists, and vocational special educators. Physical education thus, for the first time in its federal funding history, was in competition with other areas for the same funds. The effect of this change is obvious in the earlier quotes of Hillman (1983) and Bowers and Churton (1986).

The National Consortium on Physical Education and Recreation for the Handicapped has worked closely with the Senate Subcommittee for the Handicapped in strengthening the physical education sections of the EHA reauthorization (Churton, 1986b). With renewed interest in legislation, increased knowledge about OSERS, and commitment to improved communication of the value of physical education, it is likely that the new generation of adapted physical educators will create a brighter future.

Impact of Federal Funding on Adapted Physical Education

The development of adapted physical education, both as a profession and as an academic discipline, has been significantly influenced by federal legislation and funding (Hillman, 1986). PL 94-142 led to a total revision of course content. Its enactment, with the mandate that all handicapped children shall have physical education, also contributed to the trend toward teacher training programs requiring a course in adapted physical education and/or infusing information about handicapped students into all major courses.

The strong graduate level specialization in adapted physical education now available at many colleges and universities can be traced to Part D monies under EHA legislation. Without external funding, most physical education departments would never have conceptualized training teachers for handicapped children as a priority area. Just as state and local education agencies have required federal money to reduce discrimination against black children (civil rights legislation) and females (Title IX legislation), physical education departments (for the most part) have needed money as an incentive to promote positive attitudes toward the inclusion of handicapped chil-

dren in the mainstream and to provide teacher training experiences that will accomplish this goal.

Many services provided by national associations like AAHPERD can also be traced to Part D, EHA funding. Among these are the AAHPER(D) Unit on Programs for the Handicapped, which operated only as long as federal monies were available.

Funding of AAHPERD Unit

The AAHPERD Unit on Programs for the Handicapped (new name in 1968) began as a Project on Recreation and Fitness for the Mentally Retarded in 1965 with a 3-year grant from the Joseph P. Kennedy, Jr. Foundation. The voluminous work of this office, directed by Julian Stein, had much of its fiscal base in federal funding rather than the membership dues of the approximately 10% (5,000) of the total AAHPERD membership in the 1970s that checked the handicapped as one of its specific interest areas.

A brief chronology of the funding of the AAHPERD Unit on Programs for the Handicapped follows:

- *1968-1972*—funded by AAHPERD with several small grants amounting to approximately $135,000 from such sources as the Joseph P. Kennedy, Jr. Foundation, the Bureau of Education for the Handicapped, the Council for National Cooperation in Aquatics, and six different corporations. During these years Stein worked 100% for the Unit and in related projects with his salary paid 100% by AAHPERD. The BEH official primarily helpful in obtaining the first federal funding was Bobby Palk.

- *1972-1975*—funded mainly by the Bureau of Education for the Handicapped for implementation of the Physical Education and Recreation for the Handicapped Information and Resource Utilization Center (IRUC) project. During this 3-year period Stein worked 50% on the IRUC project and hence 50% of his salary was funded by BEH. The other 50% of Stein's salary was funded by AAHPERD for which he directed Unit on Programs for the Handicapped activities.

- *1975-1976*—funded by BEH for implementation of a 1-year IRUC project to develop ways of becoming a self-supporting information center. During this time Stein worked 75% on IRUC and hence 75% of his salary was funded by BEH. The other 25% was funded by AAHPERD, for which Stein directed Unit on Programs for the Handicapped services and activities. Altogether over its 4-year period of funding, IRUC received a total of $434,000 in federal money. The impact of IRUC on teacher training throughout the United States was tremendous in that it represented the only information source specifically for physical educators interested in handicapped individuals.

- *1976-1979*—funded primarily through the Leadership Development Institutes (LDI) project, which received approximately $250,000 total from BEH over the 3-year period. During this time Stein worked 75% on the LDI project, and 75% of his salary was funded by BEH. The other 25% was funded by AAHPERD for his work as Director of the Unit on Programs for the Handicapped.

- *1980-1981*—No funding was received from BEH for a new AAHPERD project on the handicapped, although grant proposals were submitted. When questioned concerning their failure to fund a new project, BEH personnel stated that AAHPERD was not indicating sufficient "in-house support" to warrant continued funding. In January, 1980, Stein was assigned to direct AAHPERD membership and computer services (50%) in addition to administration of the Unit on Programs for the Handicapped (50%).

In August, 1981, Stein resigned from AAHPERD and began teaching full time at George Mason University in Fairfax, Virginia. Mary Coscarelli, who had served as Stein's assistant during 1980-81, replaced him as acting director of the Unit. Coscarelli performed all unit duties until her resignation in the spring of 1983.

The AAHPERD Board of Directors, after receiving thousands of support letters from all over the United States, voted to extend the life of the Unit one more year (1983-84) while the issue of funding and services was studied. In 1984 the Unit ceased to function.

Summary of Services by AAHPERD Unit

During the years from 1966 to 1984 the Unit on Programs for the Handicapped made many significant contributions to professional preparation. Among these were (a) representation of AAHPERD in advocacy activities on Capitol Hill in relation to legislation for handicapped individuals; (b) publication and dissemination of activities-oriented materials, which stressed methods and materials for teaching handicapped individuals; (c) presentations at conferences and teacher training workshops; (d) sponsorship of conferences and institutes leading to the development of professional preparation guidelines and competencies; (e) promotion of self-advocacy among disabled persons (consumers) in relation to physical education and recreation; and (f) provision of free consultant services to individuals, agencies, schools, colleges, and universities—wherever and whenever information was needed.

One of the greatest contributions has been the publication of materials that focus on practical, functional approaches (methods, activities, accommodations) to integrating students with handicapping conditions through a continuum of alternative placements based on individual needs rather than traditional categorical generalizations. Included in these publications have been three newsletters (*Challenge*, 1965-1969; *Outlook*, 1969-1970; and *IRUC Briefings*, 1970-1980) and a periodical called *Practical Pointers*, which has had a variable number of volumes each year since its inception in 1968-1969. Also published by the Unit have been innumerable paperback books, including such classics as *Practical Guide for Teaching the Mentally Retarded to Swim* (1969), *Special Olympics Instructional Manual—From Beginners to Champions* (1972), *Testing for Impaired, Disabled, and Handicapped Individuals* (1975), and *Professional Preparation in Adapted Physical Education, Therapeutic Recreation, and Corrective Therapy* (1976). In addition to meeting information needs of practitioners and teachers, these publications generated monies for AAHPERD that far exceeded that needed to run the Unit and provide salaries for its personnel.

From 1972 until 1976 the Unit ran the Information and Resource Utilization Center in Physical Education and Recreation for the Handicapped (IRUC), which served our profession as a kind of specialized ERIC system. More books were published during these 4 years than any other time, making IRUC the acknowledged leader over commercial book companies in generating and disseminating adapted physical education knowledge. Although their names appear nowhere on these publications, Julian Stein and Dolores Geddes (IRUC staff member from 1973 to 1975) should be recognized as the authors of most of these volumes.

The major contributions of the Unit from 1976 until 1979, according to Stein, were the following outgrowths of the Leadership Development Institutes Project. It

> (a) provided opportunities for coordinated in-service activities and programs in 33 states where little effort of this type had previously been placed; (b) brought together representatives of organizations and individuals with various handicapping conditions in a *consumer conference* designed to get input, reactions, and recommendations from such persons about physical education, recreation, and sport activities (i.e., initiated a self-advocacy movement among disabled athletes); and (c) emphasized integration of individuals with handicapping conditions in regular physical education, recreation, and sport programs through publications, workshops, and consultations especially in 33 involved states. (Stein, 1983, personal correspondence)

Impact of AAHPERD Unit on Programs for the Handicapped. (Top left to right) Dolores Geddes-Burke (staff member from 1973-1975), Wanda Burnette (staff member from 1966-1981), and Edna Wooten-Kolan, University of Oregon. (Bottom) Julian Stein, Director of Programs for the Handicapped, 1966-1981, and bulletin board featuring Information and Resource Utilization Center (IRUC) of AAHPERD unit.

The LDI Project served all states that did not have BEH funding in physical education and recreation for the handicapped in their colleges and universities. The AAHPERD Unit on the Handicapped was therefore the major influence in upgrading existing teacher training programs and initiating new ones.

Throughout its existence the Unit worked to promote coordination of activities of the Therapeutics Council, the Adapted Physical Education Academy, and several other structures within AAHPERD that pertain to handicapped, ill, and disabled persons. In accordance with Stein's philosophy of infusion, the Unit also sought involvement of all AAHPERD structures in PL 94-142 and Section 504 implementation, thereby expanding the number of programs on handicapped individuals offered at conventions and heightening awareness of the overall AAHPERD membership. In this respect the Unit served as a catalyst and role model for state and district organizations that began adapted physical education sections while simultaneously infusing all aspects of health, physical education, recreation, and dance.

The contributions of the Unit clearly would not have been possible without the initial funding of the Joseph P. Kennedy, Jr. Foundation and the subsequent monies from BEH. In the section on professional preparation conferences that follows, the contributions of the Unit and/or its representatives are further delineated.

Impact of Funding on Major Professional Preparation Conferences

In addition to funding the Unit on Programs for the Handicapped, BEH (i.e., Part D, EHA legislation) made possible several major professional preparation conferences. These were the first of their kind, although some informal meetings had been held at AAHPERD conferences in conjunction with the Project/Unit on Programs for the Handicapped.

First BEH Conference. The first BEH conference on physical education and recreation for handicapped children and youth was convened in Washington, DC on June 26-28, 1968, to discuss implementation of PL 90-170, Title V. Conferees met in two groups, one on physical education and one on recreation services. The conference report (Gallagher, Lucito, & Hillman, 1968) indicated that both groups agreed that the highest funding priority was training at the graduate level. Research needs were listed as development of extended program research, diagnostic and evaluation tools, instructional media, and a broad-based information and retrieval system.

In essence, this conference provided in-service training in grant writing and assisted prospective grant writers in understanding training priorities. Among the physical educators who participated were Julian Stein, Lawrence Rarick, Janet Wessel, Lou Bowers, Hollis Fait, Frank Hayden, Robert Holland, Lynn McCraw, Honey Nashman, and Frank Sills.

First National Conference on Research and Demonstration Needs. A Study Conference on Research and Demonstration Needs in Physical Education and Recreation for Handicapped Children was held on February 16-19, 1969, at the University of Maryland. This conference was funded by a BEH grant to AAHPER (Julian Stein), which then subcontracted various tasks to the National Recreation and Park Association (NRPA). The 3-day conference, attended by 30 persons in physical education and recreation for the handicapped (mostly grant writers), was a first attempt to gather input from the field on research that would enhance the newly established training programs funded by BEH.

The conference report (Troester & Prezioso, 1969) summarized the major problems in research and demonstration as

- lack of basic scientific understanding of recreation and recreative activities and recreation's contribution to the growth and development of handicapped children;

- lack of effective means of increasing understanding of the problems and the potential of the handicapped child and acceptance of the importance of physical education and recreation;

- lack of basic legislation directed to physical education and recreation for handicapped children and the inhibiting effect this has on program development;

- lack of effective recruitment programs for service to handicapped children and shortcomings in training—orientation, preservice, in-service, formal education and specialized training opportunities;

- lack of reliable theory and proven methods in providing physical education and/or recreation for handicapped

children in terms of identification, rural versus urban services, cost-benefits, modes for service, integration of handicapped, professional programming for handicapped and understanding of the effects of physical education/therapeutic recreation activities on handicapped children. (Troester & Prezioso, 1969)

The major statements of need and recommendations for research and development that emerged included the need to

- develop comprehensive retrieval and dissemination procedures and systems to allow researchers and practitioners to fully utilize research findings and empirical practices;

- use sound evaluation procedures, to direct more research and demonstration to integrating the handicapped with the non-handicapped;

- encourage better coordination among various agencies and disciplines serving the handicapped, including more cooperative efforts between physical education, recreation, and special education;

- conduct multi-dimensional analyses of underlying skill functions needed as a requisite for optimizing recreation participation;

- place increased research and demonstration emphasis on programs enabling the handicapped to acquire and maintain leisure skills and attitudes. (Troester & Prezioso, 1969)

Regional Professional Preparation Institutes: Emphasis on Competencies. In 1971-1972 a series of institutes funded by BEH were held to develop guidelines for professional preparation in physical education for the handicapped. Over 120 physical educators, recreators, special educators, administrators, and others participated in one or more of these seven institutes, workshops, and meetings held between September, 1971 and August, 1972.

Two professional preparation trends of the 1970s and 1980s had their roots in these meetings: (a) the generic or noncategorical approach to handicapping conditions and (b) the competency approach to adapted physical education teacher training. The importance of practicum experience was affirmed also, as was the need for contact with recreators, special educators, and others within an interdisciplinary framework during training.

The following authors of textbooks on physical education for the handicapped participated in and were influenced by these institutes: Dave Auxter, Daniel Arnheim, Charles Buell, Alfred Daniel, Hollis Fait, Dolores Geddes, Ellen Kelly, Claudine Sherrill, Thomas Vodola, Janet Wessel, and Joseph Winnick. Influences of the institutes are evidenced also in the widespread use of these competencies by BEH project directors (Clelland, 1979).

Stein served as director of these institutes, and proceedings were published in 1973. Entitled *Guidelines for Professional Preparation Programs for Personnel Involved in Physical Education and Recreation for the Handicapped*, this book used the same terminology as BEH training grant proposals (roles, functions or tasks, competencies, and learning experiences). In so doing, it became the major resource for prospective grant writers and for university personnel who were developing adapted physical education curricula. The stage was thus set for professional preparation in adapted physical education to be competency based.

Institute participants identified three basic professional roles in adapted physical education for which students should be prepared: (a) specialist teacher; (b) supervisor; and (c) college teacher. Functions were identified for each role, after which competencies were listed for carrying out functions and possible learning experiences were stated. Table 5.7 presents the functions and competencies for the specialist teacher agreed upon by institute participants.

First National Conference on Program Development and Evaluation. On December 5-7, 1973, the first National Conference on Program Development and Evaluation in Physical Education and Recreation for Handicapped Children and Youth was held in Washington, DC. Participants were mainly BEH project directors and guests from selected national organizations. Primary purposes of the conference were to (a) allow time for each project director to present a needs statement that would be representative of his or her state's physical education and therapeutic recreation needs, (b) discuss and examine advocacy positions relative to legislation concerning the handicapped, and (c) present results of a Delphi survey conducted prior to the conference (Johnson & Nesbitt, 1973).

Findings of the Delphi survey, which focused on 24 issues and concerns, were included in the 1973 conference report by Johnson and Nesbitt. They were based upon responses from 25 BEH project directors and 8 professionals from national associations, state departments of education, and the U.S. Office of Education. The following issues were ranked as most important:

1. Educating the general public to the recreation and physical education needs of the handicapped.

2. Communicating the importance of physical education and recreation to administrators.

3. Emphasizing physical education and recreation in the special education curricula.

4. Increasing the number of recreation personnel concerned with the handicapped in public recreation departments.

5. Increasing funding from federal and state resources.

Table 5.7   1971-1972 AAHPERD Functions and Competencies for Adapted Physical Education

1. Function: Assess and evaluate the physical and motor status of individuals with a variety of handicapping conditions.

   Competencies

   (a) Identify physical and motor tolerance limits for participation in various exercises and physical activity (movement-oriented) programs.

   (b) Analyze specific movement and exercise problems/capacities.

   (c) Determine physical and motor (movement) needs of individuals.

2. Function: Develop (design, plan), implement (conduct), and evaluate diversified programs of physical education for individuals and groups with a variety of handicapping conditions.

   Competencies

   (a) Understand the general nature of specific types of handicaps and their potential effects on both learning and participating in a variety of physical activities.

   (b) Interpret and apply assessments of individuals to develop appropriate programs of exercise and physical activity (movement-oriented) programs.

   (c) Evaluate individual progress and program effectiveness.

3. Function: Participate in interprofessional situations providing special programs or services for individuals or groups, including coordination of such services for a program.

   Competencies

   (a) Identify and utilize resources of professionals in other related disciplines.

   (b) Integrate programs of individuals and/or groups with other instructional, treatment, and rehabilitation programs.

   (c) Interpret evaluations and programs of individuals to other professionals, lay persons, and families.

These issues continue to be relevant today. This conference is recognized as the first official meeting of the National Ad Hoc Committee on Physical Education and Recreation for the Handicapped, the forerunner of the National Consortium on Physical Education and Recreation for the Handicapped (NCPERH).

Conferences funded by BEH/OSE/OSEP after 1973 were mostly under the auspices of university projects. Most training projects conducted at least one conference every 3 years. Generally these were partially, rather than fully, funded.

Identification of Funding Priorities

The democratic process dictates that funds authorized by federal legislation shall be used to meet documented needs. Advisory groups comprised of national experts are generally trusted to identify these needs. Training needs in physical education and recreation for handicapped individuals were first designated by a Congressionally mandated national advisory committee and later by small groups of grant directors.

National Advisory Committee

PL 90-170, Title V, which authorized the funding of training and research in physical education and recreation for the handicapped, also provided for the appointment of a National Advisory Committee on Physical Education and Recreation for Handicapped Children to advise the Secretary of the U.S. Department of Health, Education, and Welfare concerning needs to be met. Although PL 90-170 was enacted in 1967, committee members did not meet until 1971. The following persons comprised the committee: Robert Holland, Chair, Physical Education Representative; Janet Wessel, Physical Education Representative; John Nesbitt, Recreation Representative; Fred Humphrey, Recreation Representative; George Valos, Public Representative; and William Wolfe, Special Education.

Robert Holland, Ohio State Department of Education, was the person selected 6 years earlier by the Kennedy

Foundation to serve as the first director of the AAHPERD Unit on Programs for the Handicapped; Holland was also the individual who drafted the PE-R part of the PL 90-170 legislation for Senator Kennedy. Today Holland is remembered as one of our strongest leaders. Nesbitt (1983) summarized the work of the committee as follows:

> The committee had three scheduled meetings: February 1-2, 1971; March 9-10, 1971; and May 26-27, 1971. The Committee carried out its mission by reviewing the ongoing goals and program of the U.S. Bureau of Education for the Handicapped, by assessing physical education and recreation service needs of handicapped children and youth (less than 10% were receiving service), and by formulating immediate and long range recommendations for action and for policies by the U.S. Bureau of Education for the Handicapped. (p. 326)

Although the National Advisory Committee on Physical Education and Recreation for Handicapped Children was not convened after 1971, and thus died a "natural death,"

National Advisory Committee on Physical Education and Recreation for Handicapped Children. (top left to right) Fred Humphrey, William Wolfe, John Nesbitt, George Valos; (bottom left to right) Robert Holland, Janet Wessel, and Rafer Johnson.

its work was well received by BEH, which designated physical education and recreation as funding priorities.

Janet Wessel, of Michigan State University, who now is known for *I CAN* and the *Achievement Based Curriculum*, was appointed in 1973 to the National Advisory Committee on the Handicapped (NACH), the most powerful of the BEH advisory bodies. Wessel thus became the first, and so far the only, physical educator to serve on the NACH.

BEH/OSE Advisory Group Meetings

William Hillman, Physical Education and Recreation Consultant within BEH, convened periodically with small advisory groups representing the National Consortium on Physical Education for the Handicapped (NCPERH). This organization, which began as an Ad Hoc Committee in 1973, is described in chapter 4. From 1974 onward small groups of training grant directors met with Hillman in Washington, DC to review funding in relation to training programs in physical education and recreation for the handicapped and to reassess funding priorities. Each of these meetings resulted in a memorandum from Hillman concerning training needs and was disseminated widely to grant writers and to panelists who subsequently evaluated the grants. A review of Hillman's several memoranda offers insight into emerging trends and issues within professional preparation.

Meeting 1 (November 12, 1974). In the review resulting from this advisory meeting Hillman issued the following powerful statement of need:

> It is estimated that no more than 20 percent of the nation's schools are offering physical education to handicapped children. Eighty (80) percent of the schools offering education to handicapped children have totally inadequate physical education services. (Hillman, 1974)

Six primary issues also were identified that BEH should address in its decision making:

1. Insufficient funds to provide support for currently funded projects.

2. Insufficient funds to provide support for projects in states or regions not currently funded.

3. Need to initiate doctoral level personnel preparation programs.

4. Inadequate support from special education for the provision of physical education and recreation services to handicapped children.

5. Need to involve physical education and recreation in ongoing educational services programs and new programs such as career education.

6. Lack of technical materials and basic professional and technical information services. (Hillman, 1974)

Meeting 2 (September 22-23, 1977). Physical education representatives at this meeting were Claudine Sherrill, Texas Woman's University; John Dunn, Oregon State University; Leon Johnson, University of Missouri; and David Auxter, Slippery Rock State College. Recreation representatives were Peter Verhoven, University of Maryland; David Compton, North Texas State University; Gary Robb, President, National Therapeutic Recreation Society; David Park, George Washington University; Fred Humphrey, University of Maryland; and Jerry Kelly, University of Maryland. Separate lists of priorities were drawn up for adapted physical education and therapeutic recreation.

The following eight physical education priorities were agreed upon:

1. In-service training of educational policy makers.

2. In-service training of instructional personnel.

3. In-service training of community management personnel.

4. Preparation of physical educators for rural areas.

5. Retraining and in-service of trainers of teachers.

6. In-service of paraprofessionals, volunteers, and parents related to physical education.

7. Improve dissemination procedures in physical education.

8. To assist state education agencies (SEAs) to monitor and develop physical education programs for handicapped children.

Meeting 3 (July 12-13, 1982). This advisory meeting fulfilled two purposes: (a) reassess funding priorities and training needs and (b) interact with Ed Sontag (acting director) and branch chiefs of Special Education Programs (previously known as OSE and BEH) concerning perceived funding problems. Physical education representatives included John Dunn, Oregon State University; Claudine Sherrill, Texas Woman's University; Dave Auxter, Slippery Rock State College; Mike Churton, Appalachian State University; Julian Stein, George Mason University; and Tom Songster, Joseph P. Kennedy, Jr. Foundation. Recreation representatives included Fred Humphrey, University of Maryland, and Dennis Vinton, University of Kentucky.

Nine physical education funding priorities resulted from follow-up work of the July, 1982 meeting and were developed to prepare physical education personnel:

1. To provide a cross-categorical program including severely and profoundly handicapped to conduct appropriate physical education programs for the handicapped.

2. To provide services for handicapped children in a variety of settings including regular class programs, self-contained programs, and institutional (homebound and remedial) programs.

3. To train handicapped children of various ages and disabilities in all of the defined physical education curricula areas.

4. To develop model in-service training programs that are reproducible and will bring about behavioral changes in handicapped children.

5. To develop appropriate models for incorporating the services of paraprofessionals in service delivery to handicapped children.

6. To gain knowledge and technical skill to work with parents and community personnel relative to physical education for the handicapped.

7. To communicate with local education agency (LEA) administrators relative to the appropriateness and need for physical education for the handicapped.

8. To assist state education agencies (SEAs) monitor and develop physical education programs for handicapped children.

9. To design special projects that provide research and demonstration results to strengthen the existing physical education delivery system. (Auxter & Churton, 1983, pp. 2-5)

Dunn (1983) emphasized that the preceding list evolved from concerns suggested by members of the National Consortium on Physical Education and Recreation for the Handicapped at their annual meeting in August, 1982. Priority ranking of concerns was not intended and should not be implied. This 1983 list of priorities (as compared with the 1978 list) reflected changes in philosophy and/or politics at the federal level. These priorities remain the "areas that we need to be concerned with in order to meet the challenges of quality assurance and excellence in teaching" (Churton, 1986a, p. 122). The problem of the 1980s is to create strategies for determining whether graduating students meet these standards and to examine the curricula of training programs to analyze learning experiences that contribute to the meeting of standards.

Subsequent Meetings. The development of an official position paper stating training priorities (Dunn, 1983) led to several subsequent meetings (approximately one a year) between university professors and OSERS/OSEP personnel. Whereas the meetings in the 1970s and early 1980s were initiated by BEH/OSEP personnel because they wanted input from the field, the meetings are now initiated mainly by the legislative chair and officers of the National Consortium on Physical Education and Recreation for the Handicapped. The nature of the meetings has changed also from the periodic cooperative assessment of funding priorities and training needs to that of a dialogue between funder and fundee, with the latter focusing on communication of the importance of physical education and recreation in the lives of handicapped children. The thrust of the 1980s thus has become advocacy as physical educators join special educators in trying to convince an essentially Republican administration of the importance of federal assistance to college and university programs pertaining to minority concerns.

Future Directions

Legislation, funding, and adapted physical education teacher training are inextricably linked. Because history shows the effectiveness of federal (rather than state) legislation in assuring the rights of minority groups (blacks, females, handicapped) and reducing educational inequities, it is important that physical educators continue advocacy for federal funding of EHA programs. Concurrently, it seems prudent to work toward state level EHA legislation and funding. It is crucial to ascertain that the physical education wording in federal legislation is paralleled in state statutes. Litigation may become increasingly necessary to force administrators to heed existing legislation and/or to provide needed services to school children.

The academic training of adapted physical educators must be broadened to include courses and other learning experiences in advocacy, legislation, and funding. Textbooks must be revised to include chapters on the legal bases of adapted physical education and advocacy concepts and strategies. The role of parents in helping physical educators achieve advocacy goals must receive careful attention, and undergraduate students must be exposed early to partnership projects with parents. The course work of all physical educators (not just adapted specialists) should be infused with methods of facilitating attitude change. The goal must be quality physical education for all.

References

Auxter, D., & Churton, M. (1983). Personnel preparation needs in adapted physical education. In J. Dunn (Ed.), *Training and research needs in physical education and recreation for the handicapped* (pp. 2-5). Report to OSEP from National Consortium on Physical Education and Recreation for the Handicapped. (Available from M. Churton, Appalachian State University, Boone, NC 28606.)

Ballard, J., Ramirez, B., & Weintraub, F. (Eds.). (1982). *Special education in America: Its legal and governmental foundations*. Reston, VA: Council for Exceptional Children.

Barrett, D. (1983). The who, what, when, and how of the federal funding process. *Programs for the Handicapped, 2*, 8-12.

Bowers, L., & Churton, M. (1986). *Hearing on reauthorization of the EHA discretionary programs: Prepared statement of the National Consortium on Physical Education and Recreation for the Handicapped to the U.S. Senate Subcommittee on the Handicapped.* (Available from M. Churton, Appalachian State University, Boone, NC 28606.)

Broadhead, G.D. (1981). Time passages in adapted physical education. In G. Brooks (Ed.), *Perspectives on the academic discipline of physical education* (pp. 234-252). Champaign, IL: Human Kinetics.

Burke, P. (1976). Personnel preparation: Historical perspective. *Exceptional Children, 43*(3), 144-147.

Churton, M. (1986a). Addressing personnel preparation needs to meet the challenges of the future. *Adapted Physical Activity Quarterly, 3*(2), 118-123.

Churton, M. (1986b). EHA reauthorization summary. *NCPERH Advocate, 14*(4), 2.

Clelland, R. (1979). *A survey of personnel preparation in physical education and recreation for the handicapped— The consumer's guide series: Volume VI.* Teacher Education/Special Education BEH Special Project, University of New Mexico, Albuquerque. Grant No. G007602994 from DPP/BEH.

Dunn, J. (1983). *SEP/Funding priority needs in PE/R: NCPERH Washington Committee Report to SEP.* Corvallis: Oregon State University.

Gallagher, J., Lucito, L., & Hillman, W. (1968). *Conference on physical education and recreation service for the mentally handicapped and other handicapped children.* Washington, DC: Bureau of Education for the Handicapped.

Hillman, W. (1974). *Program review: Physical education and recreation for handicapped children and youth: Memorandum.* Washington, DC: DPP/BEH.

Hillman, W. (1978). *Personnel preparation needs in recreation and physical education for handicapped children: Memorandum to BEH staff and professional personnel.* Washington, DC: Bureau of Education for the Handicapped.

Hillman, W. (1983). *To professional colleagues in physical education and recreation: Topics of interest and enclosures: Memorandum.*

Hillman, W. (1986). The role of federal government in adapted physical education. *Adapted Physical Activity Quarterly, 3*(2), 124-126.

Johnson, L., & Nesbitt, J. (1973). *A report on the national conference on program development and evaluation in physical education and recreation for handicapped children and youth in Washington DC on December 5, 1973.* Washington, DC: Ad Hoc Committee on Physical Education and Recreation for Handicapped.

Kutner, M., & Sherman, J. (1982). An intergovernmental perspective on federal education grants. *Peabody Journal of Education, 60*(1), 66-81.

LaVor, M. (1976). Federal legislation for exceptional persons: A history. In F. Weintraub, A. Abeson, J. Ballard, & M. LaVor (Eds.), *Public policy and the education of exceptional children* (pp. 96-111). Reston, VA: Council for Exceptional Children.

McNutt, R., & Wexler, H. (1983). *Introduction to the 1983 Guide to ED Programs.* Washington, DC: Office of Legislation and Public Affairs.

Mitzel, H.E. (Ed.). (1982). *Encyclopedia of educational research.* New York: Free Press.

Nesbitt, J. (Ed.). (1983). *New horizons in professional training in recreation service for handicapped children and youth.* Iowa City: Special Recreation.

Peterson, P., & Rabe, B. (1983). The role of interest groups in the formulation of educational policy: Past practice and future trends. *Teachers College Record, 84*(3), 708-729.

Sherrill, C. (1986). *Adapted physical education and recreation: A multidisciplinary approach* (3rd ed.). Dubuque: Wm. C. Brown.

Troester, C., & Prezioso, S. (1969). *Physical education and recreation for handicapped children: Proceedings of a study conference on research and demonstration needs*. Washington, DC: American Association for Health, Physical Education and Recreation/National Recreation and Park Association.

U.S. Department of Education. (1982). *New application for grants under training personnel for the education of the handicapped*. (CFDA 84.029) 1983 Grant Announcements. Washington, DC: Author.

Vodola, T. (1973). *Individualized physical education program for the handicapped child*. Englewood Cliffs, NJ: Prentice Hall.

Weintraub, F., Abelson, A., Ballard, J., & LaVor, M. (Eds.). (1976). *Public policy and the education of exceptional children*. Reston, VA: Council for Exceptional Children.

Weintraub, F., & Ramirez, B. (1985). *Progress in the education and analysis of PL 98-199: The Education of the Handicapped Act amendments of 1983*. Reston, VA: Council for Exceptional Children.

Chapter 6

Grant Writing to Fund Adapted Physical Education Teacher Training

Claudine Sherrill

*G*rantsmanship is a science, an art, and a political endeavor. The scientific aspect requires a knowledge of component parts of an application and the ability to interrelate logically all process steps. The art necessitates the interweaving of factual information about local need with evidence that the project addresses priority concerns and will impact upon a broad geographic area. And finally, the political aspect implies that the grantee will use a variety of public relations strategies to convince the proper authorities that the project will be a winner. (Vodola, 1981, p. 5)

The Division of Personnel Preparation (DDP), Office of Special Education Programs (OSEP), Office of Special Education and Rehabilitative Services (OSERS) of the U.S. Department of Education in Washington, DC is the agency that awards grants for the training of physical education and recreation personnel to educate handicapped children and youth. Funds for these grants are authorized by Part D or Subchapter IV of PL 91-230, the Education of the Handicapped Act (EHA), enacted in 1970 and amended approximately every 3 years. Grant writing therefore begins with an understanding of the Division of Personnel Preparation, its historical evolution, and the personalities that shape its policies.

The Federal Funding Agency

The Office of Special Education Programs (OSEP) was known as the Bureau of Education for the Handicapped (BEH) from its creation in 1966 through 1980, when PL 96-88, the Department of Education Act, became effective. The history of BEH is described in *Exceptional Children*, November, 1976.

Today OSEP is comprised of five divisions, each with its own administrative head, but all responsible to the same Deputy Director, Director, Assistant Secretary, and Secretary. Figure 6.1 depicts this administrative hierarchy in late 1986. It is important that the grant writer know the names of these key figures, their political party and views, and how they are appointed.

Three reference books found in most university libraries give information about the top two positions (Secretary

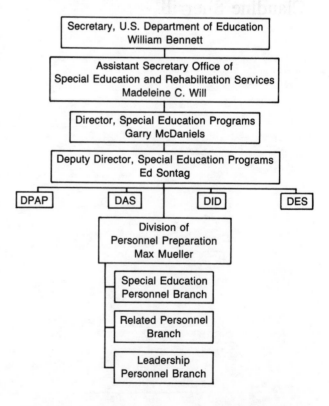

Politics is an integral part of funding and grant writing. From left to right: William Hillman, Claudine Sherrill, Louis Bowers.

Figure 6.1 Administrative chain of command influencing Division of Personnel Practice funding. *Note.* Divisions not labelled include the following: DPAP—Division of Policy Analysis and Planning; DAS—Division of Assistance to States; DID—Division of Innovation and Development; DES—Division of Educational Services.

Secretary, U.S. Department of Education
William Bennett

Assistant Secretary Office of
Special Education and Rehabilitation Services
Madeleine C. Will

Director, Special Education Programs
Garry McDaniels

Deputy Director, Special Education Programs
Ed Sontag

DPAP   DAS   DID   DES

Division of
Personnel Preparation
Max Mueller

Special Education
Personnel Branch

Related Personnel
Branch

Leadership
Personnel Branch

and Assistant Secretary) in the administrative chain of command. These are

- Brownson, C.B. (Ed.). (1985). *Congressional staff directory*. Mount Vernon, VA: Congressional Staff Directory, LTD.

- Office of the Federal Register (1985-1986). *United States government manual*. Washington, DC: U.S. Government Printing Office.

- U.S. Government Printing Office (1985-1986). *Official directory, 99th Congress*. Washington, DC: Author.

These books are revised every 1 to 2 years because individuals holding government offices frequently change.

The Secretary of Education and the Assistant Secretary of OSERS are appointed directly by the President of the United States, but such appointments must be confirmed by the U.S. Senate and House of Representatives. Moreover, the work of these persons is monitored by Congress, and they are particularly responsive to requests for information and action from congresspersons. The Secretary of Education, Assistant Secretary of OSERS, Director of OSEP, and Deputy Director of OSEP are likely to be members of whichever political party has the greater power. When the U.S. Presidency changes from one party to another, the persons occupying these top administrative positions are likely to change also. For example, Ed Martin served as Director of BEH and as the Assistant Secretary of OSERS for many years. Almost immediately after President Ronald Reagan assumed office (1981), Martin was replaced by Jean Tufts, who provided OSERS leadership until her death in 1983. Madeleine Will is currently Assistant Director of OSERS.

Grant writers need to become sensitized to the names of authority figures within federal funding agencies; to be aware of their travels, presentations, and publications; and to be able to discuss their priorities and actions with members of Congress. Ed Martin, for instance, is remembered for his strong advocacy for integration of handicapped students into regular schools. Illustrative of his writing is the following:

> Our experience with segregated societal institutions has shown them to be among our most cruel and dehumanizing activities . . . think, for a moment, about the conditions on Indian reservations, the internment of Japanese-Americans during World War II, the Willowbrooks, the jails, the racially segregated schools, and the acceptance of Cambodians and Vietnamese in our society. In each instance we have created institutions supposedly for the good of those to be incarcerated or, at least, to provide them with

human treatment. In each, however, there has been a classic pattern of neglect, isolation, rejection, and ultimate dehumanization. (Martin, 1976, p. 6)

Will, in contrast, will be known for her support of early childhood intervention and services for secondary- and postsecondary-aged handicapped persons. Testifying on OSERS priorities, Will stated,

> We have made significant strides towards our goal of full access to equal opportunity for handicapped people, but we have a long way to go. There still remains gaps as well as overlaps in what is envisioned to be a comprehensive service delivery program. Specifically two groups of handicapped youngsters can benefit from improved services. These groups are the very young children and the thousands of youngsters who are leaving our secondary schools to seek employment and independence. ("Will testifies," 1983, p. 2)

Part of the politics of grant writing is staying abreast of new funding and service priorities. Grant writers do not typically start with an original idea or personal/professional dream. Instead they study the priorities of their selected funding agency and the "pet ideas" of its administrators and staff. It is almost always advantageous to get acquainted with the staff, to solicit their input concerning proposal content, and to be a careful listener. This author, for instance, made a trip to BEH/OSEP in Washington, DC at her own expense before attempting to write a first grant. In so doing she achieved three goals: (a) became acquainted with the funding structure, (b) identified potential advisors/mentors from among the staff and initiated a sharing/working relationship with them, and (c) increased the visibility of her university as a viable prospective recipient of grant monies.

Federal Project Officers Versus Grant Negotiators

The OSEP staff members with whom the grant writer interacts the most are the project officer and the grant negotiator. It is important to understand the role of each.

The project officer is a staff member assigned to a specific geographical region and/or discretionary competition. He or she is readily available by telephone and acts as consultant/advisor in answering questions about grant writing and management. In addition to their advisory responsibilities, project officers are active in the review of proposals. They serve as chairpersons of external panels assembled to evaluate proposals and also participate in "in-house" reviews.

The grant negotiator is the staff person who telephones the grant writer and informs him or her of the grant award. The grant negotiator then goes over the budget with the writer and requests justification of monies requested for each item. Depending upon the strength of the justifications, the grant negotiator can adjust the sums allocated for each item. In grant management throughout the year, the university contacts the grant negotiator concerning problems regarding proper use of monies.

Basic Grantsmanship Concepts

OSEP training proposals are written to fund 3-year projects. This means that every 3 years the grant writer must submit a *new application* that describes in detail need, goals and objectives, program content, management plan, evaluation procedures, personnel and resources, and budget and cost effectiveness. The due date for this new application is usually October or November, after which the writer waits several months to learn whether or not the proposal has been funded. Generally this information is received in March or April. The fiscal year for training grants begins June 1, so grant directors must plan to spend at least a portion of their summer months in setting up the new project. Among the essential tasks to be accomplished as early as possible are (a) obtaining a campus budget number so the grant monies can be operationalized and spent; (b) recruiting and employing faculty, staff, and graduate assistants to be on hand when the fall academic year begins; and (c) planning cooperative training with local and state education agencies.

During the ensuing 2 years after a project is funded, the grant writer must submit *continuation proposals*. These are about half as long as the original new application and respond to slightly different criteria. The purpose of the continuation proposal is to describe annual progress made toward goals and to explain changes in project components. Typically the amount of money received for each continuation year remains the same, although budget items must be explained to the grant negotiator each spring upon notification of award just as was done for the new application.

Understanding the concept of *indirect charges* is critical for grant writers. The university as a whole (i.e., the administration) receives 8% of the total funds awarded for training grants. For other kinds of grants with other agencies the university may take more than 8% of the total, but 8% is the absolute ceiling for OSEP training grants. Often campus grants administrators are unfamiliar with OSEP training grant regulations, and the project writer/ director must play a public relations role in disseminating information about his or her particular funding agency and its regulations, rules, and priorities. Supposedly the 8% received by the university administration is for services rendered by the campus offices responsible for accounting, purchasing, facilities maintenance, and grants administration. There appears to be no way that the grant director can monitor use of this 8% (often called overhead on budget accounting sheets). In reality it is used in many ways by campus administrations.

Grant writers must also play a public relations role in obtaining as much university support for the training project as possible. This means negotiating with the departmental chair and higher level administration concerning what support (contributions) the university will provide if the proposed project is funded by the federal government. One of the most important evaluation criteria by which a new proposal is judged is promised support by the university administration. Specifically this criterion reads as follows:

> Does the application contain information on the amount of the fiscal and other effort the applicant will contribute to the program and a delineation of the procedures that will be implemented for the increase of this effort over a specified time period in relationship to the amount of Federal funds awarded for the support of the program? (U.S. Department of Education, 1986a, p. 45)

This concept of applicant (i.e., university) support is new to some campus grants administrators, university presidents, and other university decision makers because many grants are awarded by funding structures with no policy or requirement of matching or partial support from the university. OSEP does, however, require university support. The grant writer should request that the details of such support be recorded in writing by the highest level administrator possible to prevent the misunderstandings that appear to occur rather frequently between project directors and their campus superiors. Unless a grant writer has strong support from his or her administration it is foolhardy to write a proposal.

OSEP project officers and grant negotiators suggest that an applicant (university) pledge support equal to the amount requested. University support of training grants is usually in the form of salaries (hard money) for faculty who teach adapted physical education courses and other content like research, evaluation, statistics, and curriculum that may be required of graduate students specializing in adapted physical education. Other university support includes provision of office and instructional space, utilities, equipment, and custodial service. The university may also provide support by waiving all or part of the tuition for students funded by a grant, by awarding scholarships to students for which the grant is designed, by providing travel money to supplement grant travel funds, and by paying secretaries with "hard money." An unwritten policy of OSEP passed to grant writers by word of mouth is that OSEP monies may not be used for purchase of equipment. It is imperative, therefore, that the grant writer ascertains that the university will supply him or her with office equipment like typewriters and computers as well as instructional and audiovisual equipment.

Negotiations with campus administrators concerning university support of a proposed project should be completed before grant writing commences. Likewise, the grant writer should clearly understand campus policies and lines of authority pertaining to grants. It is far easier to write a federal grant than to manage the project once it has been funded. The grant writer should be assured of released time for grants management and subsequent writing before he or she commits to writing a first proposal.

Grant writers should also seek the support of their professional colleagues, both within the university and in outside agencies. Receipt of a funded project often means a shifting of job responsibilities and increased, new, or different work for several faculty members, not just the grant writer. If the faculty as a whole is not supportive of a high quality adapted physical education specialization, then the proposal should not be written.

The Grant Review Process

Before starting proposal writing, one should be familiar with the general review process. This varies somewhat from year to year but typically involves both external and in-house reviews.

External reviews are of two types. One entails the proposal being mailed to a field reader who, in turn, prepares a detailed written review of its strengths and weaknesses in accordance with the evaluation criteria stated in the grant application package. The other entails a meeting of panelists in Washington, DC. This process involves the independent reading and rating of a proposal by at least three reviewers, who then discuss its merits in a small group meeting that may include as many as eight or nine panelists. The persons assigned as first and second readers of the proposal review its content for the other panelists, who subsequently ask questions and engage in dialogue concerning the extent to which the proposal meets the evaluation criteria. Ultimately the panel agrees on a recommendation to fund or not fund the proposal.

The in-house review is conducted by the funding agency staff. It begins with a thorough review by the project officer who writes a recommendation to fund or not fund. Then the application and the project officer's recommendation are studied at the Branch, Division, and Director levels. When external and in-house reviews are in conflict, the in-house reviews naturally receive greater weight. This reality explains the importance of getting to know one's project officer and ascertaining that he or she is fully conversant with your capabilities as a grant writer and manager as well as the support of your university.

The grant review process is highly objective in that it entails numerical rating of the extent to which the proposal meets several criteria, each of which is worth

The grant review process. Panelists in 1970, from left to right, are Robert Holland, John Nesbitt, and Joseph Winnick with project officer William Hillman on right.

a set number of points. When all proposals within a discretionary competition have been scored, the proposals are placed in rank order. The project officer's funding recommendation is based on the application's rank order, field reader evaluations, panelist recommendations, and the project officer's analysis of the application.

The grant review process often includes no one with particular expertise in physical education and recreation for the handicapped. Proposals should therefore be explicit and detailed. It is better to err in the direction of writing too much than not enough.

The Grant Application Package

After becoming acquainted with the funding agency, resources for help, and the grant review process, the next step is to write or telephone for a copy of the grant application package. The grant application package provides information on all available discretionary competitions, closing dates for submission of proposals, and instructions for proposal development. It also includes the standard face page for federal applications, budget forms, and the civil rights certificate. The address and telephone number for obtaining a copy of the DPP grant application package are Director, Division of Personnel Preparation, Office of Special Education Programs, Department of Education, 400 Maryland Avenue S.W., Switzer Building, Room 4628, Washington, DC 20202, telephone 202-732-1068.

Two parts of the grant application package provide assistance in writing the program narrative for a new grant: (a) instructions for writing the program narrative and (b) the evaluation form that is used in judging the quality of the proposal. Unfortunately the two sections are not coordinated, and the naive writer is left wondering which outline is the better to follow.

Directions for Writing Program Narrative

The directions for writing the program narrative are very general. A three-part outline is recommended by the U.S. Department of Education (1986a, pp. 43-46).

1. Objectives and need for this assistance

   Describe the problem and demonstrate the need for assistance and state the principal and subordinate objectives of the project. Supporting documentation or other testimonies from concerned interests other than the applicant may be used. Projects involving training should present available data, or estimates, for need in terms of number of personnel by position type (e.g., teachers, teacher-aides) by type of handicap to

be served. Documentation by the State Education Agency (SEA) should be supplied.

2. Results or benefits expected

   Identify results and benefits to be derived. Projects should indicate the number of personnel to be trained.

3. Approach

   a. Outline a plan of action pertaining to the scope and detail of how the proposed work will be accomplished for each grant program, function, or activity provided in the budget. Cite factors which might accelerate or decelerate the work and your reason for taking this approach as opposed to others. An application for a training program should describe the substantive content and organization of the training program, including the roles or positions for which students are prepared, the tasks associated with such roles, the competencies that must be acquired, and the program staffing; and the practicum facilities including their use by students, accessibility to students and their staffing.

   b. Provide for each grant program, function, or activity, quantitative projections of the accomplishments to be achieved. Training programs should project the number of students to be trained by type of handicapping condition.

   c. Identify the kinds of data to be collected and maintained and discuss the criteria to be used to evaluate the results and successes of the project. The positions for which students are receiving training should be related to the needs as explained in 1 and 2 above.

   d. List organizations, cooperators, consultants, or other key individuals who will work on the project along with a short description of the nature of their effort or contribution. Describe the liaison with community or State organizations as it affects project planning and accomplishments.

Criteria for Evaluating Grant Proposal

Most grant writers consider the evaluation form that is used in judging the quality of the proposal to be the most important part of the grant application packet. Instead of following center headings in the directions for writing program narrative, many writers use the evaluation criteria as their center headings for developing the proposal. Field readers and panelists in the grant review process particularly like this organization because it makes everything easy to find and thus facilitates the evaluation process.

The precise wording of these criteria changes approximately every 3 to 4 years. The content, however, remains the same because these criteria are almost universally accepted as the standards by which training grants should be judged. Following are the 1986 evaluation criteria (U.S. Department of Education, 1986a, pp. 32-40).

EVALUATION CRITERIA FOR TRAINING GRANT

A. CRITERION 1—EXTENT OF NEED FOR THE PROJECT (Maximum 25 points)

Review the application for information that shows the project meets personnel training needs, consistent with the purposes of Part D of the Act. Look for information that

(1) Describes the needs addressed by the project;

(2) Describes how the project relates to

    (a) Identified personnel shortages in the field of special education, for project proposing to provide preservice training of personnel for careers in the field of special education; or

    (b) Personnel training needs, for special projects, parent, and volunteer projects and inservice projects; and

(3) Describes the benefits to be gained by meeting those personnel needs.

B. CRITERION 2—PROGRAM CONTENT (Maximum 15 points)

Review the application for information that shows

(1) The extent to which the application includes a description of competencies that each program participant will acquire and how the competencies will be evaluated;

(2) The extent to which substantive content and organization of the program

    (a) Are appropriate for the attainment of knowledge and competencies that are necessary for the provision of quality educational services to handicapped children and youth; and

    (b) Demonstrate an awareness of relevant methods, procedures, techniques, and instructional media or materials that can be used in the preparation of personnel who serve handicapped children and youth;

    (3) The extent to which appropriate practicum facilities are accessible to the applicant and are used for such activities as observation, participation, practice teaching, laboratory or clinical experience, internship, or other supervised experiences of adequate scope, combination, and length; and

    (4) The extent to which program activities are related to the education needs of handicapped children and youth.

C. CRITERION 3—PLAN OF OPERATION (Maximum 15 points)

Review the application for information that shows the quality of the plan of operation for the project. Look for information that shows

(1) High quality in the design of the project;

(2) An effective plan of management that ensures proper and efficient administration of the project;

(3) A clear description of how the objectives of the project relate to the purpose of the program;

(4) The way the applicant plans to use its resources and personnel to achieve each objective; and

(5) A clear description of how the applicant will provide equal access and treatment for eligible project participants who are members of groups that have been traditionally underrepresented, such as

    (a) Members of racial or ethnic minority groups;

    (b) Women;

    (c) Handicapped persons; and

    (d) The elderly.

D. CRITERION 4—EVALUATION PLAN (Maximum 15 points)

Review each application for information that shows the quality of the evaluation plan for the project. Look for information that shows methods of evaluation that are appropriate for the project and, to the extent possible, are objective and produce data that are quantifiable.

E. CRITERION 5—QUALITY OF KEY PERSONNEL (Maximum 15 points)

Review the application for information that shows the quality of key personnel the applicant plans to use on the project. Look for information that shows

(1) The qualifications of the project director (if one is to be used);

(2) The qualifications of each of the other key personnel to be used in the project;

(3) The time that each person plans to commit to the project; and

(4) The extent to which the applicant, as part of its non-discriminatory employment practices, encourages applications for employment from persons who are members of groups that have been traditionally underrepresented such as

(a) Members of racial or ethnic minority groups;

(b) Women;

(c) Handicapped persons; and

(d) The elderly.

To determine the qualifications of a person, consider experience and training, in fields related to the objectives of the project, as well as other information that the applicant provides.

F. CRITERION 6—ADEQUACY OF RESOURCES (Maximum 5 points)

Review the application for information that shows

(1) The applicant plans to devote adequate resources to the project;

(2) The facilities that the applicant plans to use are adequate; and

(3) The equipment and supplies that the applicant plans to use are adequate.

G. CRITERION 7—BUDGET AND COST EFFECTIVENESS (Maximum 10 points)

Review the application for information that shows that the project has an adequate budget and is cost effective. Look for information that shows

(1) The budget for the project is adequate to support the project activities; and

(2) Costs are reasonable in relation to the objectives of the project.

Length of Grant Proposal

The grant application manual indicates the recommended length of proposals. This is typically 20 to 30 pages of narrative. Additionally, most writers prepare detailed and extensive appendices. It is more important to ascertain that a proposal meets every evaluation criterion than to adhere to the recommended length. Much controversy exists concerning whether it is possible to write a good proposal in 20 to 30 pages. Prospective writers should confer with established grant directors in regard to ongoing practice in relation to proposal length.

Amount of Money Available

Most DPP project awards range between $40,000 and $70,000. The overall amount of money available to DPP to give as grants is determined by the U.S. Congress and therefore reflects politics and economic trends.

The periodic (i.e., every 3 to 4 years) authorizing EHA legislation establishes the maximum amount that each component of OSEP can receive. Then appropriations legislation determines the amounts actually received.

A list of institutions that have received physical education grants and the amounts awarded can be obtained by writing or telephoning DPP. It is often helpful to contact grant writers at other universities concerning priorities and guidelines. The National Consortium on Physical Education and Recreation for the Handicapped (see chapter 4) offers a network of individuals who can serve as resources in grant writing and management; this is the professional organization to which many grant writers belong.

Deciding on Type of Grant to be Written

Many types of training grants are available, so examination of the possible choices is the first step to be taken. These choices, called *competitions* or *priorities*, are described in detail in the grant application manual. Illustrative of such priorities are the following:

1. Special educators

2. Preparation of leadership personnel

3. Preparation of related services personnel

4. State education agency programs

5. Special projects

6. Transition projects

7. Infants

8. Rural

9. Minority

The list of priorities is generally revised when new authorizing EHA legislation is enacted. This revision is often minimal; the top four or five priorities, where most of the money is allocated, have tended to remain the same.

Physical education was listed as a separate funding priority until the early 1980s; leaders are working to regain this priority status. Until this goal is achieved, however, physical education grant writers will probably choose the *special educator* priority if the goal is baccalaureate or master's level training, or the *leadership personnel* priority if the goal is doctoral level training. In the past, few grants have been awarded for undergraduate training in physical education for the handicapped. Master's level preservice training is the area in which most universities receive funds for training physical educators to work with handicapped students.

Justifying the Need for the Project

Regardless of the type of grant to be written, much preliminary work is needed to establish the need for teacher training in adapted physical education in a particular state. It should be remembered that the purpose of federal funding is to meet state and local personnel needs, not to enhance the curriculum of the university. Proposal writers must therefore be personally acquainted with both special education and physical education administrators within their State Education Agency (SEA). Before a proposal is begun, a promise should be obtained from these individuals to write official letters documenting the need for the proposed training in their specific state.

Proposal writers should also be familiar with the state special education plan and the Comprehensive System of Personnel Development (CSPD), both of which are mandated by PL 94-142. Both of these are governed by the Special Education Component of the SEA, so it is helpful to be on the mailing list of this component. It is also advantageous to have membership in the state organization of the Council for Exceptional Children (CEC), especially the Teacher Education Division (TED) and the Council of Administrators of Special Education (CASE). These groups help determine state needs and keep their membership informed.

State Special Education Plan

Usually called the *state plan*, this is the official document that interprets how PL 94-142 is to be implemented within the state. Since 1980 the state plan has been written and approved for a 3-year period. Prior to 1980, in accordance with its description in PL 94-142, the *annual program plan* was for one fiscal year.

Proposal writers and other advocates of quality physical education for all children should be involved in the development and monitoring of the state plan because this is the legal document filed with the U.S. Department of Education as the requisite for the SEA's receiving PL 94-142 federal funds. Ascertaining that adapted physical education is defined in the state plan and that policies for employing and salarying specialists are stated maximizes the probability of state and local compliance with the intent of PL 94-142.

SEA personnel or their designates write and/or make revisions in the state plan and thus represent a major power structure. Each change, however, must be submitted to public scrutiny. This is achieved through regional hearings, open to everyone, at which oral and/or written testimony may be presented in favor of or against changes and omissions. Usually the State Board of Education approves the state plan before it is filed with the U.S. Department of Education. For physical education proposal writers the most important part of the state plan is the Comprehensive System of Personnel Development (CSPD).

Comprehensive System of Personnel Development

The CSPD is the section of the state plan that describes programs and procedures for ascertaining that sufficient numbers of personnel are trained appropriately to provide special education and related services to handicapped children and youth in compliance with PL 94-142. This section includes both preservice and in-service training. Additionally, the CSPD outlines procedures for acquiring and disseminating significant information derived from educational research, demonstration, and similar projects, and for adopting, when appropriate, promising educational practices and materials developed through these projects.

The CSPD is usually implemented by a statewide committee of educators, parents, consumers, and others concerned with PL 94-142 enforcement. Administratively the CSPD council or committee functions under the Special Education component of the SEA. This group analyzes needs assessment data compiled by the SEA and determines the number of personnel in each profession who are available versus the number who are needed.

The physical education proposal writer is tremendously affected by this analysis because he or she cannot justify funding a university training program if the SEA indicates too few adapted physical educators are needed in the year for which the proposal is being written. The SEA needs assessment data are submitted to OSEP in Washington, DC, which in turn publishes an annual report for members of Congress.

Annual Report to Congress

Official statements of need for personnel in special education, physical education, and the related services can be found in several sources. Among these is the annual report to Congress on the implementation of the Education of the Handicapped Act (U.S. Department of Education, 1986b). Beginning in 1979, this report of 200 or more pages has been published every year; it serves as official documentation of progress made in implementation of EHA legislation and of needs still unmet. Appendices include such information as the number of handicapped children and youth in each state, the number of personnel (including physical education) employed and needed, and the percent of students in the various education environments. The accuracy of this report depends, in large part, on the integrity of the state educational agencies (SEAs) that supply data. Grant writers need to read this document, not only to help them write the statement of need, but also to increase their awareness of the importance of supplying accurate physical education information to their SEA and monitoring its transmittal to the Office of Special Education Programs.

The annual report to Congress can be obtained at no cost by writing or telephoning the Division of Innovation and Development, Office of Special Education Programs, Department of Education, 400 Maryland Ave., S.W., Switzer Building, Washington, DC 20202, telephone 202-732-1106.

Copies of these reports are also available at many university libraries through the computer-based information network of the Educational Resources Information Center (ERIC). The annual reports to Congress are listed as *Implementation of Public Law 94-142; The Education of the Handicapped Act. Seventh (or whatever number) Annual Report to Congress.* The ERIC numbers for accessing the reports are ED 254 056; ED 245 526; ED 231 179; ED 215 553-554; ED 179 070; and ED 175 196. Cost of a computer-generated copy is about $30.

Research Studies of State Needs

In order to respond adequately to the proposal evaluation criteria pertaining to need for a training project, writers need information concerning the number of handicapped students in the state who are currently receiving physical education services versus the number still unserved. It is essential also to know the setting in which physical education services are delivered (integrated, separate, combination), the quality of the services, and whether or not positive change in psychomotor behaviors result. It is also important to know the qualifications of persons delivering physical education services to handicapped students, their perceptions and attitudes, and their need for additional training. Most SEAs do not collect these data as part of their CSPD, probably because they do not have the resources to do so.

Many proposal writers have therefore encouraged their graduate students to develop theses, dissertations, and

independent studies to collect such data. Illustrative of such studies are the following:

- Baber, D.J. (1984). *Service needs in physical education for handicapped students in the public schools of Georgia*. Unpublished doctoral dissertation, University of Georgia at Athens.

- Harris, J. (1977). *Compliance with PL 94-142 and its implications for physical education in Oregon*. Unpublished doctoral dissertation, Oregon State University, Corvallis.

- Jones, S.A. (1978). *Professional preparation in physical education for the handicapped in Texas: A needs assessment*. Unpublished doctoral dissertation, Texas Woman's University, Denton.

- Oakley, T. (1984). *Evaluation of physical education programs for handicapped students in the state of Arkansas*. Unpublished doctoral dissertation, Texas Woman's University, Denton.

- Stokes, B.R. (1980). *The status of physical education in Louisiana as it relates to requirements of the education for all handicapped children act of 1975*. Unpublished doctoral dissertation, University of Southern Mississippi, Hattiesburg.

Once a comprehensive needs assessment of state physical education has been conducted, it must be updated at least every 3 years to provide valid data for the serious grant writer. These updates are often found in state physical education journals (Rider, 1980; Seaman & Geddes, 1979; Sherrill & Megginson, 1982). Grant writers, whether they collect statewide data themselves or guide graduate students, must be involved in continuous research concerning physical education needs of handicapped children and youth.

Summary

This chapter has presented basic, introductory material in regard to writing training grants for submission to the Division of Personnel Preparation of OSEP. Many other types of grants are available, and once individuals become successful in writing training grants, they can usually generalize their information and skills to other sources of funding. The training grant was chosen as the focus of this chapter because it is the type most often written by university-based teacher trainers. Administrators expect doctoral level adapted physical educators to have skills in grant writing; this chapter can serve as the basis of a unit or course in grantsmanship. Additionally, cardinal principles of grant application writing appear in Appendix K.

References

Martin, E. (1976). Integration of the handicapped child into regular schools. *Minnesota Education, 2*(2), 5-7.

Rider, R. (1980). A survey of adapted physical education in Florida public schools. *Florida Association for Health, Physical Education, and Recreation Journal, 18*(3), 9-11, 14.

Seaman, J., & Geddes, D. (1979). Survey of program placement and professional preparation in adapted physical education. *California Association for Health, Physical Education, and Recreation Journal*, 16-17.

Sherrill, C., & Megginson, N. (1982). Adapted physical education in Texas: Employment options and training needs. *Texas Association for Health, Physical Education, and Recreation Journal, 50*(3), 6-7, 43-44.

U.S. Department of Education. (1986a). *New application for grants under training personnel for the education of the handicapped.* Washington, DC: Author.

U.S. Department of Education. (1986b). *To assure the free appropriate public education of all handicapped children: Eighth annual report to Congress on the implementation of Public Law 94-142.* Washington, DC: Author.

Vodola, T. (1981). *How to write and process a competitive grant proposal.* Neptune City, NJ: VEE, Inc.

Will testifies on OSERS' priorities. (1983, September/October). *Programs for the Handicapped*, pp. 2-3. (Available from the U.S. Department of Education.)

Chapter 7

Adapted Physical Educator Research Responsibilities

Geoffrey D. Broadhead

*I*n this collection of papers that seek to guide the graduate training of would-be university faculty and administrators in various community settings, the word *research* has been used frequently. Who, indeed, would deny that such graduate training should have a consistent and distinctive research orientation?

Research can be exciting, fearsome, complicated, boring, mystical, and even irrelevant. This word, *research*, can be used to denote all the creative and scholarly activities that people do, particularly in specialist establishments like universities. However, attempting to discover facts by scientific study of a subject is largely different from reviewing research literature with the objective of writing a grant proposal, updating notes for next semester's class, or helping a teacher with direct service delivery problems in a neighborhood school, separate special school, or residential institution. Certainly, in the specialization or academic discipline of adapted physical education, the more one undertakes the latter types of research, the more apparent is the need for highlighting scientific study.

Although the volume of published research in adapted physical education has increased markedly over the past 10 years, it is doubtful that significantly more is known now than before. For example, in examining recent literature on day-to-day programming for various special populations, students might find it challenging to discuss significant new information that is now available to aid in improving movement and movement-related competence. Likewise, which (new) strategies for teaching handicapped children address issues other than merely adding equipment or decreasing class size? Indeed, for those who teach courses at the graduate level, keeping up-to-date and using recent and current literature has not seemed to lessen the importance or negate the place of the classic research studies that underpin their teaching.

Current Needs in Graduate Study

An obvious interrelationship of research and teaching exists in adapted physical education. It follows, then, that the training of the graduate adapted physical educator needs to include not merely a scholarly thrust and a research project requirement for each course but also systematic training about and in the techniques of research. Degree requirements should take the form of specific courses taught in orderly sequence that provide an initial foray into the research enterprise and that include methods of research, statistics, and a thesis. Occasional theses of exceptional merit, in all probability, would meet the standards of publication.

Such a format can supply a most satisfactory blend of the basic training that should precede advanced studies.

Even when doctoral programs have a professional or applied orientation to adapted physical education, the rigors of research that underpin training should be present. While discipline-oriented doctoral programs in adapted physical education should be similar to some of the better ones that exist currently in motor behavior and exercise science, both types of program can involve exciting interdisciplinary research with faculty in cognate areas like psychology and physiology. (Is it in fact appropriate to consider program differences in any way other than those of "emphasis"?)

In this two-stage graduate training, understanding the current body of knowledge and being adept in the techniques and tools of research (having practiced them under faculty guidance) can be coordinated. Effective graduate training captures and channels the student's motivation to undertake scientific research, teach in a scholarly manner as a member of a university faculty, and use the rubric of research in administration. This inner motivation to research, almost regardless of all but the most severe of constraints, must be tapped during graduate training and utilized later if adapted physical education is to progress.

Problems With Priorities

Seemingly, the need to establish viable adapted physical education programs in public schools and improve existing services has ordered the professional priorities of university faculty and administrators alike. For administrators, the speedy expansion of services for handicapped children, as demanded by Public Law 94-142 and other legislation, has brought so many practical problems to light that research interests and desires have been overshadowed. How many of the thousands of school districts have actually mounted independently, or undertaken conjointly with universities, research projects that could produce evidence for curriculum change or curriculum stability? In universities many faculty have been drawn (willingly) into developing a very practical approach to their work, as a direct response to local community needs. This approach has often involved arranging workshops, advising teachers and principals, and actually teaching children in schools. The content and emphasis of the many new pre- or in-service courses of training have tended to meet immediate short-term needs of practitioners, but often ignore long-term needs. In short, the question asked most often with this approach has been, How quickly can I help the teacher cope with the diverse characteristics of handicapped children? Seldom will such training have incorporated more than a passing acknowledgment of research. At best, it is likely that only occasional attempts have been made to obtain data (grab while available) and produce a document worthy of dissemination. Thus the body of adapted physical education knowledge has been neither substantially used in such programs nor improved. Little has been added to the adapted physical education literature that is the product of such developments.

The place of adapted physical education in a university curriculum affects its research thrust; it also affects research productivity and dissemination. In the past it was most definitely the case, and is still so in many universities today, that adapted physical education is but one of several instructional responsibilities to be met by faculty. Serving as a generalist on a university faculty tends to deplete energy and dampen the desire to continue research begun during doctoral level specialization. The low status of adapted physical education in some universities, in part existing because of its practical thrust, may be sustained by too much faculty involvement in community service and not enough in scholarly activities. The adapted physical education knowledge base is sufficient for acceptable scholarly courses to be taught; why is it that courses are often subject to criticisms of relevance and rigor? Of course, it could be said that adapted physical education faculty themselves have aided and abetted these problems by being, perhaps, too eager to adopt the role of consultant, too eager to seek grant funds, and (can this be true?) too eager to shy away from research.

Too often faculty have emphasized personnel preparation and community-based projects rather than undertaken scientific research. Compounding this situation has been the reliance of a number of universities on the continued existence of soft, grant-generated money. Using such money to sustain temporary faculty positions beyond the usual buying-in period has placed unreasonable stress upon individual faculty and helped to delay or even prevent positions from becoming permanent. Although some faculty accrue service that does not count toward tenure, persons in tenure-earning appointments often experience difficulty meeting criteria for tenure and promotion when the relevant criteria appear to conflict with those that lead to successful completion of a funded project.

Faculty Research Thrust

Failure to establish a research program early is self-defeating for a new faculty member. In contrast, the completion of research and the communication of results at conferences, and more particularly through the process of peer evaluation in scholarly journals, sustains self-worth. Through research one gains recognition from colleagues, and this, in turn, helps to ensure a continuing involvement in research. The publish or perish ethic, often exaggerated, feared, misunderstood, and criticized,

is more than a determinant to tenure and promotion. It is a powerful motivator in developing and sustaining scholarship. Adapted physical educators can benefit from this pressure if a positive attitude is adopted to what is a feature of university life and is shared with colleagues across disciplines and across the country.

What proportion of doctoral dissertation research is thought by investigators to warrant the presentation of written work for dissemination in the public domain? Publishing dissertation work would appear to be the best and most obvious way of commencing research; it shows an understanding of the responsibility to present to colleagues the findings of research, and it shows an understanding of the responsibility to complete what has been begun.

Surely faculty understand that in conversing with students, teachers, administrators, parents and others, a data-based description of service delivery, for example, is much more satisfactory than relying upon experience and intuition alone. Because the number of researchable topics is almost endless, it should not be too difficult for many faculty to be challenged to plan projects that lead to regularly published papers. On the one hand, this sausage-machine approach, commonly called "playing the game," is of clear importance in aiding new faculty to become practiced researchers and is hard to ignore. It must not, however, supplant plans for research into longer term issues that are usually more critical.

For graduate students, even a cursory examination of the literature in physical education and related areas might prove helpful in identifying their areas of interest. For example, students may find it valuable to use their current research skills to evaluate statements about topics in adapted physical education. Several statements and suggestions for examining the statements follow:

1. Public school physical education programs for handicapped children are very successful. Just allow a small number of vaguely described handicapped students to participate in a vaguely described program for a few weeks, and all types of wondrous changes can occur.

   Suggestion:

   Assemble what you consider to be a small number of the most significant papers outlining what has been completed on this topic. Examine each paper and then decide the extent to which the statement is fair. Think carefully about program and sample descriptions, the time involved, and other issues.

2. Measuring the process and product of motor performance of nonhandicapped and handicapped students is relatively straightforward. The list of appropri-

ately constructed test items and batteries is formidable, whereas the number of assessment concerns (questions) to be addressed is relatively few.

Suggestion:

Discuss what the evaluation of process versus product involves. Compile a list of instruments by question to be answered, remembering appropriateness of test traits and age, sex, and handicap of subjects.

3. Retaining labeled, handicapped children in regular physical education classes appears to be the cause of little anxiety, whereas mainstreaming these students one at a time from specially designed classes into regular instructional settings is easily managed and usually successful.

Suggestion:

Examine and contrast the literature on special versus regular education with that on mainstreaming and least restrictive environments. What does the physical education literature tell us about this issue?

4. The understood importance of home and community influences on child performance at school has led to specific projects in adapted physical education that provide knowledge and skills to parents and guardians while they supplement school programs at home.

Suggestion:

Consider whether and how time spent at home, in the community, or at school affects the *amount* of influence shown. How is influence shown and what is known about direct and indirect influences, especially with regard to handicapped children?

Perhaps, after undertaking this task, it will be clear that our knowledge of adapted physical education is far from complete. Even allowing that the four topics outlined are multidimensional, the list is incomplete. Much more is known about each of the above topics than the literature describes; however, many seem unwilling to write.

Graduate training in adapted physical education has become increasingly rigorous over the years. New university faculty and administrators are prepared better than ever to meet the challenges that responsibilities to research pose. Their mentors are their supporters. The time is ripe, though with a touch of urgency, for a fresh approach into a reactivation of old issues and exploration

into new ones. This means planning, conducting, completing research, *and* communicating the results to others. It is important for all to share what is thought or what has been accomplished in print.

Editor's Note

Several journals now regularly publish research in adapted physical education.

- *Adapted Physical Activity Quarterly* (APAQ) is published by Human Kinetics Publishers, Champaign, Illinois. *APAQ* is a multidisciplinary journal dealing with physical activity for special populations. It includes articles originating from the disciplines of corrective therapy, gerontology, health care, occupational therapy, pediatrics, physical education, physical therapy, recreation, and rehabilitation, and deals with populations of every age. Adaptations of equipment, activity, facilities, methodology, and/or setting are all discussed within the *Quarterly*.

  APAQ includes an editorial section containing commentary on current opinion, legislative and regulatory concerns, and other professional trends; a research section reporting original and replicated research using appropriate scientific methodology, as well as analytical reviews of the literature; and an applications section containing applied investigations in settings often requiring unique methodologies, reports of case studies, programmatic developments involving strategies and techniques, and the design of equipment and facilities.

  For further information write to Geoffrey D. Broadhead, School of Physical Education, Recreation, and Dance, Memorial Gym Annex, Kent State University, Kent, OH 44242-0001.

- *Palaestra* is published by Challenge Publications, Ltd., Macomb, Illinois. The purpose of *Palaestra* is to secure and present articles discussing all aspects of human anatomy, kinesiology, physiology, psychology, and sociology that can be applied to the development of practical physical education training and competitive techniques for the recreational as well as the competitive disabled individual. Feature articles are published that focus on the activities of each disability group, including special events and national championships. Space is also devoted to presenting photo essays and human interest features. For further information, write to David Beaver, Editor-in-Chief, Challenge Publications, Ltd., P.O. Box 508, Macomb, IL 61555.

- *American Corrective Therapy Journal* is published bimonthly by the American Corrective Therapy Association and prints manuscripts of a professional and

Left. Geoffrey Broadhead, Editor of *Adapted Physical Activity Quarterly*. Middle. David Beaver, Editor and Publisher of *Palaestra*. Right. Bruce McClenaghan, Section Editor for Special Populations in *The Physical Educator*.

scientific nature in the several disciplines related to corrective therapy. Research studies, theoretical articles, and systematic reviews of special areas relating to corrective or adapted physical education, psychology, physiology, and special education are encouraged. For more information write to B. Robert Carlson, Editor, *American Corrective Therapy Journal*, Department of Physical Education, San Diego State University, San Diego, CA 92182-1900.

• *The Physical Educator* devoted one of its four issues each year from 1980 to 1985 to special populations. Topic areas included the physically, mentally, emotionally, and socially impaired, the elderly, and the gifted. Application of theory to practice in physical education and sport was stressed. The Section Editor for special populations was Bruce McClenaghan, Department of Physical Education, University of South Carolina, Columbia, SC 29208.

• *Therapeutic Recreation Journal* is published quarterly by the National Therapeutic Recreation Society of the National Recreation and Park Association. It publishes scholarly manuscripts pertaining to special populations in relation to (a) leisure needs, preferences, patterns, and attitudes; (b) effects and values of recreation; (c) integration into community recreation; (d) skill acquisition; (e) teaching methods and strategies; and (f) recreation programming. Adapted physical educators may utilize this journal as a vehicle for publishing research inasmuch as many of the goals of physical education and recreation for special populations are similar. For more information write to the editor of

Therapeutic Recreation Journal, Peter Witt, Associate Vice President for Research, North Texas State University, Denton, TX 76203.

Several regular physical education journals occasionally publish research in adapted physical education. Among these are the following:

• *Research Quarterly for Exercise and Sport*

• *Journal of Motor Behavior*

• *Journal of Human Movement Studies*

• *Journal of Sports Medicine*

• *Perceptual and Motor Skills*

• *Dance Research Journal*

• *Journal of Teaching in Physical Education*

Journals of special education, physical therapy, occupational therapy, recreation, and related disciplines all offer opportunities for publication. Adapted physical educators must accept responsibility for disseminating research findings to colleagues in other fields as well as their own. Information and instructions concerning manuscript preparation and submission to journals is printed in each journal volume. Most journals that publish adapted physical education research adhere rigidly to the directions for manuscript preparation stated in the *Publication Manual of the American Psychological Association* (APA), 3rd edition. Graduate students should be introduced to APA style early in their studies.

References

The following references should be of interest in relation to research responsibilities:

Broadhead, G. (1981). Time passages in adapted physical education. In G. Brooks (Ed.), *Perspectives on the academic discipline of physical education* (pp. 234-252). Champaign, IL: Human Kinetics.

Broadhead, G. (1986). Adapted physical education research trends: 1970-1990. *Adapted Physical Activity Quarterly, 3*(2), 104-111.

DePauw, K. (1986). Research on sport for athletes with disabilities. *Adapted Physical Activity Quarterly, 3*(4), 292-299.

Massengale, J. (1983). AAHPERD's role in perceived quality of physical education graduate faculty. *Journal of Physical Education, Recreation, and Dance, 54*(2) 57.

Massengale, J., & Sage, G. (1982). Departmental prestige and career mobility patterns of college physical educators. *Research Quarterly for Exercise and Sport, 53*(4), 305-312.

Rarick, G.L. (1981). Research in physical education—Concerns and issues. In J. Taylor, D. Compton, & T. Johnson (Eds.), *Proceedings of the National Consortium on Physical Education and Recreation for the Handicapped* (pp. 11-12). Champaign, IL: University of Illinois.

Safrit, M. (1979). Women in research in physical education. *Quest, 31*(2), 158-171.

Sherrill, C. (1981). Publications and dissemination in physical education for the handicapped. In J. Taylor, D. Compton, & T. Johnson (Eds.), *Proceedings of the National Consortium on Physical Education and Recreation for the Handicapped* (pp. 21-24). Champaign, IL: University of Illinois.

Stein, J. (1983). Bridge over troubled waters—Research review and recommendation for relevance. In R. Eason, T. Smith, & F. Caron (Eds.), *Adapted physical activity* (pp. 188-198). Champaign, IL: Human Kinetics.

Chapter 8

Evaluation and Curriculum Processes in Adapted Physical Education: Understanding and Creating Theory

Claudine Sherrill and Thomas Oakley

Research is a high hat word that scares a lot of people. It needn't. . . . It is nothing but a state of mind—a friendly, welcoming attitude toward change. . . . It is the problem-solving mind as contrasted with the let-well-enough-alone mind. It is the composer mind instead of the fiddler mind. It is the "tomorrow" mind instead of the "yesterday" mind. (Charles Franklin Kettering)

Adapted physical education specialists increasingly must understand and seek to extend the body of knowledge upon which their service delivery is based. This understanding entails continuous problem solving and initiative in research undertakings. Preliminary to field testing ideas and practices; the educator should become familiar with the structures that comprise knowledge. These structures are presented in both research and practitioner language in Figure 8.1.

Contributing to Knowledge

Contribution to the body of knowledge underlying one's specialization generally starts at the bottom of the knowledge hierarchy and moves upward. The process is first experienced by many persons while writing a thesis. The purpose, problem, hypotheses, and assumptions are in chapter 1 of the thesis, followed by a review of literature in chapter 2 and a description of research procedures in chapter 3. Data are collected and statistically treated, after which they are presented as findings (usually in tables) in chapter 4. Findings are then analyzed, and a conclusion is stated in chapter 5. Hopefully, the conclusion is original, valid, and fills some gap in existing theory. Subsequently it is incorporated into textbooks as a concept, construct, or action/strategy/technique. In time the research becomes part of the theory or practice of a profession.

Practitioners follow a similar process, although often at a subconscious or intuitive level. They may use trial and error to solve an evaluation, curricular, or instructional problem. If experienced, they are likely to engage in successive approximations (i.e., instead of randomized trial and error, each attempt more closely approximates the solution). They observe what is happening, derive facts, and arrive at a new approach, instructional strategy, action, or technique. Practitioners often change the theory and/or practice of a profession by modeling "their better way" or simply sharing the outcomes with another teacher.

Some persons seem to move more easily from theory to practice, whereas others come to understand theory through first practicing in the field. The latter know what works but have difficulty identifying and explaining the theory or principle. Ultimately, however, all graduate

Figure 8.1 The structures comprising knowledge adapted by Sherrill from content presented in Van Dalen (1979).

Thomas Oakley (left, back) and Claudine Sherrill (left, front) with Texas Woman's University alumnae. Also shown (left to right) are James Mastro, Braille Sports Foundation; Frank Mathenia, beep baseball expert; Tom Montelione, Queens College; and Nancy Megginson, Rouge River, Oregon.

students must understand theory and be able to generate and field test models.

Theories and Models

Theory can be defined as a set of related concepts that define, classify, describe, relate, and/or explain the content, principles, and practices that comprise knowledge. *Practices* are sometimes called applied theory.

Van Dalen (1979) states that some scholars contend that theories and models are the same thing; thus he lists models as one of four kinds of theories to which researchers can contribute. He indicates that both theories and models are conceptual schemes that synthesize and explain relationships. For persons who believe theories and models should not be viewed as synonymous, Van Dalen explains that models can be thought of as analogies and can tolerate some facts and concepts not in accord with reality. In contrast, theories describe only relationships that exist, are real, and can be documented. Theories are judged by truthfulness. Models are judged by usefulness; they are tools used as a basis for theory testing and/or construction.

Lockhart (1972) uses the terms *model* and *construct* interchangeably. She states,

> A model is unifying structure; thus, a model may also be a construct, an idea which unifies and makes sense out of related facts and near-facts. . . . A construct that hangs together is simpler than individual parts and, therefore, is more satisfying. The construct (model) also is more useful than its parts because it raises the level of understanding by explaining facts and providing the basis for the discovery of further facts and relationships. (p. 91)

All physical educators need to focus more attention on theory than traditionally has been the practice. Persons in relatively new areas of specialization like sport sociology, adapted physical education, and sport psychology particularly need to develop and test models that will increase understanding of their fields.

Teacher Training Model for Adapted Physical Education

Adapted physical education has been defined as the branch of physical education that focuses on individual differences, particularly on persons who perform below the 50th percentile in the psychomotor domain (Sherrill, 1986). In chapter 1 adapted physical education theory is discussed, and believing, knowing, and doing components are identified. The model illustrated in Figure 8.2 attempts to draw together these concepts in the input/process/output format used in evaluation and curriculum theory as well as in grant proposal writing (Yavorsky, 1976). The model shows that *evaluation* and/or *assessment* is the area of theory most important to the adapted physical education specialist.

Foundations of Evaluation and Curriculum Theory

Evaluation is critical to improving adapted physical education service delivery and teacher training. Since the 1950s, evaluation has evolved into a substantial body of knowledge comprised of countless concepts, theories, and models with which all educators should be acquainted. Whereas the emphasis in early physical education tests and measurements books was on evaluation of individual performance, the concept of evaluation has now become increasingly multifaceted.

One contemporary concept of evaluation comes from the *Taxonomy of Educational Objectives* (Bloom, 1956), which was developed by members of the American Psychology Association as an approach to defining and describing domains of objectives. The work of this group resulted in the widespread recognition of three domains: *cognitive* (intellectual skills), *affective* (feelings, opinions, attitudes, beliefs), and *psychomotor* (movement and fitness behaviors). Schema for these domains are explained in detail in three well-known taxonomies of educational objectives (Bloom, 1956; Harrow, 1972; Krathwohl, Bloom, & Masia, 1964).

Within the cognitive domain, *evaluation* is described as the highest order of intellectual skills (i.e., the hardest to develop and to measure). To appreciate this status, it is helpful to review the hierarchial abilities by which knowledge can be assimilated, used, and generated. These are as follows:

- *Comprehension*—The lowest level of understanding. Encompasses paraphrasing, summarizing, interpreting, and drawing implications or conclusions.

- *Application*—The use of principles, ideas, theories, and various abstract concepts. Translating theory into practice.

- *Analysis*—The breakdown of knowledge into subcomponents so as to better explain interrelationships and/or distinguish different elements from one another

INPUT   PROCESS   OUTPUT

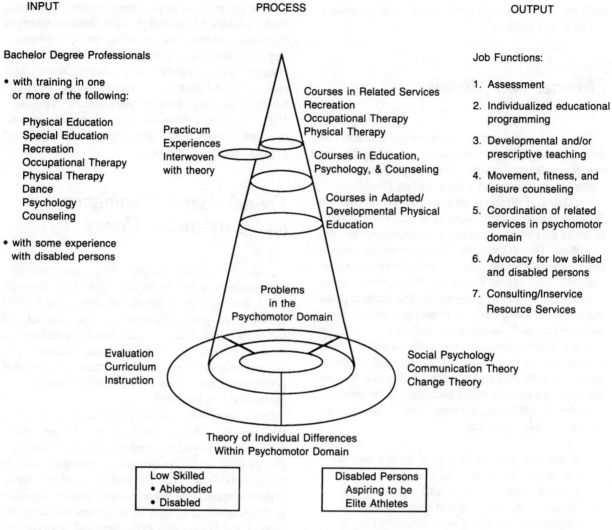

Bachelor Degree Professionals

• with training in one
  or more of the following:

    Physical Education
    Special Education
    Recreation
    Occupational Therapy
    Physical Therapy
    Dance
    Psychology
    Counseling

• with some experience
  with disabled persons

Practicum
Experiences
Interwoven
with theory

Courses in Related Services
Recreation
Occupational Therapy
Physical Therapy

Courses in Education,
Psychology, & Counseling

Courses in Adapted/
Developmental Physical
Education

Problems
in the
Psychomotor Domain

Evaluation
Curriculum
Instruction

Social Psychology
Communication Theory
Change Theory

Theory of Individual Differences
Within Psychomotor Domain

Low Skilled
• Ablebodied
• Disabled

Disabled Persons
Aspiring to be
Elite Athletes

Job Functions:

1. Assessment

2. Individualized educational
   programming

3. Developmental and/or
   prescriptive teaching

4. Movement, fitness, and
   leisure counseling

5. Coordination of related
   services in psychomotor
   domain

6. Advocacy for low skilled
   and disabled persons

7. Consulting/Inservice
   Resource Services

Figure 8.2 Cross-disciplinary teacher training model for adapted/developmental physical education specialists.

(i.e., assumptions, hypotheses, facts, concepts, theories, and principles).

• *Synthesis*—The putting together of elements and parts so as to form a whole; the construction of a model.

• *Evaluation*—Making judgments about the value of programs, materials, methods, ideas, or performance on the basis of preestablished criteria or standards. The evaluator may determine his or her own criteria or use those of others.

Evaluation then can be conceptualized as one of the several cognitive abilities of human beings. As such, it is an intellectual process that both university teachers and students should seek to develop. Improvement in the physical education profession and the theory and practice

of adapted physical education as an emerging discipline begins with evaluations (i.e., judging where we are in relation to the standards we hope to reach). Far too little time and energy in professional preparation is spent on evaluation.

The terms evaluation and assessment are often used interchangeably. A definite trend, however, appears toward using evaluation in relation to curriculum (i.e., program development and evaluation) and assessment in relation to instruction (i.e., individual and/or group needs). Both processes entail data collection (quantitative and/or qualitative) followed by making judgments about the findings in terms of preestablished goals and standards. Evaluation then can be conceptualized as an integral part of the curriculum or program development/implementation process.

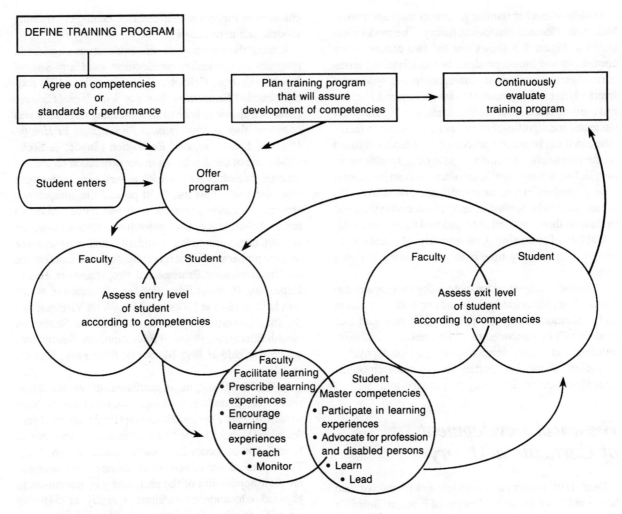

Figure 8.3 Interdependent curriculum/evaluation preservice teacher training model.

Teacher trainers need to understand the interdependence of evaluation, curriculum, instruction, and assessment. Jewett (1980) shows this interdependence in her listing of the variables that comprise curriculum and instruction in Table 8.1. Jewett differentiates between curriculum and instruction as follows:

> Curriculum is an educative agency's plan for facilitating learning. Instruction is the delivery system or the educative transactions which constitute the teaching-learning process for implementing a plan. . . . Curriculum theory provides a systematic basis for decision making in selecting, structuring, and sequencing content. . . . Instructional theory details the range of potential teacher behaviors and teacher-learner interactions; it facilitates methodological decisions. (Jewett, 1980, p. 166)

Table 8.1 Curriculum and Instruction Variables

Curriculum	Instruction
Values	Strategies (including pupil grouping and specific content progressions)
Goals/Objectives	
Content (including clustering and major decisions of sequence)	Materials and Learning Resources
Evaluation	Teaching Behaviors
	Teacher-Learner Interactions
	Class Management
	Assessment

Note. From "The Status of Physical Education Curriculum Theory" by A. Jewett, 1980, *Quest,* **32**(2), p. 166. Copyright 1980 by the National Association for Physical Education in Higher Education. Reprinted by permission.

Models of teacher training programs must encompass both evaluation and curriculum theory. The model illustrated in Figure 8.3 shows that the two processes are continuous and interdependent. In this model the terms curriculum and program are conceptualized as synonyms. Interlocking circles pertaining to assessment and teaching and learning processes are used to depict faculty, university students, and significant others as companions in facilitating in these important processes. The model is based on the philosophy that students, as well as faculty members and sometimes significant others, should be cooperatively involved in both assessment and evaluation. This means that students must be taught both curriculum and evaluation theory as well as helped to develop the cognitive ability of evaluating. Unfortunately, physical educators have spent little time in theory building in either area.

To provide background for appreciating the chapters that follow, brief historical backgrounds on both curriculum and evaluation theory are presented. It is hoped that readers will be motivated to initiate research in theory building and model development in adapted physical education. History is important because research begins with identification and study of primary sources.

Historical Development of Curriculum Theory

Jewett (1980) states that curriculum as a specialized field began in 1918 with the publication of Franklin Bobbitt's (1918) book, *The Curriculum*, and with the Commission on the Reorganization of Secondary Education's (1918) dissemination of *Ten Cardinal Principles of Education*. Also identified by Jewett as a classic is *Basic Principles of Curriculum and Instruction* by Ralph Tyler (1950). Tyler is the person to whom Benjamin Bloom and colleagues dedicated their first *Taxonomy of Educational Objectives* (1956). The dedication reads "To Ralph W. Tyler, whose ideas on evaluation have been a constant source of stimulation to his colleagues in examining, and whose energy and patience have never failed us." Tyler appears to be the first educator to give evaluation and curriculum theory development equal status.

The faculty of Teachers College, Columbia University, New York City, was also a major influence in development of curriculum theory, beginning with the seminal works of John Dewey: *School and Society* (1899) and *Democracy and Education* (1916). In each Dewey contended that curriculum should be organized to reflect the life of the larger community outside and to develop citizenship skills for equipping students to facilitate needed social changes. Sherrill continues to promote this philosophy in

chapters in this book that describe ecological training models and approaches.

Among the foremost physical education pioneers in program and curriculum development was Harry Scott of Teachers College, Columbia University, whose 1951 textbook entitled *Competitive Sports in Schools and Colleges* remains a classic in spite of its misleading title. Scott was coauthor also of *Professional Preparation in Health, Physical Education, and Recreation* (Snyder & Scott, 1954), one of the few books in our profession on teacher training. In each of these books, as well as in his teaching from the 1940s onward, Scott posited the competency approach to teacher preparation. He was active also in two national conferences that set forth recommendations for competences, principles, standards, and programs for teacher preparation; that is, (a) the National Conference on Undergraduate Professional Preparation in Health Education, Physical Education, and Recreation, which was held in 1948 at Jackson's Mill, West Virginia; and (b) the National Conference on Graduate Studies in Health Education, Physical Education, and Recreation, which was held at Pere Marquette State Park, Illinois, in 1950.

On the West Coast, major curriculum development pioneers were Camille Brown and Rosalind Cassidy, who wrote *Theory in Physical Education* (1963). Jewett (1980) describes this book as the "first systematic, comprehensive formulation of theory in physical education" (p. 165). These persons are remembered, among other reasons, for their application of the philosophy of humanism to physical education curriculum. Cassidy (1954) also wrote *Curriculum Development in Physical Education*.

Other primary sources of curriculum theory in physical education cited by Jewett (1980) include the following:

- Eleanor Metheney (1965), *Connotations of Movement in Sports and Dance*

- Muska Mosston (1966), *Teaching Physical Education: From Command to Discovery*

- Celeste Ulrich and John Nixon (1972), *Tones of Theory*

- Daryl Siedentop (1976), *Developing Teaching Skills in Physical Education*

- Ann Jewett and M. Mullan, M.R. (1977), *Curriculum Design: Purposes and Processes in Physical Education Teaching-Learning*

In adapted physical education, Janet Wessel is the acknowledged authority in curriculum development. Her basic curriculum model, on which the *I CAN* system is based, appears in Figure 8.4. Sherrill (1986) used many of Wessel's concepts in the third edition of her textbook.

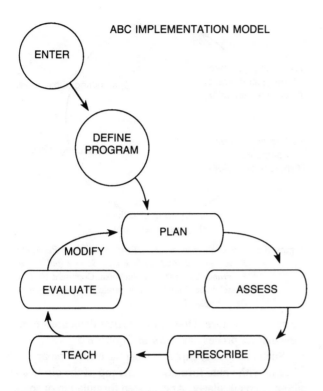

ABC IMPLEMENTATION MODEL

Figure 8.4 Achievement based curriculum (ABC) model on which I CAN is based (Wessel, 1983).

Other major shapers of curriculum theories and models in public school physical education appear in chapter 13 in this text by Walt Ersing. The contributors of other chapters in this book are considered leaders or prospective leaders in teacher training curriculum theory in adapted physical education. Chief among these persons is Julian Stein, who wrote and edited several works on adapted physical education curriculum while serving as Director of Programs for the Handicapped at the American Alliance for Health, Physical Education, Recreation, and Dance.

Development of Evaluation Theory, Trends, and Principles

Development of evaluation theory, as opposed to tests and measurements concepts, appears to have begun in the 1940s. In 1944 Maurice Troyer and Robert Pace, cooperating with the American Council on Education, published *Evaluation in Teacher Education*. This appears to be the first book of its nature.

Later, in 1954, Harry Scott and his doctoral candidate Raymond Snyder included a chapter entitled "Evaluation in the Preparation of Professional Personnel" in their classic *Professional Preparation in Health, Physical Educa-*

tion, and Recreation (Snyder & Scott, 1954). The content of this chapter is as timely today as at midcentury. Five evaluation trends were described by Snyder and Scott.

- The trend away from one-sided application of evaluation toward a *cooperative* process.

- The trend away from the pre/post measurement concept toward a *continuous* process.

- The trend away from external evaluation toward *self-study* and *self-direction.*

- The trend away from judging program effectiveness and student learning by credit hours and course content toward *assessment of competencies* in the area of specialization.

- The trend away from evaluating only the student's performance in classes toward a *comprehensive system* of evaluation in "many situations inside and outside the college. Evidence from home, laboratory and field experiences, the community, and out-of-class experiences while at college will enhance the significance and usefulness of evaluation" (p. 335).

These trends are now considered *principles* of evaluation, but educators are still searching for methods to enhance their application to practice.

Taxonomies of Educational Objectives

The first significant milestone in evaluation theory development in general education occurred when the American Psychological Association began the project directed by Bloom (1956) on classifying educational goals into taxonomies for the cognitive, affective, and psychomotor domains. The outcomes of this project are described at the beginning of this chapter.

Training in Development of Objectives

Chronologically, the next thrust of long-lasting significance was widespread emphasis on training teachers to write educational objectives to guide the instructional process. The classic book devoted exclusively to this purpose was *Preparing Instructional Objectives* by Robert Mager (1962). Written as a programmed text, the work was designed for self-study that would culminate in the ability to state *terminal objectives* for students that described the *educational intents* of the teacher.

Each terminal objective was to have three parts: (a) the conditions under which the desired behavior is to occur; (b) a verb specifying a measurable, observable act; and (c) a criterion of acceptable performance. The ability to write objectives in this manner continues to receive major emphasis in teacher education today. In fact, both evaluation and methods and materials courses begin with learning experiences in writing of objectives; Mager's book is still in demand as a text. Other similar texts with which teacher trainers should be familiar include those by Gronlund (1970), Popham and Baker (1970), and Burns (1972).

Formative and Summative Evaluation

In 1965, when Benjamin Bloom was president of the American Educational Research Association (AERA), he commissioned what appears to be the first national committee on curriculum evaluation. Its mission was "to develop guidelines for quality control model evaluation procedures to accompany the development and revision of educational curricula" (Tyler, Gagne, & Scriven, 1967, p. 11). The resulting AERA publication with chapters by these three educators as well as Robert Stake appears to be the primary source for the evolution for educational evaluation technology. In the chapter by Michael Scriven, the terms formative and summative evaluation made their first appearance and today are recognized by theorists as the two types of evaluation. Both types are operative in a training program or curricular model.

Formative evaluation is continuous, feeding back information day by day or unit by unit so changes can be made as soon as needs are identified. Formative evaluation is usually directed toward a model, a program, or a strategy. Data collection is usually structured by preestablished questions designed for each component of the model or program. Illustrative questions are (a) Have needs assessment data been collected for all groups to be affected by the new or revised program? (b) Have needs been prioritized? (c) Have the intended procedures been implemented for each component of the model? (d) Are students or trainees showing signs of responding and changing in the direction of program objectives?

The concept of formative evaluation reinforces the definition of evaluation stated by Snyder and Scott (1954), which remains applicable today.

> *Evaluation* is defined as a continuous process of judging effectiveness of learning experiences [models, programs] on the basis of an acceptable scale of values. Evaluation is not an end in itself; rather it is a means to the attainment of educational goals. It cuts across all areas of the educational program and consists of not one, but many facets. (p. 328)

The concept of formative evaluation also explains why illustrations of the evaluation process are almost always

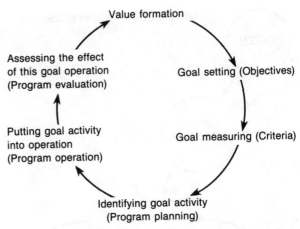

Figure 8.5   The evaluation process. From *Evaluation Research: Principles and Practice in Public Service and Action Programs*, by Edward A. Suchman. Copyright 1967 by Russel Sage Foundation. Reprinted by permission of Basic Books, Inc., Publishers.

circular in nature. One of the earliest depictions of the evaluation process appears in Figure 8.5.

Suchman (1967) explained that the evaluation process began with value formation at the top of the circle and continued circularly. At each step formulation of something (values, objectives, criteria, plans and procedures, operation, and evaluation) occurred along with implementation. Furthermore, each stage in the process was continuously assessed through formative evaluation.

Summative evaluation is assessment of the sum of results after implementation of a new program or strategy. This is traditionally achieved through comparison of entry level with exit level competencies of students in a training program. In the discrepancy evaluation model (DEM), which is popular today, summative evaluation is used to determine if conditions are closer to ideal standards at the end of a program than at its beginning.

Evaluation Models

Beginning in 1967 and throughout the 1970s, innovators of educational evaluation theories posited models for program evaluation to synthesize their ideas and guide further research. This section briefly describes four of these models and acquaints readers with primary sources.

Stake's Countenance Model

Robert Stake, Director of the Center for Instructional Research and Curriculum Evaluation at the University of Illinois, was the first educator to develop a model (see Figure 8.6). Published in the *Teachers College Record* in 1967, it was named the Countenance Model and was based on examining the "full countenance" of evalua-

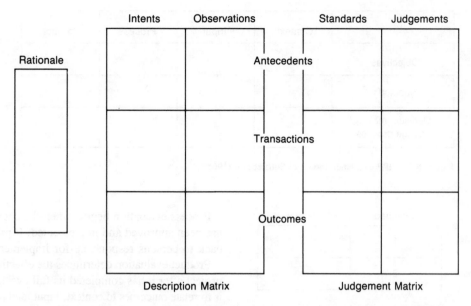

Figure 8.6 The Countenance Model. From "The Countenance of Educational Evaluation" by R. Stake, 1967, *Teachers College Record,* **68,** p. 529.

tion (both description and judgment) rather than one or the other.

Stake's model begins with writing a precise evaluation rationale in which one clarifies the philosophy underlying the planned evaluation. From this point, the evaluator implements a descriptive matrix and a judgment matrix. Regardless of purpose, descriptive or judgmental, three types of data are collected: (a) antecedents or preconditions, (b) transactions that include all the encounters that comprise the educational process, and (c) outcomes.

Within the descriptive matrix, data are classified as intents and observations. Intents are conceptualized as a priority listing of goals and objectives. Observations are what the evaluator sees, either by observation or through the use of various instruments.

The judgment matrix is comprised of standards and judgments. Standards can be relative or absolute. Relative standards infer the comparison of one program to another. Absolute standards are those established by law or policy. Judgments are made by comparing standards with what was observed to determine if congruence exists between what was intended as opposed to what the standard prescribed. Recommendations are then made from the judgments.

Two physical educators (Oakley, 1984; Stokes, 1980) have applied Stake's model in their dissertations. Both men did so to provide an objective framework for evaluating statewide physical education for the handicapped practices in relation to the standards set by PL 94-142.

Stake's model has been promoted also for use in evaluation of arts programs (Stake, 1975). The philosophy

and methodology underlying the model are now called *responsive evaluation.* Stake describes responsive evaluation as follows:

> It is an approach that trades off some measurement precision in order to increase the usefulness of the findings to persons in and around the program. . . . Responsive evaluation is less reliant on formal communication than on natural communication. . . . Responsive evaluation is an alternative, an old alternative, based on what people do naturally to evaluate things, they observe and react. . . . An educational evaluation is *responsive evaluation* if it orients more directly to program activities than program intents; responds to audience requirements for information; and if the different value-perspectives present are referred to in reporting the success and failure of the program. (p. 14)

Stufflebeam's CIPP Model

The Context, Input, Process, and Product (CIPP) Model was proposed by Dan Stufflebeam in 1968 and later refined (Stufflebeam et al., 1971). Two schematic presentations of Stufflebeam's model appear in Figures 8.7 and 8.8. He and his associates are accredited with popularizing the terms *input, process,* and *product* in relation to evaluation.

Context evaluation is the most basic type because it ultimately leads to the establishment of program goals and

	Context	Input	Process	Product
Objectives				
Methods				
Decision making/ change process				

Figure 8.7 CIPP evaluation model of Stufflebeam (1968).

	Intended	Actual
Ends (Goals)	1	3
Means (Process)	2	4

Quadrant 1. Context evaluation or needs assessment. The purpose is selection of one or more goals on which to concentrate further efforts.

Quadrant 2. Inputs evaluation (also called program planning evaluation or formative evaluation). The purpose is to identify different procedures for achieving goals agreed upon in Quadrant 1.

Quadrant 3. Process evaluation or implementation evaluation. The purpose is primarily to monitor to determine the extent that the program agreed upon has been implemented (i.e., conforms with the intended plan).

Quadrant 4. Product evaluation (also called outcome evaluation or summative evaluation). The purpose is to determine the discrepancy between what was accomplished and what was hoped for as specified in the goal statement.

Figure 8.8 Two-by-two grid by Stufflebeam et al. (1971).

objectives. Its major purpose is to define the relevant environment (context) in which change is to occur, to identify unmet needs and unused opportunities, and to diagnose problems underlying these needs and opportunities.

Context evaluation uses two methodologies: contingency and congruence. In the contingency mode, opportunities outside the system are examined to promote improvement within the system. In the congruence mode, actual and intended outputs are compared and analyzed to determine possible causes of discrepancies between actual and intended conditions. The decision-making body then recommends appropriate changes.

Input evaluation provides information for determining how to utilize resources to meet program goals and objectives. Alternative procedural designs and resources are analyzed in terms of potential costs and benefits.

Process evaluation begins when the course of action has been approved and implemented. It provides feedback to persons responsible for implementation.

Product evaluation determines the effectiveness of the project after it has completed its full cycle. Its purpose is to relate outcomes to context, input, and process information, thereby deciding whether to continue, terminate, modify, or refocus an activity.

In conclusion, the CIPP Model combines four evaluation concepts into a single generalized model. Stufflebeam et al. (1971) summarize their work by stating "Different types of evaluation are characterized by the kinds of decisions which they are intended to service—hence the acronym CIPP relating context, input, process, and product evaluation to planning, structuring, implementing, and recycling decisions, respectively" (p. 325).

Provus' DEM Model

The Discrepancy Evaluation Model (DEM) was first described by Malcolm Provus, University of Virginia, in 1969, although the book bearing this title did not appear until 1971. Provus was one of the coauthors on Stufflebeam et al.'s (1971) refined CIPP model, and in many ways DEM is an expansion of the CIPP Model. Like Stufflebeam, Provus focused evaluation on four stages of program development. Provus, however, stressed the importance of a team approach to evaluation with distinctions made between functions of an evaluation staff and a program staff. Additionally, Provus developed the planning stage of his model to a greater extent than the other innovators of his time. Likewise, he emphasized the explicit writing of standards for use in judgment making more than his contemporaries did.

DEM has had more impact on adapted physical education teacher training than any other evaluation model, primarily because the Bureau of Education for Handicapped (BEH) grant proposal writers throughout the 1970s were encouraged (indeed, almost coerced) to complete in-service training based on this model. The training was conducted by the Evaluation Center Project of the University of Virginia, which was funded by BEH to provide regional training workshops as well as evaluation materials of various kinds. The textbook used in this training was written after Provus' death by one of his disciples, Diane Yavorsky (1976). A study of primary sources by Provus (1969, 1971) reveals that Yavorsky and staff presented trainees with a simplified and somewhat modified version of DEM.

The two new constructs that Provus added to evaluation theory were (a) discrepancy and (b) continuous feedback and revision of objectives and program. The model, including these constructs, was first developed in Pittsburgh as an attempt to apply evaluation and management theory to the administration of a large public school system.

According to Provus, the purpose of program evaluation is to determine whether to improve, maintain, or terminate a program. Evaluation entails (a) agreeing upon program standards, (b) determining whether a discrepancy exists between some aspect of the actual program and its standard, and (c) using discrepancy information to identify and correct weaknesses of a program.

Evaluation is implemented in four stages.

1. *Planning*—Standards are agreed upon by all parties concerned and the actual program is defined and described in relation to the standards. Figure 8.9 (p. 134) shows Provus' use of CIPP terms *input*, *process*, and *output* as a guide in the development of a taxonomy of standards encompassing program content.

2. *Installation*—This term is used because Provus believes "the first and most common type of program in public school work is the *instant installation* variety," generally made possible by external funds that arrive too late for the careful planning of their use (Provus, 1973, p. 173). In this stage observations are made in the field regarding the installation of the program's components, and judgments are made as to whether these components are the same as planned in Stage 1.

3. *Process*—Process standards (the relationship between program processes and enabling objectives) are applied. Discrepancy information is used to redefine process and improve management and quality control procedures.

4. *Product*—Product standards (the relationship between terminal objectives and other parts of the program) are applied. Program performance information concerning staff, students, media, facilities, and other inputs and processes are measured against standards established in Stage 1.

The overall model most frequently used to depict DEM appears in Figure 8.10 (p. 134).

A major characteristic of DEM is the systematic, sequential use of questions at each procedural step comprising every evaluation stage. The same problem-solving sequence is applied each time a discrepancy is identified. In outline format this sequence is

A. Q—Why is there a discrepancy?
   C—Criterion
   I —New information
   D—Decision

B. Q—What corrective actions are possible?
   C—Criterion
   I —New information
   D—Decision

C. Q—Which corrective action is best?
   C—Criterion
   I —New information
   D—Decision

According to Provus, some 285 questions can be generated for Stage 1. These arise from 21 points of possible discrepancy between program standards and actualities and two interactive factors, time and cost. (See Figure 8.9 for the list of 21 points.) Some of the other stages lend themselves to even more questions. Provus posits that 3,420 questions may be asked and answered during the application of DEM to an educational program.

Patton's Utilization-Focused Model

In the 1980s much attention is being given to user-focused evaluation. The principle behind this approach is that the way in which information is to be used should be the driving force behind how an evaluation is designed and conducted. Several persons (Alkin, 1975; House, 1974) have contributed to the evolution of this model, but the book that most fully describes utilization-focused evaluation is by Michael Patton (1978) of the University of Minnesota Center of Evaluation.

Five principles guide the utilization-focused approach.

- Evaluation begins with the identification and organization of relevant decision makers and information users.

- Relevant evaluation questions are identified and focused.

- Evaluation methods are selected that generate useful information for identified and organized decision makers and information users.

- Decision makers and information users participate with evaluators in data analysis and data interpretation.

- Evaluators and decision makers negotiate and cooperate in dissemination efforts.

Content Specifications	Time	Costs
INPUT Staff qualifications by position Staff preprogram training Staff selection criteria Student-entry behavior Media Facilities Administrative conditions	Acquisition Time	Fixed Costs
PROCESS Student transactions with: 　Students 　Staff 　Media 　Equipment Staff transactions with: 　Staff 　Students 　Media 　Facilities 　Equipment 　Others Student-staff transactions 　relative to objectives	Operating Time	Operating Costs
OUTPUT Enabling objectives (EO) Terminal objectives (TO) Ultimate objectives (UO) Interrelationships between 　EOs, TOs, UOs	Cumulative and Storage Time	Cumulative and Storage Costs

Figure 8.9 DEM taxonomy of program content used in Stage 1 of evaluation. This taxonomy (representing standards) is compared with actual program plan/performance. Adapted from ''Evaluation of Ongoing Programs in the Public School System'' by M. Provus, 1973, in *Educational Evaluation: Theory and Practice* (p. 175) by B. Worthen and J. Sanders (Eds.), Worthington, OH: Charles A. Jones.

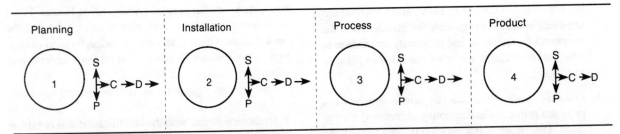

Figure 8.10 DEM flow chart showing comparisons of program performance with standards over four evaluation stages. Initials used are S, Standard; P, Performance; C, Compare; and D, Discrepancy Information. Adapted from ''Evaluation of Ongoing Programs in the Public School System'' by M. Provus, 1973, in *Educational Evaluation: Theory and Practice* (p. 174) by B. Worthen and J. Sanders (Eds.), Worthington, OH: Charles A. Jones.

No schema or diagrams are used in explaining utilization-focused evaluation. Although often referred to as a model, it appears to be more a philosophy than a paradigm. Patton (1978) concludes his book as follows:

> Utilization-focused evaluation is an approach that combines style and substance, activism and

science, personal perspective and systematic information. I have used a variety of approaches in trying to describe utilization-focused evaluation: scenarios, case examples, quotations from our federal utilization study, sufi parables, and children's studies. In the end, this approach to evaluation must also be judged by its usefulness. . . . The challenge of producing good evaluation studies that are actually used is enormous. In many ways the odds are all against utilization, and it is quite possible to become skeptical about the futility of trying to have impact on a world where situation after situation seems impervious to change. . . . The effort involved in being active, reactive, and adaptive is considerable. Utilization-focused evaluation may, indeed, be a long shot but the potential payoff is worth the risk. (Patton, 1978, pp. 290-291)

Patton's book is well worth reading. The utilization-focused approach can be combined with the models of Stake, Stufflebeam, and Provus.

Educational Accountability

Educational accountability is an aspect of evaluation that seems to have come into use in the 1960s. Leon Lessinger, superintendent of schools in San Mateo, California, and later a U.S. Associate Commissioner for Elementary and Secondary Education, wrote one of the first books on the subject. His powerful opening statement explains concerns leading to the accountability movement.

If one airplane in every four crashed between takeoff and landing, people would refuse to fly. If one automobile in every four went out of control and caused a fatal accident or permanent injury, Detroit would be closed down tomorrow. Our schools—which produce a more important product than airplanes or automobiles—somehow fail one youngster in four. And so far we have not succeeded in preventing the social and economic fatalities every school dropout represents. For each child thus failed by his school, all of us pay a price in taxes and in social unrest, and the child himself is deprived of his chance to develop to his potential. (Lessinger, 1970b, p. 3)

Lessinger's book is well worth reading in the 1980s. Many of his ideas (educational engineering, developmental capital for schools, management support, performance contracting, and educational accomplishment audits) are just now being tested by local school districts.

Definitions and Characteristics of Accountability

In 1971 Phi Delta Kappa devoted its 13th annual educational research symposium series to accountability (Gephart, 1975). William Gephart, Director of Research

Services for Phi Delta Kappa and editor of the proceedings of that meeting, summarized the confusion surrounding the accountability movement at that time.

The call for accountability in education has everyone's blessing. Like motherhood, God, and country, it is almost unassailable. How could anyone oppose something that promises that education, a necessity for our children, will produce a better product while operating at increased efficiency. . . . Simultaneous with this abundance of support, the accountability movement lacks substance. No one, yet everyone, seems to know what accountability means. . . . accountability may be said to be a goal, a direction, a framework, a process, a product, a commitment, an obligation, or a necessity. (Gephart, 1975, p. xi)

The major questions that symposium participants attempted to answer were,

- To whom is accountability directed?

- What is the object of accountability?

- How are we to attain accountability?

- Why?

By the meeting's end, the following definition was agreed upon: "Accountability is a *systematic means to seek assurance of an expected end*" (Gephart, 1975, p. xv). It was agreed also that 11 phrases would characterize the systematic means (Gephart, 1975, pp. xv-xvi).

- A set of explicitly stated constraints

- Negotiated "ends" in light of constraints

- Systematic "means"—involving negotiated responsibility *for*, responsibility *to*, and responsibility *by*

- Explicitness, clarity in negotiated means and ends

- Systematic operation, assessment, and interpretation of the goals, of the process, and of the product

- Feedback

- System adaption and recycling

- A concern for legitimacy

- A concern for social consequences

- An appropriate balance of power and authority

- Consequences related to negotiated agreements

Marvin Alkin of the Center for the Study of Evaluation at UCLA summarizes these concepts as follows: ''Accountability is (1) a negotiated relationship, (2) designed to produce increased productivity, (3) in which the participants agree in advance to accept specified rewards and costs, (4) on the basis of evaluation findings on the attainment of specified ends'' (1975, p. 23). Leon Lessinger posited a similar definition.

> Accountability is the product of a process; at its most basic level, it means that an agent, public or private, entering into a conceptual agreement to perform a service, will be answerable for performing according to agreed-upon terms, within an established time period, and with a stipulated use of resources and performance standards. (1970a, p. 218)

Few persons have published works discussing accountability in relation to physical education. Sherrill (1986) lists accountability as one of the eight characteristics of adapted physical education. Primary sources on whom she relies are Lessinger (1970), Turnbull (1975), and Vodola (1973). Seaman and Depauw (1982, p. 10) and Crowe, Auxter, and Pyfer (1981, p. 284) devote paragraphs to accountability. Clearly a need exists for more physical educators to address this issue.

A Local School District Model

Pino (1975) depicts the operational accountability model followed by the Cherry Creek school system in Colorado (see Figure 8.11). This accountability model is almost identical to many schemas denoted as evaluation models. It is increasingly evident that good evaluation assures accountability. Adapted physical educators, often responsible for screening, assessing, and programming for an entire school district, will benefit from implementation of this model.

Types and Principles of Accountability

Three types of accountability should be built into an adapted physical education accountability model: (a) goal accountability, (b) program accountability, and (c) outcome accountability. These are explained fully in the chart by Alkin (1975a, p. 27) presented in Figure 8.12. Each of these should be implemented in accordance with definitions and characteristics already presented.

Alkin identifies and discusses three principles of accountability. These principles are summarized as follows:

- *Negotiation*—It should be remembered that accountability is a cooperative enterprise in which all involved parties negotiate.

- *Explicit and clear conditions*—To hold persons accountable, the conditions of that accountability should be explicitly stated in writing and clearly understood by all parties.

- *Constraints*—The legal and financial constraints that will affect accountability should be clearly specified in writing and understood by all parties.

References

Alkin, M. (1975a). The design and implementation of accountability systems. In W. Gephart (Ed.), *Accountability: A state, a process, or a product* (pp. 21-36). Bloomington, IN: Phi Delta Kappa.

Alkin, M. (1975b). Evaluation: Who needs it? Who cares? *Studies in Educational Evaluation, 1*(3), 201-212.

Bloom, B. (Ed.). (1956). *Taxonomy of educational objectives: The classification of educational goals: Handbook I. Cognitive domain.* New York: David McKay.

Burns, R. W. (1972). *New approaches to behavioral objectives.* Dubuque, IA: Wm. C. Brown.

Crowe, W., Auxter, D., & Pyfer, J. (1981). *Principles and methods of adapted physical education and recreation* (4th ed.). St. Louis: C.V. Mosby.

Gephart, W. (Ed.). (1975). *Accountability: A state, a process, or a product.* Bloomington, IN: Phi Delta Kappa.

Gronlund, N. E. (1970). *Stating behavioral objectives for classroom instruction.* New York: Macmillan.

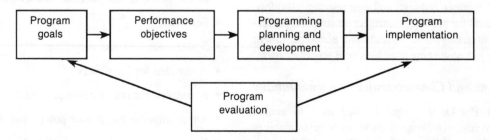

Figure 8.11 Cherry Creek School System accountability model.

Accountability Types

	Who is accountable	To whom (primary responsibility)	For what	"Procedures" for attaining accountability	"Techniques" for assessing accountability
Goal accountability	School board	Public	Goal and objective selection	Needs assessment (CSE), Delphi, objective writing	*Judge Goals and Objectives* Determine whether the goals are consistent with the desires of constituencies. Determine whether the objectives are consistent with the goals.
Program accountability	School district administration	School board	Development, modification, and/or selection of instructional programs appropriate for state objectives	Literature review, product development technology, simulation, Delphi, formative evaluation. Summative evaluation in order to establish performance standards for the programs	*Judge Programs* Compare outcomes in order to determine whether extent of achievement is satisfactory relative to objectives.
Outcome accountability	Instructional Manager (i.e., teacher)	School District Administration	Producing Program outcomes consistent with preselected objectives at a performance standard appropriate for the instructional program	Instructional Management skills PERT, CPM, interpersonal communication skills, knowledge of subject matter	*Judge Program Outcomes* Compare student outcomes to performance standards

Figure 8.12 Accountability types. From "The Design and Implementation of Accountability Systems" by M. Alkin, 1975, in W. Gephart (Ed.), *Accountability: A State, A Process, or a Product* (p. 27), Bloomington, IN: Phi Delta Kappa.

Harrow, A. (1972). *A taxonomy of the psychomotor domain*. New York: David McKay.

House, E. (1974). *The politics of educational innovation*. Berkeley, CA: McCutchan.

Jewett, A. (1980). The status of physical education curriculum theory. *Quest, 32*(2), 163-173.

Jewett, A.E., & Mullan, M.R. (1977). *Curriculum design: Purposes and processes in physical education teaching-learning*. Washington, DC: AAHPERD.

Krathwohl, D., Bloom, F., & Masia, B. (1964). *Taxonomy of educational objectives: The classification of educational goals: Handbook II. Affective domain*. New York: David McKay.

Lessinger, L. (1970a). Engineering accountability for results in public education, *Phi Delta Kappa, 52*(4), 217-225.

Lessinger, L. (1970b). *Every kid a winner: Accountability in education*. New York: Simon and Schuster.

Lockhart, A. (1972). The conceptualization of models. *Quest, 17*, 91-94.

Mager, R. (1962). *Preparing instructional objectives*. Belmont, CA: Fearson.

Oakley, T. (1984). *Evaluation of physical education programs for handicapped students and teacher training in Arkansas*. Unpublished doctoral dissertation, Texas Woman's University, Denton.

Patton, M. Q. (1978). *Utilization-focused evaluation*. Beverly Hills, CA: Sage.

Pino, E. (1975). An operational accountability model. In W. Gephart (Ed.), *Accountability: A state, a process, or a product* (pp. 9-19). Bloomington, IN: Phi Delta Kappa.

Popham, W. J., & Baker, E. (1970). *Establishing instructional goals.* Englewood Cliffs, NJ: Prentice-Hall.

Provus, M. (1969). Evaluation of ongoing programs in the public school system. In R. Tyler (Ed.), *Educational evaluation: New roles, new means. The 68th Yearbook of the National Society for the Study of Education: Part II* (pp. 242-283). Chicago: National Society for the Study of Education.

Provus, M. (1971). *Discrepancy evaluation for educational program improvement and assessment.* Berkeley, CA: McCutchan.

Provus, M. (1973). Evaluation of ongoing programs in the public school system. In B. Worthen & J. Sanders (Eds.), *Educational evaluation: Theory and practice* (pp. 170-207). Worthington, OH: Charles A. Jones. (Article originally published in 1969)

Seaman, J., & Depauw, K. (1982). *The new adapted physical education.* Palo Alto, CA: Mayfield.

Sherrill, C. (1986). *Adapted physical education and recreation: A multidisciplinary approach* (3rd ed.). Dubuque, IA: Wm. D. Brown.

Snyder, R., & Scott, H. (1954). *Professional preparation in health, physical education, and recreation.* New York: McGraw Hill.

Stake, R. (1967). The countenance of educational evaluation. *Teachers College Record,* **68**(7), 523-540.

Stake, R. (1975). *Evaluating the arts in education: A responsive approach.* Columbus, OH: Charles E. Merrill.

Stokes, B.R. (1980). *The status of physical education in Louisiana as it relates to requirements of the education for all handicapped children act.* Unpublished doctoral dissertation, University of Southern Mississippi, Hattiesburg.

Stufflebeam, D.L. (1968). Toward a science of educational evaluation. *Educational Technology,* **8**(14), 5-12.

Stufflebeam, D.L., Foley, W. J., Gephart, W. J., Guba, E.G., Hammond, R. L., Merriman, H. O., & Provus, M. (1971). *Educational evaluation and decision making.* Itasca, IL: F.E. Peacock.

Suchman, E.A. (1967). *Evaluation research: Principles and practice in public service and action programs.* New York: Russell Sage Foundation.

Troyer, M., & Pace, C. R. (1944). *Evaluation in teacher education.* Washington, DC: American Council on Education.

Turnbull, H. R. (1975). Accountability: An overview of the impact of litigation on professionals. *Exceptional Children,* **41**, 427-433.

Tyler, R. W. (1950). *Basic principles of curriculum and instruction.* Chicago: University of Chicago Press.

Tyler, R.W., Gagne, R.M., & Scriven, M. (Eds.). (1967). *Perspectives of curriculum development.* Chicago: Rand McNally.

Van Dalen, D. (1979). *Understanding educational research.* New York: McGraw Hill.

Vodola, T. (1973). *Individualized physical education program for the handicapped child.* Englewood Cliffs, NJ: Prentice Hall.

Wessel, J. (1983). *Postdoctoral training (PDT) manual: Quality physical education programs.* East Lansing, MI: Michigan State University.

Yavorsky, D. K. (1976). *Discrepancy evaluation: A practitioner's guide.* Charlottesville: University of Virginia.

Chapter 9

Professional Preparation and Public School Service Delivery

Claudine Sherrill, Janet Wessel, and Julian U. Stein

*P*rofessional preparation must be founded in the reality of public school service delivery. The purpose of this chapter is to review basic concepts related to public school finance, the structure of state education agencies (SEAs) and local education agencies (LEAs), the Comprehensive System of Personnel Development (CSPD), and advocacy at both grassroots and national organization levels.

Teacher training must not occur in a vacuum. University faculty should model a close working relationship with SEAs and LEAs for their graduate students. This relationship should be reflected in a high visibility adapted physical education service delivery program for all handicapped students, aged 3 to 21 years, in the community in which the university is located. All aspects of the local program can serve as learning experiences for graduate students. Likewise, all aspects of politics and advocacy in relation to the state plan and the CSPD can be valuable learning experiences.

Financing Public School Education: Implications for Adapted Physical Education

The bottom line in the success of adapted physical education as an emerging profession is whether LEAs will allocate monies for the employment of adapted physical education specialists. It is important to understand methods of funding public school education and problems involved in the equalization of educational opportunity for all children.

Cost of Equalizing Educational Opportunity

Everyone knows that the cost of educating handicapped students is greater than educating the nonhandicapped. Yet little research is available on special education costs. Perhaps the most authoritative source of information is the annual report to Congress on the implementation of PL 94-142 prepared by the staff of the U.S. Department of Education. The 1982 annual report summarizes findings of a major finance study by the Rand Corporation (1981), research by Rossmiller and Frohreich (1979), and a dissertation by Reger (1979).

These studies continue to be cited in subsequent reports to Congress and appear to be the major research underlying today's knowledge base. The Rand Corporation (1981) studied special education costs in 14 states during 1977-78. It documented the mix of resources used to educate handicapped children and estimated costs by handicapping condition, type of placement, and age level. The report concluded that the average cost of education per handicapped child was 2.17 times greater than

that of nonhandicapped children. Reger (1979) compared average cost per special education pupil ($3,794) with average cost per regular education student ($1,399) in Wisconsin, and Rossmiller and Frohreich (1979) analyzed special education costs in Idaho. In general, these sources agree that the cost of educating handicapped individuals is about twice that of the nonhandicapped.

Three general findings have resulted from special education finance studies (U.S. Department of Education, 1982):

> The cost of special education within any given category of handicapping condition varies considerably. The costs of providing special education are not necessarily related to the quality of the program. On the average, instructional costs for a full-time placement in a special class were higher per handicapped pupil ($1,578) than for a regular class placement with a part-time special class ($794). (p.13)

In addition to direct instructional costs, many other expenses occur in educating handicapped students: related service costs, special equipment, supplies, and facilities, transportation, and so on.

In general, the cost of service delivery is proportionate to the severity of the handicap. The Rand study (1981) indicated, for instance, the following average annual instructional costs per pupil:

$2,516—blind student
$2,336—deaf student
$ 897—educable mentally retarded student
$ 813—learning disabled student

Note that these Rand Corporation figures are not total pupil costs, just instructional costs.

A comprehensive study of special education costs was reported by Rossmiller, Hale, and Frohreich (1970), and is discussed in the sixth annual report to Congress as a model study (U.S. Department of Education, 1984). Table 9.1 presents the median per pupil cost of education and the excess cost (regular education minus special education cost). The excess cost is the amount on which controversy centers. Who should pay for this excess cost: local, state, or federal government or some combination of all three?

Use of a cost index is another approach to studying special education finance. A cost index is the ratio of average per pupil expenditure (APPE) for handicapped children to the average per pupil expenditure in the regular program. The median cost index is considered the most sound base for fiscal planning because it reflects "what might be termed average practice in a set of districts"

Table 9.1   Median Per Pupil Cost of Education and Excess Costs

Category	1970 Annual cost per pupil	Excess cost
Nonhandicapped	655[a]	—
Visually handicapped	2,197	1,542
Physically handicapped	2,113	1,458
Auditorily handicapped	2,103	1,448
Multiply handicapped	1,941	1,286
Severe learning disabled	1,757	1,102
Emotionally disturbed	1,683	1,028
Trainable mentally retarded	1,627	972
Educable mentally retarded	1,316	661
Average	—	1,187

Note. 1970 statistics based on research on five states (Wisconsin, Florida, California, Texas, and New York) by Rossmiller, Hale, and Frohreich, 1970.

[a]The 1980 annual cost per nonhandicapped student is $2,168 (Cohn, 1982b).

(Marinelli, 1976, p. 169). Table 9.2 presents illustrative cost indices for different handicapping conditions.

The use of a cost index can also be applied to per pupil cost of different delivery systems as illustrated in Table 9.3. The findings of Clemmons (1974) differ from those of the Rand Corporation (1981), which found the self-contained classroom placement to cost more than regular class placement with a part-time special class.

Research in adapted physical education is needed similar to the studies of Clemmons (1974) and the Rand Corporation (1981) to determine the relative cost of different kinds of physical education service delivery. Comparisons should be made also between the costs of physical education service and those of occupational and physical therapy, which are sometimes used illegally as substitutes for physical education. In these times of economic stress, the profession that can deliver the most for the least money is likely to get the jobs regardless of PL 94-142 constraints.

Pupil/Teacher Ratios in Relation to Cost

Per pupil costs of special education, adapted physical education, and the therapies are affected greatly by student-staff ratios. The overall pupil/teacher ratio in special education is 18:1, with the following ratios for specific handicapping conditions (U.S. Department of Education, 1982, p. 12):

> 49:1   Speech impaired
> 12:1   Emotionally disturbed

Table 9.2   Cost Indices for Different Handicapping Conditions

Handicapping condition	Rossmiller et al., 1970 5 state composite	Clemmons, 1974 Minnesota	Texas Education Agency, 1975 Texas
Physically handicapped	3.64	2.89	2.39
Auditorily handicapped	2.99	2.99	3.48
Visually handicapped	2.97	2.34	4.38
Emotionally disturbed	2.83	—	2.61
Multiply handicapped	2.73	—	—
Specific learning disabled	2.16	1.75	2.76
Trainable mentally retarded	2.10	2.03	2.22
Educable mentally retarded	1.87	1.71	2.83
Speech impaired	1.18	1.27	—
Estimated average[a]	2.45	2.14	2.95

Note. Adapted from "Financing the Education of Exceptional Children" by J. Marinelli, 1976, in F. Weintraub, A. Abeson, J. Ballard, & M. LaVor (Eds.), *Public Policy and the Education of Exceptional Children* (p. 169), Reston, VA: Council for Exceptional Children.

[a]These averages were calculated by Sherrill; in reality the average overall cost index is lower because there are many more speech impaired and MR students in an SEA than physically handicapped and sensory impaired.

Table 9.3   Per Pupil Cost for Different Delivery Systems

Delivery system	Median cost index per pupil
Regular classroom with resource room	2.00
Regular classroom with special consultant	1.86
Self-contained classroom	1.67
Part-time special education classroom	1.66
Regular classroom with itinerant teacher	1.50
Homebound or hospitalized instruction	1.34

Note. Based on research by Clemmons (1974) on six Minnesota school districts.

> 17:1   Learning disabled
> 16:1   Multihandicapped
> 4:1   Deaf blind

Pupil/teacher ratios vary tremendously by state as depicted by the following figures. Adapted physical education comparisons must therefore be made state by state (see Figure 9.1).

State	Average pupil/Teacher ratio
Alabama	18:1
California	20:1
Colorado	15:1
Connecticut	25:1
Florida	18:1
Louisiana	14:1
Minnesota	14:1
New York	13:1
Oregon	30:1
Texas	21:1
Washington	20:1

Figure 9.1   Comparison of average pupil/teacher ratios (U.S. Department of Education, 1982, p. 175).

Because of the influence of pupil/teacher ratio on per pupil costs, many state legislatures have established maximum ratios for special education. A few states, like Louisiana, have also established maximum loads for adapted physical education. In Louisiana adapted physical educators working with students with severe motor deficits are permitted an overall caseload of no more than 25:1. Adapted physical educators with students having mild to moderate conditions are assigned no more than 49 students (Cooper & Fruge, 1982). These adapted physical education caseloads can be judged cost effective in relation to the average pupil/teacher ratio of 14:1 for special educators in Louisiana.

Philosophical Concepts Underlying School Finance

In order to understand special education funding, one must know both regular physical education and special education practices. With regard to regular education funding, on the average local taxes provide 42%, states provide 50%, and the federal government contributes only about 8% ("Education: The Bold Quest," 1983, p. 65). Figures 9.2 and 9.3 show this breakdown for the APPE of regular education in 1980.

The cost required to educate a handicapped child appears to range from about one to four times that of a regular education student. The excess cost in most states is also shared by local, state, and federal governments as depicted in the figure on the opposite page.

Many persons mistakenly believe that the federal government pays the largest share of special education costs, particularly those needed for compliance with PL 94-142. Thus blame for cutting or not providing services is often directed toward the federal government's allocation of funds. This practice seems unrealistic inasmuch as most of the excess cost of special education is, and always has been, borne by the local and state governments.

Federal funding under PL 94-142 (really Part B of Education of the Handicapped Act [EHA] was designed to help with the excess cost of special education. The PL 94-142 monies are computed by formula ranging from 5 to 40% of the APPE for regular education. The exact percentage used each year depends on federal appropriations, although the original legislation authorized 40% of APPE beginning in 1982. Federal funding of education under the U.S. Constitution is justified only when such funding is needed to facilitate equal access or equal opportunity to education for all persons under the 14th amendment.

The U.S. Supreme Court asserts that equal educational opportunity is not guaranteed under the U.S. Constitution (Flygare, 1983). This decision was made in 1973 in the case of *San Antonio School District v. Rodriquez* when the U.S. Supreme Court ruled 5 to 4 that the Texas school finance program, with its heavy reliance on the local property tax, did not violate the equal protection clause of the 14th amendment. In essence, the Supreme Court reconfirmed the concept that education is a function of the local property tax base and a responsibility of the state. Thus quality and quantity of services may vary from LEA to LEA depending upon the wealth (tax base) of the community as long as education is minimally adequate. Guthrie (1983) is an excellent source on funding an adequate education. PL 94-142 has not changed this. Free, appropriate education for handicapped children and youth is the responsibility of the local and state government.

Whereas the U.S. Supreme Court refused to intervene in the unequal education of students in different LEAs, many state courts have held that unequal education expenditure is unconstitutional under their state constitution and have thus forced reforms in state education finance systems. The publication of Coons, Clune, and Sugarman (1970) is considered the primary source for this school reform. The works of Cohn (1974, 1979, 1982a, 1982b) have also been influential. Also significant in tax reform have been such phenomena as Proposition 13 in California in which voters approved reductions in local property taxes, thereby forcing the state to assume increased responsibility for schooling.

Most people believe that the expense of adapted physical education should be shared in the same way as other special education services. A model might be as indicated in Figure 9.4. To assist in LEA problem solving concerning monies for adapted physical education service delivery, physical educators must upgrade their knowledge in all aspects of school finance. The sections that follow on state aid to regular education, state aid to special education, and federal flow-through monies provide background information. This reading should be supplemented by study of the U.S. Department of Education annual report to Congress, to stay abreast of recent developments.

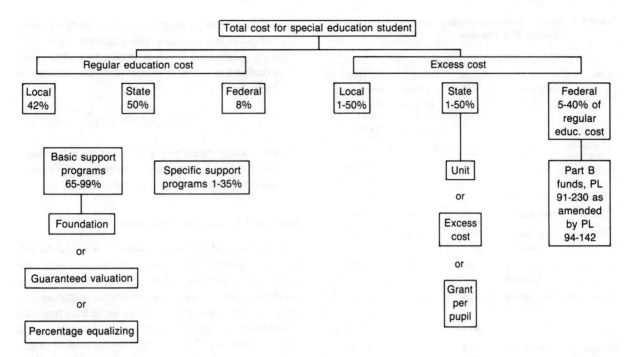

Figure 9.2 Funding sources for total cost of a special education student. Data compiled from U.S. Department of Education (1979); Cohn (1982); PL 94-142; "Education: The bold Quest" (1983).

State Aid to Regular Education

State aid to regular education is generally of two types: (a) basic support programs with funds distributed according to equalization formulas and (b) specific-support programs in which state funds are channeled for support of special needs like special education, transportation, textbooks, and capital outlays. Table 9.4 shows that three major state aid formulas are used to determine basic support to LEAs.

Table 9.4 also shows the variability among states with regard to APPE, state aid as a percentage of total education cost, and basic support as a percentage of state aid. Included in the table are most of the states considered to have good adapted physical education programs as well as the five bellwether states identified by Naisbitt (1982) as responsible for most of the social innovation in America (California, Colorado, Connecticut, Florida, and Washington). Six states in the table are below the APPE of $2,168, and six states are at or above APPE.

The three most frequently used state aid formulas for basic support can be explained as follows:

1. *Foundation plan.* A plan with state mandated minimum revenue level per pupil. The per pupil spending level is determined by state legislature. Major features of the Foundation plan include

  • foundation level (F)—the minimum expenditures necessary to support a sound educational program;

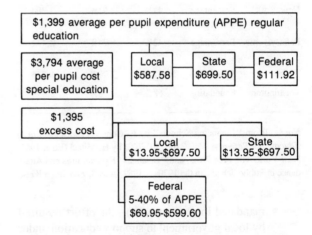

Figure 9.3 Application of data in Figure 9.2 to calculation of costs based on Reger (1979) cited by U.S. Department of Education (1982).

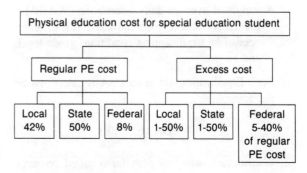

Figure 9.4 Model for sharing the expense of adapted physical education.

Table 9.4 Regular Education Funding Patterns, 1979-1980, Showing SEA Practices

States	Basic support program	State aid as % of total expenditures	Basic support programs as % of state aid	FY 1980 average per pupil expenditures (APPE)
Total 50 states plus D.C.	—	—	—	2,168
Alabama	Foundation	75%	87%	1,469
California	Guaranteed Valuation	68%	76%	2,164
Colorado	Guaranteed Valuation	45%	87%	2,353
Connecticut	Guaranteed Valuation	29%	65%	2,341
Florida	Foundation	61%	85%	1,793
Georgia	Foundation	64%	79%	1,490
Louisiana	Foundation	65%	86%	1,636
Minnesota	Foundation	67%	66%	2,300
New York	Percentage Equal	41%	91%	3,304
Pennsylvania	Percentage Equal	42%	74%	2,431
Texas	Foundation	57%	99%	1,815
Washington	Foundation	68%	76%	2,490

Note. From "Financing Schools" by E. Cohn, in *Encyclopedia of Educational Research: Vol. 2* (pp. 701-702) by H. Mitzel (Ed.), 1982, New York: The Free Press, and "Databank: Expenditures and Attendance in Public Schools in the 1970s," 1982, May 5, *Education Week.*

- mandated local tax rate (r)—the effort required by local government to support education under the local-state partnership concept;

- local wealth (V)—assessed valuations of property per pupil in the LEA; and

- weighted average daily attendance (WADA)—the LEA student count adjusted for different needs like handicapping condition, grade level, and so on.

State Equalization aid to an LEA is calculated by the formula

$$WADA\ (F - rV).$$

2. *Guaranteed valuation plan* (also called resource equalization plan). The same formula is used as for the Foundation plan except F is deleted. In its place

legislators decide on an assessed property valuation per pupil that the state will guarantee each LEA. This guaranteed level is denoted as rVG. State equalization aid to an LEA is then calculated by the formula

$$WADA\ (rVG - rV).$$

3. *Percentage equalizing plan.* This plan imposes a matching aid formula concept to encourage increased tax efforts by LEAs beyond the mandated tax rate.

State Aid to Special Education

Several methods are used by states to assist LEAs with the cost differential between special education and regular education (Thomas, 1973a, 1973b). Table 9.5 depicts the three major special education finance formulas used throughout the United States. Because federal funds are administered through SEAs, confusion often occurs as to which monies are of state origin versus federal origin. Table 9.5 presents only monies of state and local origin.

Table 9.5 reveals that from 1 to 50% of the special education APPE comes from local sources. The sum varies by state, with all states contributing substantial sums to special education APPE. The three most frequently used state aid formulas for special education APPE are as follows:

- *Unit basis.* A unit may be defined as a special education classroom having a set number of students or an administrator or other personnel category that serves a certain number of pupils daily. School districts certify the number of units, and the state reimburses them accordingly. This system tends to maximize class size to decrease per pupil cost. It therefore works best in conjunction with statutory limits on class size.

- *Excess cost pattern.* Excess cost (the differential between cost of special education and regular education for each handicapping condition) is reimbursed in some way: (a) completely, (b) partially up to a dollar amount ceiling, or (c) partially on a percentage or pro-rated basis. Theoretically, many persons consider this the best method.

- *Grant per pupil* (also called straight sum reimbursement). The state allocates a set sum, which may vary according to the handicapping condition, for each child receiving special education services in the LEA.

Federal Aid to Special Education

Federal aid to special education is generally in one of two categories: (a) *statutory*, also called entitlement and (b) *discretionary*. Funding of both is governed by

Table 9.5 Special Education Funding Patterns in 1976

States	Regular education average per pupil expenditure (APPE)	Special education finance formula	State special education funds per handicapped pupil	Estimated % of special education funds from local sources
California	1,320	Unit	838	50
Oregon	1,501	Excess cost	169	46
Indiana	1,160	Grant per pupil	343	41
Michigan	1,366	Excess cost	881	37
Minnesota	1,513	Unit	545	37
New York	2,179	Excess cost	1,061	42
South Carolina	1,030	Unit	338	1
Texas	1,422	Unit	1,001	20

Note. From U.S. Department of Health, Education, and Welfare, 1979, Appendix A.

EHA, which has been authorized approximately every three years since its enactment in 1970 as PL 91-230. Part B of EHA, the amendment known as PL 94-142, mandates various entitlement programs in which the amount of money awarded is determined by formula and thus conceptualized as permanent. In contrast, discretionary funds (i.e., those governed by other parts of EHA) are reevaluated every three years at which time the sums to be awarded are raised, lowered, or eliminated by reauthorization legislation. Discretionary funds are used to support six basic functions: personnel preparation, research and development, information dissemination, technical assistance, demonstration, and direct services to low incidence populations. For a better understanding of discretionary funding, see Table 5.3 in chapter 5.

Public school personnel are directly affected more by entitlement monies than by discretionary funding. The most important of the entitlement programs is the EHA-B State Grant Program, or PL 94-142 monies. These programs provide that federal grants be awarded to SEAs that document compliance with the law through submission of a special education state plan to the U.S. Department of Education. The amount of money distributed to each state is based on the total number of handicapped children documented as receiving special education and related services on December 1 of the previous fiscal year. These monies are called *formula* funds because PL 94-142 committed the federal government to pay a gradually escalating percentage of the APP multiplied times the number of handicapped children served. This percentage was to escalate on a yearly basis until it reached 40%.

Table 9.6 shows that entitlement funds have increased steadily from 1977 to 1985. The per child average, how-

ever, does not yet represent the 40% ceiling mandated by PL 94-142. In fact, $276 is a very small federal contribution when one remembers the average annual cost per special education student is well over $3,500 (U.S. Department of Education, 1982).

PL 94-142 protects against overlabeling and overcounting by providing a count limitation, that is, no more than 12% of the total school-age population of a state can be counted as handicapped in the funding formula. Additionally, no more than 2% of the total school-age population of a state can be counted as learning disabled.

Federal Flow-Through Monies

PL 94-142 was designed to facilitate decentralization by specifying the percentage of Part B funds to be allocated to LEAs. During the first year of PL 94-142 implementation (1978), 50% of Part B monies were allocated to SEAs and 50% to LEAs. In subsequent years the LEA entitlement was 75% and the SEA allocation was 25%.

Need for Research on Adapted Physical Education Costs

The need for research on the cost of adapted physical education service delivery parallels that of special education. The summary statement that follows is as applicable to adapted physical education as to special education.

> Research is needed to collect and analyze expenditure data and resource use in local education agencies to learn the costs of providing special education by various alternative educational placements. . . . Special education costs and finance policy can strongly influence implemen-

Table 9.6   EHA-B State Grant Program Funding, Fiscal Years 1977 to 1985

Fiscal year	EHA-B State grants (dollars)	Child count	Per-child average (dollars)
1977	251,769,927	3,485,000	72
1978	566,030,074	3,561,000	159
1979	804,000,000	3,700,000	217
1980	874,500,000	3,803,000	230
1981	874,500,000	3,941,000	222
1982	931,008,000	3,990,000	233
1983	1,017,900,000	4,053,000	251
1984	1,068,875,000	4,094,000	261
1985	1,135,145,000	4,113,312	276

Note.   The per child average is not a per capita expenditure, but represents the distribution formula on which the allocation to the states is based. From U.S. Department of Education (1986). *Eighth annual report to Congress on the Implementation of the Education of the Handicapped Act* (p. 75). Washington, DC: Author.

tations of desired special education delivery system reforms. Consequently, the issue of the cost of special education has very significant policy relevance at this time. (U.S. Department of Education, 1979, p. 139)

Importance of SEAs and LEAs

It is vital that teacher educators and graduate students possess knowledge of SEAs and LEAs. The main reason for this, of course, is that "education is a state function and LEAs are agents of the state charged with carrying out educational responsibilities" (Marinelli, 1976, p. 186). The source of the SEA's authority is explained as follows:

The powers of the federal government extend to those areas which are delegated and enumerated in the U.S. Constitution. The 10th Amendment to the Constitution provides that "the powers not delegated to the United States by the Constitution, nor prohibited by it to the State, are reserved to the States respectively, or to the people." (Marinelli, 1976, p. 182)

Many professionals have overestimated the power of PL 94-142 to improve adapted physical education service delivery. The physical education requirements of this law in reality are only as strong as SEAs and LEAs want them to be. This is because federal laws are written in broad, global language, and SEAs, through submission of state plans, specify the details for implementation. It is also because SEAs and LEAs control the financing of education.

Another reason for teacher educators and graduate

students to upgrade their knowledge and increase their involvement in SEAs and LEAs is our increasing recognition of the fact that permanent change is more likely to be initiated at LEA and SEA levels than in Washington, DC. John Naisbitt, author of the best seller *Megatrends: Ten New Directions Transforming Our Lives*, speaks eloquently to this point:

I have been overwhelmingly impressed with the extent to which America is a bottom-up society, that is, where trends and ideas begin in cities and local communities—for example, Tampa, Hartford, San Diego, Seattle, and Denver, not New York City or Washington, DC . . . trends are generated from the bottom up, fads from the top down. (1982, pp. 2–3)

Naisbitt presents evidence that most of the social invention in America comes from just five states: Florida, Connecticut, California, Washington, and Colorado. These he terms the bellwether states. In effect the other 45 states are followers. This chapter presents information on these states whenever the data are available.

A third reason for SEA and LEA focus is the megatrends away from centralization toward decentralization, from institutional help toward self-help, and from representative democracy toward participatory democracy (Naisbitt, 1982, pp. 97-188). The essence of these megatrends is captured in this statement:

Centralized structures are crumbling all across America. But our society is not falling apart. Far from it. The people of this country are rebuilding America from the bottom up into a stronger, more balanced, more diverse society.

The decentralization of America has transformed politics, business, our very culture. (Naisbitt, 1982, p. 97)

Underlying the increasing power of SEAs and LEAs is the relative strength of state and local finance as compared to federal budget deficits. All but two states (Connecticut and Vermont) must by law balance their budgets. In spite of widespread economic problems, some states (mostly the energy-producing ones) may amass surpluses. Alaska, Texas, Oklahoma, Hawaii, North Dakota, and Kansas all had surpluses of well over $100 million for both 1980 and 1981.

Structure of the SEA

The SEA is generally called the State Department of Education or the Department of Public Instruction. Just as the U.S. Department of Education is responsible to the U.S. Congress, the SEA is responsible to the state congress. It is also responsible to the State Board of Education, which generally is comprised of one official elected from each state district. University professors, as well as all advocates for educational change, should become acquainted with key SEA staff members and the power structures that influence them. A service that universities can render in this regard is development and dissemination of state directories of adapted physical education personnel, which also include names, addresses, and phone

numbers of state school board members, the Commissioner of Education, and other SEA staff members.

Figure 9.5 depicts one organizational structure of an SEA. The structure is different, of course, in every state. A commonality seems to be administrative separateness of regular education and special education. Adapted physical educators need to relate equally to both departments.

Usually, within the general education or regular education department are housed all the curriculum specialists. Among these are one or more SEA directors of physical education. These persons know their counterparts in the 50 states and thus are helpful in keeping abreast of both state and national physical education trends and issues.

Several contacts are essential within the SEA special education department. The associate commissioner or state director of special education is responsible for ascertaining that the state plan complies with PL 94-142. In this role his or her attitudes toward adapted physical education are all-important. This administrator belongs to the National Association of State Directors of Special Education (NASDE) in Washington, DC and may be influenced by the position this organization takes in regard to physical education. Also within the SEA special education department are staff members who travel about the state and monitor various LEAs in their compliance with PL 94-142. Depending upon state plan guidelines and personal attitudes and beliefs, these persons can emphasize or neglect physical education in their LEA

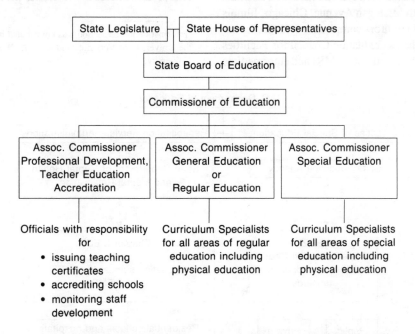

Figure 9.5 Organization of a State Education Agency (SEA). The Commissioner of Education is often chairperson of the State Board of Education. He or she is also called the Chief State School Officer and is a member of the Council of Chief State School Officers, 379 Hall of the States, 400 N. Capitol St., NW, Washington, DC 20001.

monitoring. A growing number of SEA special education departments are employing state directors and consultants in adapted physical education. Illustrative of these are Claudia Knowles at the Texas Education Agency and Janice Fruge at the Louisiana State Department of Education.

Relationship of SEAs to Residential Schools and Hospitals

In addition to responsibility for public education, SEAs also perform functions in relation to private schools and state-supported residential schools and hospitals. Often a second state structure like a Department of Mental Health and Mental Retardation is primarily responsible for state-supported residential hospitals and schools. Overlaps occur only with respect to school-aged residents. Figure 9.6 shows the relationship between this department and the SEA, the major laws and policies under which each works, and the federal office to which each reports.

Table 9.7 shows the number of persons in the United States receiving special education services under PL 94-142 (i.e., EHA-B).

Because university teacher training programs are expected to prepare teachers and staff for residential facilities as well as public and private day schools, professors and graduate students should understand the mechanics of each state structure, federal and state laws and policies under which they function, and accreditation standards. The Joint Commission on Accreditation of Hospitals (JCAH), 875 North Michigan Avenue, Chicago, Illinois 60611, issues and monitors compliance with accreditation standards of the Accreditation Council for Facilities for the Mentally Retarded (AC/FMR) and Intermediate

Care Facilities for the Mentally Retarded (IC/FMR). Periodicals published by the American Association on Mental Deficiency (AAMD) are good resources for teacher training related to severely handicapped persons found in residential facilities.

The State Plan for Special Education[1]

The state plan is a tremendously important document because it is the "blueprint" or official interpretation of how PL 94-142 is to be implemented in your state. In the past, the annual program plan was for 1 fiscal year in length and was drafted, distributed for public hearing, and submitted for approval to the Commissioner of Education annually. However, during 1980, the states were given the opportunity to submit the state plan to be implemented for a 3-year period of time.

Advocates of quality services in physical education and recreation should be involved in the development and monitoring of the state plan. The importance of this document warrants the time and energy necessary to become knowledgeable about and involved in this process. The state plan is required to be submitted for public inspection and hearings must be held to solicit input. The state is required to document these proceedings and the action taken regarding each item of public testimony in the state plan when it is submitted to Washington, DC for approval. This process insures that interested persons can be involved

---

[1]Information in this section was contributed by Larry Carmichael of the University of Vermont, and Janet A. Wessel of Michigan State University.

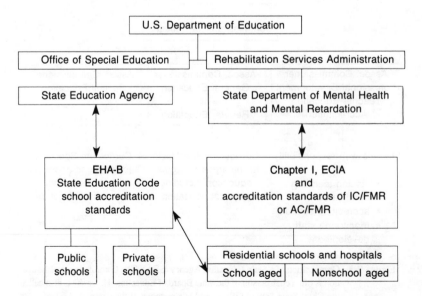

Figure 9.6 Relationship of Office of Special Education and Rehabilitation Services (OSERS) in Washington, DC to state level components responsible for special education services.

Table 9.7　Number of Handicapped Children in 1984-1985 Receiving Special Education Services Under EHA-B (PL 94-142)

Category	Ages 3-5	Ages 6-11	Ages 12-17	Ages 18-21	Total
Learning disabled	20,219	747,819	973,753	74,483	1,816,274
Speech impaired	183,021	798,887	125,139	3,666	1,110,713
Mentally retarded	20,307	198,325	328,106	75,939	622,677
Emotionally disturbed	6,245	119,538	187,847	16,778	330,408
Hard of hearing and deaf	5,456	19,424	18,571	4,695	48,081
Multihandicapped	10,697	20,129	17,336	5,981	54,063
Orthopedically impaired	7,373	17,945	17,638	4,555	47,511
Other health impaired	4,149	24,289	29,402	4,009	61,849
Visually handicapped	1,831	7,930	8,666	2,322	20,749
Deaf blind	159	380	297	151	987
Total	259,483	1,954,664	1,706,727	192,438	4,113,312

Note.　Compiled from Tables GA2–GA6, Appendix G, U.S. Department of Education (1986). *Eighth annual report to Congress on the implementation of the Education of the Handicapped Act.* This source also provides tables indicating the number of persons served under Chapter I of the 1981 Education Consolidation and Improvement Act (ECIA), previously known as PL 89-313.

in the development of the plan for services to all handicapped persons.

Figure 9.7 shows the structures involved in the development, submission, and monitoring of state and local plans for special education. Receipt of federal funds to assist with the excess cost of special education is dependent upon approval of the state plan by the Division of Assistance to States (DAS) of the Office of Special Education and Rehabilitation Services (OSERS) of the U.S. Department of Education. The SEA, in turn, is charged with approving LEA plans.

Criteria for Evaluation of State Plans

Advocates of physical education and recreation for *all* children in the least restrictive environment should consider the following when reviewing the state plan for the implementation of PL 94-142.

1. *Physical education and recreation inclusion and definition.* A basic issue is whether physical education and recreation is named as a primary or direct service (physical education) or a related service (recreation) as is stated in PL 94-142. In addition, are the appropriate definitions of these services included in this document? Obviously, the appropriate listing and interpretation of physical education and recreation will be reflected in the remainder of the document and must be checked as a necessary, but

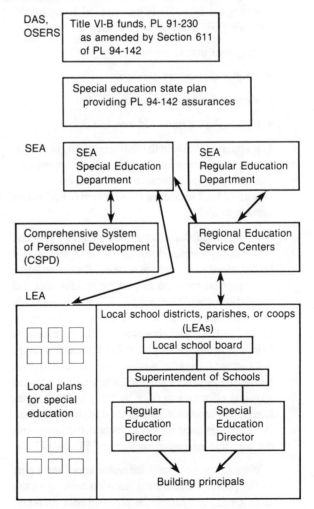

Figure 9.7　Structures involved in the development, submission, and monitoring of state and local plans for special education.

not sufficient, indication of intentions to provide these services.

2. *Reporting of services delivered in the state.* The state plan includes data regarding current and projected delivery of services to handicapped students in the state. Does this report include an indication of the number of handicapped students (by category) being served in physical education and recreation? The key to this happening is the uniform inclusion of physical education and recreation in the IEP document at the local and intermediate school levels.

3. *Monitoring and compliance.* One should determine if the plan for monitoring the compliance with the Act by school districts includes consideration for the inclusion of physical education services for each handicapped child in the IEP. Each state has a document describing the monitoring and compliance plan. Is this document consistent with the state plan?

4. *Least restrictive environment.* The state plan must specify the continuum of special education programs and services available in the state. In doing so, the following areas must be addressed:

   • Required programs

   • Required ancillary services

   • Required diagnostic services

   • Optional programs and services

Is it apparent wherein the delivery of physical education and recreation service will be provided? Also, is physical education addressed on the continuum of least restrictive environment (LRE) placement options?

5. *State organizational structure and legislative process.* The state organizational structure for education should be described in the state plan. Also, the entire legislative process for impacting on the official rules and regulations should be explained. Do you know this information and are you participating, when appropriate, in the legislative process? This process is briefly described in Figure 9.8. Physical educators must attend the public hearings and submit both oral and written testimony to facilitate optimal adapted physical education service delivery in their state. If physical education is neglected in the state plan, there appears to be no way to force compliance with the physical education sections of PL 94-142.

We must become knowledgeable about and a part of the power structure for decision making at the state level. For example, is physical education and recreation represented on

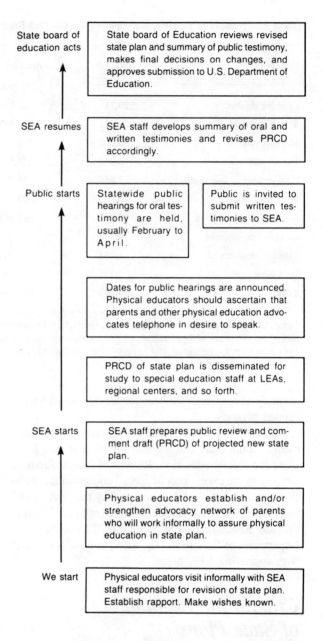

Figure 9.8   The legislative process for impacting on the rules and regulations of the state plan. This series of steps occurs every 3 years. For most states the pattern is 1985, 1988, and so forth. The resulting 3-year plan governs all aspects of SEA and LEA compliance with PL 94-142.

   • state organizational committees?

   • staff at the State Department level?

   • resource bank and manpower lists?

   • mailing lists for important notices and minutes?

Successful participation in the legislative decision-making process requires knowledge and participation in the above *plus* personal relationships with the decision-makers at various levels.

6. *Comprehensive system of personnel development (CSPD).* This is the most important section of the state plan to those of us involved in personnel development and training. Edwin Martin emphasized the importance of the CSPD as "the principal vehicle to plan for and implement the preparation of teachers and other support personnel required for the implementation of the Act" (Martin, 1980).

PL 94-142 requires each state to create a CSPD to insure cooperative statewide planning to meet personnel needs in special education, including physical education and related services. CSPD therefore sometimes refers to the written description of this system and sometimes to the persons appointed as CSPD members.

To assist SEAs in the development of CSPDs, the federal government has funded several 3-year special projects called Statewide Cooperative Planning in Special Education, which are described in lengthy reports (Schofer, 1976, 1978). The project director was Richard Schofer at the University of Missouri. Schofer, a strong advocate of physical education for the handicapped, has encouraged SEAs to include a physical educator on their CSPD. The main evaluative criterion is, Does your CSPD have physical education input?

Criteria for Evaluation of the CSPD

The CSPD is so important to teacher trainers that criteria for evaluating its worth to adapted physical education are listed separately. The CSPD outlines needs, plans, and activities in both in-service and preservice training. In light of the increasing importance to be placed on the CSPD by the Office of Special Education, several points should be considered.

1. *Participatory Planning.* Are physical education and recreation personnel involved in the planning and development of the CSPD? We need more advocates of physical education and recreation participating in the process across the nation. In Michigan, physical education representation on the State Department Council and the Committee for Planning has resulted in an Ad Hoc Committee on Physical Education and Recreation being formed to develop a 3-year plan of action to be implemented cooperatively with regular and special education. This has insured appropriate attention to our area in the state plan.

2. *Needs Assessment.* Do the needs assessment studies typically done to set priorities for preservice and in-service training in the state include physical education and recreation service personnel at four levels of training? This priority-setting is crucial as these needs become priorities with training budgets allocated to each accordingly. For example, we know that in-service training of regular physical education teachers has been identified as a priority at the national level. Is this need reflected in a continuing needs assessment for training? Can manpower data be collected as part of statewide needs assessment that will allow us to project supply and demand in our area for 3 to 5 years?

3. *Preservice Training.* PL 94-142 calls for appropriate services to be delivered to handicapped students by "qualified personnel." The definition of "qualified" is left to each state and is reflected in the teacher certification or licensing regulations. Of concern to us should be whether physical education is identified as a specialized area of programming for which personnel must be prepared with specific certification standards developed in the CSPD. This factor may require alteration of or addition to the state regulations for certification of teachers. In Michigan, a new approval category has been developed called "teacher of physical education for the handicapped," which became a part of the Special Education Code of Michigan in the fall of 1980. Practically, the next important aspect of this legislative addition (which took 2 years of almost constant monitoring and advocacy to accomplish) is that with approval status comes reimbursement to school districts from the State Department for each "approved teacher" hired. Without approval as a teacher of special education, administrations have been reluctant to hire specialists in physical education for the handicapped.

4. *In-Service Training.* Are physical education and recreation personnel involved in committees studying in-service training needs in the state? Often, these decisions are made by special educators. Physical education and recreation are not addressed as part of their deliberations. At times, somewhat aggressive action must be taken to become informed, get on appropriate mailings lists, and become involved in volunteer work. A tremendous opportunity exists for us to interpret programs and educate leaders in regular and special education through cooperative involvement by physical educators and recreators in the CSPD. Is physical education and recreation included in the competencies that will guide preservice and in-service training in your state? As a part of the CSPD in many states, core competency

Claudine Sherrill leading workshop on construction and use of homemade perceptual motor equipment.

documents are being developed by special educators— or cooperatively with regular educators—at the State Department level. When completed, these competency documents will describe the training priorities for years. It is crucial that we have input into the development of such documents.

5. *Dissemination*. Emphasis on identifying, reviewing, and disseminating promising and proven educational practices is included in the CSPD. This emphasis is not a well-known aspect of the CSPD, but it suggests a thorough assessment of practices in the state and development of resources for assistance in personnel preparation at the state and local levels. Are effective physical education and recreation programs included in this network? Are we included in human resource "banks" for training and technical assistance statewide? Are we collaborating with such nationally significant projects as the National Inservice Network, the Evaluation Training Consortium, and Project Dissemin/Action? Do you know your state facilitator as part of the National Diffusion Network?

6. *Evaluation*. As would be expected with the trend toward evidence of effectiveness of our programs

at all levels of education, evaluation is a strong component of the CSPD. The overall effectiveness of the CSPD for meeting personnel needs will be evaluated. This plan, of course, implies that physical education and recreation programs of personnel preparation (preservice and in-service) must strengthen the evaluation component to become a continuing part of this system. The national significance projects mentioned above have evaluation and evidence of effectiveness training as part of their charge and are excellent resources.

Importance of Advocacy in State Plan Process

Future trends suggest that we must move quickly to become more involved in statewide cooperative planning for education. Cooperative planning by regular and special education will be mandated. Much greater cooperative planning will occur between such agencies as the Office of Special Education Programs, the National Institute of Mental Health, Developmental Disabilities, and

Rehabilitation Services. We must be a part of these movements by being knowledgeable about and actively involved in them as they develop.

The importance of the state plan cannot be minimized for the 1980s. We have presented several criteria for the evaluation of the state plan and of the CSPD section within the state plan with particular emphasis on the implementation for physical education and recreation. The issue of active involvement in the State Department and political arenas by leaders in physical education and recreation is worthy of consideration. We must be aware of the decision-making process (as documented in the state plan) and participate actively and in large numbers if we are to maximize the delivery of appropriate services in physical education and recreation to *all* persons.

Adapted physical educators must become involved in the political process at LEA, SEA, and federal levels to assure physical education programming for all students. They must also assume initiative in teaching parents as well as professional colleagues to be advocates for physical education in the state plan legislative process. Readers are urged to follow up this section with a study of a chapter entitled "The Professional Educator and the Political Process" by Philip Jones, Department of Public Instruction, Madison, Wisconsin (Jones, 1976).

Surveys of SEA Directors Regarding Physical Education

One way of heightening awareness of adapted physical education is to periodically survey SEA directors of special education and physical education concerning service delivery in their state. Two such surveys have been conducted.

Chasey (1979) reported findings of a needs assessment survey conducted as part of his work as director of a BEH-funded special project awarded to the National Consortium on Physical Education and Recreation for the Handicapped (NCPERH). On a 25-item instrument stating characteristics of good SEA-level physical education planning and programming, significant differences ($p < .01$) were found to exist for each item between what SEA directors believed actually existed and should exist in physical education for handicapped children and youth. This research, included within the final report of the 3-year NCPERH project, was not widely disseminated. A copy of the instrument and summary of findings may be obtained from the editor of this book.

Stokes (1980) disseminated results of a 1979 survey of SEA directors conducted by the Joseph P. Kennedy, Jr. Foundation. Table 9.8 summarizes the findings of this survey and provides insight into the need for physical

educators to become more involved in the state plan legislative process. States whose SEA director answered yes to at least four of the six questions included Alabama, California, Louisiana, New Hampshire, Texas, and Wyoming. States whose SEA director answered yes to three questions included Nevada, Oregon, South Dakota, Tennessee, Utah, and Wisconsin.

In the memorandum accompanying the report from which this table was compiled, Billy Ray Stokes, Executive Director of the Programs Division of Special Education Services, Louisiana Department of Education, stated, "The results of the survey paint a bleak picture of what is taking place in the schools in regards to physical education" (Stokes, 1980, p. 1). The six questions on Table 9.7 should be posed periodically to SEA directors. Adapted physical educators within each state should be working toward a yes response to every question.

Table 9.8 Results of November 1979 Kennedy Foundation Survey of SEA Special Education Directors Regarding Physical Education Requirements of PL 94-142

Telephone interview questions	Yes	No
1. Has the state established *written* procedures, in the form of state policy or state standards, that require information concerning a child's physical education ability in its screening and/or referral process?	37%	62%
2. Has the state established *written* procedures, in the form of state policy or state standards, for conducting an evaluation in the area of physical education as part of the multi-disciplinary evaluation to determine a suspected handicapped student's physical education needs?	26%	71%
3. Do you have a written state policy or state standard that establishes a criteria for eligibility to determine when a handicapped student needs adapted or special physical education?	18%	81%
4. If evaluation results (formal or informal) indicate that a handicapped student needs special or adapted physical education, do you have established written state policy or state standards that require these needs to be addressed on the IEP?	75%	24%
5. Does your state have written certification requirements for teachers of special or adapted physical education?	9%	90%
6. Is physical education a specific written part of the state's monitoring procedures?	73%	13%

Note. This survey was based on 53 respondents: 48 states, District of Columbia, American Samoa, Guam, Virgin Islands, and Bureau of Indian Affairs (BIA). The two states that did not participate were Georgia and New Mexico. From *Memorandum Presenting Findings of November 1979 Kennedy Foundation Survey of State Special Education Directors Regarding Implementation of Physical Education Requirements of PL 94-142* by B.R. Stokes, 1980, Baton Rouge, LA: State of Louisiana Department of Education.

Annual Report of OSERS to Congress

Another method of monitoring state progress in improving adapted physical education service delivery is to review the annual report written by OSERS of the U.S. Department of Education for the U.S. Congress. The first of these reports, which range from about 150 to 200 pages, was issued in January of 1979 (U.S. Department of Health, Education, and Welfare, 1979). This

report can be obtained by contacting your U.S. Senator or House Representative or by writing OSERS. The first method is better because it creates an opportunity to encourage your congressperson to read the report and also monitor for PL 94-142 compliance.

This annual report to Congress is an excellent source of up-to-date statistics and current information about personnel needs. Illustrative of the kind of information included is Figure 9.9, which shows the increase in number of physical educators in the United States employed to teach handicapped students from 1976–1977

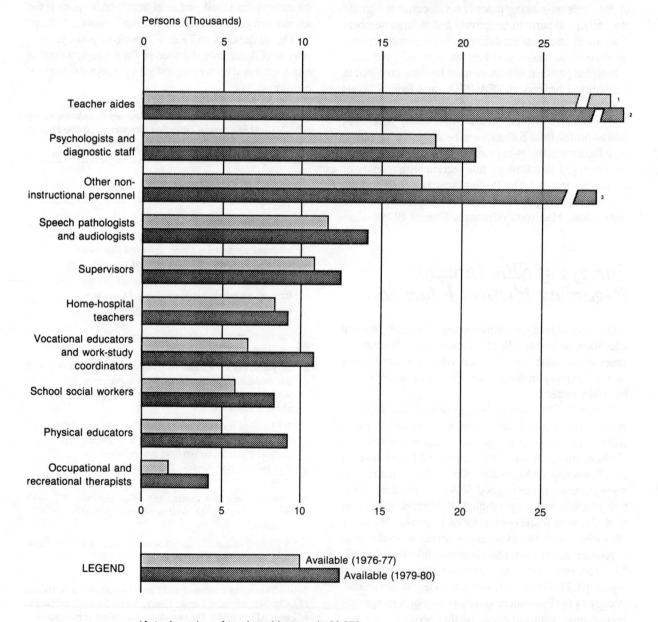

¹Actual number of teacher aides equals 66,876.
²Actual number of teacher aides equals 82,096.
³Actual number of other noninstructional personnel equals 43,459.

Figure 9.9 Total number of school staff other than special education teachers in the United States available 1976-77 as compared to 1979-80. From U.S. Department of Education, 1982, p. 11.

through 1979–1980. The statistics in the annual report often are not accurate inasmuch as they are a compilation of information included in the various state plans to OSERS. If SEA-level information on physical education needs and services is not accurate, then the input to Congress will also be incorrect. It is important, therefore, that university faculty and graduate students assist SEAs with data collection.

One section in the annual report to Congress (usually in the appendix) of particular significance to teacher trainers as well as writers of training grant proposals who must justify need for personnel in their state is the projection of personnel employed and needed. Following are excerpts from recent data (U.S. Department of Education, 1982), which shows variations within states and appears to embody gross inaccuracies that physical educators should attempt to correct. No one seems to know why the term coordinator was used rather than teacher or service deliverer.

Data such as those in Table 9.9 are used by Congress to help determine the amount of appropriations to be set aside for federal assistance to teacher training. They are also used by OSERS to estimate the number of training grants in physical education for the handicapped needed in each state. Most important, they constitute the official data source that describes the status of adapted physical education employment in public schools. Employment in private schools, residential hospitals and schools, and various agencies is another consideration as adapted physical education leaders try to estimate overall needs and services.

Some SEAs prepare annual or occasional reports to their State Congress that are similar to the annual report of OSERS to the U.S. Congress. Teacher trainers and graduate students should become informed concerning all reporting systems within LEAs and SEAs that include or should include physical education service delivery.

Advocacy Role of National Consortium on Physical Education and Recreation for the Handicapped

Advocacy for adapted physical education service delivery must be directed simultaneously upward from individuals at the grassroots level and downward from national organizations and other interest groups concerned with the formation and/or implementation of educational policy. The role of national interest groups in shaping education is particularly important before major elections and/or when the balance of power between Democrats and Republicans is relatively even (Peterson & Rabe, 1983).

Table 9.9 Physical Education Coordinators for Handicapped Students Employed and Needed in Public Schools

State	Employed 1980	Needed 1981	Needed 1982
Alabama	8	148	148
California	899	26	67
Colorado	48	3	3
Connecticut	402	11	11
Florida	100	5	7
Georgia	38	0	2
Michigan	0	0	0
Minnesota	90	39	42
New York	621	0	0
Texas	100	400	300
Washington	13	37	28
Total, all states and territories	9,271	2,146	1,683

An issue currently confronting adapted physical educators is which of several national organizations can best fulfill advocacy functions for handicapped persons. Several national groups including sport organizations for disabled persons are needed. One organization that has been particularly active in advocacy for adapted physical education is the NCPERH. One purpose of this group is to maintain rapport with the OSERS within the U.S. Department of Education and monitor its activities in physical education.

The DAS is the component responsible for dissemination of Part B, PL 94-142 monies to SEAs and for ensuring that states are carrying out the assurances provided to the federal government when they applied for forms. DAS is also responsible for approving special education state plans and for monitoring the states on their compliance with PL 94-142. From 1981 to January 1987, William Hillman was assigned to DAS. Since Hillman's retirement, this division has had no staff members whose main interest is physical education and recreation.

In its advocacy role for physical education, NCPERH recently submitted recommendations to OSERS concerning PL 94-142 implementation (Dunn, 1983). Julian Stein wrote the following section of this report, addressing eight specific ways DAS can help improve service delivery at the SEA and LEA levels.

The following represent some of the major issues, problems, and concerns for which proposed definitive actions by the DAS are requested and will be extremely helpful in ensuring compliance with Congressional intent of emphasis on physical education within The Education for All Handicapped Children Act.

1. At the present time (and in proposed regulations) there is no requirement that physical education be addressed or included in state (and consequently local) education agency plans. This creates problems because interpretations as well as the statute itself includes "instruction in physical education." Therefore it would be helpful and is certainly warranted based on legislative history and intent that the DAS require that (a) physical education be addressed in all state plans, and (b) state education agencies require local education agencies to address physical education in their plans submitted for state pass-through funds.

2. Whether physical education is formally and officially required in state plans, it is vital that the DAS include physical education in its monitoring of local education agencies. Such a procedure is necessary to ensure compliance of physical education requirements with the statute itself as well as satisfy Congressional intent for placing emphasis on physical and motor development of children with handicapping conditions in the law.

3. Few state and local education agencies include physical education on the individualized education program form. Without addressing the need for physical education services through the IEP process, it is difficult, if not impossible, for children with handicapping conditions to receive appropriate and necessary attention to physical education and their physical and motor development. In localities where physical education is addressed through the IEP form, the subject is routinely dealt with, and children are more likely to be provided with appropriate experiences as part of their guaranteed free appropriate education. Therefore, the DAS could facilitate this process by requiring that (a) physical education be included on IEP forms, (b) provisions of the position paper on IEPs be incorporated into this process, and (c) monitoring of compliance be rigidly done. In such a process, statements such as the following could be included:

- No special physical and/or motor needs; full participation in a regular physical education program.

- No special physical and/or motor needs; full participation in a regular physical education program based on listed accommodations.

- Special physical and/or motor needs necessitate listed steps and program as provided in IEP.

This procedure is consistent with the January 19, 1981, *Federal Register* position paper on IEPs (see p. 184) and leaves no doubt of what is expected or required of state and local education agencies in meeting physical education requirements under The Education for All Handicapped Children Act.

4. At the present time confusion still exists over the relationships between physical education and various therapies, including physical and occupational therapy. This confusion will undoubtedly be furthered because of changes in the proposed regulations announced August 4, 1982. The statute is very clear. "Instruction in physical education" is a defined part of special education; related services, including physical and occupational therapies, are permissible *only* if necessary for a child to benefit from a primary special education service. This statute is definitive and straightforward. The DAS would do all concerned a great service by leaving no doubts as to the intent of the statute and appropriate interpretations. Local education agencies would benefit by knowing how to handle unwarranted requests for therapy services; it would also place physical education and the therapies in intended priorities. The therapies by definitions within the statute are adjuncts to physical education, not the other way around.

5. A note after the question on physical education in the position paper on IEPs *(Federal Register*, January 19, 1981) indicated that the Department of Education was considering a position paper on physical education. The DAS would perform an important and vital need by seeing that the development of such a position paper is commissioned as soon as practically possible, followed by its release and implementation by all concerned with enforcing mandates of The Education of All Handicapped Children Act.

6. Basic to appropriate and necessary services in any area, including the physical and motor domain, is valid assessment (informal as well as formal testing). Assessment of the physical and motor characteristics and functions of children with handicapping conditions is being done (at all and/or appropriately) in too few localities. As a result many children with handicapping conditions are being misplaced in programs and activities that are inappropriate for their individual needs. It is vital that the DAS emphasize to state and local education agencies that assessment of physical and motor functions is the only way that appropriate and necessary decisions can be made about

the type of physical education program, including placement.

7. A primary need among all regular teachers, including those in physical education, is in-service opportunities. Experience has shown that regular physical education teachers are receptive to working with children having handicapping conditions when they have appropriate in-service opportunities and resource support upon which they can call. The DAS can enhance and further these processes by (a) ensuring that physical education personnel are included as integral parts of the comprehensive systems of personnel development required in the statute, and (b) encouraging implementation of the adapted/developmental/special service physical education resource specialist model to provide support services to personnel in regular education.

8. Over the years the Divisions of Personnel Preparation and Innovation and Development each had a staff person who served as a physical education advocate with responsibility for physical education and recreation programs and activities. For a short period of time such a position and responsibility was established in the DAS. The record of growth and progress in these divisions with specific and defined leadership in physical education and recreation is not debatable; it is an established fact. Similar indications of progress were noted during the time that a specific position for physical education and recreation was functioning in the DAS. It is imperative that this position be reestablished to ensure compliance in physical education at state and local levels. This position is not only justified but necessary because of the inclusion of physical education in the statute.

Summary

Throughout all of these steps and procedures, the Office of Special Education Programs in general and the DAS in particular has a great responsibility in interpreting physical education as intended and included in PL 94-142 (i.e., this is instructional, not recess, not free play, and not therapy). Physical education has been included in the statute of and for its own goals, objectives, and contributions to the growth and development of children with handicapping conditions. When physical activities are used to attain other goals and objectives, they are not fulfilling either the letter or the intent of The Education for All Handicapped Children Act. The

DAS has the responsibility of seeing that these interpretations are disseminated and implemented at state and local levels.

References

Chasey, W. (1979). *A training program in special education for SEA directors of physical education and special education* (Report No. G007603204). Washington, DC: National Consortium on Physical Education and Recreation for the Handicapped.

Clemmons, A.L. (1974). *An assessment of cost variations in selected exemplary special education programs in six selected Minnesota school districts.* Unpublished doctoral dissertation, University of New Mexico, Albuquerque.

Cohn, E. (1974). *Economics of state aid to education.* Lexington, MA: Lexington Books.

Cohn, E. (1979). *The economics of education.* Cambridge, MA: Ballinger.

Cohn, E. (1982a). Combining efficiency and equity: Optimization of resource allocation in state school systems. In W.W. McMahon & T.G. Geske (Eds.), *Financing education: Overcoming inefficiency and inequity.* Urbana, IL: University of Illinois Press.

Cohn, E. (1982b). Financing schools. In H. Mitzel (Ed.), *Encyclopedia of Educational Research: Vol. 2* (pp. 695-702). New York: The Free Press.

Coons, J., McClune, W., & Sugarman, S. (1970). *Private wealth and public education.* Cambridge, MA: Harvard University Press.

Cooper, P., & Fruge, J. (1982). *The Louisiana plan for adapted physical education.* Unpublished manuscript available from Adapted Physical Education Coordinator, Louisiana State Department of Education, Division of Special Education Services, P.O. Box 44064, Baton Rouge, LA 70804.

Databank: Expenditures and attendance in public schools in the 1970s. (1982, May 5). *Education Week.*

Dunn, J. (1983). *SEP/Funding priority needs in PE/R: National Consortium on Physical Education and Recreation for the Handicapped, Washington, DC Committee Report to SEP.* Corvallis, OR: Oregon State University.

Education: The bold quest for quality. (1983, October 10). *Time Magazine,* pp. 58-65.

Federal Register. (1981, January 19). **46**(12), 5460-5473.

Flygare, T. (1983). School finance a decade after Rodriguez. *Phi Delta Kappan, 64*(7), 477-478.

Guthrie, J. (1983). Funding an adequate education. *Phi Delta Kappan, 64*(7), 471-476.

Jones, P.R. (1976). The professional educator and the political process. In F. Weintraub, A. Abeson, J. Ballard, & M. LaVor (Eds.), *Public policy and the education of exceptional children* (pp. 284-292). Reston, VA: Council for Exceptional Children.

Marinelli, J. (1976). Financing the education of exceptional children. In F. Weintraub, A. Abeson, J. Ballard, & M. LaVor (Eds.), *Public policy and the education of exceptional children* (pp. 151-194). Reston, VA: Council for Exceptional Children.

Martin, E. (1980). *Informal letter to state directors of special education and state part b coordinators.* Washington, DC: U.S. Department of Education.

Naisbitt, J. (1982). *Megatrends: Ten new directions transforming our lives.* New York: Warner Books.

Peterson, P., & Rabe, B. (1983). The role of interest groups in the formation of educational policy: Past practice and future trends. *Teachers College Record, 84*(3), 708-729.

Rand Corporation. (1981). *Study of special education services* (ED Contract No. 300-79-0733). Santa Monica, CA: Author.

Reger, G.R. (1979). *An analysis of special education program costs in the state of Wisconsin.* Unpublished doctoral dissertation, University of Wisconsin, Madison.

Rossmiller, R., & Frohreich, L. (1979). *Expenditures and funding patterns in Idaho's programs for exceptional children.* Madison, WI: University of Wisconsin.

Rossmiller, R., Hale, J., & Frohreich, L. (1970). *Educational programs for exceptional children: Resource configurations and costs. National educational Finance Project Special Study No. 2.* Madison, WI: Dept. of Educational Administration, University of Wisconsin.

San Antonio Independent School District v. Rodriguez, 401 U.S. 1. (1973).

Schofer, R. (1976). *Statewide cooperative manpower planning in special education: A status study.* Columbia, MO: University of Missouri.

Schofer, R. (1978). *Statewide cooperative manpower planning in special education: A second status study.* Columbia, MO: University of Missouri.

Stokes, B.R. (1980). *Memorandum presenting findings of November 1979 Kennedy Foundation Survey of state special education directors regarding implementation of physical education requirements of PL 94-142.* Baton Rouge, LA: State of Louisiana Department of Education.

Thomas, M.A. (1973a). *Extent of services for exceptional children and fiscal capacity of states.* Unpublished doctoral dissertation, Indiana University, Bloomington.

Thomas, M.A. (1973b). Finance: Without which there is no special education. *Exceptional Children, 40,* 475-480.

Texas Education Agency, School Finance-Special Projects Section, Office of the Commissioner of Education. (1975). *Educational program cost differentials in Texas prepared for the Governor's office of educational research and planning.* Austin, TX: Author.

U.S. Department of Education, Office of Special Education and Rehabilitative Services. (1982). *Fourth annual report to Congress on the implementation of Public Law 94-142: The education for all handicapped children act.* Washington, DC: Author.

U.S. Department of Health, Education, and Welfare, Office of Education. (1979). *A report to Congress on the implementation of Public Law 94-142: The education for all handicapped children act.* Washington, DC: Author.

Part II

Service Delivery in the Public Schools: Functions of the Adapted Physical Education Specialist

Chapter 10

Competencies Needed to Function in the Interdisciplinary Arena

Janet A. Seaman and Lynne Heilbuth

*P*rofessionals involved in implementation of the Education for All Handicapped Children Act (PL 94-142), are well aware of the demands in this law for interdisciplinary interaction. From the onset of the service delivery process, the law requires that "the evaluation . . . be made by a multidisciplinary team" (U.S. Office of Education, *Federal Register*, 1977, section 121a.532[e]) and then suggests areas for evaluation that have implications for many professionals. The regulations further imply the interaction of groups of personnel at least yearly for the purpose of reviewing and revising each child's individualized education program (section 121a.343[d]) and at least every 3 years for reevaluation (section 121a.543[b]).

Although this legislation was passed in 1975, with the regulations signed in 1977, preparation programs have been slow to prepare future professionals for the new role of interacting in an interdisciplinary setting. In physical education, for example, the traditional model is still in effect for the beginning student teacher to locate the counselor's office, reading lab, and nurse's station. Little attention is given to learning skills required to interact with these personnel, let alone understand their philosophies and roles relative to the student. Because we are products of years of educational treatments, we supposedly *know* these concepts from firsthand experience (Christoplos & Valletutti, 1977).

The omission of interaction skills in professional preparation programs is serious enough when considering the effectiveness of future physical educators who will be serving handicapped individuals in the regular class. For adapted physical educators, this omission represents a grave injustice to future professionals who will be expected to function effectively in the interdisciplinary arena. Consider, also, the facts that special education teachers are expected to interact effectively on teams for each of their 10 to 15 students, and, physical educators often serve, on the average, 80 to 100 students (Geddes & Seaman, 1978), thereby experiencing a greater need for interaction efficiency.

Advantages of the Interdisciplinary Approach

To anyone working with individuals with special needs, serious learning problems clearly transcend the knowledge of any one individual or profession (Peters, 1977). As pointed out by Landreth, Jacquot, and Allen (1969), "A multi-faceted disability presents a complexity which must be matched with nothing less than multi-faceted remediation, the kind of remediation that only a team approach can provide" (p. 83). Under PL 94-142, in which the intent is to provide the most appropriate educa-

tion in the least restrictive environment, the collective opinion of a team should be far more prudent than the opinion of any one single professional working in isolation. As is pointed out by Kockelmans (1979), the structure of Plato's Academy was not organized according to rigidly held disciplinary boundaries. Why, then, with these educational roots, should we isolate ourselves when making decisions on mutual concerns—serving children with special needs?

Other advantages of the interdisciplinary approach described by Valletutti and Christoplos (1977) are reaped by the team members themselves. Creative approaches and professional commitment tend to be enhanced by the team interaction. Vital information for the efficacy of adapted physical education such as attending behavior, effective reinforcers, desirable practices for the use of orthotic devices, and much more can come from quality interdisciplinary interaction. Furthermore, the responsibility for decisions having ethical implications is shared by team members (Christoplos & Valletutti, 1977), bringing professionals closer together in the kindred commitment that disabilities do not occur in isolation (Landreth, Jacquot, & Allen, 1969).

Janet Seaman, California State University at Los Angeles, with Gerald Getman, optometrist and pioneer in perceptual-motor training.

Communication: The Prerequisite

Interdisciplinary communication is prerequisite to the interdisciplinary cooperation needed to identify goals for clients and to prescribe treatment priorities, sequences, strategies, implementation processes, materials, and evaluative procedures. Sharing the interdisciplinary information is an initial step toward providing a mechanism through which the collective wisdom of individual interdisciplinary team members may be marshalled for the purpose of arriving at the most logical, productive, and efficient means to remediate the difficulties that clients experience. (Valletutti & Christoplos, 1977, p. 1)

The development of awareness, knowledge, and skill in group dynamics should be prerequisite for participation on a team. Of course, specific human qualities are also needed, but these will be discussed more fully later in this chapter.

Communication skills most critical in interdisciplinary interaction include reflective listening, observing nonverbal communication, congruent message sending, and resolving the angle of a dilemma. *Communication* is defined here as shared meaning; thus, reflective listening plays an important role in assuring this outcome. A reflective listener summarizes and restates the concepts presented by the speaker to assure the speaker of having been heard. This technique further encourages the speaker to add information to his or her basic statements. The restatement tells the speaker that the meaning is being shared. Although not used all the time in a team meeting, reflective listening is invaluable when any speaker feels his or her message is not being heard.

Figures 10.1a and b graphically demonstrate the growth that can occur when professionals put forth an effort to truly communicate. The first figure (a) shows three professionals coming together for the first time using jargon and other technical language inherent in their disciplines. Such phrases may sound like this:

"He has serious artic problems."
"There is residual TLR."
"She shows serious equilibrium disorders."
"He has poor co-contraction."
"She made errors in using most plosives."
"I saw a variety of choreoform movements."

Without the use of reflective listening or each listener giving him or herself permission to ask what was meant

by a statement, there is no shared meaning. At the very least, listeners may think they understand what was said, but without checking it out, they will not know for sure. Thus professionals unable to request needed information in order to understand the message will remain at a level of communication demonstrated by Figure 10.1a.

On the other hand, individuals who are truly interested in communicating will not only define terms but will check with the listeners to determine if the definitions have been heard (and understood). Asking to be reflected (i.e., asking listeners to summarize what they understood of what was just communicated) contributes to increasing the area of shared meaning as diagrammed in Figure 10.1b and brings team members closer to a common ground for communicating.

Landreth, Jacquot, and Allen (1969) cite adequate time to discuss ideas thoroughly as being an important factor

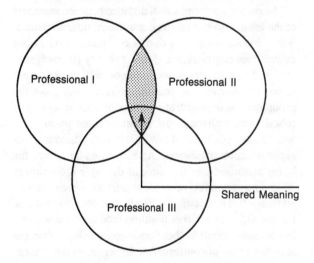

Figure 10.1a   Typical overlap of shared meaning upon entering interdisciplinary area.

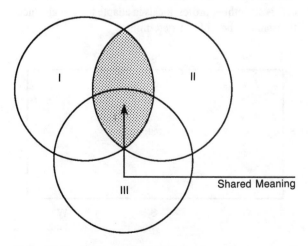

Figure 10.1b   Larger area of "jargon-free" communication after using reflective listening.

in successful team meetings. When adequate time is allowed to reflectively listen, a thorough discussion can be held. It is not uncommon for professionals using this technique to ask to be reflected or have their ideas restated if they believe the listener is not hearing the meaning of their message (Santa Clara County Superintendent of Schools, 1976). If all team members are competent in the use of this technique, far more communication takes place in considerably less time than is usually required for team meetings.

A second skill needed by team members is the ability to observe and respond to the nonverbal elements of communication. *Kinesics*, or the body language of the speaker, enhances the verbal part of the message considerably. A speaker who leans forward, gestures strongly, or is very animated in his or her facial expressions communicates much differently from one who leans back with folded arms and a straight face (Birdwhistle, 1970).

The *proximics*, or physical distance between members of the team, also can enhance or stifle group communication. Physical closeness during communication in our culture represents trust and commonality (Birdwhistle, 1970). Team members who are not willing to sit next to one another or who pull their chairs away from the group may be demonstrating a lack of trust or feeling of cohesiveness with the group. Locations in the group represent various positions of power and either encourage or suppress communication. At a rectangular table, the heads and middle of the sides of the table are stronger (s) and most conducive to communication because they allow for full eye contact with all members present (see Figure 10.2). The corner positions tend to be the weakest (w) because people in these positions are closer than the accepted range of comfortable interpersonal communication with individuals in the stronger positions; hence, their ability to take the leadership may be limited. Knowing where one feels most comfortable in a group structure and what position will most enhance ability to communicate is something professionals in adapted physical education should be able to determine.

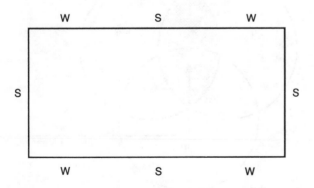

Figure 10.2 Positions of strength (S) and weakness (W) in a group.

Vocalics, or vocal intonations used by the speaker, is another aspect of nonverbal communication that should be understood by team members. Certainly the volume of speech is a quality with nearly universal meaning, but the inflections implying certainty, commitment, and competence must be understood as well. Communication is far more likely to take place when a team member states, ''I am questioning the validity of these test results because I am not convinced I got full cooperation from the child,'' than when the same message is implied while presenting scores in a faltering voice.

A third competency needed for interdisciplinary functioning is congruent message sending (Santa Clara County Superintendent of Schools, 1976). This refers to the agreement between the verbal and nonverbal aspects of the message. We have all had an experience with the familiar greeting, ''How are you today?'' knowing full well from the nonverbal aspects of the message that the speaker does not really want to know. Another example is using vocalics in saying, ''Well, don't *you* look nice today,'' when you know the speaker is mocking your attire.

Jargon or technical language should not be used unless clearly defined. ''Specialized language must not be an indirect way of saying, 'Stay out of my domain!' '' (Valletutti & Christoplos, 1977, p. 5), but often it is. The adapted physical educator should be aware that this practice often occurs and should not be afraid to ask to have words defined. Adapted physical educators must be sensitive to the congruence between the verbal and nonverbal aspects of their messages in order to be a credible part of an interdisciplinary team. Even such factors as being organized for the meeting and having each student's performance levels clearly in mind foster communication in their contribution to the congruency of the message delivered.

The *angle of a dilemma* is a situation in which team members have differing opinions on the solution to a problem. Resolving the angle of a dilemma (Santa Clara County Superintendent of Schools, 1976) incorporates all the previously discussed skills for cementing a plan for individuals with special needs brought before an interdisciplinary team. Reflective listening is needed to allow each speaker to totally explain his or her point of view and rationale for suggested solutions. Then an objectively determined list of possible solutions to the problem can be made with each team member making his or her contribution. The group can prioritize the list into the most desirable, practical, or feasible solutions until a decision is reached that all team members agree is most appropriate. Under PL 94-142, so many alternatives are available for meeting the needs of handicapped individuals that solutions should always be possible (Seaman & DePauw, 1982).

Without interdisciplinary teams to serve the handicapped, services overlap and confusion arises as to the responsibility for particular specialized services (Valletutti & Christoplos, 1977). Interdisciplinary team members should be viewed as individuals with insights and skills that are necessary to contribute to the group's functioning (Landreth et al., 1969). "Interdisciplinary intervention demands a rare virtue in human interaction—the ability to cooperate among individuals who represent different professional orientations and training experiences" (Peters, 1977, p. 140). The skills for effective interdisciplinary interaction must be based on some definable human qualities, but "To fail to communicate . . . information that is pertinent and jargon-free is to fail the purposes of an interdisciplinary team" (Peters, 1977, p. 149). Thus each of these skills should be built upon the fundamental human qualities that each future professional brings to the learning environment.

Physical educators profit immensely by taking courses in interpersonal communication and personal development and by attending seminars on transactional analysis. One rarely gets good feedback from the listener, let alone a casual observer. Further study of interpersonal interaction as found in books such as *Games People Play* (Berne, 1964), *I'm OK, You're OK* (Harris, 1969), and *Coping With Difficult People* (Bramson, 1981) will help give insight into oneself and the dynamics of human interaction.

Human Qualities

Several authors have listed human qualities or behavioral characteristics that are descriptive of either effective or ineffective communicators. Effective communicators have been characterized by "openness and security" (Landreth, et al, 1969, p. 87), as having "good will, a sense of humor and freedom from status bias" (Valetutti & Christoplos, 1977, p. 3), "a substantial degree of self-confidence and minimal defensiveness" (Valetutti & Christoplos, 1977, p. 5) and "an accepting and understanding attitude toward members on a staff conference team" (Fitzsimmons, 1977, p. 282). Bass (1974) qualified "interactive effectiveness" as "showing solidarity, raising others' self-esteem, giving help and reward, showing tension release, joking, laughing, showing satisfaction, agreeing, accepting, concurring and complying" (p. 25). In summary, an effective communicator might be characterized as being open, supportive, sincere, and secure.

For example, the following is a description of productive interdisciplinary communication between an adapted physical educator, a regular physical educator, and a special educator.

PE: Susie is really doing well in my class.

SpEd: Oh really? She usually doesn't want to go to PE because she says she doesn't know what to do.

PE: She doesn't know what to do? Now that you mention it, she does sort of hang back in soccer and really doesn't get involved in the game.

SpEd: I can understand why she would hang back. She has difficulty understanding verbal instructions and, because she learns well visually, she is probably waiting to see what the others are doing.

APE: I could work with Susie more in my class on the sequence of play and strategy of the game.

PE: (to APE) Well, if you could give her extra help on the sequence and strategy, then you and I could talk before my class to see what you covered and I could use more demonstration to reinforce it.

SpEd: (to PE and APE) Could you two coordinate teaching the sequence and strategy using more demonstration? (they acknowledge) Then, when we play soccer and other games at recess, we could act out some of the rule violations to help her learn the rules better.

In this exchange, the physical educator used reflective listening that brought out more information from the special education teacher. The adapted physical educator demonstrated a true understanding of Susie's learning disorder by contributing a strategy that would work only in a smaller class executed by someone knowledgeable of the game. The special educator reflected what the other two had offered, letting them know she had heard and understood the message. All three were sincerely interested in facilitating Susie's learning. Through positive and open communication, the key factors influencing the child's performance in physical education were brought forth and discussed, resulting in appropriate program decisions.

Ineffective communicators have been characterized as "defensive" (Gibb, 1974, p. 327), "manipulative and nonempathetic" (Gibb, 1974, p. 330), "nonaccepting," and "ascending over one or more" (Fitzsimmons, 1977, p. 282). Bass (1974) described "interactive ineffectiveness" as characterized by "disagreement, rejection, withholding help, withdrawing, showing antagonism, deflating others' esteem, acting defensive or self-assertive" (p. 25). An ineffective communicator, then, might be characterized as being defensive, derisive, hypocritical, and insecure.

Following is an example of ineffective interdisciplinary communication. The purpose of the meeting, as described by the adapted physical educator, was to evaluate the child's progress in regular physical education class. The special education teacher had reported that the child did not like going to PE class.

PE: Susie is just average in skills and is always looking around not paying attention. When her team gets the soccer ball, she's always way behind trying to catch up.

SpEd: Well, Susie has problems with auditory reception, primarily with lexicon and sequencing, so she's probably trying to learn visually.

PE: Well, she just can't keep up with the other students in my class, so I think she should either be scheduled into a class with younger kids or placed in adapted PE.

APE: Susie isn't eligible for adapted PE, and besides, she needs to be in a class with other students her age.

PE: Well, she can't stay in my class. I'm going to ask for an IEP team meeting and have her placement reviewed. This just isn't working!

APE: Well, I suppose she could go into my adapted class that hour. It's a small class.

This appears to be a situation in which the adapted physical educator is withholding help (perhaps based on previous experiences) and has allowed the physical educator to dominate. The physical educator seems to be nonempathetic, dominating, and perhaps defensive about Susie's not wanting to go to class. The special educator flowered her input with jargon, then withdrew from the conversation when it was evident that there was little room for meaningful input. Neither physical educator asked the special educator what was meant by the description of Susie's learning problems, nor did the special educator ask if they understood the technical language used. Thus it appears there was little shared meaning of the implications of Susie's handicaps and how they might have been manifested in her motor behavior. This communication further afforded an inappropriate decision, which may result in placement of Susie into an adapted physical education class that is not least restrictive and will not appropriately meet her needs.

Important questions to ask ourselves, then, are, As a communicator, who am I? What qualities do I bring to a communication setting? Am I open or defensive, supportive or derisive, sincere or hypocritical, secure or insecure? Am I an asset or a detriment to an interdisciplinary team? Probably, I am not one or the other but am on a continuum affected by my perceptions of the past, present, and future (B. Myers, personal communication, August, 1979). I may also interact differently in different situations, relative to different team members or different students.

Our perceptions of past experiences—the impressions made upon us—influence our psychological set, our attitude toward present and future circumstances that we perceive as similar. More specifically, if one perceives past interdisciplinary communication experiences to be, for example, threatening, one is likely to be on guard or defensive during the next interchange (Gibb, 1974). Or, if one has experienced group interchange where one or more group members exert power over the rest of the group, one could establish a pattern of withdrawal or could rebel by being overly assertive the next time or in the next group.

Our perceptions and anticipations of the future also influence the present psychological set. One who seeks power or position may be reluctant to speak opinions that differ from persons perceived as having higher status or may be overanxious to assert views beyond what is needed to accomplish the group goal.

One's present psychological set is not only influenced by past experiences and future expectations, but by the present environment. Interdisciplinary team members who display, through verbal and nonverbal language, acceptance and respect toward other team members (toward the members' professions, knowledge, and potential contributions) inspire effective group participation by all members of the team. A supportive group communication environment fosters equal participation of members, a broad and thorough expression of knowledge from many and varied sources, creative thinking and planning, and cooperative and sound decision making. A nonsupportive group communication environment may foster unequal participation of members, a base of expressed knowledge from a few sources, narrow or status quo thinking and planning, and decision making that is limited in its effectiveness and appropriateness.

Professionals working in an interdisciplinary context must share the goal of working effectively—communicating openly, sincerely, and with a willingness to give and take. Each must be able to look at him- or herself objectively and insightfully and judge whether or not he or she is making the best possible contribution. Each must be willing to apply the criteria of an effective communicator—

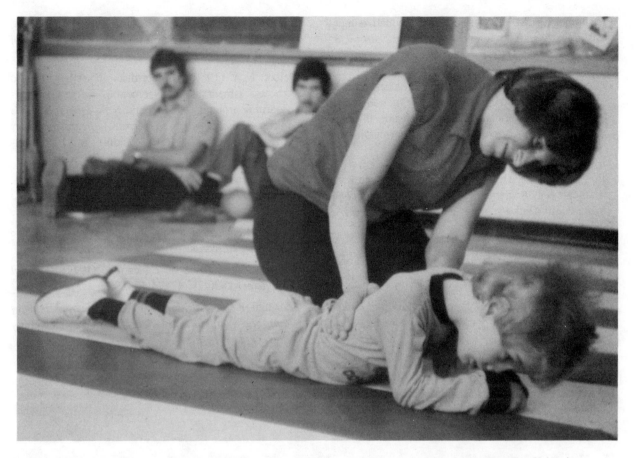

Lynne Heilbuth, Texas public school adapted physical education specialist until 1987, now teaching at San Diego State University.

open, secure, with a sense of humor, confident, non-defensive, accepting, understanding, supportive, and sincere. Once this evaluation is complete, each must be willing to improve on those qualities found lacking. In the absence of such an evaluation, objectivity, or willingness, then careful consideration should be given to reevaluating one's career goals.

Who are we? What do we offer interdisciplinary communication? Do we possess the knowledge and techniques of effective communication coupled with human qualities that enable us to be competent, capable persons in the interdisciplinary arena? Whether our role is that of practitioner in the field involved in interdisciplinary teamwork, or that of a trainer of practitioners, or both, are we not obligated to direct ourselves and facilitate others toward effective interdisciplinary communication? Whether a practitioner or a trainer of practitioners, the ultimate concern is to offer the best service for the handicapped individual. Effective interdisciplinary communication provides a process for holistic education for a whole child. A process is stated by Landreth et al. (1969) in which we "match the dynamic inner structure of the

child with an equally dynamic team structure'' (p. 25). The whole truly *can* be more than the sum of the parts.

References

Bass, B. (1974). The definition of a "group." In R.S. Cathcart & L.A. Samovar (Eds.), *Small group communication* (2nd ed., pp. 19-27). Dubuque, IA: Wm. C. Brown.

Berne, E. (1964). *Games people play.* New York: Grove Press.

Birdwhistle, R.L. (1970). *Kinesics and context.* Philadelphia: University of Pennsylvania Press.

Bramson, R.M. (1981). *Coping with difficult people.* New York: Ballantine Books.

Christoplos, F., & Valletutti, P.J. (1977). Education. In F. Christoplos & P.J. Valletutti (Eds.), *Interdisciplinary approaches to human services* (pp. 81-92). Baltimore: University Park Press.

Fitzsimmons, R.M. (1977). Fostering productive inter-disciplinary staff conferences. *Academic Therapy, 3*, 281-287.

Geddes, D., & Seaman, J.A. (1978). *Competencies of adapted physical educators in special education.* Reston, VA: American Alliance for Health, Physical Education, Recreation and Dance, Information and Research Utilization Center.

Gibb, J.R. (1974). Defensive communication. In R.S. Cathcart & L.A. Samovar (Eds.), *Small group communication* (2nd ed., pp. 327-333). Dubuque, IA: Wm. C. Brown.

Harris, T.A. (1969). *I'm ok, you're ok.* New York: Harper & Row.

Kockelmans, J.J. (1979). *Interdisciplinary and higher education.* University Park, PA: Pennsylvania State University Press.

Landreth, G.L., Jacquot, W.S., & Allen, L. (1969). A team approach to learning disabilities. *Journal of Learning Disabilities, 2*, 82-87.

Peters, N.A. (1977). An interdisciplinary approach to the assessment and management of severe language-learning problems. In W. Otto, N.A. Peters, & C.W. Peters (Eds.), *Reading problems: An interdisciplinary perspective* (pp. 140-150). Reading, MA: Addison-Wesley.

Santa Clara County Superintendent of Schools. (1976). *Communication and other good things.* San Jose, CA: Author.

Seaman, J.A., & DePauw, K.P. (1982). *The new adapted physical education.* Palo Alto, CA: Mayfield.

United States Office of Education. (1977). *Federal Register, 163*(42), 42474-42518.

Valletutti, P.J., & Christoplos, F. (1977). *Interdisciplinary approaches to human services.* Baltimore: University Park Press.

Chapter 11

Assessment: A Foundation

Janet A. Seaman

No area of professional preparation is more important in adapted physical education than assessment. In this chapter, the relationship of assessment to the various responsibilities of the adapted physical education specialist is described, including implementation of legislative mandates, funding, research, and in-service training. Also presented in this chapter is a model to explain the relationship between testing, measurement, and assessment and decision making in the PL 94-142 evaluation process.

Generally speaking, adapted physical educators use assessment, evaluation, and measurement to classify students according to ability, exempt students from some activities, predict future ability, determine achievement, measure improvement, motivate students, assign grades, evaluate teaching, justify programs, and evaluate the curriculum (Barrow & McGee, 1979; Baumgartner & Jackson, 1981; Safrit, 1980). Safrit also mentions the diagnosis of motor and fitness weaknesses as a purpose of measurement. Barrow and McGee go further in suggesting the use of measurement to identify individual differences and reveal individual needs. The chronology suggested by Barrow and McGee is compatible with the mandates of legislation. They state, ''When needs have been identified, a program can be planned to meet them. Thus, measurement is indispensable in planning a program to meet individual needs, . . . and in recognizing when such needs have been met'' (1979, p. 10).

Legislative Mandates

Public Law 94-142, Education for All Handicapped Children Act of 1975, is the first federal mandate involving physical education service delivery and one of the few pieces of legislation calling for accountability of educational services to the consumer. One of the striking features of this law is that it requires that educational services be determined and delivered on the basis of each child's individual needs rather than on the basis of predetermined, categorical age- or sex-linked needs recommended in professional educational literature. Each child's individual needs are to be determined by a variety of methods, including an assessment of current levels of performance.

The requirements of PL 94-142 include the use of tests and materials ''tailored to assess specific areas of educational need . . . including motor abilities'' (U.S. Office of Education, *Federal Register*, 1977, section 121a.532). The results of the measurement must be used to make ''(a) A statement of child's present levels of educational performance; and (b) A statement of annual goals, in-

Janet Seaman administering fine motor test to 3-year-old. Seaman is senior author of *The New Adapted Physical Education*.

cluding short term instructional objectives" (section 121a.346). This section of regulations, of course, implies that the results of measurement must be interpreted in order to project reasonable levels of expectation for 1 year hence. The section goes further to require, "(c) A statement of the specific special education . . . services" (section 121a.346) of which physical education is a part. Finally, the regulations require "(e) Appropriate objective criteria and evaluation procedures . . . for determining . . . whether the short term objectives are being achieved" (section 121a.346).

This concept of using test results for determining a student's approximation to stated objectives is a relatively new concept to most physical educators and an application of measurement given only the most cursory treatment in many texts. The establishment of a new direction in assessment of individual needs is viewed, by this author, as one of the most pressing issues confronting adapted physical education today. Without the ability to quantify and justify the place of motor performance in the lives of handicapped children, the resolution of other issues in the discipline of adapted physical education is purely academic.

PL 94-142 mandates that all children between the ages of 3 and 21 years who meet the criteria for at least 1 of 11 categories of handicapping conditions receive physical education services. Each child must first be given the opportunity to participate in the regular physical education program unless she or he is either (a) enrolled full-time in a separate facility, or (b) needs specially designed physical education, as prescribed in the child's individualized education program (IEP) (*Federal Register*, August 23, 1977, section 121a.346).

The IEP must include the child's current level of performance as well as annual goals and short-term objectives. The current level of performance is determined by a process of data gathering and interpretation, but the law is unclear as to what this process is because the terms *testing* and *measurement* are also used in the legislation. The model described in this chapter is an attempt to clarify the meaning of these terms in relation to adapted physical education service delivery.

Clarification of Terms

The use of the term *evaluation* in PL 94-142 does not follow the classic definition found in professional literature. Section 121a.500 states that "Evaluation" means "procedures used . . . to determine whether a child is handicapped and the nature and extent of the special education and related services that the child needs. The term means procedures used selectively with an individual child and does not include basic tests administered to or procedures used with all children in a school, grade, or class."

The term *assessment*, which is often used interchangeably with *evaluation*, is not defined in the regulations. In order to bridge the gap between the law's explanation of evaluation, definitions in professional literature, and practices in the field, adapted physical educators need a model depicting interpretation and application of such terms as evaluation, assessment, measurement, testing, decision making, planning, and implementation. Once the use and relationship of these terms can be generally agreed upon, more effective communication can take place. Ultimately, a certain amount of universality will improve the credibility of adapted physical education as an emerging discipline and enhance its chance for permanence in the broad spectrum of educational services.

The terms traditionally associated with quantifying motor performance include testing, measurement, and evaluation. These terms historically have been used to describe the processes of classifying, grading, and diagnosing students. Classification of students occurs in general physical education classes when grouping students for teams. Ultimately, classifications become grades that are assigned as summative forms of evaluation at the end of a reporting period such as a semester or school year. Diagnosing has historically taken the form of identifying students with problems for the purpose of directing them out of general physical education and into such specialized programs as education or providing for exemption.

Evaluation, the one term defined in the law, has been identified by most authors in physical education as including testing and/or measurement (Barrow & McGee, 1979; Baumgartner & Jackson, 1981). Testing has been uniquely defined for use in adapted physical education as a data-gathering technique that uses tools or specific procedures for systematizing observations (Seaman & DePauw, 1982). This definition is much broader than the conceptualization of the term that is often used in physical education. As used here, *testing* includes data gathered from teacher or parent observation, self-reports, direct measures, and anecdotal records as well as scores obtained from formal testing. *Measurement*, also a technique of evaluation, is the result of the use of the testing technique. "Measurement determines the degree to which an individual possesses a defined characteristic" (Baumgartner & Jackson, 1981, p. 1). The evaluation process occurs when the results of measurement are compared with established standards to facilitate rational decisions. In this regard, some authors use the terms *evaluation* and *assessment* interchangeably (Barrow & McGee, 1979) just as the regulations of PL 94-142 do.

Safrit (1980) is one of the few authors in physical education who distinguishes between assessment and evaluation. She uses *assessment* as the larger, global process that includes measurement and evaluation. The use of the term *evaluation* as the global process encompassing assessment, measurement, testing, and decision making seems more appropriate in the implementation of PL 94-142 than the term *assessment*.

Several authors in recent years have attempted to develop a precise language relative to the process of assessment. Bruininks (1982) considers assessment as the process that improves precision in decision making. Seaman and DePauw (1982) state, "assessment involves *interpreting* the results of measurement for the purpose of making decisions about placement, program planning, and performance objectives. As used with students with special needs, assessment is formative in nature" (p. 147). More recently, Werder and Kalakian (1985) "regard assessment as the necessary link in planning instruction" (p. v). They further go on to state that "Assessment thus becomes the key component in fulfilling the letter and spirit of PL 94-142" (p. 7). Assessment means the interpretation of the results of measurement generated through testing, for the purpose of decision making, planning, and evaluation.

A Model of Relationships

Figure 11.1 presents a graphic representation of the relationship between testing, measurement, assessment, and decision making in the PL 94-142 evaluation process as it has been operationalized by some adapted physical educators. First introduced as a model by Seaman (1979), this

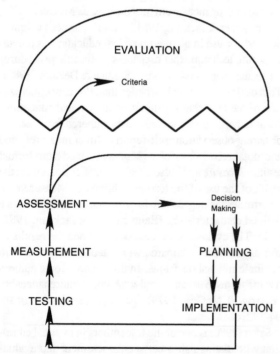

Figure 11.1   A model to explain the relationship between testing, measurement, and assessment and decision making in the PL 94-142 evaluation process. *Note.* From *The New Adapted Physical Education* (p. 144) by J. Seaman and K. DePauw, 1982, Palo Alto, CA: Mayfield.

representation has incorporated assessment as a "necessary link"—that step in improving the precision for decision making leading to planning and implementing an individualized program or comparison with external criteria for the purpose of evaluation. The data gathering act results in a measurement of a specific parameter. These results are then interpreted relative to known laws, principles, and theories. In some instances, the results are judged to be significant enough to be considered facts or criteria and can be used in the future as the foundation for evaluation. In most instances, however, the interpretation of results yields questions about which decisions must be made. This is the assessment process. Again, known laws, principles, and theories must be considered, including any new discoveries since the process was begun. A plan or revised plan is developed and implemented, and the assessment process begins again. As stated by Womer, "The ultimate goal of assessment is to provide information that can be used to benefit the educational process through improved decision making" (1970, p. 1). This, of course, is the goal of adapted physical education as well.

A Model for Interpretation

With the foregoing model in mind, it is possible to further interpret, communicate, and apply other sections of the law to field use. Some elements on which the law is very clear can be found in section 121a.532, Evaluation Procedures.

> State and local educational agencies shall insure, at a minimum, that:
>
> (a) Tests and other evaluation materials:
>
> (1) Are provided and administered in the child's native language or other mode of communication, unless it is clearly not feasible to do so;
>
> (2) Have been validated for the specific purpose for which they are used; and
>
> (3) Are administered by trained personnel in conformance with the instructions provided by their producer.

The meaning of the word *tests* in this PL 94-142 passage is the same as that used in Figure 11.1 to refer to any and all data-gathering procedures. The use of the word *validated*, however, is vague as to whether the validation is to apply to the evaluation process or the assessment process. Some data-gathering procedures (tests) have enormous validity for measuring a specific parameter among nonhandicapped populations, but questionable validity for handicapped students. As an evaluation tool, the procedure may be perfectly appropriate but of little value for decision making if used as part of the assessment process.

PL 94-142 goes on to state that the tests and other evaluation materials and procedures should include those that were tailored to assess specific areas of educational need and not just yield a general score of overall ability such as an intelligence quotient. The data collection instruments must also be selected and administered to best measure what the tests purport to measure and not reflect the child's impaired sensory, manual, or speaking skills unless these are the parameters being measured (this was discussed in the previous paragraph). Furthermore, no single procedure is to be used "as the sole criterion for determining an appropriate educational program for a child" (U.S. Office of Education, *Federal Register*, 1977, section 121a.532[d]). The evaluation is, of course, to be made by a multidisciplinary team having at least one member who is knowledgeable in the area of suspected disability. Part (f) of this section concludes that the child should be assessed in all areas related to the suspected disability, including motor abilities. The use of the terms *evaluation* and *assessment* in this section of PL 94-142 appears to refer to the decision-making step in those processes. Clearly, a multidisciplinary team is to take the measurements obtained by each of them and collectively make a decision about each child's program. To assess in all areas related to the suspected disability implies gathering data and making decisions about each aspect of each child's program, including motor abilities.

Certain protections are built into the assessment process cited in section 300.533 of PL 94-142, which require that, in interpreting assessment data and in making placement decisions, each public agency shall

- draw upon information from a variety of sources, including aptitude and achievement tests, teacher recommendations, physical condition, social or cultural background, and adaptive behavior;

- ensure that information obtained from all these sources is documented and carefully considered;

- ensure that the placement decision is made by a group of persons, including persons knowledgeable about the child, the meaning of the assessment data, and the placement options; and

- ensure that the placement decision is made in conformity with the least restrictive environment rules in sections 300.550 to 300.554 (California State Department of Education, 1983).

Here again the use of the term *assessment data* goes a bit afield of its usual application. The section obviously

refers to the data provided for making decisions and may be obtained in a variety of ways.

A Model for Further Development

To enhance the status of the discipline of adapted physical education in the academic community, quantitative thinking must permeate the profession. Just as accounting is the language of business, so must assessment be the language of adapted physical education in order for concrete results to be identified with its domain. The accountant provides quantitative information about a business to both consumers and managers of the business so they can make rational decisions. In the case of the consumers, the decision may focus on whether or not to buy more stock in the business. In the case of the managers, the decision may involve whether or not to market a new product. Without such quantifiable information, the decision making process will be less sound. Thus the assessment model presented earlier in Figure 11.1 must be applied to all responsibilities of adapted physical educators in order to facilitate more rational, quantitative decision making.

Assessment for Funding

The area of funding covers a broad spectrum of issues and therefore is addressed first. Nearly all agencies, public and private, administering grant programs require the demonstration of need or rationale for any project submitted. So-called expert opinion or even consumer support is far less weighty justification than hard data. The assessment of needs, trends, and issues is important documentation for nearly any project submitted for funding.

Funding sources supporting personnel preparation demand records of the numbers who are going to be affected by the proposed project. The cascading influence of the proposed preservice or in-service project should realistically reflect the number of handicapped individuals who will ultimately profit from the project should the monies be awarded. Therefore, a needs assessment should include data on the personnel who make up the target population, incidence figures, and actual prevalence of conditions.

Proposed research on various methods and techniques needed to implement current legislation requires an assessment of the results of other similar research. In addition, the measurement and evaluation of the efficacy of the proposed treatment plan through a pilot study of ongoing programs can greatly enhance the credibility of the proposed project.

Other types of funded projects such as the development of criteria for placement, demonstration projects for the delivery of services, and research pertaining to the social issues surrounding the education of handicapped students all require the gathering and interpretation of data. With this assessment process and its influence on decision making for the purpose of planning new, fundable projects, the grant writer may find help in making order out of chaos in the world of external funding.

Assessment for Research

One can readily see, by looking at the model in Figure 11.1, that the research undertaking is a definite kin. Whether the research is funded, of personal interest to the investigator, or a student project, it still contains the elements of assessment previously discussed. Adapted physical educators must, however, begin producing research that will take our unique body of knowledge one step further toward conclusive findings in order to generate criteria for evaluation.

Philosophically, we must prepare ourselves to accept and value replicated research in adapted physical education. This research must be done in order to test theories that have been floating around the discipline for years, but have never been established as principles. We would never think of taking medication that has been shown to be effective in 95% of the cases in one study of 20 white, male rats. Why, then, do we continue to accept as fact results of one human study in which a theory of motor learning has been tested using one group of institution-alized mentally retarded individuals? We must be prepared to use the assessment process in research, as used by great scientists before us, to interpret the results of research, make appropriate decisions for revision, and then retest the theory. Until this cycle has been repeated many times, we will never generate criteria for evaluation in which we can put a high degree of confidence.

Furthermore, we must be patient in our search for criteria. We must be willing to manipulate only one variable at a time in efficacy studies, for example, in order to separate out the factors of change. Most master's and even doctoral level research results in raising more questions than are answered. The aura that has permeated educational research somehow precludes investigators, in most cases, from replicating their research after manipulating the variable or conditions that caused them to raise the questions. Scientists whose names are attached to laws and various other phenomena of our universe are people who tested and retested their theories under a multitude of conditions until their measurement of the phenomenon consistently showed the same results that could then serve as criteria for evaluation.

Assessment for In-Service Training

Assessment as a foundation for in-service training is actually required by law. Section 121a.382 of the regulations for PL 94-142, requires that each state conduct "an annual needs assessment to determine if a sufficient number of qualified personnel are available" (U.S. Office of Education, *Federal Register*, 1977, section 121a.382 [b] [1]) to determine what their needs are and to use that information to initiate personnel development programs. The states are further directed to "enter into contracts with institutions of higher education" (U.S. Office of Education, *Federal Register*, 1977, section 121a.382 [d]) and/or other agencies to carry out experimental or innovative programs, develop or modify instructional materials, and disseminate information from research and demonstration projects.

Although this requirement of assessment is made of each state, the concept should be embraced by all who speak on behalf of adapted physical education. Whether you are a university professor planning formal in-service sessions for physical educators or an adapted physical educator planning in-service sessions for classroom teachers, the process is the same. You must somehow do a needs assessment in order to decide how to plan your presentation. When reporting test results to parents, for example, you essentially follow the same process. You describe the data in different terms to parents, however, than you would to a colleague. In the field of speech communication, this process is called audience analysis. Although it may be done using qualitative rather than quantitative data, it still fits under the general rubric of assessment.

Summary and Conclusions

For an emerging discipline like adapted physical education, it is essential to establish sound methods and procedures and utilize mechanical and technical tools that are tested and respected by related disciplines (Nixon, 1967). Adapted physical educators must embrace quantitative thinking in order to generate an identifiable domain, a unique integrity, and a precise language in order to meet these and other criteria of a discipline (Nixon, 1967).

The link between measurement and decision making involving the interpretation of data is assessment. An assessment model is presented that has application to all issues confronting adapted physical educators today and attempts to broaden the application of the terms *testing* and *assessment*. Heretofore, testing has referred to a formal procedure of data gathering with the resulting measurement most commonly used to measure pupil performance. The term evaluation has been reserved for a more global critique of program effectiveness or comparison of measurements against predetermined criteria or standards.

The proposed model provides the adapted physical educator with a mechanism for decision making and planning that is vital to all aspects of adapted physical education. This mechanism is the interpretation of measurements called assessment. The use of more quantifiable procedures, too, will help move the discipline closer to the establishment of criteria for evaluation. The use of time-worn respected technology offers much to enhance the status of adapted physical education within the spectrum of special education and related services. Therefore, we must seek to quantify our existence if we are to pursue new directions and emerge as a respected discipline.

Editor's Note

This chapter by Seaman illustrates the work involved in creating, explaining, and justifying a model (see chapter 7 for additional information on this process). A model depicting relationships between testing, measurement, assessment, decision making, and evaluation is shown in Figure 11.1. Do you agree or disagree with this model? Can you write a scholarly paper justifying your beliefs?

Most authorities believe that adapted physical education specialists should complete one or more graduate courses specifically in evaluation and assessment in adapted physical education. Such a course should include units on program evaluation and assessment of opinions and attitudes (see chapter 17) as well as testing, measuring, and assessing handicapped and clumsy students. Most adapted physical education textbooks include strong units or chapters on assessment of individual students. Additionally, two books are available.

- American Alliance for Health, Physical Education, Recreation, and Dance (1976). *Testing for impaired, disabled, and handicapped individuals*. Washington, DC: Author.

- Werder, J., & Kalakian, L. (1985). *Assessment in adapted physical education*. Minneapolis: Burgess.

A major problem in developing a course on assessment is determining which data collection instruments should be covered and in how much detail. Table 11.1, based on a national survey by Ulrich (1985), lists the 12 standard-

Table 11.1 Standardized Assessment Tests Most Frequently Used by Physical Educators Working With Handicapped Students (Ulrich, 1985)

Rank	Assessment test
1	Bruininks-Oseretsky Test of Motor Proficiency (Bruininks, 1978)
2	AAHPER Special Fitness Test for Mildly Mentally Retarded (AAHPER, 1976)
3	Brigance Diagnostic Inventory (Brigance, 1978)
4	Hughes Basic Gross Motor Assessment (Hughes, 1979)
5	Project ACTIVE (Vodola, 1976)
6.5	Purdue Perceptual Motor Survey (Roach & Kephart, 1966)
6.5	AAHPERD Health Related Fitness Test (AAHPERD, 1980)
8	I CAN (Wessel, 1976)
9.5	OSU-SIGMA (Loovis & Ersing, 1979)
9.5	AAHPERD Youth Fitness Test (AAHPERD, 1976)
11	Denver Developmental Screening Test (Frankenburg & Dodds, 1967)
12	AAHPERD Fitness Test for Moderately Retarded (Johnson & Londeree, 1976)

ized assessment tests most frequently used by physical educators working with handicapped students. Other tests, too new to be well known, that merit consideration include

- Folio, M.R., & Fewell, R. (1983). *Peabody developmental motor scales and activity cards*. Allen, TX: DLM Teaching Resources.

- Ulrich, D. (1985). *Tests of gross motor development*. Austin, TX: Pro-Ed Publishers.

- Winnick, J., & Short, F. (1985). *Physical fitness testing of the disabled: Project UNIQUE*. Champaign, IL: Human Kinetics.

Supplementary texts for assessment courses recommended because of their strong coverage of assessment methodology are

- Dunn, J., Morehouse, J., & Fredericks, H.D.B. (1985). *Physical education for the severely handicapped: A systematic approach to a data based gymnasium*. Austin, TX: Pro-Ed Publishers.

- Morris, G.S.D. (1980). *How to change the games children play* (2nd ed.). Minneapolis: Burgess.

Sources for standarized tests most frequently used by physical educators working with handicapped students (see Table 11.1) are included in the following list:

- American Alliance for Health, Physical Education, and Recreation. (1976). *AAHPER youth fitness test manual*. Washington, DC: Author.

- American Alliance for Health, Physical Education, Recreation and Dance. (1980). *Health related physical fitness test manual*. Washington, DC: Author.

- American Alliance for Health, Physical Education, and Recreation. (1976). *Special fitness test manual for the mildly mentally retarded* (2nd ed.). Washington, DC: Author.

- Brigance, A. (1978). *The Brigance diagnostic inventory of early development*. Worburn, MA: Curriculum Associates.

- Bruininks, R.H. (1978). *Bruininks-Oseretsky test of motor proficiency manual*. Circle Pines, MN: American Guidance Service.

- Frankenburg, W., & Dodds, J. (1967). The Denver developmental screening test. *The Journal of Pediatrics*, **71**, 181-191.

- Hughes, J. (1979). *Hughes basic gross motor assessment manual*. Yonkers, NY: G.E. Miller.

- Johnson, L., & Londeree, B. (1976). *Motor testing manual for the moderately mentally retarded*. Washington, DC: American Alliance for Health, Physical Education, and Recreation.

- Loovis, M., & Ersing, W. (1979). *Assessing and programming gross motor development for children* (2nd ed.). Loudonville, OH: Mohigan.

- Roach, E., & Kephart, N. (1966). *The Purdue Perceptual-Motor Survey*. Columbus, OH: Charles C. Merrill.

- Ulrich, D. (1985). *Standardized motor assessment tests used by adapted physical education teachers*. Unpublished manuscript available from author at Physical Education Department, Indiana University, Bloomington, IN 47401.

- Vodola, T. (1976). *Project ACTIVE maxi-model kit*. Oakhurst, NJ: Township of Ocean Park.

- Wessel, J. (1976). *I CAN: Locomotor and rhythmic skills*. Northbrook, IL: Hubbard Scientific.

- Wessel, J. (1976). *I CAN: Object control*. Northbrook, IL: Hubbard Scientific.

References

Barrow, H.M., & McGee, R. (1979). *A practical approach to measurement in physical education* (3rd ed.). Philadelphia: Lea and Febiger.

Baumgartner, T.A., & Jackson, A.S. (1981). *Measurement for evaluation in physical education* (2nd ed.). Boston: Houghton Mifflin.

Bruininks, R.H. (1982, September 23). Presentation delivered to statewide annual leadership conference on adapted physical education. Camp Courage, Mable Lake, MN.

California State Department of Education. (1983). *California special education programs: A composite of laws*. Sacramento: Office of Special Education.

Nixon, J.E. (1967). The criteria of a discipline. *Quest*, **9**, 42-48.

Safrit, M.J. (1980). *Evaluation in physical education: Assessing motor behavior* (2nd ed.). Englewood Cliffs, NJ: Prentice-Hall.

Seaman, J.A. (1979). *Assessment: A foundation*. Unpublished manuscript.

Seaman, J.A., & DePauw, K.P. (1982). *The new adapted physical education*. Palo Alto, CA: Mayfield.

United States Office of Education. (1977). Education of handicapped children. *Federal Register*, **42**(163), 42474-42518.

Werder, J.K., & Kalakian, L.H. (1985). *Assessment in adapted physical education*. Minneapolis: Burgess.

Womer, F.B. (1970). *What is national assessment?* Denver: National Assessment of Educational Progress.

Chapter 12

Individualized Educational Programming

Claudine Sherrill

*I*ndividualized educational programming (IEP) is one of several broad service areas for which adapted physical education specialists are responsible. Although the importance of individualizing and personalizing physical education instruction has long been recognized, it was the enactment of PL 94-142 that made individualized educational programming a legal requirement in the education of handicapped students. The August 23, 1977, issue of the *Federal Register* provides the following information about IEPs under Subpart C (Services).

INDIVIDUALIZED EDUCATION PROGRAMS

121a.340   Definition

121a.341   State educational agency responsibility

121a.342   When individualized education programs must be in effect

121a.343   Meetings

121a.344   Participants in meetings

121a.345   Parent participation

121a.346   Content of individualized education program

121a.347   Private school placements

121a.348   Handicapped children in parochial or other private schools

121a.349   Individualized education program—accountability (*Federal Register*, 1977, p. 42477)

Adapted physical educators should know what the federal law and their state plan says about each of these topics. They should also know procedural safeguards that must be followed and understand due process.

Definitions of IEP

IEP may refer to either the individualized education program or plan (a written statement) or to individualized educational programming (a planning process or management system, see Figure 12.1). The legal bases for these varying uses of the term are found in PL 94-142.

- *As a written statement.* Section 121a.340 of the *Federal Register* states: "As used in this part, the term 'individualized education program' means a written statement for a handicapped child that is developed and implemented in accordance with 121a.341-121a.349." The content of this written statement is specified in section 121a.346 as follows:

(a) A statement of the child's present levels of educational performance

(b) A statement of annual goals, including short term instructional objectives

(c) A statement of the specific special education and related services to be provided to the child, and the extent to which the child will be able to participate in regular educational programs

(d) The projected dates for initiation of services and the anticipated duration of the services

(e) Appropriate objective criteria and evaluation procedures and schedules for determining, on at least an annual basis, whether the short term instructional objectives are being achieved

The IEP is thus an official special education document. By law, it must encompass physical education. Thus inclusion is generally a mention of the type of physical education placement (regular, adapted, or some combination) under (c) and a description of psychomotor functioning under (a). Most IEP forms do not have space for a complete delineation of physical education goals, objectives, and services. Many physical educators therefore develop physical education IEPs to include such detail. The physical education IEP discussed in several textbooks (Geddes, 1981; Sherrill, 1986; Wessel, 1977) should not be confused with the legally mandated IEP.

- A *planning process* or *sequence of procedures*. Mandated by PL 94-142 and directed toward finding unserved handicapped students, admitting them to the school district's special education program, providing special services, reviewing progress periodically (at least once annually), and subsequently dismissing students from special education. Figure 12.1 describes this process as it relates to adapted physical education.

- As a *management system* or *philosophical approach*. For individualizing instruction based on the assessed needs of each learner. This does not refer to a 1:1 pupil/teacher ratio but rather to a system for individualization within a group or class setting. Among the physical educators who have used this meaning are Thomas Vodola and Janet Wessel in Projects ACTIVE and I CAN respectively.

Responsibility of LEA and SEA

Regardless of whether IEP is conceptualized as a process, a management system, or a written statement, it is governed by special education (usually the special education director of the local education agency [LEA]). This person

Phase 1 Child Find	District-wide screening process for all children in all school subjects. (1) Usually done by mainstream physical education instructor or classroom teacher.	(2) Usually conducted at beginning of school year but can occur anytime. (3) Often informal, resulting from observation and/or conference with parent.	(4) Parent can initiate process instead of teacher.
Phase 2 Initial Data Collection and Pre-IEP Meeting	Begins with referral for further testing to determine if adapted physical education/special ed services are needed. (1) As result of Phase 1, Child Find, anyone can request special education director to determine pupil's eligibility for special services.	(2) Contact parents for consent to test and/or collect eligibility data. (3) Data collection usually done by mainstream physical education instructor	(4) Pre-IEP meeting to determine need for more extensive testing. (5) Written report of findings.

Phase 3 Admission to Special Education, including Adapted Physical Education	**Comprehensive Individual Assessment**
	Initiated by written report signed by referral committee—see Phase 2.
	(1) Special education director assigns persons to do assignment.
	(2) Notification of rights to parents.
	(3) Obtain parent consent for comprehensive assessment by multidisciplinary team.
	(4) Comprehensive individual assessment with psychomotor part done by adapted physical education specialist.
		IEP Meeting
		(1) procedural safeguards must be observed in planning meeting.
		Consider
		(a)—who must be present
		(b)—time and place and
		(c)—native language
		(2) Presentation and analysis of assessment data by different team members
		(3) Agreement on present level of functioning
			(4) Decision making concerning
			(a)—goals and objectives
			(b)—services
			   (i)—educational placement
			   (ii)—interventions
			   (iii)—et cetera
			(c)—dates, timeline
			(d)—evaluation plan
			(5) Write IEP
			(6) Sign IEP

Phase 4 Program implementation with Annual Program Review			

Figure 12.1 Individualized educational programming process as required by PL 94-142 adapted to show roles of mainstream and adapted physical education instructors. From *Adapted Physical Education and Recreation: A Multidisciplinary Approach* (p. 15) by C. Sherrill, 1981, Dubuque, IA: Wm. C. Brown.

is responsible to the Special Education Division of the state education agency (SEA) for having a written IEP on file for every student who is receiving special education and related services and for following the IEP process as specified in PL 94-142 for screening, referral, assessment, planning meeting, placement, and annual program review. To assure compliance with PL 94-142 and the state plan, the SEA periodically has staff members visit and monitor LEAs. In at least 73% of the states, physical education is a specific written part of the SEA's monitor-

ing procedures (Stokes, 1980). A goal for the 1980s is to achieve this status in every state.

The responsibility of the SEA for IEP is described in a different section of the *Federal Register* from other references to the idea. Specifically, the *Federal Register* states under section 121a.130, Individualized education programs:

(a) Each annual program plan must include information which shows that each public agency in the State maintains records of the individualized education program for each handicapped child, and each public agency establishes, reviews, and revises each program as provided in Subpart C.

(b) Each annual program plan must include:

(1) A copy of each State statute, policy, and standard that regulates the manner in which individualized education programs are developed, implemented, reviewed, and revised, and

(2) The procedures which the State educational agency follows in monitoring and evaluating those programs. (20 U.S.C. 1412 (4). (*Federal Register*, 1977, p. 42482)

This section shows the importance of each adapted physical educator owning a copy of the state plan (annual program plan) and advocating for physical education to be addressed in state statutes, policies, and standards.

Compliance monitoring of LEAs by the SEA is discussed in an excellent article by Smith and Tawney (1983). Included is reference to the *PARC v. Scanlon* litigation (1981) that charged the Philadelphia School District with failure to adequately serve severely handicapped students and the Commonwealth of Pennsylvania to adequately monitor implementation of PL 94-142. Also included is research on the use of parents in the monitoring process.

Regulations Relating to Dates

PL 94-142 requires that an IEP must be in effect *before* a handicapped student can receive special education, including adapted physical education services or related services. The IEP must be in effect because the IEP process is the means by which eligibility for services is determined and educational placement is assigned.

Parental consent is required before comprehensive individual assessment for special education can be begun. Once this consent is obtained, most states require that the IEP process be completed in 30 to 60 days. Seaman and DePauw (1982) state 35 school days as the specific requirement.

In its annual report to Congress, the U.S. Department of Education states,

PL 94-142 does not define timelines for completing the evaluation process, and thus there is no standard definition of what constitutes a delay.

However, many SEAs have established their own timelines. . . . It was found that 27 of them developed their own time period for performing the sequence of functions that takes place between referral and the determination of a student's eligibility for special education. . . . These timelines typically allowed 30 to 60 days for a school district to complete its evaluation process. (U.S. Department of Education, 1982, p. 52)

PL 94-142 states that LEAs are responsible for initiating and conducting an IEP meeting for each newly identified more frequent reviews. The purpose of these reviews is to analyze the student's educational progress and make revisions in the IEP.

IEP Meetings and Participants

PL 94-142 states that LEAs are responsible for initiating and conducting an IEP meeting for each newly identified student who needs special education or related services within 30 days of the determination of need. The timing of IEP meetings for students already receiving services is left to the discretion of each agency as long as a meeting is held at least once a year.

PL 94-142 is very specific about participants in the IEP meeting. It states in section 121a.344, Participants in meetings:

(a) General. The public agency shall insure that each meeting includes the following participants (*Federal Register*, 1977, p. 42490):

(1) A representative of the public agency, other than the child's teacher who is qualified to provide, or supervise the provision of, special education.

(2) The child's teacher.

(3) One or both of the child's parents subject to 121a.345.

(4) The child, where appropriate.

(5) Other individuals at the discretion of the parent or agency.

(b) Evaluation Personnel. For a handicapped child who has been evaluated for the first time, the public agency shall insure:

(1) That a member of the evaluation team participates in the meeting; or

(2) That the representative of the public agency, the child's teacher, or some other person is present at the meeting, who is knowledgeable about the evaluation procedures used with the child and is familiar with the results of the evaluation. (20 U.S.C. 1401 (19); 1412 (2) (B), (4), (6); 1414 (a) (5).)

In general, it can be noted that participants in IEP meetings represent four types of roles: (a) parental, (b) administrative, (c) instructional, and (d) diagnostic. Most adapted physical education authorities believe that a physical educator should be present at the IEP meeting to provide input concerning performance and needs in the psychomotor domain. Research seems to indicate, however, that attendance of physical educators at IEP meetings varies by state. Heilbuth (1983) reported that 59.7% of 77 adapted physical educators in Texas regularly attended IEP meetings, whereas Gilliam (1979) and Gilliam and Coleman (1981) made no mention of physical educators.

Research (Gilliam & Coleman, 1981) indicates that the following persons participate most often in IEP meetings in Michigan: special education teachers, directors, supervisors, and consultants, regular education teachers, psychologists, guidance counselors, social workers, parents, principals, reading teachers, speech therapists, curriculum consultants, and school nurses. In this study 130 participants in 27 IEP meetings (average attendance of five) were asked to evaluate themselves and other participants on influence and contributions to five IEP functions: (a) diagnosis, (b) planning, (c) placement, (d) implementation, and (e) due process. Findings revealed that the psychologist was perceived to have the most influence in diagnosis; the special education teacher in planning and implementation; the director, in placement; and the supervisor, in due process decisions.

In addition to this research, several studies have focused on the role of regular educators (Pugach, 1982) and parents (Goldstein, Strickland, & Turnbull, 1980; Goldstein & Turnbull, 1982; Scanlon, Arick, & Phelps, 1981; Yoshida, Fenton, Kaufman, & Maxwell, 1978) in an IEP meeting. Findings reveal that attendance and participation of both groups should be increased. This increase is particularly important to the inclusion of appropriate physical education placement and programming in that these groups can be taught to advocate for physical education (Sherrill, 1986). Consumer satisfaction in relation to PL 94-142 compliance and implementation promises to be an in-

creasingly good subject for research (Polifka, 1981). Research designs on the role of regular educators and parents in the IEP process should be applied to study the role of regular and adapted physical educators in IEP.

IEP in Private and Parochial Schools

LEAs may contract with private schools for special education services. When this occurs, the LEA must conduct an IEP meeting with a representative of the private school present *before* the handicapped child is referred to or placed in the private school. The LEA and SEA are responsible for ascertaining that private schools implement the IEP process, including the annual review of written programs.

These same policies apply to parochial schools that receive special education or related services from LEAs. Recently, education of handicapped students in private schools has received considerable attention (Audette, 1982; Bajan & Susser, 1982; Grumet & Inkpen, 1982).

IEP and Accountability

Although LEAs must provide special education and related services in accordance with the IEP, PL 94-142 states "Part B of the Act does not require that any agency, teacher, or other person be held accountable if a child does not achieve the growth projected in the annual goals and objectives" (*Federal Register*, 1977, p. 42491). Although litigation in relation to PL 94-142 accountability cannot be directed toward teachers, agreement is widespread that the IEP encourages accountability behaviors in physical educators and classroom teachers (Seaman & DePauw, 1982; Sherrill, 1986; Wessel, 1977). Wessel states in this regard:

> Teacher, student, parent, school and community accountability are all necessary for planning, implementing, and evaluating the IEP. Accountability consists of a clearly defined set of procedures. It is a six-step process which is done *with* people, not to them: (a) setting program goal, (b) establishing sequential performance objectives for students to achieve stated goals, (c) assessing student needs, (d) planning the instructional program based on the assessed needs of each student, (e) continuously measuring and evaluat-

ing each student's progress; and (f) recommending and implementing changes indicated by evaluation. (1977, p. 7)

IEP and Due Process

Due process, defined as "the right of an individual to receive fair play" (Appenzeller, 1983, p. 115) is guaranteed under the fifth and 14th amendments to the U.S. Constitution. The fifth amendment, which applies only to federal government, states, "No person . . . shall be deprived of life, liberty, or property without due process of law." The 14th amendment extends this concept to state government operations, stating, "nor shall any State deprive any person of life, liberty, or property without due process of law." Appenzeller (1983, p. 116) points out that the 14th amendment due process rights are guaranteed only to public school students. Pupils in private schools are protected instead under contract theory as specified in *Dixon v. Alabama State Board of Education* (1961).

In general, law distinguishes between two types of due process: substantive and procedural. *Substantive* due process requires that a state have a valid goal, like protection from disease, before it can deprive an individual of the right to life, liberty, or property, as in requiring vaccinations before children can attend school. *Procedural* due process is the type referred to most often in school and everyday life. The following conditions comprise procedural due process (Appenzeller, 1983, pp. 115-116):

- An individual must have proper notice that he is about to be deprived of life, liberty, or property.

- An individual must be given the opportunity to be heard.

- An individual must be afforded a fair trial or hearing.

A large part of PL 94-142 focuses on procedural due process. An outline of Subpart E, Procedural Safeguards, from the *Federal Register* (1977, p. 42477), shows the importance of due process in the law and acquaints readers with the broad areas under which due process is addressed.

DUE PROCESS PROCEDURES FOR PARENTS AND CHILDREN

121a.500   Definitions of "consent," "evaluation," and "personally identifiable"

121a.502   General responsibility of public agencies

121a.503   Independent educational evaluation

121a.504   Prior notice; parent consent

121a.505   Content of notice

121a.506   Impartial due process hearing

121a.507   Impartial hearing officer

121a.508   Hearing rights

121a.509   Hearing decision; appeal

121a.510   Administrative appeal; impartial review

121a.511   Civil action

121a.512   Timeliness and convenience of hearings and reviews

121a.513   Child's status during proceedings

121a.514   Surrogate parents

PROTECTION IN EVALUATION PROCEDURES

121a.530   General

121a.531   Preplacement evaluation

121a.532   Evaluation procedures

121a.533   Placement procedures

121a.534   Reevaluation

LEAST RESTRICTIVE ENVIRONMENT

121a.550   General

121a.551   Continuum of alternative placements

121a.552   Placements

121a.553   Nonacademic settings

121a.554   Children in public or private institutions

121a.555   Technical assistance and training activities

121a.556   Monitoring activities

CONFIDENTIALITY OF INFORMATION

121a.560   Definitions

121a.561   Notice to parents

121a.562   Access rights

121a.563   Record of access

121a.564   Records on more than one child

121a.565   List of types and locations of information

121a.566   Fees

121a.567　Amendment of records at parent's request

121a.568　Opportunity for a hearing

121a.569　Result of hearing

121a.570　Hearing procedures

121a.571　Consent

121a.572　Safeguards

121a.573　Destruction of information

121a.574　Children's rights

121a.575　Enforcement

121a.576　Office of Education

OFFICE OF EDUCATION

121a.580　Opportunity for a hearing

121a.581　Hearing panel

121a.582　Hearing procedures

121a.583　Initial decision; final decision

121a.589　Waiver of requirement regarding supplementing and supplanting with Part B funds

121a.590　Withholding payments

121a.501　Reinstating payments

121a.592　Public notice by state and local educational agencies

121a.593　Judicial review of Commissioner's final action on annual program plan

This list, however, can be misleading. Saunders and Sultana (1979, 1980), in research concerning the knowledge of teachers about due process, indicated only six correct response categories: (a) evaluation, (b) placement, (c) examination of records, (d) hearing, (e) appeal to civil court, and (f) appointment of surrogate.

It is easy for beginners in the study of law to confuse due process rights with components of PL 94-142 that are not due process provisions. According to Saunders and Sultana (1979, 1980), incorrect responses of teachers include the rights of free education, individualized educational programs, and least restrictive environments. Wording is very important in discussing due process. For instance, due process rights refer to placement but not to least restrictive environment; to certain components of the IEP process like evaluation and placement, but not to the IEP per se. Due process must always refer to life, liberty, or property (i.e., not all rights are due process rights).

Of the due process rights most important to physical educators is the requirement that schools must give parents written notice that their child has been referred for special education, including adapted physical education assessment, and that parents must give written consent before such assessment can be undertaken. The written notice to parents should include reasons for the referral, information about who will administer tests, names and descriptions of tests or data collection protocols, and a statement of parents' rights. In most school systems this paperwork is under the jurisdiction of the director of special education. Physical educators should obtain copies of all official school district forms relating to due process and ascertain that physical education assessment is included.

Due process rights concerning the opportunity to be heard and to be afforded a fair trial or hearing are detailed in regard to required participants in IEP meetings and procedures to be followed when parents wish to challenge the school's decisions or quality of service to their child. Appenzeller (1983, p. 117) suggests that parents should follow PL 94-142 due process procedures if they believe

- the evaluation was not appropriate,

- parents' opinions concerning the child's education were not considered or addressed in planning conferences,

- the IEP was not appropriate based on evaluation findings,

- the school is not implementing the services specified in the IEP,

- the school has delayed implementation of any service specified in the IEP,

- the child is not showing any progress in the educational setting, and

- racial, cultural, or disability biases appear to have led to development of an inappropriate IEP.

Appenzeller (1983, pp. 117-118) reports six legal actions available for challenging the school.

- Appeal to the local officials.

- Request an independent evaluation.

- Request a hearing from an independent and neutral hearing officer.

- File an administrative appeal.

- File a complaint to the Federal Office for Civil Rights.

- File a lawsuit.

Appenzeller (1983) discusses due process in detail and gives excerpts from illustrative cases. Procedural safeguards are also addressed in the annual reports to Congress on the implementation of PL 94-142 by the U.S. Department of Education.

Research Pertaining to IEP and/or PL 94-142

Adapted physical educators need to undertake research pertaining to the IEP process, the inclusion of physical education in the IEP written statement, and PL 94-142. Familiarity with special education research helps in the design of needed studies. Illustrative published research not yet mentioned in this chapter includes studies by Anderson, Barner, and Larson (1978): Budoff, Orenstein, and Abramson (1981); Cobb and Phelps (1983); Morgan and Rhode (1983); Polifka (1981); Price and Goodman (1980); and Tymitz (1981). Each of these research designs could be replicated with emphasis on physical education rather than special education.

Length of IEPs and Time Spent

In a national survey conducted under contract with the U.S. Department of Education, it was reported that 47% of the IEPs reviewed were three pages or less in length. The U.S. Department of Education (1981) indicated that the federal IEP requirements can usually be met in a one to three page form. Research conducted in 1981 revealed that most LEAs had IEP practices that exceeded PL 94-142 requirements. For instance, IEPs in the school districts studied included from 13 to 150 short-term objectives, with medians of 22 and 27 objectives in two different studies (U.S. Department of Education, 1982). Federal officials noted that "such a large number of objectives seems to be more than needed to meet the intent of PL 94-142" (p. 29).

Price and Goodman (1980) investigated the amount of time spent developing IEPs. The average IEP for 85 teachers representing 22 school districts in Pennsylvania required 390 minutes. Of this, 265 minutes were taken from the school day and 125 minutes came from teachers' personal after school time. Six activity categories were analyzed: (a) gathering diagnostic data, (b) telephone calls, (c) IEP conferences, (d) interprofessional conferencing, (e) writing the IEP document, and (f) other. Writing the IEP required more time than any of the other tasks. This paper work is sometimes cited as a source of bad attitudes toward IEPs and PL 94-142 in general.

Morgan and Rhode (1983) reported studies of teachers' attitudes toward IEPs in 1978 and 1980. A 27-item attitude questionnaire is included in their paper. Among the findings is the importance of support from parents, regular educators, and others in the IEP process.

Inclusion of Physical Education in the IEP

Because of its tremendous time demands, special educators are often reluctant to include anything in the IEP that is not required. A frequently asked question is, When must physical education be described or referred to in the IEP? In a 14-page *Federal Register* section (1981, p. 5471) specifically on IEPs, the following answer was given:

Section 300.307(a) provides that *physical education services, specially designed if necessary, must be made available to every handicapped child receiving a free appropriate public education.* The following paragraphs (1) set out some of the different PE program arrangements for handicapped students, and (2) indicate whether, and to what extent, PE must be described or referred to in an IEP:

a. *Regular PE with non-handicapped students.* If a handicapped student can participate fully in the regular PE program without any special modifications to compensate for the student's handicap, it would not be necessary to describe or refer to PE in the IEP. On the other hand, if some modifications to the regular PE program are necessary for the student to be able to participate in that program, those modifications must be described in the IEP.

b. *Specially designed PE.* If a handicapped student needs a specially designed PE program, that program must be addressed in all applicable areas of the IEP (e.g., present levels of educational performance, goals and objectives, and services to be provided.) However, these statements would not have to be presented in any more detail than the other special education services included in the student's IEP.

c. *PE in separate facilities.* If a handicapped student is educated in a separate facility, the PE program for that student must be described or referred to in the IEP. However, the kind and amount of information to be included in the IEP would depend on the physical-motor needs of the student and the type of PE program that is to be provided.

Thus, if a student is in a separate facility that has a standard PE program (e.g., a residential school for the deaf), and if it is determined—on the basis of the student's most recent evaluation— that the student is able to participate in that program without any modification, then the IEP need only note such participation. On the other hand, if special modifications to the PE program are needed for the student to participate, those modifications must be described in the IEP. Moreover, if the student needs an individually designed PE program, that program must be addressed under all applicable parts of the IEP. (See paragraph "b" above.)

This official response confirms that physical education is generally only a small part of the total IEP. Adapted physical education authorities typically recommend that adapted physical education service providers take the initiative in offering to do psychomotor assessments and to write the physical education portions of the IEP. This relieves special educators of an extra burden but more

Heather Seaver (top), blind athlete from Colorado, in national track meet showing benefit of high quality individualized educational programming. Adult CP athlete (bottom) serves as model for elementary school students in wheelchair soccer (also called team handball).

importantly assures that the writing is done by the better qualified person.

Importance of the Mention

If physical education is not mentioned in the IEP, there is no legal basis for adapted physical education service delivery and/or modifications in the regular physical education program. If a school district has high quality regular physical education instruction with small class sizes, no modification may be needed. To benefit optimally from instruction, handicapped pupils need approximately the same pupil/teacher ratio in physical education and classroom settings. The average ratio of the number of handicapped students to special education teachers is 18:1, with 12:1 for emotionally disturbed students, 13:1 for mentally retarded students, 17:1 for learning disabled, and 21:1 for other health impaired (U.S. Department of Education, 1982). Often the class size in regular physical education is the one modification that should be specified. Grading and/or criteria for success is another modification often needed for handicapped students in regular classes.

The most common other modifications of regular physical education that should be written on the IEP are the following (Masters, Mori, & Lange, 1983, p. 88):

• Changes in equipment

• Changes in communication, demonstration, and instructional techniques

• Alterations in facilities

• Alterations of activity expectancy levels

• Alterations in accuracy and intensity requirements for games and sports

Still another modification in regular physical education practice to be requested is instruction by a certified specialist in physical education who has had adapted physical education training rather than by the classroom teacher, coach, or nonspecialist utilized in many school districts.

In most instances these modifications will not be written into IEPs unless parents are taught characteristics of good physical education and refuse to sign their child's IEP until such physical education is written in. Research is needed to document the differences that modifications such as small class size, instruction by a specialist, and changes in teaching methods, equipment, and facilities make.

A Loophole in the Requirement

In a few states physical education is not required, especially at the elementary level, of all students. Even if it is required, some LEAs do not implement the requirement. If nonhandicapped students in a community do not receive physical education, then handicapped students with comparable psychomotor functioning (i.e., no identified special needs) cannot be required to have instruction. PL 94-142 mandates, however, that handicapped students with identified physical education needs be provided specially designed instruction if, indeed, parents ascertain that the need is written into the IEP.

William Wilson, previously a consultant within the Division of Assistance to States, Office of Special Education Programs, U.S. Department of Education, explains how this loophole occurred.

> The Congress of the United States assumed that all children received physical education. Therefore, all handicapped children should also receive physical education with one exception—if a local school district does not have a general physical education program, we presently do not have the authority to require physical education. I do not know of too many communities where this is the case. (Wilson cited in French & Jansma, 1982, p. 361)

The IEP and Physical Education Placement Criteria

Inasmuch as one of the main purposes of the IEP is to designate placement in the least restrictive environment for each instructional area in which there is a special need, adapted physical education specialists have recently begun to recognize the importance of placement criteria. Ideally these placement criteria should be included in the special education state plan as well as state statutes and policies.

Among the states that have adopted criteria or specific guidelines for adapted physical education placement are Alabama, Georgia, Minnesota, and Louisiana. The following are those used by Alabama. Georgia's guidelines are almost identical.

(a) Perform below the 30th percentile of standardized tests of:

    (i)   motor development,
    (ii) motor proficiency,
    (iii) fundamental motor skills and patterns,
    (iv) physical fitness,
    (v) game/sports skills,
    (vi) perceptual-motor functioning, and
    (vii) posture screening;

(b) exhibit a developmental delay of 2 or more years based on appropriate assessment instruments;

(c) function within the severe or profound range as determined by special education eligibility standards; and

(d) possess social/emotional or physical capabilities that would render it unlikely for the student to reach his or her physical education goals without significant modification or exclusion from the regular physical education class.

The Minnesota guidelines are as follows:

There are no specific rules on placement according to formal assessment results; however, some general guidelines follow:

a. Developmental Age

(1) 1 to 2 years below chronological age— take a close look at the situation

(2) 2 or more years below chronological age—some type of program should be initiated

b. Percentile Rank

(1) 16th-25th percentile—take a close look at the situation

(2) under the 15th percentile—some type of program should be initiated

The Louisiana criteria are as follows:

The criteria developed by the committee addressed two categories of exceptional students. In the first, students below the age of 6 years demonstrating at least a 6-month delay in motor development would become eligible for services. A two-step process was developed for students ages 6-21. Step 1 called for evidence of a motor deficit as demonstrated by performance at least 1 standard deviation below the mean on an instrument measuring both fine and gross motor abilities. In addition, the older students would be administered a physical education competency test derived from the state physical education curriculum. Students meeting 30 to 80% of the competencies would be identified as mildly/moderately motor deficient. Students meeting 29% or less would be identified as severe.

Research is needed to determine what other states are doing with regard to physical education placement criteria, the types of tests and data collection instruments that are being used in screening and individual assessment, problems, and solutions. Sherrill, who strongly advocates writing class size and specialist teacher modifications into regular physical education placement on the IEP of almost all handicapped pupils, suggests the following criteria:

- Score below 50th percentile or the mean on standardized test

- Score below 4th stanine

- Perform consistently below average as documented in independent observations by two physical education specialists on three different days

Sherrill conceptualizes adapted physical education occurring in the mainstream as well as separate settings and recommends team teaching by regular and adapted physical educators in the mainstream and/or resource room setting for children scoring below the mean. She also recommends combined placements with, for example, 3 days in the mainstream and 2 days in an 8:1 pupil/teacher class size setting. Pyfer (1982) is one of the few persons to devote an entire article to criteria for physical education placement. She states,

Areas in which performance falls one standard deviation below the mean or the 25th percentile need concerted attention. . . . Annual goals and accompanying objectives should be selected for a reasonable number (3-5) of physical functions found to be below the acceptable standard. These goals and objectives should be written in behavioral terms on the IEP. (Pyfer, 1982, p. 13)

Until state plans establish placement criteria, adapted physical educators should work at the grassroots level for agreement on criteria and guidelines by the LEA. Many LEAs with high quality programs are providing leadership in serving both handicapped and nonhandicapped students who exhibit low motor skill, fitness, or other special needs.

Job Functions of the Adapted Physical Educator

Little research is available on the IEP role of adapted physical educators. In her survey of job functions of 77 adapted physical education specialists in Texas, Heilbuth

(1983) reported several IEP responsibilities. Among these were the following: 66.2% of the adapted physical educators participated in LEA screening; 89.6% were involved in assessment of student abilities; 58.4% served as a member of an assessment team; 87% wrote objectives for IEPs, and 59.7% regularly attended IEP meetings. Megginson (1982) asked administrators, physical educators, special educators, and parents to rate current and desired status on several conditions believed to characterize good LEA adapted physical education in relation to IEP. On a 6-point scale, with 6 highest, these ratings are reported in Table 12.1. For each condition a significant difference ($p < .01$) existed between current and desired status. Adapted physical education specialists would more than likely rate the desired status of each of these conditions as a "6" (out of 10). Increasing emphasis must be given to communicating the job functions and competencies of adapted physical educators.

In relation to working with the multidisciplinary team in the IEP process, American Alliance for Health, Physical Education, and Recreation (1977, pp. 8-9) lists 10 suggestions to be followed:

1. Ensure that physical education is included in each child's IEP when necessary and appropriate.

2. Volunteer input about the child's physical and motor development and social, emotional, and personal characteristics to the team for preparation of the IEP.

3. Be available to participate in planning conferences and show a personal interest in actively contributing to this process.

4. Make sure that children who need specially designed physical education programs receive them and are not inappropriately placed in regular programs.

5. Make sure that children are not programmed for specially designed physical education when their needs can be adequately and appropriately met in regular programs.

6. Remind the committee that every handicapped child does not need, want, or require specially designed physical education.

7. Remind the committee that certain specially designed physical education programs can be accomplished in regular classes, some with additional support and others without any supplementary assistance.

8. Primarily remember the specific nature of physical education as IEPs are planned and implemented.

9. See that placement flexibility is maintained so that the child participates in regular physical education activities where possible and in specially designed programs as necessary.

10. Remember that individualized education and one-to-one relationships are not synonymous.

The Physical Education IEP

In addition to writing the physical education part of IEPs required by PL 94-142, several authorities believe adapted physical educators should write physical education (or psychomotor) IEPs for all of their students (Geddes, 1981; Sherrill, 1986; Wessel, 1977). This provides the opportunity to write out more about students than the small space allocated to each curricular area on the official IEP. Whereas regular physical educators devote time to writing lesson plans for classes, adapted physical educators should use this time on IEPs to ensure individualized and personalized instruction, whether it occurs in a 1:1 ratio, a small group, or a mainstream setting.

Sherrill, who admittedly is an idealist, would like to see mainstream physical education personalized and individualized for all students. She therefore believes regular physical educators, as well as adapted physical educators, should be taught to write IEPs and held accountable for basing daily instruction on the assessed needs of students. In this regard, Sherrill states,

> We have long recognized the principle of readiness—starting each class where the students are. This principle implies assessment of the

Table 12.1   Comparison of Current and Desired Conditions in LEA Adapted Physical Education Relating to IEP

Conditions	Group	Current M	Desired M
1. Specially trained PE personnel participate in the IEP process and/or other interdisciplinary planning.	ADM	3.92	5.05
	PE	3.58	4.83
	SPED	3.41	5.19
	PAR	3.67	5.50
2. Appropriate PE placement is discussed and agreed upon by school personnel and parents at the initial IEP meeting and thereafter.	ADM	4.71	5.37
	PE	3.87	4.92
	SPED	3.67	5.37
	PAR	4.42	5.92
3. PE programming is based on IEPs that include present levels of motor performance, long-range goals, and short-term objectives.	ADM	3.75	4.81
	PE	3.63	4.76
	SPED	3.82	5.16
	PAR	3.90	5.80
4. Motor assessment in IEP process is done by a physical educator specially trained in motor evaluation who utilizes appropriate motor assessment tools.	ADM	4.06	5.03
	PE	3.69	4.89
	SPED	4.23	5.23
	PAR	3.90	5.70

level of psychomotor performance—formal or informal. The IEP simply exends the practice of determining where the whole class is to determining the needs of individuals in the class. Likewise, teachers have always written into lesson plans (or at least had in mind) long-range goals and short-term objectives for their students. These have served as the criteria for selecting learning activities (called services in the IEP). Good teachers have always subjected their programs to periodic evaluation. Thus good physical education teachers have been writing IEPs (at least in their minds) for years. (Sherrill, 1986, p. 135)

Illustrative physical education IEPs are provided in many texts. In other texts, examples labelled as the physical education part of the legal IEP are too long to realistically be incorporated into the legal IEP, which is typically only three pages long and includes all curricular areas. These examples might more appropriately be labelled physical education IEPs. Wessel (1977) and Geddes (1981) are among the best sources for methodology relating to physical education IEPs.

References

American Alliance for Health, Physical Education, and Recreation. (1977). Individualized educational programs. *Practical Pointers*, **1**(6), 8-9.

Anderson, L., Barner, S., & Larson, H. (1978). Evaluation of written individualized education programs. *Exceptional Children*, **45**, 207-208.

Appenzeller, H. (1983). *The right to participate: The law and individuals with handicapping conditions in physical education and sports*. Charlottesville, VA: The Michie Company.

Audette, D. (1982). Private school placement: A local director's perspective. *Exceptional Children*, **49**(3), 214-219.

Bajan, J., & Susser, P. (1982). Getting on with the education of handicapped children: A policy of partnership. *Exceptional Children*, **49**(3), 208-212.

Budoff, M., Orenstein, A., & Abramson, J. (1981). Due process hearings: Appeals for appropriate public school programs. *Exceptional Children*, **48**(2), 180-182.

Cobb, R.B., & Phelps, L.A. (1983). Analyzing individualized education programs for vocational components; An exploratory study. *Exceptional Children*, **50**(1), 62-64.

Dixon v. Alabama State Board of Education, 294 F. 2nd 150 (5th Cir. 1961)

Federal Register. (1977, August 23). **42**(163), 42477-42491.

Federal Register. (1981, January 19). **46**(12), 5460-5473.

French, R., & Jansma, P. (1982). *Special physical education*. Columbus, OH: Charles E. Merrill.

Geddes, D. (1981). *Psychomotor individualized educational programs*. Boston: Allyn and Bacon.

Gilliam, J. (1979). Contributions and status rankings of educational planning committee participants. *Exceptional Children*, **45**(6), 466-468.

Gilliam, J., & Coleman, M. (1981). Who influences IEP committee decisions? *Exceptional Children*, , **47**(8), 642-644.

Goldstein, S., Strickland, B., Turnbull, A., & Curry, L. (1980). An observational analysis of the IEP conference. *Exceptional children*, **46**, 278-286.

Goldstein, S., & Turnbull, A. (1982). Strategies to increase parent participation in IEP conferences. *Exceptional Children*, **48**(4), 360-361.

Grumet, L., & Inkpen, T. (1982). The education of children in private schools: A state agency's perspective. *Exceptional Children*, **49**(3), 200-206.

Heilbuth, L. (1983). *Psychomotor job functions of Texas public school adapted physical education teachers, occupational therapists, and physical therapists*. Unpublished doctoral dissertation, Texas Woman's University, Denton.

Joiner, L., & Sabatino, D. (1981). A policy study of PL 94-142. *Exceptional Children*, **48**(1), 24-33.

Masters, L., Mori, A., & Lange, E. (1983). *Adapted physical education: A practitioners guide*. Rockville, MD: Aspen System Corporation.

Megginson, N. (1982). *Adapted physical education needs assessment: A cooperative manpower planning model for the local school district*. Unpublished doctoral dissertation, Texas Woman's University, Denton.

Morgan, D., & Rhode, G. (1983). Teachers' attitudes toward IEPs: A two year follow-up. *Exceptional Children*, **50**(1), 64-67.

Polifka, J. (1981). Compliance with Public Law 94-142 and consumer satisfaction. *Exceptional Children*, **48**(3), 250-253.

Price, M., & Goodman, L. (1980). Individualized educational programs: A cost study. *Exceptional Children*, **46**(6), 446-454.

Pugach, M. (1982). Regular classroom teacher involvement in the development and utilization of IEPs. *Exceptional Children, 48*(4), 371-374.

Pyfer, J. (1982). Criteria for placement in physical education experiences. *Exceptional Education Quarterly, 3*(1), 10-16.

Saunders, M., & Sultana, Q. (1979). Educational due process rights of handicapped: Familiarity of professionals. *Education Unlimited, 1*(5), 13-15.

Saunders, M., & Sultana, Q. (1980). Professionals' knowledge of educational due process rights. *Exceptional Children, 46*(7), 559-561.

Scanlon, C., Arick, J., & Phelps, N. (1981). Participation in the development of the IEP: Parents' perspective. *Exceptional Children, 47*(5), 373-374.

Seaman, J., & DePauw, K. (1982). *The new adapted physical education*. Palo Alto, CA: Mayfield.

Sherrill, C. (1986). *Adapted physical education and recreation: A multidisciplinary approach* (3rd ed.). Dubuque, IA: Wm. C. Brown.

Smith, J., & Tawney, J. (1983). Compliance monitoring: A dead or critical issue. *Exceptional Children, 50*(2), 119-127.

Stokes, B.R. (1980). *Memorandum presenting findings of 1979 Kennedy Foundation Survey of state special education directors regarding implementation of physical education requirements of PL 94-142*. Baton Rouge: State of Louisiana Department of Education.

Tymitz, B. (1981). Teacher performance on IEP instructional planning tasks. *Exceptional Children, 48*(3), 258-260.

U.S. Department of Education. (1982). *Fourth annual report to Congress on the implementation of Public Law 94-142*. Washington, DC: Author.

Wessel, J. (Ed.). (1977). *Planning individualized education programs in special education*. Northbrook, IL: Hubbard.

Yoshida, R., Fenton, K., Kaufman, M., & Maxwell, J. (1978). Parental involvement in the special education pupil planning process: The school's perspective. *Exceptional Children, 44*, 531-533.

Chapter 13

Program Models in Adapted Physical Education: Implications for Teacher Training

Walter F. Ersing

*O*f the many challenges facing adapted physical education in the 1980s, the ability to provide excellence in instructional programming for students with special needs is foremost. Pressures from various sources force us to examine the nature and emphasis of our instructional programs and to be accountable for the effects of such programming on each student.

Recognizing the significance of the role of instructional programs, it becomes imperative that professional preparation programs in physical education assure that future regular physical education teachers as well as specialists in adapted physical education become aware and knowledgeable of the developments in curriculum and programming for the handicapped. The purpose of this chapter is to provide an overview of such program developments by reviewing a number of nationally validated or regionally recognized instructional programs that have emerged since the mid-1970s.

Several adapted physical education models have developed in response to the need for individualized approaches to instructional programming, commonly referred to as individualized education programs (IEPs), as mandated within PL 94-142. Included among these approaches are the diagnostic-prescriptive model, the modular systems approach, peer tutoring, a behavior modification program strategy, a movement education model, and the task card system.

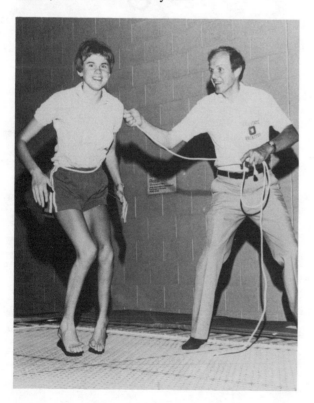

Walter Ersing, Ohio State University, working with learning disabled child on trampoline.

This chapter presents a description of several models and includes for each the target audience, the nature of the instructional model, the program content, training materials available for the model, and reference information on the program. Additionally, recognition is given to programs with approval of the U.S. Office of Education Joint Dissemination Review Panel (JDRP), an accrediting agency for exemplary educational programs (National Diffusion Network Division of Educational Replication, Room 805, Reviere Building, 1832 M. Street, N.W., Washington, DC 20036).

Project ACTIVE

Project ACTIVE (All Children Totally Involved Exercising) is a nationally validated program that provides diagnostic and prescriptive data-based physical education for handicapped individuals aged 6 to 60 and nonhandicapped students in grades K-12. ACTIVE has been approved by the Joint Dissemination Review Panel (JDRP) of the Department of Education (Vodola, 1976; Karp, 1987). This packaged program offers direct programming information for personalized-individualized instruction through the use of a comprehensive curriculum and a variety of teacher strategies.

The program is designed to serve all handicapped individuals but is also applicable to normal, slow learners, and gifted children. Specifically, the curriculum is designed to address special needs of the mentally retarded, learning disabled, orthopedically handicapped, visually impaired, hearing impaired, malnourished, asthmatic, and students with postural abnormalities and postoperative problems.

The seven programmatic components that cut across the various handicapped populations consist of low motor ability, low physical vitality, postural abnormalities, nutritional deficiencies, breathing problems, motor disabilities or limitations, and communication disorders. Each program component is addressed in an individual manual and provides the teacher with assessment, curriculum, resource activities, and administrative information necessary for the implementation of the individualized diagnostic and prescriptive model.

In addition to the seven curriculum manuals, in-service materials in the form of filmstrips and five manuals for the purpose of providing in-service training on the program are available. Included among the manuals are an administrator's guide, a manual on state and national resources and services, a competency-based teacher training manual, a monograph with a synthesis of all ACTIVE research studies and findings, and a norms manual with motor ability and physical fitness data for normal, mentally retarded, learning disabled, and emotionally disturbed individuals.

Project ACTIVE was directed by Thomas Vodola until 1981 when NDN funding was disrupted by enactment of the Education Consolidation and Improvement Act. When funding of NDN projects was restored in 1986, Joe Karp, a public school physical educator in Kelso, Washington, became the new director.

I CAN

I CAN (Individualize Instruction, Create Social Leisure Competence, Associate All Learnings, Narrow the Gap Between Theory and Practice) is an example of the modular systems approach to individualized instruction and is a nationally recognized instructional program with JDRP approval (Wessel, 1979). I CAN is also an example of the diagnostic-prescriptive model. The I CAN model consists of three separate instructional programmatic systems, Preprimary Skills, Primary Skills, and Sport, Leisure, and Recreation Skills, each of which utilizes a systems approach applied to an objective-based instructional program model. All programs have been designed for use by the physical education, special education, or classroom teacher who works with children, adolescents, or adults with special needs in a special or integrated school or community environment.

The implementation of the I CAN instructional model uses a process consisting of five major curriculum tasks, each of which is achieved through a prescribed number of special substeps. The major tasks include (a) planning program goals, objectives, content, and schedule times; (b) assessing the student; (c) prescribing instructional activities; (d) developing teaching strategies for the instructional materials; and (e) evaluating and reviewing the effectiveness of the instructional program. In the early 1980s Wessel began using the term Achievement-Based Curriculum (ABC) Model to describe an instructional system based on these five tasks. A 3-year postdoctoral leadership training project (1983-1986) was awarded to Wessel to develop teacher training modules for implementation of ABC in physical education, and many university personnel began using the terms *I CAN* and *ABC* interchangeably. A book describing ABC is now available (Wessel & Kelly, 1985).

To assist the teacher in implementing individualized instruction, each module includes a curriculum guide for every subarea with performance objectives for specific skills, criterion levels to assess the student's performance level, and teaching strategies. Other materials included in each module are a game book and class and individual score sheets for recording and reporting progress. An implementation guide provides the teacher with the neces-

sary information to develop the competencies needed to plan and teach within the curriculum. Field testing evidence on the program and onsite in-service training are available. Figure 13.1 presents modules comprising the I CAN/ABC system.

Project PEOPEL

Project PEOPEL (Physical Education Opportunity for Exceptional Learners) is a nationally JDRP-accredited program that focuses on handicapped and nonhandicapped peer-tutors for grades 9 through 12 and may be used for middle and elementary school. The primary program focus is a one-on-one individualized success-oriented learning experience for handicapped individuals through peer tutoring utilizing student aides (Long, 1979). The program is for students who because of some physical, mental, social, or emotional exceptionality will benefit more from a prescriptive program than from a regular physical education class.

The student aides are prepared for the role through the means of in-service programs as prescribed in a Student Aide Training Manual and administered by the physical education teacher. Additional assistance in terms of administrative and instructional considerations, as well as short- and long-term planning, is provided to the physical education teacher through an Administrative Guide Manual.

Materials in the PEOPEL Teacher's Guide consist of 35 separate Units of Instruction in a variety of individual, dual, and team activities. Each instructional unit has been developed with task-analyzed objectives for six content areas consisting of skill progression, safety terminology, rules, history, and etiquette. The individualized program includes a pretest to determine entry skill level based on performance objectives within the Unit of Instruction. Program implementation is flexible according to the needs of students, a class, a school, or a district. No special equipment or facilities are required for program implementation. Data on program effectiveness over a 3-year period showed significant statistical gains in fitness and attitudes of experimental PEOPEL students.

A Data-Based Gymnasium

A data-based gymnasium provides, through a behavior modification approach, a systematic strategy to designing curriculum for low-incidence severely and profoundly handicapped children enrolled in the National Model Program for Severely Handicapped Children in Monmouth, Oregon (Dunn, Morehouse, & Fredericks, 1985). The essence of this approach is that the physical education teacher systematically makes maximum and efficient use

Preprimary	Primary	Sport, leisure, and recreation	
Body management	Body management	Backyard/Neighborhood activities	
• Body control	• Body control	• Croquet	• Badminton
	• Body awareness	• Horseshoes	• Roller skating
		• Tetherball	
Fundamental skills	Fundamental skills	Outdoor activities	
• Locomotor	• Locomotor and rhythm	• Backpacking	• Camping
• Object control	• Object control	• Cross-country skiing	• Hiking
Health/Fitness	Health/Fitness	Dance and individual sports	
• Physical fitness	• Physical fitness	• Bowling	• Gymnastics
	• Postural	• Folk dance	• Track and field
Play participation	Aquatics	Team sports	
	• Basic skills	• Basketball	• Softball
	• Swimming and entry	• Kickball	• Volleyball
Play equipment			

Figure 13.1 The essential instructions and program materials needed to implement I CAN/ABC tasks are contained in each program module of the Preprimary, Primary, and Sport, Leisure, and Recreation instructional systems.

of the environment to assist a child in learning a behavior or to assist a child in extinguishing an undesirable behavior.

The behavior management principles utilized in physical education programming for the handicapped are achieved through a seven-step process: (a) pinpointing and accurately defining the behavior; (b) baselining the behavior; (c) establishing terminal objectives; (d) designing and implementing the behavior program; (e) analyzing the data; (f) modifying the program as necessary; and (g) insuring that the behavior change is maintained over time. The intent of the process is to provide a bridge between therapeutically oriented programs and the more advanced physical education experiences that include highly organized game, sport, and physical fitness skills. Emphasis is placed on the importance of individualized and data-based instruction.

The content of the physical education curriculum consists of four areas. The first area, Movement Concepts, focuses on movement through one's immediate space to movement in more complex environments. The second area emphasizes skills found in many of the popular elementary games, and the third area addresses physical fitness skills essential for survival in our present society.

The last area of the curriculum focuses on select popular lifetime leisure skills.

Task analysis is applied to skills in the four curriculum areas. The specific skill within each area is organized into a terminal objective, prerequisite skills that are stated in behavioral terms and progressively arranged in phases from a simple to complex order, suggested additional materials, and teaching notes.

The entire model is provided in a single manual form. Besides an overview of the philosophy and principles of behavior management that govern implementation of the curriculum and the content of the curriculum, the manual provides instruction for the teacher on topics such as gymnasium management; recording student progress; training and utilizing volunteers; teaching small group activities for low-functioning, severely handicapped youngsters; utilizing medical support services; and facilitating parent involvement.

Every Child a Winner

The focus of this program is an individualized movement-education approach for the purpose of providing mainstreaming and success experiences for all children in K-6 regardless of physical and mental ability (Owens, 1974). A JDRP-approved project, the program is designed to be conducted by classroom teachers and physical educators with a class ratio of 1:30.

The program utilizes the themes and concepts of space awareness, body awareness, quality of body movement, and relationships. The themes are provided through developmental movement experiences consisting of creative games, creative dance, and educational gymnastics. The project supports competition in that "winning" occurs as each child does his or her best and is found in the program only when child-designed.

Curriculum materials consist of lesson plans for 31 behaviorally stated objectives. Each lesson plan provides the teacher the necessary instructional information to implement and meet the objective. Each lesson is designed to enhance the child's self-concept and to improve academic skills as well as motor skills.

A two-phase, 5-day in-service training program for teachers is available. Phase I (3 days) includes an accountability model for program implementation, teaching techniques, and public relations. Phase II provides training on refining students' movement skills and assistance in implementing the program in grades 4-6. Program materials consist of a training manual and a lesson plan book designed for each teacher/participant. A resource book list and equipment list are supplied in the materials. Evidence on program effectiveness with students in grades 1-6 over a 3-year period showed improvement in all areas, with physical fitness and motor skill behaviors being elevated significantly.

The Ohio State Individual Motor Program

The Ohio State Individual Motor Program promotes an individualized program approach to the development of fundamental motor skills by directly linking assessment activities to programmatic elements, namely the Ohio State University (OSU) Scale of Intra Gross Motor Assessment (SIGMA) and the Performance-Based Curriculum (PBC). The Individual Motor Program (Loovis & Ersing, 1979) is designed for mentally retarded children from preschool through the remainder of the developmental period. The program is applicable also to other handicapping conditions such as learning disabilities and autism and to normal children with motor delay or coordination problems from 3 to 9 years of age.

The OSU SIGMA is the assessment element of the program and is a criterion reference tool for 11 fundamental motor skills, namely, walking, stair climbing, running, throwing, catching, jumping, hopping, skipping, strik-

ing, kicking, and ladder climbing. Each SIGMA skill has four levels of performance with Level 1 being the least mature and Level 4 being the mature. The assessment process consists of determining which of four sets of criteria represents the child's present level of performance for a given skill.

The programmatic component of this model is the PBC, which consists of a sequence of instructional progressive motor experiences designed for each level within each skill of the SIGMA. Instructional experiences consist of behavioral objectives, each of which are accompanied by a list of sequential and progressive teaching-learning activities designed to achieve the specific objective. Supplemental activities for the mature functional level of behavior are provided for each fundamental motor skill. The development of the OSU SIGMA and the PBC resulted from research and has been subjected to field testing (Ersing, Loovis, & Ryan, 1982).

Project MOBILITEE

Project MOBILITEE is a program intended to impact on the moderately and severely handicapped by providing regular physical educators and special education teachers with directions for administering, scoring, and interpreting curriculum-embedded physical education assessment. The two main components of Project MOBILITEE (Hopewell Special Education Regional Resource Center, 1982) are an Assessment Guide and a Curriculum Guide. The content of each is based largely on OSU SIGMA and PBC (Loovis & Ersing, 1979).

The Assessment Guide focuses on three performance areas: physical/motor fitness, fundamental motor skills, and games/sport skills. The assessment items are intended to be administered during a regular physical education class for the purpose of identifying general areas of motor needs and determining a student's level of performance for each area. The assessment component provides a baseline or beginning information and is intended only to identify the general motor/physical needs of a student.

The Curriculum Guide is designed to complement the assessment component in that it provides programming suggestions based on the level of motor performance of the child as determined by the assessment component. A task analysis approach is utilized in the curriculum component and includes annual goals, short-term objectives, and suggested activities. These include the name, equipment, formation, procedure, variations, and additional references for each illustrative activity. The activities in the assessment and curriculum component are intended to provide individualized physical education programming in the least restrictive environment.

AIMS

The primary approach in *AIMS* (Assessment of Individual Motor Skills) is diagnostic/prescriptive. AIMS is designed for children with developmental delays in the motor skills area. Two major curriculum materials have been developed, the Assessment Manual and the Activities Manual (Strauss & DeOreo, 1979). Both materials have been designed to help the classroom or physical education teacher and systematically assessing the sensorimotor skills of children in implementing an individualized program of prescriptive motor activities.

The Assessment Manual describes three major functions for the teacher. First, it provides an overview of normal development in order for the teacher to understand and identify subnormal development in children. This orientation covers four areas of motor development: postural and body integration, body awareness, locomotor skills, and visual-motor skills. Secondly, it provides training in screening techniques through a motor screening checklist that serves to identify those children performing ''below'' expected developmental standards. The final section of this manual focuses on assessment of motor skills. This section includes all the assessment protocols, scoring, and interpretation. It permits the teacher to do more in-depth assessment of inappropriate motor behaviors as pinpointed in the screening checklist. Testing procedures utilize both normative and criterion reference approaches.

The programmatic component of AIMS consists of an Activities Manual and focuses on the same four motor development areas as its assessment companion. An individualized program of prescriptive motor skills is achieved through a curriculum that offers activities designed to progress sequentially from a very basic level to a mature functional skill level. The proposed activities are relatively simple, require a minimum of equipment, and are not intended to be all-inclusive. The manual further assists the teacher with program development by providing behavioral objectives for specific subareas of the four motor development areas, with suggested activities to achieve the prescribed behavior.

Other Instructional Models

In addition to the programs discussed, other instructional models have physical education programming possibilities for handicapped children. The IPI (Individually Prescribed Instructional System) provides an overall individualized learning model that utilizes a task card system with the moderately retarded (Auxter, 1971). Through the use of coded language on task cards, appropriate physical education activity information on such variables as the nature of the response to be performed, equipment required, direction of action, and time constraint is communicated to the child.

An instructional model currently in its formative stage that will directly impact on special populations within a mainstream environment is *Project COMPAC* (Reams, 1981). Management guides on curriculum and equipment modification allow visually impaired and orthopedically impaired students to be served in the regular physical education program in grades 1-12.

Other program models have emerged as part of a multidisciplinary intervention approach or in conjunction with an assessment process. One among the multidisciplinary group is *Project Success*, which is a JDRP-approved prescriptive program and classroom delivery system designed for pupils in grades 1-4 with specific language disabilities (Metteer, 1973). This structural linguistic language program with a multisensory approach integrates motor perception training into language activities. The motor dimension relates movement to learning in the areas of muscular strength, dynamic balance, body awareness, and spatial awareness.

Instructional motor programs to be implemented by parents have emerged as well. One such program that focuses on a variety of developmental motor activities for the mentally retarded is entitled *Let's Play to Grow* (Joseph P. Kennedy, Jr. Foundation, 1977). These program materials span the entire developmental period and consist of a series of guides that provide introductory information and activities in the areas of basic movement, rhythms, creative tasks, fundamental motor skills, outdoor pursuits, swimming, basic ball skills, bowling, volleyball, basketball, kicking sports, and softball. Another parent intervention program is *Moving and Doing*, a multisensorimotor program for visually impaired children that focuses on the developmental motor areas of body awareness, spatial relationships, balance, gross motor, fine motor, locomotor, and rhythmic activities (Muste & Fellows, 1982).

In terms of instructional materials that focus specifically on sport skill development, the new Sports Instruction Skill Program developed by the Joseph P. Kennedy, Jr. Foundation represents one effort in this area. These materials provide both the lay and professional person with information on skill techniques and training approaches for the Special Olympics program and are available through each state director of Special Olympics or the Kennedy Foundation.

Conclusion

As one surveys the programmatic directions as presented in current adapted physical education textbooks and the more recently developed instructional program models previously discussed, certain observations seem evident. First, the instructional programs are linked in some manner to an assessment function. This function generally is represented by a process that involves assessing the present level of motor performance of a child and then linking specific intervention activities to short-term instructional objectives designed to facilitate performance change. Both normative and criterion reference testing procedures are evident in the assessment function of the various models.

Secondly, a trend has occurred to develop motor activities based on the task analysis process, regardless of the approach utilized within the instructional model. The use of task analysis in developing curriculum experiences has resulted in the presentation of activities in a sequential and progressive manner of simple to complex. Such an analytical arrangement of activities permits a wide range of entry levels of skills and thus an individualized approach to instructional programming in adapted physical education in either a special or integrated class environment.

A third observation of the instructional models is that targeted populations vary by program. Some programs focus on a single categorical condition, whereas others address multicategories. Still others have used a noncategorical approach with emphasis on the type of functional motor/physical problems rather than the specific categorical condition.

Another observation evident is that not only do a variety of programs and curriculum models exist in adapted physical education, but many such programs have been validated as to their effectiveness to produce motor and physical performance changes in the handicapped child. Finally, the instructional models not only address the problems of the common categories such as mental retardation, developmental disabilities, the physically handicapped, and other health-impaired conditions, but also focus on problems of the nonhandicapped group in the areas of motor coordination, fitness, sensorimotor and motor skill development.

This chapter has provided an overview of the more recently developed models of physical education programming for handicapped children. It is hoped the overview will assist the regular educator and physical educator to better understand the kinds of instructional materials presently available.

References

Auxter, D. (1971). *Perceptual motor development programs for an individually prescribed instructional system*. Slippery Rock, PA: Slippery Rock State College.

Dunn, J., Morehouse, J., & Fredericks, H.D.B. (1985). *Physical education for the severely handicapped: A systematic approach to a data-based gymnasium*. Austin, TX: Pro-Ed Publishers.

Ersing, W.F., Loovis, E.M., & Ryan, T.M. (1982). On the nature of motor development in special populations. *Exceptional Education Quarterly,* **3**(1), 64-72.

Hopewell Special Education Regional Resource Center. (1982). *Project MOBILITEE*. Hillsboro, OH: Author.

Karp, J. (1987). *ACTIVE Newsletter*. (Available from Project ACTIVE, 601 Crawford, Kelso, WA 98626, Telephone (206) 577-2463).

Joseph P. Kennedy, Jr. Foundation. (1977). *Let's Play-to-Grow*. (Available from 1350 New York Avenue, N.W., Suite 500, Washington, DC 20005).

Long, E. (1979). *Project PEOPEL*. Phoenix, AZ: Phoenix Union High School System.

Loovis, E.M., & Ersing, W.F. (1979). *Assessing and programming gross motor development for children* (2nd ed.), Londonville, OH: Mohica.

Metteer, R. (1973). *Project Success*. Wayne, NY: Wayne Middle School.

Muste, J., & Fellows, R.R. (1982). *Moving and doing*. (Available from Comprehensive Eye Center, Children's Hospital, 700 Children's Drive, Columbus, OH 43205).

Owens, M.F. (1974). *Every child a winner*. Ocilla, GA: Irwin County Schools.

Reams, D.N. (1981). *Project COMPAC*. Hialeah, FL: Dade County Public Schools, Exceptional Student Division.

Strauss, R.N., & DeOreo, K. (1979). *AIMS, assessment manual and activities manual*. Austin, TX: Education Service Center.

Vodola, T. (1976). *Project ACTIVE*. Oakhurst, NJ: Township Ocean School District.

Wessel, J. (1979). *I CAN—Sport, leisure and recreation skills*. Northbrook, IL: H. Hubbard.

Wessel, J., & Kelly, L. (1985). *Achievement-based curriculum development in physical education*. Philadelphia: Lea & Febiger.

Chapter 14

A Service Delivery Model in Adapted Physical Education: An Ecological Approach

Michael Churton and James R. Tompkins

A service delivery system that is appropriate and serves the needs of the exceptional child is the first step in contributing to long-term growth and development of programs in the public schools. Programs that tend to be revised or reduced because of financial cutbacks are programs that have not established a broad service delivery system (i.e., they are limited in terms of their impact on individuals, schools, and the community). Historically, physical education programs have tended to focus only on public schools. Physical education teaching has failed to affect resources that could maintain or facilitate programs. Subsequently, the teaching of physical education in the public schools has been the scapegoat for budget reductions within the past several years (Churton, 1979).

With the emergence of PL 94-142, physical education is considered an integral part of a child's special education program. The monitoring of the motor education of exceptional children, however, has not been as keenly enforced as in other service areas. If physical education programs for the handicapped are to survive budget cutbacks, then appropriate service delivery models must be developed to ensure long-term growth and development.

A model that has been widely accepted relative to the treatment of children with emotional disturbance is the ecological model (Barker, 1968; Barker & Wright, 1955;

Bronfenbrenner, 1979; Hobbs, 1966; Paul, 1968; Rhodes, 1962, 1967, 1970). The ecological model as used in special education focuses upon the interrelationships between a child and various social structures (i.e., family, community, neighborhood, and school) within his or her environment. Figure 14.1 depicts a child's ecosystem. The goal of the ecological model is to make the ecosystem work in the interest of the child's total development (Hobbs, 1979). The arrow in Figure 14.1 emphasizes that the ecosystem changes with time.

The ecological model is applicable to both adapted physical education service delivery and teacher training (Churton, 1979; Sherrill, 1981a, 1981b). Churton first tested the ecological model in a federally funded in-service training project at the University of Southern Mississippi, whereas Sherrill (1981a) proposed ecological orientation as one of eight characteristics that distinguish adapted from regular physical education. In this regard, Sherrill emphasizes that success of handicapped students in mainstream physical education depends not only on improving motor skill and fitness but on the teacher's ability to change the ecosystem so as to eliminate attitudinal, aspirational, and architectural barriers in the environment.

More attention needs to be given to the ecological model relative to adapted physical education (Churton, 1979).

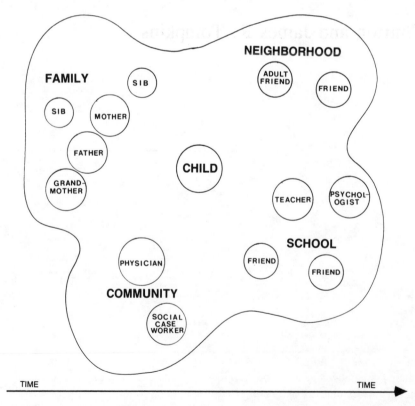

Figure 14.1   Diagram of an ecosystem of a child. From Families, schools and communities: An ecosystem for children (p. 193), by N. Hobbs, 1979, in H. Leichter (Ed.), *Families and communities as educators*. New York: Teachers College Press. Reprinted by permission.

This chapter therefore examines a philosophical orientation and the programmatic outcomes that will facilitate the development and implementation of comprehensive adapted physical education programs for children with special needs relative to the ecological model.

Ecological Model: Overview

The underlying philosophical position of the ecological model espouses that every child is born with a genetic blueprint. The fulfillment of the possibilities included in that blueprint are minimized or maximized by the environment or human arrangements that affect the child's growth. When the blueprint and the arrangements do not "fit," the potential for behavioral discordance between the child and his or her environment may evolve. This trouble is often resolved by the eventual extrusion of the child from meaningful programs to endue a calm in the transactions of that environment.

The ecological point of view is concerned with one's adaptation. It is concerned with the relationship between children and environments. It is not, therefore, a static model that assumes that by holding constant one set of factors (psychobiological needs of children, psychodynamic needs of children, environmental needs of children, etc.) and then operating on these isolated factors, that solutions to human problems are resolved. Rather, it searches for solutions that are constant, continual, and dynamic between child and environment, or more accurately, between children and environments.

The ecological model treats the individual and his or her setting or environment as a complex interactive system. The ecological point of view identifies human discordance in the typical exchanges that occur between the child and the environment in which he or she lives. The model views the critical problem as the quality of the interaction or the lack of interaction between the child and the various entities that affect or influence his or her life. Although traditionally applied to emotional disturbance, the overall philosophical position can be applied to any disability that experiences discordance.

Ecological Model and Program Implications

Based on the ecological position, our broad task is to provide children with the opportunity for transactions that maximize their potential for growth and development. This position implies that the extrusion of children from needed enriching programs and "regular" environments on which they are not dependent for most of their cognitive, affective, and psychomotor learnings

(home, school, community, etc.) is a manifestation of suboptimal transactions between children and their academic, social, and physical environments.

Three general goals seem appropriate to the model:

1. To create environments in which "fits" between child and environments are consistently arranged, and the process of extrusion from needed environments does not occur.

2. To create or facilitate in a community or neighborhood interventions that reduce the extrusion of children from their regular environments or secure maximal gains for the child.

3. To identify an individual whose responsibility is to insure the minimization of the extrusion process.

Achievement of these goals will require design and implementation of a purposeful system for intervening in and modifying current and future child-environment transactions. As a purposeful and comprehensive system, it must be directed toward defined goals. As a system to meet human needs, the system must be capable of change in response to changing needs. Furthermore, the mechanism for reassessment and modification and design of child-environment transactions will require constant inquiry about needs, alternative definitions, effectiveness of activities, new arrangements, and so forth (Tompkins, 1972).

Ecological Model and Programmatic Objectives

Programs that focus on the interaction between children and their environments must stress compatibility so as to minimize the effects of discordance. In this pursuit, program developers must be able to recognize the conditions that have produced the present pattern of service models, to define the ecological view of child development, and to formulate plans that will maximize the possibility of a child reaching optimal growth and development.

Motor Needs and Exceptional Children

The blueprint for handicapped children relative to their genetic potential in the psychomotor domain is directly affected by the influence of the environment and the educational setting in which the child is placed. The misfit between the child and his or her psychomotor needs develops when the personnel responsible for programming are either unprepared or lack the competencies to plan an appropriate program. Individuals responsible for the child's psychomotor development are those who have a direct role in planning, implementation, and evaluation. If these individuals are qualified, they prevent what Rhodes (1962) refers to as "behavior discordance" or in this particular model "psychomotor discordance."

The adapted physical education ecological model includes four specific resources who directly affect the handicapped child's psychomotor development. Resources include teachers, support personnel, administrators, and parents and community (see Figure 14.2). Collectively, these resources provide a comprehensive plan by which the handicapped child can achieve his or her psychomotor potential. If the handicapped child's psychomotor potential is to be optimized, then the aforementioned resources must realize their roles and responsibilities in the child's overall motor development.

Teachers

In order to prevent the process of discordance relative to a handicapped child's psychomotor needs, an individual must be identified who will assume responsibility for program development, implementation, and evaluation. A leadership role must be assumed that will not only consider the needs of the child, but also review the competencies of individuals who directly affect the development of the child's psychomotor blueprint. The prevention of psychomotor discordance is contingent upon qualitative evaluation and program development. The leadership role, therefore, can best be realized generally by the classroom teacher and specifically by the adapted physical education specialist. Because of the interdisciplinary emphasis placed on the education of the handicapped, teachers (as a resource) are classified as a trichotomy that includes special, regular, and physical education teachers.

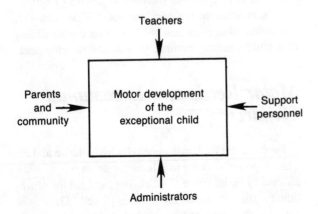

Figure 14.2   Ecosystem depicting persons who impact most on the motor development of an exceptional child.

Adapted Physical Education Teachers

The bottom line in the proposed ecological model for the development and evaluation of appropriate physical education programs for the handicapped is the adapted physical education specialist. In order for comprehensive psychomotor program assessment, development, implementation, and evaluation to occur, the adapted physical education specialist must assume a leadership role. This leadership will have a direct effect not only on the handicapped child's psychomotor program but also on the competencies and effectiveness of the resource personnel (paraprofessionals, administrators, parents, and community) as defined by this ecological model service delivery system.

Ideally, an adapted physical education specialist should be working in each school that serves handicapped students. Realistically, however, this may prove financially impossible. On the other hand, every school system will benefit greatly from employing at least one specialist in adapted physical education if it uses the ecological service delivery system. By employing a specialist trained in the ecological service delivery approach, a school system is assured of at least minimally meeting the psychomotor needs of handicapped children.

Responsibilities of the adapted physical educator should include not only a direct practitioner's role but also administrative duties of in-service training, needs assessment, curriculum development, and program evaluation. Specialists should be the key individuals who provide in-service training for other physical education teachers as well as special and regular education teachers in the system.

The proposed ecological model for psychomotor development supports a service delivery system dependent upon what Lewis (1973) refers to as a scanner process (i.e., a "manager" is identified who insures the effective and efficient operation of the system). The adapted physical education specialist is the "scanner" within the context of this model. By scanning the psychomotor programming of handicapped children within the system, the specialist insures the effectiveness and efficiency of this service delivery model.

Regular Physical Education Teachers

Because of the "least restrictive environment" concept, regular physical education teachers are becoming more involved with the psychomotor education of handicapped children. The preparation of the regular physical education teacher has been adequate to meet the psychomotor needs of handicapped children whose motor behaviors are similar to the nonhandicapped. However, some handicapped children require adapted and/or remedial programming. Most regular physical educators have not been properly trained to meet this need.

Mike Churton, Appalachian State University, discussing legislative affairs with Tommy Oakley, Dallas Public Schools, on left and Gail Webster, Virginia Tech University on right.

A school that does not have the services of an adapted physical educator must provide alternative training to mainstream teachers so as to insure that each handicapped child is receiving an appropriate physical education program. Methods that have been used include in-service training, workshops, and continuing education. The regular physical educator role in the ecosystem is to provide an appropriately planned physical education program for all children. Assistance is provided by the other resource personnel, including the adapted physical education specialist, in the ecosystem.

Special/Regular Education Teachers

Regular and special education teachers are often directly involved in the psychomotor education of handicapped children. The need to enroll all prospective teachers in courses that emphasize the motor aspects of children has long been recognized. Preservice training in the psychomotor domain, however, often has not been provided, and thus in-service training is needed.

The classroom teacher's role in the ecological model is to facilitate the implementation process. After completion of a comprehensive in-service training program, the classroom teacher should be competent to assist the adapted physical educator in assessing the motor needs of the child and in developing an appropriate psychomotor curriculum. Based upon identified motor needs, implementation of the program can be directed by the classroom teacher with close supervision by the adapted physical education specialist. The child, therefore, is given a program that facilitates his or her psychomotor needs within the ecological system.

Support Personnel

According to the ecological service delivery model, the second source having impact on the motor development of exceptional children is that of paraprofessionals and related services. Utilizing support personnel to alleviate some of the direct and indirect teaching responsibilities of certified teachers is a definite trend. Ecological service delivery models consider the category of support personnel as a trichotomy that includes aides, volunteers, and related services (e.g., physical therapy, occupational therapy, and recreation therapy).

Aides

Educational aides have long been used by public schools as a means of distributing daily workloads with a minimum of expenses and without sacrificing efficiency. Descriptions of job responsibilities are usually written so as to allow the aide to assist the classroom teacher in both noninstructional and instructional responsibilities. Often aides substitute for the classroom teacher during break time, recess, and free play periods.

The educational backgrounds of aides are varied. Usually aides do not have a degree in education and possess little knowledge of the psychomotor area. The ecological model stresses that, if aides are impacting on the psychomotor development of children, then they must be made aware of children's psychomotor requirements. Aides, therefore, should receive special training in the psychomotor development of exceptional children.

Volunteers

Increasingly, school systems are utilizing the services of the community through the volunteer system. Volunteers are nonpaid personnel who usually contract or agree to work a set number of hours a week. This provides for consistency of services and reduction of overload situations within the schools. Often, volunteers are individuals who at some point in time have held teaching credentials and are intrinsically motivated to initiate change.

Responsibilities of the volunteer are quite similar to the responsibilities assigned to the educational aide. Educational background may not include competencies in the psychomotor domain. Dunn, Morehouse, and Fredericks (1985) include an entire chapter on the training and use of volunteers with severely handicapped students.

Related Services

With the impact of PL 94-142, several ancillary services have been providing psychomotor skill development to exceptional children. Physical therapy, occupational therapy, and therapeutic recreation demonstrate a prominent role in public schools relative to the therapeutic treatment of handicapped children. As part of the ecological team concerned with the motor development of exceptional children, related service personnel can strengthen physical education programming. It is imperative, therefore, that the related service personnel not only be included in the ecosystem, but also have the necessary competencies to work within an educational milieu (Thomas & Marshall, 1977).

Administrators

The key to long-term growth and development of any program in the public schools is directly dependent upon the positive support and involvement of the school administration. Within the context of the ecological model, administrators are considered to have a direct influence upon the motor development of exceptional children relative to program development, implementation, and continuance. Administrators within the scope of this model include superintendents, principals, and special and physical education coordinators.

Superintendents

The superintendent of education, serving as the chief administrator of the school system, provides the necessary administrative direction to facilitate the development of the program. Implementation procedures, however, are usually relegated to the principal of the school in which the program is to be conducted. Although policy is deter-

mined by the school board, the superintendent assumes a role that is translative and in many instances dictatorial relative to program continuance.

In addition to the approval role, the decision-making process is affected by the reaction of parents to various programs. It is important for superintendents to be cognizant of PL 94-142 relative to the psychomotor development of handicapped children. In-service training conducted or assisted by the adapted physical educator specialist can foster this awareness. The superintendent, therefore, indirectly plays a role in the psychomotor development of exceptional children and is significant within the ecosystem of delivering psychomotor services.

Principals

Administratively, the principal of a school plays a direct role in the assurance of long-term growth and development of a program. The principal is responsible for the provision of scheduling, facilities, equipment, personnel, and operating expenses for their schools. This provision in turn has a direct impact on programming within the system. The principal must also be made cognizant of the need for appropriate physical education programs for handicapped students. The support of the principal for psychomotor development of exceptional children is critical for program continuance within the ecological model.

Coordinators (Physical and Special Education)

Although the superintendent and principal within a school system determine policy, the implementation of policy is usually delegated to the coordinators of particular programs. Coordinators, namely those in special education and physical education, are the individuals within the ecosystem who are most knowledgeable concerning federal, state, and local policies relative to programs for the handicapped. Subsequently, coordinators are responsible for insuring that every handicapped child is receiving an appropriate psychomotor program.

The coordinator's role within the ecosystem is one of program implementation and advocacy. Because coordinators advise superintendents and principals, their knowledge and support of psychomotor programming are critical for development, implementation, and continuance of psychomotor programs.

Parents and Community

Parents

The fourth area of concern in this ecological model includes the resources of parents and the community. Parents of exceptional children can play a significant role in psychomotor development (Bishop & Horvat, 1984; Folsom-Meek, 1984; Fredericks, Baldwin, McDonnell, Hofmann, & Harter, 1971; Horvat, 1982).

By utilizing the time period after school, on weekends, and on various vacation periods, parents can promote psychomotor growth and development. Parents can be trained effectively through various parental organizations, in-service training, or through homebound instruction to assist in the psychomotor development of their children.

Further, parents provide an advocacy base that can exert influence on the local education agencies. Parental support for a program can facilitate its development and implementation within the school. The adapted physical education teacher must therefore involve parents in the training, development, and implementation of psychomotor programs (Sherrill, 1981b).

Community

The community in which the child lives is also important within the ecosystem. Recreational programs, social clubs, and various public facilities offer opportunities for handicapped children to participate in activities that stress psychomotor development. The personnel associated with community programs are responsible for the organization and development of recreational programs for all children. If the programs involve psychomotor skills, then the staff must address the psychomotor needs of the participants in an appropriate and comprehensive manner. The ecological system proposed by this service delivery model includes the community personnel as a resource that significantly affects the psychomotor development of exceptional children.

Summary

This chapter has described generic roles for resource personnel who affect handicapped children motorically. The adapted physical education specialist provides the leadership and direction for comprehensive programming. The ecological model offers, through preservice and in-service training, an opportunity to ensure that every handicapped child within a given system is provided with an appropriate psychomotor program. The model ensures that the individuals who have influence over the child's educational program are competent in the psychomotor domain.

References

Barker, R. (1968). *Ecological psychology.* Stanford, CA: Stanford University Press.

Barker, R. (1968). *Ecological psychology.* Stanford, CA: Stanford University Press.

Barker, R., & Wright, H.F. (1955). *Midwest and its children: The psychological ecology of an American town.* New York: Harper.

Bishop, P., & Horvat, M.A. (1984). Effects of home instruction on the physical and motor performance of a clumsy child. *American Corrective Therapy Journal,* **38**(1), 6-10.

Bronfenbrenner, U. (1979). *The ecology of human development: Experiments by nature and design.* Cambridge, MA: Harvard University Press.

Churton, M.W. (1979). *Final report: USM motor development in-service training program.* University of Southern Mississippi, Hattiesburg, MS.

Dunn, J., Morehouse, J., & Fredericks, H.D.B. (1985). *Physical education for the severely handicapped: A systematic approach to a data-based gymnasium.* Austin, TX: Pro-Ed Publishers.

Folsom-Meek, S. (1984). Parents: Forgotten teacher aides in adapted physical education. *Adapted Physical Activity Quarterly,* **1**(4), 275-281.

Fredericks, H.D., Baldwin, V.L., McDonnell, J.J., Hofmann, R., & Harter, J. (1971). Parents educate their trainable children. *Mental Retardation,* **9**(3), 24-26.

Hobbs, N. (1966). Helping disturbed children: Psychological and ecological strategies. *American Psychologist,* **21**, 1105-1115.

Hobbs, N. (1979). Families, schools, and communities: An ecosystem for children. In H. Leichter (Ed.), *Families and communities as educators* (pp. 192-202). New York: Teachers College Press.

Horvat, M.A. (1982). Effect of a home learning program on learning disabled children's balance. *Perceptual and Motor Skills,* **55**, 1158.

Lewis, W.W. (1973). *Environmental intervention in emotional disturbance.* Paper presented at the Missouri Conference on Environmental Intervention for Emotionally Disturbed Children and Youth, University of Missouri, Columbia, MO.

Paul, J. (1968). *Atlantic Beach Conference Document.* Raleigh, NC: North Carolina Department of Mental Health.

Rhodes, W.C. (1962, April). *Discordant child behavior.* Paper presented at the annual meeting of the Council for Exceptional Children, Columbus.

Rhodes, W.C. (1967). The disturbing child: A problem in ecological management. *Exceptional Children,* **33**, 449-455.

Rhodes, W.C. (1970). A community participation analysis of emotional disturbance. *Exceptional Children, 36*, 309-314.

Sherrill, C. (1981a). *Adapted physical education and recreation—A multidisciplinary approach* (2nd ed.). Dubuque: Wm. C. Brown.

Sherrill, C. (1981b). An ecological approach to needs assessment for inservice training. *Resources in Education*, SPO 18467; ED 204306.

Thomas, E., & Marshall, M. (1977). Clinical evaluation and coordination of services: An ecology model. *Exceptional Children, 44*, 16-22.

Tompkins, J.R. (1972). Child services: A child's advocate's view. In J. Nesbitt, C. Hansen, B. Bates, & L. Neal (Eds.), *Training needs and strategies in camping for the handicapped* (pp. 73-78). Eugene, OR: University of Oregon Press.

Chapter 15

Perceptual-Motor Programming in the School: Application

Jean L. Pyfer

*T*hrough the years we educators have become very proficient in eliciting desired outcomes from "normal" learners. We understand how to organize optimum learning environments, sequence material for mastery, and reinforce appropriate responses. If the child is teachable, we capitalize on the opportunity.

Unfortunately, we haven't been so successful with those "other" children. Many of those other children demonstrate the same intellectual capacity as their peers, but despite our best teaching efforts, they persist in responding with inadequate or inappropriate behaviors. Usually when it becomes apparent children are not progressing along expected developmental lines, we begin to search for alternate strategies for teaching them. Most of the strategies we traditionally select involve altering visual and/or auditory stimuli in their teaching. Any one of us is occasionally very successful with these "developmentally delayed" children, but more often we demonstrate only partial effectiveness. The end result is frustration for the teacher, the child, and the parent.

Perceptual-motor theories represent an attempt to utilize unique techniques to facilitate learning. Most con-

temporary perceptual-motor theories are founded on Piaget's (1963), Bruner's (1967), and Gagne's (1965) precepts that cognitive thought builds on a sensorimotor base. In their opinion the more varied and rich the sensorimotor experiences, the greater the possibility for eventual qualitative abstract thought. The perceptual-motor theorist embraces the contemporary learning theories, but rather than relying solely on traditional teaching methodology, he or she attempts to expand the pedagogical experience to include a wider variety of sensorimotor stimulation for the child. These efforts have generated excitement, discussion, research, and often rejection. Interestingly enough, though Piaget is still regarded in most circles as an intellectual giant, many perceptual-motor theories have been rejected as minimally effective. However, a growing body of research strongly supports that certain aspects of perceptual-motor intervention may indeed be more promising to the slowly developing learner than early studies suggested.

In this chapter I will review some of the more widely known perceptual-motor theories, organize their theoretical components into a unified model, and share some of our research findings with you. It is my hope to leave you with a new way of looking at perceptual-motor possibilities and some desire to explore the area further.

Classic Perceptual-Motor Theories

One of the earliest classical studies done in perceptual-motor programming was that of Itard and Seguin in the 1800s. Any of you who have read *The Wild Boy of Aveyron* share in the accomplishments and frustration of Itard (1932) as he used sensory stimulation techniques in an attempt to heighten the awareness and hence functioning of the boy who had been raised by a pack of wolves in the Aveyron Forest.

Maria Montessori (1965) reinforced the idea of sensory stimulation in the early 1900s with her work with children living in deprived conditions in Italy. She advocated development of the senses as a basis for later intellectual functioning. Montessori schools all over the world have kept the importance of a stimulating sensory environment alive.

The emergence of Kephart's theory (1960) in the 1960s introduced a rich proposition concerning the importance of motor experience and integration to cognitive functioning. He argued that through movement a child learns to match sensory inputs and construct perceptual components vital to cognition. A contemporary of Kephart, Getman (1965) reinforced the perceptual processing postulate while emphasizing importance of vision to intellectual functioning.

Jean Pyfer, Texas Woman's University, coauthor with Dave Auxter of *Principles and Methods of Adapted Physical Education.*

Marianne Frostig broadened the available list of visual perception components believed to contribute to cognition and, working with Phyllis Maslow, proposed several aspects of movement experience and auditory perception believed important to performance output (Frostig & Maslow, 1970).

A theory that continues to emerge in our country is that of A. Jean Ayres (1979). Ayres is best known for her advocacy of sensory integration stimulation as a means of facilitating cognitive processing. Her efforts have made us aware of the reflex, kinesthetic, tactile, and vestibular sensory input components and their contributions to integration processes in the central nervous system. Ayres postulates that maturation of each sensory modality is somewhat dependent upon maturation of the other sensory modalities; thus sensory modality perception develops in an interdependent manner. Among other things, she proposes that auditory and visual system maturation are dependent upon tactile and vestibular maturation; tactile functioning affects emotional development; and proprioception is necessary for efficient movement to occur.

Anyone who is familiar with the specific studies (Alley, 1967; Belmont & Birch, 1965; Hammill), 1971) done on these theories knows that the research evidence of their effectiveness is mixed. Most studies show that application of any given theory with a group of developmentally delayed learners results in improvement of motor performance but little, if any, gain in academic behaviors. Because of such studies (most of which were done in the 1960s and early 1970s), the vast majority of special educators in the United States concluded that the techniques were worthless for improving classroom behaviors and thus rejected the theories. That attitude still permeates special education in our country. Why, then, does research in perceptual-motor programming continue?

Methodological Problems in Perceptual-Motor Research

When one examines studies done in the 1960s, several methodological problems become apparent. The most prominent of these is that the studies were carried out with a wide range of students demonstrating a variety of problems. For example, readers with good reading speed but poor comprehension were grouped with slow readers with poor word attack skills. Youngsters with persisting word and letter reversal problems were included with children with no directionality problems but who showed inefficient visual tracking skills. In essence, lemons were grouped with oranges, and then we complained that the lemonade tasted funny.

However, studies that have divided learners into more discrete categories have produced very promising results. Broxterman and Stebbins (1981) completed a study in which, with the use of any eye track camera, children with poor visual fusion who were also having a variety of reading problems were identified. A specially designed program to promote eye fusion was initiated, and specific reading gains that resulted were categorized. Ayres (1976) conducted a series of studies on the use of sensory-integrative stimulation on children with reading problems who also demonstrated hypo, hyper, or normal nystagmus. Her findings show promise for the child with hyponystagmus. Four studies completed in the last 6 years demonstrated that swimming lessons designed to promote bilateral integration significantly reduced reading problems for the child who has midline problems (Miller & Haley, 1978). None of the 1960s studies sorted out children with visual tracking, sluggish vestibular function, and midline problems from those with no such difficulties; thus the design of the studies rather than the validity of the theory under investigation may have been at fault.

A second problem inherent in the studies of the 1960s was that investigators had little, if any, knowledge of the sequential nature of motor development. Programs requiring rather sophisticated levels of performance were applied with children who may have lacked prerequisite motor abilities. Rider (1972), at the University of Kansas, has reported that children with reflex abnormalities demonstrate a significantly greater incidence of learning disabilities than do children with normal reflex development. Another study completed 4 years later showed that children with three or more abnormal reflexes do poorly on the balance and posture and the body image and differentiation portions of the Purdue Perceptual Motor Survey (Werbel, 1975). Yet, not one of the studies testing Kephart's theory attempted to sort out children with reflex problems. Failure to attain significant cognitive gains could have resulted from the fact that the perceptual-motor training program used was too advanced for the children included in the studies.

Other methodological problems with the early studies were age of the subjects, length of intervention, and size of the groups. We have found that the sooner you identify abnormal motor development and intervene with an appropriate program, the greater the probability the child will develop normally. Length of program depends upon the severity of a child's problem. When we continue a perceptual-motor program until a child is performing to normal age expectation standards, that child performs in the classroom just as ably as any other child. How long the program should be depends on how many perceptual-motor problems the child has. The greater the number of abnormalities, the longer the intervention. Optimal size of groups for programming is still an unknown. All of our work has been done one-on-one with programs designed around the specific difficulties of the child. I am confident, however, that group activities can be used effectively. In elementary schools in our country where movement education programs are used in grades K-3, we find our lowest incidence of perceptual-motor dysfunctions. Those programs seem to contain elements that promote perceptual-motor development. It should be possible to sort out components that would be applicable to given developmental delays.

The perceptual-motor theories may be of more benefit to disabled learners than original studies led us to believe, but I don't believe that the 1960s studies should bear the brunt of the criticism. Those studies investigated emerging theories that represented the first attempts to define how cognitive functioning develops. Although the writings of each of those theorists is biased toward a certain aspect of development, inherent within each theory is the acceptance that behavior is dependent upon sensory input into the central nervous system, some type of internal processing, an observable outcome, and a feedback system.

Perceptual-Motor Development Components

The relationships between the components proposed by the majority of perceptual-motor theories is diagrammed in Figure 15.1. All perceptual-motor theorists, regardless of individual biases, seem to agree that when attempting to elicit a given behavior, it is important to control sensory input, facilitate appropriate processing within the central nervous system, and provide feedback about the outcome to the sensory input systems. If we understand the role of the sensory input components and processing functions that occur within the learner, we increase the probability of eliciting desired outcomes.

Some of the studies we have completed bear out the fact that if the developmental components found in the theories are extracted and each is fit into this model, an overview results that enables one to sort out important aspects of development. In addition to visual and auditory input, other components that fit into the initial level are reflexes and vestibular, kinesthetic, tactile, olfactory, and gustatory components. Internal processes found in the various theories include laterality, directionality, bilateral integration, form perception, spatial awareness, balance, and visual and auditory figure ground. Incorporating those components and adding traditionally accepted behaviors into the model results in perceptual-motor development as illustrated in Table 15.1.

This model is not meant to be all encompassing but does include many components found to be important, and

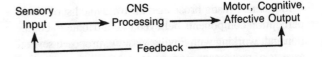

Figure 15.1 Diagram of the relationships among the components proposed by the majority of perceptual-motor theories.

it has provided an orderly process for delineating learning problems. What it suggests is that if the perceptual-motor theorists, Piaget and his contemporaries, are correct, a child with sensory input or processing delays should experience learning difficulties. Even though the exact relationship between all of these developmental components is not yet clear, research is beginning to substantiate that some individuals with output problems do indeed demonstrate underlying perceptual-motor deficits.

Findings of Recent Research

Through the use of a variety of test and observation techniques, descriptive studies (Broxterman & Stebbins, 1981; Pyfer, 1983; Pyfer & Alley, 1978; Werbel, 1975) reveal the following:

- *Intelligence*—Children who have both sensory input and integration processing deficits demonstrate IQ score discrepancies. Our studies have shown that the performance IQ score is approximately 15 points below the verbal IQ score.

- *Reading*—There is 99% chance that young children who demonstrate delayed reflex and vestibular development will have difficulty learning to read. Children who have bilateral integration problems often have reading comprehension difficulty.

- *Math*—Children who have spatial awareness problems are identified by inefficient movement patterns when moving backward, slowness in learning to tell time,

Table 15.1 Perceptual Motor Development

Sensory input level	Integration level	Output level
Reflex	Bilateral integration	Walking
Vestibular	Laterality	Running
Visual	Directionality	Skipping
Auditory	Balance	Writing
Kinesthetic	Form perception	Reading
Tactile	Spatial awareness	Spelling

inability to solve math computation problems (particularly when there are more than two or three on one page), and severe problems in learning their multiplication tables.

- *Attention Span*—Children with tactile input problems have difficulty sitting still for any length of time, have short attention spans, and cannot tolerate prolonged contact with another individual.

- *Self-Concept*—Children with severe perceptual-motor problems have poor self-concepts that result in withdrawal or aggressive behaviors.

- *Motor*—Children whose eyes do not coordinate precisely have depth perception difficulties and demonstrate the following behaviors: They continue to go down steps one at a time, turn their heads and tend to use a scooping motion when catching a ball, refuse to attend to fine motor tasks such as desk activities for any length of time, and have difficulty following the printed word on a page. Children with severely delayed reflex and vestibular development move in an awkward, clumsy manner, fall easily, have trouble learning to ride a bike, and are slow in developing fine motor skills. Children with bilateral integration problems cannot skip, cannot coordinate their hands at the midline of the body, and are delayed in establishing handedness.

Other more subtle inappropriate behaviors are also demonstrated by the child with perceptual-motor problems, but the preceding examples make the point clear: The individual with output functioning difficulties may also have a variety of input and integration process dysfunctions. Keep in mind that the cited studies do not prove a dependency relationship; they may simply describe pervasive depressions that are casual rather than causative in nature. To answer the question of whether treating a perceptual-motor problem can benefit output behaviors, one must look to intervention studies, many of which I've already cited.

The following findings have been observed clinically or resulted from statistical treatment (.05) after individually designed intervention programs for children having very specific types of problems were completed.

- *Intelligence*—When sensory input and integration processing deficits are resolved through intervention programs, the discrepancy between IQ scores disappears. That is, the performance IQ increases to a point equal to the verbal IQ. As a result, the total IQ score improves.

- *Reading*—This involves facilitating a bilateral integration comprehension gain equal to that brought about through individual reading tutoring. Studies designed to improve eye-tracking performance of 9- to 12-year-old boys show a significant improvement in reading ability.

- *Math*—For the child with spatial awareness problems, if math problems are separated into individual spaces on a page, computation skill improves. When spatial awareness problems are eliminated through movement programs, a child improves in ability to tell time.

- *Attention Span*—Resolving tactile input problems results in calmed behavior and increased in-seat behavior.

- *Self-Concept*—Resolving severe perceptual-motor problems increases a child's motor ability and his self-concept.

- *Motor*—Resolving a child's eye coordination problems results in improving locomotor skills to age-level expectancies. Facilitating reflex and vestibular development has a direct positive effect on static and dynamic balance. Facilitating bilateral integration results in the ability to skip and coordinate hands at the midline and contributes to establishment of handedness. Resolving all of a child's sensory input and integration developmental delays results in raising motor performance to age level. The child then continues to develop to age level expectations.

Conclusion

Today it is becoming increasingly apparent that developmentally delayed children can benefit from perceptual-motor intervention programs. Research has always demonstrated that some motor gains are possible even when intervention programs are selected at random; however, in the last decade more precise evaluation techniques have resulted in greater selectivity in programming. We are now capable of identifying exact developmental component dysfunctions, intervening at the level of dysfunction, and sequencing activities to promote development at each successive level of functioning. Children destined to reach adulthood as "klutzes" can now look forward to mastery of motor skills. Cognitive gains are also resulting from precisely designed perceptual-motor programs; however, exact relationships between sensorimotor components of intellectual functioning are still somewhat unclear. A tremendous amount of research is needed to sort these complexities out. While that puzzle is being unraveled, children can be afforded the motor gains known to accrue from perceptual-motor programming.

Motor development specialists should be as involved in our school systems as school psychologists and special education resource personnel are. Children with motor development delays should be identified as early as possible, and intervention programs should be designed to resolve those deficiencies. Children could be screened for perceptual-motor functioning upon entry to school. Those youngsters with severe delays could be referred to the motor development specialist for in-depth diagnostic testing. Once the precise dysfunctions are identified, the specialist could meet with the child's teachers and define cognitive, psychomotor, and affective problems the child would be expected to demonstrate. An intervention program could be designed with each professional taking responsibility for an appropriate part. Large motor activity might be carried out in the gym; visual tracking or desk work could appropriately be done in the classroom; psychological needs could mandate small group counseling or a behavior management program to be carried out in school and at home. Each professional could contribute to a distinct part of the child's total development.

Perceptual-motor programming does promote normal motor development; cognitive gains may also be realized. But to deny a child the possibility of a normal movement potential because the academic benefits are not yet clear-cut cannot be justified. To read, write, and spell can help a person *become* someone in this world, but to move with confidence and poise is to *be* someone in this world.

Editor's Note

See chapter 3 for additional background on the evolution of perceptual-motor training in physical education. History and the current status of perceptual-motor theory are also covered in adapted physical education textbooks by Auxter and Pyfer (1985), Seaman and DePauw (1982), and Sherrill (1986). Figure 15.2 presents a chronological summary of contributors to perceptual-motor theory who appear to have most influenced adapted physical education practice.

A survey of adapted physical education teacher trainers (*N* = 111) indicated that perceptual-motor training or sensory integration was the programming area of the greatest strength in 48.6% of the respondents (Sherrill & Tymeson, 1979). Among learning disabled populations, perceptual-motor training was the most popular method of education from 1936 through 1970 (Hallahan & Cruickshank, 1973). Although the acceptance of perceptual-motor training among special educators has changed greatly since the 1970s, authors of adapted physical education textbooks are divided in their opinions concerning perceptual-motor training and sensory integration as a goal of adapted physical education (Sherrill, 1985). Additionally, much confusion exists about the definitions of terms. Auxter and Pyfer (1985) explain the difference as follows:

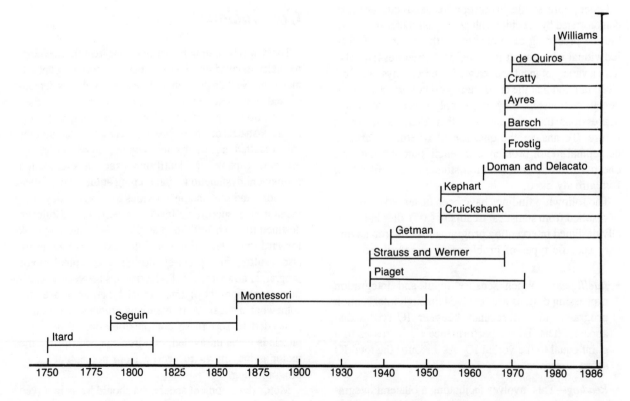

Figure 15.2 Chronology of leaders influencing Perceptual-Motor Training. *Note.* Adapted from figure in *The New Adapted Physical Education* (p. 22) by Janet Seaman and Karen DePauw, 1982, Palo Alto, CA: Mayfield.

A perceptual-motor program is usually made up of activities believed to promote development of balance, body image, spatial awareness, laterality, directionality, cross-lateral integration, and so on. Sometimes intact perceptual-motor programs such as those developed by Kephart or Frostig and Maslow are used. Other times physical educators select perceptual-motor activities from a variety of sources.

A sensory integration program is made up of activities believed to promote processing of sensory stimuli. The activities used are based on Ayres' theory of sensory integration. (p. 229)

To clarify their beliefs about perceptual-motor training and sensory integration, professionals need to study primary sources and read articles that will enable them to understand both sides of the perceptual-motor issue. The best references I have found on the history and philosophy of perceptual-motor training are

Cratty, B.J. (1972). *Physical expressions of intelligence.* Englewood Cliffs, NJ: Prentice-Hall.

Hallahan, D., & Cruickshank, W. (1973). *Psychoeducation foundations of learning disabilities.* Englewood Cliffs, NJ: Prentice-Hall.

Both books review research on the efficacy of perceptual-motor training. Few such research studies are being published today. Why? Is there no longer a need?

Some particularly interesting articles concerning perceptual-motor training include

Davis, W. (1983). An ecological approach to perceptual-motor learning. In R. Eason, T. Smith, & F. Caron (Eds.), *Adapted physical activity: From theory to application* (pp. 162-171). Champaign, IL: Human Kinetics.

Keogh, J.F. (1978). Movement outcomes as conceptual guidelines in the perceptual-motor maze. *Journal of Special Education,* **12,** 321-330.

Mann, L. (1970). Perceptual training: Misdirections and redirections. *American Journal of Orthopsychiatry,* **40,** 30-38.

Reid, G. (1981). Perceptual-motor training: Has the term lost its utility? *Journal of Health, Physical Education, Recreation and Dance,* **52,** 38-39.

A trend in teacher training appears to be increasing emphasis on theory, particularly as it relates to intersensory and intrasensory perception and sensory integration. Among the newer references are

Carterette, E., & Friedman, M. (Eds.). (1978). *Perceptual ecology.* New York: Academic Press.

Cratty, B.J. (1978). *Perceptual and motor development in infants and children* (2nd ed.). New York: Macmillan.

Dember, W., & Warm, J. (1979). *Psychology of perception* (2nd ed.). New York: Holt, Rinehart, & Winston.

DeQuiros, J. B., & Schrager, O. L. (1978). *Neurological fundamentals in learning disabilities.* Novata, CA: Academic Therapy Publications.

Geert, P. (1983). *The development of perception, cognition, & language: A theoretical approach.* Boston: Routledge & Kegan Row.

Pick, A. (Ed.). (1979). *Perception and its development.* Hillsdale, NJ: Lawrence Erlbaum Associates.

Walk, R., & Pick, H. (Eds.). (1978). *Perception and experience.* New York: Plenum.

Walk, R., & Pick, H. (1981). *Intersensory perception and sensory integration.* New York: Plenum.

Williams, H., & DeOreo, K. (1980). Perceptual-motor development. In C. Corbin (Ed.), *A textbook of motor development* (2nd ed., pp. 135-196). Dubuque, IA: Wm. C. Brown.

Williams, H. (1983). *Perceptual and motor development.* Englewood Cliffs, NJ: Prentice-Hall.

Much confusion exists about the early pioneers who contributed to perceptual-motor theory and practice. Following is a list of references, offering a beginning work plan for persons interested in in-depth study of history and philosophy.

Illustrative Primary Sources Reflecting the Chronology of Perceptual-Motor and Sensory Integration Theory

Jean Marc Itard (1775-1837), a French physician, gained prominence by describing innovative sensorimotor training program for Victor, a 12-year-old found mute, naked, and uncivilized in the forests of France on January 9, 1800. Itard's reports of 1801 and 1806 are available in English in an inexpensive but unreliable version, *The Wild Boy of Aveyron,* translation by G. Humphrey and M. Humphrey (New York: Appleton-Century-Crofts, 1932). The original French texts can be found in Lucien Malson's *Les Enfants Sauvages* (Paris: 10/18, 1964), translated as *Wolf Children and* *the Problem of Human Nature* (New York: Monthly Review Press, 1972).

Edouard Seguin (1812-1880) was Itard's student. He immigrated to the United States in 1848 and received his MD degree from the City College of New York in 1861. His book, *Idiocy and Its Treatment by the Physiological Method*, published in the United States in 1866, described in detail Itard's work.

Maria Montessori (1870-1952), the first woman to receive an MD degree in Italy, strongly influenced the education of both normal and mentally retarded children with such statements as, "The education of the senses should be begun methodically in infancy, and should continue during the entire period of instruction which is to prepare the individual for life in society" (Montessori, 1912). Many of her works were not widely disseminated in the United States until the 1950s and 1960s. Primary sources are

> Montessori, M. (1912). *The Montessori method* (A. George, Trans.). New York: Stokes.
>
> Montessori, M. (1917). *The advanced Montessori method: Scientific pedagogy as applied to the education of children from seven to eleven years*. London: Heinemann.

Jean Piaget (1896-1980) served as codirector of the Institute of Education Science in Geneva and Professor of Experimental Psychology at the University of Geneva. Piaget published research for more than 40 years, beginning in 1923. Among his earliest works are

> (1926). *The language and thought of the child* (M. Worden, Trans.). New York: Harcourt, Brace & World. (Original French edition, 1923)
>
> (1929). *The child's conception of the world* (J. & A. Tomlinson, Trans.). New York: Harcourt, Brace & World. (Original French edition, 1926)
>
> (1930). *The child's conception of physical causality* (M. Worden, Trans.). New York: Harcourt, Brace & World. (Original French edition, 1927)
>
> (1932). *The moral judgment of the child* (M. Worden, Trans.). New York: Harcourt, Brace & World.
>
> (1952). *The origins of intelligence in children* (M. Cook, Trans.). New York: International Universities Press. (Original French edition, 1936)

Alfred A. Strauss (1897-1957) and **Heinz Werner** (1890-1964), German psychologiests who migrated to the United States in the 1930s to escape Hitler, are recognized as the first American perceptual motor theorists. Both eventually settled in Michigan, where they conducted the pioneer research on brain-injured, mentally retarded children that formed the basis for almost all early learning disabled practices. Illustrative of their early works are the following:

> Strauss, A.A., & Werner, H. (1938). Deficiency in the finger schema in relation to arithmetic ability (finger agnosia and acalculia). *American Journal of Orthopsychiatry, **8**, 719-725.
>
> Strauss, A.A., & Werner, H. (1942). Disorders of conceptual thinking in the brain-injured child. *Journal of Nervous and Mental Disease, **96**, 153-172.
>
> Werner, H. (1948). *Comparative psychology of mental development*. New York: International Universities Press.
>
> Werner, H., & Strauss, A.A. (1941). Pathology of figure-background relation in the child. *Journal of Abnormal and Social Psychology, **36**, 236-248.

Newell C. Kephart (1911-1973), a professor at Purdue University, Lafayette, Indiana, during most of the years he wrote about perceptual-motor development and remediation, was influenced greatly by Werner and Strauss and Piaget as well as several other theorists described by Hallahan and Cruickshank (1973). His classic book *The Slow Learner in the Classroom* (1960) still serves as the guide for many perceptual-motor practitioners. Kephart's earliest publications were with Strauss. Best known of these is

> Strauss, A.A., & Kephart, N. (1955). *Psychopathology and education of the brain-injured child*. New York: Grune and Stratton.

Illustrative research studies that have tested the Kephart approach are

> Alley, G., & Carr, D. (1968). Efforts of systematic sensory-motor training on sensory-motor, visual perception, and concept formation performance of mentally retarded children. *Perceptual and Motor Skills, **27**, 451-456.
>
> Edgar, C., Ball, T., McIntyre, R., & Shotwell, A. (1969). Effects of sensory-motor training on adaptive behavior. *American Journal of Mental Deficiency, **73**, 713-720.
>
> Haring, N., & Stables, J. (1966). The effect of gross motor development on visual perception and hand-eye coordination. *Journal of the American Physical Therapy Association, **46**, 129-135.
>
> Maloney, M., Ball, T., & Edgar, C. (1970). Analysis of the generalizability of sensory-motor training.

American Journal of Mental Deficiency, **74**, 458-469.

Maloney, M., & Payne, L. (1970). Note on the stability of changes in body image due to sensory-motor training. *American Journal of Mental Deficiency,* **74**, 708.

Gerald Getman (1913-   ), an optometrist, appears to be the first theorist to translate ideas into practical activities for remediation of perceptual-motor problems (balance beam, trampoline, creeping through tunnels made of barrels, angels in the snow, and other exercises), although Kephart (1960) is often accredited with this contribution. Getman's first book, *How to Develop Your Child's Intelligence* (1965), was first published privately in 1942, 18 years before Kephart's *The Slow Learner in the Classroom*. Cratty (1972) incorrectly indicated the publication date of *How to Develop Your Child's Intelligence* as 1952. Getman also included these activities in a teacher's manual, which outlined a visual-motor-tactile (VMT) program.

> Getman, G.N., Kane, E., Halgren, M., & McKee, G. (1966). *Developing learning readiness.* New York: McGraw-Hill.

Closely associated with Arthur Gesell at the Yale University for several years, Getman was also a contributor to the classic book by A. Gesell, F. Ilg, G. Bullis, G. Getman, and F. Ilg (1949), entitled *Vision: Its Development in Infant and Child* (New York: Hoeber).

Illustrative research studies that have tested the Getman approach to perceptual-motor remediation are

> Goodman, L., & Hammill, D. (1973). The effectiveness of the Kephart-Getman activities in developing perceptual-motor and cognitive skills. *Focus on Exceptional Children,* **4**, 1-10.

> Halgren, A. (1961). Opus in see sharp. *Education,* **81**, 369-371. This study is critiqued by Hallahan and Cruickshank (1973), and many possible sources of error are identified.

William Cruickshank (1915-   ), for many years professor of psychology at the University of Michigan, was strongly influenced by Strauss and Werner and by work with a doctoral student, **Jane Dolphin**, whose dissertation focused on the perceptual-motor problems of cerebral palsied individuals. Among their contributions to the literature are

> Cruickshank, W.M. (1967). *The brain-injured child in home, school and community.* Syracuse, NY: Syracuse University Press.

> Cruickshank, W.M., Bice, H.V., & Wallen, N.E. (1957). *Perception and cerebral palsy.* Syracuse, NY: Syracuse University Press.

> Dolphin, J.E., & Cruickshank, W. (1951a). The figure-background relationship in children with cerebral palsy. *Journal of Clinical Psychology,* **7**, 288-331.

> Dolphin, J.E., & Cruickshank, W. (1951b). Visuo-motor perception of children with cerebral palsy. *Quarterly Journal of Child Behavior,* **3**, 198-209.

> Dolphin, J.E., & Cruickshank, W.M. (1952). Tactual motor perception of children with cerebral palsy. *Journal of Personality,* **20**, 466-471.

Primary sources for other pioneers listed in Figure 15.2 include the following:

> Ayres, A.J. (1965). Patterns of perceptual-motor dysfunction in children: A factor analytic study. *Perceptual and Motor Skills,* **20**, 335-368.

> Ayers, A.J. (1972). *Sensory integration and learning disorders.* Los Angeles: Western Psychological Press.

> Barsch, R. (1965). *Achieving perceptual-motor efficiency, a space-oriented approach to learning.* Seattle: Special Child Publications.

> Delacato, C. (1959). *Treatment and prevention of reading problems.* Springfield, IL: Charles C. Thomas.

> Frostig, M. (1963). *Marianne Frostig developmental test of visual perception* (3rd ed.). Palo Alto, CA: Consulting Psychologists Press.

> Frostig, M., & Maslow, P. (1970). *Movement education: Theory and practice.* Chicago: Follett.

References

Alley, G.R. (1967). *The effects of systematic sensory motor training on sensory motor, visual perception and concept formation of mentally retarded children.* Unpublished manuscript, University of Iowa, Iowa City.

Auxter, D., & Pyfer, J. (1985). *Adapted physical education and recreation* (5th ed.). St. Louis: Times Mirror/Mosby.

Ayres, A.J. (1976). *The effect of sensory integrative therapy on learning disabled children: The final report of a research project.* Pasadena, CA: The Center for the Study of Sensory Integrative Dysfunction.

Ayres, A. J. (1979). *Sensory integration and the child.* Los Angeles: Western Psychological Services.

Belmont, L., & Birch, H. G. (1965). Lateral dominance, lateral awareness and reading disability. *Child Development, 36*, 57-71.

Broxterman, J., & Stebbins, S. (1981). A study of the significance of visual training in the treatment of reading disabilities. *American Journal of Corrective Therapy, 35*(5), 122-126.

Bruner, J. S. (1967). *Studies in cognitive growth.* New York: John Wiley & Sons.

Frostig, M., & Maslow, P. (1970). *Movement education: Theory and practice.* Chicago: Follett.

Gagne, R. M. (1965). *The conditions of learning.* New York: Holt, Rinehart & Winston.

Getman, G. N. (1965). The visuomotor complex in the acquisition of learning skills. In J. Hellmuth (Ed.), *Learning disorders* (pp. 105-108). Seattle, WA: Special Child Publications.

Hallahan, D., & Cruickshank, W. (1973). *Psychoeducational foundations of learning disabilities.* Englewood Cliffs, NJ: Prentice-Hall.

Hammill, D. (1971). *Training visual perceptual processes.* Paper presented at the Annual Convention of the Council for Exceptional Children, Miami Beach, FL.

Itard, J.M.G. (1932). *The wild boy of Aveyron.* New York: Appleton-Century-Crofts.

Kephart, N.C. (1960). *The slow learner in the classroom.* Columbus, OH: Charles E. Merrill.

Miller, D., & Haley, A. (1978). *Effects of the front crawl swimming stroke on reading and on bilateral integration.* Unpublished manuscript, University of Kansas, Lawrence.

Montessori, M. (1965). *Spontaneous activity in education.* New York: Schoken Books.

Piaget, J. (1963). *The origins of intelligence in children.* New York: W.W. Norton.

Pyfer, J.L., & Alley, G. (1978). *Sensory-perceptualmotor dysfunction of learning disabled children.* Presentation at the Council of Exceptional Children, First World Congress, Stirling, Scotland.

Pyfer, J.L. (1983). *Translating assessment into action: Research studies that emphasize the problems that face us.* Presentation at the Therapeutics Council and Adapted Physical Education Conference, National Convention of American Alliance for Health, Physical Education, Recreation and Dance, Minneapolis, MN.

Rider, B. (1972). Relationship of postural reflexes to learning disabilities. *American Journal of Occupational Therapy, 26*(5), 239-243.

Seaman, J., & DePauw, K. (1982). *The new adapted physical education.* Palo Alto, CA: Mayfield.

Sherrill, C. (1985). *Working paper on ranking of perceptualmotor function and sensory integration as an adapted physical education goal.* Unpublished manuscript, Texas Woman's University, Denton.

Sherrill, C. (1986). *Adapted physical education and recreation: A multidisciplinary approach* (3rd ed.). Dubuque, IA: Wm. C. Brown.

Sherrill, C., & Tymeson, G. (1979). *Directory of resources in physical education and recreation for the handicapped.* Denton, TX: Texas Woman's University.

Werbel, V. (1975). *Reflex dysfunction and perceptualmotor performance.* Unpublished master's thesis, University of Kansas, Lawrence.

Chapter 16

Advocacy: Perspectives on Theory and Practice

Wanda Rainbolt and Claudine Sherrill

*A*dvocacy has many faces. Every action taken in behalf of a cause is an advocate action. Jane Addams, one of the social work pioneers, once said that action was the one medium man had for appropriating and expressing the truth. Advocacy may thus mean action to achieve a better life for children from infancy to adulthood. (Lourie, 1975, p. 71)

Advocacy is action aimed at promoting, maintaining, or defending a cause. Adapted physical educators need to be advocates toward two causes: (a) the right of all children and youth to high quality physical education service delivery and (b) the elimination of attitudinal, aspirational, and architectural barriers that handicapped persons experience in sport, dance, aquatics, and fitness activities. Advocacy, as used in this paper, is action based on such areas of knowledge as

- law;
- human relations and communication theory with particular emphasis upon legislation, litigation, and rules/

regulations/procedures that affect the rights and opportunities of "different" persons;

- social psychology and attitude theory with emphasis on techniques for fighting prejudice, promoting integration, and helping persons understand, appreciate, and accept themselves and others; and
- humanistic philosophy and psychology.

Today advocacy is recognized as an integral aspect of professionalism in many disciplines. Specifically, adapted physical educators (Rainbolt, 1985; Sherrill, 1981a, b; Winnick, 1984), therapeutic recreation specialists (Edginton & Compton, 1975; Hillman, 1972), classroom teachers (Lilly, 1982), special educators (Frith, 1981; McGregor, 1982), social workers (Darling & Darling, 1982), and mental health/mental retardation personnel (Berlin, 1975; Kurtz, 1975; Wolfensberger, 1973) have all been identified as responsible for advocacy activities.

Although used frequently in the other helping professions, the term advocacy is not often heard in physical education. Sherrill (1986), however, proposes that advocacy is one of the six major tasks that comprise adapted physical education service delivery. The other tasks are (a) individualized educational planning, (b) assessment, (c) developmental and/or prescriptive teaching, (d) counseling, and (e) coordination of resources and services. The rationale for the inclusion of advocacy is the time and energy that adapted physical educators spend consulting with and acting as resources to mainstream physical educators and classroom teachers (as well as students) in facilitating the implementation of PL 94-142 and related legislation. Adapted physical educators are also involved in changing the attitudes and aspirations of administrators, families, and others regarding rights and opportunities of handicapped persons. Such allocation of time and energy deserves recognition, and achievement of advocacy goals generally requires special training. This chapter is therefore a first effort toward consideration of advocacy as an area of knowledge with both theoretical and practical aspects.

Theoretical Basis for Advocacy in Adapted Physical Education Service Delivery

The major theoretical basis for advocacy in this stage of our evolving thought is *ecological psychology* and the *ecological model*. The initial use of these terms is accredited to Herbert Wright and Roger Barker, whose work at the Midwest Psychological Field Station at the University of Kansas can be traced back to the 1950s (Barker, 1963, 1968; Barker & Gump, 1964; Barker &

Wanda Rainbolt (left) and Claudine Sherrill (right) discussing role of *Adapted Physical Activity Quarterly* and *Palaestra* in advocacy activities.

Wright, 1951, 1955; Wright & Barker, 1950). Both men were psychologists with strong Gestalt backgrounds. Barker indicates that their theoretical base was the work of Kurt Lewin (1951) on psychological environment (i.e., "life-space, the world as a particular person perceives and is otherwise affected by it" [Barker, 1968, p. 1]). Ecological psychology, as defined by Barker (1968), is "concerned with both the psychological environment . . . and the ecological environment (the objective, preperceptual context of behavior; the real-life setting within which people behave" (p. 1).

Many authors have described ecological models, each in a slightly different way. Goodlad (1979), for instance, states,

> A useful theoretical model for viewing and improving educational conditions in schools is what, for want of a better term, I call an ecological perspective. . . . An ecological model of schooling is concerned primarily, then, with interactions, relationships, and interdependencies with a defined environment. . . . The metaphoric use of ecological concepts is obviously helpful in promoting our conceptual grasp of education as a system larger than, but including, schools. (pp. 76-77)

Hobbs (1975, 1979), well known among special educators for his advocacy of ecological strategies, believes that the only way to help students with problems is

> to involve the child, his family, his school, and his community in a cooperative assessment of the problem and a shared design for its solution. Schools that take their educational tasks seriously know now that they must extend their efforts to the family and to the earliest years of the child's life. (1979, pp. 195, 197)

Hobbs proposes that teachers direct their service delivery toward the ecosystem rather than the individual student. The ecosystem is comprised of the student and all of the significant others in family, community, neighborhood, and school.

The adapted physical educator who advocates for the rights of a handicapped student among the individuals in his or her family, community, neighborhood, and school is implementing an ecological model. Inherent in this model is work directed toward changing the opinions, beliefs, and attitudes of individuals in the various ecosystems. Often efforts are also needed to change the self-concept and aspirations of the handicapped student in regard to fitness, physical activity, and leisure time choices.

An ecological model can also be conceptualized as a multidisciplinary, interdisciplinary, or cross-disciplinary model in that professionals from several disciplines work together in assessment, placement, service delivery, and follow-up. If PL 94-142 is implemented, parents, and when appropriate the handicapped student, are involved in decision making concerning these processes. In many schools, representatives and/or consultants from the community are also involved and facilitate the integration of handicapped students in community recreation and sport programs. If integration is not recommended, such nonschool personnel often provide sport training and competition (e.g., activities of the U.S. Cerebral Palsy Athletic Association, the National Wheelchair Basketball Association, or Special Olympics). The interactions, relationships, and interdependencies among school and nonschool personnel, the family, and significant others determine, in large part, the quality of physical education service delivery. Minner, Prater, and Beane (1984), for example, discuss dilemmas that occur concerning whether students should be recommended for adapted physical education services. Much research is needed in relation to the ecological model of adapted physical education service delivery. An understanding of history and current status as well as knowledge of primary sources may help in planning such research and in extending advocacy theory.

History of the Advocacy Movement

Concepts of professional advocacy, citizen and child advocacy, and consumer advocacy have emerged primarily during the past 2 decades, affecting both professional preparation and service delivery. Prior to the 1960s, the only profession to use the term *advocacy* was law. A lawyer, or legal advocate, has always been known as one who pleads the cause of another. In the past few years, however, the meaning of advocacy has broadened to encompass social and political action directed toward improving quality of life and protecting rights of children (Berlin, 1975; Darling & Darling, 1982; Mearig, 1978), mentally retarded persons (Kurtz, 1975; Strichart & Gottlieb, 1980; Wolfensberger, 1972, 1973), cerebral palsied persons (Wyeth, 1983), and other individuals in need of health, educational, and social services (Buscaglia & Williams, 1979; Mann, 1976; Neufield, 1979).

Citizen Advocacy

Although the roots of citizen and professional advocacy can both be traced to the mid-1960s, citizen advocacy (particularly that of parents) seems to have evolved first.

Kurtz (1975) states that the starting point for current ideas about advocacy for mentally retarded persons was the founding of the parent-sponsored National Association for Retarded Children (NARC) in 1950. The development of the citizen advocacy movement paralleled the social movements of deinstitutionalization and normalization.

The foremost spokesperson for citizen advocacy has been Wolf Wolfensberger, most of whose books have been published by the National Institute on Mental Retardation in Toronto, Canada (Wolfensberger, 1972, 1973). Wolfensberger believes strongly that advocates must be volunteers rather than professionals. He defines an advocate as

> a mature, competent citizen volunteer representing, as if they were his own, the interests of another citizen who is impaired in his instrumental competency, or who has major expressive needs which are unmet and which are likely to remain unmet without special intervention. (Wolfensberger, 1973, p. 11)

In this definition *instrumental competency* pertains to daily living skills, and *expressive needs* refers to friendship, communication, warmth, and support.

Wolfensberger believes that volunteer efforts should be supported by a network of advocacy offices. He reports that the first of these offices was opened in Lincoln, Nebraska, in 1969, funded partly by United Fund and partly by federal social security monies. By 1975, NARC revealed that 117 local and 10 state citizen advocacy programs were operating in 30 states. Local associations for retarded citizens were responsible for 75% of these programs. Approximately 3,000 pairings of one-to-one advocates and protégés had been established by 1975 (Strichart & Gottlieb, 1977).

The term *citizen advocacy,* in the past, has been mostly associated with mental retardation services. It has influenced volunteerism in Special Olympics and recreation programming for this and other populations. The broad scope of citizen advocacy can be described as follows:

> Advocacy roles can range from minor to major, from formal to informal, and from short-term to long-term or even life-long. Formal advocacy roles might include adoptive parenthood, guardianship, and trusteeship for property. Informal roles include friend and guide. Some advocacy roles emphasize close relationships and exchange of affection and concern. Others are more involved with practical problem-solving. Many roles fulfill both types of need. (Wolfensberger, 1972, p. 219)

Research on reasons for becoming a citizen advocate, advocates' perceptions of their protégés, and the nature of interaction between advocates and their protégés is reported by Strichart and Gottlieb (1977). Further research is needed. It is evident, however, that

> citizen advocacy provides an opportunity for citizen advocates, their friends, families, neighbors, and coworkers to learn about people with developmental disabilities; to learn that people with developmental disabilities are unique individuals who cannot be labeled, categorized, or stereotyped. (McGlamery & Malavenda cited in Strichart & Gottlieb, 1977, p. 243)

Adapted physical educators today are seeking to extend the concepts of citizen advocacy to all disabled populations. Helping handicapped and nonhandicapped students to become friends is a major objective of adapted physical education. This approach is supported by Wolfensberger, who states, "At a certain point, a person needs a friend and not a law, and no law can create, nor any amount of money buy the freely-given dedication of one person to the welfare of another" (Wolfensberger, 1973, p. 10). Adapted physical educators may act as either citizen or professional advocates. As citizens, they should have some close friends who are disabled. As citizens also, adapted physical educators are involved in fighting for legislation and budgetary commitments favorable to optimal services for persons with disabilities.

Professional Advocacy

Professional advocacy, while now sanctioned by many disciplines, has been supported most strongly by the National Association of Social Workers (NASW) and the Council for Exceptional Children (CEC). Both organizations have taken the stand that, in instances of conflict between demands of employer and needs of student or client, the professional's obligation to the child takes primacy (Darling & Darling, 1982). The child advocacy movement of NASW and similar organizations can be traced back to reports of the Joint Commission on the Mental Health of Children (1970) and the White House Conference on Children and Youth (1971). Recommendations were made in both reports for advocacy related to the "prevention of disease and disorder and the provision of health, mental health, and social services" (Lourie, 1975, p. 69). Thereafter several federal actions reflected the new emphasis on advocacy. The Office of Child Development within the United States Department of Health, Education, and Welfare designated child advocacy as the main function of one of its structures. The United States Office of Education and the National

Institute of Mental Health began offering jointly funded grants for child advocacy projects.

Professional preparation of mental health and mental retardation personnel changed accordingly, and service delivery systems increasingly stressed the elimination of physical, cultural, and social barriers. Darling and Darling (1982) summarize the philosophical stance that professionals should act as advocates:

> If professionals do not act as advocates, who will? Society simply does not have enough interested, knowledgeable, altruistic citizens. Professionals who work closely with the handicapped and their families and who are committed to a "collectivity orientation" (involvement in all aspects of a client's life rather than only in-class instruction) are natural advocates for their clients. Unresponsive systems must somehow be changed to eliminate the "advocacy dilemmas" that are so prevalent in the professional role today. Even professionals who do not choose to become directly involved in advocacy themselves can become effective organizers of parent action. (Darling & Darling, 1982, p. 253)

The advocacy dilemma has been featured in several recent issues of *Exceptional Children* (Frith, 1981; Heshusius, 1982; McGregor, 1982). The issues confronting special educators are applicable also to adapted physical education service providers. Frith, for instance, cites a case in which a child needed adapted physical education and physical therapy, but no such services were made available by the school system. The administrator requested the teachers involved to omit these items from the individual education program (IEP) and not to discuss them with the parents. The dilemma of whether to comply with the administrator's wishes or to advocate for the child's needs is frequently experienced in the real world. Fortunately, creative teachers can find many ways to act as advocates.

Consumer Advocacy

The consumer and self-advocacy movement is also a product of the 1970s. Mostly it has been facilitated by organizations of and for disabled persons and their families, such as the American Coalition of Citizens with Disabilities, the President's, Governor's, and Mayor's Committees on Employment of the Handicapped, and the Developmental Disabilities (DD) Councils that now exist in every state as mandated by law. The first White House Conference on Handicapped Individuals (WHCHI), held in 1976, was instrumental in this movement as was the International Year of the Disabled in 1981. Many national

and state organizations like United Cerebral Palsy Associations, Inc. have consumer affairs offices or branches staffed by disabled persons.

Athletes in the various sport organizations for disabled persons are among the most vocal. Among these are Charles Buell, Harry Cordellos, and Jim Mastro of the United States Association for Blind Athletes, and Duncan Wyeth, Wendy Shugol, and Nancy Anderson of the United States Cerebral Palsy Athletic Association. These persons demonstrate their effectiveness as self-advocates not only through speeches and publications but also through their life-styles and commitment to high level competition and risk-recreation as rights of all persons. The chapter by Julian Stein later in this book elaborates on the consumer advocacy of athletes.

Teacher Training for the Advocacy Role

In teaching adapted physical education courses, university educators should strive to develop attitudes and habits of advocacy as well as knowledge about handicapping conditions and service delivery. A first step in achieving this goal is to help physical education majors to become personally acquainted with disabled persons. In addition to practica that entail teaching or coaching handicapped students, Sherrill (see illustrative course outline in chapter 21) requires that persons enrolled in the introductory course in adapted physical education spend at least 2 hours a week recreating and socializing with handicapped persons of equal status (i.e., as friends and peers rather than as consumers who need services). The purpose of this requirement is to promote positive attitudes and habits of advocacy. Classroom orientation encompassing the following suggestions is generally needed.

Stein (1978) provides suggestions from several sources for advocates relating to handicapped persons. These suggestions appear in *Practical Pointers* (pp. 7-8):

1. Offer help when it looks as though it might be needed, but do not insist on it if an individual refuses aid;

2. When handicapped persons fall, take it easy. Wait for them to give you a cue. If individuals can get up by themselves, they may prefer doing that. If they need a lift, they will tell you which is the easiest way to get them back on their feet;

3. No matter what you do, if you are friendly and kind, the handicapped person is going to like you;

4. Talk about the same things you would with any other person. A physical impairment or disability does not necessarily limit interests or dampen a sense of humor;

5. Let common sense and consideration be your guide and you will never err seriously. Disabled individuals are just like you, only with a physical difference that does not have to make them feel or think differently;

6. Do not assume that the way you help an individual with an impairment or disability will be the same for all people with similar conditions. Always ask what is the best way to help that individual;

7. Do not be afraid to ask a handicapped person to repeat what he/she said. Most handicapped individuals would rather repeat what they said than to have an able-bodied person fake understanding and subsequent communication;

8. Be sensitive to the fact that some handicapped people get tired of asking for help and may forget to say please and thank you. They are not necessarily being impolite.

As part of course requirements, university students often write or speak about handicapped persons. It is important, therefore, that adapted physical educators learn early to adhere to the following criteria when portraying individuals with disabilities (Media Project, 1984):

1. Do not refer to a disability unless it is crucial to a story.

2. Avoid portraying persons with disabilities who succeed as superhuman. This implies that persons who are disabled have no talents or unusual gifts.

3. Do not sensationalize a disability by saying afflicted with, victim of, and so on. Instead, say *person who has multiple sclerosis, person who had polio*.

4. Avoid labeling persons into groups, as in the disabled, the deaf, a retardate, an arthritic. Instead, say *people who are deaf, person with arthritis, persons with disabilities*.

5. Where possible, emphasize an individual, not a disability. Say *people* or *persons with disabilities* or *person who is blind* rather than disabled persons or blind person. [Authors of this chapter do not feel strongly about this criterion when an entire paper focuses on disabilities; too many *with* phrases and *persons who are* phrases make awkward reading.]

6. Avoid using emotional descriptors such as unfortunate, pitiful, and so on. Emphasize abilities, such as *uses a wheelchair/braces* rather than confined to a wheelchair, *walks with crutches/braces* rather than is crippled, *is partially sighted* rather than partially blind.

7. Avoid implying disease when discussing disabilities. A disability such as Parkinson's disease may be caused by a sickness, but it is not a disease itself, nor is the person necessarily chronically ill. Persons with disabilities should not be referred to as patients or cases unless they are under medical care.

In relation to sport events, adapted physical educators should advocate that athletes with disabilities be treated as athletes and not as outstanding achievers with disabilities whose stories are told in sections of the newspaper other than sports. This guideline also applies to media coverage. Teaching the media how to portray handicapped students humanistically is one way that adapted physical educators can act as advocates. The university newspaper is a good place to begin.

Because sport has been found to be a viable way to arouse public interest in persons with disabilities and to increase the effectiveness of fund-raising campaigns, physical educators should be taught guidelines for participating in telethons and related events. Telethons are controversial among self-advocacy groups of disabled persons, and adapted physical educators should find out how persons in their particular community feel. Illustrative of guidelines acceptable to many disabled persons are the following, disseminated by the National Consumer Activities Committee of the United Cerebral Palsy Associations, Inc. (Wyeth, 1983, p. 2):

1. Both adults and children should be shown on the telethon and in demonstrations of programs and services.

2. Disabled individuals appearing on the telethon should be typical of the different degrees of disability and the variety of living situations represented among persons with cerebral palsy.

3. Talent appearing on the telethon should be thoroughly informed about the nature of

cerebral palsy and appropriate terminology to be used in referring to cerebral palsy. Such negative terms as "victims," "disease," "poor," "crippled," "unfortunate," "tragedy," and other words that arouse pity rather than respect for human beings should be avoided.

4. Asking viewers to give out of thankfulness that their own children were born healthy should be avoided, as this implies that cerebral palsy is hopeless and leaves those who have it without the capacity for leading meaningful lives.

5. Children's marches or other demonstrations placing undue emphasis on walking and talking as goals for persons with cerebral palsy should be avoided. Too much emphasis on walking and talking can lead to unrealistic expectations on the part of the public and do damage to the self-image of persons with cerebral palsy who will never be able to do either.

6. Attention should be given to the United Cerebral Palsy's advocacy role in helping the disabled realize their rising expectations; for example, mainstreaming into public education, barrier free buildings, accessible transportation, independent living, and productive employment. This may be accomplished by depicting persons with cerebral palsy accomplishing with pride what others take for granted, once physical and psychological barriers are removed.

The guidelines stated by Wyeth can be used as criteria for evaluating media and other events. Through experiences in such evaluation, graduate students and professionals become better advocates for disabled persons. Teacher trainers should use every possible means to activate university students in actions aimed at promoting, maintaining, and defending quality physical education for disabled persons.

Adapted physical educators, as well as other professionals, must become increasingly involved also in political advocacy. Stedman (1977) states,

> Advocacy is a form of political behavior. It rests on values, a predisposition to change, an ability to maintain a broad perspective, a tolerance for ambiguity, and the ability to delay gratification. . . . No advocate can be successful for very long without a road map of state and local government and some idea of how to develop alternative strategies for negotiating the various routes between the influence and the power centers. (pp. 53, 62)

Physical educators need to understand the difference between laws that *authorize* and those that *appropriate* monies. PL 94-142 authorized the expenditure of monies for the handicapped. New laws are needed year by year to actually appropriate the money for use.

Following is a list of strategies that physical educators can use in advocating for needed legislation. To implement these strategies most graduate students need special classroom training.

1. Get to know your state and federal legislators. Let them know you vote for them specifically because they support legislation favorable to education and equal opportunity for handicapped persons.

2. Visit your legislator in his or her office in the Capitol. Get to know the legislator's staff by name and personality; usually they are the ones responsible for compiling materials, reading and answering letters sent to the legislator, and keeping him or her informed.

3. Make frequent contacts with legislators. The best communication is face-to-face, but telephone calls, telegrams, and letters are crucial when bills are ready for a vote.

4. Do not mail form letters; make contents brief and personal. Be sure to mention the law by name and number and state specifically which passage you wish to retain or change.

5. Develop parent advocacy corps for physical education. Take different kinds of stationery to Special Olympics and other sport practices and ask parents who are waiting to jot letters to their legislator. Offer to speak at meetings of parent groups, inform them about PL 94-142, and ask them to visit, telephone, and write legislators specifically on behalf of physical education.

6. Become a member of parent and other advocacy groups for handicapped persons and encourage them to invite legislators to speak at their meetings. Volunteer to be program chairperson and you can make this happen for sure. Legislators, as well as candidates running for office, are particularly willing to speak during election years.

7. Become personal friends with handicapped persons and encourage them to advocate for physical education. A physical educator and a handicapped adult who believes in physical education make a powerful partnership in facilitating change.

8. When you write to a legislator, be sure to ask for an answer in which he or she states intent to support or not support your request. When you speak to a legislator, do the same.

9. Invite legislators, with the approval of your administration, to visit your adapted physical education program and to be a dignitary in the opening or closing ceremonies of Special Olympics, Cerebral Palsy Sports, or other events.

10. Keep abreast of funding issues, especially which parties and which persons support federal and state funding favorable to education. Find out how your legislator votes on critical issues by reading newspapers or the *Congressional Record* or by telephoning his or her office. Let him or her know when you approve as well as when you disapprove.

11. Get to know the state directors of physical education and special education and their staff, all of whom are part of the SEA, and encourage them to communicate with legislators.

12. Be sure local and state meetings of physical educators include legislative updates concerning action that may affect adapted physical education. Exhibit bulletin boards showing progress made in implementation of laws. Encourage officers of local and state physical education organizations, as well as members, to maintain close contact with their legislators.

Teacher trainers need to experiment with ways of infusing advocacy training into required courses and practica. Contract teaching is one approach that can be used with a preestablished number of points earned for each advocacy action. Sherrill's experience in teaching graduate students how to write letters to congresspersons led to the development of the following criteria (see Figure 16.1). Fulfillment of the assignment could lead to 25 to 50 points that were applicable to the overall grade in the course and equal in value to points earned on a 50-point quiz or essay paper. From 47 to 50 points resulted in a grade of A, and at least 43 points were needed for a B.

While the criteria in Figure 16.1 may seem rather arbitrary, they were developed and field tested over a period of 10 years. Obviously developed during the era when advocates were working to retain PL 94-142, the format and procedures are applicable to any law as well as to input at hearings in relation to changes of state educational policy. Writing letters is a first step for many persons in the development of advocacy habits. Research is needed on methods, procedures, and approaches for teaching advocacy and for measurement of attitudes and habits.

Summary

Development of attitudes and habits is an integral part of adapted physical education teacher training. The body of knowledge underlying action aimed at promoting, maintaining, and defending a cause such as quality physical education for disabled students can be conceptualized as advocacy theory. This chapter presents perspectives of both advocacy theory and practice; the approach is elementary because advocacy, as a job function, is relatively new to the thought processes of many physical educators.

References

Barker, R. (Ed.). (1963). *The stream of behavior*. New York: Appleton.

Barker, R. (1968). *Ecological psychology*. Stanford, CA: Stanford University Press.

Barker, R., & Gump, P. (1964). *Big school, small school*. Stanford, CA: Stanford University Press.

Barker, R., & Wright, H.F. (1951). *One boy's day*. New York: Harper.

Barker, R., & Wright, H.F. (1955). *Midwest and its children: The psychological ecology of an American town*. New York: Harper.

Berlin, I.N. (Ed.). (1975). *Advocacy for child mental health*. New York: Brunner/Mazel.

Buscaglia, L., & Williams, E. (1979). *Human advocacy and PL 94-142*. Thorofare, NJ: Charles B. Slack.

Darling, R., & Darling, J. (1982). *Children who are different* (pp. 247-258). St. Louis: C.V. Mosby.

Edginton, C., & Compton, D. (1975). Consumerism and advocacy: A conceptual role for the therapeutic recreator. *Therapeutic Recreation Journal*, **9**(1), 26-31.

Frith, G. (1981). "Advocate" vs "professional employee": A question of priorities for special educators. *Exceptional Children*, **47**(7), 486-492.

Goodlad, J.L. (1979). *What schools are for*. Los Angeles: University of California.

Heshusius, L. (1982). At the heart of the advocacy dilemma: A mechanistic world view. *Exceptional Children*, **49**(1), 6-13.

Hillman, W. (1972). Therapeutic recreational specialist as advocate. *Therapeutic Recreation Journal*, **6**(2), 50.

Hobbs, N. (1975). *The futures of children*. San Francisco: Jossey-Bass.

Hobbs, N. (1979). Families, schools, and communities: An ecosystem for children. In H. Leichter (Ed.),

Dr. Sherrill
Texas Woman's University

Criteria for Evaluating Letter to Legislator or Hearing Officer

Good Intent—25 points

You wrote the letter, mailed it, kept a copy for your files, and submitted a copy to (professor's name) by assigned deadline.

Content—13 points, 1 point for each criterion

1. Mention PL 94-142 or the issue of concern in first paragraph.

2. Indicate position of "against changes" in PL 94-142 or the law or issue of concern clearly in first paragraph.

3. State specific section number (121a.14) that you most care about.

4. State specific section by content (physical education) that you most care about.

5. Identify self in your most *credible* role—teacher of handicapped and/or member/officer of advocacy groups, not as a graduate student.

6. Indicate number of handicapped persons you serve as a professional, volunteer, and/or parent who will be negatively affected by proposed changes.

7. Indicate number of handicapped persons in your school district or city or state who will be negatively affected, that is, be specific with regard to *impact*—will others (families, nonhandicapped) be affected also?

8. & 9. Give two more reasons *why* you are against the proposed changes (one point for each).

10. State reasons clearly and specifically. For instance, state, "If the 121a.14 definition of physical education is eliminated, then _____ may occur."

11. Request a specific action. Ask him or her to talk to/influence the President, a specific Subcommittee, the Dept. of Education, or to vote a specific way.

12. Request an answer. Ask where he or she stands, what he or she is doing.

13. Make letter dignified, respectful, and sincere.

Mechanics—12 points, 1 point for each criterion

1. Use personal stationery or blank paper, not business stationery.

2. Include your return address in upper right-hand corner.

3. Give date under return address.

4. Give correct address for person you are writing.

5. Use correct greeting—Dear _____:

6. Type single-spaced format.

7. Limit content to one page.

8. Limit paragraphs to 10 lines or less than one third of a page.

9. Double space between paragraphs or numbered points.

10. Ascertain no spelling or proofreading errors.

11. Ascertain no grammatical or sentence composition errors.

12. Include your *work title* under signature at end of letter, not title of graduate student. Also good to put your voter registration number.

Figure 16.1 Handout explaining evaluation criteria to graduate students.

Families and communities as educators (pp. 192-202). New York: Teachers College Press.

Joint Commission on Mental Health of Children. (1970). *Crisis in child mental health*. New York: Harper & Row.

Kurtz, R. (1975). Advocacy for the mentally retarded: The development of a new social role. In M.J. Begab & S.A. Richardson (Eds.), *The mentally retarded and society: A social science perspective* (pp. 377-394). Baltimore: University Park Press.

Lewin, K. (1951). *Field theory in social science*. New York: Harper & Row.

Lilly, S. (1982). The education of mildly handicapped children and implications for teacher education. In M. Reynolds (Ed.), *The future of mainstreaming: Next steps in teacher education* (pp. 54-70). Reston, VA: Council for Exceptional Children.

Lourie, N. (1975). The many faces of advocacy. In I.N. Berlin (Ed.), *Advocacy for child mental health* (pp. 68-80). New York: Brunner/Mazel.

Mann, P. (Ed.). (1976). *Shared responsibility for handicapped students: Advocacy and programming*. Coral Gables, FL: Training and Technical Assistance Center at Miami University.

McGregor, D. (1982). Readers respond: The advocacy dilemma. *Exceptional Children, 49*(1), 14-15.

Mearig, J. (Ed.). (1978). *Working for children*. San Francisco: Jossey-Bass.

Media Project. (1984). *Guidelines for reporting and writing about people with disabilities*. (Pamphlet available from Media Project, Research and Training Center on Independent Living, 348 Haworth Hall, University of Kansas, Lawrence, KS 66045)

Minner, S., Prater, G., & Beane, A. (1984). Provision of adapted physical education. A dilemma for special educators. *Adapted Physical Activity Quarterly, 1*(4), 282-286.

Neufield, G. (1979). The advocacy role and functions of developmental disabilities. In R. Wiegerink & J. Pelosi (Eds.), *Developmental disabilities: The DD movement* (pp. 45-60). Baltimore: Paul H. Brookes.

Rainbolt, W. (1985). Advocacy and coordination of services. *Adapted Physical Activity Quarterly, 2*(1), 8-15.

Sherrill, C. (1981a). *Adapted physical education and recreation: A multidisciplinary approach* (2nd ed.). Dubuque, IA: Wm. C. Brown.

Sherrill, C. (1981b). An ecological approach to needs assessment for inservice training. *Resources in Education*, SPO 18467; ED 204306.

Sherrill, C. (1986). *Adapted physical education and recreation: A multidisciplinary approach* (3rd ed.). Dubuque, IA: Wm. C. Brown.

Stedman, D. (1977). Politics, political structures, and advocacy activities. In J. Paul, D. Stedman, & G. Neufield (Eds.), *Deinstitutionalization: Program and policy development* (pp. 53-62). New York: Syracuse Press.

Stein, J. (1978). Tips on mainstreaming: Do's and don'ts in activity programs. *Practical Pointers, 1*(10), 1-16.

Strichart, S., & Gottlieb, J. (1980). Advocacy through the eyes of citizens. In J. Gottlieb (Ed.), *Educating mentally retarded persons in the mainstream* (pp. 231-250). Baltimore: University Park Press.

White House Conference on Children and Youth. (1971). *Recommendations and resolutions*. Washington, DC: U.S. Government Printing Office.

Winnick, J. (1984). *A special physical education preparation program: Competencies required of graduate students at SUNY at Brockport*. Unpublished manuscript.

Wolfensberger, W. (1972). *The principle of normalization in human service*. Toronto: National Institute of Mental Retardation.

Wolfensberger, W. (1973). *Citizen advocacy and protective services for the impaired and handicapped*. Toronto: National Institute of Mental Retardation.

Wright, H.F., & Barker, R.G. (1950). *Methods in psychological ecology: A progress report*. Lawrence, KS: University of Kansas.

Wyeth, D. (1983). *Guidelines for conducting telethons*. New York: United Cerebral Palsy Associations, Inc.

Chapter 17

Opinion and Attitude Assessment: The First Step in Changing Public School Service Delivery

Jo E. Cowden and Nancy Megginson

*T*he implementation of Public Law 94-142 is largely dependent upon increasing the knowledge of administrators and significant others concerning desirable adapted physical education practices and changing their attitudes in regard to integration of handicapped and nonhandicapped students. To facilitate the achievement of these goals, professionals must have access to valid and reliable assessment instruments that determine status quo and measure change. The purpose of this chapter is to present selected instruments, describe their validity and reliability, and briefly review pioneer research. The following instruments are included at the end of this chapter (pp. 235-255).

- National Consortium on Physical Education and Recreation for the Handicapped (NCPERH) State Needs Assessment (Chasey, 1979)

- Cowden Administrator Survey of Opinions Toward Adapted Physical Education (Cowden, 1980)

- Mainstreaming Attitude Inventory for Physical Educators (Jansma & Shultz, 1982)

- Physical Educators' Attitude Toward Teaching the Handicapped Inventory (Rizzo, 1984)

- Survey of Adapted Physical Education Needs (Sherrill & Megginson, 1984)

Definitions of Terms

Attitude is defined as "an enduring organization of motivational, emotional, perceptual, and cognitive processes with respect to some aspect of the individual's world" (Krech & Crutchfield, 1948, p. 152). Thus attitudes involve (a) cognitive structures, (b) affect, and (c) behavioral intentions. The cognitive component (i.e., the idea that generally involves categorizing as good or bad, belonging or not belonging, and the like) develops first (Triandis, 1971). Next the affective component (i.e., the emotion that charges the idea) evolves. Often affect is at a subconscious level, and thus it is difficult to measure affect separate from cognition. Last, the behavioral component (i.e., the predisposition to action) emerges.

Some theorists use such terms as attitude, opinion, and belief interchangeably. Others (Abelson & Karlins, 1959; Krech & Crutchfield, 1948) differentiate between formative and enduring cognitions, stating that the cognitive component of attitude has two parts: opinions and beliefs. *Opinions* are "relatively superficial, changeable, and limited" (Gould & Kolb, 1964, p. 477), whereas *beliefs* are enduring and hard to change. Changing opinions, then, is considered the first step in altering beliefs and ultimately modifying attitude. Most of the instruments reviewed in this chapter seem to assess opinion rather than belief. As these instruments are subjected to further study and new surveys are developed, attitude theory should receive increased attention.

Approaches to Assessment of Attitudes and Opinions

Many approaches to the measurement of attitudes are described in research textbooks. Each of the instruments reviewed in this chapter, however, employs a Likert-type scale (Likert, 1932) in the rating of statements. In a Likert-type scale, each statement is responded to in terms of agreement or disagreement. Although Likert used five categories (strongly approve, approve, undecided, disapprove, and strongly disapprove), fewer or more categories can be used. Each category is assigned a point value (e.g., 1 to 5), and the highest value is always the one showing the greatest favorableness toward the phenomenon. This approach does not assume that the distance between scale values is equal.

Three of the five instruments reviewed (Chasey, 1979; Cowden, 1980; Sherrill & Megginson, 1984) follow the needs assessment model of Educational Systems Associates, Inc. (1974) and Schipper and Wilson (1975). *Needs assessment* is defined as follows:

> . . . a technique for identifying those goals which most merit accomplishment in a given situation. A needs assessment is accomplished by performing a discrepancy analysis between the current and desired status with respect to an existing goal. (Educational Systems Associates, 1974, p. 1)

A needs assessment instrument is comprised of statements that represent goals or ideal conditions or services. Typically, each statement is rated twice, once indicating an opinion about the extent the goal is presently being implemented, and again, indicating an opinion about the extent the goal should be implemented. Additionally, the Cowden instrument requires a third rating of each statement, indicating the extent of intent to change conditions. Figure 17.1 depicts the format of a typical needs assessment instrument.

Statistics in needs assessment methodology are kept simple so that they are easily understood by parents, teachers, and others interested in more closely approximating ideal conditions within a state, school district, or school. The purpose of needs assessment is action directed toward change rather than data collection per se. Thus attention is focused on testing the hypothesis of no significant difference between actual and desired conditions in

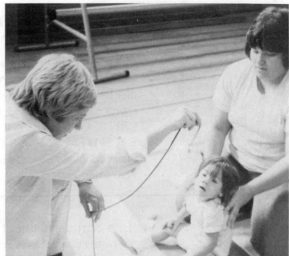

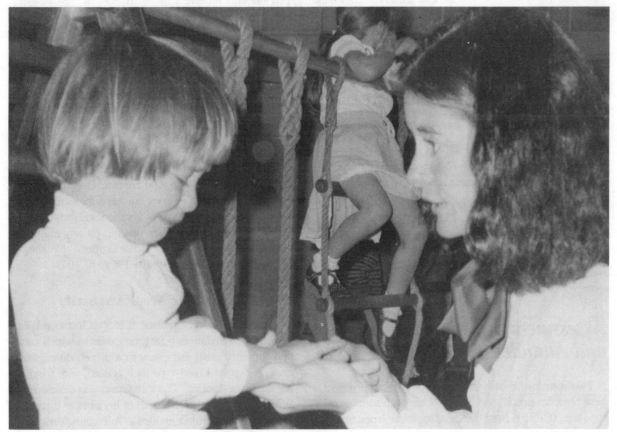

Jo E. Cowden (top), University of New Orleans. Nancy Megginson (bottom), Rouge River, Oregon.

order to determine which require change. When several target groups rate the same statements (Megginson, 1982; Schipper & Wilson, 1975), group means are compared using statistical methods to test such hypotheses. Because special educators, physical educators, and parents often differ in ratings, needs assessment methodology offers the

following criteria for resolving differences and deciding priorities for change.

1. First Priority Need (+)—*Should exist* item mean is above, grand mean, and *now exists* item mean is below its grand mean.

GIVE YOUR OPINION NOW EXIST	SURVEY OF ADAPTED PHYSICAL EDUCATION NEEDS (SAPEN)	GIVE YOUR OPINION SHOULD EXIST

| 6—Completely agree 5—Mostly agree 4—Slightly agree 3—Slightly disagree 2—Mostly disagree 1—Completely disagree | Please circle in the lefthand column the number that you feel best represents the services that *now exist* in your school district. Circle in the righthand column the number that represents your opinion about what *should exist*. IT IS CRITICAL THAT YOU CIRCLE A NUMBER FOR EACH ITEM IN EACH COLUMN. Once you have completed, double check to see if you have responded to every item using both columns. | 6—Completely agree 5—Mostly agree 4—Slightly agree 3—Slightly disagree 2—Mostly disagree 1—Completely disagree |

6 5 4 3 2 1   1. A curriculum manual describing physical education instruction/services for the handicapped is available.   6 5 4 3 2 1

6 5 4 3 2 1   2. Elementary school handicapped students receive 150 minutes of physical education instruction each week.   6 5 4 3 2 1

6 5 4 3 2 1   3. Administrative personnel understand that adapted physical education services are separate and different from those provided by a physical, occupational, or recreational therapist.   6 5 4 3 2 1

Figure 17.1 Format of a typical needs assessment instrument.

2. Second Priority Need (+ +)—*Should exist* item mean is above both its grand mean and *now exists* item mean.

3. Third Priority Need (+ + +)—*Should exist* item mean is below its grand mean but above *now exists* item mean.

4. Nonpriority Status (−)—*Should exist* item mean is below *now exists* item mean.

Assessment of Opinions and Attitudes of Administrators

Two instruments utilizing needs assessment protocol have been developed specifically for use with administrators: the NCPERH State Needs Assessment, specifically for use with state education agency (SEA) personnel, and the Cowden Administrator Survey of Opinions Toward Adapted Physical Education (CASAPE), specifically for use with public school administrators. The philosophy underlying this emphasis upon administrators is the following:

> Contrary to general opinion, administrators and not teachers are effective change agents for educational innovations. The teacher is not an independent professional who is free to decide what he will teach to whom at what time or

what price. As long as he remains inside the classroom, he is in total control. Once outside the classroom, he does not have the authority to propose a new type of instructional program. Therefore, the decision making for any major education innovation is determined by the administration. (Brickell, 1961, p. 107)

The NCPERH State Needs Assessment

This instrument is comprised of 25 goal statements, each of which is rated on two factors: extent to which condition currently exists and extent to which condition should exist. A 5-point Likert-type scale is used, with 5 indicating the highest rating. The instrument was developed by William Chasey in 1975 as part of his work as director of a 3-year special project entitled, "A Training Program in Special Physical Education for State Education Directors of Physical Education and Special Education." Chasey (1979) did not describe procedures for development of the instrument or measures of validity and reliability. Oakley (1984) verified the content validity of the NCPERH State Needs Assessment by two methods. Documentary analysis of the 25 items revealed that each embodied a mandate of PL 94-142 and/or AAHPERD guidelines (American Alliance for Health, Physical Education, and Recreation, 1973, 1976a, 1976b). A panel of experts (three SEA personnel) also attested to validity; independent validity ratings resulted in 21 of the items receiving a 4 or higher on a 6-point scale. Oakley (1984) also investigated the reliability of Chasey's instrument. Alpha coefficients of .76 and .93 for the now exists and should exist scales, respectively, were reported.

Chasey (1979) reported the findings of a study using this instrument to survey SEA special education and physical education personnel in the 50 states, District of Columbia, Puerto Rico, Virgin Islands, Guam, and Samoa. A 73% response rate was achieved. Chasey's statistical treatment, like that of Schipper and Wilson (1975), included calculation of the mean, standard deviation, and variance for real and ideal ratings of each condition. A paired *t* test was computed for each statement to determine if a significant difference existed between the mean ratings on the two scales.

Chasey's findings revealed that significant differences (*p* < .01) between means of real and ideal ratings were present in each of the 25 conditions. He concluded that a significant discrepancy exists between actual conditions and beliefs of SEA directors concerning desired physical education conditions in their states.

Oakley (1984) reported opinions of SEA physical education and special education personnel (*N* = 8) in Arkansas concerning statewide adapted physical education service delivery. On the 5-point scale, the mean ratings for existing conditions ranged from 1.00 to 3.00 with a grand mean of 1.78. These ratings were interpreted to mean that direct service delivery conditions and services believed important by Chasey (1979) were mostly or completely absent in Arkansas in the opinion of SEA personnel. The mean ratings for desired conditions and services ranged from 3.00 to 4.63 with a grand mean of 3.87. These ratings were interpreted to mean that, for the most part, the SEA personnel mostly or completely agreed that conditions and services believed important by Chasey (1979) should exist in Arkansas. Oakley concluded that considerable discrepancy exists in opinions concerning existing versus desired conditions in adapted physical education in Arkansas.

The Cowden Administrator Survey of Opinions Toward Adapted Physical Education (CASAPE)

CASAPE is comprised of 36 goal statements, each of which is rated on three scales: degree to which services/conditions now exist, degree of importance of each item, and the strength of intent to implement. A 4-point Likert-type scale is used with 4 as the highest rating. Content validity of CASAPE was established by six experts who reviewed individual items and agreed that each represented an ideal condition, was clearly stated, and measured what it purported to measure. Study of the reliability of CASAPE is in progress.

Cowden (1980) used CASAPE as the pre- and posttest measure of the effectiveness of three in-service education workshops in adapted and developmental physical education for 25 public school administrators in Fort Bend Independent School District in Texas. The administrators represented 10 job descriptions, including building principals, coordinators and directors of special education, and coordinators and directors of elementary and secondary instruction. The workshops were presented in three one-half-day sessions spaced over a 3-week period.

The statistical treatment was similar to that of Chasey (1979). A paired *t* test was computed between pre- and posttest means for each of the three measures on the CASAPE. Significant differences were found at the .01 level for the degree to which services and conditions now exist, indicating that administrators became increasingly aware of adapted physical education as a result of the workshops. All posttest means increased over pretest means, but the *t* values for degree of importance and strength of intent to implement were not significant at the .05 level.

Even though all subjects were administrators, many, because of their job classifications and delimited areas of management, did not believe they could implement specific aspects of the adapted physical education program. Many administrators indicated they could comment only for their own buildings and not for the entire school district regarding their intent to implement changes in programs for handicapped students. Confusion and discrepancy characterized the ratings of administrators as to what services and conditions existed and which were the most important when prioritizing needed improvements.

Assessment of Attitudes Toward Integration

Attitudes of teachers toward handicapped students and toward mainstreaming contribute to potential physical education success or failure of many exceptional individuals. Two attitude instruments for use by physical educators are reviewed in this chapter: The Mainstreaming Attitude Inventory for Physical Educators (Jansma & Shultz, 1982) and the Physical Educators' Attitude Toward Teaching the Handicapped Inventory (Rizzo, 1984).

The Mainstreaming Attitude Inventory for Physical Educators (MAIPE)

This instrument is comprised of a half-page vignette that describes a 10-year-old boy with special needs who has just been assigned to mainstream physical education for the first time and includes 20 statements pertaining to this placement. Each statement is rated, using a 6-point

Likert-type scale, with 1 specified as the most favorable attitude. A total attitude score is derived; the range of possible scores is 20 (best attitude) to 120 (worst attitude).

Jansma and Shultz (1982) report the validity and reliability of MAIPE as well as its use as a pretest/posttest measure of the effectiveness of in-service training workshops. Validity is based on the fact that it parallels the Watson and Hewett (1976) Learning Handicapped Integration Inventory, which is comprised of six vignettes, each followed by the same 29 statements to be rated. The content validity of the Watson and Hewett instrument was established by 10 experts. Content validity of MAIPE was established by ratings of seven experts (mean of 7 on a 10-point scale, mode of 8). Construct validity was established by factor analysis. Test-retest reliability for MAIPE, using Hoyt's two-way analysis of variance, was .82 for 74 physical education administrators. Jansma and Shultz (1982) administered MAIPE to directors of physical education in New York State. Four in-service institutes were developed to provide training for the experimental groups ($n = 46$) of randomly selected administrators. The control groups ($n = 33$) of administrators (also selected randomly) did not attend the in-service training. The subjects completed the MAIPE prior to the in-service institutes and at the end of the 2-day sessions.

A two-way ANOVA was applied to data collected from the four in-service institutes, and no significant differences were found. A factorial ANOVA with repeated measures was then applied to the combined data from all institute participants. The results indicated a significant difference at the .01 level for the main effects of the treatment and for the time dimension. Although several potential threats to the internal validity of the study existed, overall participant attitude toward handicapped students did not change in a positive direction. Jansma and Shultz cautioned that, although statistical significance was obtained in the study, many individual differences existed among subjects, even within the same groups. This finding supports the variability of subjects cited in other studies, but does not imply that in-service training is not a viable means for educating teachers. This study demonstrated that short sessions of in-service training could affect teacher attitudes, the change could remain over periods of time, and the MAIPE appears to be an appropriate tool for measuring attitude change among physical educators.

The Physical Educators' Attitude Toward Teaching the Handicapped Inventory (PEATH)

The PEATH Inventory assesses teacher attitudes according to the specific handicaps of the students and the grade level. The instrument, which contains 20 belief statements, is based on Fishbein and Ajzen's (1980) model of the Theory of Reasoned Action. Teachers respond on a 5-point Likert-type scale according to extent of agreement or disagreement. The instrument is based on the premise that beliefs underlie attitudes and "the assumption that five to seven salient beliefs, when taken collectively, approximate attitude toward a behavior. Thus, attitude scores were computed by summing response scores to 20 belief statements" (Rizzo, 1984, p. 269). Reliability of the PEATH, determined by computing an alpha coefficient, was .97. A panel of six experts established content validity, which included face and sampling validity.

Rizzo (1984) reported findings of a study in which the PEATH was used to measure the attitudes of 194 physical education teachers from a large Midwestern urban school district. A 2×3 randomized block factorial design was used to determine the physical educator's attitude toward teaching handicapped pupils by grade level and handicapping condition. Results indicated a significant main effect for the handicapping condition, $F (1, 193) = 26.92$, $p \leqslant .001$, and grade level, $F (2, 386) = 51.42$, $p \leqslant .001$. Interaction between handicapping condition and grade level was not significant. To identify the nature of differences between grade levels, the Tukey Honestly Significant Difference Test was applied to the data. Significant differences were demonstrated.

Rizzo concluded that attitudes of physical educators are more positive for the lower grade levels, and teachers become less favorable to accepting the students as the grade level increases. Physical educators were also found to be more accepting with regard to mainstream placement of pupils with learning problems than pupils with physical impairments.

Rizzo is continuing refinement of PEATH. Before using this instrument, readers should contact him at the Physical Education Department, State University College at Cortland, Cortland, NY 13045.

Assessment of Opinions Toward School District Services

To provide quality services in adapted physical education, the first step toward program change must be to determine the specific needs of the school district or parish. To assist school personnel, Sherrill and Megginson, in 1981, developed an opinion survey to assess needs in regard to adapted physical education service delivery; research pertaining to this was published in 1984. Use of this instrument, called the Survey of Adapted Physical Education Needs (SAPEN), was a small part of Megginson's dissertation (1982), which had as its main purpose the development and field testing of a comprehensive needs assessment model for use in local school districts. Oakley (1984) extended the research of Megginson by developing and field testing a model applicable to an entire state; he also used SAPEN as a small part of his dissertation.

Survey of Adapted Physical Education Needs (SAPEN)

The 50-item Survey of Adapted Physical Education Needs (SAPEN) was developed for use by administrators, physical educators, special educators, and parents. SAPEN encompasses five categories: (a) significance of physical education, (b) assessment, placement, and IEP, (c) instruction and programming, (d) personnel, and (e) other. Persons respond to the survey by rating items on two 6-point Likert-type scales for services that *now exist* and services that *should exist*. Needs are prioritized according to procedures established by Schipper and Wilson (1975).

Validity and reliability of SAPEN are reported by Sherrill and Megginson (1984). Content validity of SAPEN was determined by five national experts (i.e., textbook authors) in adapted physical education. Items were independently analyzed and placed in the five categories of SAPEN. The Spearman rank correlation technique, utilized to determine test-retest reliability, yielded *r* values ranging from .46 to .97 for the now exists column and .62 to .96 for the should exist column. To determine internal reliability of the instrument, the alpha correlation technique was used. It yielded the following alpha values for the now exists and should exist scales, respectively: (a) significance of physical education—.76 and .90; (b) assessment, placement, and IEP—.73 and .91; (c) instruction and programming—.79 and .93; (d) personnel—.80 and .91; and (e) other—.84 and .93. The lower alpha values for the now exists ratings again point out the uncertainty and low awareness levels of persons concerning existing adapted physical education service delivery.

Megginson (1982) used SAPEN in conjunction with the development and field testing of a comprehensive needs assessment model for use in local school districts. The SAPEN was administered to 238 administrators, physical educators, special educators, and parents in a selected school district in the Fort Worth-Dallas area. Grand means for these four target groups ranged from 3.52 to 4.01 on the now exists scale and from 4.93 to 5.51 on the should exist scale. Research and statistical hypotheses were examined in order to determine the effectiveness of the needs assessment model. Megginson concluded that the needs assessment model met 12 of 13 objective criteria and was therefore effective.

Oakley (1984) used SAPEN as one aspect of the evaluation of direct service delivery in physical education for handicapped students in the state of Arkansas. SAPENs were mailed to supervisors of special education in every school district ($N = 100$), and a 61% return resulted. Mean ratings on a 6-point scale for existing conditions ranged from 1.44 to 5.07, with a grand mean of 2.79. These ratings indicate that conditions believed important by adapted physical education authorities were partly or mostly lacking according to opinions of special education supervisors. Mean ratings for desired conditions ranged from 4.44 to 5.71 with a grand mean of 5.08. These ratings indicate that special education supervisors in Arkansas mostly desire to adhere to direct service delivery conditions believed important by authorities. Chi-square analysis was used to examine the hypothesis of no significant difference between frequencies of 1 to 6 ratings of existing conditions and of desired conditions. The null hypothesis was rejected for 44 of the 51 goal statements.

In summary, the SAPEN represents a viable approach to self-study by school personnel and parents. It has been used in school districts of various sizes. The now exists scale of SAPEN offers a good observation tool for use by graduate students and others who may be visiting and/or evaluating local school district adapted physical education programs. Tom Montelione, Physical Education Department, Queens College, New York City, can be contacted for information regarding computerization of SAPEN data.

Summary

The intent of this chapter was to describe assessment instruments used to measure opinions of school administrators, teachers, and parents. Instruments have been discussed for use in conjunction with comprehensive assessment models (Megginson, 1982; Oakley, 1984), as well as for individual and small group purposes (i.e., research, self-study within school districts, effectiveness of in-service training, and the like).

References

Abelson, H., & Karlins, M. (1959). *Persuasion: How opinions and attitudes are changed*. New York: Springer.

American Association for Health, Physical Education, and Recreation. (1973). *Guidelines for professional preparation programs for personnel involved in physical education and recreation for the handicapped*. Washington, DC: Author.

American Alliance for Health, Physical Education, and Recreation. (1976a). *Adapted physical education guidelines: Theory and practices for the seventies and eighties*. Washington, DC: Author.

American Alliance for Health, Physical Education, and Recreation. (1976b). *Professional preparation in adapted physical education, therapeutic recreation, and corrective therapy*. Washington, DC: Author.

Brickell, H.M. (1961). A study of the dynamics of instructional change in the elementary and secondary schools of New York with recommendations for improved organization. In State Education Department (Ed.), *Organizing New York State for educational change*. Albany, NY: Author.

Chasey, W. (1979). *A training program in special education for SEA directors of physical education and special education* (Report No. G007603204). Washington, DC: National Consortium on Physical Education and Recreation for the Handicapped.

Cowden, J. (1980). *Administrator inservice training for program implementation in adapted and developmental physical education* (ED 204 29 B). Washington, DC: Educational Resources Information Center (ERIC).

Educational Systems Associates, Inc. (1974). *Needs assessment procedures manual*. Austin, TX: Author.

Fishbein, M., & Ajzen, I. (1980). *Understanding attitudes and predicting behavior*. Englewood Cliffs, NJ: Prentice-Hall.

Gould, J., & Kolb, W. (Eds.). (1964). *A dictionary of the social sciences*. New York: The Free Press.

Jansma, P., & Shultz, B. (1982). Validation and use of a mainstreaming attitude inventory with physical educators. *American Corrective Therapy Journal, 36*, 150-157.

Krech, D., & Crutchfield, R. (1948). *Theory and problems of social psychology*. New York: McGraw-Hill.

Likert, R. (1932). A technique for the measurement of attitudes. *Archives of Psychology, 22*, 5-43.

Megginson, N. (1982). Adapted physical education needs assessment: A cooperative manpower planning model for the local school district. *Dissertation Abstracts International, 43*, 2928A. (University Microfilms No. 83-03114)

Oakley, T. (1984). *Evaluation of direct service delivery and teacher training in physical education for handicapped students in Arkansas*. Unpublished doctoral dissertation, Texas Woman's University, Denton.

Rizzo, T. (1984). Attitudes of physical educators toward teaching handicapped pupils. *Adapted Physical Activity Quarterly, 1*(4), 267-273.

Schipper, W., & Wilson, W. (1975). *A survey of opinions on the training of teachers of exceptional children* (No. ED 115 037). Arlington, VA: ERIC Documentation Reproduction Service.

Sherrill, C., & Megginson, N. (1984). A needs assessment instrument for local school district use in adapted physical education. *Adapted Physical Activity Quarterly, 1*(2), 147-157.

Triandis, H. (1971). *Attitude and attitude change*. New York: John Wiley.

Watson, P.C., & Hewett, F.M. (1976). *The learning handicapped integration inventory: Assessing regular classroom teachers' perception of the effect of integrating mildly handicapped children*. Unpublished Technical Report SERP.

National Consortium on Physical Education and Recreation for the Handicapped

(NCPERH) State Needs Assessment on Adapted Physical Education

(Chasey, 1979)

You are participating in a needs assessment survey regarding the adapted physical education service delivery in your state. This survey was developed and validated specifically for use by State Education Agency (SEA) personnel in special education and physical education. Statements on the survey are directed toward conditions which presently exist or those which you feel should exist.

Directions

Please circle in the lefthand column the number which you feel best represents the conditions that now exist in your state. Circle in the right-hand column the number which represents your opinion about what *should exist*. IT IS CRITICAL THAT YOU CIRCLE A NUMBER FOR EACH ITEM IN EACH COLUMN. When you are completed, double check to see if you have responded to every item using both columns. Completion of the information below regarding permission and confidentiality of information will be appreciated.

Permission

I, _____, give my permission for these answers to be used for research and/or educational purposes. I understand that my name and that my state will be kept confidential.

Business mailing address: _____

_____
              City   State   Zip Code

Home Telephone: ( )_____ Work Telephone: ( )_____

_____

Continued

Continued

GIVE YOUR OPINION NOW EXIST					NCPERH STATE NEEDS ASSESSMENT ON ADAPTED PHYSICAL EDUCATION	GIVE YOUR OPINION SHOULD EXIST				
5—To a very large extent	4—To a fairly large extent	3—To a moderate extent	2—To a slight extent	1—Not at all	Please circle in the lefthand column the number which you feel best represents the conditions that *now exist* in your state. Circle in the righthand column the number which best represents your opinion about what *should exist*. IT IS CRITICAL THAT YOU CIRCLE A NUMBER FOR EACH ITEM IN EACH COLUMN. Once you are completed, double check to see if you have responded to every item using both columns.	5—To a very large extent	4—To a fairly large extent	3—To a moderate extent	2—To a slight extent	1—Not at all
5	4	3	2	1	1. The State Education Agency sets specific guidelines for assessment and evaluation in physical education for handicapped children.	5	4	3	2	1
5	4	3	2	1	2. The State Advisory Panel includes a member from the adapted physical education field.	5	4	3	2	1
5	4	3	2	1	3. Physical education is a significant part of the education curriculum for all handicapped children.	5	4	3	2	1
5	4	3	2	1	4. Teacher-pupil ratios are adequate in providing for special education needs within regular physical education classes.	5	4	3	2	1
5	4	3	2	1	5. The State Education Agency monitors physical education programming for handicapped children in local school districts.	5	4	3	2	1
5	4	3	2	1	6. Specially trained physical education personnel are effectively used in the IEP planning process to determine appropriate physical education programming.	5	4	3	2	1
5	4	3	2	1	7. Program resources (instructional materials and media) are available for effective and efficient conduction of physical education programs for handicapped children.	5	4	3	2	1
5	4	3	2	1	8. Physical education designed as a developmental program of instruction is available to all handicapped children.	5	4	3	2	1
5	4	3	2	1	9. The state education plan contains specific planning for physical education programming for handicapped children.	5	4	3	2	1
5	4	3	2	1	10. Sufficient numbers of qualified personnel to meet the physical education requirements of PL 94-142 are available throughout the state.	5	4	3	2	1
5	4	3	2	1	11. Staff development programs are provided for special education/regular education teachers to acquaint them with relevant methods, procedures, and techniques that can be used in physical education programming for handicapped children.	5	4	3	2	1
5	4	3	2	1	12. Physical education programs impact upon other related programs in the community, schools, and institutions.	5	4	3	2	1

Continued

Continued

GIVE YOUR OPINION NOW EXIST					NCPERH STATE NEEDS ASSESSMENT ON ADAPTED PHYSICAL EDUCATION	GIVE YOUR OPINION SHOULD EXIST				
5	4	3	2	1	13. Special education/regular education teachers provide adapted physical education instruction when required in a handicapped child's IEP.	5	4	3	2	1
5	4	3	2	1	14. Preservice curricula for special education teachers contain a unit in adapted physical education.	5	4	3	2	1
5	4	3	2	1	15. Certified adapted physical education specialists serve as resource persons to special education personnel.	5	4	3	2	1
5	4	3	2	1	16. In-service training is adapted physical education for regular/special educators in a high priority.	5	4	3	2	1
5	4	3	2	1	17. Special educators and physical educators work together to develop appropriate physical education programs for handicapped children.	5	4	3	2	1
5	4	3	2	1	18. Regular physical education teachers adjust adequately to problems arising from the integration of handicapped children in regular classes.	5	4	3	2	1
5	4	3	2	1	19. The State Education Agency provides leadership in identifying physical education personnel preparation needs, both at preservice and in-service.	5	4	3	2	1
5	4	3	2	1	20. Parents are directly involved in the decision-making process regarding adapted physical education programs.	5	4	3	2	1
5	4	3	2	1	21. Public schools employ adapted physical education teachers.	5	4	3	2	1
5	4	3	2	1	22. As much emphasis is given to physical education programs for the handicapped as is given other curriculum areas.	5	4	3	2	1
5	4	3	2	1	23. Physical education and special education administrators in the State Education Agency work together to develop the physical education component of state education plans.	5	4	3	2	1
5	4	3	2	1	24. The special education division of the State Education Agency employs a consultant in physical education for the handicapped.	5	4	3	2	1
5	4	3	2	1	25. National technical assistance in physical education is provided to State Education Agency personnel within the state.	5	4	3	2	1

Cowden Administrator Survey of Opinions Toward Adapted Physical Education (CASAPE)

(Cowden, 1980)

You, as a public school administrator, are participating in in-service education sessions and in an opinion survey regarding Adapted and Developmental Physical Education services in your school district. Statements are directed toward services and/or conditions which presently exist or those which you feel should be included in the future.

Degree to which services/ conditions NOW EXIST	Please circle the selection which you feel best represents the existing services in your school/school district and the corresponding columns for those services which you feel should exist in the future. Please mark through statements which are not applicable.	Degree of importance	Strength of intent to implement
0—Undecided 1—Rarely 2—Occasionally 3—Usually 4—Almost always		0—Undecided 1—Very little 2—Little 3—Much 4—Very much	0—Undecided 1—Very weak 2—Weak 3—Strong 4—Very strong
0 1 2 3 4	1. Handicapped students at the elementary level receive daily physical education services.	0 1 2 3 4	0 1 2 3 4
0 1 2 3 4	2. Handicapped students at the secondary level receive daily physical education services.	0 1 2 3 4	0 1 2 3 4
0 1 2 3 4	3. A student-teacher ratio of 1 to 5 or less is maintained in physical education for severe/profound handicapped students.	0 1 2 3 4	0 1 2 3 4
0 1 2 3 4	4. Regular mainstream physical education classes with handicapped children in them have a student teacher ratio of 1 to 30 or less.	0 1 2 3 4	0 1 2 3 4
0 1 2 3 4	5. Teacher aides are used to supplement the delivery of services to handicapped students by regular physical education/ adapted physical education teachers.	0 1 2 3 4	0 1 2 3 4
0 1 2 3 4	6. Teachers of physical education classes for the handicapped possess the necessary competencies and knowledges in adapted and developmental physical education techniques.	0 1 2 3 4	0 1 2 3 4
0 1 2 3 4	7. Teacher's aides in physical education are provided sufficient in-service training regarding instructional techniques for the handicapped.	0 1 2 3 4	0 1 2 3 4
0 1 2 3 4	8. Regular physical education personnel in mainstream settings are provided at least one session of in-service training each year on current instructional techniques by specialists in adapted and developmental physical education.	0 1 2 3 4	0 1 2 3 4

Continued

Continued

CASAPE

Degree to which services/ conditions NOW EXIST	Please circle the selection which you feel best represents the existing services in your school/school district and the corresponding columns for those services which you feel should exist in the future. Please mark through statements which are not applicable.	Degree of importance	Strength of intent to implement
0—Undecided 1—Rarely 2—Occasionally 3—Usually 4—Almost always		0—Undecided 1—Very little 2—Little 3—Much 4—Very much	0—Undecided 1—Very weak 2—Weak 3—Strong 4—Very strong
0 1 2 3 4	9. The school district budgets proportionately for equipment needed in classes of physical education for the handicapped as compared with regular physical education instructional classes.	0 1 2 3 4	0 1 2 3 4
0 1 2 3 4	10. Adequate facilities are allocated for instruction of students enrolled in physical education classes for the handicapped.	0 1 2 3 4	0 1 2 3 4
0 1 2 3 4	11. Physical education teachers with mainstreamed classes evaluate handicapped students on psychomotor skills and record the results in permanent records.	0 1 2 3 4	0 1 2 3 4
0 1 2 3 4	12. Individual education programs include short-term physical education objectives and a statement of psychomotor performance.	0 1 2 3 4	0 1 2 3 4
0 1 2 3 4	13. A curriculum manual describing services provided in physical education for the handicapped is available.	0 1 2 3 4	0 1 2 3 4
0 1 2 3 4	14. Early childhood programs include appropriate daily physical education activities for motor development.	0 1 2 3 4	0 1 2 3 4
0 1 2 3 4	15. Kindergarten programs include appropriate daily physical education activities for motor development.	0 1 2 3 4	0 1 2 3 4
0 1 2 3 4	16. Administrators are knowledgeable about statements in Public Law 94-142 regarding physical education instruction for handicapped students.	0 1 2 3 4	0 1 2 3 4
0 1 2 3 4	17. Administrators are knowledgeable about statements in the State Education Agency Handbook, *Policies and Administrative Procedures for the Education of Handicapped Students*, regarding physical education instruction for handicapped students.	0 1 2 3 4	0 1 2 3 4
0 1 2 3 4	18. Facilities used in physical education instruction for the handicapped student are architecturally accessible.	0 1 2 3 4	0 1 2 3 4
0 1 2 3 4	19. Physical education teachers for self-contained classes of severely handicapped students evaluate psychomotor skills and record the results in their permanent records.	0 1 2 3 4	0 1 2 3 4

Continued

Continued

CASAPE

Degree to which services/ conditions NOW EXIST 0—Undecided 1—Rarely 2—Occasionally 3—Usually 4—Almost always	Please circle the selection which you feel best represents the existing services in your school/school district and the corresponding columns for those services which you feel should exist in the future. Please mark through statements which are not applicable.	Degree of importance 0—Undecided 1—Very little 2—Little 3—Much 4—Very much	Strength of intent to implement 0—Undecided 1—Very weak 2—Weak 3—Strong 4—Very strong
0 1 2 3 4	20. Administrators are knowledgeable about current employment alternatives for hiring adapted and developmental physical education instructors.	0 1 2 3 4	0 1 2 3 4
0 1 2 3 4	21. Administrators use the same scheduling practices for physical education classes as for classes in other subjects.	0 1 2 3 4	0 1 2 3 4
0 1 2 3 4	22. Administrators are knowledgeable about alternatives for mainstreaming and about meeting the needs of students in their least restrictive environment.	0 1 2 3 4	0 1 2 3 4
0 1 2 3 4	23. The school district sponsors and funds Special Olympics athletic competition for mentally retarded students.	0 1 2 3 4	0 1 2 3 4
0 1 2 3 4	24. The school district sponsors and funds special athletic competition for other handicapped students.	0 1 2 3 4	0 1 2 3 4
0 1 2 3 4	25. Administrative personnel understand that adapted and developmental physical education services are separate from those services provided by a physical therapist or occupational therapist.	0 1 2 3 4	0 1 2 3 4
0 1 2 3 4	26. Administrators are aware of the curriculum content of a diversified adapted and developmental physical education program.	0 1 2 3 4	0 1 2 3 4
0 1 2 3 4	27. Administrators are aware of the various alternatives for the delivery of services by an adapted physical education instructor/consultant.	0 1 2 3 4	0 1 2 3 4
0 1 2 3 4	28. Self contained units of handicapped students receive daily physical education services appropriate to their needs.	0 1 2 3 4	0 1 2 3 4
0 1 2 3 4	29. Children who can experience success in the least restrictive environment are mainstreamed in regular physical education classes.	0 1 2 3 4	0 1 2 3 4
0 1 2 3 4	30. Administrators allow and encourage physical education instructors to attend professional meetings in order to strengthen their competencies in adapted physical education.	0 1 2 3 4	0 1 2 3 4

Continued

Continued

CASAPE

Degree to which services/ conditions NOW EXIST	Please circle the selection which you feel best represents the existing services in your school/school district and the corresponding columns for those services which you feel should exist in the future. Please mark through statements which are not applicable.	Degree of importance	Strength of intent to implement
0—Undecided 1—Rarely 2—Occasionally 3—Usually 4—Almost always		0—Undecided 1—Very little 2—Little 3—Much 4—Very much	0—Undecided 1—Very weak 2—Weak 3—Strong 4—Very strong
0 1 2 3 4	31. Evaluative criteria are available to guide administrators in monitoring the quality of adapted physical education programs.	0 1 2 3 4	0 1 2 3 4
0 1 2 3 4	32. Physical education personnel participate regularly on IEP committees and/or other interdisciplinary planning sessions concerned with education of handicapped children.	0 1 2 3 4	0 1 2 3 4
0 1 2 3 4	33. Administrators can cite the competencies an adapted physical education specialist should possess and can state the tasks he/she should perform.	0 1 2 3 4	0 1 2 3 4
0 1 2 3 4	34. Parents of handicapped students are made aware of adapted physical education services in the school district through a variety of techniques, including special meetings focusing upon adapted physical education.	0 1 2 3 4	0 1 2 3 4
0 1 2 3 4	35. Students with medical excuses to exempt them from regular physical education classes must have these medical excuses reevaluated/renewed periodically.	0 1 2 3 4	0 1 2 3 4
0 1 2 3 4	36. Students with medical excuses to exempt them from regular physical education are scheduled for alternative adapted physical education programs.	0 1 2 3 4	0 1 2 3 4

Mainstreaming Attitude Inventory
for Physical Educators

(Jansma & Shultz, 1982)

Instructions

(If read previously, please skim)

Below you will find a brief description or vignette of Robert, a child with exceptional learning needs. Please read it carefully. Following the vignette are 20 statements concerned with the possible effects of placement of a child like Robert into your regular class. You are to rate each statement in terms of your degree of agreement or disagreement with it. An example will be provided below. There are no right or wrong answers to any statement. Please use your best *subjective judgement* in rating each item. Remember, your responses will be confidential.

It is possible that you may not find all the information within the vignette that you would like in order to respond knowledgeably to certain items. However, since many teaching decisions are made with only limited information, you are asked to use your best judgement based on what information is provided.

Please indicate your response to each statement on the following pages by placing a check above the rating that corresponds to the degree to which you agree or disagree with the statement.

Example:

It is hot in Chicago in the summer _____   _____   _____   _____   _____ $\sqrt{}$

	strongly disagree	disagree	slightly disagree	slightly agree	agree	strongly agree

The teacher in this example considers Chicago to be *very* hot in the summer and so has placed a check to indicate a position of strong agreement with the statement. Remember, each statement that follows will refer to the effects of having a child like Robert in your regular class. Even though you may not actually teach in a class at the age level of the child, please assume for the moment that you do and respond to each item accordingly.

ROBERT

Robert is a 10-year-old boy whose home is in a middle class suburban area. He lives with his mother and father and a 12-year-old sister who is an average student in the sixth grade. Robert however has an obvious handicap. Robert has spent two of his last four years in a self-contained segregated special education classroom. The local committee on the handicapped has recently decided that Robert could be safely and successfully placed in your school including your physical education class.

Robert has now been placed full-time in your regular physical education class. Please read and respond to each of the 20 statements that follow as described in the instructions.

PLEASE RESPOND TO ALL STATEMENTS

1. A pupil like Robert will maintain satisfactory _____ _____ _____ _____ _____ _____
   attendance in your class.

	strongly disagree	disagree	slightly disagree	slightly agree	agree	strongly agree

2. A pupil like Robert will likely form a positive _____ _____ _____ _____ _____ _____
   relationship with you, the teacher.

	strongly disagree	disagree	slightly disagree	slightly agree	agree	strongly agree

Continued

Continued

3. With a pupil like Robert in your class, there will be an increase in the number of behavior problems among the other pupils.

strongly disagree	disagree	slightly disagree	slightly agree	agree	strongly agree

4. There will be more problems with the parents of a pupil like Robert than with the parents of the other pupils.

strongly disagree	disagree	slightly disagree	slightly agree	agree	strongly agree

5. Placement of a pupil like Robert in your class will likely result in his becoming socially withdrawn.

strongly disagree	disagree	slightly disagree	slightly agree	agree	strongly agree

6. A pupil like Robert will develop a more positive self-concept as a result of being placed in your class.

strongly disagree	disagree	slightly disagree	slightly agree	agree	strongly agree

7. Teaching a pupil like Robert will increase your overall teaching competence.

strongly disagree	disagree	slightly disagree	slightly agree	agree	strongly agree

8. The experience of being in your class will increase the chances of a pupil like Robert attaining a more productive and independent place in society.

strongly disagree	disagree	slightly disagree	slightly agree	agree	strongly agree

9. As a result of placement in your class, a pupil like Robert will develop a more positive attitude toward school.

strongly disagree	disagree	slightly disagree	slightly agree	agree	strongly agree

10. The presence of a child like Robert in your class will be a cause for complaints from the parents of the other pupils.

strongly disagree	disagree	slightly disagree	slightly agree	agree	strongly agree

11. It is unlikely that any of the other pupils in your class will form a friendship with Robert.

strongly disagree	disagree	slightly disagree	slightly agree	agree	strongly agree

12. A visitor to your class would not be able to pick out a pupil like Robert on the basis of his behavior.

strongly disagree	disagree	slightly disagree	slightly agree	agree	strongly agree

13. A pupil like Robert will not respond even to your best teaching efforts.

strongly disagree	disagree	slightly disagree	slightly agree	agree	strongly agree

14. A pupil like Robert will be disruptive in your class.

strongly disagree	disagree	slightly disagree	slightly agree	agree	strongly agree

15. A pupil like Robert in your class will adversely affect the other pupils' motivation to learn.

strongly disagree	disagree	slightly disagree	slightly agree	agree	strongly agree

Continued

Continued

16. A pupil like Robert will be motivated to learn in your class.

strongly disagree	disagree	slightly disagree	slightly agree	agree	strongly agree

17. The other pupils in your class will be apt to make a scapegoat of a pupil like Robert.

strongly disagree	disagree	slightly disagree	slightly agree	agree	strongly agree

18. A pupil like Robert will be able to safely participate in your class.

strongly disagree	disagree	slightly disagree	slightly agree	agree	strongly agree

19. A pupil like Robert will be able to successfully participate in your class.

strongly disagree	disagree	slightly disagree	slightly agree	agree	strongly agree

20. Assignment of a pupil like Robert to your class is a wise administrative decision overall.

strongly disagree	disagree	slightly disagree	slightly agree	agree	strongly agree

Physical Educators' Attitude Toward Teaching the Handicapped (PEATH) Inventory

(Rizzo, 1984)

Directions

This questionnaire is concerned with how the physical educator feels about teaching the learning and physically handicapped pupil in the regular class setting. Read each statement carefully and using the scale below indicate for each statement the extent of your agreement or disagreement by writing in each box:

SA if you *strongly agree* with the statement;
A   if you *agree* with the statement;
U   if you are *undecided* about your opinion;
D   if you *disagree* with the statement;
SD if you *strongly disagree* with the statement.

For example, if you were asked your opinion about teaching learning and physically handicapped pupils, the question may read like this:

Learning and/or physically handicapped pupils should be taught in the regular physical education class whenever possible.

	K-3	4-6	7-8
Learning Handicapped:			
Physically Handicapped:			

If you strongly believe that learning handicapped pupils should not be taught in the regular class, but you do agree that physically handicapped pupils should be taught in grades K-3 and 4-6 but not in grades 7-8, you would mark the scale like this:

	K-3	4-6	7-8
Learning Handicapped:	SD	SD	SD
Physically Handicapped:	A	A	D

PLEASE RESPOND TO EACH STATEMENT.
DO NOT LEAVE ANY BOXES BLANK.
MARK ONLY ONE RESPONSE IN EACH BOX.

LEARNING HANDICAPPED: REFERS TO PUPILS TYPICALLY IDENTIFIED AS LEARNING DISABLED, EDUCABLE MENTALLY HANDICAPPED OR EDUCATIONAL MALADJUSTMENT RELATED TO SOCIAL OR EMOTIONAL CIRCUMSTANCES.

PHYSICALLY HANDICAPPED: REFERS TO PUPILS TYPICALLY IDENTIFIED AS HAVING: SENSORY DEFICITS (e.g., HEARING & VISION, etc.); A PHYSICAL DISABILITY (e.g., AMPUTEE, CEREBRAL PALSY, CLUB FOOT, etc.); OR PERCEPTUAL DEFICITS (e.g., NO OBVIOUS DISABILITY BUT WHOSE ABILITY TO PERFORM SKILLED, PURPOSIVE MOVEMENT IS IMPAIRED).

PLEASE TURN THE PAGE AND BEGIN

Continued

Continued

1. One advantage of teaching learning and/or physically handicapped pupils in regular physical education classes with nonhandicapped pupils is that all pupils will learn to work together toward achieving goals.

	K-3	4-6	7-8	
Learning Handicapped:				4-6
Physically Handicapped:				7-9

2. There will be more discipline problems if I have to teach learning and/or physically handicapped pupils in my regular physical education classes.

	K-3	4-6	7-8	
Learning Handicapped:				10-12
Physically Handicapped:				13-15

3. Teaching learning and/or physically handicapped pupils in regular physical education classes will motivate nonhandicapped pupils to learn to perform motor skills.

	K-3	4-6	7-8	
Learning Handicapped:				16-18
Physically Handicapped:				19-21

4. Learning and/or physically handicapped pupils will learn more rapidly if they are taught with their nonhandicapped peers.

	K-3	4-6	7-8	
Learning Handicapped:				22-24
Physically Handicapped:				25-27

5. Teaching learning and/or physically handicapped pupils in regular physical education classes will increase the acceptance of individual differences on the part of nonhandicapped pupils.

	K-3	4-6	7-8	
Learning Handicapped:				28-30
Physically Handicapped:				31-33

6. Learning and/or physically handicapped pupils should be taught with nonhandicapped pupils in physical education classes whenever possible.

	K-3	4-6	7-8	
Learning Handicapped:				34-36
Physically Handicapped:				37-39

7. Learning and/or physically handicapped pupils will develop a more favorable self-concept as a result of learning motor skills in physical education classes with nonhandicapped pupils.

	K-3	4-6	7-8	
Learning Handicapped:				40-42
Physically Handicapped:				43-45

8. Learning and/or physically handicapped pupils will not be accepted by their nonhandicapped peers in regular physical education classes.

	K-3	4-6	7-8	
Learning Handicapped:				46-48
Physically Handicapped:				49-51

Continued

Continued

9. Teaching learning and physically handicapped pupils in physical education classes with nonhandicapped pupils may require additional special equipment.

	K-3	4-6	7-8	
Learning Handicapped:				52-54
Physically Handicapped:				55-57

10. Teaching learning and/or physically handicapped pupils in physical education classes with nonhandicapped pupils will disrupt the harmony of the class.

	K-3	4-6	7-8	
Learning Handicapped:				58-60
Physically Handicapped:				61-63

11. Having to teach learning and/or physically handicapped pupils in physical education classes with nonhandicapped pupils places an unfair burden on teachers.

	K-3	4-6	7-8	
Learning Handicapped:				64-66
Physically Handicapped:				67-69

12. Teaching learning and/or physically handicapped pupils in physical education classes will slow down the rate of learning motor skills for nonhandicapped pupils.

	K-3	4-6	7-8	
Learning Handicapped:				70-72
Physically Handicapped:				73-75

13. In general, physical education teachers do not have the sufficient training necessary to teach learning and/or physically handicapped pupils and nonhandicapped pupils together in physical education classes.

	K-3	4-6	7-8	
Learning Handicapped:				76-78
Physically Handicapped:				4-6

14. The best way to meet the needs of learning and/or physically handicapped pupils is through special, separate physical education classes.

	K-3	4-6	7-8	
Learning Handicapped:				7-9
Physically Handicapped:				10-12

15. There is not enough time during the physical education class period to deal satisfactorily with the different needs of both the nonhandicapped and learning and/or physically handicapped pupils.

	K-3	4-6	7-8	
Learning Handicapped:				13-15
Physically Handicapped:				16-18

16. Teaching learning and/or physically handicapped pupils in physical education classes with nonhandicapped pupils means more work for the teacher.

	K-3	4-6	7-8	
Learning Handicapped:				19-21
Physically Handicapped:				22-24

Continued

Continued

17. Both learning and/or physically handicapped pupils and nonhandicapped pupils benefit from participating together in physical education classes.

	K-3	4-6	7-8	
Learning Handicapped:				25-27
Physically Handicapped:				28-30

18. Learning and/or physically handicapped pupils should not be taught in physical education classes with nonhandicapped pupils because they will require too much of the teacher's time.

	K-3	4-6	7-8	
Learning Handicapped:				31-33
Physically Handicapped:				34-36

19. Learning and/or physically handicapped pupils can actively participate in most physical education class activities with their nonhandicapped peers.

	K-3	4-6	7-8	
Learning Handicapped:				37-39
Physically Handicapped:				40-42

20. Teachers will need inservice training before they will be able to teach a physical education class of learning and/or physically handicapped pupils and nonhandicapped pupils.

	K-3	4-6	7-8	
Learning Handicapped:				43-45
Physically Handicapped:				46-48

Now, I would like to know how you think other people (associated with your school) might feel about you teaching learning and physically handicapped pupils in your regular physical education classes. For items 21-33 please circle the response that most accurately describes your feelings.

	Strongly Disagree	Disagree	Not Sure	Agree	Strongly Agree	
21. Most people who are important to me at school think that I should teach handicapped pupils in my regular physical education class.	1	2	3	4	5	49
22. Principals in public schools think that handicapped pupils should be taught in regular physical education classes.	1	2	3	4	5	50
23. Generally speaking, I will cooperate with what my principal thinks that I should do to educate handicapped pupils in my regular class.	1	2	3	4	5	51
24. Other physical educators do not think that handicapped pupils should be taught in regular classes.	1	2	3	4	5	52
25. Generally speaking, I will go along with what other physical educators think that I should do to teach handicapped pupils in my regular classes.	1	2	3	4	5	53
26. Special education teachers think that handicapped pupils should be taught in regular physical education classes.	1	2	3	4	5	54

Continued

Continued

	Strongly Disagree	Disagree	Not Sure	Agree	Strongly Agree	
27. Generally speaking, I will cooperate with what special educators think I should do to teach handicapped pupils in my regular classes.	1	2	3	4	5	55
28. Most parents of handicapped pupils think that their children should be taught in regular physical education classes.	1	2	3	4	5	56
29. Generally speaking, I do not go along with what parents of handicapped pupils think I should do to teach handicapped pupils in my regular classes.	1	2	3	4	5	57
30. Regular classroom teachers do not think that handicapped pupils should be taught in reguarl physical education classes.	1	2	3	4	5	58
31. Generally speaking, I will go along with what regular classroom teachers think I should do to teach handicapped pupils in my regular classes.	1	2	3	4	5	59
32. Most parents of nonhandicapped pupils think that handicapped pupils should be taught in regular physical education classes.	1	2	3	4	5	60
33. Generally speaking, I will go along with what parents of nonhandicapped pupils think I should do to teach handicapped pupils in my regular classes.	1	2	3	4	5	61

Finally, just a few background questions about yourself.

34. Are you a male or female? Please circle the appropriate response.

Male.......................1
Female....................2   62

35. How many years have you been teaching physical education?

Number of years teaching_____
63-64

36. What is the highest degree that you have earned? Please circle the appropriate response.

Bachelor's.................1
Master's...................2
Doctorate.................3   65

37. In what year were you born?

Year 19____   66-67

38. How many undergraduate or graduate courses have you taken that have dealt specifically with physical education for handicapped pupils?

Number of courses: _____68-69
No courses: _____

39. How many undergraduate or graduate courses have you taken (outside of physical education, e.g., special education) that have dealt specifically with handicapped pupils?

Number of courses: _____70-71
No courses: _____

40. Have you had teaching experiences with handicapped pupils? Please circle the appropriate response.

Yes..........................1
No 2   72

41. Assuming that you might have some handicapped pupils entering your physical education class what type(s) of support service(s) (e.g., training, equipment, class management techniques, etc.) may be of most benefit to help you teach your classes?

Survey of Adapted Physical Education Needs (SAPEN)

(Sherrill & Megginson, 1984)

You are participating in a needs assessment survey regarding the adapted physical education service delivery in your school district or cooperative. Statements on the survey are directed toward conditions that presently exist or those that you feel should exist.

Directions

Please circle in the lefthand column the number that you feel best represents the services that *now exist* in your school district or cooperative. Circle in the righthand column the number which represents your opinion about what *should exist*. IT IS CRITICAL THAT YOU CIRCLE A NUMBER FOR EACH ITEM IN EACH COLUMN. Once you have completed, double check to see if you have responded to every item using both columns. Completion of the information below regarding permission and confidentiality of information will be appreciated.

Permission

I, _____, give my permission for these answers to be used for research and/or educational purposes. I understand that my name will be kept confidential.

Home mailing address: _____

_____
City   State   Zip Code

Home Telephone: _____   Work Telephone: _____

GIVE YOUR OPINION NOW EXIST						**SURVEY OF ADAPTED PHYSICAL EDUCATION NEEDS (SAPEN)**	**GIVE YOUR OPINION SHOULD EXIST**					
6—Completely agree	5—Mostly agree	4—Slightly agree	3—Slightly disagree	2—Mostly disagree	1—Completely disagree	Please circle in the lefthand column the number that you feel best represents the services that *now exist* in your school district. Circle in the righthand column the number that represents your opinion about what *should exist*. IT IS CRITICAL THAT YOU CIRCLE A NUMBER FOR EACH ITEM IN EACH COLUMN. Once you have completed, double check to see if you have responded to every item using both columns.	6—Completely agree	5—Mostly agree	4—Slightly agree	3—Slightly disagree	2—Mostly disagree	1—Completely disagree
6	5	4	3	2	1	1. A curriculum manual describing physical education instruction/services for the handicapped is available.	6	5	4	3	2	1
6	5	4	3	2	1	2. Elementary school handicapped students receive 150 minutes of physical education instruction each week.	6	5	4	3	2	1
6	5	4	3	2	1	3. Administrative personnel understand that adapted physical education services are separate and different from those provided by a physical, occupational, or recreational therapist.	6	5	4	3	2	1
6	5	4	3	2	1	4. Regular physical education classes with handicapped students in them have a student-staff ratio of 30 to 1 or less.	6	5	4	3	2	1

Continued

Continued

| GIVE YOUR OPINION NOW EXIST | SURVEY OF ADAPTED PHYSICAL EDUCATION NEEDS (SAPEN) | GIVE YOUR OPINION SHOULD EXIST |

Please circle in the lefthand column the number that you feel best represents the services that *now exist* in your school district. Circle in the righthand column the number that represents your opinion about what *should exist*. IT IS CRITICAL THAT YOU CIRCLE A NUMBER FOR EACH ITEM IN EACH COLUMN. Once you have completed, double check to see if you have responded to every item using both columns.

6—Completely agree
5—Mostly agree
4—Slightly agree
3—Slightly disagree
2—Mostly disagree
1—Completely disagree

6 5 4 3 2 1   5. Evaluative criteria are available to guide administrators in monitoring the quality of adapted physical education programs.   6 5 4 3 2 1

6 5 4 3 2 1   6. Administrators are utilizing current funding alternatives for hiring adapted physical education specialists.   6 5 4 3 2 1

6 5 4 3 2 1   7. Parents of handicapped students are made aware of adapted physical education services through a variety of techniques, including special meetings focusing on adapted physical education.   6 5 4 3 2 1

6 5 4 3 2 1   8. Adapted physical education classes designed specially for the severely handicapped have a student-staff ratio of 5 to 1 or less.   6 5 4 3 2 1

6 5 4 3 2 1   9. Students with medical excuses to exempt them from regular physical education classes have these medical excuses re-evaluated/renewed annually.   6 5 4 3 2 1

6 5 4 3 2 1   10. Handicapped students take field trips to recreation and health/fitness facilities in the community and learn to use these resources as part of their school physical instruction.   6 5 4 3 2 1

6 5 4 3 2 1   11. Specially trained physical education personnel participate in the IEP planning process and/or other interdisciplinary planning sessions concerning education of handicapped children.   6 5 4 3 2 1

6 5 4 3 2 1   12. Appropriate physical education placement is discussed and agreed upon by school personnel and parents at the initial IEP meeting and at each program review thereafter.   6 5 4 3 2 1

6 5 4 3 2 1   13. The curriculum content of adapted physical education classes is diversified and includes opportunities to learn movement patterns, games, sports, dance, and aquatics adapted to individual abilities.   6 5 4 3 2 1

6 5 4 3 2 1   14. Physical education teachers of handicapped students seek cooperation from and maintain communication with parents.   6 5 4 3 2 1

Continued

Continued

GIVE YOUR OPINION NOW EXIST	SURVEY OF ADAPTED PHYSICAL EDUCATION NEEDS (SAPEN)	GIVE YOUR OPINION SHOULD EXIST

Please circle in the lefthand column the number that you feel best represents the services that *now exist* in your school district. Circle in the righthand column the number that represents your opinion about what *should exist*. IT IS CRITICAL THAT YOU CIRCLE A NUMBER FOR EACH ITEM IN EACH COLUMN. Once you have completed, double check to see if you have responded to every item using both columns.

Column key (both sides): 6—Completely agree, 5—Mostly agree, 4—Slightly agree, 3—Slightly disagree, 2—Mostly disagree, 1—Completely disagree

6 5 4 3 2 1 — 15. Handicapped students in regular physical education classes receive comparable attention and instruction as regular students. — 6 5 4 3 2 1

6 5 4 3 2 1 — 16. Secondary school handicapped students receive 200 minutes of physical education instruction each week. — 6 5 4 3 2 1

6 5 4 3 2 1 — 17. Kindergarten handicapped students receive 100 minutes of physical education/motor development instruction each week. — 6 5 4 3 2 1

6 5 4 3 2 1 — 18. Teacher's aides are provided at least one session of in-service training each year by an adapted physical education specialist on physical education instructional techniques. — 6 5 4 3 2 1

6 5 4 3 2 1 — 19. The school district has specific eligibility standards for placement of students in adapted physical education. — 6 5 4 3 2 1

6 5 4 3 2 1 — 20. Persons who teach physical education are knowledgeable about federal and state legislation/policies/guidelines regarding physical education for handicapped students. — 6 5 4 3 2 1

6 5 4 3 2 1 — 21. Program resources (instructional materials, equipment, and media) are available for effective physical education instruction for handicapped. — 6 5 4 3 2 1

6 5 4 3 2 1 — 22. Administrators in physical education, special education, and other areas work together effectively in the promotion of physical education for the handicapped. — 6 5 4 3 2 1

6 5 4 3 2 1 — 23. Early childhood handicapped students receive 100 minutes of physical education/motor development instruction each week. — 6 5 4 3 2 1

6 5 4 3 2 1 — 24. Facilities used in physical education for handicapped students are architecturally accessible. — 6 5 4 3 2 1

6 5 4 3 2 1 — 25. Comparable facilities are allocated for instruction of physical education classes for handicapped as for regular physical education programs. — 6 5 4 3 2 1

6 5 4 3 2 1 — 26. Handicapped students are adequately prepared for optimal leisure and lifetime sports through physical education programs. — 6 5 4 3 2 1

Continued

Continued

| GIVE YOUR OPINION NOW EXIST | SURVEY OF ADAPTED PHYSICAL EDUCATION NEEDS (SAPEN) | GIVE YOUR OPINION SHOULD EXIST |

GIVE YOUR OPINION NOW EXIST

6—Completely agree
5—Mostly agree
4—Slightly agree
3—Slightly disagree
2—Mostly disagree
1—Completely disagree

SURVEY OF ADAPTED PHYSICAL EDUCATION NEEDS (SAPEN)

Please circle in the lefthand column the number that you feel best represents the services that *now exist* in your school district. Circle in the righthand column the number that represents your opinion about what *should exist*. IT IS CRITICAL THAT YOU CIRCLE A NUMBER FOR EACH ITEM IN EACH COLUMN. Once you have completed, double check to see if you have responded to every item using both columns.

GIVE YOUR OPINION SHOULD EXIST

6—Completely agree
5—Mostly agree
4—Slightly agree
3—Slightly disagree
2—Mostly disagree
1—Completely disagree

6 5 4 3 2 1 — 27. Teacher's aides and volunteers are used to supplement the delivery of services to handicapped students by regular and adapted physical education teachers. — 6 5 4 3 2 1

6 5 4 3 2 1 — 28. Administrators are knowledgeable about federal and state legislation/policies/guidelines regarding physical education for handicapped students. — 6 5 4 3 2 1

6 5 4 3 2 1 — 29. Teachers of regular physical education are as accountable for their handicapped students in terms of motor assessment, appropriate developmental teaching techniques, and keeping written IEP records as teachers of adapted physical education. — 6 5 4 3 2 1

6 5 4 3 2 1 — 30. Special educators and physical educators work together to develop optimal physical education programs for handicapped students. — 6 5 4 3 2 1

6 5 4 3 2 1 — 31. The local school district employs at least one adapted physical education specialist full time to provide assessment, IEP, and instructional services for the handicapped and to assist regular educators in these tasks. — 6 5 4 3 2 1

6 5 4 3 2 1 — 32. Teachers of handicapped students in physical education possess the necessary adapted physical education competencies and knowledges. — 6 5 4 3 2 1

6 5 4 3 2 1 — 33. Regular physical education personnel are provided at least one in-service training session each year on adapted physical education by specialists in this area. — 6 5 4 3 2 1

6 5 4 3 2 1 — 34. Physical education teachers have as an educational goal strengthening the self-concept of handicapped students. — 6 5 4 3 2 1

6 5 4 3 2 1 — 35. The IEPs of handicapped students include present level of *motor and physical* performance, physical education goals and short-term objectives, and specific physical education services to be provided. — 6 5 4 3 2 1

6 5 4 3 2 1 — 36. Nonhandicapped students with medical excuses to exempt them from regular physical education are provided adapted physical education instruction/services. — 6 5 4 3 2 1

Continued

Continued

GIVE YOUR OPINION NOW EXIST

SURVEY OF ADAPTED PHYSICAL EDUCATION NEEDS (SAPEN)

GIVE YOUR OPINION SHOULD EXIST

Please circle in the lefthand column the number that you feel best represents the services that *now exist* in your school district. Circle in the righthand column the number that represents your opinion about what *should exist*. IT IS CRITICAL THAT YOU CIRCLE A NUMBER FOR EACH ITEM IN EACH COLUMN. Once you have completed, double check to see if you have responded to every item using both columns.

6—Completely agree	5—Mostly agree	4—Slightly agree	3—Slightly disagree	2—Mostly disagree	1—Completely disagree		6—Completely agree	5—Mostly agree	4—Slightly agree	3—Slightly disagree	2—Mostly disagree	1—Completely disagree
6	5	4	3	2	1	37. The physical education curriculum for grades K-12 creates positive attitudes toward people who "differ" from the norm.	6	5	4	3	2	1
6	5	4	3	2	1	38. Physical educators provide special counseling on fitness, weight control, and use of leisure time for handicapped students and their families to facilitate increased involvement in home and community activities.	6	5	4	3	2	1
6	5	4	3	2	1	39. Certified physical education teachers and/or adapted physical education specialists deliver physical education instruction/services to handicapped students.	6	5	4	3	2	1
6	5	4	3	2	1	40. Handicapped students who experience success in regular physical education and athletics are given the opportunity to do so.	6	5	4	3	2	1
6	5	4	3	2	1	41. Administrators understand the components which adapted physical education specialists should possess and know whom to contact for additional assistance and/or in-service training assistance.	6	5	4	3	2	1
6	5	4	3	2	1	42. Sufficient numbers of qualified personnel to meet the physical education requirements in PL 94-142 are available in the school district.	6	5	4	3	2	1
6	5	4	3	2	1	43. Physical education programming is based on individual education programs (IEPs) which include present levels of motor performance, long range goals, and short-term objectives.	6	5	4	3	2	1
6	5	4	3	2	1	44. The Local Education Agency (LEA) monitors physical education programming for the handicapped students.	6	5	4	3	2	1
6	5	4	3	2	1	45. Motor assessment in IEP process is done by a physical educator specially trained in motor evaluation who utilizes appropriate assessment tools of motor performance.	6	5	4	3	2	1
6	5	4	3	2	1	46. Administrators encourage persons who teach physical education to attend professional meetings, workshops, and seminars in order to strengthen such adapted physical education competencies as assessment, IEP, and developmental techniques.	6	5	4	3	2	1

Continued

Continued

GIVE YOUR OPINION NOW EXIST						SURVEY OF ADAPTED PHYSICAL EDUCATION NEEDS (SAPEN)	GIVE YOUR OPINION SHOULD EXIST					
6—Completely agree	5—Mostly agree	4—Slightly agree	3—Slightly disagree	2—Mostly disagree	1—Completely disagree	Please circle in the lefthand column the number that you feel best represents the services that *now exist* in your school district. Circle in the righthand column the number that represents your opinion about what *should exist*. IT IS CRITICAL THAT YOU CIRCLE A NUMBER FOR EACH ITEM IN EACH COLUMN. Once you have completed, double check to see if you have responded to every item using both columns.	6—Completely agree	5—Mostly agree	4—Slightly agree	3—Slightly disagree	2—Mostly disagree	1—Completely disagree
6	5	4	3	2	1	47. The school district has an effective screening program for the identification of students with motor, physical, and/or other problems which need special programming in physical education.	6	5	4	3	2	1
6	5	4	3	2	1	48. Handicapped persons who have achieved success in sports, dance, or aquatics are employed as consultants, teachers, or aides to provide physical education instruction and serve as role models for handicapped students.	6	5	4	3	2	1
6	5	4	3	2	1	49. The school district works with parents and other groups in promoting Special Olympics and/or special athletic programs for handicapped students.	6	5	4	3	2	1
6	5	4	3	2	1	50. School and community personnel work together to facilitate integrated and special community-based recreation and health/fitness programs on weekends and after school for handicapped individuals.	6	5	4	3	2	1

Chapter 18

Counseling in Adapted Physical Education

Glenda Adams and Trudy Younger

Counseling is spontaneous encounter, a happening, a changing to meet the needs of those being helped. It is not something confined to an office setting, nor is it a specific occurrence. Counseling can happen throughout a school whether it be in the gymnasium, lunchroom, classroom, library, or wherever. Counseling can occur on a one-to-one basis or in a group. In any of these situations the counselor accepts a person as he or she is, never stereotyping the person with judgmental or labeling language. This philosophy should hold true for all educators in that they should maintain a belief in the worth and dignity of every individual.

Because counseling is spontaneous and can happen anywhere, it is an excellent tool for all teachers. Physical educators can benefit greatly from a course that teaches counseling skills that emphasize communication and personal growth. Some say that it is the school counselors' job to counsel. The statement is true; yet, with the ratio of one counselor to 350 students, obviously not every student receives the individual counseling he or she needs. Teachers have the opportunity to see students on a daily basis and to build a relationship of trust and understanding. Counselors, on the other hand, often work with crisis situations or have other responsibilities that prevent their seeing the same student on a daily basis.

Team Approach to Educating Handicapped Students

In schools that employ a team approach to education, all staff members are interested in the total student and in his or her achieving the following goals: proficiency in academic subject matter, workable coping skills, ability to relate and share feelings with others, knowledge of how to spend leisure time, maintenance of physical fitness, learning parenting skills, and knowledge of how to develop a career plan. In the team approach everyone has a hand in the nurturing of all students, whether it be through direct involvement in teaching, counseling, or extracurricular activities or indirectly through the establishment of programs.

The philosophy is the same for handicapped students as they spend 12 to 14 years moving through the public

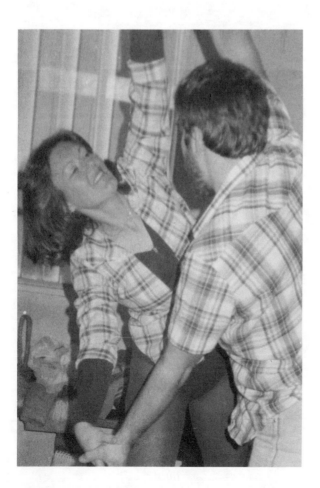

Trudy Younger (left) and Glenda Adams (right) depict nonverbal and verbal therapeutic approaches, respectively. Both are from Colorado public schools.

school system. These students often require a more intense and unified team approach than nondisabled peers. Usually the team working with a handicapped student is varied and includes classroom teachers, counselors, an adapted physical education teacher, an itinerant teacher, aides, a school nurse, a psychologist, and a social worker. The approach this chapter follows is to look at the adapted physical education teacher as a member of the school team and to focus on his or her role as seen through a guidance and counseling concept. Discussion includes techniques of counseling that physical educators can use in various situations, including fitness and leisure-time counseling, providing resource people for the teacher, and some ideas that have proven successful in helping students with special needs in several secondary schools.

Importance of Counseling Skills for Teachers

Humanistic theory posits that when students learn it is because they have responded to the teacher as a person—a person who relates to students with an attitude of acceptance, empathy, concreteness, and personal genuineness (Aspy & Roebuck, 1977). These are the same qualities that make an effective counselor. This helps promote the idea that teaching is a therapeutic experience to promote human growth (Belkin, 1975). This theory closely resembles that of Carl Rogers' client-centered theory (Rogers, 1951), which is based on the principle of an open and accepting attitude toward individuals.

A background in basic counseling skills is beneficial to many professionals and especially teachers because their work focuses exclusively on people. Counseling techniques can be used in many situations dealing with students or for that matter with other staff or team members. An adapted physical education teacher uses counseling techniques in promoting fitness as a way of life. Teachers explore with students (individually or in small groups) attitudes or misconceptions they have toward themselves, exercise, and fitness in general. Through skills in listening and observing, the teacher helps students to discover reasons for their attitudes or behavior in relation to fitness.

Counseling Skills Needed by Adapted Physical Educators

The characteristics of a healthy counseling relationship are active listening, understanding the other's point of view, acceptance, willingness to become committed and involved, and genuineness. Active listening is one of the most important ingredients in helping others. Basic techniques used in counseling to indicate that you are involved in listening are (a) squarely facing the individual who is talking, (b) maintaining an open posture (i.e., not crossing the arms or legs because such gestures suggest a closing-off from the respondent), (c) establishing and maintaining eye contact, (d) slightly leaning toward the student to indicate you are ready to move in to help and not pull away from him or her, and (e) remaining as relaxed and as natural in this attending posture as possible. Attending or listening to a student who is speaking is important because it demonstrates that all of your attention is focused on him or her.

Active listening builds the foundation for understanding. Putting yourself in the student's situation and relating to his or her feelings involves true understanding. It is important to hear what is being said, but it is even more important to *understand what is being felt*.

When students share their concerns, the teacher should not only focus on the content of what is said but also identify the feelings underlying the student's message. Several responses can be used to facilitate a counseling situation. The most common technique used to interact with a student is to use minimal encouragers such as "uh-huh," "go on," "yes," "and then," and so forth. This technique is beneficial when there is a need for a sympathetic listener only; however, a continuation of only minimal encouragers does nothing to facilitate growth and understanding in a counseling situation because counseling is a verbal process. Techniques that better facilitate the situation are paraphrasing and reflection of feelings.

Paraphrasing is a technique used to identify the content of the message and then to restate the message in your own words. For example, should a handicapped individual state, "There are a lot of things I can't do in physical education," the teacher could paraphrase with, "Sounds as though you are seeing some things in physical education as really difficult." This allows the student to hear what he or she has just said and gives the opportunity to clarify the response if that was not what he or she truly meant to say.

The most facilitative response is to reflect not only the content of the message, but also the feeling underlying the message. For example, if a student should say, "I get frustrated because it takes me so long to get the ball," the teacher could respond by identifying the stated feeling word *frustrated* and reply with, "You're telling me that you get mad at yourself because you get the ball too slowly." This helps the student to know that he or she is being understood and accepted and is not being judged or criticized. This sets up a caring atmosphere and opens the way for further discussion.

Another important characteristic related to helping others is acceptance, or recognizing the person as unique and worthy of respect. The self-concept of the handicapped student can be enhanced if nonthreatening situations are created. If, as a teacher, you are accepting, nonlabeling, and nonjudgmental, then an environment free from threat is created. Genuine acceptance and respect are not freely given in today's society to individuals who are different. The tendency is to ignore, stand off from, and/or reject people who are unusual or different. Acceptance means we look at another with no strings attached or we accept them for what they are and who they are, not for their thoughts or behaviors. Acceptance recognizes the student as unique. As we assist in that uniqueness, we help them to realize that they are ultimately responsible for their attitudes and behaviors.

A helping situation can take place only when the student and the teacher are committed to working together. The teacher must care enough to get involved—personally involved—and this caring is best demonstrated by spending time and energy with the student. Without caring and commitment, the teacher experiences fatigue and the student feels frustration.

Teachers must be genuine in their dealing with students. Teachers should be themselves in the relationship and assume no roles. If the teacher is not genuine, it causes the person being helped to be suspicious and places him or her on the defensive.

Humanistic Approach to Adapted Physical Education Service Delivery

Although counseling skills are beneficial to all teachers, these skills are essential for physical educators and adapted physical educators in particular. The subject area lends itself to a humanistic approach to teaching because it provides opportunities for a more relaxed learning atmosphere than the classroom setting. Counseling also offers opportunities for the development of mutual trust and understanding between teacher and student (i.e., before and after class or between activities). Adapted physical education teachers can develop special rapport with a student through daily contact. This often leads the student to respond with friendship and trust. The environment of a physical education class offers students the chance to share thoughts, to relate to others, and to create emotional ties made stronger through shared physical activities. It offers students the chance to challenge and test themselves, which, in turn, can lead to greater confidence or to self-doubt. Either situation may call for a counseling session.

Situations arise whereby students, both handicapped and nonhandicapped, ask the teacher for help in solving a problem or working through a situation. These are excellent opportunities for the teacher to help a student with coping and decision-making skills and in making other needed adjustments in personal growth areas. These are not times when advice is needed. Too often students are looking for a quick solution or a "tell me what to do" answer. It is important that the teacher be able to discuss the situation and listen to the student and yet not offer advice or solutions to the problem. Students must work out answers for themselves. This is especially true when counseling handicapped students, who may be accustomed to people handling their problems for them. For example, the student may not want to change clothes for physical education class or he or she may not want to participate in activities that day. It is important to find out the reasons why students feel and/or act. The adapted physical education teacher, in coping with such issues, is engaged in the counseling process.

Counseling is time-consuming, but it is a caring time. When a person spends time discussing a problem or an issue, he or she is in effect saying, "I care enough about you to listen to you and to spend time with you." Giving advice is like a quick fix to a problem. It is essentially saying, "I don't have the time to listen to you—the problem is not that important to take time to listen." It is probably wise to remember that because people are individuals, they address problems differently. Advice may only confuse the issue.

Leisure Counseling in Adapted Physical Education

Counseling concerning leisure activities can help to provide balance to the handicapped student's life (Gunn & Peterson, 1978). The manner in which people express themselves during leisure time depends on the resources they have developed for free time. Individuals have a tendency to pursue during free time those activities that are familiar or those things that have brought them feelings of success, accomplishment, or pleasure.

Counseling handicapped individuals with respect to enjoyable and constructive use of leisure time is vital (Iso-Ahola, 1980). Often handicapped students do not understand the difference between structured and unstructured free time. They have not consciously thought about the manner in which free time is spent. Many are very aware, however, that during unstructured time they suffer from boredom and depression. In assisting the handicapped to understand the concept of leisure time, the first step is to help them differentiate between necessary activities and those that are freely chosen. Sherrill (1986) describes several instruments that can be used in leisure counseling.

One counseling technique the adapted physical educator can use to facilitate exploration of the handicapped individual's free time is to ask open-ended questions—

questions that cannot be answered by a simple "yes" or "no" but ones that solicit longer, more detailed responses. Such questions can include, "What do you like to do in your free time?" "What are your hobbies?" "How much time do you spend with friends?" Questions beginning with who, where, what, when, and how are especially good. Beginning a question with "why," however, can appear too judgmental and tends to stifle response because it can be received in a defensive manner (i.e., "Why don't you have any hobbies?"). Open-ended questions help to reveal to the teacher and to the student the types of activities that occupy most of the student's leisure time. Leisure counseling provides opportunities to look critically at activities to see if they are meaningful and serve as an important part of life or are seen as something separate and apart from the life-style of the student. For example, a handicapped student might see basketball as something that other children play when they have free time but not an activity he or she can choose. Handicapped individuals should learn and grow as much in leisure-time activities as they do in other moments of life.

Carefully selected leisure activities can provide excellent opportunities for the handicapped individual to grow socially. Socialization is considered to be one of the most important contributions adapted physical education can make in the affective domain (Oliver, 1972; Sherrill, 1986). Providing experiences in cooperative learning, competitive behavior, and appreciation of laws and rules are compatible objectives for both physical education and leisure-time activities.

As adapted physical education enhances socialization and increases physical awareness, a broader frame of reference is established for the handicapped individual as choices are made concerning leisure activities. Because handicapped children often become adults with an abundance of leisure time, the handicapped need guidance, stimulation, and suggestions to help structure leisure time activities (Sherrill, 1986).

Resource Persons to Assist With Counseling

The following resource people are usually available within a school; however, their time commitments and other assignments will vary from school to school. The school nurse can be an excellent resource in working with adapted physical educators. Most nurses will gladly give lectures concerning health and fitness. If teachers do not feel that they have an adequate understanding of the student's physical education capabilities, the school nurse can be very helpful in interpreting the physician's recommendations and in contacting the physician when more information is necessary or when a reevaluation

is needed. The nurse is also available to consult with parents and to participate in other planned team efforts on behalf of the student.

Both the school psychologist and social worker are excellent resources. The psychologist assists the physical educator in determining where a student is academically and the extent to which he or she can understand and interpret verbal instructions. The school psychologist may offer family therapy to families in need of intensive counseling. This type of family therapy can have a tremendous impact on the handicapped student. The school social worker functions as a liaison between the home and school. He or she often makes home visits to bridge the gap that can exist between the home and school environments.

Aides within a school can be invaluable with physically handicapped students. The aides are assigned to help handicapped students take notes, eat meals, assist with bathroom needs, help change clothes for physical education class, and help with other needs. These aides are also a good contact source for obtaining personal insight into the student.

The itinerant teacher is usually involved with physically handicapped students inasmuch as he or she acts as coordinator of all services (including aide help, transportation, etc.) within the school setting. The itinerant teacher can be valuable to the adapted physical education teacher in relating important background information on students' home environments, past academic and physical performances, and health needs. The itinerant teacher also helps in locating and preparing special equipment for the physical education class.

The school counselor is in a position to work closely with the adapted physical education teacher in implementing direct services to students. In situations requiring extended one-to-one counseling in which the teacher may not have sufficient time to spend, the counselor should be of help. The counselor may help also with small group fitness counseling or parent group counseling. The counselor should be available for consultation.

Counseling Approaches That Work in Adapted Physical Education

Each teaching situation within a given school is unique, and yet some ideas and methods already in use have proven their worth. For example, many schools with adapted physical education programs and those with regular physical education programs have instituted student aide programs. Often classes in today's public schools number more than 30 students, and it becomes the teacher's reponsibility to be innovative in his or her approach to the situation. A student assistant can be assigned to work individually with a student in need of special help. The student assistant should possess certain qualities such as sensitivity, empathy, and a caring attitude. The assistant should receive training from the teacher in order to be more effective with the handicapped student and should receive credit for work during the semester or year. Using student assistants allows handicapped students more individual help and permits the teacher more freedom to work with larger numbers of students. Project PEOPEL (Long, Irmer, Burkett, Glasenapp, & Odenkirk, 1980) is one example of the use of student assistants who serve as both peer teachers and counselors. In many schools, however, the approach is individualized.

In one high school a student assisted an entire year in a body mechanics and weight lifting class by working with a young lady who had cerebral palsy. The assistant, under the direction of the teacher, worked with the student on a planned exercise program including weights on a daily basis, game skills, prescribed exercises, plus a lot of understanding conversation and companionship. This type of one-to-one commitment cannot be implemented by a teacher in a class situation; however, it is very feasible with student assistants.

The counselor is in an excellent position to help screen for students interested in helping handicapped students as he or she discusses career plans with students. Career planning usually includes discussing interests in working with people, data, or things and other pertinent information that would help a counselor know if the student would be a good choice for the program. In the student assistant program the teacher still must write the weekly program of planned activities for the handicapped student; however, the time commitment is well worth the reward of personalized physical and personal growth for the handicapped student.

The use of peer counselors within the total education system has increased greatly over the past several years (Gray & Tindall, 1978; Jenkins & Jenkins, 1981). The basic premise of the program is that peer counselors are an extension of the school's guidance and counseling program. A further concept is that often students feel more comfortable discussing some problems with students nearer their own age. Peer counselors are trained over a period of time (anywhere from 9 to 18 weeks) in such areas as techniques of counseling, communication skills with an emphasis on listening, confrontation and conflict resolution, and decision-making skills. During training, peer counselors are involved in extensive personal growth because such students must be in tune with themselves before they can venture out to help others.

After training, the peer counselors work out of the counseling center and usually receive referrals from parents, teachers, and students themselves. Sometimes they begin work without referrals on what can be termed peer counselor "intuition." The peer counselor is trained to be observant of fellow students who appear lonely, exhibit negative body language, or in any way seem to need help. Because of his or her sensitivity and caring for others, the peer counselor can attempt to help this type of student and yet not take it personally if rebuked. Peer counselors work with all types of students with the only criteria being that of accepting the person as he or she is, being genuine with the person, and trying to understand what he or she is saying by looking at the situation through his or her eyes. A common phrase for this counseling approach is "walking a mile in the other person's moccasins."

Peer counselors are trained in group processes. Most are skilled facilitators or leaders. A peer counselor can be helpful in an adapted physical education or regular class with handicapped students as an aide or helper in teaching or in facilitating groups on a weekly or biweekly basis. This is an excellent approach when the teacher does not feel comfortable with handling groups and when he or she wants to divide the class and have half the class in an activity and the other half in a counseling group and then switch the next class time. This is not suggesting that group work or counseling replace activities for handicapped students in physical education; instead, it is an opportunity to have the students learn more about themselves and their actions as directly related to such areas as self-concept, body image, use of leisure time, and fitness considerations. It is a time for students to do a sort of perception check on how they see themselves and how others see them.

Illustrative of this is the self-actualization group. In it a teacher or peer counselor can have a greater impact on more students than can be achieved by working with only one individual at a time. The group also creates a more realistic setting than one-to-one dialogue for certain kinds of problem solving. Groups provide students with a safe place in which to try out new attitudes, beliefs, and behaviors. The activities for a group in self-actualization can assist students in personal development, communication, and decision-making skills. It is best to have students volunteer for the group; however, teachers can recommend or place students in the group.

The following is an example of setting up a group using "The Magic Circle" technique:

A. Place the students in a circle—if some are in wheelchairs, it might be best for all to sit in chairs. If those in chairs can sit on the floor, then sitting on the floor can be more relaxing.

B. Use a warm-up to get the students to talk.

1. Say your name and I want (to eat lunch, to take a trip, anything).

2. Say your name and a descriptive adjective starting with the same letter of the first name (I'm Jumping Judy); the next person must name all people before him or her and then him- or herself.

C. Go over ground rules with the group for each meeting in the circle.

1. Everyone gets a turn to share, including the leader.

2. You can skip your turn.

3. Listen to the person who is sharing.

4. The time is shared equally.

5. No put-downs, interruptions, probing, or gossip.

6. Stay in your own space.

7. Bring only yourself to the circle.

D. Facilitate communication in the circle.

1. Set the tone through a nonthreatening manner, and make the students feel safe to say whatever they want.

2. Review the ground rules.

3. Introduce the topic (e.g., self-actualization).

a. State it and possibly define it: Self-actualization means to act in such a way that we become better persons. We become better in the sense that we begin to develop and use our unique potentialities. The process of striving to become what we are capable of becoming is self-actualization.

b. Elaborate on the topic: Few people, if any, ever become fully self-actualized because there is always more room for growth and personal development.

c. Restate the topic: We all have within us the power to become more self-actualized and fulfilled than we are now. What is required is a personal awareness of our own potentiality and how it can be nurtured and developed. We also need to become aware of and skilled in practicing those deeds and actions that can enable us to become more self-actualized and fulfilled persons.

d. Provide a 30-second silence so that each person can think about the topic.

4. Lead the participation phase. It is up to the leader as to how structured to make the group and whether he or she wants to stimulate discussion by tossing out ideas or whether he or she wants the group to come up with ideas and thoughts to share.

5. Lead the cognitive summary. This is the opportunity to draw all the ideas together and have students say what they have learned or observed. It is also an opportunity for the leader to relate some thoughts as to how this topic relates to leisure, fitness, health, or any other area.

6. Terminate the circle. Everyone is given an opportunity to speak a last time or summarize the session if he or she wishes. The leader may want to remind the students that things said are confidential within the group. The leader may do a check to see if the students would like to meet again.

An intramural program for handicapped students also creates a situation conducive to counseling. Intramurals give students an opportunity for extra activity and the feel of limited competition. One school had a group of students with such handicapping conditions as cerebral palsy, muscular dystrophy, and juvenile rheumatoid arthritis who got together a soccer team to compete with other teams. Some of the students were in wheelchairs and some were on crutches, but they played soccer in the gymnasium on a weekly basis. The group became known as the "Not So Fragiles" and eventually played non-disabled students who competed in wheelchairs to even up the affair. Usually the Not So Fragiles won. It was very exciting for the handicapped students to have the thrill of competition and the appreciation of a student body audience.

Intramural activities and programs of this type lend themselves to mutual caring and sharing situations among sponsors, participants, officials, and audience. Some faculty members may be interested in teaching or working in a recreational setting on a weekly basis during their unscheduled time. A school may consider special events or intramurals in conjunction with such organizations as Key Club, which is a community and school service organization nationally affiliated with Kiwanis Clubs of America. These groups sponsor dance-a-thons for muscular dystrophy, marathon races for the March of Dimes, blood drives, and health fairs. It is a way of bringing the handicapped and nonhandicapped into a relationship of helping each other and working together.

In conclusion, all educators should be exposed to at least one class in guidance and counseling during their professional preparation program. A class that stresses communication skills seems essential for adapted physical educators as they work with students, striving not only to make academic gains, but also to open doors for fuller participation in the larger society.

Recommended Reading for Adapted Physical Educators

Following is a list of references on counseling that may help the adapted physical educator.

Anderson, E. (1970). *Helping the adolescent with the hidden handicap*. Belmont, CA: Fearon Publishers/ Lear Siegler.

Ayrault, E. (1971). *Helping the handicapped teenager mature*. New York: Association Press.

Buscaglia, L. (1975). *The disabled and their parents: A counseling challenge*. Thorofare, NJ: Charles B. Slack.

Dinkmeyer, C., & Dreikurs, R. (1963). *Encouraging children to learn: The encouragement process*. Englewood Cliffs, NJ: Prentice-Hall.

Eagan, G. (1975). *The skilled helper: A model for systematic helping and interpersonal relating*. Monterey, CA: Brooks/Cole.

Egg, M. (1969). *The different child grows up*. New York: The John Day Company.

Gallagher, J. (1975). *The application of child development research to exceptional children*. Reston, VA: Council for Exceptional Children.

Huckaby, H., & Daly, J. (1979, September). Got those PL 94-142 blues. *Personnel and Guidance Journal*, pp. 70-72.

Johnson, D.W. (1972). *Reaching out*. Englewood Cliffs, NJ: Prentice-Hall.

Johnson, D.W., & Johnson, F.P. (1975). *Joining together: Group theory and group skills*. Englewood Cliffs, NJ: Prentice-Hall.

Myrick, R.D., & Erney, T. (1978). *Caring and sharing: Becoming a peer facilitator*. Minneapolis, MN: Educational Media Corporation.

Nelson, E.S. (1979, December). Counseling the handicapped in the secondary school under PL 94-142. *The High School Journal*, pp. 109-113.

Ohlsen, M. (1977). *Group counseling*. New York: Holt, Rinehart and Winston.

Reynolds, M. C. (Ed.). (1980). *Social environment of the schools*. Reston, VA: Council for Exceptional Children.

Sherrill, C. (1986). *Adapted physical education and recreation* (3rd ed.). Dubuque, IA: William C. Brown.

Valett, R. (1974). *Self-actualization*. Niles, IL: Argus Communications.

Wright, B.A. (1983). *Physical disability—A psychosocial approach* (2nd ed.). New York: Harper and Row.

References

Aspy, D., & Roebuck, F. (1977). *Kids don't learn from people they don't like*. Amherst, MA: Human Resource Development Press.

Belkin, G. S. (1975). *Practical counseling in the schools*. Dubuque, IA: William C. Brown.

Gray, H. D., & Tindall, J. (1978). *Peer counseling: An in-depth look at training peer helpers*. Muncie, IN: Accelerated Development.

Gunn, S., & Peterson, C. (1978). *Therapeutic recreation design: Principles and practices*. Englewood Cliffs, NJ: Prentice-Hall.

Iso-Ahola, S. (1980). *The social psychology of leisure and recreation*. Dubuque, IA: William C. Brown.

Jenkins, J., & Jenkins, L. (1981). *Cross age and peer tutoring: Help for children with learning problems*. Reston, VA: Council for Exceptional Children.

Long, E., Irmer, L., Burkett, L., Glasenapp, G., & Odenkirk, B. (1980). PEOPEL. *Journal of Physical Education and Recreation*, **51**, 28-29.

Oliver, J. (1972). Physical activity and the psychological development of the handicapped. In J. E. Kane (Ed.), *Psychological aspects of physical education and sport* (pp. 187-208). Boston: Routledge & Kegan Paul.

Rogers, C. (1951). *Client-centered therapy*. Cambridge, MA: Riverside Press.

Sherrill, C. (1986). *Adapted physical education and recreation: A multidisciplinary approach* (3rd ed.). Dubuque, IA: William C. Brown.

Chapter 19

Instructional Accountability in Adapted Physical Education: A Review of Research

Claudine Sherrill

*A*dapted physical education is a comprehensive service delivery system designed to meet the unique needs of students with problems in the psychomotor domain. Adapted physical education is to regular physical education what special education is to mainstream instruction; they have many elements in common, yet are very different. Regular physical educators generally cite fitness and motor proficiency as their most important goals (Rosentswieg, 1969), whereas many adapted physical education personnel believe that self-actualization, particularly as it relates to self-concept, peer acceptance, socialization, and perceptual-motor functioning, is the primary goal of movement work with handicapped and clumsy students (Sherrill, 1986; Sherrill & Montelione, 1983).

To assure instructional accountability in adapted physical education, it is important that teachers conceptualize and subsequently prioritize long-range instructional goals. To facilitate this task, Sherrill (1982) developed the Goals of Adapted Physical Education Scale (GAPES), a paired comparison instrument in which each of nine goals is ranked individually against every other goal in round robin fashion. Table 19.1 presents preliminary findings based on the administration of this scale to regular and

adapted physical educators (Sherrill & Montelione, 1983); analysis of data from more than 700 respondents is under way. The definitions of the goals as stated on GAPES were formulated through a group process approach by the following persons: Dave Auxter, Walter Ersing, Janet Seaman, Claudine Sherrill, Julian Stein, and Robert Strauss. Although there will probably never be 100% agreement on definitions of goals, these definitions represent the combined efforts of several experts over 2 to 3 hours.

Physical education instruction can contribute to development in all three of the commonly recognized domains of behavior: *cognitive* (intellectual skills); *affective* (feelings, opinions, attitudes, beliefs, values, interests, and desires); and *psychomotor* (movement skills and fitness). Figure 19.1 presents the many values that students can derive from carefully planned and properly conducted physical education programs. These values have been substantiated by research and comprise the rationale for required physical education instruction in the public schools. The model presented in Figure 19.1 was developed in conjunction with GAPES, using the definitions of that instrument. The most controversial of the nine goals is probably perceptual-motor function and sensory integration. This is perhaps because some persons conceptualize this as

Table 19.1   Ranking of Long-Range Goals of Adapted Physical Education by 152 Teachers From Ohio, Minnesota, and Texas

Rank	Long-range goal and definition used in paired comparison procedure
Highest	
1	POSITIVE SELF-CONCEPT. To develop a positive self-concept and body image through activity involvement; to increase understanding and appreciation of the body and its capacity for movement; to accept limitations that cannot be changed and to learn to adapt to the environment so as to make the most of strengths (i.e., to work toward self-actualization).
2	SOCIAL COMPETENCY. To learn appropriate social behaviors (i.e., how to interact with others—sharing, taking turns, following, and leading). To reduce social isolation, to learn how to develop and maintain friendships, to demonstrate good sportsmanship and self-discipline in winning and losing, and to develop other skills necessary for success in the mainstream.
3	MOTOR SKILLS & PATTERNS. To learn fundamental motor skills and patterns; to master the motor skills indigenous to games, sport, dance, and aquatics participation; to improve fine and gross motor coordination for self-care, school, work, and play activities.
4	PHYSICAL & MOTOR FITNESS. To develop the cardiovascular system, promote ideal weight, increase muscular strength, endurance, and flexibility, and improve postures.
5	PERCEPTUAL-MOTOR FUNCTION AND SENSORY INTEGRATION. To enhance visual, auditory, tactile, vestibular, and kinesthetic functioning; to reinforce academic learnings through games and perceptual-motor activities; to improve cognitive, language, and motor function through increased sensory integration.
6	LEISURE TIME SKILLS. To learn to transfer PE learnings into habits of lifetime sport, dance, and aquatics; to become acquainted with community resources for recreation; to expand repertoire of individual and group games and sport, dance, and aquatic activities and/or to refine skills.
7	FUN/TENSION RELEASE. To have fun, recreation, happiness; to release tensions in a healthy, socially acceptable manner; to reduce hyperactivity and learn to relax; to improve mental health and attitude toward exercise and/or physical education.
8	PLAY & GAME SKILLS. To learn to play (i.e., to progress through developmental play stages from solitary and parallel play behaviors up through appropriate cooperative and competitive game behaviors). To promote contact and interaction behaviors with toys, play apparatus, and persons; to learn basic game formations and mental operations needed for play; to master rules and strategies of simple games.
9 Lowest	CREATIVE EXPRESSION. To increase creativity in movement and thought. When posed a movement problem, to generate *many* responses, *different* responses, *original* responses. To learn to imagine, to embellish and add on, to risk experimentation, to devise appropriate game strategy, and to create new games, dances, and movement sequences.

a prerequisite to fundamental motor skills and patterns, whereas others believe it is a continuous, ongoing process in motor control and development. Figure 19.1 assumes the latter stance, that is, that instruction directed at perceptual-motor functions, sensory integration, and motor skills and patterns can occur concurrently, and thus goals may need to be written for each on the individualized education plan (IEP).

Whereas regular physical educators approach changing psychomotor behaviors in a general way, adapted physical educators spend much time in assessment, identifying the specific problems that are interfering with or preventing success in the mainstream setting or in community recreation or in home and neighborhood play. Once the problems are identified, they are prioritized and stated on IEPs as long-range goals that can be broken down into short-term behavioral objectives. For the severely handicapped child, goals may need to be in the areas of play and game

skills (simply learning to play), perceptual-motor function and sensory integration, and body image. For a hypo- or hyperactive child, goals may need to be in the areas of fun and tension release, self-concept, and social competency and peer acceptance.

This chapter presents nine broad areas in which physical education, properly planned and conducted, can be of value to all students. It is not possible, however, to achieve all goals at the same time. Adapted physical educators must choose two or three goals at a time and carefully plan their implementation. They must dare to be different from regular physical educators in prioritizing their goals because their students *are* different. If their students did not have unique and special instructional needs, they would already be experiencing success in the mainstream.

This chapter also reviews selected published research studies that document that the hypothesized values of

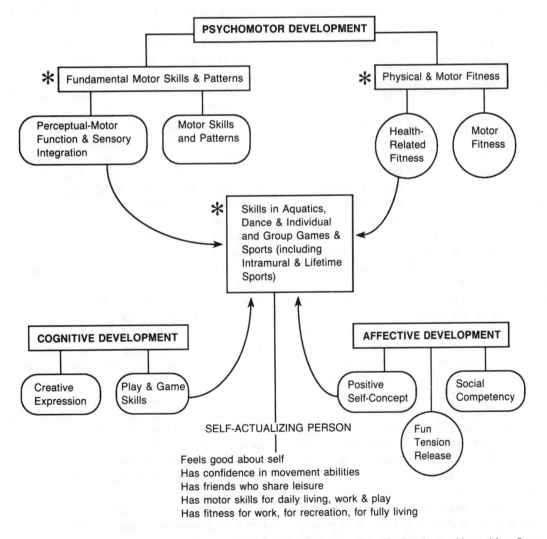

Figure 19.1 Psychomotor behaviors for which the physical educator is responsible. The three boxes with asterisks reflect the PL 94-142 definition of physical education (*Federal Register*, August 23, 1977, **42**, pp. 42474-42798). The circles and ovals represent the long-range goals that appear most often in IEPs of handicapped students (Sherrill, 1982).

physical education can be achieved with disabled students. Research needs are evident in the many areas where little published research can be found. For adapted physical education to acquire status as a viable discipline or sub-discipline, it must amass a substantial body of research. This chapter presents, therefore, the state of the art in the early 1980s with regard to experimental research.

The idea for this chapter evolved from the need to justify adapted physical education as a viable part of the curriculum to public school administrators. Their questions centered about goals and instructional accountability. Do we, as professionals, *know* what we want to accomplish? Do we have research that documents that we are successful and accountable?

What physical education can do for the handicapped student depends upon his or her psychomotor needs as determined by the individualized educational program (IEP) process. Comprehensive assessment may reveal deficits in many areas. For the purpose of this chapter, the nine areas depicted in Figure 19.1 will be discussed. These areas may be conceptualized as the values of physical education or its long-range goals.

Physical and Motor Fitness

The value or goal of physical and motor fitness includes developing the cardiovascular system, promoting ideal body weight, increasing muscular strength and endurance, maintaining or increasing range of motion (flexibility), and improving postures. The American Alliance for Health, Physical Education, Recreation, and Dance (AAHPERD) recognizes two kinds of fitness: (a) health-related and (b) motor or physical. Health-related fitness refers to the aspects of physiological and psychological functioning that are believed to offer protection against such degenerative diseases as obesity and coronary heart disease (our nation's Number 1 killer). It focuses upon the aspects of functioning necessary to carry out daily living tasks, without pain and undue fatigue, with ample energy for a balanced life of work, recreation, and self-care. Physical or motor fitness refers to the traditional concept of optimal strength, endurance, flexibility, power, and other abilities needed for athletic success and generally measured by school fitness tests.

Clearly, health-related fitness is a more realistic and relevant goal for most handicapped students than motor fitness. Health-related fitness for all students emphasizes cardiovascular function, body composition, strength and endurance of the abdominal muscles, and range of motion of the lower back muscles and hamstrings. For the severely handicapped, it encompasses the functioning of the postural reflex mechanism; adequate strength to maintain the head and trunk erect against the pull of gravity, to roll over, sit, and ambulate in some manner; and sufficient range of motion (flexibility) to engage in self-care, play, and other activities requisite to learning, growing, and developing.

Health-related fitness, particularly in the severely handicapped, is a prerequisite to learning and benefitting from certain kinds of instruction (vocational training, special education, and regular physical education). The typical mentally retarded employee is required to use physical rather than intellectual skills (Coleman, Ayoub, & Friedrich, 1976; Leighton, 1966; Nordgren & Bäckström, 1971) and thus vocational training focuses on domestic work, light industry, manual labor, and agriculture. Many retarded persons lack the fitness to engage in work tasks more strenuous than sewing, sweeping, and parts assembly (Coleman et al., 1976). Not only does this limit their training but it seriously reduces job eligibility and work stability. Most special education requires the postural strength and flexibility to sit for long periods of time and to manipulate paper, pens, and other learning materials. Regular physical education instruction is directed toward students with average or better fitness with low grades assigned to those who cannot keep up. Health-related fitness is thus an important outcome of an adapted physical education program designed to prepare students for mainstream instruction and life in general.

Physical activity is particularly important to bone and muscle growth during ages 0 to 21. Research shows that exercise increases bone width and mineralization, whereas recumbent inactivity and cast immobilization decrease bone mineralization, making the skeletal system weaker and more brittle. Likewise, physical activity is necessary for normal muscle growth. Whereas nondisabled children often derive sufficient physical activity from daily play to promote normal growth and development, handicapped children (particularly the nonambulatory and those who learn to walk late) tend not to have enough exercise unless it is built into their IEP. The stunted growth of many severely handicapped persons can be attributed, at least in part, to lack of physical activity. Likewise, the limited range of movement and contractures found so often among cerebral palsied persons can be ameliorated by daily stretching exercises as part of a well-rounded physical education program.

Physical activity is necessary also for the normal growth, development, and functioning of such internal organs as the heart and lungs. The well-documented sedentary lives of most handicapped children after school, on weekends, and during summer substantiate the vital need for school-oriented exercise programs. Without normal heart and lung functions, children receive insufficient oxygen for the mental alertness requisite to academic and preacademic learning.

Although much research documents the inferiority of handicapped to normal students on measures of fitness

(Buell, 1950; Francis & Rarick, 1959; Hayden, 1964; Winnick & Short, 1984), few experimental studies have been conducted to show that physical education instruction can improve the fitness of handicapped students. Oliver (1958) reported significant differences in the 50-yard dash, standing broad jump, and distance throw favoring the experimental group after a 10-week intensive training program in which all school subjects except mathematics and English were replaced by physical education. His subjects were boys aged 13 to 15 years, with a mean IQ of 70. Other researchers who have compared physical education training for the mentally retarded with no training and who report significant differences favoring the training group include Corder (1966), Solomon and Pangle (1966), Carter (1966), Brown (1968), Chasey (1970), Funk (1971), Campbell (1974), and Brown (1977). Two particularly large and outstanding studies are those by Rarick, Dobbins, and Broadhead (1976) and Vodola (1978).

Rarick et al. (1976) reported findings of a 20-week experimental physical education program (35 minutes daily) on 49 classes of special education children in the Galena Park, Pasadena, and Deer Park school districts of Texas. The subjects (275 EMR and 206 minimally brain injured) ranged in age from 6 to 13 years. A four-group experimental design was used to compare individualized PE instruction, group PE instruction, art instruction, and no instruction. The two physical education groups produced the greatest gains in motor fitness as measured by the AAHPER Youth Fitness Test for EMR Youth, with a tendency for greatest gains to occur in all areas within the individualized instructional program.

Vodola (1978) reported six studies that documented the efficacy of Project ACTIVE programs in improving the physical fitness of children exhibiting low physical vitality, neurological impairment, and emotional disturbance. The individualized-personalized teaching approach of Project ACTIVE produced more significant improvement in fitness than the traditional approach.

A review of research studies indicating that the fitness of other special populations can be increased through physical training is presented by Loovis (1978). Included are findings on youth with cerebral palsy, polio, asthma, diabetes, epilepsy, and paraplegics who use wheelchairs. More recently studies by such researchers as Bundschuh and Cureton (1982), Tomporowski and Jameson (1985), and McCubbin and Shasby (1985) have appeared.

Motor Skills and Patterns

Motor skills and patterns include learning fundamental motor skills and patterns; mastering the motor skills indigenous to games, sport, dance, and aquatics participa-

tion; and improving fine and gross motor coordination for self-care, school, work, and play activities.

Delayed or abnormal motor development is a major problem among handicapped individuals. The mean age of walking, for instance, is 4.2 years in Down's syndrome children and 3.2 years for other types of mentally retarded youngsters (Molnar, 1978).

Many severely retarded and orthopedically impaired children do not learn to walk until age 7 or 8. The fundamental motor skills and patterns on which adapted physical educators focus include rolling, crawling, creeping, walking, running, jumping, climbing, hanging, balancing, throwing, striking, catching, and kicking. Handicapped children must be carefully taught the motor behaviors that evolve naturally in normal children, and these must be practiced repeatedly before learning (a permanent change acquired through practice) can occur. In many instances, physical educators must work on reflexes and balancing reactions to promote motor development and learning.

The adapted physical educator facilitates learning of whatever motor skill is needed—lifting the head, rolling over, crawling, creeping, sitting, or changing from one position to another. Ball-handling skills and patterns for the severely handicapped may be conceptualized as teaching object awareness, eliciting approach and avoidance reactions to objects, and developing reach, grasp, hold, and release mechanisms. These abilities, which do not evolve normally in the severely handicapped, are prerequisite to the use of academic learning materials like paper and pencil manipulations.

Children on crutches or in braces or wheelchairs need assistance in learning to adapt their mobility abilities to the games and play activities of their peers. For such students to participate in mainstream physical education, much help is needed. Additionally, such students have the right to separate instruction in wheelchair sports that will enable them to experience competition adapted to their special abilities and needs. Persons who ambulate with a limp or generally use crutches are eligible for wheelchair sports. Authorities are increasingly emphasizing the importance of beginning wheelchair sport training early in any mobility-impaired child who does not have a chance at winning in the regular physical education setting (Jones, 1984; Labanowich, 1978; Sherrill, 1986). Recent research on the discrepancy between what exists and what is desired in physical education by handicapped children revealed winning to be the Number 1 wish of handicapped children (Megginson, 1982). Adapted physical education, with opportunities to participate with and compete against athletes of equal ability levels, is clearly needed by most handicapped children in addition to some mainstream experience.

In adapted physical education, children can learn early the opportunities available to them through the United

Instructional techniques that result in behavioral change when used to achieve specific individual objectives.

States Cerebral Palsy Athletic Association, the United States Association for Blind Athletes, the National Wheelchair Athletic and Basketball Associations, the American Athletic Association for the Deaf, and Special Olympics. Sport is part of the American culture, and handicapped children can experience this culture as participants rather than spectators by training in the motor skills indigenous to sports adapted to their abilities or sports created specifically for them like beep baseball, wheelchair soccer, and bocci ball. The 1978 Amateur Sports Act (PL 95-606) recognized the official sport organizations representing various handicapped groups and made them part of the United States Olympic Committee (USOC), with their athletes eligible for the same support and training as all other athletes. State, national, and international sport opportunities are available to all handicapped persons, regardless of the severity of their condition, who have had quality early sport training to develop their motor skills and patterns optimally (Sherrill, 1985).

Although the benefits of physical education instruction to the improvement of motor skills and patterns are obvious, little published experimental research exists to document these benefits. For the mentally retarded four studies are usually cited, those of Oliver (1958), Lillie (1968), Ross (1969), and Chasey and Wyrick (1971). Oliver (1958) reported significant differences favoring the experimental group (*n* = 19) on athletic ability as measured by the Metheney-Johnson Test after 10 weeks of daily intensive training. His subjects were 13 to 15 years of age with IQs from 57 to 86. Lillie (1967) provided mildly retarded preschool children (aged 57 to 70 months; IQs of 50 to 85) with 65 sequential motor training lessons; the findings revealed a significant difference favoring the experimental group on fine motor proficiency as measured by the Lincoln-Oseretsky Motor Development Scale. Ross (1969) showed that an experimental motor skills training program of 6 months duration (three times a week, 20-25 minutes each session) was effective in improving general motor ability as measured by the Brace Test and such fundamental motor skills as hitting, throwing, catching, running, jumping, and hopping. Her subjects were 40 EMR children from preschool and primary classes from three school districts. Chasey and Wyrick (1971) demonstrated that 15 weeks (daily, 1 hour a day) of one-to-one physical education instruction provided by university students could significantly improve motor proficiency as measured by the Lincoln-Oseretsky Motor Development Scale. Their subjects were from the Austin State School, ranged in age from 6 to 12 years, and had IQs of 50 to 85.

Other published experimental research documenting significant changes in motor skills as a result of physical education, including dance instruction, are studies by Berrol (1978), Duehl (1979), Reber and Sherrill (1981), Beuter (1983), and Karper, Martinek, and Wilkerson (1985). Additional research is reported in theses and dissertations that can be ordered through interlibrary loan.

Positive Self-Concept and Healthy Body Image

Development of a positive self-concept and healthy body image through activity includes increasing understanding and appreciation of the body and its capacity for movement, accepting limitations that cannot be changed, and learning to adapt the environment so as to make the most of strengths (i.e., working toward self-actualization).

Body image problems among handicapped children are well documented: Centers and Centers (1963) on amputees; Myklebust (1964) on the deaf and hearing impaired; Cratty and Sams (1968) on the blind; Guldager (1970)

on the deaf-blind; Weininger, Rotenberg, and Henry (1972) on persons with spina bifida; Bailey, Shinedling, and Payne (1970) on the obese; Fisher and Cleveland (1968) on the mentally ill and emotionally disturbed; Wysocki and Wysocki (1973) on the mentally retarded; and Ayres (1972), Kephart (1971), and Johnson and Myklebust (1967) on the learning disabled. Whereas normal children usually become conscious of their bodies, internalize these perceptions, and acquire a healthy body image without help, handicapped students experience many of the following problems: (a) inability to separate self from environment (I from not I); (b) inability to identify body parts and surfaces; (c) inability to make right-left discriminations on self and others; (d) difficulty in distinguishing between male and female body types, proportions, and features; (e) problems in matching one's own somatotype and body parts to those of models; (f) distortions in perception of body and its parts; and (g) inability to accept missing, distorted, or malfunctioning parts. The development of a healthy, mature body image is widely recognized as the first stage in the evolution of the self-concept (Freud, 1927; Piaget, 1955). Thus much of early childhood and adapted physical education instruction focuses on body image. Depending upon the IEP, the teacher may work to promote image development or to remedy specific problems.

Published experimental research showing that physical education and movement can improve the body image of mentally retarded students includes studies by Daw (1964); Ball and Edgar (1967); Hill, McCullum, and Sceau (1967); Maloney, Ball, and Edgar (1970); Chasey, Swartz, and Chasey (1974); and Franklin (1979). Most of these investigators used Kephart as the primary source for their developmental activities.

Published experimental research documenting changes in body image in other populations is very sparce. Studies include Auxter, Zahar, and Ferrini (1967) on the emotionally disturbed; and Galloway and Bean (1974) on deaf preschoolers.

Self-concept is believed by many persons, especially special educators, to be the most important dimension in handicapped youth to which good physical education can contribute. Self-concept, what a person thinks and feels about his or her appearance, abilities and resources, background and origins, and relationships with peers and significant others, is the frame of reference through which he or she interacts with the world. Self-concept, in early childhood and among many handicapped persons of all ages, is related to what they can do with their bodies and how they think others perceive their movement competence. Of the 80 items comprising the Children's Self-Concept Scale (CSCS) (Piers & Harris, 1969), 11 relate specifically to physical appearance and motor abilities. Of these as many as 50% of children with motor problems answer yes to "Are you the last to be chosen in games?";

31% answer yes to "In games do you watch instead of play?"; and 30% respond affirmatively to "Are you clumsy?" (Cratty & Martin, 1969, p. 214).

A major value of properly conducted adapted physical education is to change such negative feelings about the self by building success into movement experiences until such a time that the child becomes secure enough to react normally to occasional failures. Several theorists posit that self-concept, movement confidence, motivation, and motor skill are intricately related (Bandura, 1977; Griffin & Keogh, 1982; Harter, 1978). Only one experimental research study (Hedrick, 1985) could be found, however, relating competence theory, physical education, and disability. Measurement instruments by Harter (1978, 1982) hold much potential for physical education researchers.

Another value of properly conducted adapted physical education is help and support in learning to accept body and movement limitations in a friendly, nonthreatening setting where individual differences are celebrated as good, and the teaching methodology emphasizes "try another way." Adapted physical education typically has a small enough pupil-teacher ratio that the focus can be on assisting students to find physical activities in which they personally can excel rather than the traditional practice of instructing everyone in the same skills, games, and sport. Self-concept is thus enhanced by a growing feeling of movement competence and continuous involvement in values clarification concerning the perceptions and expectations of self and others in relation to the body and what it can do.

This kind of physical education is especially important for handicapped children. Abundant research reveals that the self-concepts of handicapped and clumsy persons are lower than those of their peers. Among the best works in this area are Wright (1960) on the physically handicapped and Lawrence and Winschel (1973) on the mentally retarded.

Published experimental research showing that physical education programs can change self-concepts of handicapped children is sparce. Oliver (1960) reported significant differences favoring the experimental group on the CSCS after 6 weeks of training. His subjects were mentally retarded. Fretz, Johnson, and Johnson (1969) reported a significant decrease in discrepancy between actual and ideal height in 74 subjects, aged 4 to 17 years, after 6 weeks (2 days a week, 1 to 2 hours daily) of physical education. The subjects included 28 emotionally disturbed, 31 mentally retarded, and 15 brain-damaged people treated statistically as a one-group design. Cratty (1974) indicated that mentally retarded children showed improvement on items relating to physical attractiveness, physical appearance, and school after 5 months of motor training. Simpson and Meaney (1979) reported a significant difference favoring the experimental group ($n = 14$) on the Self-

Concept Scale for Children (Lipsitt, 1958) after participation in a 5-week ski program (five group lessons each week of 1.5 hours each). The subjects were trainable mentally retarded youth (IQs 40 to 60) aged 14 to 20 years. Mancini, Develin, and Frye (1980) reported significant improvement on the Martinek-Zaichkowsky Self-Concept Scale (1977) favoring the experimental group ($n = 20$) after 8 weeks (1 hour daily) of instruction in specific contingency management skills. Their subjects were elementary school children who had been identified as disruptive by their physical education teachers. Barton (1982) in a one-group experimental study of 21 mildly retarded students aged 6 to 16 years, reported a significant difference in self-concept after 8 weeks of aerobic dance training (3 times a week, 45-minute sessions). Wright and Cowden (1986) reported improved self-concept of mentally retarded youth after participation in Special Olympics swimming.

Perceptual-Motor Function and Sensory Integration

This value or goal includes enhancing visual, auditory, tactile, vestibular, and kinesthetic functioning; reinforcing academic learnings through games and perceptual-motor activities; and improving cognitive, language, and motor function through increased sensory integration. Most physical educators believe that sound perceptual-motor function is a prerequisite or cocondition for the acquisition of motor skills and mental operations for successful participation in games, sport, dance, and aquatics (Cratty, 1980; Crowe, Auxter, & Pyfer, 1981; Seaman & DePauw, 1982; Sherrill, 1986). Additionally, many educators have stressed perceptual-motor programming because of its hypothesized relationship to cognitive learning and academic achievement (Bruner, 1964; Frostig & Maslow, 1970; Kephart, 1971; Montessori, 1912; Piaget, 1955). Sensory integration, a newer term promoted by Ayres (1972), is generally used as a goal for severely disabled children and considered a prerequisite to perceptual-motor function.

The Pyfer model for perceptual-motor development in chapter 15 helps to clarify the specific areas for which goals and objectives may be written (see Figure 19.2). The early development of body image (recognition of self vs. not self, of body parts, and of where the body is in space) is also an outcome of sound perceptual-motor functioning. Likewise, an understanding of game formations (circle vs. square), of directions of movement in games and dance, and of position play is dependent upon perceptual-motor function. Success in the teaching-learning partnership relates largely to a child's ability

Perceptual-Motor Development

Sensory Input Level	Integration Level	Output level
Reflex	Bilateral Integration	Walking
Tactile	Laterality	Running
Vestibular	Directionality	Skipping
Kinesthetic	Balance	Writing
Visual	Form Perception	Reading
Auditory	Spatial Awareness	Spelling

Figure 19.2   Model by Jean Pyfer (see chapter 15) showing levels for which long-range goals and short-term objectives should be written.

to process the auditory (words) and visual (demonstration) input of the teacher as well as the feedback of his or her own body (tactile, vestibular, and kinesthetic) after attempting a new skill.

Sound perceptual-motor function develops normally, without the help of school programming, in most children. A high incidence of perceptual-motor problems, however, appears to be among children classified as mentally retarded, cerebral palsied, and learning disabled.

Illustrative research documenting that perceptual-motor training can remedy these problems and improve cognitive, language, and motor functioning include the following.

For mentally retarded students.   Haring and Stables (1966) found significant differences favoring the experimental group ($n = 13$) on a perceptual-motor test after 7 months (30 minutes daily) of specific training; the mean age of their subjects was 10 years, 7 months. Hill, McCullum, and Sceau (1967) used Frostig and other visual-motor activities with 12-year-olds for 4 months, 5 days a week, 20 minutes a day, and reported significant improvement in directional awareness. Edgar, Ball, McIntyre, and Shotwell (1969) reported a significant improvement in motor, language, and social development in children aged 3 to 8 years after 8 months of Kephart-type activities, 3 days a week, 20 minutes a day. Maloney, Ball, and Edgar (1970) reported a significant improvement in perceptual-motor development and body image with students having a mean age of 14 years after 2 months of Kephart training, 3 days a week, 40 minutes a day. Webb (1969) indicated that a variety of sensorimotor training techniques provided over a period of 5.5 to 10.5 months could improve the social maturity and sensorimotor development of profoundly retarded students aged 2.5 to 17.5 years. Morrison and Pothier (1972) reported significant differences in gross motor and language functioning, favoring the sensorimotor training group, in nursery school children after a 6-month, daily, 20- to 30-minute training program.

For learning disabled students.   Halgren (1961), using the Getman program and other visual training techniques with ninth-grade boys for 10 weeks, 5 days a week, reported inprovement in IQ and reading achievement. Ames (1969) indicated substantial gains on the Gesell Developmental Test in second graders after 6 months of daily training, 30 minutes a day. Fretz, Johnson, and Johnson (1969) showed that 8 weeks of one-to-one instruction conducted by university students could significantly improve the perceptual-motor functioning of males aged 5 to 11 years. Martin and Ovans (1972) reported that children aged 3 to 7 years could improve their percentile ranks on Cratty's Six-Category Gross Motor Test and Caldwell's Preschool Inventory after 5 weeks of daily training, 2 hours a day. Lamport (1974) showed that a 16-week perceptual-motor program could significantly improve static balance for 8- and 9-year-old boys, dynamic balance for 7- and 8-year-old children, manual dexterity and speed for 7-year-old girls, and coordination of the upper limbs for 9-year-old girls. Ottenbacher, Short, and Watson (1979) reported that sensory integrative therapy over a 6-month period could enhance the vestibular and proprioceptive systems of children aged 4 to 10 years.

Fun and Tension Release

Fun and tension release focuses upon fun, recreation, and happiness. This goal includes releasing tensions in a healthy, socially acceptable manner; reducing hyperactivity and learning to relax; and improving mental health and attitude toward exercise and physical education.

This potential value of adapted physical education relates to students on either extreme of the physical activity continuum—the *hyperactive*, with problems of motor impulsivity and self-control, and the *hypoactive*, who tend to be lethargic and sluggish. Either extreme may dislike or feel uncomfortable in a structured physical education class that demands movement at a particular pace or rhythm. Adapted physical education for such students should be directed toward normalizing their energy expenditure and motor output level. Thus an appropriate objective for a hyperactive student might be to demonstrate the ability to perform selected motor activities, like walking a 12-foot line, in twice the number of seconds required in the baseline measurement (i.e., learn self-control in moving as slowly as possible). For the hypoactive child, the objective is reversed.

Because attitudes toward physical activity are critical to the formation of desired exercise habits and the maintenance of good mental health, students who score low on any of the standardized measures of attitudes toward physical education should receive specialized individual or small-group training directed toward changing these attitudes. Physical education and selected forms of daily exercise like jogging or cycling should be fun, pleasurable, and satisfying. If they are not, as may be the case with an obese or asthmatic student, then a carefully planned combination of counseling and progressive fitness training with many kinds of reinforcement should be implemented.

Van Andel and Austin (1984) offer an excellent review of research on mental health and fitness. Clearly, mental health influences motivation and helps determine whether physical education is fun or drudgery.

Handicapped persons, because their disability unduly tires them out, slows them down, or creates unusual stress in learning situations, may need relaxation training more than their peers. Several adapted physical education textbooks include whole chapters on teaching relaxation (Cratty, 1980; Crowe, Auxter, & Pyfer, 1981; Sherrill, 1986).

Although some research on the benefits of relaxation training has been conducted on the mentally retarded (Harvey, 1979) and other groups, few of these studies relate to motor learning (Brandon, Eason, & Smith, 1986). Cratty's various books include chapters on the adjustment of arousal level and improvement of attention (1969) and on intellectual ability, activation, and self-control (1972). These review research from other disciplines primarily in relation to learning disabilities and hyperactivity. The efficacy of physical education in relation to this broad goal has received little attention; this constitutes a major research need.

Creative Expression

Creative expression emphasizes increasing creativity in movement and thought (i.e., learning to generate *many* responses, *different* responses, and *original* responses when posed a movement problem). It includes learning to imagine, to embellish and add on, to risk experi-

mentation, to devise appropriate game strategy, and to create new games, dances, and movement sequences.

Increased verbal (ideas, thoughts, words) and nonverbal (movements, actions, rhythms) creativity is an important outcome of the movement education approach to physical education instruction. Research shows the relationship between creative thinking and intelligence and between creativity and motor ability is low and nonsignificant; there appears no reason to believe that handicapped children cannot be helped to become highly creative. The continuous process of adapting that handicapped persons undergo in coping with architectural, attitudinal, and aspirational barriers demands considerable creativity (i.e., problem solving, the discovery of alternative ways, and the appreciation of individual differences). Creativity expression is important also as a socially acceptable means of letting off steam because limited fitness, mobility, and skill often prevent releasing frustrations and anxiety through vigorous physical activity as much of the normal population does. Assistance with creative thinking may help handicapped persons become more aware of the world around them, able to see things in many different ways, and thus more interesting conversationalists and companions. Creativity training can be used also to remedy specific problems of conceptual rigidity that seem to characterize some mentally retarded, learning disabled, and emotionally disturbed students.

Developmentally, children seem to move from imaginative play to fantasy play to creative play (Piaget, 1962). Handicapped children who are delayed in their progression through these play stages and/or are repetitious and mechanical in their use of play objects can be helped also by creativity training. Creativity seems directly related to breadth and depth of play and movement experiences; it seems also to be a forerunner of a rich, full leisure life with abundant ideas for interesting use of free time.

Little research has been conducted on handicapped children's potential for creativity; existing studies have been reviewed by Sherrill (1979). Whereas handicapped children are generally found inferior to their normal peers on verbal measures of creativity, often no significant difference is shown between the handicapped and the normal on nonverbal measures. Movement thus seems an ideal means for facilitating creative development. Experimental research documenting that movement education approaches can improve creativity in mentally handicapped children is limited to studies by Carter, Richmond, and Bundschuh (1973), Rowe (1976), and Crumbliss and Wenger (1978). Lubin and Sherrill (1980) and Reber and Sherrill (1981) document the improvement of creativity in deaf preschoolers and hearing-impaired adolescents, respectively, as a result of movement education and dance. Jackson-Glass and Reid (1981) indicated work with the motor creativity of physically handicapped children.

Leisure Time Skills

Leisure time skills include learning to transfer physical education learnings into habits of lifetime sport, dance, and aquatics; becoming acquainted with community resources for recreation; expanding one's repertoire of individual and group games and sport, dance, and aquatic activities; and refining motor skills.

Work toward achievement of this value is especially important because most adult handicapped persons have far more leisure time than their nondisabled peers. The U.S. Department of Education reports that 80% of the handicapped population is, within 1 year of leaving school, at best underemployed with most being unemployed, or dependent on welfare and/or under total care (*Training Educators for the Handicapped*, 1976). Razeghi and Davis (1979) report that 40% of all disabled adults are employed as compared with 74% of the nondisabled. Moreover, the U.S. census statistics show that 80% of the disabled have annual incomes of less than $7,000. Of these, 52% make less than $2,000 a year.

Research indicates also that the recreation of handicapped adults during this abundant enforced leisure is typically impoverished (Edgerton, 1967; Heimark & McKinnon, 1971; Katz & Yekutiel, 1974; Redding, 1979; Sherrill & Ruda, 1977; Stanfield, 1973). Stanfield reported, for instance, that only 23% of his sample (*n* = 120) had friends to visit, that only 10% traveled about the community at large, and that most spent their enforced leisure at home watching television, listening to records or the radio, or looking at books and magazines. Concerning adults in group home community placement, Sherrill and Ruda (1977) reported that most spent their leisure time watching television or ''alone napping or daydreaming or just sitting and looking in small groups in which no conversation was occurring'' (p. 33). It was obvious that they did not have the skills and interests to permit use of leisure time in physical activity. Matthews (1979), comparing elementary school aged retarded and non-retarded children, all living at home, indicated that the major difference in recreation interests and patterns at this early age was in community recreation involvement. Clearly, the handicapped must be taught how to use community resources. Transfer of learning from the school physical education setting to lifelong use of community recreation resources cannot be expected without careful instruction directed specifically toward transfer.

Almost no research has been conducted on the relationship between school physical education training and adult habits of physical activity. Foss (1981) compared active

with inactive normal adult females and reported that a significantly greater proportion of actives than inactives had (a) physical education training, especially in elementary school and junior high, (b) had swimming instruction in elementary school, (c) had instruction in dance and leisure time sport, (d) had coeducational physical education classes in high school, and (e) remembered enjoyment of physical education during high school years. Ervin (1980) reported that, although most blind adults expressed satisfaction with their school physical education programs, 47% had no knowledge of community recreation programs. Rarick (1978) investigated the effects of Special Olympics upon participants as viewed by parents, teachers, administrators, and civic leaders. Approximately 25% of the parents indicated a change toward greater participation in various recreational pursuits by their children after Special Olympics involvement.

Of the 925,000 persons who participate in Special Olympics, 47% are 18 years or older. Transfer of learning from school-based Special Olympics training to adult involvement apparently does occur in this particular sport program. On the other hand, approximately 123 million mentally retarded adults over age 21 live in this country and all are eligible to engage in Special Olympics. Clearly, the goal of training for transfer needs stronger emphasis.

Play and Games Skills

Play and games skills focus on learning to play (i.e., progressing through the developmental play stages from solitary and parallel play behaviors up through appropriate cooperative and competitive game behaviors). They also include promoting contact and interaction behaviors with toys, play apparatus, and persons; learning basic game formations and mental operations needed for play; and mastering the rules and strategies of simple games.

Play is critical in the facilitation of cognitive, emotional, and social development of handicapped as well as normal children (Levy, 1978; Piaget, 1962; Wehman, 1977). Play is also important to good mental health and a requisite to understanding leisure and using free time wisely. Instead of engaging spontaneously in play activities as normal children do, severely handicapped students (regardless of age) may simply lie or sit and stare into space (Benoit, 1955). When presented with toys, they may mouth, shake, pound, or throw them. Most handicapped children appear to be delayed in their progression through the development play stages (autistic or unoccupied, onlooker, solitary, parallel, associative, cooperative) and some remain frozen at the lower levels throughout life. Piaget emphasizes that play is the main ingredient in the development of sensorimotor and preoperational intelligence (i.e., the predominant force from birth to 2 years and tremendously important from 2 to 7 years of age). Play is also the medium through which infants learn to recognize and relate to objects as well as human beings. Play also facilitates the development and use of language, particularly as the child progresses to the cooperative play stage and wishes to interact verbally in dramatic or imitative activities.

An important value of adapted physical education is learning to play and developing increasingly mature play behaviors. Research documenting the efficacy of physical education in changing play behaviors is sparce because physical education training was not required for the early childhood handicapped prior to the enactment of PL 94-142. Likewise, adapted physical education as a discipline has only recently begun to focus on assessment and programming of the severely handicapped. Research demonstrating changes in play behaviors does, however, exist.

Illustrative of experimental research concerning the play of autistic and emotionally disturbed children are the following. Maurer (1969) reported the success of Peek-A-Boo in establishing eye-to-eye recognition in a 6-year-old autistic male. Richer and Nicoll (1971) reported that use of a specially constructed playroom increased social interactions and decreased stereotyped behaviors in 10 autistic or emotionally disturbed children aged 4 to 11 years. Koegel, Firestone, Kramme, and Dunlap (1974) showed that spontaneous play could be increased in two autistic children aged 6 to 8, as a result of suppressing self-stimulatory behaviors. Romanczyk, Diament, Goren, Trunell, and Harris (1975) demonstrated the effectiveness of play intervention in increasing isolate and social play in four severely disturbed children aged 5 to 7 years.

Illustrative of experimental research documenting changes as a result of play instruction and/or therapy with severely retarded children is the following. Paloutzian, Hasazi, Streifel, and Edgar (1971) were among the first to demonstrate that severely retarded children could be trained to imitate motor and social responses that could then form the framework for instruction in play. Physical prompting, with fading and social reinforcement, were used to shape the following: (a) passing a beanbag, (b) walking to another child and gently stroking his or her face, (c) pulling a peer in a wagon, (d) pushing another child in a swing, and (e) rocking another child in a rocking chair or hobby horse. Pre- and posttest scores, favoring the experimental group, indicated significant improvement in social behavior as measured by social interactions in a free-play setting. Flavell (1973) reported that prompting, verbal and candy reinforcement, and involvement in a pegboard game decreased stereotyped behaviors to 0 and increased play responses in three severely retarded males aged 8 to 14 over a 5-day period with each receiving 15 minutes of individual instruction daily. Morris and Dolker (1974)

compared the effectiveness of three approaches in the development of cooperative play in six severely retarded children aged 4 to 7. The cooperation task involved two children seated on the floor rolling a 4-inch ball back and forth between them. The greatest amount of cooperative play was facilitated by a combination of shaping with the pairing of the child with the trainer or a high-interacting child; candy and verbal praise were used in all three experimental conditions.

Improved functioning on the Denver Developmental Screening Scale, which measures gross motor, fine motor, language, and personal-social behaviors, was the outcome of two studies that used play therapy with mildly and moderately retarded institutionalized children aged 5 to 11 (Morrison & Newcomer, 1975; Newcomer and Morrison, 1974). The play therapy was divided into directive (similar to one-to-one instruction) and nondirective approaches (child used materials and toys he or she desired). No differences were found between the two approaches.

Two other studies are generally cited as classics. Knapczyk and Yoppi (1975) found a token-praise-feedback procedure with an ABAB design was effective in increasing both cooperative and competitive play in five EMR children aged 8 to 10, all residing in the same cottage. Children were praised and given points each time they emitted the target behavior of "playing together nicely." Points could be banked for a special prize (e.g., model car or field trip) at the end of the experiment or used to rent games that were not previously available. Wehman, Karan, and Rettie (1976) reported that a combination of manual and verbal prompting, modeling, and social reinforcement for appropriate play over 35 days in a multiple baseline across individuals design was successful in increasing social interactions and decreasing stereotypic rocking. The subjects were three women aged 29 to 32 years with IQs between 22 and 26. The training was part of a work-activity program and included exposure to marble games, push-pull toys, books, clay, view finders, balls, and musical instruments.

Most of the research documenting the efficacy of training in play seems to rely heavily upon behavior management techniques. Two other approaches, however, appear in the literature. Shotick and Thate (1960) reported the responses of eight EMR children aged 10 to 15 years to instruction in low organized games and rhythmic activities, including simple dances like LaRaspa, Virginia Reel, and Oh Johnny. Over 4 months, responses were recorded in three categories: level of enthusiasm for each activity, response to instruction (degree to which they could follow instructions), and social interactions during activity. The findings allowed the ranking of activities as to degree of difficulty. For instance, students could follow direction in fox and geese, swat tag, steal the bacon, and newcomb better than in stealing sticks, nose tag, freeze, and kickball. Bowers (1975, 1979) has been the leading researcher in demonstrating how playground design and arrangement of apparatus can affect play behaviors in all children, including the mentally retarded (IQs 22 to 52, 45 to 96), the cerebral palsied, and the emotionally disturbed. Among the principles of playground design that promote play development are (a) be accessible to all children; (b) provide safe distance between levels; (c) incorporate a variety of inclines on which the children can move at their own level of ability; (d) provide partially closed spaces through which children can safely move; (e) be complex and stimulating—color, texture, and types of material; (f) use interconnected play areas to produce higher levels of continuous play; and (g) combine sound design with strong materials and quality construction.

In addition to mentally retarded and autistic or emotionally disturbed children, other special populations need instruction to learn age-appropriate play and game skills. Strong documentation of this need appears for deaf and hearing impaired children in whom communication deficits contribute to delays in play and social development (Darbyshire, 1977; Higginbottam, Baker, & Neill, 1980). No published experimental research on this value, however, has been identified for the deaf or other special populations.

Social Competency and Peer Acceptance

Social competency and peer acceptance focus on learning appropriate social behaviors (i.e., how to interact with others—sharing, taking turns, and following and leading). They include reducing social isolation, learning to develop and maintain friendships, demonstrating good sportsmanship and self-discipline in winning and losing, and developing other personal-social skills necessary for success in the mainstream.

Handicapped children and youth generally experience more problems in individual and social adjustment than do their normal peers. Such factors as overprotection of parents and teachers, exclusion from peer play and social activities, and the ambivalence or rejection of significant others all affect social maturation. Placement of children in regular physical education without providing them with the social skills that are critical to peer acceptance may result in increased social isolation. A major outcome of adapted physical education, if carefully planned and properly conducted, can be preparation of handicapped students for the mainstream and their successful continuation in this setting.

Unless specific conditions that promote social interaction and peer acceptance are present, however, research has shown unequivocally that nonhandicapped and handicapped students interact with one another very little in the mainstream setting (Gresham, 1981). Some research

even shows that integrated physical education instruction reduces peer acceptance. Stein (1966), for instance, collected pre- and postdata on the AAHPER Youth Fitness Test and the Cowell Personal Distance Scale from 189 junior high school boys, of whom 24 were retarded and integrated within six different physical education classes. After an 8-month experimental period, Stein reported that the mentally retarded students remained the most rejected in each class. Specifically, Stein stated, ''They had become further isolated socially and had lost in acceptance significantly more than other IQ groups over the 8-months experimental period'' (p. 242). Much literature documents the teasing and often times mental cruelty that occurs during unstructured, integrated play settings like recess and before and after school (Wright, 1960). This teasing is generally directed toward the handicapped, the clumsy, the overweight, and boys dubbed sissies by their peers. Likewise, many traditional physical education games result in elimination of the poorly skilled (dodgeball, basketball shooting games, three strikes in softball) rather than facilitating inclusion and acceptance with adaptations to minimize individual differences.

The social isolation and loneliness of handicapped persons is well documented in autobiography, biography, and research. The relationship between motor impairment and social development is also well established (Smoll, 1974). Children with poor movement skills tend to have low social prestige and are likely to be left out of play activities. Motor competence during childhood and youth, particularly among boys, plays a large part in popularity and social acceptance (Aloia, Beaver, & Pettus, 1978; Cowell, 1960; Smith & Hurst, 1961). It appears, therefore, that handicapped students must reach a criterion level of motor competence before placement in mainstream physical education classes, or the nature of the mainstream physical education instruction must be geared to teaching social values rather than fitness and fundamental motor skills.

Prior to the late 1970s, little research investigated the efficacy of physical education in increasing peer acceptance and promoting social development in handicapped students. Only four published studies reported success (i.e., significant differences).

Corder and Pridmore (1966) found significant differences favoring the experimental group in sociometric status after 4 weeks of physical education training (daily, 1 hour a day). The subjects were 16 EMR boys aged 14 to 17 divided into two groups of eight each and equated on IQ and CA. Sociometric status was measured by the Cowell Personal Distance Scale.

Adams (1971) studied changes in social adjustment of three groups of EMR girls organized in adapted, mainstream, and control physical education settings. At the end of one semester she concluded that social adjustment as assessed through teachers' ratings and peer acceptance appears to be achieved better through participation in an adapted physical education program than through retention in regular physical education.

McDaniel (1970) investigated the effects of an extracurricular program of basketball and square dancing on the social acceptance of EMR boys and girls aged 13 to 15. At the end of the 6-week period (daily, 1 hour) the experimental group was higher than the control group, which experienced no extracurricular program.

Nezol (1971) investigated the relationships between sociometric status, quality of physical education programs, and choices of active over sedentary activities and social over solitary activities for 60 blind secondary school youth integrated with sighted youth for their physical education. Significant intercorrelations occurred between high sociometric status, high quality physical education offerings, and choice of active over sedentary recreation activities.

After the passage of PL 94-142, with its mandated least-restrictive placement of handicapped students, physical education was increasingly conceptualized by special educators as a prime setting to promote peer acceptance among handicapped and nonhandicapped and to facilitate optimal social development. Several research studies have demonstrated that physical education *can* accomplish these goals but only under certain conditions. The following reviews highlight these conditions.

Three studies that used the games analysis intervention of Morris in *How to Change the Games Children Play* (1976) have resulted in significant differences in the affective domain. The games analysis model entails the changing of game components within six categories so as to ensure success for the players. Implementation of the model begins with assessment to determine the progression (easy to difficult) at which each student is functioning in the fundamental motor skills. The changes are then decided upon cooperatively by teacher and students in the following categories: players, equipment, movement pattern, organizational pattern (formation), limitations (rules), and purpose.

Marlowe, Algozzine, Lerch, and Welch (1978) reported that 6 weeks of games analysis intervention (daily, 30 minutes) significantly reduced feminine game choices of 11 emotionally disturbed boys as compared to their matched pairs in a control group. The subjects were third, fourth, and fifth graders who scored 1 *SD* or more above normal in feminine game choices on the Sutton-Smith Games Choice Test.

Marlowe (1980) reported success with the games analysis model in reducing the social isolation of 12 fifth-grade children assigned randomly to an experimental group ($n = 7$ integrated with 6 normal children) and to a control group ($n = 5$ integrated with 18-24 normal children). The criterion of "social isolated" was stated as the two

least preferred children of each sex in three different classrooms. Each group was instructed for a 5-week period, 30 minutes daily. Marlowe concluded "that games analysis training is effective in increasing the sociometric status of socially isolated children" (p. 425). He stated also,

> The games analysis instruction appeared to foster reciprocity between children. Children considered the feelings and capabilities of their playmates in changing the game environments. This may have assisted the children in more effectively exploring and coping with their environment, physically and mentally. (p. 425)

Aloia et al. (1978) studied selections of partners and opponents by seventh- and eighth-grade students to determine factors that influenced social interaction between EMR and normal youth in a game setting. The game entailed tossing three beanbags over a screen onto floor targets that varied in value from 2 to 5 points. Partners were chosen for the cooperative game method to help the subject accumulate 15 points. Opponents were chosen for the competitive method to compete with the subject as to whom could win the higher score. The findings showed that the subjects' selections of partners and opponents were based primarily on competency rather than handicapping condition. Aloia et al. (1978) concluded that the "expressed interaction of EMR and nonretarded children can be facilitated to some degree by increasing the competency of EMR children and by providing alternative structures in which to allow the interaction to occur" (p. 579). This supports the need for good adapted physical education to bring handicapped children up to a criterion motor competency level before placement in mainstream physical education.

Two other studies have focused upon alternative organizational structures (cooperative vs. individual) in promoting interpersonal interaction through participation in physical education activities. Martino and Johnson (1979) observed interactions during nine swimming lessons spaced over a 3-week period. Instruction lasted 45 minutes followed by 15 minutes of free swim time, during which data were collected on interactions among three learning disabled and three normal children, all from the second and third grades. The cooperative condition entailed assignment of a normal-progress "buddy" to each learning disabled child with directions for them to help each other learn to swim. In the individual condition subjects were not paired, and they were told to pay no attention to one another. The findings showed that the cooperative condition produced significantly more interactions during the free swim time than individual instruction did.

Cooperative, competitive, and individualistic organizational structures for recreational bowling were compared to determine which promoted optimal positive inter-actions among trainable Down's syndrome youth and nonhandicapped teenagers aged 13 to 15 years (Rynders, Johnson, Johnson, & Schmidt, 1980). Each bowling group was comprised of six nonhandicapped and four Down's syndrome students. They were told they would be bowl-ing together for 8 weeks (1 hour a week) and would be rewarded with prizes for improvement in performance. In the cooperative condition, the students were instructed to maximize their group bowling score by 50-plus over the previous week and to offer each other verbal encourage-ment, reinforcement, and help in ball handling. In the competitive condition, the students were instructed to outperform the other students in their group by maximiz-ing their own scores. In the individualistic condition, the students were to maximize their own score by 10 points over the previous week. The findings favored the cooperative condition, showing it produced significantly more positive interactions than the other conditions. The implication, of course, is that physical education conducted to promote mainstreaming and peer acceptance must utilize a cooperative class structure rather than the traditional games that encourage individual skill development and competition.

Peer and cross-age teaching and modeling also have been used successfully to increase peer acceptance. Project PEOPEL (Physical Education Opportunity Program for Exceptional Learners) has documented its efficacy in promoting peer acceptance through the National Diffusion Network (NDN) system. The PEOPEL approach differs from regular physical education in three ways: (a) the use of trained student aides—a 1:1 ratio, (b) smaller class sizes—24 maximum, and (c) use of task-analyzed learning sequences and individualized instruction (Long, Irmer, Burkett, Glasenapp, & Odenkirk, 1980).

Whereas PEOPEL focuses on secondary school instruc-tion, Project PERMIT (Physical Education Resources for Mainstreaming and Inservice Training) in Tennessee has documented the success of peer teaching at the elementary school level in mainstreaming handicapped children into regular classes of 30 or more students (Folio & Norman, 1981). In PERMIT, upper elementary grade children are trained to be peer or cross-age tutors through four mini-workshops (each 1/2 hour) during which similarities between the handicapped and normal are stressed. "New games" are used that emphasize sharing and cooperation rather than competition. Other features of Project PERMIT include (a) a personal space concept—each child has his or her own space on the gymnasium floor; (b) movement exploration—this teaching style focuses upon "try another way" with all ways accepted; (c) personal equipment—the size, shape, and weight of equipment are adapted to individual abilities; (d) station training—stations are developed for teaching different skills, and

students progress from station to station at their own rate; and (e) positive interaction—behavior management tech-niques are utilized with approval, disapproval, and ignoring used under specified conditions.

Behavior management techniques have been demon-strated to be useful also, documenting that teacher praise specifically for social interaction is a necessary condition for its success. Santomier and Kopczuk (1981) compared three types of teacher praise and intervention on nine dyads (one TMR and one normal child, aged 12 to 14 years), with three dyads randomly assigned to each of the following conditions: (a) teacher praise on motor skill performance, (b) teacher praise and intervention on motor skill, and (c) teacher praise and intervention on social interaction. The experimental period was 8 weeks (15 minutes daily) conducted within an integrated physical education setting. The findings indicated that social interaction rates can be increased significantly through the use of assigned buddies and consistent, frequent praise for social interactions maintained for 3 or more seconds.

Behavior management can be used also to decrease or eliminate personal behaviors that contribute to the social isolation of handicapped students. Allen (1980), for instance, demonstrated that 5 to 10 minutes of jog-ging at the beginning of each school day over a 6-week period reduced disruptive classroom behaviors by half in 12 boys, grades 1 to 6, in a self-contained classroom because of their behavioral and perceptual disorders. Features of this program believed to contribute to its effectiveness were (a) teacher jogging with pupils; (b) awards given as individuals reached 10-, 25-, and 50-mile goals; (c) structured routines of warm-up and cool-down; (d) emphasis on competition against self in increased distance and stamina rather than against others; and (e) promotion of camaraderie among runners.

Several other unpublished research studies have been conducted on the use of behavior management, particu-larly contingent reinforcement, in reducing inappropriate social behaviors in the physical education setting. These studies are reviewed by Loovis (1980). Also recommended (but not tested by research) are the use of reality training (Jansma, 1980) and transactional analysis (Jansma & French, 1979) for improving social competency through physical education experiences.

Concluding Observations

The purposes of regular and adapted physical education are the same: to change behaviors in the psychomotor domain. The long-range goals are the same also: a positive self-concept and healthy body image, physical and motor fitness, leisure time skills, play and game skills, social tency and peer acceptance, motor skills and patterns, fun and tension release, perceptual-motor function and sensory integration, and creative expression. Why then is adapted physical education emerging as an independent specialization and/or a separate discipline?

Two hypotheses support the need for special training in adapted and developmental physical education as a separate and different body of knowledge from regular physical education. One hypothesis is that adapted physical educators focus on children and youth who usually fail (i.e., score below the 50th percentile on standardized tests or appear *different* from others—weaker, clumsier, slower, fatter). In contrast, regular physical educators tend to gear their lessons toward the average or better performer, children who generally already have good self-concepts and who conceptualize themselves as able to become highly skilled and fit, if they choose to work hard enough. The second hypothesis is that adapted physical educators prioritize the long-range goals differently from regular physical educators because the needs of handicapped and clumsy students demand this. Research is needed to support or negate these hypotheses.

Continuing research is needed also on the accountability of physical educators in implementing goals. The purpose of this chapter was not to analyze strengths and weaknesses of existing research but to increase awareness of what exists.

References

Adams, K.O. (1971). The effects of adapted physical education upon the social adjustment and motor proficiency of educable mentally retarded girls. *American Corrective Therapy Journal, 25,* 64-67.

Allen, J. (1980). Jogging can modify disruptive behaviors. *Teaching Exceptional Children, 12*(2), 66-70.

Aloia, G., Beaver, R., & Pettus, W. (1978). Increasing initial interactions among integrated EMR students and their nonretarded peers in a game-playing situation. *American Journal of Mental Deficiency, 82,* 573-579.

Ames, L.B. (1969). Children with perceptual problems may also lag developmentally. *Journal of Learning Disabilities, 2,* 205-208.

Auxter, D., Zahar, E., & Ferrini, L. (1967). Body image development of emotionally disturbed children. *American Corrective Therapy Journal, 21,* 154-155.

Ayres, A.J. (1972). *Sensory integration and learning disorders.* Los Angeles: Western Psychological Services.

Bailey, W., Shinedling, H., & Payne, I. (1970). Obese individuals: Perception of body image. *Perceptual and Motor Skills, 31,* 617-618.

Ball, T.S., & Edgar, C.L. (1967). The effectiveness of sensory-motor training in promoting generalized body image development. *Journal of Special Education, 1,* 387-395.

Bandura, A. (1977). Self-efficacy: Toward a unifying theory of behavioral change. *Psychological Review, 84,* 191-215.

Barton, B. (1982). Aerobic dance and the mentally retarded: A winning combination. *The Physical Educator, 39*(1), 25-29.

Benoit, E.P. (1955). The play problem with retarded children: A frank discussion with parents. *American Journal of Mental Deficiency, 60,* 41-55.

Berrol, C. (1978). The effects of 2 remedial movement programs on selected performance criteria using 1st graders with learning and motor problems. In C.B. Corbin (Ed.), *AAHPER Research Consortium Papers: Movement Studies: Vol. 1. Book 3* (pp. 57-61). Washington, DC: AAHPER.

Beuter, A. (1983). Effects of mainstreaming on motor performances of intellectually normal and trainable mentally retarded students. *American Corrective Therapy Journal, 37*(2), 48-52.

Bowers, L. (1975). *Play learning centers for preschool handicapped children* (BEH Research and Demonstration Project Report). University of South Florida, Tampa.

Bowers, L. (1979). Toward a science of playground design: Principles of design for play centers for all children. *Journal of Physical Education and Recreation, 50,* 51-53.

Brandon, J., Eason, R., & Smith, T. (1986). Behavioral relaxation training and motor performances of learning disabled children with hyperactive behaviors. *Adapted Physical Activity Quarterly, 3*(1), 67-79.

Brown, B.J. (1977). The effect of an isometric strength program on the intellectual and social development of trainable retarded males. *American Corrective Therapy Journal, 31,* 44-48.

Brown, J. (1968). The effect of a physical education program on the muscular fitness of trainable retarded boys. *American Corrective Therapy Journal, 22,* 80-81.

Bruininks, V., & Bruininks, R. (1977). Motor proficiency of learning disabled and nondisabled students. *Perceptual and Motor Skills, 44,* 1131-1137.

Bruner, J. (1964). The course of cognitive growth. *American Psychologist, 19,* 1-15.

Buell, C. (1950). Motor performance of visually handicapped children. *Journal of Exceptional Children, 16,* 69-72.

Bundschuh, E., & Cureton, K. (1982). Effect of bicycle ergometer conditioning on the physical work capacity of mentally retarded adolescents. *American Corrective Therapy Journal,* **36**(6), 159-163.

Campbell, J. (1974). Improving the physical fitness of retarded boys. *Mental Retardation,* **12**, 31-35.

Carter, J.L. (1966). The status of educable mentally retarded boys on the AAHPER youth fitness test. *TAHPER Journal,* **34**(3), 8, 29-31.

Carter, K., Richmond, G., & Bundschuh, E. (1973). The effect of kinesthetic and visual-motor experiences in the creative development of mentally retarded students. *Education and Training of the Mentally Retarded,* **8**(1), 24-28.

Centers, L., & Centers, R. (1963). A comparison of the body image of amputee and non-amputee children as revealed in figure drawings. *Journal of Projective Techniques,* **27**, 158-165.

Chasey, W.C. (1970). The effects of clinical physical education on the motor fitness of educable mentally retarded boys. *American Corrective Therapy Journal,* **24**, 74-75.

Chasey, W., Swartz, J., & Chasey, C. (1974). Effect of motor development on body image scores for institutionalized mentally retarded children. *American Journal of Mental Deficiency,* **78**, 440-445.

Chasey, W., & Wyrick, W. (1971). Effects of a physical developmental program on psychomotor ability of retarded children. *American Journal of Mental Deficiency,* **75**, 566-570.

Coleman, A.E., Ayoub, M.M., & Friedrich, D. (1976). Assessment of the physical work capacity of institutionalized mentally retarded males. *American Journal of Mental Deficiency,* **80**(6), 620-635.

Corder, W.O. (1966). Effects of physical education on the intellectual, physical, and social development of EMR boys. *Exceptional Children,* **32**, 357-364.

Corder, W.O., & Pridmore, H. (1966). Effects of physical education on the psychomotor development of educable mentally retarded boys. *Education and Training of the Mentally Retarded,* **1**(4), 163-167.

Cowell, C. (1960). The contributions of physical activity to social development. *Research Quarterly,* **31**, 286-306.

Cratty, B.J. (1972). *Physical expressions of intelligence.* Englewood Cliffs, NJ: Prentice-Hall.

Cratty, B.J. (1974). *Motor activity and the education of retardates* (2nd ed.). Philadelphia: Lea & Febiger.

Cratty, B.J. (1980). *Adapted physical education for handicapped children and youth.* Denver: Love Publishing.

Cratty, B.J., & Martin, M.M., Sr. (1969). *Perceptual-motor efficiency in children.* Philadelphia: Lea & Febiger.

Cratty, B.J., & Sams, T.A. (1968). *The body-image of blind children.* New York: American Foundation for the Blind.

Crowe, W., Auxter, D., & Pyfer, J. (1981). *Principles and methods of adapted physical education and recreation* (4th ed.). St. Louis: C.V. Mosby.

Crumbliss, K., & Wenger, L. (1978). *Creative movement for retarded children* (ERIC Document Reproduction Service No. ED 157343). Durham, NC: Authors.

Darbyshire, J.O. (1977). Play patterns in young children with impaired hearing. *Volta Review,* **79**, 19-26.

Daw, J.F. (1964). The effect of special exercises on body image in mentally retarded children—A tentative exploration. *The Slow Learning Child,* **11**(2), 109-116.

Duehl, A.N. (1979). The effect of creative dance movement on large muscle control and balance in congenitally blind children. *Journal of Visual Impairment and Blindness,* **73**, 127-133.

Edgar, C., Ball, T., McIntyre, R., & Shotwell, A. (1969). Effects of sensorymotor training on adaptive behavior. *American Journal of Mental Deficiency,* **73**, 713-720.

Edgerton, R. (1967). *The cloak of competence: Stigma in the lives of the mentally retarded.* Berkeley: University of California Press.

Elstein, A. (1976). *Effects of physical education on the physical fitness, social adjustment, and self-concept of learning disabled students.* Unpublished doctoral dissertation, Temple University.

Ervin, S. (1980). *Visually impaired adults: Opinions about physical education and recreation.* Unpublished master's thesis, Texas Woman's University, Denton.

Fisher, S., & Cleveland, S. (1968). *Body image and personality.* New York: Dover Publications.

Flavell, J. (1973). Reduction of stereotypes by replacement of toy play. *Mental Retardation,* **11**(4), 21-23.

Folio, M.R., & Norman, A. (1981). Toward more success in mainstreaming: A peer teacher approach to physical education. *Teaching Exceptional Children,* **13**, 110-114.

Foss, P. (1981). Impact of previous physical education experiences on current physical activity habits of urban adult females. *Abstracts of 1981 AAHPERD Conference.* Reston, VA: American Alliance for Health, Physical Education, Recreation and Dance.

Francis, R.J., & Rarick, G.L. (1959). Motor characteristics of the mentally retarded. *American Journal of Mental Deficiency,* **63**, 792-811.

Franklin, S.B. (1979). Movement therapy and selected measures of body image in the trainable, mentally retarded. *American Journal of Dance Therapy,* **3**, 43-50.

Fretz, B.R., Johnson, W.R., & Johnson, J.A. (1969). Intellectual and perceptual motor development as a function of therapeutic play. *Research Quarterly,* **40**, 687-691.

Freud, S. (1927). *The ego and the id.* London: Hogarth Press.

Frostig, M., & Maslow, P. (1970). *Movement education: Theory and practice.* Chicago: Follett.

Funk, D.C. (1971). Effects of physical education on fitness and motor development of trainable mentally retarded children. *Research Quarterly,* **42**, 30-33.

Galloway, H.F., & Bean, M.F. (1974). The effects of action songs on the development of body-image and body-part identification in hearing-impaired preschool children. *Journal of Music Therapy,* **11**, 125-134.

Gresham, F. (1981). Social skills training with handicapped children: A review. *Review of Educational Research,* **51**(1), 139-176.

Griffin, N.S., & Keogh, J. (1982). A model for movement confidence. In J. Kelso & J. Clark (Eds.), *The development of movement control and coordination* (pp. 213-236). New York: Wiley.

Guldager, V. (1970). *Body image and the severely handicapped rubella child.* Watertown, MA: Perkins School for the Blind.

Halgren, A. (1961). Opus in see sharp. *Education,* **81**, 369-371.

Haring, N.G., & Stables, J.M. (1966). The effect of gross motor development on visual perception and eye-hand coordination. *Physical Therapy,* **46**, 129-135.

Harter, S. (1978). Effectance motivation reconsidered: Toward a developmental model. *Human Development,* **21**, 34-64.

Harter, S. (1982). The perceived competence scale for children. *Child Development,* **53**, 87-97.

Harvey, J. (1979). The potential of relaxation training for the mentally retarded. *Mental Retardation,* **17**(2), 71-76.

Hayden, F. (1964). *Physical fitness for mentally retarded.* Toronto: Metropolitan Association for Mentally Retarded.

Hedrick, B.N. (1985). The effect of wheelchair tennis participation and mainstreaming upon perceptions of competence of physically disabled adolescents. *Therapeutic Recreation Journal,* **19**(2), 34-46.

Heimark, R., & McKinnon, R. (1971). Leisure preferences of mentally retarded graduates of a residential training program. *Therapeutic Recreation Journal,* **5**, 67-68, 93.

Higginbottam, D.J., Baker, B., & Neill, R. (1980). Assessing the social participation and cognitive abilities of hearing impaired preschoolers. *Volta Review,* **82**(5), 261-271.

Hill, S.D., McCullum, A., & Sceau, A. (1967). Relation of training in motor activity to development of right-left directionality in mentally retarded children: Exploratory study. *Perceptual and Motor Skills,* **24**, 363-366.

Jackson-Glass, K., & Reid, G. (1981). Motor creativity of physically disabled children. *Abstracts of Third International Symposium on Adapted Physical Activities.* New Orleans: University of New Orleans.

Jansma, P. (1980). Reality therapy: Another approach to managing inappropriate behavior. *American Corrective Therapy Journal,* **34**(3), 64-69.

Jansma, P., & French, R. (1979). Transactional analysis: An alternative approach to managing inappropriate behavior. *American Corrective Therapy Journal,* **33**(5), 155-162.

Johnson, D., & Myklebust, H. (1967). *Learning disabilities: Educational principles and practices.* New York: Grune & Stratton.

Jones, J.A. (Ed.). (1984). *Training guide to cerebral palsy sports* (1st ed.). New York: National Association of Sports for Cerebral Palsy.

Karper, W., Martinek, T., & Wilkerson, J. (1985). Effects of competitive/non-competitive learning on motor performance of children in mainstreamed physical education. *American Corrective Therapy Journal,* **39**(1), 10-15.

Katz, S., & Yekutiel, E. (1974). Leisure time problems of mentally retarded graduates of training programs. *Mental Retardation,* **12**, 54-57.

Kephart, N. (1971). *The slow learner in the classroom* (2nd ed.). Columbus, OH: Charles E. Merrill.

Knapczyk, D., & Yoppi, J. (1975). Development of cooperative and competitive play responses in developmentally disabled children. *American Journal of Mental Deficiency,* **80**, 245-255.

Koegel, R., Firestone, P., Kramme, K., & Dunlap, G. (1974). Increasing spontaneous play by suppressing self-stimulation in autistic children. *Journal of Applied Behavior Analysis,* **7**, 521-528.

Labanowich, S. (1978). Psychology of wheelchair sports. *Therapeutic Recreation Journal,* **12**, 11-17.

Lamport, L.C. (1974). *The effects of a specific perceptual-motor physical education program on the self-concept of children with learning disabilities.* Unpublished doctoral dissertation, University of New Mexico, Albuquerque.

Lawrence, E., & Winschel, J. (1973). Self-concept and the retarded: Research and issues. *Exceptional Children,* **39**, 310-319.

Leighton, J. (1966). The effect of a physical fitness developmental program on the self-concept, mental age, and job proficiency in the mentally retarded. *Journal of the Association for Physical and Mental Rehabilitation,* **20**, 4-11.

Levy, J. (1978). *Play behavior.* New York: John Wiley & Sons.

Lillie, D.L. (1968). The effect of motor development lessons on mentally retarded children. *American Journal of Mental Deficiency,* **72**, 803-808.

Lipsitt, L.P. (1958). A self-concept scale for children and its relation to the children's form of the manifest anxiety scale. *Child Development,* **29**, 463-472.

Long, E., Irmer, L., Burkett, L., Glasenapp, G., & Odenkirk, B. (1980). PEOPEL. *Journal of Physical Education and Recreation,* **51**, 28-29.

Loovis, E.M. (1978). Effect of participation in sport/physical education on the development of the exceptional child. *American Corrective Therapy Journal,* **32**, 167-179.

Loovis, E.M. (1980). Behavior modification: Its application in physical education motor development for children with special needs. *American Corrective Therapy Journal,* **34**(1), 19-24.

Lubin, E., & Sherrill, C. (1980). Motor creativity of preschool deaf children. *American Annals of the Deaf,* **125**, 460-466.

Maloney, M.P., Ball, T.S., & Edgar, C.L. (1970). Analysis of the generalizability of sensory-motor training. *American Journal of Mental Deficiency,* **74**, 458-469.

Mancini, B., Devlin, G., & Frye, P. (1980). Teaching contingency management skills to disruptive elementary students: Its effects on student self-concept and student influence on physical education behaviors. *Abstracts of 1980 AAHPERD Convention.* Reston, VA: AAHPERD.

Marlowe, M. (1980). Games analysis intervention: A procedure to increase peer acceptance of socially isolated children. *Research Quarterly for Exercise and Sport,* **51**, 422-426.

Marlowe, M., Algozzine, G., Lerch, H.A., & Welch, P.D. (1978). Games analysis intervention: A procedure to decrease the feminine play patterns of emotionally disturbed boys. *Research Quarterly,* **49**, 484-490.

Martin, S.M., & Ovans, P. (1972). Learning games are pathways to cognizance for young handicapped children in therapeutic recreation. *Therapeutic Recreational Journal,* **6**, 153-157, 171.

Martinek, T., & Zaichkowsky, L. (1977). *Manual for the Martinek-Zachkowsky Self-Concept Scale for Children.* Jacksonville, IL: Psychologists and Educators.

Martino, L., & Johnson, D. (1979). Cooperative and individualistic experiences among disabled and normal children. *Journal of Social Psychology,* **107**, 177-183.

Matthews, P. (1979). The frequency with which the mentally retarded participate in recreation activities. *Research Quarterly,* **50**(1), 71-79.

Maurer, A. (1969). Peek-a-boo: An entry into the world of the autistic child. *Journal of Special Education,* **3**, 309-312.

McCubbin, J., & Shasby, G. (1985). Effects of isokinetic exercise on adolescents with cerebral palsy. *Adapted Physical Activity Quarterly,* **2**(1), 56-64.

McDaniel, C. (1970). Participation in extracurricular activities, social acceptance, and social rejection among educable mentally retarded students. *Education and Training of the Mentally Retarded,* **5**(1), 4-14.

Megginson, N. (1982). *Cooperative manpower planning in local adapted physical education needs assessment.* Unpublished doctoral dissertation, Texas Woman's University, Denton.

Molnar, G. (1978). Analysis of motor disorder in retarded infants and young children. *American Journal of Mental Deficiency,* **83**, 213-221.

Montessori, M. (1912). *The Montessori method* (A. George, Trans.). New York: Stokes.

Morris, G.S.D. (1976). *How to change the games children play.* Minneapolis: Burgess.

Morris, R., & Dolker, M. (1974). Developing cooperative play in socially withdrawn retarded children. *Mental Retardation,* **12**, 24-27.

Morrison, D., & Pothier, P. (1972). Two different remedial motor training programs and the development of mentally retarded preschoolers. *American Journal of Mental Deficiency,* **77**, 251-258.

Morrison, T., & Newcomer, B. (1975). Effects of directive vs. nondirective play therapy with institutionalized mentally retarded children. *American Journal of Mental Deficiency,* **79,** 666-669.

Myklebust, H.R. (1964). *The psychology of deafness* (2nd ed.). New York: Grune & Stratton.

Newcomer, B., & Morrison, T. (1974). Play therapy with institutionalized mentally retarded children. *American Journal of Mental Deficiency,* **78,** 727-733.

Nezol, A.J. (1972). Physical education for integrated blind students: Its relationship to sociometric status and recreational activity choices. *Education of the Visually Handicapped,* **4,** 16-18.

Nordgren, B., & Bäckström, L. (1971). Correlations between muscular strength and industrial work performance in mentally retarded persons. *Acta Paediatrica Scandinavica* (Suppl.), **217,** 122-126.

Oliver, J.N. (1958). The effect of physical conditioning exercises and activities on the mental characteristics of educationally subnormal boys. *British Journal of Educational Psychology,* **28,** 155-165.

Oliver, J.N. (1960). The effect of physical conditioning on the sociometric status of educationally subnormal boys. *Physical Education,* **52,** 38-40.

Ottenbacher, K., Short, M.A., & Watson, P.J. (1979). Nystagmus duration changes of learning disabled during sensory integrative therapy. *Perceptual and Motor Skills,* **48,** 1159-1164.

Paloutzian, R., Hasazi, J., Streifel, J., & Edgar, C. (1971). Promotion of positive interaction in severely retarded young children. *American Journal of Mental Deficiency,* **75,** 519-524.

Piaget, J. (1955). *The language and thought of the child.* New York: World Publishing.

Piaget, J. (1962). *Play, dreams, and imitation in childhood.* London: Routledge and Kegan Paul.

Piers, E., & Harris, D. (1969). *The Piers-Harris children's self-concept scale.* Nashville, TN: Counselor Recordings and Tests.

Rarick, G.L. (1978). Adult reactions to the Special Olympics. In F.L. Smoll & R.E. Smith (Eds.), *Psychological perspectives in youth sports* (pp. 229-246). New York: Halstead Press.

Rarick, G.L., Dobbins, D., & Broadhead, G. (1976). *The motor domain and its correlates in educationally handicapped children.* Englewood Cliffs, NJ: Prentice-Hall.

Razeghi, J.A., & Davis, S. (1979). Federal mandates for the handicapped: Vocational education opportunity and employment. *Exceptional Children,* **45**(5), 353-359.

Reber, R., & Sherrill, C. (1981). Creative thinking and dance/movement skills of hearing impaired youth: An experimental study. *American Annals of the Deaf,* **26**(9), 1004-1009.

Redding, S.F. (1979). Life adjustment patterns of retarded and nonretarded low functioning students. *Exceptional Children,* **45,** 367-369.

Richer, J., & Nicoll, S. (1971). A playroom for autistic children and its companion therapy project: A synthesis of ideas from ethology, psychology, nursing, and design. *The British Journal of Mental Subnormality,* **17,** 132-143.

Romanczyk, R., Diament, C., Goren, E., Trunell, G., & Harris, S. (1975). Increasing isolate and social play in severely disturbed children: Intervention and post-intervention effectiveness. *Journal of Autism and Childhood Schizophrenia,* **5,** 57-70.

Rosentswieg, J. (1969). A ranking of the objectives of physical education. *Research Quarterly,* **40,** 783-787.

Ross, S. (1969). Effects of an intensive motor skills training program on young educable mentally retarded children. *American Journal of Mental Deficiency,* **73,** 920-926.

Rowe, J. (1976). Motor creativity of mildly mentally retarded preschool children. Unpublished doctoral dissertation, Texas Woman's University, Denton.

Rynders, J., Johnson, R., Johnson, D., & Schmidt, B. (1980). Producing positive interaction among Down's Syndrome and nonhandicapped teenagers through cooperative goal structuring. *American Journal of Mental Deficiency,* **85,** 268-273.

Santomier, J., & Kopczuk, W. (1981). Facilitation of interactions between retarded and nonretarded students in a physical education setting. *Education and Training of the Mentally Retarded,* **16,** 60-23.

Seaman, J., & DePauw, K. (1982). *The new adapted physical education: A developmental approach.* Palo Alto, CA: Mayfield.

Sherrill, C. (Ed.). (1979). *Creative arts for the severely handicapped.* Springfield, IL: Charles C. Thomas.

Sherrill, C. (1980). Posture training as a means of normalization. *Mental Retardation,* **18**(3), 135-138.

Sherrill, C. (1982). *Development of paired-comparison instrument for prioritizing long range adapted physical education goals.* Unpublished manuscript, Texas Woman's University, Denton.

Sherrill, C. (Ed.). (1985). *Sport and disabled athletes.* Champaign, IL: Human Kinetics.

Sherrill, C. (1986). *Adapted physical education and recreation: A multidisciplinary approach* (3rd ed.). Dubuque, IA: Wm. C. Brown.

Sherrill, C., & Montelione, T. (1983). *Ranking of adapted physical education goals: A preliminary study.* Unpublished manuscript, Texas Woman's University, Denton.

Sherrill, C., & Ruda, L. (1977). A time to listen: Leisure interests and practices of mentally retarded adults. *Parks and Recreation, 12*(11), 30-33.

Shotick, S., & Thate, C. (1960). Reactions of a group of educable mentally handicapped children to a program of physical education. *Exceptional Children, 26*(5), 248-252.

Simpson, J.M., & Meaney, C. (1979). Effects of learning to ski on the self-concept of mentally retarded children. *American Journal of Mental Deficiency, 84*(1), 25-29.

Smith, J.R., & Hurst, J.G. (1961). The relationship of motor abilities and peer acceptance of mentally retarded children. *American Journal of Mental Deficiency, 66*(1), 81-85.

Smoll, F. (1974). Motor impairment and social development. *American Corrective Therapy Journal, 28*(1), 4-7.

Solomon, A., & Pangle, R. (1967). Demonstrating physical fitness improvement in the EMR. *Exceptional Children, 34*, 177-181.

Stanfield, J. (1973). What happens to the retarded child when he grows up? *Exceptional Children, 39*, 548-552.

Stein, J. (1966). *Physical fitness in relation to intelligence quotient, social distance, and physique of intermediate school mentally retarded boys.* Unpublished doctoral dissertation, George Peabody College for Teachers, Nashville, TN.

Tomporowski, P., & Jameson, L. (1985). Effects of a physical fitness training program on the exercise behavior of institutionalized mentally retarded adults. *Adapted Physical Activity Quarterly, 2*(3), 197-205.

Training educators for the handicapped: A need to redirect federal programs (Report to Congress by the Comptroller General of the United States) (1976, September 28). Washington, DC.

Van Andel, G., & Austin, D. (1984). Physical fitness and mental health: A review of the literature. *Adapted Physical Activity Quarterly, 1*(3), 207-220.

Vodola, T. (1978). *ACTIVE research monograph: Competency-based teacher training and individualized-personalized physical activity.* Oakhurst, NJ: Township of Ocean School District.

Webb, R. (1969). Sensory-motor training of the profoundly retarded. *American Journal of Mental Deficiency, 74*, 2.

Wehman, P. (1977). *Helping the mentally retarded acquire play skills.* Springfield, IL: Charles C. Thomas.

Wehman, P., Karan, O., & Rettie, C. (1976). Developing independent play in three severely retarded women. *Psychological Reports, 39*, 995-998.

Weininger, O., Rotenberg, G., & Henry, A. (1972). Body image of handicapped children. *Journal of Personality Assessment, 36*, 248-253.

Winnick, J., & Short, F. (1984). The physical fitness of youngsters with spinal neuromuscular conditions. *Adapted Physical Activity Quarterly, 1*(1), 37-51.

Wright, B. (1960). *Physical disability—A psychological approach.* New York: Harper & Row.

Wright, J., & Cowden, J.E. (1986). *Changes in self-concept and cardiovascular endurance of mentally retarded youth in a Special Olympics swimming program. Adapted Physical Activity Quarterly, 3*(2), 177-183.

Wysocki, B.A., & Wysocki, A.C. (1973). The body image of normal and retarded children. *Journal of Clinical Psychology, 29*, 7-10.

Part III

Adapted Physical Education Teacher Training Approaches, Programs, and Pedagogies

Chapter 20

Vintage Years: Competency, Certification, and Licensure in Adapted Physical Education

Karen P. DePauw and Ernest Bundschuh

Just as standards are required for the production of quality wines, so there must be standards in adapted physical education. The winemaker continually strives to improve upon traditional methods in quest of superior wines. By this improvement, an enhanced technology is developed through which wines of fine vintage are produced. As the demands of the consumer increase, so must the standards be improved to enhance the quality of wine. This is also the case in adapted physical education. One such standard is the minimum level of competency required of those teaching adapted physical education. Certification, licensure, and endorsement can be utilized in an attempt to assure that competency is developed and maintained.

Improving Technology

Competencies and competency-based education are terms that are not new in education; they have been used in reference to standards, expected performances, and requirements to be satisfied for preparation in a given field of study. For at least the last decade, professionals in adapted physical education have used the term *competencies* in discussion of teacher training programs.

Because competencies in adapted physical education have been identified (American Alliance for Health, Physical Education, and Recreation, 1973; Hurley, 1981), it is important that professionals in adapted physical education understand the meaning of competencies and their application to the discipline as a field of study. To insure relevance, professionals need to understand and use the appropriate terminology.

In regular and adapted physical education, the term *competencies* has been used more frequently than competency-based education. The use of the term may lead one to think in terms of either expected performances or competency-based education. Are these concepts dichotomous? Is there a continuum along which these would be found? How are the terms being used in adapted physical education?

Competency-Based Education

Andersen (1973) has chosen to define a competency-based program in its simplest form, as "one which specifies the objectives for training of teachers in an explicit form, and then proceeds to hold the prospective teachers accountable for meeting those objectives" (p. v). Hall and Jones (1976) viewed competency-based education as both a means and an end: "a process for change . . . and . . . a set of tools for building new programs" (p. 22). They stated that competency-based education can be a "catalytic process for change and program development that embodies guidelines and ways of specifying . . . outcomes" (p. 23). They viewed it as "education that focuses on . . . acquisition of specific competencies" (p. 10). Competency-based education is an attempt to place emphasis upon demonstrated competencies necessary

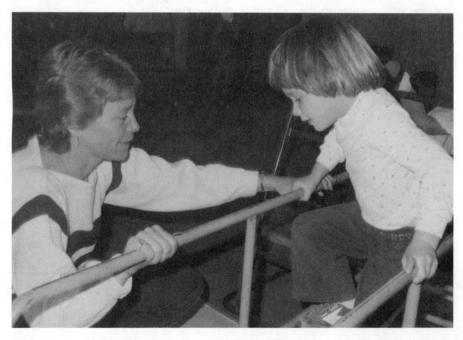

Karen DePauw, Washington State University in Pullman, who is coauthor of *The New Adapted Physical Education*.

in a given field of study in an effort to establish, challenge, change, and hold accountable the professionals in the profession. Competencies make up the cornerstone of competency-based education.

As is evident by the many and varied programs, models, and projects in use today, there is general agreement that competency-based education can take almost any form necessary to get the job done in any given environment, for any given purpose, and for any given field of study. When put into practice, competency-based education may utilize many different structures and/or models such as modules, learning resource centers, or field experiences. Regardless of form, the application reflects a conceptual approach to competency-based education. The application of the basic concept and constructs is and shall continue to be widely diverse. The concept underlying competency-based education presents an extremely viable approach to education, physical education, and adapted physical education.

Over the years when professionals in adapted physical education have spoken of competencies for preparation in adapted physical education, they alluded to the underlying constructs of competency-based education. Thus it followed that professionals would seek to establish competencies for the professional preparation of adapted physical educators—not through a specific model but through a conceptual approach to competency-based education.

Competencies

Before utilizing a conceptual approach to competency-based education, one must look at the specification and levels of competencies. According to Hall and Jones (1976), competencies are "composite skills, behaviors, or knowledge that can be demonstrated . . . and are derived from explicit conceptualizations of the desired outcomes of learning" (p. 11). Competencies comprise just one level of the scope of learning outcomes.

Although other authors have alluded to levels and many have defined goals, competencies, and objectives, Hall and Jones (1976) have written extensively on the identification of competencies, goals, and objectives. Goals are understood as the broadest outcome statements; objectives as the most specifically identified statements. Competencies are found midway between the ends of the continuum from goals to objectives. Competency statements encompass and include a description of "performances that are based on the acquisition, integration, composite building, and application of a set of related skills and knowledge" (Hall & Jones, 1976, pp. 29-30). Thus emphasis is placed upon a growth process and the development and demonstration of overall performance rather than the acquisition of specific skills.

Historical Perspective on Competencies

Evelyn Davies (1950) was the first person to state teacher training competencies in adapted physical education (then called correctives). Her dissertation, directed by Josephine Rathbone at Teachers College, Columbia University, focused specifically on competencies needed to work with orthopedically impaired students. Davies, like other graduates of Columbia University, was influenced strongly by Harry Scott, who emphasized competency-based education in all of his courses and was coauthor with his doctoral candidate, Raymond Snyder, of the first book on professional preparation in health, physical education, and recreation (Snyder & Scott, 1954). This text included more than 50 pages that stated competencies needed to perform selected functions. The organization of this pioneer work is illustrated in Table 20.1. Many adapted physical educators subsequently were influenced by the competency-based education movement in regular physical education throughout the 1950s and 1960s.

Not until 1971-1972, however, did a nationwide effort to develop competencies especially for adapted physical education occur. During that year a series of institutes funded by the Bureau of Education for the Handicapped resulted in lists of competencies needed to fulfill the functions required of specialist teachers, supervisors, and college teachers in adapted physical education (see appendix B). More than 120 physical educators, recreators, special educators, administrators, and others participated in the development of these competencies. Julian Stein served as director of these institutes and as editor of the resulting proceedings that published these competencies (American Alliance for Health, Physical Education, and Recreation, 1973). Throughout the 1970s these competencies played an important role in shaping adapted physical education (see review of Clelland research [1979] in chapter 3). Of 34 adapted physical education teacher training projects studied by Clelland (1979), 27 were competency-based. When read the 78 competencies stated in the 1973 Proceedings, from 63 to 81% of the project directors indicated intent to develop every competency in their graduate students. During the late 1960s and 1970s, the literature included several articles specific to competencies in adapted physical education (American Alliance for Health, Physical Education, Recreation, and Dance, 1976a, 1976b; Bird & Gansneder, 1979; California State Task Force on Standards for Professional Preparation in Adapted Physical Education, 1978; DePauw, 1979; French, Jansma, & Winnick, 1978; Geddes & Seaman, 1978; Stein, 1969; Vodola, 1978). All of this information was quite valuable in the identification and establishment of competencies for the professional preparation of adapted physical education specialists.

Table 20.1   Organizational Plan for Competency-Based Education

Problems to be met by student	Selected competencies needed to meet the problem	Selected experiences to develop the competencies	Resource areas
To comprehend the needs of children of different age-grade groups	Appreciates the hereditary factors in child growth and development	Studies the latest medical findings concerning the needs of children.	Foundations of education.
	Looks upon behavior as the result in the individual attempting to satisfy his needs.	Analyzes the behavior of a number of children in an effort to understand their needs.	Laboratory and field experiences
	Understands the developmental tasks of children.	Plans with staff members a program to meet the needs of students.	Health appraisals
	Understands the field theory of psychology and appreciates the "organism in its setting" concept.	Experiments with the Wetzel grid as a means of discovering how growth factors are affected.	Child growth and development
	Understands all the factors of child growth and development and how they affect behavior.	Weighs and measures children for the teacher and considers the importance of changes in the height and weight.	

Note. From *Professional Preparation in Health, Physical Education, and Recreation* (p. 144) by R.A. Snyder and H.A. Scott, 1954, New York: McGraw-Hill.

Conceptual Approach to Competencies in Adapted Physical Education

As an emerging discipline, adapted physical education has a unique and identifiable body of knowledge in which goals, competencies, and objectives can be determined. Although one or more goal statements for adapted physical education could be written, the task would be an academic exercise. Whatever words each professional or group of professionals might select to state the goals, one goal statement would undoubtedly reflect the notion of adequately prepared, competent teachers of physical education for individuals with disabilities.

Pioneer Work on Competencies in Adapted Physical Education

Individuals in California were among the first to undertake the task of establishing standards through the identification of competencies for the professional preparation of adapted physical educators. A Task Force on Standards for the Professional Preparation in Adapted Physical Education was established in 1977. The Task Force, chaired by Karen P. DePauw, included professionals in adapted physical education from colleges and universities, school districts employing adapted physical education specialists, and representatives from the State Department of Education. After a year of meetings,

several revisions of the original document, and hours of testimony at hearings around the state, the scope and content of the Guidelines for Academic Preparation in Adapted Physical Education were approved in late 1978. The approved guidelines became an integral part of the "first ever" required California Emphasis Credential in Adapted Physical Education. An outline of the areas of academic preparation and percentage of time to be spent in each follows:

1.0 Biological Foundations (20%)

    1.1 Physical Growth and Development

    1.2 Kinesiology

    1.3 Physiology of Exercise and Motor Functioning

    1.4 Neurological Bases

2.0 Sociological Foundations (5%)

    2.1 Recreation and Leisure in the Community

3.0 Psychomotor Foundations (20%)

    3.1 Motor Learning

    3.2 Self-Realization

    3.3 Personality Dynamics

    3.4 Behavior Management

4.0 Foundations and Understandings (10%)

    4.1 Historical Aspects

4.2 Philosophical Aspects

4.3 Issues and Trends

4.4 Interdisciplinary Concept

5.0 Assessment and Evaluation (20%)

    5.1 Performance Assessment

    5.2 Program Goals and Objectives

    5.3 Individualizing Instruction

    5.4 Program Evaluation

6.0 Instructional Subject Matter (20%)

    6.1 Psychomotor Skills, Rules, and Strategies

7.0 Health and Safety Concepts (5%)

    7.1 Physical Activity and Health

    7.2 Factors Affecting Health

    7.3 Safety

After 1973, The American Alliance for Health, Physical Education, Recreation and Dance (AAHPERD) became increasingly involved in the process of establishing standards for professional preparation, the identification of competencies, and the encouragement of certification, licensure, and endorsement in adapted physical education. In 1979, a task force on adapted physical education was established and charged with the development of teaching competencies (Hurley, 1981).

The task force consisted of 14 representatives from the three structures of AAHPERD (Unit on Programs for the Handicapped, the Therapeutics Council of ARAPCS, and the Adapted Physical Education Academy of NASPE). The members included Ernie Bundschuh, Emilo DaBramo, Karen DePauw, John Dunn, Sue Grosse, Robert Holland, Joseph Huber, Dianne Hurley, Larry Irmer, Ellen Lubin Curtis Pierce, Robert Roice, Julian Stein, and Robert Strauss.

The first meeting was held in July, 1979, in Kansas City. The initial draft of the guidelines was subsequently presented at state and district conventions and published in the January, 1980 *IRUC Briefings* for reaction, response, and feedback from the professionals across the nation. In response to the feedback, the task force revised the guidelines prior to the 1980 AAHPERD convention in Detroit. The resulting guidelines included the competencies necessary for both the regular physical education generalist and the adapted physical education specialist. The competencies for the specialist were approved by AAHPERD, while those identified for the generalist were submitted to a NASPE task force for inclusion within the guidelines for the undergraduate professional preparation curriculum. The competencies as identified by the task force are presented in Appendix B of this textbook. A major issue facing the emerging discipline of adapted physical education is the identification of learning activities, evaluation techniques, and performance criteria associated with established competencies and the implementation of such as standards on the state and local levels.

Certification, Licensure, and Endorsement

Certification, licensure, or endorsement by a state education agency (SEA) is essential to quality control of individuals employed to deliver adapted physical education services in the public schools. Excellence in adapted physical education teacher training programs is meaningless if the SEA does not establish and enforce standards for employment in a given profession.

Although PL 94-142 mandates that all handicapped school children shall receive physical education, it does not specify who is qualified to deliver such services. This decision is therefore made at the state and local education agency levels. Who can teach adapted physical education is often written into the SEA Special Education State Plan. It is imperative, therefore, that adapted physical education university personnel and public school leaders work with special educators at the state level in ascertaining that policies regarding adapted physical education employment and service delivery are consistent with teacher training goals and standards.

The adapted physical education curricula of a teacher training facility should be closely correlated with the SEA Special Education State Plan and vice versa. University teachers should interact frequently with both the Special Education and Teacher Education Divisions of their respective SEAs. Among the competencies that university teachers should develop is knowledge concerning procedures for changing SEA teacher certification, licensure, or endorsement.

Procedures for changing teacher certification, licensure, or endorsement are different in each state, as are the definitions of these terms. In general, a *certification, licensure,* or *credential* is earned in a broad area of specialization like special education, physical education, or mathematics and requires a minimum of 30 semester hours in the specialization plus 12 to 18 credits in education and student teaching courses. In contrast, *endorsement* usually refers to new competencies documented by 9 to 18 semester hours of course work, which are added onto an existing teacher credential and thus extend employment opportunities.

Adapted physical education leaders are unanimous in their belief that SEAs should offer endorsement, licensure, or certification specifically in adapted physical education. There is not agreement, however, as to whether this should be available to graduate students who already have a broad background in physical education and/or special education or to undergraduate students. Once leaders within a state resolve this issue and concur on the competencies and content to be required, they should cooperatively develop a written request for the new certification that includes the following:

1. Present or emerging need for new certification plan. This statement should include the number of persons presently employed in such positions within the state and an estimate of the number still needed. It should also present the advantages of having such certification and the disadvantages of not having certification.

2. Name of group(s) sponsoring the request for certification.

3. Suggested nature of the training program.

4. Role of persons who would be eligible for certification.

5. Certification practices in other states for similar positions.

6. A list of names of people (including relevant organizations to which they belong) who would be willing to appear before the appropriate SEA structure and answer questions.

To facilitate the establishment of adapted physical education teacher certification plans in every state, this chapter presents the requirements of selected states that have already met the certification goal. Most of these plans appear to be endorsements as the term is defined in this paper, but the actual language of each SEA is used. With the exception of Louisiana, all of the plans specify competencies rather than course titles.

Louisiana Requirements for Adapted Physical Education Endorsement[1]

Directed by the Louisiana Department of Education, a committee composed of university personnel and local school system officials developed the requirements for the new certification. As an endorsement to the regular physical education certification, the adapted certification required an additional 12 credit hours that included practical experience. The courses were titled and approved by the Office of Teacher Certification as follows:

- Introducing Physical Education for All Handicapped Children

- Behavior Impairment and Physical Education
- Chronic Disability and Physical Education
- The Physical Education Curriculum for All Handicapped Children

The 1979 Louisiana Legislature appropriated state funds to allow local education agencies to employ adapted physical education teachers. However, until fully certified, teachers were required to sign a Plan of Professional Development and file it with the Department of Education. The Professional Plan of Development was equivalent to a temporary certificate in adapted physical education. Teachers could then be employed by the local agencies while pursuing certification. The new certification was fully approved by the Board of Education in August, 1979.

Georgia Standards for Endorsement in Adapted Physical Education[2]

An endorsement in adapted physical education may be added to the T-4, T-5, TS-6, D-7, PBT-4, PBT-5, PBTS-6, and PBT-7 certificates in Health and Physical Education by completing the requirements outlined below. This endorsement may be carried to higher levels of certification.

Twenty quarter hours of graduate credit is deemed a minimum standard for endorsement in adapted physical education. The T-4 certification level in health and physical education currently requires only the survey course in special education. Many teachers from professional preparation programs out of state lack that requirement. Furthermore, formal training or associated field experiences specifically in adapted physical education are lacking. The minimum of 20 quarter hours as an endorsement in adapted physical education would allow competencies to be developed across the eight categories of handicapped students that have been identified as needing specially designed physical education.

Foundations of Adapted Physical Education. The special education survey course required by HB 671 may not be applied to this area.

Five graduate quarter hours in physiological, psychological, and motor characteristics of handicapped children and/or youth as related to programs designed to improve motor performance of these students are required. Current trends in social and philosophical issues as related to physical education and special education should be included. The course should have an associated field experience.

[1]Submitted by Patrick Cooper and Janice Frugé, Louisiana Department of Education.

[2]Submitted by Ernest Bundschuh, University of Georgia.

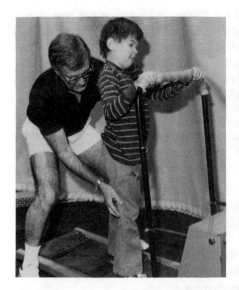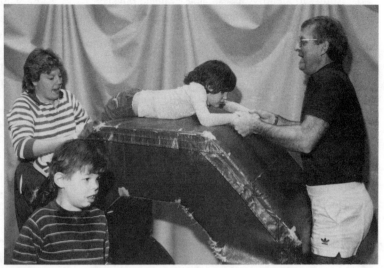

Ernie Bundschuh at the Georgia Retardation Center in Athens, where he has taught University of Georgia students for many years.

Curriculum and Methods in Adapted Physical Education. Ten graduate quarter hours in adapted physical education curriculum and methods stressing assessing, developing, and implementing individualized education plans and knowledge of appropriate physical education curriculum and programs are required. Additional emphasis should be given to the roles and functions of the adapted physical education specialist serving in an interdisciplinary manner. These hours should have associated field experiences.

Practicum in Adapted Physical Education. Five graduate quarter hours of supervised practicum experience in a physical education environment serving youth and/or children whose handicaps necessitate adapted physical education are required.

Minnesota Requirements for Licensure in Developmental/Adapted Physical Education[3]

A. All candidates recommended for licensure to teach Developmental/Adapted Physical Education (grades prekindergarten-12) shall

1. hold a baccalaureate degree,

2. hold a valid license as a teacher of physical education, grades K-12,

3. satisfactorily complete core skill area requirements in special education enumerated in 5 MCAR paragraph 3.0901, and

4. satisfactorily complete a Developmental/Adapted Physical Education teacher preparation program, approved by the Minnesota Board of Teaching, consisting of at least 27 quarter hours, or the equivalent.

B. Each program leading to the licensure of teachers of Developmental/Adapted Physical Education (grades prekindergarten-12) shall provide candidates recommended for licensure with knowledge, skills, and understandings in all of the following:

1. Theoretical foundations of developmental/adapted physical education consisting of the sciences of biology, anatomy, and/or human physiology, which shall include the following:

   a. Understanding of sequences of motor development from early childhood through adolescence, including typical and atypical patterns of development.

   b. Understanding of physically handicapping conditions that interfere with motor function.

   c. Understanding of physical rehabilitation as applied to physical education programs for handicapped and special needs students.

2. Organization and management of instruction, consisting of planning, implementing, and evaluating physical education instruction for handicapped and special needs students (grades prekindergarten-12), which shall include the following:

   a. Understanding of scope, sequence, and implementation of developmental/adapted physical education curriculum.

[3]Submitted by Lief "Curly" Bollesen, Rochester Public Schools.

b. Ability to identify, assess, and evaluate physical and motor development of handicapped and special needs students.

c. Ability to develop, adapt, select, and utilize a variety of instructional resources to implement a developmental/adapted physical education curriculum.

d. Knowledge of the application of research to developmental/adapted physical education curriculum.

e. Ability to adapt physical education activities and curriculum for handicapped and special needs students.

f. Ability to select and adapt facilities and equipment for handicapped and special needs students.

g. Ability to supervise nonlicensed personnel in the delivery of developmental/adapted physical education programs for handicapped and special needs students.

h. Teaching experiences with handicapped and special needs students, including students in regular physical education classes and students in self-contained special education classes, and experiences in two or more of the handicapped categories set forth in M.S. 120.03.

C. An institution applying to the Board of Teaching for approval of its Developmental/Adapted Physical Education preparation program (grades prekindergarten-12) shall meet the provisions of 5 MCAR paragraph 3.141. All approved programs leading to the licensure of teachers of developmental/adapted physical education shall include a description of the way in which practicing teachers may have their teaching experience and teacher preparation in those areas enumerated in A. and B., above, evaluated, and credited by an institution maintaining an approved program leading to the licensure of teachers of developmental/adapted physical education. Such evaluation shall include previous teaching experience and previous teacher preparation.

D. Provisional licensure. A provisional license shall be issued to an applicant who meets the requirements of A.1. and A.2., above, who has completed a minimum of 15 quarter hours or the equivalent selected from B.1. and B.2., above, in a program approved by the Minnesota Board of Teaching leading to the licensure of teachers of developmental/adapted physical education. Previous teaching experience and/or previous teacher preparation evaluated according to the provisions of C., above, may apply toward provisional licensure. The provisional license shall be valid for 2 years, after which full licensure as specified in A., above, shall be required. Provisional licensure shall remain in effect until July 1, 1990, at which time provisional licensure shall be repealed without further action by the Minnesota Board of Teaching.

E. Continuing licensure. The continuing license shall be issued and renewed according to rules of the Board of Teaching governing continuing education and relicensure.

F. This rule is effective July 1, 1985, for all applicants for licensure to teach developmental/adapted physical education (grades prekindergarten-12).

Michigan Requirements for Certification as a Teacher of Physical Education for the Handicapped[4]

A teacher of physical education for handicapped individuals shall possess a valid Michigan teaching certificate with approval in physical education, special education or both, and shall complete all of the following:

A. A minimum of 9 semester hours or 12 term hours in special education courses leading to the acquisition of all of the following competencies:

1. Knowledge of the causes of various handicapping conditions and the effects of those conditions on learning.

2. Ability to assess physical education skills of individuals exhibiting various handicapping conditions.

3. Knowledge of special education teaching models that employ assessment-prescriptive techniques.

4. Ability to use community and staff resources within the special education environment.

B. A minimum of 9 semester hours or 12 term hours in special physical education courses leading to the acquisition of all of the following competencies:

1. Ability to write in behavioral terms and assess instructional objectives for physical education for the handicapped.

2. Knowledge of motor characteristics, behaviors, and development sequences associated with various handicapping conditions in relation to normal motor development.

3. Knowledge of anatomy, kinesiology, and neurology that pertains to normal and abnormal motor control and sensorimotor integration for teaching

---

[4]Submitted by Janet Wessel, Michigan State University.

physical education to severely handicapped and nonambulatory students.

4. Ability to adapt teaching methods, materials, and techniques for physical and motor fitness, gymnasium use, fundamental motor skills, aquatic skills, dance, individual and group games, and lifetime sport skills for the needs of the handicapped.

5. Ability to analyze, adapt, and implement physical education curriculum in providing appropriate programs for a variety of handicapping conditions.

C. A directed field experience in teaching physical education with handicapped persons in a school setting.

Alabama Requirements for Certification and Employment of Adapted Physical Education Teachers[5]

1. The Local Education Agency must have on file written documentation from a university that the adapted physical education teacher has successfully completed the 12 semester hours (20 quarter hours) of course work as described in number 3.

2. Universities preparing students to become adapted physical education specialists must submit, in writing, the proposed courses that will fulfill the 12 semester hours (20 quarter hours) of course work to the State Department of Education, Program for Exceptional Children and Youth for approval. Approval must be obtained prior to providing any written documentation to Local Education Agencies regarding the completion of their program by individual students.

3. Adapted Physical Education teachers (employed after the approval of the rules of this section) must possess the following qualifications in order to be paid from special education funds.

   a. The teacher must be certified in physical education or special education;

   b. The teacher must have met a practicum requirement in adapted physical education of at least 100 hours in either a practicum course or in selected approved courses that include the following:

   (1) Knowledge of appropriate techniques for managing behavior.

   (2) Ability to function successfully as a team member with other direct service providers, that is, occupational therapists, classroom teachers, physical education teachers, and so on.

   (3) Ability to apply adapted physical education strategies learned for assessing, identifying, and prescribing specific learning experiences and implementing IEP or other individualized approaches for youth with disabilities.

   c. The teacher must have completed a minimum of 12 semester hours (20 quarter hours) of course work leading to the following competencies:

1.0 Sociological Foundations

1.1 Sport, Dance, and Play

1.1.1 Demonstrate ability to analyze the role and significance of sport, dance, and play in the lives of individuals with disabilities.

1.1.2 Demonstrate understanding of roles and significance of lifetime physical activities for individuals with disabilities.

1.1.3 Demonstrate understanding of influences of community social agencies on sport, dance, and play in lives of individuals with disabilities.

1.2 Cooperative/Competitive Activities

1.2.1 Demonstrate ability to apply understanding of potential for human interaction and social behavior occurring in cooperative/competitive activities for individuals with disabilities.

1.2.2 Demonstrate ability to work and cooperate with organizations that conduct adapted sport, dance, and play programs and activities for individuals with disabilities.

1.3 Social Development

1.3.1 Demonstrate ability to apply understanding of the potential that sport, dance, and play provides for social interaction among individuals with and without disabilities.

2.0 Psychological Foundations

2.1 Human Growth and Development

2.1.1 Demonstrate ability to apply understanding of deviations in normal human growth.

2.1.2 Demonstrate ability to apply understanding of atypical motor development to individuals with disabilities.

2.2 Motor Learning

2.2.1 Demonstrate ability to apply principles of motor learning to individuals with specific physical and motor needs.

---

[5]Submitted by Glenn Roswal, Jacksonville State University.

2.2.2 Demonstrate ability to apply principles of motivation on development of motor skills by individuals with disabilities.

2.3 Self-Concept and Personality Development

2.3.1 Demonstrate understanding of how participating in physical and motor activities contributes to positive self-concepts of individuals with disabilities.

2.3.2 Demonstrate ability to apply understanding of how interpersonal relationships are affected by participation in physical and motor activities.

2.3.3 Demonstrate ability to apply skills and techniques to assist individuals with disabilities overcome additional barriers that can affect interpersonal relationships and development of positive self-concepts.

2.4 Management Behavior

2.4.1 Demonstrate ability to apply appropriate techniques for managing behavior (i.e., behaviorism, existentialism, humanism).

2.4.2 Demonstrate ability to apply techniques of motivation to enhance acceptable behavior and promote motor performance.

3.0 Biological Foundations

3.1 Kinesiology

3.1.1 Demonstrate ability to apply understanding of motor dysfunctions and their implications to adapted physical education programs.

3.1.2 Demonstrate ability to apply understanding of neurological disorders and their implications to motor functioning.

3.1.3 Demonstrate ability to apply understanding of deviations from normal physical growth and development to analyses of motor skills.

3.1.4 Demonstrate proficiency in evaluating and analyzing motor skills.

3.1.5 Demonstrate ability to apply understanding of unique structures of individuals with disabilities to individualized instruction in adapted physical education.

3.1.6 Demonstrate ability to apply biomechanical principles that affect motor functioning to wheelchair, crutch, braces, and artificial limb use.

3.1.7 Demonstrate ability to apply biomechanical principles that affect motor functioning to posture, and neurological, muscular, and other specific physical health needs.

3.2 Physiology of Exercise

3.2.1 Demonstrate knowledge of how dysfunctions affect physiological responses to exercise.

3.2.2 Demonstrate ability to design instructional physical education programs in accordance with essential physiological considerations and principles specific to individuals with disabilities.

3.2.3 Demonstrate proficiency in conducting instructional physical education programs in accordance with essential physiological considerations and principles specific to individuals with disabilities.

3.2.4 Demonstrate ability to apply research findings in the area of exercise physiology specific to individuals with disabilities.

3.3 Physiological and Motor Functioning

3.3.1 Demonstrate ability to apply an understanding of physiological functioning of individuals with physical, mental, sensory, neurological, and other specific health needs to programs designed to improve motor performances of these individuals with disabilities.

3.3.2 Demonstrate ability to apply an understanding of physiological motor characteristics for individuals with physical, mental, sensory, neurological and other specific health needs to programs designed to improve motor performance of these individuals with disabilities.

3.3.3 Demonstrate ability to apply techniques for the prevention and care of injuries specific to individuals with specific disabilities.

4.0 Assessment and Evaluation

4.1 Program Goals and Objectives

4.1.1 Demonstrate ability to apply goals and objectives of adapted physical education.

4.1.2 Demonstrate ability to develop instructional objectives that lead to fulfillment of physical education goals in psychomotor, affective, and cognitive domains by individuals with disabilities.

4.2 Screening and Assessment

4.2.1 Demonstrate proficiency in applying appropriate instruments and procedures for measuring levels of physiological, biomechanical, and psychomotor functioning of individuals with disabilities.

4.2.2 Demonstrate proficiency in applying appropriate criteria in constructing assessment instruments for measuring physical and motor performances of students with disabilities.

4.2.3 Demonstrate proficiency interpreting assessment results of students with disabilities in terms of physical education goals and objectives.

4.3 Evaluation

4.3.1 Demonstrate proficiency in applying appropriate instruments in determining physical and motor needs of individuals with disabilities.

4.3.2 Demonstrate proficiency in applying principles of evaluation in determining student progress in adapted physical education.

5.0 Curriculum Planning, Organization, and Implementation

5.1 Program Planning

5.1.1 Demonstrate proficiency in planning instructional programs to meet needs of students with disabilities emphasizing the following areas:

• Physical and motor fitness

• Fundamental motor skills and patterns

• Skills in aquatics, dance, individual and group games and sports, including lifetime sport and leisure skills.

5.1.2 Demonstrate ability to plan individual physical education programs based on goals and objectives established by an interdisciplinary team.

5.1.3 Demonstrate ability to adapt physical and motor fitness activities, fundamental motor skills and patterns, aquatics and dance, and individual and group games and sports, including lifetime sport and leisure skills, to accommodate needs of individuals with disabilities.

5.1.4 Demonstrate understanding of organizations that govern adapted sport and games.

5.2 Individual Instruction

5.2.1 Demonstrate ability to apply strategies for individualizing instruction for students with disabilities in a variety of instructional settings.

5.2.2 Demonstrate ability to apply task analysis techniques in the process of individualizing instruction.

5.2.3 Demonstrate ability to implement appropriate physical education programs for individuals with disabilities based on each student's current level of performance.

5.3 Program Implementation

5.3.1 Demonstrate ability to implement appropriate physical education curricula for individuals with disabilities based upon adequate supportive factors (i.e., administrative policies, facilities, equipment, faculty, and community).

5.3.2 Demonstrate ability to function effectively as a member of an interdisciplinary team.

5.3.3 Demonstrate ability to apply appropriate techniques for facilitating interdisciplinary communication among all persons working with individuals with disabilities.

5.4 Safety Considerations

5.4.1 Demonstrate ability to apply principles of safety to wheelchair transfers, lifts, and assists needed when individuals with disabilities participate in physical activities.

5.4.2 Demonstrate understanding of scientific bases for specifically contraindicated exercises and activities for individuals with disabilities.

5.5 Health Considerations

5.5.1 Demonstrate ability to apply principles of appropriate health practices to participation in physical and motor activities by individuals with disabilities.

5.5.2 Demonstrate understanding of effects of medication, fatigue, and illness on mental, physical, and motor performances of individuals with disabilities.

5.5.3 Demonstrate understanding of implications of personal hygiene, posture, and nutrition for individuals with disabilities.

Most of the states that offer adapted physical education teacher certification require that additional course work be added to an existing physical education or special education certificate. The minimum number of hours of credit specifically in adapted physical education for this endorsement is 9 semester hours (12 quarter hours). Most states, however, require at least 12 semester hours (20 quarter hours) and specify the competencies/content to be covered.

Future Directions

During the decade of the 1970s, the need for professional preparation in adapted physical education was well established as an issue. The trend continues toward the training of competent physical education personnel. Competencies in adapted physical education have been established at the national, state, and local levels. Future directions may lead to national registration or certification in addition to the certification, licensure, or endorsement in adapted physical education, which are well under way in some states.

Although the impact of legislation may have brought adapted physical education into the forefront recently, the move toward the establishment of professional preparation standards was well on its way earlier in history. Standards for the training of competent adapted physical educators have been discussed over the last 25 years and are finally coming to fruition. During the decade of the 1980s, adapted physical educators have and will continue to make a strong commitment to the discipline and its standards for professional preparation; focus will be placed upon the quality of service delivery to individuals with disabilities. During the challenge of the 1980s, professionals in adapted physical education will have to direct attention not only to providing training for the ever-changing profile of the specialist in adapted physical education but also to the competency of the generalist in physical education who will deliver service in an integrated instructional environment.

As C.H. McCloy (1927) challenged the physical education profession in the 1900s with his call for new wine in new bottles, so might adapted physical education be challenged today. As professionals in adapted physical education, we should continually seek a variety of grapes, experiment with the fermentation process and procedures, and taste and evaluate the wine for acceptability. It is through this process that we may succeed in producing wines of good vintage. Wines of good vintage are most pleasing to the consumer and satisfying to the winemaker. Although the labels, the ingredients in the wine, and the bottles may have already changed over the years, our vintage years are now and in the near future.

References

American Association for Health, Physical Education and Recreation. (1973). *Professional preparation in adapted physical education, therapeutic recreation and corrective therapy*. Washington, DC: Author.

American Alliance for Health, Physical Education, and Recreation. (1976a). *Adapted physical education guidelines: Theory and practices for the seventies and eighties*. Washington, DC: Author.

American Alliance for Health, Physical Education, and Recreation. (1976b). *Professional preparation in adapted physical education, therapeutic recreation, and corrective therapy*. Washington, DC: Author.

Andersen, D.W. (1973). *Competency based teacher education*. Berkeley, CA: McCutchan.

Bird, P., & Gansneder, B. (1979). Preparation of physical education teachers as required under Public Law 94-142. *Exceptional Children, 45*, 464-466.

California State Task Force on Standards for Professional Preparation in Adapted Physical Education. (1978).

Scope and content statement in adapted physical education. Los Angeles: California State University.

Clelland, R. (1979). *A survey of personnel preparation and recreation for the handicapped—The consumer's guide series, Vol. VI*. BEH Special Project, University of New Mexico, Albuquerque.

Davies, E.A. (1950). *An analysis of corrective physical education in schools with implications for teacher education*. Unpublished doctoral dissertation, Teachers College, Columbia University, New York.

DePauw, K. (1979). Nationwide survey of professional preparation in adapted physical education. *California Association for Health, Physical Education, and Recreation Journal/Times, 42*(2), 28.

French, R.W., Jansma, P., & Winnick, J.P. (1978). Preparing undergraduate regular physical educators for mainstreaming. *American Corrective Therapy Journal, 32*, 43-48.

Geddes, D., & Seaman, J.A. (1978). Competencies of adapted physical educators in special education. *IRUC Briefings*. Washington, DC: American Alliance for Health, Physical Education and Recreation.

Hall, G.E., & Jones, H.L. (1976). *Competency-based education: A process for the improvement of education*. Englewood Cliffs, NJ: Prentice-Hall.

Hurley, D. (1981). Guidelines for adapted physical education. *Journal of Physical Education, Recreation and Dance, 52*, 43-44.

McCloy, C.H. (1927). New wine in new bottles. *Journal of Physical Education, 25*, 43-52.

Snyder, R.A., & Scott, H.A. (1954). *Professional preparation in health, physical education, and recreation*. New York: McGraw-Hill.

Stein, J.U. (1969). Professional preparation in physical education and recreation for the mentally retarded. *Education and Training of the Mentally Retarded, 4*, 101-108.

Vodola, T. (1978). *A.C.T.I.V.E. research monograph: Competency-based teacher training and individualized personalized physical activity*. Oakhurst, NJ: Township of Ocean School District.

Chapter 21

Teaching the Introductory Adapted Physical Education Course

Paul Jansma

*T*he introductory course in adapted physical education has now come of age and has almost universally been embraced in the United States as an integral component of professional preparation in departments of physical education.[1] As a result, most physical education professional preparation programs among the 3,200 colleges and universities across the country offer an introductory adapted physical education course taught by instructors of varying orientation and competence. This course is also attended by a variety of students affected, in part, by State Board of Education mandates.

This chapter focuses on essential factors related to the teaching of the introductory adapted physical education course. Such factors include an analysis of course enrollees (the consumers), approaches to selecting course content, grading, practicum experiences, course methodology, course materials, and attitude formation and change. As a synthesis of these factors, two introductory adapted physical education course models are presented. These models have been field tested, one in Ohio and one in Texas.

Course Enrollees

The most typical enrollee in an introductory adapted physical education course is the undergraduate regular physical education major who needs attitudes, knowledge, and skills with which to provide appropriate mainstreamed physical education programs. Other physical education major enrollees might also attend the class as part of the core requirements for an undergraduate concentration in adapted physical education or for a graduate level specialization in adapted physical education. A number of undergraduate and graduate level nonphysical education majors might also be in attendance because adapted physical education is related to their professional endeavors. Such students might be majoring in such related fields as special education, recreation, dance, early childhood education, elementary education, or allied medicine.

Selecting Course Content

The scope of the introductory adapted physical education course content should entail a survey approach to teaching physical education to high incidence handicapped pupils. High incidence handicaps or categories include those types of handicaps that a person teaching regular physical education will probably see in pupils. Mentally retarded, learning disabled, orthopedically handicapped,

and emotionally disturbed are the primary categories of high incidence handicap most relevant to the teaching of physical education. Examples of low incidence handicapping conditions include the visually impaired, deaf and hard of hearing, deaf-blind, multihandicapped, and other health impaired.

As critical as a high incidence categorical approach, a noncategorical, nonlabeling, or generic theme to the teaching of physical education to all types of pupils is appropriate in the course because the same physical education objectives essentially exist for both handicapped and nonhandicapped pupils. This eliminates the overemphasis on labeling pupils (e.g., mentally retarded) and instead places the course training focus on such areas as testing, assessing, prescribing, instructing, evaluating, following up, using team approaches, and individualizing educational programs. A noncategorical orientation further entails a developmental approach to teaching whereby all pupils are viewed as being placed on the same psychomotor developmental continua. Some pupils just happen to be further down these developmental ladders in comparison to other pupils of the same chronological age.

This commitment to a noncategorical theme also transcends the psychomotor domain. Behavior management issues should be addressed in the introductory course because discipline is the Number 1 problem among teachers, especially new ones. Behaviors must be managed before one can teach, and the best physical educators are the best behavior managers. Some believe that all behavior management training should take place in special education and psychology courses. On the contrary, behaviors in unstructured movement settings (gymnasium, pool, and playground) with a stretched teacher/pupil ratio need to be addressed in the physical education curriculum, too. Last, beyond the essential modules of instruction discussed above, a few topics may also be introduced at purely an awareness level such as laws, historical trends, organization and administration of adapted physical education programs, and extracurricular activities for handicapped students.

In summary, when selecting course content for the introductory adapted physical education course, the following components and subcomponents should be considered:

Categorical
  Mentally retarded
  Learning disabled
  Orthopedically handicapped
  Emotionally disturbed
Noncategorical
  Behavior management
  Testing (gather data)

---

[1]The author prefers the term *special physical education* but is using *adapted physical education* to maintain consistent terminology within the text.

Assessing (analyze data)

Prescribing

Instructing developmentally

Evaluating

Follow-up

Team approaches

Individualizing education programs

Laws and historical trends

Organization and administration

Extracurricular activities

In practice, instructors of the introductory adapted physical education course will always vary relative to the selection of content for their courses. This is a function of their orientation, training, and direct experiences. Rarely is a course presented strictly from only a categorical or noncategorical perspective. The large majority of courses taught involve both approaches, that is, a combined approach. Only the percentages of emphasis vary. Examples of courses employing a combined approach are contained in the two models presented later in the chapter. Additionally, the major textbooks currently used in introductory adapted physical education courses are analyzed with respect to their categorical and/or noncategorical nature.

A Competency-Based Approach to Grading

Specific teaching competencies should be addressed and graded in this introductory course. Bundschuh (1976) suggests that competencies for future teachers of physical education in a mainstreamed setting should include those related to foundations, specific impairments, and program development. French, Jansma, and Winnick (1978) have gathered data that suggest that those competencies that relate to direct benefits for pupils are the most crucial to develop. A few specific examples of these include the following:

- An understanding of and ability to apply sound first aid and safety procedures in the conduct of physical education activities for special pupils

- An understanding of the effect of physical activities on the physical, social, emotional, and intellectual development of pupils with special needs

- An understanding of normal and abnormal growth and development

- An ability to modify traditional physical education activities for pupils with special needs

- An ability to use numerous motivating and reinforcing techniques to obtain changes in behavior of special pupils

- A knowledge of appropriate facilities and equipment utilized in adapted physical education

Most recently, Hurley (1981) has summarized the competency guidelines suggested for physical education generalists and adapted physical education specialists as determined by the American Alliance for Health, Physical Education, Recreation and Dance. The 59 generalist competencies fall under the headings Biological Foundations; Sociological Foundations; Psychological Foundations; Historical-Philosophical Foundations; Assessment and Evaluation; and Curriculum Planning, Organization, and Implementation.

But can all of these suggested competencies be developed in one survey course? Even development of all regular physical educator mainstreaming competencies cannot occur in one introductory survey course. Such competency development should also occur and be reinforced through their infusion into other undergraduate and graduate physical education courses. For example, the tests and measurements course should include some coverage of psychomotor tests for pupils with special needs. This training should, however, be spearheaded by the introductory course in adapted physical education.

Practicum Experiences

The scope of the introductory course should include a required field experience or practicum because the application of knowledge is critical to an understanding of theory. Hands-on experiences not only have the potential to reinforce theory but can improve teaching skills and positively affect attitudes of future teachers toward handicapped students. Such a practical experience could ideally include both one-to-one and group instruction in a segregated and mainstreamed setting.

A theoretical base for the importance of practical experiences for all those preparing to teach handicapped students has been well established (Heward & Orlansky, 1984). As a reflection of this importance in the field of physical education specifically, the American Alliance for Health, Physical Education, Recreation and Dance has outlined a series of adapted physical education practicum-oriented competencies that physical education generalists and adapted physical education specialists are urged to acquire via preservice or in-service experiences (Hurley, 1981). Physical education state certification requirements are also beginning to recognize the critical importance of precontract practical experiences with handicapped pupils. For example, in California, varied practicum experiences are required of any potential adapted physical education teacher. California state certification in adapted physical education is awarded only upon evidence of satisfactory completion of this requirement.

Course Methodology

The introductory adapted physical education course may be characterized by any or possibly all of the following: lecture, discussion, audiovisual aids, role playing, homework assignments, reading of texts and articles, guest lectures (including presenters with handicapping conditions), simulation of handicaps, student presentations, and observation of mainstreamed and segregated physical education programs in the field.

Of singular importance is one or more hands-on practical experiences in connection with the introductory course. These experiences could involve only a social element or both a physical education and social thrust.

Paul Jansma, Ohio State University, who is coauthor (with Ron French) of *Special Physical Education.*

At the Ohio State University, the author teaches an introductory adapted physical education course to a class consisting of mainly nonphysical education majors. The specific methods that are used to address this introductory course's scope are varied. In attempting to most adequately serve the students, a 5-credit sequence is offered. A 2-credit practicum (10 weeks) is offered the quarter immediately after a 3-credit lecture/discussion class (10 weeks) has been completed. This system permits all enrollees to amalgamate the information over a longer period of time so as to better prepare them for their hands-on experience. This experience, in turn, helps to lessen their commonly felt apprehensions about teaching a nonmajor subject and about working with a child who might look, move, and act differently from the norm. Using this 5-credit system, observations of practicums in action might be scheduled, if possible, during the 3-credit course. The course outline for the lecture portion is contained in one of the models offered at the end of the chapter.

The practicum experience offered in connection with this course is provided on Thursday nights. This developmental laboratory incorporates a combination of gymnasium and aquatics instruction. Both one-to-one teaching and group activities are offered. There is also a culminating experience in the form of a "mini-Olympics" with parent participation in the gymnasium and pool. Furthermore, course enrollees each write weekly lesson plans, a case study, and the physical education part of each child's individualized educational plan (IEP) for use by the next practicum teacher or by local school district personnel.

Practicum children with a variety of handicapping conditions are signed up on a quarterly basis at no cost to the parents. A waiting list is typically the case because the clients are recruited from a large urban setting (Columbus, the state capital) and because a combination of adapted physical education laboratories at the university has gained a certain reputation for service over the last 20 to 30 years.

Course Materials

Students in the introductory adapted physical education course must have access to appropriate permanent products that they can use during and after course completion. Textbooks, articles, reference lists, and varied handouts are included here.

The primary course material is the required textbook. Almost 30 different adapted physical education-related texts have been published with a copyright date of 1975 or later. A selected listing of those that appear appropriate for the introductory course follows. They are grouped according to whether they seem to be basically categorical, noncategorical (generic), or combined in content.

Categorical

Adams, R.C., Daniel, A.N., McCubbin, J.A., & Rullman, L. (1982). *Games, sports and exercises for the physically handicapped* (3rd ed.). Philadelphia: Lea & Febiger.

Arnheim, D.D., & Sinclair, W.A. (1975). *The clumsy child* (2nd ed.). St. Louis: C.V. Mosby.

Buell, C.E. (1983). *Physical education for blind children* (2nd ed.). Springfield, IL: Charles C. Thomas.

Colvin, N.R., & Finholt, J.M. (1981). *Guidelines for physical educators of mentally handicapped youth: Curriculum, assessment, IEPs*. Springfield, IL: Charles C. Thomas.

Geddes, D. (1978). *Physical activities for individuals with handicapping conditions* (2nd ed.). St. Louis: C.V. Mosby.

Geddes, D. (1981). *Psychomotor individualized education programs for intellectual, learning, and behavioral disabilities*. Boston: Allyn and Bacon.

Moran, J.M., & Kalakian, L.H. (1977). *Movement experiences for the retarded or emotionally disturbed child* (2nd ed.). Minneapolis, MN: Burgess.

Noncategorical (generic)

Cratty, B.J. (1975). *Remedial motor activity for children*. Philadelphia: Lea & Febiger.

Masters, L.F., Mori, A.A., & Lange, E.K. (1983). *Adapted physical education: A practitioner's guide*. Gaithersburg, MD: Aspen Systems Corporation.

Miller, A.G., & Sullivan, J.V. (1982). *Teaching physical activities to impaired youth*. New York: John Wiley & Sons.

Seaman, J., & DePauw, K. (1982). *The new adapted physical education: A developmental approach*. Palo Alto, CA: Mayfield.

Combined

Arnheim, D.D., & Sinclair, W.A. (1985). *Physical education for special populations: A developmental, adapted, and remedial approach*. Englewood Cliffs, NJ: Prentice-Hall.

Auxter, D., & Pyfer, J. (1985). *Principles and methods of adapted physical education and recreation* (5th ed.). St. Louis: C.V. Mosby.

Clarke, H.H., & Clarke, D.H. (1978). *Developmental and adapted physical education* (2nd ed.). Englewood Cliffs, NJ: Prentice-Hall.

Cratty, B.J. (1980). *Adapted physical education for children and youth*. Denver: Love.

Daniels, A.S., & Davies, E.A. (1975). *Adapted physical education* (3rd ed.). New York: Harper and Row.

Eichstaedt, C.B., & Kalakian, L.H. (1987). *Developmental/adapted physical education: Making ability count* (3rd ed.). Minneapolis, MN: Burgess.

Fait, H.F., & Dunn, J.M. (1982). *Special physical education: Adapted, corrective, developmental* (5th ed.). Philadelphia: W.B. Saunders.

French, R.W., & Jansma, P. (1982). *Special physical education*. Columbus, OH: Charles E. Merrill.

Sherrill, C. (1986). *Adapted physical education and recreation: A multidisciplinary approach* (3rd ed.). Dubuque, IA: William C. Brown.

Vannier, M. (1977). *Physical activities for the handicapped*. Englewood Cliffs, NJ: Prentice-Hall.

Wheeler, R.H., & Hooley, A.M. (1976). *Physical education for the handicapped* (2nd ed.). Philadelphia: Lea & Febiger.

Winnick, J.P. (1979). *Early movement experiences and development: Habilitation and remediation*. Philadelphia: W.B. Saunders.

Wiseman, D.C. (1982). *A practical approach to adapted physical education*. Reading, MA: Addison-Wesley.

Attitude Formation

A problem in adapted physical education is the formation and maintenance of appropriate attitudes toward handicapped students by preservice trainees. This attitude development is especially important for regular physical education undergraduate majors. Some information on strategies to influence preservice teacher attitudes toward the handicapped might therefore be extremely beneficial. Numerous strategies do exist for potential use in the introductory adapted physical education course.

Perhaps the most significant experience that a preservice student can have to influence attitudes is direct contact with handicapped persons. This contact would naturally occur in a structured practicum provided as part of an introductory adapted physical education course. Careful attention therefore has to be paid to all practicum details. Such details include what match up will be made (course enrollee and handicapped student) and the timing of the practicum. Regarding match ups, perhaps an autobiography from the course enrollee or direct conversation with him or her will yield helpful information with regard to a preferred handicapped student's sex, age, and handicapping condition. Relative to practicum timing, perhaps a formal teaching experience could be planned after the didactic adapted physical education experience is completed. This experience is similar in nature to the regular student teaching experience at the undergraduate level, whereby elementary and secondary methods courses are completed prior to registering for formal student teaching. An adapted physical education practicum given after the lecture classes may serve as a more effective attitude formation enabler. This idea is rarely used, however, in the teaching of the introductory adapted physical education course. At present most practicums are offered concurrent with introductory course lectures.

A series of additional secondary attitude-influencing tactics are readily available for use in an introductory adapted physical education course. Speakers who themselves have handicapping conditions can be effectively utilized. The simulation of handicaps can also leave a lasting impression. In a gymnasium, playground, or pool, students can have their eyes or ears covered, limbs can be placed in a temporary splint, students can be required to move in a wheelchair, distractions can be intentionally imposed, and various frustrations can be simulated momentarily. Further, course enrollees can be required to observe individuals with handicapping conditions in a physical education environment or elsewhere. Special readings and audiovisual materials related to attitudes and handicapped people can be assigned to all class members, and several phrases can be memorized and discussed. For example, "label jars, not people"; "labeling is disabling"; "I don't want a second chance, just the first"; and "prejudice is being down on something you're not up on."

Last, the course instructor is an integral component in the attitude formation sphere. An appropriate attitude can be contagious and unfortunately, so can an inappropriate attitude. An increasing positive correlation probably exists between appropriate instructor attitudes and his or her training in adapted physical education coupled with direct adapted physical education teaching experience.

Course Models

To assist in synthesizing this discussion on factors related to teaching the introductory adapted physical education course, two course outline models in current use are presented here. It is not intended that either would be used verbatim by another instructor because situations are different from institution to institution.

An Ohio State University Alternative Model

Introductory Special Physical Education Course
P.E. 662E
1st Term Summer Quarter
Tues & Thurs 9–11:30 a.m.
Larkins 120

TEXT: French, R., & Jansma, P. (1982). *Special Physical Education*. Columbus, OH: Charles E. Merrill.

I.   Course Description—Analysis of historical trends, evolving definitions and current resource information on physical education for the handicapped. Survey of individuals with disabilities, their related needs, and adjustment problems. Stress upon day-to-day programming in physical education for the handicapped and relationships to diagnosis/prescription, the educational team, behavior management, teaching methodology, organization/administration, and extracurricular activities. P.E. 662E is the prerequisite for P.E. 631, Special Physical Education Practicum (Fall Quarter).

II. Course Objectives

A. To understand basic concepts related to physical education for the handicapped (historical trends, legislation, definitions, current resources).

B. To understand handicapping diseases/conditions and their relationship to physical and motor performance.

C. To understand the limitations, abilities, and needs of disabled and nondisabled pupils.

D. To develop a rudimentary understanding of diagnostic/prescriptive techniques to be incorporated in individualized education programs (IEPs).

E. To understand the role of physical education for the handicapped and the roles of the special physical educator as a member of the total educational team.

F. To understand behavior management techniques.

G. To understand the foundation for teaching methods particularly relevant to physical education for the handicapped.

H. To understand various organizational and administrative tactics in elementary and secondary school special physical education programs.

I. To understand extracurricular offerings for special populations.

III. Course Modules—Noncategorical

A. Basic needs, adjustment problems, and nature of the handicapped (pp. 10–12, pp. 33–37)

B. Historical perspectives, roles, laws (ch. 1 & 2; pp. 46–49; ch. 15)

C. Behavior management (pp. 180–183)

D. Testing (ch. 16)

E. Teaching using the developmental approach (pp. 37–42)

F. General techniques (pp. 42–55)

G. Organization & administration (ch.18)

H. Extracurricular activities for special populations (ch. 17)

Course Modules—Categorical

A. Emotional disabilities (ch. 8)

B. Mental retardation (ch. 7)

C. Learning disabilities (ch. 9)

D. Physical—Organic—Sensory disabilities (readings will be assigned), including orthopedic, posture, auditory, visual, cardiac, cerebral palsy, epilepsy, and other topics of class interest if time permits

IV. Methods of Instruction

A. Lecture

B. Audio/visual techniques

C. Small and large group discussion

D. Independent study—readings, discussion

V. Methods of Grading

A. Midterm	30%
B. Final exam (comprehensive)	50%
C. Class participation	20%

NOTES:

1. Attendance at lecture will not be required; however, participation is a factor in grading (see above). In addition, some material in class will not be from the course text and, therefore, class attendance is strongly encouraged.

2. Incompletes will be reluctantly allowed on an individual basis.

Letter/Number Final Grade Conversions:

A	= 94–100	C+	= 76– 78
A–	= 92– 94	C	= 72– 75
B+	= 89– 91	C–	= 69– 71
B	= 82– 88	D+	= 66– 68
B–	= 79– 81	D	= 62– 65
		E	= 61 and below

VI. Academic Dishonesty

Please be assured and forewarned that cheating will not be tolerated in this course. All cases of confirmed or suspected academic dishonesty will be referred to the University's Committee on Academic Misconduct. This action is required by all instructors as outlined in the Faculty Handbook. Regarding the consequences of being found guilty of dishonest academic practice, The Ohio State University Bulletin states that "the student will generally be denied credit for the course and could be subject to suspension or dismissed from the University."

The Texas Woman's University Model

PHED 3623, Introductory Adapted and Developmental Physical Education Course

Course Description: Adapted physical education service delivery in accordance with PL 94-142; characteristics of selected handicapping conditions with implications for physical education; psychomotor assessment and individualized educational programming; adapting mainstream physical education to meet the needs of handicapped students. Three lecture hours a week. Three semester credits.

Text: Sherrill, C. (1986). *Adapted physical education and recreation: A multidisciplinary approach* (3rd ed.). Dubuque, IA: Wm. C. Brown.

Course objectives stated as competencies

1. Can define adapted physical education and discuss five aspects of direct service delivery: (a) assessment; (b) individualized educational programming; (c) developmental teaching; (d) motor, fitness, and leisure counseling; and (e) coordination of services.

2. Can explain the humanistic and legal bases of adapted physical education.

3. Can describe five stages in the historical development of adapted physical education with emphasis on the transition from the medical to the educational model.

4. Can explain normal curve theory and relate it to individual differences in the cognitive, affective, and psychomotor domains.

5. Can name and describe outstanding disabled persons at local, state, and national levels who serve as models in sport, dance, aquatics, and/or enrich leisure use. Can identify factors contributing to their success.

6. Can discuss the psychosocial problems typically experienced by persons with handicapping conditions and clumsiness and suggest solutions for problems.

7. Can list the 11 handicapping conditions defined in PL 94-142 and discuss each in terms of eligibility for adapted physical education placement and services, including appropriate assessment instruments and protocol.

8. Can explain the least restrictive placement continuum and discuss it in terms of teaching styles and various organizational plans for instruction and competition.

9. Can discuss individual differences within the 11 handicapping conditions in terms of self-concept/body image; intelligence; adaptive behaviors; fitness; motor performance; postures; leisure-play behaviors; sociometric status; attitudes toward physical education and physical activity and discuss each in terms of adapting assessment and instruction.

10. Can discuss the 11 handicapping conditions in relation to motor development (normal, abnormal, or delayed).

11. Can identify and discuss sport organizations and special programs for disabled persons; classification systems for competing; and resources for coaching/teaching techniques.

12. Can state the five parts of a written IEP. When given assessment data, can write the psychomotor portion of an IEP, demonstrating beginner teacher competence level.

13. Can identify 16-plus factors that can be manipulated in adapting instruction to learner needs. Can discuss these in relation to specific psychomotor problems.

14. Can explain task analysis and apply it to the teaching of selected skills and activities.

15. Can explain behavior management and apply it to the teaching of selected skills and activities (beginner teacher competency level).

16. Can relate principles of motor development, motor learning, fitness development, and biomechanics to persons with psychomotor problems.

17. Can describe a good adapted physical education program in terms of resources, effectiveness of service delivery, and educational accountability. Can cite examples at the local and state level.

18. Can identify methods and techniques for facilitating social acceptance of low-skilled and/or handicapped students and making mainstreaming work.

Course Units

1. Foundations of adapted physical education: chapters 1, 2, 3, 4.

2. Getting acquainted with disabled and low-skilled persons: Assigned readings of autobiographies, biographies, and articles; guest lecturers who are disabled.

3. Individual differences and adaptation: chapters 4–7; with chapters 17–25 and appendix for reference as needed.

4. Principles of motor development, motor learning, exercise physiology, and biomechanics applied to individual differences in assessment, IEP, and programming: chapters 7–16.

5. Components of good adapted, regular, and combined programs—Making the dream work: Student reports of programs observed and supplementary lecture material.

Course Requirements

1. Read the textbook and master the contents. Give particular attention to the *generic* half of the book, chapters 1–16. Use the *categorical* half, chapters 17–25, as resource material to support observations and practical experiences. Demonstrate mastery by: (a) Passing periodic 25-question quizzes with a score of 20 or better for grade of C, and (b) Passing 100-question multiple choice test with score of 76 or better for grade of C.

2. Go through the Subject Index of the textbook, pp. 589–596, and be able to talk at least 60 seconds on every subject listed. Demonstrate this by periodic oral quizzes in which you randomly draw a topic from the box and speak.

3. Spend at least 2 hours a week recreating and socializing with handicapped persons—just for fun—and for the kind of sensitivity and advocacy training that no course can give. Demonstrate this through oral contributions in class and talks with the instructor.

4. Observe at least three public school adapted physical education programs and two residential school programs (approximately 1/2 day each or longer). Demonstrate this through oral contributions in class and talks with the instructor.

Exams, papers, and quizzes will be graded on the following scale:

Letter grades	100 questions	50 questions	35 questions	25 questions	15 questions
A	93–100	47–50	32–35	23–25	14–15
B	86– 92	43–46	29–31	21–22	12–13
C	76– 85	38–42	26–28	18–20	10–11
D	70– 75	35–37	24–25	15–17	8– 9
F	Below 70	Below 35	Below 24	Below 15	Below 8

Conclusion

An introductory survey course in adapted physical education is an integral aspect of the overall college or university physical education department curriculum. This chapter has provided both background information for such an introductory course and specific ideas about the conduct of such a course with respect to enrollees, course content, grading, practicum experiences, course methodology, materials, and attitude formation. In addition, two course outline models are offered. This is not meant to suggest that all courses should operate similarly because situations are obviously varied across the country. Many of the ideas and concepts presented here are considered, however, to be quite exportable, and they are offered in that light in the interest of handicapped pupils everywhere.

References

Bundschuh, E.L. (1976). Preparation of undergraduate physical education majors for mainstreaming. In the

National Association for Physical Education of College Women (NAPECW) and the National College Physical Education Association for Men (NCPEAM) (Eds.), *Mainstreaming Physical Education: Briefings,* **4**, pp. 46-55, Champaign, IL: Human Kinetics.

French, R.W., Jansma, P., & Winnick, J.P. (1978). Preparing undergraduate regular physical educators for mainstreaming. *American Corrective Therapy Journal,* **32**, 43-48.

Heward, W.L., & Orlansky, M.O. (1984). *Exceptional children* (2nd ed.). Columbus, OH: Charles E. Merrill.

Hurley, D. (1981). Adapted physical education guidelines. *Journal of Physical Education, Recreation, and Dance,* **52**(6), 43-45.

Chapter 22

Practicum Experiences for Reinforcing Theory and Changing Attitudes

Glenn M. Roswal

*T*he preservice preparation of physical education, special education, and adapted physical education students should involve opportunities for expansion of the knowledge base through application of theory. The provision of an appropriate practicum allows the student to accept or reject principles on the basis of hands-on experience with disabled and clumsy individuals. Thus theoretical issues may be directly related to practical applications in the classroom, gymnasium, or agency. The practicum then is used to reinforce classroom theory.

The practicum is also an excellent medium by which to elicit changes in attitude among preservice students. It is apparent that increasing the knowledge base by itself does not affect a change in attitude. Students need to be exposed to a significant experience that causes them to voluntarily seek additional knowledge in deriving solutions to problems. This is consistent with the Significant Experience Model (Hall, 1980).

Research Concerning Practicum Experience

Programs that provide both classroom and practicum experience components have been found to elicit greater changes in student/teacher behavior than programs emphasizing classroom academics. Neumann and Daniel (1980) postulated that learning tasks must be structured to provide a thread between self-theory and curricular develop-

ment. This theory is consistent with literature directly relating the development of self-concept to further academic achievement in students (Berretta, 1970; Epstein, 1973; Fitts, 1972; Jersild, 1969; Johnson, 1962; Sebeson, 1970; Wylie, 1974). Additionally, studies have indicated that self-concept can be improved through physical and motor programs (Fretz & Johnson, 1973; Platzer, 1976; Puretz, 1973; Roswal, Frith, & Dunleavy, 1984; Wright & Cowden, 1986).

Neumann and Daniels (1980), in their Self-Awareness Curriculum Theory, proposed that learning programs must (a) meet the needs and interests of learners, (b) provide interaction between the learner and the environment, and (c) allow internalization of experiences. The learner must be given an active role in the development of curriculum, thus assuring the curriculum has relevance to the learner. This is also stipulated in the Significant Experience Model (Hall, 1980). Johnson proposed that students are best motivated when they are an active part of the learning program (Johnson, 1972; 1978; 1981).

Reynolds, Reynolds, and Mark (1982) reported that programs stressing student involvement with disabled individuals have impact on attitudes toward the disabled. Naor and Milgram (1980) reported that preservice training that provides for contact with a variety of exceptional children in conjunction with traditional classroom lecture/discussion methodology was found to have an advantage over traditional classroom methodology in promoting attitudinal and behavioral changes in preservice students. Yates (1973) used a laboratory/ experiential approach to increase the amount of special education information processed by regular education classroom teachers. The laboratory approach, in contrast to the traditional classroom approach, also increased teacher perception that handicapped students could be successfully integrated into the regular classroom environment.

Organization of the Practicum Program

An effective practicum program enables students to directly relate classroom theory and practical application. Hence, a prerequisite to the practicum should be the presentation of appropriate content and methodology in the classroom. It is the direct relationship between content and application that provides access to the Significant Experience Model (Hall, 1980), that is, the changing of student attitudes through a significant and meaningful experience. Subsequently, the knowledge base is expanded when theories are reinforced in the applied setting.

The practicum may be infused within the course construct or provided as a separate motor laboratory experience.

Glenn Roswal, Jacksonville State University in Alabama.

Two programs are described in this text. The Jacksonville State University Children's Motor Development Program described in this chapter is an example of a program infused into adapted physical education and special education course work. The Trinity University Motor Behavior and Learning Laboratory (see chapter 23) is an example of a separate motor laboratory experience that is conducted as an adjunct to theoretical course work.

Support

The initial steps in the organization of a program determine (a) the attitude of the university toward community/student based programs, (b) the availability of clients, and (c) the needs of university students in conjunction with specific coursework. It is difficult to imagine any university administration being unreceptive to a request to provide quality educational experiences to its students in conjunction with positive publicity in the community.

The first step in structuring the practicum involves soliciting college or university administration support. Traditionally, most institutions of higher education are less than sensitive to the needs of disabled individuals. However, they are quite cognizant of the positive publicity that accompanies community-based programs. In initial steps, it is important that the director proceed carefully, gaining access to each level of administrative hierarchy through the proper channels. Emphasis should be placed upon the positive publicity the program will bring to the university by providing a sound community service. Of course, it is extremely important that, after program commencement, the administration receive positive publicity. Descriptions of the program should appear in local and campus newspapers and on local television and radio.

Additional support can be solicited through letters from parents, school personnel, directors of community agencies, and local and state legislators acknowledging the university in providing needed community services. Such individuals also appreciate a connection with a service-oriented program that benefits the local community.

Although it is ideal to initiate a practicum with a substantial university endowment, it is often best policy to begin by promoting the practicum as a cost-free program for the university. Emphasis should be placed on using existing facilities at times normally not needed for university functions.

Clients

Client availability is critical to the organization of the practicum. Contacts with local schools and agencies should be established. Considerations of transportation must be addressed. It is sometimes difficult for school-based programs to gain access to funds and permission to transport clients to the practicum's site. It may be most feasible to conduct the practicum at the local school site. Of prime importance is matching the university student's educational needs with the client population. The Jacksonville State University program uses different methods of securing clients. For clients with transportation, components of the program are conducted at the University. Other components are held as practica at the local school site or agency. Some programs are held during the school day, and others after school hours when parents are available. Some practica focus on preschool children, others on adults. Some practica are motor development–oriented programs, whereas others stress coaching and sport. By providing flexibility in the program structure, client selection and availability become more manageable.

University Students

The university student is the focal point of the practicum. The program should be designed for the student and with student input. Programs should be structured to provide learning experiences and assignments that facilitate a change in behavior in accordance with the Significant Experience Model (Hall, 1980). Programs should benefit student performance while fostering growth and independence in clients.

The practicum should be organized in conjunction with appropriate classroom activities. Students are recruited by emphasizing the direct relationship between theory and application in an innovative setting. The success of the practicum often depends upon the extent to which this goal is successful. If students perceive that the program is being structured around their needs and interests, their input is solicited and used, and the success of the program is directly affected by their performance, the program will flourish. On the other hand, if the program is perceived as a medium for faculty and university success, student interest will quickly subside.

Securing student volunteers for in-class practica is handled by aggressively recruiting students for course offerings. Attracting students for a separate motor laboratory experience involves (a) determining times of availability for students, (b) determining times of availability for clients, and (c) determining times of facility access. Additionally, the type of practica affects recruiting. The director should advertise the practicum through departments of physical education, recreation, dance, health, special education, psychology, sociology, art, music, drama, nursing, and the like, emphasizing the generic nature of the program in facilitating understanding of growth and development and other areas common to all disciplines.

Recruiting should stress the student-oriented focus of the program. Word will quickly spread from student to student that the practicum is an enjoyable means of developing skills, a way of meeting and working with others of similar interests, a valuable community service, and a viable resource in future employment. Publicity should be general enough to attract all interested persons, but specific enough to allow students the opportunity to recognize the relevance of the program to their own professional and educational goals. The Jacksonville State University program began as a Saturday morning laboratory experience. With student support, it has grown to include 10 courses with associated practica.

Critical to the success of the program is the provision of structured, meaningful learning experiences for students. Students must perceive the program as relevant to their educational needs. The practicum should provide structured learning tasks in a supervised setting. Faculty must always be at hand to explain, demonstrate, and modify both client and student behavior.

Funding

A multitude of sources of funding are available, including federal, state, and local grants, university budgets, and community donations. The Jacksonville State University program receives no funding from the university. Yet the program is financially sound. About half of the budget is supplied through in-kind contributions from community businesses, student contributions, and self-generated funds. Services and goods are often solicited from businesses. This not only meets the short-range goal of providing services to clients and practicum to university students, but also accomplishes the long-range goal of involving the community in the program.

Approximately one half of the Jacksonville program budget is derived from student projects. Students seeking an excellent rating for the course (grade of ''A'') must complete an outside project. One option is to design and construct a piece of instructional or assessment equipment for use in the practicum.

Self-generated funds provide capital for future improvements, equipment, consultants, and the like. Illustrative of these are tuition fees or a student practicum manual. The Children's Motor Development Program at Jacksonville State University is funded through local grants, tuition fees for the summer version of the program, Camp Help, and proceeds from the student practicum manual. The manual (Roswal, Harper, & Roswal, 1985) describes program philosophy and procedures as well as all student learning tasks and the assignments to be submitted at program completion. The manual is required of all students involved in courses with practica.

Facilities

Securing facilities is often the easiest of all tasks associated with establishing a practicum program. Virtually all universities and colleges have facilities adequate for practicum use. By conducting the practicum at times when the facilities are least used, the program often has access to excellent facilities. Facilities to consider are basketball courts, gymnasiums, swimming pools, classrooms, large rooms, rooms with mats, dance studios, outdoor playing fields, weight rooms, gymnastic areas, and so forth.

Practicum Environment

Eleven variables should be considered in shaping the practicum environment. These include (a) a client-centered approach, (b) a nonthreatening environment, (c) labeling, (d) self-concept development, (e) a teaching model, (f) a developmental approach, (g) parents, (h) safety procedures, (i) emergency procedures, (j) a client-student relationship, and (k) student assignments and learning tasks.

Client-Centered Approach

The practicum environment should be client centered, using an enjoyable approach to developing fundamental skills in disabled individuals. Activity environments should be arranged to promote active participation by clients as opposed to passive manipulation by student clinicians. Hence, the clients can become active participants in their own education. Johnson (1972) used this approach in the University of Maryland Children's Health and Developmental Clinic, where clinicians were trained to provide instruction and guidance while clients selected from prescribed activities.

A client-centered approach permits individualization of programs to each client's needs and interests. It stresses curriculum planning by client needs rather than being based on broad stereotypes and labels. Individualized programs are designed after careful evaluation of each client's abilities and potential.

Nonthreatening Environment

A nonthreatening environment, for both students and clients, promotes maximum use and enjoyment of the activity milieu. Achievement is promoted but never at the expense of success. Clients and students are made to feel they want to achieve rather than they must achieve. Failure, often contrived, does occur, but is used as a medium for promoting further success. Many young clients equate a failing experience with overall failure. University students are asked to help modify such beliefs.

Activities that involve direct competition should be selectively employed. Emphasis should be placed upon self-testing activities that challenge clients but do not make them losers. Games that result in winners and losers can be little fun, particularly for the losers. Activities should be structured to take advantage of the activity environment without creating unnecessary failure.

Labeling

The use of a noncategorical approach as opposed to traditional educational and medical labeling is recommended. Students should be trained to view clients as people and to structure individualized programs to foster development regardless of a label. Client applications and case histories should not contain information regarding general labels. Labeling adds little to the knowledge of the client's abilities, promotes education by disability, hides individuals behind labels, and predetermines behavior.

Self-Concept Development

The primary focus of any practicum should be the encouragement of a positive self-concept of both students and clients. Self-concept may be described as the way individuals perceive their environment in relation to (a) the way they feel about themselves and (b) the way they think others feel about them. Learning activities should be structured to promote self-concept development through affective skills. In many disabled clients, self-concept is perceived largely in terms of movement abilities. Individuals who move well often exhibit higher self-concepts than those with movement handicaps. Hence, activities should be aimed at improving self-concept by increasing confidence in a broad base of motor activities.

Self-concept improvement is promoted through program activities developed on the principles of *success, fun,* and *safety*. Success is the element that encourages progression to the next developmental stage. Each experience should be challenging yet allow for an element of success, no matter how small. Most individuals functioning at low skill levels have experienced considerable failure in previous tasks. The phenomenon results in a "failure syndrome." Previous failures frequently yield a negative self-concept. Low self-concept can result in additional failure. Overcoming the failure syndrome requires successful experiences over time. The greater the negative self-concept, the greater the number of successful experiences required. Once freed from the failure syndrome bond, clients should be able to improve risk-taking behavior (that is, the willingness to attempt new tasks without an overbearing fear of failure). This pattern encourages the development of a new cycle that promotes a more positive self-concept. Positive self-concept and risk-taking behaviors are essential prerequisites for learning new tasks.

Fun facilitates motivation. If activities are not fun, why should the client participate? Physical activities should always contain an element of fun. No rationale exists for prescribing monotonous calisthenics when creative self-testing activities are comprised of similar skills. Fun is

undoubtedly a crucial element in motivating individuals toward task completion.

Safety allows participation without fear of injury. Clients who must negotiate a difficult environment are not free to enjoy prescribed activities. All activities should provide an element of challenge and risk. However, risks should be controlled by the student and not dictated by the environment.

Teaching Model

A systematic teaching model should form the basis of the practicum. The Achievement Based Curriculum (Sherrill, 1986; Wessel & Kelly, 1984) is appropriate for use in conjunction with the practicum. The Achievement Based Curriculum Model (see Figure 8.4 in chapter 8) emphasizes program planning, diagnosis by assessment, prescription based upon assessment, instruction of prescribed activities, counseling integrated with teaching, evaluation of program activities and goals, and modification based upon evaluation.

Developmental Approach

In a traditional, categorical approach, analysis of potential is predicated on assumptions made regarding specific handicapping conditions. Discrete activities are then prescribed based on the particular handicapping condition. In the developmental approach, prescription is based on the developmental level of the individual, as determined by educational diagnosis rather than handicapping condition. Developmental sequences are held constant for all individuals; only the rate and inherent potential differ. Once generalized developmental sequences are learned, this approach allows students to assess the level of functioning of the client and prescribe appropriate activities. Students focus on the clients and their abilities rather than on disabilities associated with handicapping conditions. The developmental approach is recommended for use in practicum settings.

Parents

It is sound policy to invite parents to participate in the progress of their children to the maximum extent possible. Students should be encouraged to meet parents and discuss successful experiences and situations. Discussion should be of a positive nature, emphasizing abilities and capabilities rather than disabilities and limitations. Students should be asked not to talk to parents about clients while the client is present.

Safety Procedures

Motor phases of the practicum should be conducted in one-to-one or small group interaction. The individualized approach allows relaxation of many traditional safety procedures, but students should be instructed to follow two rules:

- Students must stay close enough to their assigned client to touch him or her at all times. This is particularly true for the swimming pool area.

- Common sense should prevail in prescribing activities safely. The decision regarding the safety of any activity for a particular client is the responsibility of each student.

Emergency Procedures

Students should be instructed in basic emergency techniques. Training may include CPR, first aid, and seizure procedures. In the event of an injury or illness, students should be instructed to

- remain calm;

- speak softly and reassure the client;

- have another student call for the director; and

- not leave a client unattended.

Staff of the university infirmary or hospital should be aware of the practicum and be on call in case of emergency.

Client-Student Relationship

Beginning students should be assigned only one or two clients. Some experienced students may work with small groups. Students should be responsible for (a) establishing a constructive relationship with the client(s) assigned to them, (b) assessing interests, skills, and abilities, (c) prescribing sequential activities, and (d) providing evaluative feedback. A fundamental concern of students should be to facilitate independence in the clients. The students ensure success, fun, and safety in all activities. They make mistakes and failures part of the fun of playing. They show the clients that to fail does not make a person a failure. Students help bring others into the fun, while always focusing attention on their particular clients, ensuring they are special.

Student Assignments and Learning Tasks

Student learning tasks should be carefully planned, sequential, and clearly identified. At Jacksonville State University, all students in adapted physical education purchase the *Children's Motor Development Programs and Camp HELP: Practicum Guidelines and Procedures Manual* (Roswal, Harper, & Roswal, 1985). The manual clearly stipulates the purpose, philosophy, and format of the program as well as all student responsibilities. The

manual contains learning tasks, resource information, and all forms that must be completed for credit in the practicum (see Appendices A through F at the end of this chapter).

Evaluation and Grading

The practicum should be a nongraded learning experience. The student should be evaluated on a pass-fail performance scale. The pass-fail criteria should be based upon completion of structured learning tasks and assignments. Assigning a letter grade to practicum performance violates the concept of the nonthreatening environment. Student motivation becomes extrinsic to the evaluation rather than intrinsic to the relation of theory and application. Student achievement is perceived in terms of letter grade requirements.

Additionally, the practicum should be structured as a student practice experience. Students should be given the freedom to attempt new skills and procedures. They should be allowed the freedom to fail in their experiences, reevaluate their performance, and try again without the pressure of external grading. Providing the student with the opportunity to fail without a fear of failure will promote greater motivation and experimentation and hence a greater possibility of achievement.

Program evaluation may be accomplished through parent and student feedback (Appendices H and I at the end of this chapter), systematic research of program effects, and student behavior changes and client achievement (Roswal, 1980; Roswal & Frith, 1983; Roswal, Frith, & Dunleavy, 1984; Roswal & Harper, 1985).

An Illustrative Practicum Program

The Children's Motor Development Program (CMDP) and the summer version, Camp HELP, at Jacksonville State University, are an extension of an earlier model initiated at the University of Maryland (Johnson, 1972). The CMDP and Camp HELP are designed to provide experiential learning opportunities for university students by offering experiences in educational, social, behavioral, and motor environments. The program provides opportunities for (a) experiences for student clinicians in dance, physical education, recreation, special education, and related areas; (b) research with preschool, elementary school age, and special children; (c) supplemental programming for local education agencies; (d) increased parental participation in the children's educational endeavors; (e) improvement in the psychosocial and psychomotor behaviors of children; and (f) volunteer work by citizens of the community. The program provides a direct community service to persons and agencies involved with the care and education of preschool, elementary school age, and disabled children.

The Children's Motor Development Program (CMDP)

The fall and spring CMDP are conducted as the practicum phase of courses in physical education, special education, motor development, and dance. Programs included are the (a) Nursery School Program, (b) Wellborn Special Education Program, (c) Cerebral Palsy Center Program, (d) Cerebral Palsy Center Satellite Program, (e) Parents and Children Together (PACT) Program, (f) Kitty Stone Elementary School Program, and (g) Sports for Disabled Coaching Practicum. The programs consist of in-course orientation and training and a series of client-student practicum sessions. All client-student assignments are on a small group or one-to-one basis. Clinicians may use the motor lab, swimming pool, and physical education Coliseum facilities. Students participating in the Kitty Stone Elementary School or Cerebral Palsy Center Satellite Programs use the facilities at those sites. The director and supervising teachers are always available for supervision and assistance. Class sessions are reserved to discuss program problems and occurrences.

The **Nursery School Program** is held at the physical education complex 1 hour a week over a 10-week period. Students work with preschool children in a one-to-one relationship. The program is conducted during regularly scheduled class time.

The **Wellborn Special Education Program** is held at the physical education complex 1 hour a week for 10 weeks. Clients are moderately handicapped students from the special education program at Wellborn High School. Students work with clients in a one-to-one relationship as a part of the regularly scheduled class time.

The **Cerebral Palsy Center Program** is conducted 1 hour a week for 10 weeks with preschool multihandicapped children. Students work with children in a one-to-one relationship at the physical education complex during the regularly scheduled class time. The **Cerebral Palsy Center Satellite Program** is conducted at the Cerebral Palsy Center.

The **Parents and Children Together (PACT) Program** provides graduate students with experiential learning opportunities with preschool children and their parents. Students direct developmental activities for parents, who actively assist in the activities with their children. Parents also receive supplemental parenting information in special sessions. The program is conducted at the physical education complex, 1 hour a week for 8 weeks, during regularly scheduled evening class time.

Students work with small groups of parents and their children.

The **Kitty Stone Elementary School Program**, in addition to serving as a practicum for JSU students, is designed to provide quality physical education instruction to kindergarten through sixth-grade students in a reduced teacher-student ratio. Students schedule 1 hour a week outside of class time. Each student works with eight elementary school children in regular physical education or in a one-to-one relationship in adapted physical education.

The **Sports for Disabled Coaching Program** is conducted at the physical education complex as a part of regularly scheduled class time in a course designed for training and competition for disabled individuals. Each student works in a one-to-one coaching relationship with a disabled individual. The practicum involves training, simulated competition, and interscholastic competition. The practicum culminates in state level athletic competition.

Camp HELP

Camp HELP is conducted daily during summer session I (June–July) in conjunction with several courses in special physical education and special education. The program consists of a 1-week orientation and 3 weeks of child-clinician interaction. Camp HELP meets daily (Monday–Friday), 8:30 a.m. to 12:00 p.m. Child-clinician assignments are based on clinician gender, major field of study, and stated preferences. Assignments are on a one-to-one and small group (one or two children) basis. Participants are typically 50 to 60 handicapped and nonhandicapped children, 3 to 15 years of age, referred to Camp HELP through physicians, local school systems, and child-based agencies. Children range from gifted to severely handicapped.

Clinicians work in Camp HELP on either a full-time or a part-time basis. Full-time clinicians are community volunteers or students enrolled in special physical education or special education courses. They are required to work daily in all program phases. Part-time clinicians work only in selected program phases depending upon the time of attendance.

At selected periods through the program, special events are conducted. These include trips to the museum, a picnic trip, and fishing and canoeing trips. Special events are generally held on Fridays.

All facilities and equipment used during the regular CMDP are available during the Camp HELP program. Supervising teachers are always available for assistance. At scheduled times a physical therapist is also on site. In-service sessions are scheduled prior to Camp HELP and daily at 8:30 a.m. and 12:00 to 1:00 p.m. during Camp operation.

Practicum Student Responsibilities

Students participating in the CMPD and the Camp HELP program are expected to complete a series of structured practicum learning tasks. The student clinician's responsibilities for each practicum program are identified in the practicum manual (Roswal, Harper, & Roswal, 1985). Illustrative responsibilities follow.

- Report to class on time to meet the assigned child.

- Remain the entire period to work with the assigned child.

- Obtain a copy of the CMDP/Camp HELP Manual (Roswal, Harper, & Roswal, 1985) and become familiar with all procedures and requirements.

- Report to class in dress that allows freedom to move without constraint. Wearing jewelry, watches, and so forth is not recommended. Swimming suits and towels should also be available.

- Prepare the case history (Appendix 22A)[1] of the assigned child.

- Assess the child using (a) the Language Check List, (b) the Behavioral Rating Scale, (c) the Bruininks-Oseretsky Test of Motor Proficiency or Motor Skills Evaluation (or the Davis and Texas Revisions of Basic Skills Evaluation), (d) I CAN or the OSU SIGMA, (e) the Dynamic Balance Test or Fitness Battery, (f) the Sequence of Swimming Skills, and (g) the Martinek-Zaichkowsky Self-Concept Scale for Children (see Appendix 22B for references).

- Prepare an individualized program (Appendix 22C) addressing each motor unit (locomotor, manipulative, balance, fitness, aquatics, dance) for at least one session.

- Prepare a lesson plan (Appendix 22D) for each program session.

- Complete the daily log sheets (Appendix 22E).

- Complete the summary sheet (Appendix 22F).

- Attend the weekly sessions regularly, and meet the attendance requirements of the specific course practicum.

- Inform supervisor if not able to attend a session.

- Serve as a resource clinician if the assigned child is absent.

- Clean up and set up motor lab.

---

[1]Appendix 22A to 22I are located at the end of this chapter.

Summary

The practicum is a beneficial component to the adapted physical education preservice program. Programs involving college and university students provide positive public relations for both the adapted program and the institution. In many areas, such service-oriented programs cast the university in a benevolent role. The practicum also brings publicity to the program itself, allowing it to often stand above other programs that are entirely academic in nature. The practicum, designed and conducted with student input, provides students with meaningful experiences that assist in reinforcing classroom theory and shaping attitudes toward disabled individuals.

References

Berretta, S. (1970). Self-concept development in the reading program. *Reading Teacher, 24*, 232-238.

Brigance, A. (1978). *Brigance Diagnostic Inventory.* North Billerica, MA: Curriculum Associates.

Bruininks, R.H. (1978). *Bruininks-Oseretsky Test of Motor Proficiency.* Circle Pines, MN: American Guidance Service.

Davis, W. (1981). *Special physical education program handbook.* Champaign, IL: University of Illinois Press.

Dunn, J.M., Morehouse, J.W., & Fredericks, H.D. (1985). *Physical education for the severely handicapped: A systematic approach to a data based gymnasium* (2nd ed.). Austin, TX: Pro. Ed Publishing.

Epstein, S. (1973). The self-concept revisited. *American Psychologist, 28*(5), 404-416.

Fitts, W.H. (1972). *The self-concept and performance. Dede Wallace Center Research Monograph No. 5.* Nashville, TN: Counselor Recordings and Tests.

Fretz, B.R., & Johnson, W.R. (1973). Behavioral changes in children participating in a physical developmental clinic. *Perceptual and Motor Skills, 36*, 855-862.

Hall, J. (1980). A working model for curricular modification: Infuse. In D.P. Mood (Ed.), *Infuse workshop proceedings* (pp. 1-9). Boulder: University of Colorado.

Jersild, A.T. (1969). *In search of self.* New York: Columbia University, Teachers College Press.

Johnson, W.R. (1962). *Some psychological aspects of physical rehabilitation: Toward an organismic theory.* Paper presented at the Tri-Scientific and Clinical Conference, Buffalo.

Johnson, W.R. (1972). A humanistic dimension of physical education. *Journal of Health, Physical Education, and Recreation, 43*, 31-35.

Johnson, W.R. (1978). The resort model. *Journal of Health, Physical Education, and Recreation, 49*, 42.

Johnson, W.R. (1981). Parent education in clinical physical education and recreation. *Journal of Physical Education, Recreation, & Dance, 52*, 34-36.

Loovis, E.M., & Ersing, W.F. (1979). *Assessing and programming gross motor development for children*. Cleveland Heights, OH: Ohio Motor Assessment Associates.

Martinek, T.J., & Zaichkowsky, L.D. (1977). *The Martinek-Zaichkowsky self-concept scale for children*. Jacksonville, IL: Psychologists and Educators.

Naor, M., & Milgram, R.M. (1980). Two preservice strategies for preparing regular class teachers for mainstreaming. *Exceptional Children, 47*, 126-129.

Ness, R. (1974). *The standardization of the basic movement performance profile for profoundly retarded institutionalized residents*. Unpublished doctoral dissertation, North Texas State University, Denton.

Neumann, M.E., & Daniel, C. (1980). *The self-awareness curriculum theory*. (Available from C. Daniel, Department of Physical Education, Western Kentucky University, Bowling Green, KY)

Platzer, W.S. (1976). Effect of perceptual motor training on gross motor skill and self-concept of young children. *American Journal of Occupational Therapy, 30*, 422-428.

Puretz, S.L. (1973). *A comparison on the effects of dance and physical education on the self-concept of selected disadvantaged girls*. Unpublished doctoral dissertation, New York University, New York.

Reynolds, B.J., Reynolds, J.M., & Mark, F.D. (1982). Elementary teachers' attitudes toward mainstreaming-EMR students. *Education and Training of the Mentally Retarded, 17*, 171-176.

Roswal, G.M. (1980). *The effects of a children's program on the social-emotional behaviors of mildly and moderately handicapped children*. (Available from G. Roswal, Department of HPERD, Jacksonville State University, Jacksonville, AL)

Roswal, G.M., FLoyd, R., Jessup, G.P., Pass, A.L., & Hanson, G. (1985). *Special Olympics Sports Skills Battery*. Montgomery, AL: Alabama Special Olympics.

Roswal, G.M., Floyd, R., Roswal, P.M., Jessup, G.P., Pass, A.L., Klecka, L.A., Montelione, T., Vaccaro, P., & Dunleavy, A.O. (1985). *Alabama Special Olympics Fitness Battery*. Montgomery, AL: Alabama Special Olympics.

Roswal, G.M., & Frith, G.H. (1983). The effect of a developmental play program on the motor proficiency of mildly handicapped children. *American Corrective Therapy Journal, 37*, 105-108.

Roswal, G.M., Frith, G.H., & Dunleavy, A.O. (1984). The effect of a developmental play program on the self-concept, risk-taking behaviors, and motoric proficiency of mildly handicapped children. *The Physical Educator, 41*, 43-50.

Roswal, G.M., Harper, C.H., & Roswal, P.M. (1985). *Children's motor development programs and Camp HELP: Practicum guidelines and procedures manual*. Jacksonville, AL: Jacksonville State University.

Roswal, G.M., & Jacobs, D. (1984). *Kitty Stone Elementary School Fitness Battery*. (Available from D. Jacobs, Department of Physical Education, University of Alabama, University, AL)

Sebeson, L. (1970). Self-concept and reading disabilities. *Reading Teacher, 23*, 460-463.

Sherrill, C. (1986). *Adapted physical education and recreation: A multidisciplinary approach* (3rd ed.). Dubuque, IA: William C. Brown.

Wessel, J.A. (1976). *I CAN*. Northbrook, IL: Hubbard Scientific.

Wessel, J.A., & Kelly, L. (1984). *Achievement based curriculum model*. East Lansing, MI: Michigan State University.

Wright, J., & Cowden, J.E. (1986). Changes in self-concept and cardiovascular endurance of mentally retarded youth in a Special Olympics swimming program. *Adapted Physical Activity Quarterly, 3*(2), 177-183.

Wylie, R.C. (1974). *The self-concept: A review of methodological considerations and measuring instruments*. Lincoln, NE: University of Nebraska Press.

Yates, J.R. (1973). Model for preparing regular classroom teachers for mainstreaming. *Exceptional Children, 39*, 471-472.

Acknowledgment

Appreciation is extended to Benjie L. Duvall and Lynn A. Klecka in the preparation of this chapter.

Appendix 22A
Case History

Child's Name _____

Sex _____Male_____ Age _____9_____

Name Child Prefers _____Jamie_____

Emergency Telephone _____555-1142_____

Medical Information

Seizures: _____ yes ___x___ no

Other: Jamie has *no* history of frequent high temperatures, headaches, colds, allergies, skin problems, other infections, diabetes, heart problems, or missing limbs. However, he is extremely nearsighted and at present he wears soft contact lenses to correct his vision.

Medication:

None

Physical and Motor Development

No information was supplied concerning this area on the child's application form.

Social and Emotional Development

Behavior: In a classroom or school setting, teachers have had difficulty in persuading Jamie to "participate in organized games."

Personality: At home, Jamie is described as being "generally cooperative and happy." However, at school, he is "often deviant" in that he refuses to complete his assigned work, and will not participate in games.

Educational Development

No information was supplied concerning this area on the child's application form.

Self-Help Skills

Jamie has difficulty in the self-help skills of tying his shoes and buttoning some buttons.

Appendix 22B
CMDP Assessment Instruments

Instrument	Component	Age
ASO Fitness Battery (Roswal et al., 1985)	Fitness	8–19
ASO Sports Skills Battery (Roswall, Floyd, Jessup, Pass, & Hanson, 1985)	Sport skills	10+
Brigance Diagnostic Inventory (Brigance, 1978)	Comprehensive	All
Bruininks-Oseretsky Test of Motor Proficiency (Bruininks, 1978)	Motor proficiency	4.5–14.5
Behavioral Rating Scale (Davis, 1981)	Behavior	All
Davis Revision of Basic Motor Skills Evaluation (Davis, 1981)	Motor skills	SH
Dynamic Balance Test	Balance	All
Data Based Gymnasium (Dunn, Morehouse, & Fredericks, 1985)	Motor skills	SH
I CAN (Wessel, 1976)	Motor skills	All
KSE Fitness Battery (Roswal & Jacobs, 1984)	Fitness	5–12
Language Checklist (Davis, 1981)	Language	All
Martinek-Zaichkowsky Self-Concept Scale (Martinek & Zaichkowsky, 1977)	Self-concept	5–14
OSU SIGMA (Loovis & Ersing, 1979)	Motor skills	All
Motor Skills Evaluation (Roswal, Harper, & Roswal, 1984)	Motor skills	All
Sequence of Swimming Skills (Davis, 1981)	Swimming skills	All
Texas Revision of Basic Motor Skills Evaluation (Ness, 1974)	Motor skills	SH

Note. See references on pp. 318–319 for primary sources where these instruments can be found.

Appendix 22C
Individualized Education Program

ALABAMA INDIVIDUALIZED EDUCATION PROGRAM: Implementation Plan for _____Jamie_____

(Name of Student)

_____

LEA/OTHER AGENCY: _____CMDP_____ SCHOOL _____ YEAR _____Fall, 1984_____

VOCATIONAL EDUCATION OCCUPATIONAL GOAL (IF APPLICABLE): _____

SPECIAL GOALS AND OBJECTIVES	TYPE EVALUATION	DATE
AREA: _____Balance_____	Informal Observation	12/84
ANNUAL GOAL: Jamie will be able to walk backward heel-to-toe on a 4 inch beam placed 4 inches off the floor with assistance.	Balance Beam	
OBJECTIVE: Jamie will walk a designated line on the gym floor backward as assessed by clinician observation.	Dynamic Balance Test	
OBJECTIVE: Jamie will walk a 4 inch beam placed on the floor backward with assistance assessed by clinician observation.		
AREA: _____Locomotion—Jumping_____	Informal Observation	12/84
ANNUAL GOAL: Jamie will jump 3 feet using correct horizontal jumping form.		
OBJECTIVE: Jamie will jump to designated spots placed one foot apart using correct form 4 out of 5 times.	Motor Skills Evaluation	
OBJECTIVE: Jamie will jump to designated spots placed 2 feet apart using correct form 3 out of 5 times.		
AREA: _____Manipulation—Catching_____	Informal Observation	12/84
ANNUAL GOAL: Jamie will catch a ball from a distance of 20 feet using correct form.	I CAN	
OBJECTIVE: Jamie will stop a large, propelled ball from a distance of 20 feet using any body parts 5 out of 5 times.		
OBJECTIVE: Jamie will catch a large ball from a distance of 20 feet using hands, arms, and chest 4 out of 5 times.		

Appendix 22D
Lesson Plan Format

Unit: Manipulative: Throwing for accuracy and striking

Grade/Age Level: 2nd Grade

Objective: The children in the class will be able to do the prescribed activities (throwing and striking) with 80% accuracy as assessed by clinician's observation.

Facilities: Area outside gym

Equipment: 32 bean bags   8 nylon tennis rackets
          2 bean bag targets   8 fluff tennis balls

Activities and Schedule:

5 minutes	warm up stretching routine to music
10 minutes	Bean bag partner tosses & instruction Bean bag target practice & instruction Bean bag target team competition
10 minutes	Fluff tennis ball practice & instruction Fluff tennis ball cooperative team play
5 minutes	Clean up, cool down, line up

Parent Cues and Activities (PACT): Parents serve as child's partner, constantly rewarding child with success and positive praise.

Evaluation: Informal observation

Appendix 22E
Daily Log

Child's Name _____ Jamie _____

Session Number ____ #4 ____ Date _____ June 17, 1984 _____

Activities: Jamie was extremely active in the pool today. He moved short distances on his own initiative; he seemed more confident in moving about the pool. Today, he chose to jump off the edge into the pool with no coaxing. We worked on floating on his back with assistance and kicking his feet while holding onto a float. During motor development, we completed the Special Olympics Sports Skills Battery. His attention span was a little short today, so we did several things in art: we made python snakes from clay, then pictures of them with finger paints (the figures were basic curving lines). Later we painted a stick horse with a big face and an "H" for hay. We also spent some time with the musical instruments and singing with records. During educational session we worked on completing the Brigance Inventory.

Child's Response: At the start of the day, Jamie was very active. During art he was very distractible. He did well on the assessments, although he wanted to do too many things at once. He has shown a consistent interest in the musical instruments and with singing, clapping hands, tapping feet, and so on. He also responded well to communication skills while using puppets. He expressed an interest to go swimming again tomorrow.

Parent Involvement/Responses: I talked with Jamie's mother for a few minutes at pick-up. She is very pleased with his swimming interest. Jamie is also very proud to show his mother the art work he creates.

Appendix 22F
Summary Sheet

Instructions: Write a clear and concise summary of your child's experiences during the CMDP/CAMP HELP. Emphasize all program phases and all phases of development, that is, social, emotional, enrichment, and motor areas. Summaries should reflect knowledge of program philosophy and concepts.

In the last 3 weeks I have noticed a definite change in Jamie. His creative play skills have improved in that he is independent in his initiative toward others. He has involved himself in group activities and loves to play with others. His motor skills have improved, particularly in the areas of balance and manipulative skills. Throwing and catching skills have improved from Level II to Level III on the OSU test. Although his basic locomotor skills are good, he still has difficulty with hopping, galloping, sliding, and skipping. His balance has improved remarkably, largely due to an increased confidence in trying new activities. He progressed from being afraid of the water to actually jumping off the side of the pool without assistance. He expressed interest in learning to jump off the diving board next year. He also learned to put his face in the water for 2 to 3 seconds and to perform a back float with minimal assistance. An important note is that several times we were unable to complete swimming skills due to Jamie's contact lenses. I suggest he wear a good pair of eye goggles that fit tightly against his head. During arts and crafts, Jamie would often become very creative. He enjoyed painting and especially enjoyed showing his mother his art. Although Jamie did not seem to enjoy dancing, he did like to sing, particularly when puppets were involved. His speech would often improve when he was involved in puppet play. During the program, Jamie learned to tie his shoes. Initially he had difficulty in handling the laces. I brought a dark blue tennis shoe with a long red shoe lace and worked with Jamie on tying one step at a time. I suggested to his mother that she put some longer, cotton shoe laces in his shoes and by the 5th week he was tying his shoes. Jamie's social skills improved to the point he began to play with other children in group activities. However, he became easily frustrated and we would withdraw to a more isolated activity before attempting group activity again.

The attention on self-concept in this program was a real asset for Jamie. Although his skills are not very good, Most problems seem to relate to his resistance to try new activities due to his fear of failure. I feel I was somewhat successful in helping Jamie to feel better about himself and in attempting new tasks with success.

Appendix 22G
Student Teacher Evaluation Form

STUDENT

Name _____

Date _____

EVALUATION	*POINTS*
E = Excellent	7
G = Good	5
F = Fair	3
P = Poor	1

1. Enthusiasm _____

2. Concentration on child _____

3. Rapport with child _____

4. Adaptability to new activities _____

5. Ability to initiate new activities _____

6. Cooperation with others in program _____

7. Knowledge of characteristics of children _____

8. Knowledge of program philosophies and procedures _____

9. Resourcefulness and creativity _____

10. Confidence in working with children and peers _____

11. Establishment of specific goals according to child's needs _____

12. Ability to motivate child _____

13. Follows safety procedures _____

14. Actively involved with child and activities _____

15. Activities are in line with program goals and philosophies _____

16. Well prepared _____

17. Promptness _____

18. Assessment completed correctly _____

19. IEP completed correctly _____

20. IEP and actual activities are in agreement _____

Appendix 22H
Clinician's Evaluation Form

1. Generally speaking, did you find Camp HELP a valuable experience?

    _____ excellent _____ good _____ fair _____ poor

2. Did you find working with the children enjoyable?

    _____ very much _____ somewhat _____ no

3. What were the strongest features of the camp?

    _____

    _____

    _____

4. Were there particularly bad features of Camp HELP that need correction?

    _____ yes _____

    _____ no _____

5. Do you feel your experience with Camp HELP is likely to influence your future behavior as a parent?

    _____ yes _____ no

6. Do you feel your experience with Camp HELP is likely to influence your future behavior as a teacher?

    _____ very much _____ somewhat _____ no

7. Did you find the daily logs concerning your child's progress satisfactory?

    _____ very much _____ somewhat _____ no

    Suggestions for improvement:

    _____

    _____

8. Did you talk with your child's parents?

    _____ several times _____ once or twice _____ not at all

9. Generally speaking, do you think the camp was valuable to your child?

    _____ very much _____ somewhat _____ not at all

10. Has your child's self-concept improved?

    _____ very much _____ somewhat _____ no

11. Does your child seem to be trying more new things now?

    _____ very much _____ somewhat _____ no

12. Has your child's motor skill ability improved? (play skills, coordination, gross and fine motor skills)

    _____ very much _____ somewhat _____ not at all

13. Has your child's social skill ability improved?

    _____ very much _____ somewhat _____ not at all

Appendix 22I
Parent's Evaluation Form

1. Generally speaking, did you find Camp HELP valuable to your child?

    _____ yes   _____ no

2. Which areas were of value?

    _____ therapeutic play   _____ self-help skills

    _____ therapeutic swimming   _____ academics

    _____ dance and music   _____ arts and crafts

    _____ feeding   _____ special activities

3. Were there any particular features about the camp that you would like to see changed?

    _____

    _____

4. Has the camp influenced your child's role in your family?

    _____ yes   _____ no

5. Did you talk with any of your child's clinicians?

    _____ several times   _____ once or twice   _____ not at all

6. How was your relationship with your child's clinicians?

    _____ excellent   _____ good   _____ fair   _____ poor

7. How would you rate the clinician's performance?

    _____ excellent   _____ good   _____ fair   _____ poor

8. What do you consider to be your child's attitude toward the camp?

    _____ excellent   _____ good   _____ fair   _____ poor

9. What was your child's attitude toward his/her clinicians?

    _____ excellent   _____ good   _____ fair   _____ poor

10. Did your child get:

    Less from the camp than you hoped _____

    More from the camp than you hoped _____

    About what you had hoped   _____

11. Do you think Camp HELP helped your child feel better about his/her abilities?

    _____ very much   _____ somewhat   _____ not at all

12. Does your child seem to be trying more new things?

    _____ very much   _____ somewhat   _____ not at all

Chapter 23

Motor Behavior and Learning: A Multidisciplinary Practicum for Undergraduate Students

Robert Strauss

Undergraduate professional preparation programs must assume greater responsibility in providing course and practicum work for individuals pursuing careers helping children who demonstrate various motor behavior and learning disabilities. To help meet this challenge, practical experience in developmental, diagnostic, and prescriptive techniques must be provided.

Many children who demonstrate motor behavior and learning disabilities are mainstreamed. All physical education personnel must therefore be able to provide appropriate programs for mainstreamed children as well as those who qualify for adapted physical education.

Many undergraduate physical education professional preparation programs offer only one 3-credit course in adapted physical education with no, or at most, limited provision for practical experience. Because most physical education teachers in the public schools have only acquired the undergraduate degree, it is no wonder many of them shy away or complain when children demonstrating motor behavior disabilities are mainstreamed into their classes.

Development of a Practicum Site

The need for qualified personnel prompted the Health, Physical Education, and Athletic Department at Trinity University, San Antonio, Texas, to develop a Motor Behavior and Learning Laboratory (MBLL) as a practicum site for its students. The main objectives of this laboratory are preparing prospective teachers/clinicians and conducting research with children demonstrating motor behavior and learning disabilities. In addition to theoretical courses, Trinity University undergraduate students receive practical experience in assessing, diagnosing, planning, and implementing prescriptive programs and coordinating programs with other related services within the MBLL. The MBLL also provides services to local schools and community agencies.

The MBLL functions within an interdisciplinary context in assessing and developing prescriptive instructional interventions within the psychomotor domain. Emphasis is placed on the development of motor behavior competencies as they relate to motor, cognitive, and affective skills. The MBLL provides an enjoyable and effective learning center for future teachers/clinicians as well as children with motor behavior and learning disabilities.

A Multidisciplinary Approach

Providing an effective educational program for children demonstrating various motor behavior and learning disabilities requires teamwork of the professional staff. Administrators, teachers, and related personnel must be prepared to assume and meet their responsibilities if programs are to comply with the legislative mandates of PL 94-142.

In order to establish a cooperative team and initiate the correct program for each child, qualified personnel must be prepared. These individuals must be knowledgeable about the physiological, psychological, sociological, and educational needs of all special children.

Trinity University students from different disciplines have been involved in the MBLL serving as instructors, evaluators, and researchers. The MBLL and its involvement have broadened in an interdisciplinary fashion to embrace studies in a number of related fields (i.e., language, reading, arithmetic, and other related behavioral disorders).

These are multifaceted problems requiring multidisciplinary solutions. The Psychology and Special Education Departments have been involved in each of the prime areas, bringing their perspective and skills to further the potential usefulness of the MBLL.

Psychology Department

To maximize the effectiveness of the MBLL (programs, training, research, and client service), the Psychology Department provides valuable help in the areas of evaluation (psychological and neuropsychological) and consultation (to both staff and parents).

Graduate clinical psychology students (under the supervision of the MBLL staff clinical psychologist) are trained to administer neuropsychological evaluations oriented toward the child with motor or learning disabilities. They are trained to evaluate psychological problems that result from such disorders as well as neuropsychological deficits and lags that create such problems. They are also taught consultation and methods of working in the multidisciplinary approach.

Undergraduate psychology students, in addition to serving as student instructors, observe what the psychologists do, how the tests are used, and how to apply the results to the target population at the MBLL. Students from other disciplines (regular education, special education, regular physical education, and adapted physical education) are taught how to use the psychologists as support for their prescriptive programs and as consultants for clients who have psychological problems.

Special Education Department

The Special Education Department plays an integral role in the functioning of the MBLL because many of the children attending the lab have specific learning disabilities in addition to motor difficulties. Undergraduate students enrolled in selected special education courses serve as student instructors in the MBLL. In addition to the motor development program, they provide individual-

Scenes from the Trinity University Motor Behavior and Learning Laboratory directed by Robert Strauss.

ized instruction to the children in areas of reading, auditory and visual perception, language, and fine perceptual-motor skills (manuscript and cursive writing).

Because Trinity University students come to the MBLL from various disciplines with a variety of specialized skills in their respective areas of study, additional training in the motor development area is needed. Each student instructor receives, in addition to their respective classes, 20 hours of intensive training in working in the lab. This enables students serving as instructors to learn how to work in the motor behavior develop-

mental area (sensorimotor, perceptual-motor, manipulative, and fine-motor). Additional facets of the MBLL, such as the Reading Program, are handled under the supervision of the Special Education Department.

Physical Education Department

Physical education (regular and adapted) undergraduate students learn through their respective courses how to assess the motor behavior development of children. Two courses, Motor Development and Adapted Physical

Education, are required of all undergraduate physical education majors. Each involves the MBLL as a practicum site. In addition to theoretical material covered in each class, 30 hours of lab practicum are also provided.

The Motor Development course provides the undergraduate student with experience in dealing with children demonstrating various perceptual-motor dysfunctions who are mainstreamed into the regular physical education classes. The Adapted Physical Education course provides the undergraduate student with experience in working with the more severely involved motor disabled children who qualify for adapted physical education programming in the public schools. They are taught how to work in a multidisciplinary setting in developing prescriptive motor behavior training based upon test evaluations provided by psychologists, educational diagnosticians, adapted physical educators, and other related services. The adapted physical education undergraduate is also taught how to assess, develop, and implement physical activities for children with a variety of handicapping conditions.

An additional course, Advanced Developmental/Adapted Physical Education, is offered for elective credit to those students wanting more in-depth work in providing services to children demonstrating various motor behavior disabilities. In addition to attending regularly scheduled seminars, students conduct a research project and serve as assistant program coordinators. These students (under the supervision of the MBLL director and program coordinator) become involved in the operation of the MBLL. This involvement provides them with practical experience in admitting children to the MBLL, assessing, diagnosing, developing and writing individual prescriptive programs, assisting in parental conferences, training student instructors in program implementation, and conducting staff meetings for student instructors.

Children Enrolled in the MBLL

Children who attend the MBLL are referred by the local schools (public and private), physicians (pediatricians, neurologists, and ophthalmologists), psychologists, optometrists, and other related community services. The MBLL works cooperatively with referral agencies by utilizing the agency's test information in addition to its own assessment. The MBLL serves as an adjunct to the schools; therefore, consultation with the classroom teacher and other related personnel is an ongoing function of the staff.

The children attend the MBLL for three 1-hour sessions per week for 10 weeks. Children needing special work

in reading attend the Reading Lab for one 1-hour session and the MBLL for two 1-hour sessions. Individualized prescriptive programming within a small group setting is provided (one student per three children). When necessary and prescribed by the staff, individual one-to-one instruction is provided.

Major Contributions of an On-Campus Practicum Site

An on-campus multidisciplinary practicum site like the MBLL provides undergraduate students with a unique learning experience. Some of the goals of such an educational program are presented in the following list.

• To encourage and promote the continuation and further development of cooperative interdisciplinary teaching and research opportunities among faculty from a variety of disciplines

• To provide resources and faculty for any student interested in pursuing studies concerning motor behavior and learning disabled children

• To provide students with the opportunity to work with motor behavior and learning disability children in a multidisciplinary setting

• To pursue both basic and applied research with particular emphasis on meeting the needs of motor behavior and learning disabled children

• To provide services to a limited number of children experiencing motor behavior and learning disabilities

• To provide services to schools, community agencies, organizations, and individuals who seek assistance with the motor behavior and learning of children

• To provide evaluation and diagnostic services for children who are experiencing motor behavior and/or learning difficulties

This practicum experience, in addition to classroom instruction, prepares future teachers and clinicians to recognize, assess, diagnose, plan, and implement prescriptive programs for children demonstrating various motor behavior and learning disabilities. Futhermore, on-campus practicums afford faculty greater opportunity for supervision and monitoring progress of the children. Providing the undergraduate with practical experience makes classroom instruction meaningful and applicable.

Chapter 24

Leadership Training in Adapted Physical Education

Claudine Sherrill

*T*he preservice program at Texas Woman's University is designed as a graduate program in adapted and developmental physical education. Since 1972, the program has received funding from the federal government under Part D (Subchapter IV) of the Education of the Handicapped Act. The emphasis is on doctoral and postdoctoral studies, although large numbers of master's candidates also seek training.

Ecological Training Model

The training model used at Texas Woman's University during the 1970s and early 1980s was ecological in nature, stressing interrelationships between graduate students, faculty, and the community at large. The primary source for the model was *Ecological Psychology* by Roger G. Barker (1968), which presents concepts and methods for studying the environment of human behavior. The basic premise of the model is that graduate students learn more about disabled children and youth by interacting with them and their parents in everyday environments than by exclusive study of theory. Likewise, graduate students learn more about professionalism, leadership, and research through close relationships with faculty and peer role models who serve as catalysts and mentors than by reading about leadership and planning for the future.

Students are thus taught to conceptualize themselves as a professional family, each with a responsibility to one another and to the disabled persons they are learning to serve. Moreover, feelings of caring, accepting, prizing, and sharing that characterize the learning and living environment of the present are linked gradually with the past as graduate students are taught to take pride in the college's alumnae and with the future as they help select each year's new graduate assistants. Past, present, and future TWU alumnae are brought together also by their sharing of the same handicapped children and youth who participate year after year in practica that are cooperatively sponsored by the university, the public schools, and the Denton Association for Retarded Citizens. Since the early 1970s, TWU adapted physical education graduate students have conducted a year-round training program in Special Olympics. Now, with the evolution of new sport organizations for the disabled, graduate students are increasingly involved in sport with cerebral palsied, blind, and spinal cord–injured athletes.

Another tenet of the ecological training model is that prospective teachers/leaders should be interacting daily with equal-status adult disabled peers. To facilitate this belief, at least one graduate assistant each year since the mid-1970s has been disabled. These have included a double leg amputee, a USABA Class B$_2$ blind athlete, and Class 2 and 7 cerebral palsied athletes. Faculty members as well as graduate students learn much from these interactions, many of which are extracurricular and social.

The ecological training model presupposes that everything within the environment, not just class attendance and homework, is relevant. Thus many experiences are

Leadership training includes attending conferences and meeting leaders in the field such as Eunice Shriver (right), founder of Special Olympics. From left to right are Randy Foederer, Linda Johnstone, Patricia Putman, Claudine Sherrill, Joy Camplin, and Martha Stinson.

required for which no course credit is given. These learning opportunities are designated as Participation-Advocacy-Leadership (PAL) competencies and depicted in Figure 24.1.

PAL Competencies

The acronym PAL conveniently relates to being a pal to disabled children and youth as well as to one's professional colleagues. All TWU students receive training in this generic PAL role. *Participation* refers to involvement in the community and in professional organizations, supporting events by and for the handicapped. *Advocacy* activities encompass public relations, legislation, and research documenting that adapted physical education

programming does cause positive change in the handicapped. *Leadership* entails working on committees, holding office, writing for publication, and presenting at meetings.

The PAL competencies reflect the belief that university teacher training should facilitate values training (Freiberg & Foster, 1979) and that such training should aim toward achievement of the objectives comprising the affective domain (Krathwohl, Bloom, & Masia, 1964). Adapted physical education training at Texas Woman's University attempts to guide graduate students through the taxonomy continuum from receiving levels (awareness) through responding levels (believing and acting commensurate with beliefs) and valuing levels (implementing the ecological approach and growing commitment). The level that each graduate student reaches

A Generic Role

Participation—Advocacy— Leadership (PAL) Competencies

Association Membership and Conference Participation

Effective Speaking, Interacting, and Disseminating

Writing and Public Relations Influencing Legislation and Awareness

1. Join at local and state levels CEC and at least two parent and consumer organizations (DARC, DACLD, DCEH, PTA) at local level. Attend at least 50% of local level meetings.

2. Join at local, state, and national levels AAHPERD and/or NTRS and attend at own expense at least one state (all students) and one national (PhD only) conference each year. Attempt to get on program for maximum advocacy.

3. Assist with OSE Project Drop-In Center or Booth at at least two conferences.

4. Name and recognize officers and key persons in each organization at local, state, and national levels; give evidence of some social or professional interaction with leaders.

1. Give at least one off-campus workshop or speech each semester on PE-R for handicapped for parents, volunteers, or consumer groups.

2. Conduct at least two in-service education sessions in schools or school districts and follow up with needed developmental assistance (PhDs only).

3. Give evidence of socializing at a friendship level with handicapped citizens and/or their parents.

4. Chair and/or document involvement with one of the six off-campus OSE Committees within the Ecological Model Structure.

5. Prepare and present publicly one videotape, film, or slide presentation.

1. Vote knowledgeably in all elections and support legislation favorable to the handicapped.

2. Know names of state and national congressmen and give evidence of correspondence with at least one of them.

3. Attend at least one session of State Legislature in Austin and sign in at the office of your local congressman.

4. Assume responsibility for newspaper publicity for at least one event.

5. Submit one article on physical education and recreation for the handicapped to a state or national journal of your choice (*PhD students only*).

Figure 24.1 Special tasks required of OSE funded students in adapted physical education designed to develop habits, commitment, and competencies.

differs depending on entry level competencies and behaviors, time available to learn, and many other factors.

Other Roles for Which the Program Prepares Personnel

Personnel roles for which master's level students are prepared include the following:

• *Direct service delivery* to handicapped students and their families. This includes psychomotor assessment, individualized educational programming, developmental and/or prescriptive teaching, counseling, and coordination of related services and resources.

• *Administration* of a school adapted physical education program. This includes management, supervision, program development, accountability, grant writing, and consulting.

• *In-service training* for mainstream physical education teachers, special educators, and elementary school teachers who may have responsibility in physical education for the handicapped.

Personnel roles for which doctoral level students are prepared include the above and the following additions:

• *Preservice training*. This entails teaching others to deliver adapted physical education services, grant writing for university-based projects, and grant management.

• *Research*. This entails learning to conduct research, make research presentations, and write papers for publication.

Philosophy of Training Program

Master's and doctoral training extends beyond the traditional school day and university-based theory program. It aims to develop in graduate students a life-style of commitment, leadership, and continuous learning. This is achieved largely through giving students good faculty and graduate assistant models to follow and involving them, as part of their competency training, in as many and diverse practicum experiences as possible.

Specific beliefs underlying this philosophy include the following:

• That graduate degrees should be comprised of courses and practica specifically designed to teach trainees how to work with handicapped children and youth

• That graduate degrees should emphasize generic training but include some learning experiences specifically addressing the special needs of severely handicapped students

• That theory and practice should be integrated in graduate training with approximately 50% of the homework of all courses in practicum experiences; that overall all graduate students should document a minimum of 480 hours of practica

• That graduate students be trained to deliver in-service and staff development services as well as to teach handicapped children and/or university-based classes

Tasks Associated With Direct Service Role and Instructional Program That Facilitates Learning

Both master's and doctoral students train for the role of direct service delivery but for different reasons. Master's level trainees do so because most of the jobs available to them are in direct service delivery. Doctoral and postdoctoral trainees do so in order to feel confident as models as they return to their colleges and universities and teach others to teach.

Direct service delivery is broken down into five subroles or task areas. Each of these is defined, and the courses are specified that address specific competency development. Courses with one asterisk are required of doctoral students, and courses with two asterisks are required of both master's and doctoral students. In addition to required courses, students must elect a specified number of courses in their specialization.

Assessment

Assessment is the combined process of testing, measuring, and evaluating. To comply with individualized education program (IEP) requirements, every adapted physical education program must begin with assessment of the *present level of psychomotor functioning* of the handicapped student. Moreover, evaluation procedures must be established for periodically determining the effectiveness of the physical education program. Thus assessment is an integral part of the teaching-learning process and occurs continuously.

The following courses are suggested:

• ** PHED 5013—Evaluation in HPER

• * PHED 5853—Appraisal of Psychomotor Functions in APE

- * PHED 6593—Neurological Bases of Motor Dysfunctions

- PHED 6853—Neurological Bases of Motor Control

Also recommended are graduate courses in biomechanics, cinematography, exercise physiology, and motor learning for application of their techniques to assessment.

Counseling

In adapted physical education, counseling refers to the process of assisting handicapped and clumsy persons to understand and accept themselves in various dimensions of the psychomotor domain. Guidance and counseling books describe counseling as a *helping process* that utilizes specific facilitation techniques. These may be primarily *verbal* as in leisure counseling or *nonverbal* as in dance/movement therapy.

Physical education adapted counseling (PEAC) is a helping process that facilitates changes in the affective/psychomotor domains, helping the person to feel and be more whole, more integrated, and more self-actualizing. The process focuses upon reducing the discrepancies between the ideal self and the actual self in levels of motor performance and fitness, use of leisure, and acceptance of body and self (physical appearance, weight, body proportions, missing limbs or parts, distorted or twisted parts, etc.). To engage effectively in such a helping process, the adapted physical educator should take courses in guidance and counseling such as the following:

- EDPS 5513—Counseling Theory and Practice

- PHED 5733—Psychology of Motor Learning II

All adapted physical education courses emphasize guidance and counseling techniques as an integral part of assessment and teaching. TWU has a Department of Counseling and Personnel Services within its College of Education. This department offers both master's and doctoral level work.

Individualized Educational Programming

The individualized educational programming process is a sequence of procedures, prescribed by Public Law 94-142, directed toward finding unserved handicapped children, *admitting* them to the school district's special education program, *referring* them for special services, and hopefully remediating their problems and subsequently *dismissing* them from special education. These same procedures apply to adapted physical education eligibility and programming. Physical educators are expected to contribute their expertise with regard to the identification, analysis, and solution of problems in the psychomotor domain.

Required courses include the following:

- ** PHED 5123—Professional Affiliation

- * PHED 5853—Appraisal of Psychomotor Functions in APE

- * PHED 6853—Practicum: IEP

Most adapted physical education courses include a module on writing IEPs specifically related to their content.

Developmental and Prescriptive Teaching

Developmental and prescriptive teaching are the processes in adapted physical education whereby psychomotor behaviors are changed and optimal growth and development are promoted. Adapted physical education is considered prescriptive teaching because the long-term goals and short-term objectives in each student's IEP are agreed upon by a multidisciplinary committee, including one or both parents and (where appropriate) the handicapped student. This agreement constitutes an educational prescription. Adapted physical education is also considered developmental teaching because the physical educator adapts the learning activities or interventions to the developmental motor, fitness, or play level of the student.

The course load is as follows:

- ** PHED 5833—Adapted & Therapeutic Physical Education

- * PHED 5923—Administration and Service Delivery in Adapted Physical Education

- ** PHED 5603—Motor Development: Normal and Abnormal

- PHED 5763—Sports/Athletics for Handicapped

- PHED 5823—Elementary PE—Methods for Mainstreaming

- PHED 5933—Adapted Physical Education Early Childhood Intervention

- PHED 5873—Aquatics for Special Populations

- DNCE 5263—Dance for Handicapped

- DNCE 5273—Adapted Dance

- * PHED 5863—Diagnostic—Prescriptive Teaching for Severely Handicapped

- * PHED 5793—Perceptual Motor Learning

- * PHED 5883—Mainstreaming in HPER

- PHED 5903—Special Topics Used for Summer School Institutes

Coordination of Resources and Services

In order for physical education to improve the quality of life, it must be carried over in daily living activities and leisure. The adapted physical educator therefore identifies community, home, and agency resources that can be used by handicapped persons during after-school and weekend hours and then facilitates and coordinates the use of such resources as they relate to adapted physical education.

All adapted physical education courses emphasize resources and services. The noncredit PAL competencies support this area. Additionally, most master's candidates and many doctoral students complete 12 or more credits in special education.

Tasks Associated With Administration Role and Instructional Program That Facilitates Learning

All graduate students, particularly graduate assistants, learn administrative skills through executing responsibilities for diverse assignments, including the following:

- Organizing both on-campus and off-campus practica in which undergraduate students work one-to-one with handicapped children and youth. Graduate students serve as supervisors of these practica and are responsible for recruitment of undergraduates, providing them with in-service training, and supervising them.

- Organizing and conducting on-campus workshops, seminars, and special events. In executing these assignments they learn conference management skills, ranging from registration through evaluation.

- Inventorying equipment and supplies, arranging for repairs, and making out requisitions for purchase of new items.

- Evaluating campus facilities with respect to architectural barriers and assessing compliance with Section 504 in all aspects of university life.

Content pertaining to administration is covered in PHED 5123, Professional Affiliation, and in PHED 5923, Administration and Service Delivery in Adapted Physical Education. Most content, however, is learned in relation to the PAL role in which advanced students and faculty serve as models, mentors, and one-to-one tutors in cooperative implementation of administrative tasks. Illustrative administrative competencies, tasks, and functions include the following:

- Demonstrate understanding of breadth, scope, and nature of administrative activities: (a) personnel functions, (b) policy formulation, (c) program planning, (d) decision making, (e) budget and finance, (f) facilities design and maintenance, (g) equipment management, (h) office management, (i) public relations, (j) trouble shooting, (k) attendance at meetings, (l) communication, and (m) evaluation.

- Demonstrate knowledge of theories and philosophies of administration: (a) traditional (democratic, laissez-faire, and autocratic), (b) systems theory, including Management by Objectives (MBO), (c) human behavior theory—group dynamics, human motivation, interpersonal relations, and (d) eclectic.

- Show skill in conducting meetings according to *Robert's Rules of Order*, writing minutes, planning agendas, and completing committee work assignments.

- Demonstrate skill in recruitment, selection, orientation, and in-service training of various groups: (a) undergraduates to work in practica with handicapped children and in related volunteer projects, (b) new university students, including graduate assistants for the subsequent year, and (c) parents and community volunteers for various tasks.

- Demonstrate knowledge of standards for making physical education facilities accessible for persons with various kinds of disabilities.

- Demonstrate skill in removing architectural, attitudinal, and aspirational barriers that interfere with equity and mainstreaming.

- Demonstrate understanding of the legal and humanistic bases for adapted physical education and skill in conveying these to others.

- Demonstrate ability to work effectively with power structures that influence program development and evaluation both within and outside the university.

- Demonstrate knowledge of supervision, including qualifications needed by supervisory personnel, basic principles of supervision, evaluation approaches and instruments, and the role of interpersonal relations.

- Demonstrate understanding of litigation in regard to compliance with federal laws, negligence, tort, and equipment and facilities liability.

- Demonstrate knowledge of the relationship between economics, law, and funding of adapted physical education services including (a) grant writing and management, (b) fund raising, and (c) fiscal and program accountability.

- Demonstrate understanding of the processes of program accreditation and teacher certification, licensure, and endorsement in relation to quality control of personnel and programs.

- Demonstrate understanding of processes for effecting change, including participation in (a) federal and state legislation, (b) shaping regulations in the *Federal Register*, (c) hearings, (d) the Comprehensive System of Personnel Development (CSPD), and (e) the SEA Special Education State Plan.

- Demonstrate understanding of the megatrends that are affecting U.S. government and education as a whole and their influence on adapted physical education.

- Demonstrate knowledge of national studies of education, the impact they have at state and local levels, and their relevance for adapted physical education.

- Demonstrate knowledge of needs assessment and evaluation models, processes, and procedures.

- Demonstrate skills in consulting, staff development, in-service training, and conference planning and management.

Tasks Associated With In-Service Training Role and Instructional Program That Facilitates Learning

Graduate assistants at both master's and doctoral levels receive intensive training and practice in the role of *in-service training and developmental assistance*. This training is especially important because adapted physical educators often receive requests from public schools and education service centers. These requests are not surprising because the State Board of Education of Texas considers staff development as one of its statewide priorities. The Texas Education Code, Section 16.055, specifies that 10 days are to be used in the public schools every year for "inservice education and preparation."

These competencies are developed in the Tuesday–Thursday afternoon, 1:00–4:00 p.m. seminar block, conducted for PHED 5123, *Professional Affiliation* credit. Other class work is scheduled Tuesday and Thursday mornings and evenings so that OSEP-funded graduate assistants have Monday, Wednesday, and Friday free to gain practice in in-service training as well as to engage in other types of practica.

Content pertaining to conducting in-service training is included also in PHED 5923, Administration and Service Delivery in Adapted Physical Education. Special Friday and Saturday seminars in which professional leaders are brought to campus to conduct workshops provide models for graduate students to emulate. Attendance at off-campus workshops and conferences also reinforces content to be learned. Graduate students are urged not only to appreciate content presented at such sessions but to observe and evaluate the pedagogy of in-service training.

1. *Planning for In-Service Training*

   Planning necessitates the following knowledge and understanding:

   - Demonstrate an understanding of in-service training, cite principles that should be followed in its conduct, and be able to document research and literature describing "programs that work" that serve as the basis for the principles cited.

   - Be able to discuss five in-service training models that work and to identify and analyze the factors operative in their success.

   - Demonstrate knowledge of OSEP-funded in-service training programs in adapted physical education.

   - Cite criteria for evaluation of adapted physical education in-service and be able to evaluate ongoing programs on the basis of those criteria and to suggest needed changes.

   - Know state law and SEA policies with regard to in-service and staff development.

   - Know who are considered the state's authorities and leaders in in-service and be able to cite model in-service projects within the state.

   - Be able to cite state needs in in-service training, including those of the Comprehensive System of Personnel Development (CSPD) of the Special Education Department (SEA).

   - Demonstrate knowledge of state geography, population densities, special multicultural or minority needs, and historical and cultural factors that influence in-service training.

2. *Needs Assessment Skills*

   - Demonstrate ability to use *Texas School Directory*, the *Texas Almanac*, and other reference and resource systems to identify names, addresses, and telephone numbers of administrators.

   - Demonstrate competence in learning about a school system or district before making initial telephone or visitation contact.

   - Demonstrate competence in making at least one planning visit: (a) establish rapport; (b) obtain administrator's assessment of adapted physical education in-service needs; (c) engage in cooperative planning of in-service with persons who plan to attend; (d) observe handicapped children in classes of teachers who plan to attend the in-service; ask them which children are their greatest problems and why; (e) observe physical education and adapted physical education public school classes in session and determine equipment and space resources and limitations; (f) determine time, place, and specific objectives of the workshop; acquaint persons who will attend with evaluation forms to be used at the in-service training; and (g) apply needs assessment process to yourself to ascertain what you specifically wish to learn by conducting adapted physical education in-service and what preparation you need to undertake.

- Demonstrate ability to cooperatively plan in-service training objectives with school personnel during the planning visit.

- Demonstrate knowledge of the evaluation forms used by the school district in assessing the success of in-service training. Obtain a copy of this form during the planning visit and discuss it with the administrator responsible for setting up the workshop.

3. *Designing and Planning Workshops*

- Analyze specific objectives of the in-service training, and break these down into behavioral terms.

- List and put into sequence tasks that you need to perform with respect to each behavioral objective in terms of preparation, implementation, evaluation, and follow-up.

- Determine instructional materials needed, whether they are already available, or whether you need to develop them, including (a) overheads; (b) slide-tape shows; (c) films; (d) sample homemade equipment; (e) bulletin board materials, and (f) books, journals, and so forth for display.

- Determine take-home materials to be disseminated, their cost in duplication, and method for reimbursement.

- Consider a wide variety of presentation alternatives, with emphasis on maximum involvement of trainees—be sure to include some kind of warm-up activity.

- Determine what kinds of demonstrations are needed, whether children are needed, and (if so) decide on procedures for obtaining children, get-

ting permissions, providing tangible thanks or recognition.

- Determine your workshop format and practice each part of the presentation; ask other graduate students to observe and evaluate you; refine presentation skills as necessary; double check time and space requirements.

- Type out workshop program with specific objectives to be achieved and timeline for each part of the workshop delineated. Send this to the public school administrator or his or her designate for approval.

- Submit in writing your workshop space and equipment needs and ascertain time, place, and directions for driving there.

4. *Implementation and Evaluation Skills*

- Demonstrate success in workshop presentation as determined by written evaluations by participants.

- Document at least two in-service workshops that you have presented each year by turning in a report, including your evaluation data.

5. *Follow-Up Skills*

- Document at least one follow-up visit to school districts during which you visit with participants and receive verbal input.

- Apply a needs assessment model for conducting follow-up. See Borich (1980).

- Continue adapted physical education developmental assistance as needed with the school or school district during the remainder of the year.

Tasks Associated With the Preservice and University Teaching Role and Instructional Program That Facilitates Learning

Doctoral students prepare also for the role of preservice training—teaching others to deliver adapted physical education services, including the subroles of on-campus teacher training, off-campus practica supervision and field operations, curriculum development and evaluation, research, and other service to the profession. Tasks for each of these are listed; competency is demonstrated by proficiency in performing each task. All courses except those in the research block with an asterisk are elective.

1. *On-Campus Teacher Training*

   • Teach theory and activity courses

   • Conduct on-campus practicum experiences for students

   • Engage in selective recruitment and retention of students

   • Perform guidance and counseling tasks

   • Participate in multidisciplinary/interdisciplinary campus committees and training activities

   • Develop curriculum materials and media for pre-service training program

   • Plan off-campus learning activities

   Courses

   • EDFD 5393—Higher Education in the United States

   • EDFD 5403—Problems in College Teaching

   • EDFD 5513—Production of Instructional Media

   • EDFD 5543—Instructional Systems and Design

   • PSY   5543—Counseling Techniques

2. *Off-Campus Practica Supervision and Field Operations*

   • Select off-campus practicum sites in accordance with established criteria

   • Orient and train off-campus practicum supervisors and cooperating teachers

   • Assign students to practicum sites in accordance with their individual training needs and monitor their development of behavioral objectives they wish to achieve

   • Supervise and evaluate students at practicum sites in accordance with their preestablished behavioral objectives

   • Perform consultant role in answering needs for technical assistance in the field

   • Plan, conduct, and evaluate in-service education activities in the field

   • Assume responsibility for placement of graduates and follow-up (including visits to their schools and provision of technical assistance as needed)

   • Serve as liaison between university training program and parent-professional organizations like the Parent-Teacher's Association, Association for Retarded Citizens, and Association for Children and Adults with Learning Disabilities, providing assistance as needed

   Courses

   • PHED 5103—Presentation of Activities to the Public

   • PHED 5143—Group Dynamics in the Professions

   • PHED 6103—Advanced Seminar in Group Dynamics

   • PSY   6813—Consultation Methods

   • PHED 5123—Professional Affiliation

   • SOCI 5643—Racial & Minority Group Relations

3. *Curriculum Development and Evaluation*

   • Develop evaluation methodology for all components of training program

   • Implement evaluation methodology and write periodic reports

   • Use evaluation data as part of annual needs assessment to determine needed curricular changes

   • Arrange for input from alumnae and various advisory groups concerning programmatic strengths and weaknesses

   • Develop and validate curricular materials and media

   • Monitor instructional resources, including ordering of new library books, periodicals, films, and equipment

   • Develop new courses and facilitate their acceptance by departmental, college, and university curriculum committees

   • Maintain close contact with state education agency and work for needed changes in state teacher certification

   • Monitor SEA Special Education State Plan and ascertain that changes made are supportive of high-quality adapted physical education service delivery

   Courses

   • PHED 5013—Evaluation in HPER

- PHED 5773—Physical Education in the Curriculum

- EDCI 5123—Curriculum Building

- EDFD 5253—Evaluation: Primary Principles and Practices

- EDFD 5263—Evaluation of Educational Programs, Projects, and Materials

- EDFD 5713—The Adult Learner

- SOCI 5653—Sociometry

- EDFD 5633—Understanding the Culturally Different Learner

4. *Research and Other Service to the Profession* (This task can be subdivided into the following activities for which doctoral candidates are preparing.)

- Direct graduate students in theses and dissertations

- Conduct own research and submit articles regularly to research journal and report at research sections of professional meetings

- Engage in creative thinking, writing, and speaking and submit articles to periodicals; write textbooks

- Perform committee work for campus assignments and off-campus professional organizations

- Serve as chairperson of committees and/or officer of organizations

Courses

- PHED 6143—Research Design in HPER (doctoral students only)

- PHED 6573—Research Techniques in Human Performance

- PHED 6713—Research Design & the Motor Learning Laboratory

- PHED 6103—Advanced Seminar in Group Dynamics & Research Theory

- PHED 5033—Applied Statistical Principles (doctoral students only)

- PHED 5043—Statistical Inference (doctoral students only)

- MATH 5073—Computer Science

- MATH 5744—Microcomputer Systems

- MATH 5783—Computer-Assisted Instructional Systems

- MATH 5673—Statistical Computer Packages (doctoral students only)

The instructional program that facilitates learning of tasks in these four broad areas (preservice and university teaching, off-campus practica supervision and field operations, curriculum development and evaluation, and research and other service to the profession) is almost entirely elective (except for research and statistics courses). Each doctoral student's program is highly individualized, and a strong academic counseling program is directed toward motivating doctoral students to select courses that meet personal needs rather than enrolling in courses because they are required.

Leadership Training in Research

Modeling faculty members who have ongoing research programs and regularly publish and report findings at professional meetings is perhaps the best means of providing leadership training in research. Although the faculty's research interests at Texas Woman's University are varied, several data pools have been developed and are shared with graduate students who have the needed computer skills to access data from the university's mainframe computer. Campus computer services are free, and students may work in numerous computer labs or may access on the mainframe through a modem in their home. Computer competencies are stressed as a first step in research leadership training, and several doctoral students have recently chosen computer science as their minor.

Chapter 34 offers excellent suggestions for both graduate students and faculty on organization of time and energy so as to find the extra hours for research and other leadership activities. High-quality teaching and community services should never be considered a substitute for research productivity. Illustrative of articles that stress the importance of research are those by Baker and King (1983), Massengale (1983), and Safrit (1979).

Importance of Leadership Training in Adapted Physical Education

Leadership training is especially important in adapted physical education for many reasons. First, the theory of adapted physical education largely encompasses change. Leadership skills are needed to become a successful change agent. Second, leadership is essential in the evolution of a new specialization and its eventual acceptance as a profession and/or academic subdiscipline. Third, leadership skills are indispensible to successful grant writing and project management.

Almost all doctoral level graduates of adapted physical education are expected to write training grants. If funded, these grants thrust their writers into administration of the most difficult kind. Whereas departmental chairpersons are answerable to one set of superiors (the university administration), the grant project director is simultaneously responsible to the funding agency, the university administration, and the departmental chairperson. These three sets of superiors often have different value systems. The director of a training grant needs a strong repertoire of leadership attitudes, beliefs, and skills to cope and survive.

Grant writing and subsequent management of resources tend to change relationships with peers (i.e., the other faculty). Sometimes jealousy is to be overcome. More often there is the growing loneliness of not having the time and energy to maintain friendships and social contacts of the more relaxed pregrant era of teaching.

Doctoral candidates cannot wait until the on-the-job experience of their first university teaching position to acquire leadership training. Nor can necessary attitudes, knowledge, and skills be developed in theory courses. The PAL competencies described earlier in this chapter have therefore been developed by using the 20 hours a week for which graduate assistants are salaried for work in leadership skill training. Whether the specific assignment is direct service delivery at a practicum site, data collection and analysis for a research project, or conducting in-service training, the hidden agenda in the work hours is development of leadership and administrative skills.

This hidden agenda (or underlying, all-pervasive goal) is often difficult for graduate students to grasp. John Loy, in the foreword to Kroll's book on graduate study and research in physical education, describes the problem to be resolved:

> The transition from undergraduate study to graduate study causes "cultural shock" for many students. Newly admitted graduate students quickly discover that they are required to play a different academic game. This game has a different set of objectives, more stringent rules, better qualified players, more demanding coaches, a greater degree of competition, more sophisticated equipment, and last but not least, this game has a highly uncertain outcome wherein each player has more at stake. (Kroll, 1982, p. ix)

The transition from master's to doctoral study is often as traumatic as that from undergraduate to graduate. Whereas undergraduate and master's levels of study emphasize transmission of existing knowledge and mastery of beginning research skills for producing new knowledge, doctoral programs stress research productivity, leadership, and administration. Much has been written about research productivity (Baker & King, 1983; Kroll, 1982; Massengale, 1983; Safrit, 1979). Little attention, however, has been given to the development of leadership and administrative skills in doctoral candidates.

Distinction Between Leadership and Administration

Many persons use the terms *leadership* and *administration* as synonyms, but theoretically each embodies a different concept. Leadership comes from the Anglo Saxon word *laedan*, meaning to go, and is defined as guiding, conducting, preceding, or being foremost among. Administration comes from the Latin word *administrare*, meaning to serve, and is defined as managing or directing the execution, application, or conduct of some activity.

Leadership has a broader meaning than administration in that many persons are leaders but not administrators. In contrast, it is generally assumed that good administrators are leaders. Leadership, broadly defined, is usually volunteer; one leads because he or she believes in an idea, cause, or activity and chooses to invest time, energy, and self in it. Administration, on the other hand, is typically a salaried position with set goals to be achieved.

Two definitions of administration clarify the role. Frost and Marshall (1981) define administration as follows:

> Administration consists of the leadership and guidance of individuals, the procuring and manipulation of resources, and the coordinating of many diverse efforts so effective progress can be made toward the achievement of the goals and purposes of an organization. (p. 1)

This definition, like the next, indicates that the goals and purposes are established; an administrator is employed to facilitate goal achievement, not to set or prioritize goals. Orway Tead, author of the classic *The Art of Administration*, writes,

> Administration is the comprehensive effort to direct, guide, and integrate associated human strivings which are focused toward some specific end or aims. For immediate . . . purposes, administration is conceived as the necessary activities of those individuals (executives) in an organization who are charged with ordering, forwarding, and facilitating the associated

efforts of a group of individuals brought together to realize certain defined purposes. (1951, pp. 3–4)

Leadership, in contrast to administration, often involves goal setting and goal changing. A person committed to an idea, cause, or activity like equity, for instance, models behaviors that others follow. Leadership implies being the first to speak out or act. It also embodies willingness to take the consequences for one's initiative in that the first to champion a cause often does so at personal, social, and financial sacrifice.

Leadership is a gift bestowed by one's followers. It usually stems from respect, admiration, and appreciation. Ideally it cannot be bought by persuasion, authority, or power. Leadership in educational circles is usually measured in the following ways:

- Quantity and quality of offices held in professional organizations, including chairing of work committees

- Quantity and quality of publications

- Quantity and quality of original ideas or knowledge generated as evidenced in their use by others (citations, quotations, acknowledgments, etc.)

- Quantity and quality of changes in law, policy, or human behavior that can be related to a person's term of office, publications, presentations, or teachings

- Quantity and quality of volunteers a person can recruit and retain in activity directed toward achievement of some idea, cause, or action

- Quantity and quality of other resources (money, equipment, facilities) a person can generate for achievement of some goal

- Quantity of votes a person can generate for a motion, law, or candidate

In summary, *leadership* can be defined as

- being the first to recognize a need, identify a cause, dream a dream, evolve an idea, or innovate a plan of action;

- demonstrating an enduring commitment to one or more causes, ideas, or dreams; and

- speaking, writing, teaching, and living in ways that draw others to the same commitment.

Leadership and Commitment

In adapted physical education leadership is needed in the broad areas of equity, humanism, and normalization—persons with strong commitment to the right of *all* persons to physical education of optimal quality, to the dignity and worth of all human beings, and to the right of all individuals to be in the normalizing mainstream rather than separated away into categories. In physical education, in general, commitment is needed to our profession, our discipline, and our integrated community of scholars, researchers, teachers, and service deliverers. In education, commitment is needed to nurture academic qualities in ourselves and our students. These qualities include the following:

regularly displaying the character, disposition, or capacity to be academic: being disciplined, studying, learning, finding the facts, teaching oneself, both thinking and acting more or less reflectively, being patient, paying attention to detail, taking little for granted, researching, discovering, and creating, and aiming at seeing connections between things that have not been seen before. (Harper, 1980, p. 175)

Leadership training, then, begins with nurturing commitment. One must *value* an idea, cause, or action before he or she is willing to invest time, energy, and self in the leadership of others.

Pedagogical Approaches to Leadership Training

The essential problem in teaching education is, What pedagogies best develop leadership qualities? At Texas Woman's University we believe that leadership can be taught and/or facilitated. One approach to leadership training is through values clarification and education in accordance with the Krathwohl, Bloom, and Masia (1964) taxonomy for the affective domain. The highest level of this taxonomy is *characterization by a value or value complex* (see chapter 1 for the full taxonomy). This values characterization level is described as follows:

At this level of internalization the values already have a place in the individual's value hierarchy, are organized into some kind of internally consistent system, have controlled the behavior of the individual for a sufficient time that he has adapted to behaving this way. (Krathwohl, Bloom, & Masia, 1964, p. 184)

In other words, a leader *knows* what he or she believes and *lives* these beliefs. Through this living, modeling (conscious or unconscious) occurs. If others are affected by this modeling and drawn to the same beliefs, eventually reaching the values characterization levels themselves, then leadership is occurring.

This leadership training approach appears to be consistent with the findings of Massengale and Sage (1982) concerning the importance of a professional mentor in doctoral level success. Persons with similar values concerning equity, humanism, and normalization tend to cluster together and to promote the career mobility of younger professional colleagues who are modeling the same values.

McIntyre (1981) approaches leadership training in a different but entirely compatible way. He states that leadership skills are generated in three ways: (a) through lectures and reading, (b) through practice in an artificially created environment, and (c) through on-the-job training. McIntyre, citing Mintzberg (1973) as his primary source, discusses eight skills associated with successful educational leadership: (a) peer skills, (b) leadership skills, (c) conflict-resolution skills, (d) information-processing skills, (e) skills in decision making under ambiguity, (f) resource-allocation skills, (g) entrepreneurial skills, and (h) skills of introspection. These skills are all better taught in on-the-job training than through lectures and simulated practice.

The heavy emphasis on practica in doctoral level training within the Texas Woman's University adapted physical education specialization is to teach and/or reinforce these leadership skills as well as to refine pedagogical and research techniques. In conjunction with practica in which hidden agendas are to be achieved, weekly seminars appear to be important. The two self-evaluation instruments that appear at the end of this chapter are helpful in assisting graduate students to understand hidden agendas of seminars and practica.

Use of these instruments seems to facilitate the openness and sharing needed in leadership training. Heller (1974) emphasizes: "Openness does not mean blunt, tactless opinioning. It means a curiosity, a willingness to work with alternatives, a love of people. Honesty and integrity must be the overriding values" (p. 41).

Use of these instruments also seems to promote the conditions necessary for graduate study discussed by Harper (1980): (a) academic quality, (b) time to fiddle, (c) a baggy idea of truth, and (d) a sense of community. Readers are encouraged to peruse the works of both Harper and Heller and to develop their own position papers on leadership training.

References

Baker, J., & King, H. (1983). Leading physical education doctoral programs: What characteristics do they have in common? *Journal of Physical Education, Recreation, and Dance,* **54**(2), 51-54.

Barker, R.G. (1968). *Ecological psychology.* Stanford, CA: Stanford University Press.

Borich, G. (1980). A needs assessment model for conducting follow-up studies. *Journal of Teacher Education,* **31**(3), 39-42.

Freiberg, H.J., & Foster, D. (1979). Who should facilitate values education? *Journal of Teacher Education,* **30**(3), 37-40.

Frost, R., & Marshall, S. (1981). *Administration of physical education and athletics.* Dubuque, IA: Wm. C. Brown.

Harper, W. (1980). Some conditions for graduate study. *Quest,* **32**(2), 174-183.

Heller, M. (1974). *Preparing educational leaders: New challenges and new perspectives.* Bloomington, IN: Phi Delta Kappa Educational Foundation.

Krathwohl, D., Bloom, B., & Masia, B. (1964). *Taxonomy of educational objectives: Affective domain.* New York: David McKay.

Kroll, W. (1982). *Graduate study and research in physical education.* Champaign, IL: Human Kinetics.

Massengale, J. (1983). AAHPERD's role in the perceived quality of physical education graduate faculty. *Journal of Physical Education, Recreation, and Dance,* **54**(2), 57-64.

Massengale, J., & Sage, G. (1982). Departmental prestige and career mobility patterns of college physical educators. *Research Quarterly for Exercise and Sport,* **53**(4), 305-311.

McIntyre, M. (1981). Leadership development. *Quest,* **33**(1), 33-41.

Mintzberg, H. (1973). *The nature of managerial work.* New York: Harper & Row.

Safrit, M. (1979). Women in research in physical education. *Quest,* **31**(2), 158-171.

Tead, O. (1951). *The art of administration.* New York: McGraw-Hill.

SELF-EVALUATION FORM FOR INTERRELATING THEORY AND PRACTICE

Identify your major practicum experience settings this semester and indicate approximate number of hours in each.

_____   _____

_____   _____

_____   _____

_____   _____

_____   _____

1. To what extent did you gain knowledge of psychomotor development and motor and fitness performance in handicapped children and youth?

   Extensive   A lot   Some   A little   None

2. To what extent did you gain or refine competencies in assessment, IEP, teaching, and counseling handicapped students?

   Extensive   A lot   Some   A little   None

3. To what extent did you increase knowledge/skill regarding a particular type of educational setting and interpersonal relations?

   Extensive   A lot   Some   A little   None

4. To what extent did you read and/or seek out research to give direction and support to your practicum experiences (i.e., relate theory to practice)?

   Extensive   A lot   Some   A little   None

5. To what extent did you initiate sharing in our graduate seminar of your practicum experiences and/or direct attention to the knowledge base and research needs of your handicapped students/clients?

   Extensive   A lot   Some   A little   None

6. To what extent did you integrate and/or relate other course work (statistics, research, evaluation, biomechanics, computer, word processing, whatever) to your practicum experiences?

   Extensive   A lot   Some   A little   None

7. To what extent did you develop papers/products/tangibles to be shared with others from your practicum experiences: audiovisuals like slide shows, overheads, films, videotapes; instructional materials/manuals; assessment tools; research papers; nonresearch articles; poems/stories?

   Extensive   A lot   Some   A little   None

8. To what extent did you share your practicum experiences with your advisor/administrator outside of seminar class?

   Extensive   A lot   Some   A little   None

SELF-EVALUATION FORM:
DESIRED OUTCOMES OF A SEMINAR

1. Gradutate student will

demonstrate increased self-initiative and direction about handicapped individuals and adapted physical education (i.e., the habit of continuous self-directed learning that becomes part of one's life style and continues after formal schooling is completed).

Evidenced by	High				Low
(a) identifying own needs in relation to competencies established for the program	5	4	3	2	1
(b) designing a reading plan to meet needs	5	4	3	2	1
(c) designing an experiential plan to meet needs	5	4	3	2	1
(d) designing a plan to improve writing skills	5	4	3	2	1
(e) designing a plan to improve speaking/presenting skills	5	4	3	2	1
(f) implementing one's own learning plans	5	4	3	2	1
(g) creating a file of resource material	5	4	3	2	1
(h) sharing one's learning plan and the activities being implemented with administrator (seminar teacher)	5	4	3	2	1

2. Graduate student will

demonstrate increased leadership in his or her profession and in advocacy for handicapped persons.

Evidenced by

	High				Low
(a) membership and participation in selected professional organizations (i.e., supporting these organizations and their officers and actively seeking to improve them)	5	4	3	2	1
(b) advancing the knowledge base of one's discipline through continuous involvement in research	5	4	3	2	1
(c) reporting one's own research or synthesizing other persons' research findings through					
• sharing with peers in seminar setting	5	4	3	2	1
• presenting at workshops and meetings	5	4	3	2	1
• publishing in nonresearch journals	5	4	3	2	1
• publishing in research journals	5	4	3	2	1
• giving a demonstration or conducting a meet or event	5	4	3	2	1
(d) participating in the legislative process through					
• presenting oral and/or written testimony at hearings for the state plan and/or for legislation	5	4	3	2	1
• visiting with and writing congresspersons	5	4	3	2	1
• voting and encouraging others to vote	5	4	3	2	1

3. Graduate student will

demonstrate increased colleagueship and good interpersonal skills, including a growing feeling of responsibility for self as part of a community of scholars and service providers

Evidenced by

	High				Low
(a) contributing to effectiveness of seminar by arriving early or on time, getting into circle, focusing in on needed topics, taking initiative in shaping direction of seminar interaction	5	4	3	2	1
(b) assisting in making the seminar a meaningful sharing time, talking, contributing ideas, helping to relate practice to theory	5	4	3	2	1
(c) supporting others in their sharing, listening, expressing interest, asking questions of one another	5	4	3	2	1
(d) motivating and helping to facilitate each other's growth in class and out	5	4	3	2	1
(e) engaging in cooperative problem solving, including identification of problems and/or sources of conflict, misunderstanding, and discontent and taking initiative in ameliorating them	5	4	3	2	1
(f) assisting one another with work and/or learning activities, taking initiative—asking, How can I help?	5	4	3	2	1

Chapter 25

Teacher Training to Enhance Motor Learning by Mentally Retarded Individuals

Gail M. Dummer

A recent task force of the American Alliance for Health, Physical Education, Recreation, and Dance (AAHPERD) emphasized the importance of motor learning competencies for adapted physical education specialists by including two competency statements in their list of teacher training guidelines (Hurley, 1981). The task force indicated that the adapted physical education specialist should "demonstrate ability to apply principles of learning to individuals with specific physical and motor needs" and "demonstrate ability to apply principles of motivation on development of motor skills by individuals with disabilities" (p. 44). Unfortunately, these motor learning competencies are difficult to address within adapted physical education teacher training curricula. This dilemma exists primarily because of a limited knowledge base in motor learning characteristics of atypical populations.

Rationale for Motor Learning Competencies

The problem of an inadequate knowledge base is perhaps most critical to physical educators who teach mentally retarded children. Mentally retarded children seldom attain the same degree of proficiency at motor

Gail M. Dummer, Michigan State University, a specialist in the combined areas of motor learning, aquatics, and adapted physical education.

skills as do nonretarded children of the same chronological age (Bruininks, 1974; Francis & Rarick, 1959; Malpass, 1960, 1963; Mann, Burger, & Proger, 1974; Rarick, 1973). Educable mentally retarded children generally score 2 to 3 years behind nonretarded peers, while trainable mentally retarded children lag 3 to 5 years behind nonretarded children on motor tests (Rarick & Dobbins, 1972; Rarick & McQuillan, 1977). Furthermore, the motor deficits of mentally retarded children become progressively greater with increasing age (Francis & Rarick, 1959; Rarick, Widdop, & Broadhead, 1970; Sloan, 1951).

The motor performance of mentally retarded individuals is marked by qualitative as well as quantitative deficits in motor performance. Variability of performance is characteristic both of individual performers (Baumeister & Kellas, 1968a; Dummer, 1978; Dunn, 1978; McGown, Dobbins, & Rarick, 1973; Rarick & Dobbins, 1972; Rarick & McQuillan, 1977) and of the mentally retarded population as a whole (Bensberg & Cantor, 1957; Bruininks, 1974; Caffrey, Jones, & Hinkle, 1971; Heath, 1942; Karrer, Nelson, & Gailbraith, 1979; Rarick, 1973). Whereas nonretarded persons typically adapt learned motor skills to meet changing task demands, the mentally retarded individual seems unable to employ already acquired skills in new situations (Belmont & Butterfield, 1977; Borkowski & Cavanaugh, 1979; Brown, 1974).

Although the motor performance deficits of mentally retarded children have been documented by numerous investigators, little is known about the motor educability or motor learning potential of these children. The retardate's apparent inability to transfer skills from familiar to unfamiliar situations and the trait of high intraindividual variability of performance among retardates suggest that they do not learn motor tasks readily. Although some investigators have demonstrated that retardates do learn motor tasks with sufficient instruction and practice (Bankhead, 1976; Holman, 1933; Horgan, 1980; Kahn & Burdett, 1967; Lillie, 1967; Mann, Burger, & Proger, 1974; Rarick, 1973; Ross, 1969; Wade, 1977a), others have found that mentally retarded children are less efficient learners than their nonretarded peers, given similar instruction and practice (Anwar, 1981; Nideffer & Fowler, 1981; Wyrick & Owen, 1970).

Clearly, mentally retarded students could benefit from the skills of physical educators who are well versed in principles of motor learning. Although teacher training in motor learning is obviously important for adapted physical education teachers who work with mentally retarded populations, few guidelines suggest the optimal nature of such teacher training. At the present time, common sense would dictate that the student of adapted physical education should be exposed to existing motor learning curricula as well as courses concerned with the learning characteristics of the mentally retarded. Extensive research will be required before specific course work in motor learning for the mentally retarded can be developed.

Outline of Chapter

A review of existing research literature on the motor learning characteristics of the mentally retarded reveals numerous research needs. Extant research literature, the implications of this research for teaching practices, and future research needs are discussed in the remaining sections of this chapter. In this review, more attention will be given to research based upon the information processing model of motor learning than upon psychophysiological research. Although psychophysiological research may ultimately yield definitive explanations of motor learning that are valid and useful in the classroom setting, at this time results of information processing research have more implications for teaching motor skills to mentally retarded individuals. Because relatively little research has been published that directly addresses motor learning by mentally retarded individuals, pertinent findings describing verbal learning by retardates are included also.

Information Processing in the Acquisition of Motor Skills by Mentally Retarded Individuals

Information processing refers to the mental or cognitive operations involved in the input, decision-making, output, and feedback aspects of performance. Some scholars (e.g., Marteniuk, 1976) define motor learning as changes in the information processing component of motor skill performance. Learning occurs and motor skill levels improve when appropriate information processing strategies are used (Rothstein, 1981).

Research has revealed numerous developmental differences in information processing abilities. Young children process information less efficiently than older children or adults (Clark, 1978; Wade, 1977b), and retarded individuals process information less efficiently than nonretarded persons (Belmont, 1978; Belmont & Butterfield, 1977; Brown, 1974, 1975; Brown & Campione, 1978; Mercer & Snell, 1977). Some evidence shows that information processing may be a function of mental age (MA). If so, retardates should exhibit similar learning abilities as do nonretarded children of equal MA. While the equal MA hypothesis has received considerable attention in the verbal learning literature (Belmont, 1978;

Brown, 1975), few investigators have compared the information processing abilities of MA-matched retarded and nonretarded subjects on motor learning tasks (Dummer, 1979; Poretta, 1982; Sugden, 1977, 1978).

Developmental differences typical of mentally retarded and equal MA nonretarded children have been noted in each aspect of information processing in verbal learning tasks. Some of these differences have been noted also in motor learning tasks. Additional research is needed to determine the exact nature of developmental differences in information processing in motor learning as well as ways in which such developmental differences might be remediated. Until such time as the knowledge base of developmental motor learning is expanded, the adapted physical educator should become aware of the demonstrated developmental differences in input, decision-making, output, and feedback aspects of information processing and should use common sense in applying principles of motor learning to teaching activities.

Input

Input consists of all information that is considered by the performer when making a decision. Factors that are important in the input stage of information processing include the ability to focus attention on task dimensions, concentrate on relevant internal or external stimuli and ignore irrelevant stimuli, maintain attention, predict event outcomes on the basis of a few early cues, and be aware of changing events in the environment (Rothstein, 1981).

Mentally retarded individuals frequently exhibit deficiencies in input skills. In a review of Zeaman and House's attention theory of retardate learning difficulties, Mercer and Snell (1977) cited evidence indicating that the retardate's primary learning difficulty is an inability to sample the stimulus field and select the relevant stimuli. In the Zeaman and House discrimination learning experiments, the subjects' initial task was to discover relevant dimensions of two stimuli and determine which stimulus object was associated with a reward. Nonretarded subjects made this discrimination rapidly. In contrast the number of trials of chance-level responding among retardates increased as a function of decreasing MA. Once the discrimination was made, the rate of incidental learning was similar for all subjects, regardless of MA.

Other attentional deficits also contribute to the retardate's poor learning abilities. Krupski (1979) found that retarded children spent less time on task, more time out of seat, and more time looking busy but not working than nonretarded children during academic tasks. Although retarded children were less attentive than others during academic tasks, this disctractibility did not carry over to nonacademic tasks. Another point of view was proffered by Baumeister and Kellas (1968), who reviewed numerous studies on reaction time performance in which retardates exhibited slower reaction times than nonretarded subjects. Baumeister and Kellas concluded that retardates show an arousal deficiency or attentional lag to stimuli presented in reaction time experiments.

Motor learning texts offer many suggestions as to how teachers can help students to develop input skills; however, few of these suggestions have been tested with retarded students in motor learning tasks. These suggestions include (a) manipulating the familiarity, complexity, and uncertainty of environmental stimuli; (b) manipulating task difficulty; (c) providing verbal cues about where to focus attention; (d) enhancing relevant cues and reducing the intensity of less important cues; (e) changing the ratio of important to unimportant cues; (f) providing advance warnings about what to expect; (g) motivating students to attend by use of reward systems; (h) gradually returning manipulated task conditions back to normal as learning occurs; and (i) once learning has occurred, providing a variety of practice conditions (Rothstein, 1981).

Although common sense dictates that use of these teaching strategies should enhance the motor learning of mentally retarded students in many situations, research evidence indicating the applicability of these suggestions to retarded students is sparse. Gold (1972, 1973a, 1973b) employed several of these teaching strategies in an effort to improve discrimination learning by retardates. Gold and his associates taught retardates to assemble a 10-speed bike brake in part by manipulating task difficulty, telling subjects where to focus attention, and increasing the intensity of important task cues. Gold and Pomerantz (1978) also point out the importance of task analysis as an approach to reducing task difficulty.

Research by Baumeister and Hawkins (1966) and Surburg (1981) indicates that mentally retarded subjects perform best when they know what to expect in a reaction time task. Subjects in both studies performed best when a consistent temporal interval existed between the onset of a warning signal and the presentation of the reaction time stimulus. Baumeister, Hawkins, and Kellas (1965) found reaction time of retardates to be faster under conditions of high stimulus intensity. Hasazi and Allen (1973, 1975) confirmed the facilitating effects of stimulus intensity and also concluded that monetary reinforcements improve attention and performance in the reaction time task.

In addition to the motor learning studies cited above, numerous investigations of the verbal learning abilities of mentally retarded individuals have involved the use of these teaching strategies. When discussing Zeaman and House's attention theory, Mercer and Snell (1977) cited several studies that demonstrated the effectiveness of these teaching methods with retarded populations in verbal learning tasks. Before concluding that such teaching strategies will work in motor learning situations, these verbal learning studies must be replicated using motor learning tasks.

Decision Making

Decision making refers to the executive plan the performer generates for a movement response to meet specific task requirements. The executive plan consists of instructions to the body about the planned movement response. It is a flexible plan designed specifically for the task at hand and includes information about the timing and sequence of subroutines needed for that response. Subroutines are standard practiced movement sequences that are always performed in exactly the same way. The quality of the movement decision or executive plan depends upon the quality of input information. The performer with good input skills who has a good memory of experience in similar situations should generate better decisions.

The primary factors related to improvement in the decision-making segment of information processing are the use of strategies to retain input information in short-term memory long enough for the decision-making process to occur and the use of strategies designed to retain subroutines in long-term memory for use in future movement decisions. Other factors of importance in decision making are the ability to develop general rules or schema to guide the planning and selection of movements to meet task demands, the ability to execute subroutine movements without conscious attention, and the ability to integrate and analyze complex information (Rothstein, 1981).

Mentally retarded students exhibit considerable difficulty in the decision-making aspect of information processing. The characteristics of retardate learning and memory that have received the most attention in verbal learning are deficiencies in the production and use of memory strategies (Belmont, 1978; Belmont & Butterfield, 1977; Borkowski & Cavanaugh, 1979; Brown, 1974, 1975; Ellis, 1970; Friedman, Krupski, Dawson, & Rosenburg, 1977; Glidden, 1979; Mercer & Snell, 1977; Spitz, 1966). Strategies typically used by nonretarded persons to remember input information in verbal learning tasks include labeling, grouping or categorizing stimulus materials, cues, simple rehearsal, cumulative rehearsal, imagery, and verbal elaboration. Retardates are generally less likely than nonretarded persons to use any of these strategies (Glidden, 1979). In addition, retardates lack what Belmont and Butterfield (1977) call executive function, the ability to select, coordinate, and sequence the most effective learning strategies for a particular situation. Furthermore, mentally retarded persons are deficient in metamemory, or knowing about knowing (Brown, 1975; Friedman et al., 1977).

The performance of retardates on many verbal learning tasks that require the production or use of memory strategies or require metamemory is similar to that of equal MA nonretarded children (Brown, 1975). As would be expected, the level of performance among retardates on such tasks is generally found to be a function of MA. When the use of memory strategies is not required or is prevented by experimental manipulation, retardates often perform near the level of nonretarded persons of equal chronological age (CA).

Retardates apparently exhibit these developmental differences in the generation or use of appropriate learning strategies in motor learning tasks. Sugden (1977, 1978) found that equal CA normal and educable subnormal boys performed similarly on a linear positioning task when rehearsal of positioning information was prevented but that normal boys out-performed the retarded boys on trials during which information rehearsal was possible. Sugden attributed these differences to nonuse of mnemonic strategies by retarded boys. Kelso, Goodman, Stamm, and Hayes (1979) and Reid (1980) described similar results concerning the short-term motor memory of mentally retarded individuals. Kelso et al. (1979) also indicated that short-term motor memory may be a function of MA in that older educable retardates performed better than younger educable retardates.

Other investigators have attempted to facilitate motor learning among mentally retarded children through the use of verbal elaboration or verbal mediation. Luria (1963) asked young children to talk their way through a multipart task. He observed that the use of language helped the children to remember what to do next. Wacker, Carroll, and Moe (1980) and Rotundo and Johnson (1981) used a similar verbalization strategy to assist trainable mentally retarded children to learn an assembly task.

Research is needed to determine the nature of other memory strategies (e.g., mental practice) that may facilitate decision making by mentally retarded persons. In addition, information is needed on the executive functioning ability of retardates in motor learning tasks before researchers and teachers can consider ways of improving the decision-making abilities of retarded individuals.

Motor learning research from investigations involving nonretarded subjects suggests that teachers can help students to develop better decision-making skills by (a) providing verbal cues to help the performer to "chunk" environmental cues and attend to internal proprioceptive cues, (b) providing the student with a general plan to guide decision making, (c) specifying various subroutine movements and their temporal and spatial organization for the performer, (d) modeling the task to be performed, (e) judiciously using the whole and part methods of practice to facilitate learning of subroutines, (f) providing extensive practice to facilitate learning of subroutines,

(g) providing variability of practice conditions to enhance schema development, and (h) providing feedback about performance outcomes to help enable the performer to update schema rules (Marteniuk, 1976; Rothstein, 1981).

Few investigations have been performed to determine the validity of these teaching suggestions to improve decision making in motor learning situations by mentally retarded populations. Chasey (1971, 1977) determined that overlearning of gross motor skills improved retention of those skills over an 8-week period. Presumably, motor skills experience retained in long-term memory should facilitate decision making in similar situations.

Dummer (1979) conducted two experiments to determine whether variable practice conditions facilitate schema development and whether instruction in movement strategies improves performance among trainable mentally retarded children and nonretarded children of equal MA. Neither variability of practice nor instruction resulted in improved performance levels by trainable retardates in the Dummer studies. Although Dummer did not produce evidence of the efficacy of variable practice conditions, Poretta (1982) did find variable practice conditions to be superior to constant practice conditions for educable mentally retarded boys on a kicking for accuracy task. More research is needed to determine the optimal nature of practice conditions for mentally retarded learners.

Research evidence from verbal learning studies is more voluminous. These studies indicate that although retarded individuals may be trained to use efficient learning strategies, decision making may be the most difficult aspect of information processing for the retardate to develop. Studies performed by Belmont and Butterfield (1977) and by Butterfield, Wambold, and Belmont (1973) were concerned with demonstrating that retarded people will benefit from executing good memory programs and also that normal adult's memory will suffer as a consequence of doing what self-programmed retarded people do by way of memorizing. Belmont and Butterfield (1977) demonstrated that retarded people were capable of using appropriate learning strategies when instructed to do so, but failed to produce or use such strategies spontaneously. Brown (1974, 1975) and Brown and Campione (1978) found similar results with both retarded subjects and equal MA nonretarded children.

Borkowski and Cavanaugh (1979) also noted the retardate's apparent inability to transfer, generalize, or maintain strategies across tasks. Based upon a review of relevant literature, Borkowski and Cavanaugh (1979) concluded that an inability to produce or use appropriate strategies may be an instructional problem rather than a retardate deficit. They noted the importance of the students' readiness to learn as an instructional variable. (Some scholars have suggested the use of Piagetian stages as indices of learning readiness. See reviews by Kahn, 1979; Klein & Safford, 1977; Sternlicht, 1981; Weisz & Yeates, 1981; Woodward, 1979.) Borkowski and Cavanaugh (1979) further suggested that maintenance of learning strategies may be better when learning materials are physically manipulated by the performer.

Glidden (1979) reviewed the efforts of her colleagues and noted that efforts to improve the production and use of strategies by retarded persons have not been particularly economical. Glidden commented that "while it is of theoretical interest that remediation of a production deficiency is possible by training a strategy, it is of little practical importance if the training involves 25 PhD-level person hours for 20% improvement in 50% of the subjects, lasting for only 48 hours" (p. 647). Glidden's comment serves as a caveat to her colleagues. Cost-effective teaching methods for use with retarded populations still need to be developed.

Output

Output refers to the performer's ability to execute the planned movement sequence. The ability to move the body as planned depends upon the integrity of neurological, physiological, sensory, and structural systems of the body, as well as upon practice.

Most mildly mentally retarded individuals possess the neurological, physiological, sensory, and structural integrity necessary for the execution of motor skills. Individuals with moderate, severe, and profound levels of retardation and certain subpopulations of mentally retarded persons typically experience movement difficulties. These difficulties may stem from delayed development (e.g., interference from dominating reflexes), anomalies associated with a specific etiology (e.g., short stature of Down's syndrome children), or impairments associated with an accompanying handicap (e.g., cerebral palsy). Such movement deficits may also have unknown etiology. The effects of such deficiencies upon motor performance by retardates have been reviewed elsewhere.

Motor learning research concerned with improving the execution of movement sequences indicates that practice is the primary ingredient for improvement (Rothstein, 1981). The physical educator should consider the efficacy of the following methods in deciding upon the nature of practice sessions: massed versus distributed practice, speed versus accuracy tradeoff, and physical versus mental practice.

Chasey (1976) investigated the distribution of practice effects on learning retention and relearning by retarded boys. He found that subjects in distributed practice groups needed fewer trials to criterion than subjects in

massed practice groups on a stabilometer task. Longer rest intervals between trial blocks were associated with better performance. Chasey also noted that no difference existed between massed and distributed practice groups with respect to retention or relearning of the balance skill.

Additional research is clearly needed to determine ways of improving movement execution by retarded persons. Teachers may also need to be concerned with helping retarded students to alter movement patterns to conform with individual differences in ability.

Feedback

Feedback refers to knowledge about the results of a planned movement or movement sequence. Knowledge of results may be ascertained by the performer on the basis of proprioceptive, sensory, or environmental cues. Information about performance can be obtained also from a teacher or other observer. Performers with good information processing skills are able to use feedback constructively to improve future decisions about movement and to improve the actual execution of planned movements.

The major factors related to improvement in the use of feedback are the ability to determine which internal and external cues provide information about the relative success of a performance, the ability to interpret the meaning of feedback, and the ability to determine needed adjustments to correct decision or movement errors (Rothstein, 1981).

Although some investigators have failed to demonstrate that retardates may benefit from knowledge of results (Knowles, 1974), most investigators have found that the motor performance of retardates improves when information about performance results is provided. Nideffer and Fowler (1981) found that nonretarded subjects were more capable of using visual and proprioceptive feedback on a force production task than were equal MA retarded children. Retarded subjects in the Nideffer and Fowler study improved more under conditions of visual feedback than when using proprioceptive feedback.

Levy (1974) concluded that mentally retarded children performed better on a pursuit rotor task when knowledge of results was provided than when knowledge of results was not provided, regardless of reinforcement contingencies. Horgan's (1980) educable mentally retarded subjects also improved on a pursuit rotor task when knowledge of results was provided. Horgan noted that tactile and auditory feedback were more effective than visual feedback in improving performance, and that knowledge of results was more effective when subjects were informed about successful rather than unsuccessful performance attempts.

Karrer et al. (1979) reviewed studies indicating that retardates could benefit from highly sophisticated forms of feedback. Studies were cited in which retardates learned to use electromyographical feedback and other forms of biofeedback to reduce the incidence of seizures.

Although some performers are capable of using feedback to improve performance without the assistance of a teacher or coach, others need help to benefit from cues that provide information about the relative success of their efforts. Motor learning experts (Rothstein, 1981) suggest that teachers can assist students in using feedback by (a) providing verbal cues to direct the performer's attention to important feedback information, (b) enhancing feedback cues, (c) providing feedback in a form that is clear to the performer, (d) providing precise quantitative or qualitative knowledge of results rather than general statements about effort, (e) providing reinforcement to encourage the performer to attend to feedback cues, (f) demonstrating or teaching about cause and effect relationships, and (g) informing the performer of movement adjustments that are needed to correct errors.

Several investigators have found various types of reinforcements to be helpful in improving performance by mentally retarded learners on motor tasks. Holland, Friedrich, and Hawkins (1974) discovered that the pursuit rotor performance of educable mentally retarded children improved when monetary rewards were employed. Furthermore, retardates improved performance more than nonretarded children under these monetary reward conditions.

Although reinforcement is apparently effective in improving the motor performance of retardates, some investigators have discovered that knowledge of results plus reinforcement is more effective than reinforcement alone. Heitman, Justen, and Gilley (1980) studied educable mentally retarded children as they learned a marble placement task. Subjects performed better under conditions of praise than with silence or general conversation. Knowledge of results also elevated performance levels; however, the combination of knowledge of results plus praise was the most potent condition for improvement of performance by the Heitman et al. subjects. Levy (1974) similarly noted that reinforcement plus knowledge of results was the most effective type of feedback. In the Levy study, retarded subjects responded better to tangible rewards than social reinforcements.

Whereas the teaching strategy of pairing reinforcement with knowledge of results has received considerable attention by researchers, other teaching suggestions designed to facilitate use of feedback cues by retardates have not been investigated. Research is needed to determine the utility of these teaching strategies with mentally retarded populations.

Understanding the Psychophysiological Bases of Motor Learning by Mentally Retarded Individuals

Psychophysiological research involves the study of psychological events in terms of physiological activity of the central and autonomic nervous systems (CNS and ANS). The purpose of psychophysiological research is generally to determine lawful relationships between behavior and physiological events during various affective, cognitive, and motor activities. Karrer et al. (1979) indicate that "the determination of the effects of these variables on the physiological systems is an essential step in the elucidation of the black box and is an interface with more molecular neuroscience" (p. 231). Typical dependent variables in psychophysiological research include electroencephalograms (EEGs) and event-related potentials (ERPs) as indices of CNS function and cardiovascular, electrodermal, and respiratory activity as indices of ANS function.

Knowledge of psychophysiological characteristics of mentally retarded individuals is available from studies of both motor learning and verbal learning. Most reported psychophysiological research in motor learning has involved the assessment of physiological activity during performance of various reaction time tasks. Researchers in verbal learning have employed a variety of tasks and experimental conditions when studying psychophysiological phenomena among retarded persons. Several comprehensive reviews of psychophysiological research involving mentally retarded subjects are available to the interested reader, including those by Berkson (1963), Clausen (1977), and Karrer et al. (1979). Continued research effort in this area may help determine whether the organization of cortical activity in mental retardation follows the same developmental sequence as in the nonretarded population, or whether some etiology-specific factors may exist in neurological functioning and motor learning characteristics.

Conclusion

At the outset of this chapter, it was suggested that AAHPERD's motor learning competencies (AAHPERD, 1980) are difficult to address within adapted physical education teacher training curricula because of a limited knowledge base in the motor learning characteristics of handicapped populations. The preceding review of research on the information processing and psychophysiological characteristics of retardates attests to the validity of that premise with respect to mentally retarded individuals. Relatively little is known about the motor learning characteristics of retardates, and even less is known about how to remediate the identified motor learning deficits of retarded students. A review of extant literature on the learning and memory characteristics of persons with other handicapping conditions may reveal a similar lack of knowledge.

How then can students of adapted physical education be trained and prepared to "demonstrate ability to apply principles of learning to individuals with special physical and motor needs" (Hurley, 1981, p. 44)? The importance of a secure knowledge base on motor learning characteristics of handicapped students is obvious. Research to expand that knowledge base is needed before teacher training efforts in motor learning for the handicapped can succeed. Perhaps AAHPERD should add competency statements pertaining to research skills to their adapted physical education teacher training guidelines.

References

Anwar, F. (1981). Visual-motor localizations in normal and subnormal development. *British Journal of Psychology, 72*, 43-57.

Bankhead, I. (1976). Task difficulty and motor performance in severe subnormality. *Journal of Mental Deficiency Research, 20*, 261-265.

Baumeister, A., & Hawkins, W. (1966). Variations of the preparatory interval in relation to the reaction times of mental defectives. *American Journal of Mental Deficiency, 70*, 689-694.

Baumeister, A., Hawkins, W., & Kellas, G. (1965). Reaction speed as a function of stimulus intensity in normals and retardates. *Perceptual and Motor Skills, 20*, 649-652.

Baumeister, A., & Kellas, G. (1968a). Distribution of reaction times of retardates and normals. *American Journal of Mental Deficiency, 72*, 715-718.

Baumeister, A., & Kellas, G. (1968b). Reaction time and mental retardation. In N.R. Ellis (Ed.), *International review of research in mental retardation* (Vol. 3, pp. 163-194). New York: Academic Press.

Belmont, J.M. (1978). Individual differences in memory: The cases of normal and retarded development. In M. Gruenbert & P. Morris (Eds.), *Aspects of memory* (pp. 153-185). London: Methuen.

Belmont, J.M., & Butterfield, E.C. (1977). The instructional approach to developmental cognitive research. In R. Kail & J. Hagen (Eds.), *Perspectives on the development of memory and cognition* (pp. 437-481). Hillsdale, NJ: L. Erlbaum.

Bensberg, G.J., & Cantor, G.N. (1957). Reaction time in mental defectives with organic and familial etiology. *American Journal of Mental Deficiency, 62*, 534-537.

Berkson, G. (1963). Psychophysiological studies in mental deficiency. In N.R. Ellis (Ed.), *Handbook of mental deficiency: Psychological theory and research* (pp. 556-573). New York: McGraw-Hill.

Borkowski, J.G., & Cavanaugh, J.C. (1979). Maintenance and generalization of skills and strategies by the retarded. In N.R. Ellis (Ed.), *Handbook of mental deficiency: Psychological theory and research* (pp. 569-618). Hillsdale, NJ: L. Erlbaum.

Brown, A.L. (1974). The role of strategic behavior in retardate memory. In N.R. Ellis (Ed.), *International review of research in mental retardation* (Vol. 7, pp. 55-111). New York: Academic Press.

Brown, A.L. (1975). The development of memory: Knowing, knowing about knowing, and knowing how to know. In H.W. Reese (Ed.), *Advances in child development and behavior* (Vol. 10, pp. 103-152). New York: Academic Press.

Brown, A.L., & Campione, J.C. (1978). Memory strategies in learning: Training children to study strategically. In H. Pick & H. Stevenson (Eds.), *Applications of basic research in psychology* (pp. 85-99). New York: Plenum Press.

Bruininks, R.H. (1974). Physical and motor development of retarded persons. In N.R. Ellis (Ed.), *International review of research in mental retardation* (Vol. 7, pp. 209-261). New York: Academic Press.

Butterfield, E.C., Wambold, C., & Belmont, J.M. (1973). On the theory and practice of improving short-term memory. *American Journal of Mental Deficiency, 77*, 654-669.

Caffrey, B., Jones, J., & Hinkle, B. (1971). Variability in reaction times of normal and educable mentally retarded children. *Perceptual and Motor Skills, 32*, 255-258.

Chasey, W.C. (1971). Overlearning as a variable in the retention of gross motor skills by the mentally retarded. *Research Quarterly, 42*, 145-149.

Chasey, W.C. (1976). Distribution of practice effects on learning, retention and relearning by retarded boys. *Perceptual and Motor Skills, 43*, 159-164.

Chasey, W.C. (1977). Motor skill overlearning effects on retention and overlearning by retarded boys. *Research Quarterly, 48,* 41-46.

Clark, J.E. (1978). Memory processes in the early acquisition of motor skills. In M.V. Ridenour (Ed.), *Motor development: Issues and applications* (pp. 99-112). Princeton, NJ: Princeton Book.

Clausen, J. (1977). Psychophysiology of mental retardation. In N.R. Ellis (Ed.), *International review of research in mental retardation* (Vol. 9, pp. 85-126). New York: Academic Press.

Dummer, G.M. (1979). Information processing in the acquisition of motor skills by mentally retarded children. *Dissertation Abstracts International, 40,* 152A.

Dunn, J.M. (1978). Reliability of selected psychomotor measures with mentally retarded adult males. *Perceptual and Motor Skills, 46,* 295-301.

Ellis, N.R. (1970). Memory processes in retardates and normals. In N.R. Ellis (Ed.), *International review of research in mental retardation* (Vol. 4, pp. 1-32). New York: Academic Press.

Francis, R.J., & Rarick, G.L. (1959). Motor characteristics of the mentally retarded. *American Journal of Mental Deficiency, 63,* 792-811.

Friedman, M., Krupski, A., Dawson, E.T., & Rosenberg, P. (1977). Metamemory and mental retardation: Implications for research and practice. In P. Mittler (Ed.), *Research to practice in mental retardation: Education and training* (Vol. 2, pp. 99-104). Baltimore: University Park Press.

Glidden, L.M. (1979). Training of learning and memory in retarded persons: Strategies, techniques, and teaching tools. In N.R. Ellis (Ed.), *Handbook of mental deficiency: Psychological theory and research* (pp. 619-658). Hillsdale, NJ: L. Erlbaum.

Gold, M.W. (1972). Stimulus factors in skill training of the retarded on a complex assembly task: Acquisition, transfer and retention. *American Journal of Mental Deficiency, 76,* 517-526.

Gold, M.W. (1973a). Factors affecting production by the retarded: Base rate. *Mental Retardation, 11,* 41-44.

Gold, M.W. (1973b). Research on the vocational habilitation of the retarded: The present, the future. In N.R. Ellis (Ed.), *International review of research in mental retardation* (Vol. 6, pp. 97-148). New York: Academic Press.

Gold, M.W., & Pomerantz, D.J. (1978). Issues in prevocational training. In M.E. Snell (Ed.), *Systematic instruction of the moderately and severely handicapped.* Columbus: Charles E. Merrill.

Hasazi, J.E., & Allen, R.M. (1973). Signal intensity and reinforcement effects on reaction time in brain-damaged and familial retardates. *Perceptual and Motor Skills, 36,* 1227-1233.

Hasazi, J.E., & Allen, R.M. (1975). Differential reinforcement of reaction times in developmental retardates. *Perceptual and Motor Skills, 41,* 631-634.

Heath, S.R., Jr. (1942). Railwalking performance as related to mental age and etiological type among the mentally retarded. *American Journal of Psychology, 55,* 240-247.

Heitman, R.J., Justen, J.E., & Gilley, W.F. (1980). Effects of mental age, knowledge of results and social reinforcement on motor performance. *American Journal of Mental Deficiency, 85,* 200-202.

Holland, J.M., Friedrich, D., & Hawkins, W.F. (1974). Effects of incentive on rotary pursuit performance by normals and retardates. *Perceptual and Motor Skills, 39,* 491-494.

Holman, P. (1933). The relationship between general mental development and manual dexterity. *British Journal of Psychiatry, 23,* 279-283.

Horgan, J.S. (1980). Pursuit rotor learning of mildly retarded children under supplementary feedback conditions. *Perceptual and Motor Skills, 50,* 1219-1228.

Hurley, D. (1981). Guidelines for adapted physical education. *Journal of Physical Education, Recreation, and Dance, 52,* 43-44.

Kahn, H., & Burdett, A.D. (1967). Introduction of practice and rewards on motor performance of adolescent mental retardates. *American Journal of Mental Deficiency, 72,* 422-427.

Kahn, J.V. (1979). Applications of the Piagetian literature to severely and profoundly mentally retarded persons. *Mental Retardation, 17,* 273-280.

Karrer, R., Nelson, M., & Galbraith, G.C. (1979). Psychophysiological research with the mentally retarded. In N.R. Ellis (Ed.), *Handbook of mental deficiency: Psychological theory and research* (pp. 231-288). Hillsdale, NJ: L. Erlbaum.

Kelso, J.A., Goodman, D., Stamm, C.L., & Hayes, C. (1979). Movement coding and memory in retarded children. *American Journal of Mental Deficiency, 83,* 601-611.

Klein, N.K., & Safford, P.L. (1977). Application of Piaget's theory to the study of thinking by the mentally retarded: A review of research. *Journal of Special Education, 11,* 201-216.

Knowles, C.J. (1974). The effect of extrinsic feedback on the learning of gross motor skills by mildly and moderately retarded males. *Dissertation Abstracts International, 34,* 5690A.

Krupski, A. (1979). Are retarded children more distractible? Observational analysis of retarded and nonretarded children's classroom behavior. *American Journal of Mental Deficiency, 84,* 1-10.

Levy, J. (1974). Social reinforcement and knowledge of results as determinants of motor performance among educable mentally retarded children. *American Journal of Mental Deficiency, 78,* 752-758.

Lillie, D.L. (1967). The effects of motor development lessons on mentally retarded children. *American Journal of Mental Deficiency, 72,* 803-808.

Luria, A.R. (1963). Psychological studies of mental deficiency in the Soviet Union. In N.R. Ellis (Ed.), *Handbook of mental deficiency: Psychological theory and research* (pp. 253-387). New York: McGraw-Hill.

Malpass, L.F. (1960). Motor proficiency in institutionalized and noninstitutionalized retarded and normal children. *American Journal of Mental Deficiency, 64,* 1012-1015.

Malpass, L.F. (1963). Motor skills in mental deficiency. In N.R. Ellis (Ed.), *Handbook of mental deficiency: Psychological theory and research* (pp. 602-631). New York: McGraw-Hill.

Mann, L., Burger, R.M., & Proger, B.B. (1974). Physical education intervention with the exceptional child. In L. Mann & D. Sabatino (Eds.), *The second review of special education* (pp. 193-250). Philadelphia: J.S.E. Press.

Marteniuk, R.G. (1976). *Information processing in motor skills.* New York: Holt, Rinehart, and Winston.

McGown, C.M., Dobbins, A.D., & Rarick, G.L. (1973). Intra-individual variability of normal and educable mentally retarded children on a coincidence timing task. *Journal of Motor Behavior, 5,* 193-198.

Mercer, C.D., & Snell, M.E. (1977). *Learning theory research in mental retardation: Implications for teaching.* Columbus: Charles E. Merrill.

Nideffer, F.D., & Fowler, S.C. (1981). Nonretarded and mentally retarded children's performance on a manual-control task with and without visual feedback. *American Journal of Mental Deficiency, 85,* 521-529.

Poretta, D.L. (1982). Motor schema formation by EMR boys. *American Journal of Mental Deficiency, 87,* 164-172.

Rarick, G.L. (1973). Motor performance of mentally retarded children. In G.L. Rarick (Ed.), *Physical activity: Human growth and development* (pp. 227-256). New York: Academic Press.

Rarick, G.L., & Dobbins, D.A. (1972). *Basic components in the motor performance of educable mentally retarded children: Implications for curriculum development* (Grant No. OEG-0-70-2568-610). Washington, DC: U.S. Office of Education.

Rarick, G.L., & McQuillan, J.P. (1977). *Factor structure of motor abilities of trainable mentally retarded children* (Grant No. OEG-0-73-5170). Washington, DC: U.S. Office of Education.

Rarick, G.L., Widdop, J.H., & Broadhead, G.A. (1970). The physical fitness and motor performance of educable mentally retarded children. *Exceptional Children, 36,* 509-519.

Reid, G. (1980). Overt and covert rehearsal in short-term motor memory of mentally retarded and nonretarded persons. *American Journal of Mental Deficiency, 85,* 69-77.

Ross, S.A. (1969). Effects of an intensive motor skills training program on young educable mentally retarded children. *American Journal of Mental Deficiency, 73,* 920-926.

Rothstein, A. (1981). *Motor learning: Basic stuff series I.* Reston, VA: American Alliance for Health, Physical Education, Recreation and Dance.

Rotundo, N., & Johnson, E.G. (1981). Verbal control of motor behavior in mentally retarded children: A re-examination of Luria's theory. *Journal of Mental Deficiency Research, 25,* 281-298.

Sloan, W. (1951). Motor proficiency and intelligence. *American Journal of Mental Deficiency, 55,* 394-406.

Spitz, H.H. (1966). The role of input organization in the learning and memory of mental retardates. In N.R. Ellis (Ed.), *International review of research in mental retardation* (Vol. 2, pp. 29-56). New York: Academic Press.

Sternlicht, M. (1981). The development of cognitive judgement in the mentally retarded: A selective review of Piagetian-inspired research. *Journal of Genetic Psychology, 139,* 55-68.

Sugden, D.A. (1977). The relation of visual motor short term memory to age and intelligence. *Dissertation Abstracts International, 38,* 2707A.

Sugden, D.A. (1978). Visual motor short term memory in educationally subnormal boys. *British Journal of Educational Psychology, 48,* 330-339.

Surburg, P.R. (1981). Effects of uncertainties of time and occurrence on reaction time of mentally handicapped students. *Perceptual and Motor Skills, 53,* 355-360.

Wacker, D.P., Carroll, J.L., & Moe, G.L. (1980). Acquisition, generalization, and maintenance of an assembly task by mentally retarded children. *American Journal of Mental Deficiency,* **85**, 286-290.

Wade, M.G. (1977a). Categories of disabilities and their influences on the motor performance of children. In R.E. Stadulis (Ed.), *Research and practice in physical education* (pp. 77-84). Champaign, IL: Human Kinetics.

Wade, M.G. (1977b). Developmental motor learning. In J.F. Keogh & R.S. Hutton (Eds.), *Exercise and sport sciences reviews* (Vol. 4, pp. 375-394). Santa Barbara, CA: Journal Publishing Affiliates.

Weisz, J.R., & Yeates, K.O. (1981). Cognitive development in retarded and nonretarded persons: Piagetian tests of the similar structure hypothesis. *Psychological Bulletin,* **90**, 153-178.

Woodward, W.M. (1979). Piaget's theory and the study of mental retardation. In N.R. Ellis (Ed.), *Handbook of mental deficiency: Psychological theory and research* (pp. 169-196). Hillsdale, NJ: L. Erlbaum.

Wyrick, W., & Owen, G. (1970). Effects of practice on simple reaction time of trainable mental retardates. *American Corrective Therapy Journal,* **24**, 176-179.

Editor's Note: For additional information and references, see

Hoover, J., & Wade, M. (1985). Motor learning theory and mentally retarded individuals: A historical review. *Adapted Physical Activity Quarterly,* **2**(3), 228-252.

Chapter 26

Personnel Preparation in Physical Education and Litigation

David Auxter and Charles Jelley

*T*he right to education litigation of the early 1970s (*Lau v. Nichol*, 1974; *PARC v. Commonwealth of Pennsylvania*, 1972, also called the PARC Consent) challenged fundamental educational practices of the time: (a) exclusion of handicapped children from educational services, (b) education in the most integrated setting, (c) individualized instruction, and (d) parent participation in determining the outcomes of education for handicapped children. These early cases required major changes in educational practices. Changes in instructional practices required techniques for individualizing instruction for heterogenous groups of children of which handicapped children were a part. The states then went to the federal government for assistance in delivering the previously denied constitutional right to an appropriate education under the equal protection clause of the United States Constitution. Testimony given to the Congress in the formulation of PL 94-142 emphasized the fact that all children could learn through the application of a body of scientifically and empirically validated practices to educate the handicapped. Thus the obligation of colleges and universities who train physical education personnel to teach the handicapped through individualized instruction with the nonhandicapped requires application of training technology that imparts validated scientific practices from research and demonstration.

Senator Stafford (1975) asserted on the floor of Congress the benefits of providing public education for all handicapped children.

> This is the day that handicapped children and their parents can point to and say that this Congress—their Congress—recognized as matter of National

policy, the equal protection under the law that they have always deserved.

In this Nation, in this society, a right to an education is not a great deal to ask. That right should be guaranteed. For those estimated 7 million unserved handicapped children and their parents, it should be an everyday fact, not a legal matter. It is a pattern that every normal child expects to wake up and find five days a week. So should the handicapped child.

It is part of the rhythm of life in this country, an unconscious assumption, that our children will be educated. So should it be for the handicapped child and his parents. It must not be, for them, a court battle.

Those children have hopes and dreams and desires to achieve in some measure, just as do their normal peers. They should not have to go to court—as they have had to in 27 states—to assure for themselves something that for everyone else is part of the pattern, the rhythm and assumption of everyday life.

I think that today Congress makes a very important statement. It makes a necessary statement of principle about how we intend our handicapped children to be treated in the educational process. Unfortunately, we cannot, by that or any other statement, change the attitudes of those who would equate ''handicap'' with ''inferior.''Attitudes and prejudices cannot be legislated away. They will only be changed by the good will of men. This statement that we make will help because it is designed to bring

Dave Auxter (center), Slippery Rock State University, with Joseph Winnick, Brockport State University, on his left. Auxter is senior author of *Principles and Methods of Adapted Physical Education and Recreation* and a prolific writer from the 1960s onward.

our children together, those with and without handicaps, to try to undo the prejudices in education. (p. 20403)

Impact of PL 94-142 on Intended Outcomes

The intended outcome of PL 94-142 for handicapped children was maximization of skills that enhance self-sufficient living in the community. It was intended that state of the art technology would be employed to reach this goal. As a result, there were significant rule changes in the manner that physical education teachers were to conduct instruction. The Pennsylvania litigation (*Armstrong v. Kline*, 1979; *Fialkowski v. Pittenger*, 1976; *PARC v. Commonwealth of Pennsylvania*, 1972; and *PARC v. Scanlon*, also called PARC Enforcement, 1982) indicates that handicapped children have made few gains over a 10-year period as a result of the introduction of state and federal legislation and regulations. New laws govern the rules of operating programs; however, as Gallanter (1972) points out:

> Our analysis suggests that change at the level of rules is not likely in itself to (bring) redistributive outcomes. Rule change in itself is likely to have little effect because the system is so constructed that changes in the rules can be filtered out unless accompanied by changes at other levels. The system has a capacity to change a great deal at the level of rules without corresponding changes in everyday patterns of practice or distribution of tangible advantages.

Thus subsequent litigation to the PL 94-142 has indicated that the delivery system has not changed much with respect to rule changes in laws. A great need exists to train teachers with skills that enable practices commensurate with the state of the art and that provide legal entitlements to the handicapped.

Changes in the practices of special physical education must be developed from outside and inside the system. The role of the colleges and universities to deliver adapted and/or special physical education at the local level is critical.

The mission of teacher training programs in physical education for the handicapped is simple and straightforward: It is to provide teachers with skills to conduct individual education programs (IEPs) in the least restrictive environment. Special education is specially designed instruction as set forth in the IEP (U.S. Congress, 1975). Physical educators should be trained, therefore, to first conduct the IEP in physical education and in the regular class if possible. The PARC Enforcement 1982 litigation reveals that attempts under court order by teachers in Pennsylvania have failed to deliver legitimate services. The issues of litigation to fulfill the constitutional guarantee under the equal protection clause of the 14th Amendment of the United States Constitution primarily address omitted teacher behavior while conducting the IEP. Colleges and universities must verify that teachers are adequately trained to resolve these issues while conducting instruction. The particulars of this litigation indicate the following list of noncompliance issues that relate to teacher preparation in individual education programming:

- In not assessing, evaluating, and training in natural environments, thereby wrongly relying on skills to be transferred from one environment to the other

- In not task-analyzing skills to be taught in such a way that they are broken down into each component and subcomponent part for instruction

- In not planning, providing, and refining assessments and reassessments that distinguish precisely an individual student's strengths and needs, learning styles, behavior management needs, and life skill needs

- In not planning, providing, and refining instruction and behavior management that distinguish precisely an individual's strengths and needs

- In not developing, using, and applying a relevant data system, giving staff an accurate assessment of successes of cues and reinforcers, interaction, and external stimuli

- In not providing the effective sequencing and integration of instructional tasks, and in assessment, planning, design, delivery, evaluation, and redesigning of each child's education

- In not providing systematic concurrent teaching strategies reducing ''dead time''

- In not reducing routinized instruction by techniques, high levels of expectations for students, and use of promising educational practices from research and demonstration

Each of the particulars listed above has impact on the training of physical education teachers for the handicapped.

Clearly, when the handicapped are identified, they are deemed a risk to society for dependence upon government and/or others. Thus in addition to providing equal education opportunity to the handicapped, the school's ultimate mission is to teach skills for independent functioning in society. State of the art technology employed through the IEP is to maximize this opportunity. The central focus of personnel preparation of physical education teachers should be teaching the handicapped recreational, domestic, and community-based motor skills that direct learning toward self-sufficiency. To achieve this mission, teachers must be trained to assess pupil behaviors that are needed to function in natural environments, teach behaviors in natural environments, and evaluate utilization of physical and motor skills in the natural environment.

Technology Commensurate With State of the Art: Use of Promising Practices From Research and Demonstration

The litigation strategies of the early right to education cases indicate that educational law and the advancement of instructional technology are interrelated. In the PARC Consent 1972, plaintiffs used the precedent from *Caroline Products Company v. United States* (1938) in which the court declared, ''The constitutionality of a statute predicated upon the existence of a particular set of facts—in this case, exclusion of any statutes based on uneducability of certain persons, may be challenged by showing that those facts cease to exist'' (the advancement of new instructional techniques open through testimony of the profession, which make education possible). Following this legal doctrine in *Stanley v. Illinois* (1972), the court wrote, ''When (a procedure) explicitly disdains realities in deference to past formalities (exclusion of the handicapped from education) . . . it can not stand.''

Laski (1979) makes it clear that when presented with the choice of technologies, present legal responsibility requires that the best technology be chosen consistent with the state of the art (Hooper, 1932).

This same legal doctrine has been adopted by the Supreme Court. Justice Powell, in writing the unanimous decision in the Davis case, stated,

> Technological advances can be expected to enhance opportunities to rehabilitate the handicapped. Such advances also may enable attainment of these goals without imposing undue financial and administrative burdens upon a state. Thus, situations may arise where a refusal to modify an existing program might become unreasonable and discriminatory. Identification of those instances where a refusal to accommodate the needs of a disabled person amounts to discrimination against the handicapped continues to be an important responsibility of HEW. (*Southeastern Community College v. Davis*, 1979).

In the Congressional finding of fact and purpose related to the enactment of the Education for All Handicapped Children Act (1975), Congress found that

> developments in the training of teachers and in diagnostic and instructional procedures and methods have advanced to the point that state and local educational agencies can and will provide effective special education to meet the needs of handicapped children.

Case law is clear that refusal to recognize advances in state of the art application of instructional and behavioral technology is a discriminatory act. This refusal to recognize new practices, with the refusal to modify programs, is a violation of handicapped persons' rights. Personnel preparation programs have an obligation to train teachers to use state of the art practice verified through research and demonstration.

To ensure that advancements in technology would be made available to teachers, Congress required a comprehensive system of personnel development conditional with the acceptance of federal monies. The comprehensive system of personnel development mission is directed toward documentation and adoption of promising educational practices.

> The development and implementation of a comprehensive system of personnel development which shall include detailed procedures to assure that all personnel necessary to carry out the purposes of this Act are appropriately and adequately prepared and trained, and effective procedures for acquiring and disseminating to teachers and administrators of programs for handicapped children significant information derived from educational research, demonstration, and similar projects and adopting, where appropriate, promising educational practices and materials development through such projects. (U.S. Department of Health, Education and Welfare, August 23, 1977)

Effective and promising practice in physical education should be incorporated in physical education personnel preparation curricula. These technical practices embodied in laws are discussed later in this chapter.

Assessment, Training, and Evaluation in Natural Environments

The fundamental purpose of the Education for All Handicapped Children Act of 1975 was not merely to provide the opportunity for educational participation of the handicapped in physical education but rather to provide handicapped children with skills for self-sufficient living in the community. To achieve such a purpose it is necessary to assess, train, and evaluate children in natural environments where they live as well as in instructional settings.

> The legislative history of the act has convinced numerous courts that the aim of the Education for All Handicapped Children Act is an educational program leading to self-sufficiency in behavioral patterns. (See *Armstrong v. Kline*, 1979.)

Judge Newcomer in the *Armstrong v. Kline* (1979) decision summarizes,

> As do educators of normal children, teachers often articulate the goal of education as being the attainment of the child's highest potential. But, of course, when they discuss the potential of handicapped children as compared to non-handicapped children, it is clear that there are differences both in expectations and reality. While an educator may anticipate that a normal child will become a doctor, professor, musician . . . , these are not the sights set for SPE and SED children. Generally, educators speak of their students' potential in terms of attaining the highest level of self-sufficiency that the child can achieve, whether that be acquiring additional self-help skills, avoiding institutionalization or attaining that level of independence with regard to self-care that he or she can live in a community living arrangement or at home.

The purpose of this act as a vehicle for self-sufficiency was also expressed by congresspersons.

> With proper education/habilitation, many would be able to become productive citizens, contributing to society instead of being forced to remain burdens. Others through such services would increase their independence, thus reducing their dependence on society. (Congressional Record— Senate, 1975, pp. 10-11)

And in the House, Congressman Harkin (1976) reiterated these thoughts when he stated,

> With proper education services provided . . . these children can become productive citizens contributing to society instead of being left as burdens on our society. . . . As noted throughout the Congressional debates there is a strongly expressed concern for securing through education/ habilitation the handicapped person's achievement of self-sufficiency. This legislative history convinces the court that Congress recognized self-sufficiency as a goal of an appropriate education/habilitation for the handicapped and sought to secure it by enacting PL 93-112, PL 94-103, and PL 94-142. The court concluded, therefore, that the unique needs that must be met by education/habilitation programs include those that, if satisfied, allow the person within the limits of his or her handicap to become self-sufficient. . . . The congressional intent was to provide for that education/habilitation which would leave these persons as independent as possible from dependency on others, including the state.

Refined Assessments That Distinguish Life Skill Needs

Assessment of the physical education needs of the handicapped for self-sufficiency in natural environments begins with determining the skills needed for self-sufficiency in the community environment where a handicapped person lives. The discrepancy between the skills needed and the skills possessed becomes the central thrust of the goals of the individual program. These goals must be stated in behavioral terms so refined assessments of prerequisite and subsequent programs and task analysis can be made. When instruction begins at the present level of educational performance, readiness to learn the task is not a problem. Thus a beginning point exists for instruction for each child on each task. Refinement of assessment should focus on functional skills that will contribute to self-sufficient living. Such refined assessment of life skill needs in physical education is an important part of a personnel preparation program.

Teacher Practices in Identification of the Handicapped

Once handicapped children are identified, they are entitled to adapted or special physical education in the least restrictive environment (U.S. 94th Congress, 1975). Physical educators must be trained in procedures for identification of handicapped children. Federal regulations define the behavioral characteristics of a disorder to be something "which adversely affects educational performance." Dual criteria exist for most handicapping conditions. To determine adverse education performance, assessments must be made of the children in regular physical education classes. Educational tasks with curriculum standards and testing procedures are needed by regular physical educators to make judgements as to which children's educational performance is adversely affected. If a judgement is made that the child is performing adversely in physical education and this is substantiated by psychological or medical data, the child is handicapped and entitled to an IEP in special (physical) education in the least restrictive environment. The results of research and demonstration have not been incorporated adequately into teacher training programs so that handicapped children receive appropriate education.

General Problems With Implementing the Individual Education Program in Physical Education for the Handicapped

The PARC Consent (1972) indicates technical procedures for the conduct of programs by which all children can learn. The PARC Enforcement (1982) litigation reveals that over a 10-year span, teachers still have not acquired the skills to provide appropriate education to handicapped children. If appropriate education cannot be delivered to handicapped children over a 10-year period under court order, it is doubtful that handicapped children who are not under a court order receive appropriate education. Other litigation points to the inability of teachers to conduct appropriate education. In *Armstrong v. Kline* (1979) defendants (State of Pennsylvania) argued that regression of children in extended school layoffs was due to incompetent teachers. Circuit Judge Vance, in the *Campbell v. Talladega County Board of Education* (1981) case, noted that the plaintiff's teachers were "minimally trained." Inappropriate teacher responses to instructional problems are indicated as follows:

Joseph's program suffers from its lack of individualization. Created from commercially prepared program materials, the program had not been shaped to Joseph's specific needs. This problem is compounded by the lack of detailed evaluation and record keeping. Since it is very difficult for a student of Joseph's abilities to acquire a skill, it is vital that time be usefully spent, that approaches which persistently fail be dropped and that achievements be built upon. Records of progress in a skill must be kept in order to assess the steps already accomplished. Even Joseph's IEP itself, however, was practically unchanged from one year to the next.

Teacher practices like failing to utilize educational technology in IEPs, ignoring behavioral defects, allowing children to regress through poor teaching strategies, and failing to decrease dead time in a classroom are inappropriate and discriminatory in operation. Physical education teachers must acquire skills for assessing handicapped and nonhandicapped children on tasks of *the regular curricula and skills to conduct community-based assessments of specific behaviors that lead to self-sufficiency in specific natural environments.*

Task Analysis and Programming of Skills

Skills that are to be taught to handicapped children through the special education process should be task analyzed or converted to programmed instruction (*PARC v. Scanlon*, 1982; *Fialkowski v. Pittenger*, 1976). Teachers must be trained in these instructional procedures. Litigation has identified instructional technology that enables severely handicapped children to learn. This technology has been embodied in the conduct of the IEP where goals, short-term instructional objectives, and present levels of education performance are required. The work of Gold (1975) is descriptive of the application of instructional technology in the implementation of an individual education program. In 20 trials Gold taught a person who was legally blind, deaf, physically handicapped, and mentally retarded with an IQ of 28 to assemble a complex 14-part Bendix bicycle brake. Implicit in the implementation procedures were observing the learner performing the task (preevaluation), identifying what the learner can do (present level of educational performance), identifying what the learner cannot do (short-term objectives), and teaching those components of the task that are unlearned to reach the goal (the bicycle brake assembly in this case).

Instructional tasks are to be broken down into teachable components. They may be broken down through task analysis, programmed instruction, or concept analysis. Unless teachers are trained to the state of the art practices with these techniques, many handicapped children will not have opportunities to learn physical education tasks.

Programmed Instruction

Programmed instruction may be used to refine instruction and distinguish individual needs. This technique is based on the psychological principle of shaping (Lindvall & Bolvin, 1967). The testimony of Gallagher, Steadman, and Goldberg in *Fialkowski v. Pittenger* (1976) clearly indicates the need for programmed instruction. Their testimony indicates the need for structure to distinguish individual needs upon which the programming is based. Gallagher (1976) states,

> You cannot expect a retarded child to really respond effectively to merely providing a good environment. What you have to have is programmed instruction, programmed learning for this particular youngster, so that specific goals are set down as to what he can accomplish if they are carried out with trained personnel. . . . These results are evaluated so that...the retarded child reaches the level of performance he is capable of. A program developed by trained personnel seems to be required. The average child may be able to make his way through a program that is not structured . . . most will agree . . . that structured programming is required in this case. But it is possible, and both research and practice have shown that even in the severely retarded youngster it is possible to get measurable gains if you have a specific objective, if you have a trained person who lays out a schedule and a program of activities to reach these particular goals, so it is possible to move these youngsters further along.

Ignacy Goldberg and Donald Steadman (1976) articulate the same theme in the same litigation by saying,

> I think the (handicapped) children will profit through this highly organized and structured educational intervention. They will profit having their varieties of abilities raised. We are talking about a process which sets goals and develops strategies and moves toward them (the children),

a process . . . that involves, engineering by trained personnel.

The Department of Education curriculum guide, which was developed to conform with the *PARC v. Commonwealth of Pennsylvania* (1972) litigation, indicated that "the degree to which a desired behavior is sequenced depends upon the developmental level of the child." Further, the guide indicates that it is important to apply the following generalities to sequencing: (a) make the steps small enough to provide more success than failure and (b) make sure the student has mastered all prerequisite skills before proceeding. The present technology for implementing the IEP is well defined in the relief prescribed by the courts in the Pennsylvania litigation. The mission, therefore, of personnel preparation programs is to train teachers to conduct physical education instruction commensurate with practices defined by the courts.

Application of a Relevant Data System to Provide Accurate Assessment of Success

Instruction for handicapped children involves refinement in which tasks are broken down into teachable components. A data base must be kept that enables all parties involved with the child to determine what has and has not been learned. With this knowledge, instruction can proceed so needed objectives and skills are acquired. Such procedures require detailed recording. The precedent for law on reassessment of ongoing behavior can be found in *Armstrong v. Kline* (1980). A more detailed and technical explanation of the process of continual reassessment of educational behavior can be found in Bellamy's testimony in *Fialkowski v. Pittenger* (1976). Bellamy testifies that measurement is an integral part of education when utilizing those instructional procedures "in which antecedents and consequences are changed through continuous evaluation." To apply appropriate procedures that are commensurate with the abilities of the child there must be a process of continuous ongoing measurement. He further states that

> record keeping should all be done during the period of instructional time. In a period of very short time teachers are observing students' responses to an incredibly large number of tasks. It is difficult, if not impossible, for teachers to remember 100 or 200 bits of information and write them down later. They must keep ongoing records of short-term instructional objectives achieved.

Judge Newcomer, in *Armstrong v. Kline* (1979), reviews the process of implementing the IEP that incorporates the need for a data base.

> Although specific methods of teaching . . . may vary . . . teachers usually employ the "diagnostic-prescriptive model" as a teaching guide. The model, which is endorsed by the DOE's curriculum guide for retarded children, first instructs the teacher to determine the child's level of functioning and needs. Based upon that assessment, appropriate long- and short-term goals should be set, as well as criteria for determining whether the goals are attained. The educator may teach the child the goal in small discrete steps that build one on another and must be achieved to reach the goal. The small steps are taught by way of practice sessions or "trials" until they are learned. To evaluate the child's learning the small steps and reaching the goals, the teacher may employ the data-based teaching method, which requires that the child's responses to each trial be recorded and then reviewed. If the child fails to progress as anticipated, the plan is modified.

Clearly, the outcome of a personnel preparation program should be a trained teacher who can keep a data base of the outgoing developmental progress of handicapped children as they acquire behaviors that make them more self-sufficient for independent community living.

Effective Sequencing of Instructional Tasks

Longitudinal skill sequences are the basis of the physical education program for handicapped children. Motor skills are selected by physical educators because they contribute to self-sufficient living. These skills are then divided or analyzed into subskills until the present level of educational performance is determined for a specific handicapped child. As Riechle, Williams, Vogelsberg, and Williams (1980) indicate, hierarchies or progressions of behavior advance from zero or very limited skills. Effective sequencing of instructional tasks requires the identification of hierarchies with subsequent application of task analysis or programmed instruction for documentation of ongoing development.

Skill sequences provide a framework for assessment and programming that meet individual learner needs. Some of the advantages of skill sequences delineated by

York and Williams (1977) are as follows: (a) They identify what skills learners do and do not perform and what skills may be taught next; (b) they eliminate a need for the concept of "readiness"; (c) they facilitate the individualization of instruction; (d) they facilitate coordination of assessment, selection of instructional objectives, and program evaluation; (e) they help minimize the deleterious effects of learner transfer to other environments and personnel; and (f) they facilitate the development of a more efficient curriculum.

Reduction of Dead Time

Dead time refers to activity in which there is no acquisition or maintenance programming objectives on the IEP for handicapped children. Unless children are on a learning task, instructional time is not relevant for the development of skills for self-sufficient living. The management of task behavior that is individualized to meet the unique needs of the learner requires refined and technical management skills of teachers. Therefore, an important part of personnel preparation programs is training teachers to reduce dead time and yet conduct instructional formats that enable the implementation of IEPs.

Generalization Training for Self-Sufficiency

Handicapped children must generalize skills attained in physical education to natural community living environments if they are to become self-sufficient. Thus instruction in physical education in the classroom is only part of the education process. For the more severely handicapped persons, it is desirable to train teachers to master a three-step process that involves (a) assessing the needed behaviors for self-sufficiency in the community, (b) training handicapped children to acquire the behaviors in the physical education instructional setting, and (c) planning for generalization of attained skills in the school instructional setting back into the community. This procedure is articulated in the *Armstrong v. Kline* (1979) decision that follows.

> When the child achieves the criterion for learning a goal, he or she should continue to practice it so that the child will generalize it and perform it naturally in a variety of environments for a variety of people. The more related the goals and small steps are to the child's routine outside the classroom, the easier it will be for

the child to generalize what has been taught. When the behavior has been generalized, it is considered mastered. (*Armstrong v. Kline*, 1979)

Physical education personnel preparation programs to train teachers of the severely handicapped must provide practica and training in which instructional skills of the handicapped are generalized and expressed in natural community living environments.

Least Restrictive Environments

Handicapped children are to receive special education and related services in the least restrictive environments (PL 94-142). Section 504 of the Rehabilitation Act of 1973 (U.S. Department of Health, Education and Welfare, 1977) also specifies educational benefits are to be received by handicapped children in their least restrictive environments. Not only must handicapped children benefit from their education, but it must be as effective as that provided to the nonhandicapped. Section 504 indicates that for education to be equally effective, however, an aid or service need not produce equal results. Each must merely afford an equal opportunity to achieve equal results. This process is intended to encompass the concept of equivalent (as opposed to identical) services and to acknowledge the fact that adjustments or accommodations to regular programs may sometimes be necessary. Equal treatment and equal opportunity are not synonymous. In fact, equal treatment of handicapped persons can be discriminatory. Equality of opportunity for every handicapped person is the key consideration in this process.

In the case of *Lau v. Nichol* (1974) the Supreme Court ruled that the provision of schooling in the English language alone to children from non-English-speaking families was tantamount to the denial of schooling altogether and hence was illegal. Regarding equally effective programs, Supreme Court Justice Berger wrote in response to a unanimous court decision,

Congress has now required that the posture and conditions of the . . . seeker be taken into account and the criterion of services may not provide equality of opportunity merely in the sense of the fable which offers milk to the fox in a long-necked pitcher and the stork in a shallow pitcher, but must provide the vessel in which the milk is offered in one all seekers can use.

Equally effective service (physical education for the handicapped) should provide for accommodation of the individual as needed to attain maximum benefits. This implies that there be compensatory aids, services, or adjustments in regular programs. Thus individualization of instruction provides accommodation and is essential for equally effective services to the handicapped.

The theme of consideration for the individual again was sounded in the case of *Frederick v. Thomas* (1976). The Eastern District Court of Pennsylvania ruled that the placement of a learning disabled child in a regular class with no provision for individual accommodation was tantamount to no education at all and may even have been harmful. It is clear that handicapped children placed in regular classes must participate in IEPs that meet their unique needs.

Implications for Teacher Training

Teachers should possess skills to individualize instruction for both the handicapped and the nonhandicapped. Technology has been developed to accommodate the individual differences of all children in a class and it can be applied to physical education (Auxter, 1971). As Reynolds (1975) states,

The emergence of individual priority over institutional convenience and the measurement of programs in terms of individual rather than social reward has spread. . . . The emphasis in educational measurement and monitoring is tending to shift to the individual: Journals accept studies based on N = 1; new management systems, such as Individually Guided Education (IGE), stress individual development; curricula stress individual adaptations, as in Individual Prescribed Instruction (IPI); and innumerable systems for individualizing instruction through computerized assistance have been developed.

Reynolds (1975) identifies technical systems for individualizing instruction for the nonhandicapped and handicapped in an integrated setting.

Thus an instructional technology for individualizing instruction for all children (handicapped and nonhandicapped) in an integrated setting has been developed. Teacher training institutions should train teachers to use this technology to individualize the needs of each student in a group rather than plan content for classes based on assumptions of mutual sameness.

A necessary condition of an adequate, effective, and appropriate education for each handicapped child in the least restrictive environments are teachers trained to accommodate both handicapped and nonhandicapped children. The legislative history of PL 94-142 demonstrates Congress's major concern for continuous training of teachers.

> If the integration of handicapped children into the classroom is to be accomplished, several important changes must take place. . . . Teachers will be responsible for the management of the handicapped children in the classroom.
>
> The Committee is aware that there is a shortage of fully qualified personnel trained to serve all handicapped in educational programs. Therefore, the Committee has determined that a program's continuous in-service training be undertaken to provide general and support personnel with basic requirements needed to serve handicapped children in (the) classroom. (Congressional Record, 1975)

Senator Mondale (1975) and Senator Randolph (1975) both expressed concern for the need to train professionals in the field. Senator Randolph, on the floor of Congress, stated that

> continuous training is vitally necessary, particularly if children are to be mainstreamed into the classroom. Teachers must receive training that not only provides technical assistance necessary to teach handicapped children, but also deals with the potential problem of "attitude barriers." (1975, p. 19482)

Justification

A certified teacher of physical education for the handicapped must possess skills to instruct the handicapped and nonhandicapped to self-instruct and self-evaluate themselves in regular class. White (1971) indicates that it is possible for normal children who function at the kindergarten level and trainable mentally retarded persons who have reached a mental age of 5 years to direct their own learning through the use of programmed learning materials. The ability of teachers to construct hierarchical programmed instruction and manage the individual learning of each child as he or she progresses through the behavioral learning sequences is central to accommodating the individual needs of all children in an integrated educational setting.

Effective personnel preparation in physical education should include training that assures that personnel are appropriately and adequately prepared so that they have a working command of necessary educational skills, knowledge, and techniques. This requires continuous training. Significant information derived from educational research and demonstration should be incorporated into training (Laski, 1979). Physical education services should be continually upgraded through improved content based on research and demonstration related to physical education for the handicapped.

References

Armstrong v. Kline (Civil Action 78-132, 133, 172) in the 3rd Circuit Court, U.S. Eastern District, (Findings of act and conclusion of law) (June 21, 1979).

Auxter, D. M. (1971). Integration of the mentally retarded with norms in physical and motor fitness training programs. *Journal of Health, Physical Education and Recreation, 41,* 61-62.

Bellamy, T. (1976). Testimony in Fialkowski v. Pittenger (1976), in the U.S. District Court for the Eastern District of Pennsylvania, Civil Action 74-2262.

Campbell v. Talledega County Board of Education in the U.S. District Court for the Northern District of Alabama, Civil Action No. 79-M-277 (1981).

Caroline Products Company v. United States 304, United States 144, 152-153, N. 4 (1938).

Congressional Record, Senate Report (Senate Report No. 94168, pp. 10-11). (1975, June 2).

Fialkowski v. Pittenger, in the U.S. District Court for the Eastern District of Pennsylvania, Civil Action 74-2262 (1976).

Frederick v. Thomas, 419 F. Supp. 960 (1976).

Gallanter, L. (1972). *A working paper in the Yale Law School program for modernization.* New Haven, CT: Yale University.

Gallagher, J. (1976). Testimony in Fialkowski v. Pittenger (1976), in the U.S. District Court for the Eastern District of Pennsylvania, Civil Action 74-2262.

Gold, M.V. (1975). *Task analysis: A statement and example using acquisition and production of a complex assembly task by the retarded blind.* Urbana, IL: Institute for Child Behavior and Development, University of Illinois.

Goldberg, I., & Steadman, D. (1976). Testimony in Fialkowski v. Pittenger (1976), in the U.S. District

Court for the Eastern District of Pennsylvania, Civil Action 74-2262.

Griggs v. Duke Powers, 401 U.S. 424 (1971).

Harken, T. (1976). *Congressional Record-House of Representatives Report*.

Hooper, T.J., 60 F 2d 3 737-740, 3rd Cir. (1932).

Laski, F. (1979). Petitions of the Fialkowskis', Advocates for the Developmentally Disabled and the Police and Fire Association for Handicapped Children, Civil Action 71-42 3rd Circuit Court of the Eastern District of Pennsylvania (1979).

Lau v. Nichol, 414:563 (1974).

Lindvall, C.M., & Bolvin, J.D. (1967). Programmed instruction in the schools: An application of programming principles in individually prescribed instruction. In *Sixty-sixth yearbook of the National Society of the Study of Education*. Chicago, IL: University of Chicago Press.

Mondale, W. (1975, June 18). *Congressional Record-Senate* (Vol. 121, p. 19483).

PARC v. Scanlon, in the U.S. District Court for the Eastern District of Pennsylvania, Civil Action 71-42, 1982.

PARC v. Commonwealth of Pennsylvania, 343 F. Supp. 279 (Eastern District of Pennsylvania) (1972).

Randolph, J. (1975, June 18). *Congressional Record-Senate* (Vol. 121, p. 19482).

Riechle, J., Williams, W., Voglesberg, T., & Williams, F.O. (1980). Curricula for the severely handicapped: Components and evaluation criteria. In *Quality education for the severely handicapped: The federal investment*. Washington, DC: U.S. Department of Education, Office of Special Education.

Reynolds, M. (1975). *Trends in special education in domain-referenced testing in special education*. Reston, VA: Council for Exceptional Children.

Southeastern Community College v. Davis, 442 U.S. 397 (1979).

Stafford, R. (1975). *Congressional Record* (Vol. 121, p. 20403).

Stanley v. Illinois, 405 U.S. 645-657 (1972).

U.S. Department of HEW. (1976, December 30). Regulation for the Education for All Handicapped Children Act of 1975. *Federal Register*.

U.S. Department of HEW. (1977, May 4). Regulations for the Rehabilitation Act of 1973. *Federal Register*, 42-22676-22702.

U.S. 94th Congress. (1975, November 29). Public Law 94-142.

U.S. Department of HEW. (1977, May 4). *Federal Register*, 42-22676-22702.

U.S. Department of HEW. (1977, August 24). *Federal Register*, Vol. 4.

White, C. (1972). *Acquisition of lateral balance between trainable mentally retarded children and kindergarten children in an individually prescribed instructional program*. Unpublished master's thesis, Slippery Rock State College, Slippery Rock, PA.

York, R., & Williams, W. (1977). Curricula and ongoing assessment for individualized programming in the classroom. In B. Wilcox, T. Kohl, T. Voglesberg, B. Reguly, & M. Hagen (Eds.), *The severely and profoundly handicapped child*. Champaign, IL: Statewide Institute for Educators of Severely and Profoundly Handicapped.

Chapter 27

CAFIAS: A Systematic Observation Tool to Improve Teaching Behaviors

Sarah M. Rich, Deborah A. Wuest, and Victor H. Mancini

A developing area in the field of education is the application of systematic observation to explore the scientific basis underlying the art of teaching. Not only can systematic observation be used to describe teaching behaviors, it can also be used as an intervention technique to assist teachers in improving their instructional strategies. Specifically, systematic observation can be used by preservice and in-service teachers as a technique for "identifying, observing, classifying, and/or quantifying specific classroom behaviors" (Murray, 1970, p. 3).

Observation Systems for Interaction Analysis

Many observation instruments have been developed that describe the dynamic interaction between participants in the learning process. These instruments are designed to provide an objective, rather than subjective, measure of the instructional act. Relevant behaviors are categorized according to the underlying theoretical rationale of the system into discrete categories. Using live or videotaped observations, the observer classifies the behaviors into the appropriate category. Tallies may be recorded for every behavioral change and/or may be temporally paced, depending on the system employed.

Many observation systems trace their roots to the work of Anderson (1939), who developed a system to assess the classroom climate by measuring the teachers' integrating and dominating behaviors and their effects on student behavior. Other researchers—Withall (1949), Bales (1950), Flanders (1960), Hough (1964), and Galloway (1968)—developed additional observational techniques for measuring classroom interactions.

The most widely used interaction analysis system is the Flanders' Interaction Analysis System (FIAS) (Flanders, 1960). This instrument has been used by researchers to describe the verbal classroom behaviors in terms of indirect and direct teacher behaviors, student behaviors, and interaction patterns. Several researchers adapted

Victor Mancini (left), one of the authors of *Systematic Observation: Instrumentation for Physical Education*, and Sarah Rich, one of the first adapted physical education specialists to use systematic observation in research. Both are from Ithaca College in New York.

FIAS for use in the physical education milieu (Anderson, 1975; Cheffers, 1972; Dougherty, 1971; Nygaard, 1975). As rationale for modification of FIAS, Cheffers (1972) cited three major limitations in the use of FIAS in the physical education domain.

- FIAS measures only verbal behaviors.

- FIAS considers the teacher as the sole teaching agent.

- FIAS allows description of only traditional class structure.

With a view to addressing these shortcomings and desiring to develop an instrument to be used in the physical education setting, Cheffers (1972) developed the Cheffers' Adaptation of Flanders' Interaction Analysis System (CAFIAS). In his system, he provided a means to (a) code both verbal and nonverbal behaviors; (b) identify various teaching agents—the teacher, other students, and the environment; (c) allow for differences in class structure; and (d) expand the types of student response that could be coded (Cheffers, Mancini, & Martinek, 1980). Table 27.1 describes the CAFIAS categories. The observer, having mastered CAFIAS, records the appropriate category number every 3 seconds or every change of behavior. Computer analysis of the data recorded provides the researcher and/or teacher with the percentage of use of each category, identifies the major teaching pattern, and combines the categories into parameters that permit further analysis of teacher-student interaction.

Table 27.2 lists the major CAFIAS parameters, which, if used, provide a more complete description of the components of the teaching process in the physical education setting.

Investigators have used CAFIAS extensively. Through modifications such as subscripting and elaboration of categories (Darst, Mancini, & Zakrajsek, 1983), researchers have developed CAFIAS into a versatile tool

Table 27.1 Categories of CAFIAS

Verbal behavior	Nonverbal behavior	Concurrent verbal and nonverbal behavior	Description of behavior
2	12	②	Praise, encouragement, joking
3	13	③	Acceptance of student ideas
4	14	④	Question
5	15	⑤	Lecture, information giving
6	16	⑥	Directions
7	17	⑦	Criticism
8	18	⑧	Rote student response
8	18	⑧	Analytic student response
9	19	⑨	Unpredictable or initiative student response
10	20		Silence, confusion

Note. The numbers have no mathematical value but are used as symbols for classifying communication events, not judging them.

Table 27.2 Major CAFIAS Parameters

Parameters	Statistic
Teacher contribution, verbal	Percentage
Teacher contribution, nonverbal	Percentage
Total teacher contribution	Percentage
Student contribution, verbal	Percentage
Student contribution, nonverbal	Percentage
Total student contribution	Percentage
Silence	Percentage
Confusion	Percentage
Total silence and/or confusion	Percentage
Teacher use of questioning, verbal	Ratio
Teacher use of questioning, nonverbal	Ratio
Teacher use of questioning, total	Ratio
Teacher acceptance and praise, verbal	Ratio
Teacher acceptance and praise, nonverbal	Ratio
Teacher acceptance and praise, total	Ratio
Pupil initiation, teacher suggested verbal	Ratio
Pupil initiation, teacher suggested nonverbal	Ratio
Pupil initiation, teacher suggested total	Ratio
Pupil initiation, student suggested verbal	Ratio
Pupil initiation, student suggested nonverbal	Ratio
Pupil initiation, student suggested total	Ratio
Content emphasis	Ratio
Teacher as teacher	Percentage
Other students as teacher	Percentage
The environment as teacher	Percentage
Verbal emphasis	Percentage
Class structure whole	Percentage
Class structure group or individualized	Percentage
Class structure no teacher influence	Percentage
Teacher empathy to student emotions	Tally

that is capable of describing a wide spectrum of instructional approaches and is sensitive to individual differences in student populations.

Review of Related Research

Because of the inherent flexibility of CAFIAS, it is particularly suitable for use in adapted physical education classes. Mawdsley (1977) used CAFIAS to describe the interaction patterns of physical education teachers in regular and adapted physical education classes. Mawdsley's findings indicated that teaching behaviors in adapted and regular classes were similar; however, the teachers were more accepting of student feelings and exhibited more praise and encouragement in the adapted classes. Bechtold (1976) used CAFIAS to study the effect of a tutorial relationship between high school volunteers and peer-aged moderately retarded students as they interacted in individually prescribed physical education programs. The investigator found that tutor-student interactions became more positive as the sessions progressed and that nonverbal communication was the predominant mode of interaction exhibited. Bechtold also reported an increase in the amount of teacher praise and in the amount of student-initiated nonverbal response. Rich (1981) used CAFIAS to describe the teaching behaviors of physical educators interacting with nonmainstreamed classes of physically handicapped and moderately mentally retarded students. She found the teachers did not vary greatly in their teaching-interaction patterns between the two classes. Generally, the teachers gave verbal and nonverbal directions, which led to rote student responses that the teacher verbally and nonverbally praised and accepted. This pattern tended to be repeated through the lessons by all teachers. The results seemed to indicate that the teachers' interaction patterns were direct and structured and that the nonverbal domain played an important role in classroom interaction.

The use of CAFIAS has not been limited to the description of teaching behaviors. It also has been used successfully in the training of preservice physical education teachers. Van der Mars, Mancini, and Frye (1981) summarized research on the effect of training in CAFIAS and changes of teaching behaviors (Getty, 1977; Hendrickson, 1975; Inturrisi, 1979; Rochester, 1976; Van der Mars, 1979; Vogel, 1976). They reported that teaching behaviors became more indirect as a result of training in CAFIAS. An increase in the amount of praise, questioning, and student-initiated response was shown in classes where the teacher had received instruction and supervision using CAFIAS as an intervention technique.

Wuest (1980), using CAFIAS and other systematic observation instruments, demonstrated that the flow of student involvement can be charted and teaching behaviors identified that promote involvement. On this basis, teachers can be trained through the use of CAFIAS to employ instructional strategies that have the greatest probability of eliciting the desired student response.

These intervention studies lend credence to the idea that teachers can be successfully taught to modify their teaching behaviors by receiving instruction and supervision in the use of CAFIAS. In addition to modifying behaviors, CAFIAS can be used to encourage teachers to broaden their repertoire of teaching behaviors, thus enabling them to better meet the individual needs of their students. Because of the diversity of students' needs encountered in adapted physical education classes, this concept is of particular importance. By becoming aware of their own teaching behaviors, potential adapted physical educators can learn to select the teaching behaviors that most closely correspond to the needs of their students, thereby maximizing student learning and interest.

Suggestions for Use in Preservice Programs

Although a wide variety of approaches can accomplish this goal, the following suggestions are offered for use in preservice adapted physical education programs:

- Videotape (20 minutes minimum) the preservice teachers as they interact with handicapped students in a physical education setting.

- In the classroom, describe and discuss the concept of interaction analysis as a descriptive, rather than an evaluative, system. Describe the CAFIAS categories and parameters. In a micropeer teaching setting, practice the CAFIAS behaviors. Introduce the preservice teachers to the coding process and have them observe the coding of a demonstration tape. Assist the preservice teachers in the interpretation of the data provided by the computer printout. Based on the data, provide feedback on the lesson observed and suggest methods for the modification of teaching behaviors.

- Code and provide individual feedback to the preservice teachers on their initial practicum teaching observation.

- Provide opportunities to practice, with supervision, the appropriate behaviors identified through the analysis of the CAFIAS data.

- Videotape the preservice teacher in the same practicum setting as the initial observation.

- Code data and provide feedback to the preservice teacher.

- Continue to monitor the preservice teacher's progress using CAFIAS until the desired behaviors are demonstrated consistently.

- Encourage the preservice teacher to apply his or her knowledge in a variety of adapted physical education settings.

Systematic observation techniques have enabled educators to gain a more accurate knowledge of the components involved in the teaching-learning process. This knowledge has allowed educators to design and improve instructional resources and to develop teaching skills that facilitate student learning. Providing meaningful and successful learning experiences for handicapped individuals is a challenge to physical educators teaching in the adapted realm. The teacher can be assisted in meeting this challenge through the use of systematic observation instruments such as CAFIAS, which can be used to develop a variety of teaching skills. By possessing a broad range of teaching behaviors, the physical educator will be more likely to adjust instructional strategies to meet the individual needs of the students, thus making the educational experience more rewarding for all those involved in the learning process.

Recommendations for Future Research

To date, little research using systematic observation instruments has been undertaken in the adapted physical education realm. Thus this area is a fertile area for research. One source of the various systematic observation instruments that the researcher(s) may wish to use in this endeavor is the text, *Systematic Observation: Instrumentation for Physical Education* by Darst, Mancini, and Zakrajsek (1983). Ideas for future research in adapted physical education using CAFIAS as well as other systematic observation instruments are listed below.

- Investigate the teaching behaviors used with different populations, different age groups, and/or different sexes.

- Compare physical educators' teaching behaviors in different settings—regular classes, mainstreamed classes, and segregated classes for handicapped students.

- Investigate the effects of various teaching approaches on students' behaviors.

- Investigate the relationship between teachers' behaviors and students' behaviors.

- Identify the effects of receiving feedback generated from systematic observation instruments on preservice and in-service teachers' behaviors.

- Compare teachers' verbal and nonverbal emphasis and the changes with respect to different handicapping conditions and the severity of these conditions.

- Investigate the effectiveness of using systematic observation techniques for self-analysis and improvement of one's own teaching behaviors.

- Evaluate the effectiveness of grants, projects, and special programs in changing behaviors of teachers and/or students.

References

Anderson, H.H. (1939). The measurement of domination and of socially integrative behavior in teachers' contacts. *Child Development,* **10**(2), 73-89.

Anderson, W.G. (1975). Videotape data bank. *Journal of Physical Education and Recreation,* **46**(7), 31-34.

Bales, C.F. (1950). A set of categories for the analysis of small group interaction. *American Sociological Review,* **15**, 181-187.

Bechtold, W. (1976). *A study of the effect of a tutorial relationship between volunteer high school students and moderately retarded peer-aged students participating in an individualized program.* Unpublished doctoral dissertation, Boston University, Boston.

Cheffers, J.T.F. (1972). *The validation of an instrument designed to expand the Flanders system of interaction, different varieties of teacher behavior, and pupil responses.* Unpublished doctoral dissertation, Temple University, Philadelphia.

Cheffers, J.T.F., Mancini, V.H., & Martinek, T. (1980). *Interaction analysis: An application to nonverbal activity.* St. Paul, MN: Association for Productive Teaching.

Darst, P.W., Mancini, V.H., & Zakrajsek, D.B. (1983). *Systematic observation: Instrumentation for physical education.* Champaign, IL: Leisure Press.

Dougherty, M.J. (1971). A plan for the analysis of teacher-pupil interaction in physical education classes. *Quest,* **15**, 39-50.

Flanders, N.A. (1960). *Interaction analysis in the classroom: A manual for observers.* Minneapolis: University of Minnesota.

Galloway, C.M. (1968). Nonverbal communication. *Theory Into Practice, 7*, 172-175.

Getty, H.L. (1977). *Effects of instruction and supervision in interaction analysis on the teaching behavior of student teachers.* Unpublished master's thesis, Ithaca College, Ithaca, NY.

Hendrickson, C.E. (1975). *The use of Cheffers' adaptation of Flanders' interaction analysis system in a preservice training program of physical education teachers.* Unpublished master's thesis, Ithaca College, Ithaca, NY.

Hough, J.E. (1964). *An observational system for the analysis of classroom interactions.* Unpublished manuscript, Ohio State University, Columbus.

Inturrisi, E. (1979). *The effects of feedback and interpretation of interaction analysis on the attitudes and teaching behaviors of student teachers.* Unpublished master's thesis, Ithaca College, Ithaca, NY.

Mawdsley, R.H. (1977). *Comparison of teacher behaviors in regular and adapted movement classes.* Unpublished doctoral dissertation, Boston University, Boston.

Murray, C.K. (1970). The systematic observation movement. *Journal of Research and Development in Education, 4*(2), 3-7.

Nygaard, G.A. (1975). Interaction analysis of physical education classes. *Research Quarterly, 46*, 351-357.

Rich, S.M. (1981). *Teaching behavior in physical education for the handicapped: An interaction analysis.* Unpublished doctoral dissertation, Texas Woman's University, Denton.

Rochester, D.A. (1976). *The effects of supervision and instruction in the use of interaction analysis on the teaching behavior and effectiveness of preservice teachers.* Unpublished master's thesis, Ithaca College, Ithaca, NY.

Van der Mars, H. (1979). *The effects of instruction in and supervision through interaction analysis on the relationship between perceived and observed teaching behaviors of preservice physical education teachers.* Unpublished master's thesis, Ithaca College, Ithaca, NY.

Van der Mars, H., Mancini, V.H., & Frye, P.A. (1981). Effects of interaction analysis training on perceived and observed teaching behaviors. *Journal of Teaching in Physical Education, 1*, 57-65.

Vogel, R.D. (1976). *The effects of and supervision in Cheffers' adaptation of Flanders' interaction analysis system and the teaching behavior of student teachers.* Unpublished master's thesis, Ithaca College, Ithaca, NY.

Withall, J. (1949). The development of a technique for the measurement of social-emotional climate in classrooms. *Journal of Experimental Education, 17*, 347-361.

Wuest, D.A. (1980). *Social and psycho-physiological concomitants of interaction and involvement in pedagogical processes: A multidimensional analysis.* Unpublished doctoral dissertation, Boston University, Boston.

Chapter 28

Of Bits, Bytes, and Boxes: Using Simulations and Games in Professional Preparation of Adapted Physical Educators

Sue Gavron

T he battle cry has been sounded, and its theme is "Excellence in Education." When considering the continuum of education, which ranges from infant stimulation to teacher preparation programs and adult education, the battle to be enjoined takes on a whole new perspective. The task at hand requires changes not only in physical and environmental aspects of schools and classrooms but also in curriculum content and teacher preparation for all facets of the continuum (see Figure 28.1). When newly graduated physical educators leave their teacher education institutions, they may fit into any one small (bit) of the whole; this is especially true of specialists in adapted physical education. Not only must they be flexible enough to fit within various points on the continuum, but they must have "a wide repertoire of methods at their disposal and the competence to select the most appropriate methods for the task" (Megarry, 1981, p. 25).

The use of innovative instructional systems has grown tremendously during the past decade. A myriad of methodological approaches to learning are available that include simulations, games, and computers. It is important that these significant approaches be understood and used by both teacher trainers and teachers in the field. Megarry (1981) has identified the more common kinds of simulations on a continuum (see Figure 28.2).

Definitions of Simulation and Gaming

A difference exists between a simulation and a game. However, simplistic though this statement appears, during the 1960s and early 1970s much disagreement existed as to the meanings of these two words. In some places today the two terms have evolved into one: simulation game.

Abt (1970) defined the term *serious games* in the following manner: "A game is an activity among two or more independent decision makers seeking to achieve their objective in some limiting context; a game is a contest with rules among adversaries trying to win objectives" (p. 27). Conflict and/or cooperation may also be components of the game.

Usually formalized games come in boxes with pre-planned marketing procedures. In the areas of health, physical education, and recreation, Konnan (1972) developed *Thumbs Up*, a decision-making game in the area of recreation. In adapted physical education, Gavron (1976) developed *Movement Mosaics* for training physical education teachers to work with moderately mentally retarded persons in physical education. In 1978, Toner developed and marketed *Fun and Fitness, The Fun-Filled Physical Fitness Game*.

Many simulation games have been developed in special education by either curriculum specialists or special education teachers. Semmel (1971) developed a set of games with seven variations entitled *Anticipation* for prospective teachers of educable mentally retarded children. The psychomotor domain was not included. Windell (1975) developed a game module for special education trainees concerned with determining pupils' instructional reading levels. Zuckerman (1975) developed the *Label Game*, a role-playing board game in which special education teacher trainees experienced the effects of the labeling process.

Simulation has been characterized by Greenblat and Duke (1975) as "entailing abstraction and representation from a larger system. Central features must be identified and simplified, while less important elements are omitted from the model" (pp. 12-13). The term *model* appears within this context but not in gaming. Raser (1969) characterized a simulation in the following manner:

1. People engaged in role playing, crisis gaming, economic modeling, and scenario construction

2. A fancy term for imitation

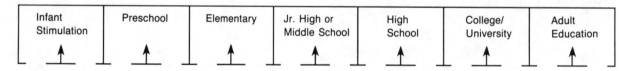

Figure 28.1 The educational continuum.

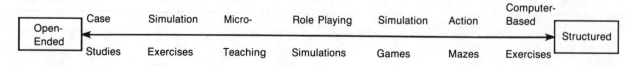

Figure 28.2 The structure dimension in stimulation. Adapted from "Simulations, Games and the Professional Education of Teachers" by J. Megarry, 1981, *Journal of Education for Teaching,* **7**(1), p. 29.

3. A reproduction of characteristics of something else, in some respects, yet still a little different. (pp. 4-5)

More recently, Megarry (1981) defined a simulation as "aspects of the educational world are replicated or recreated. The school, classroom or social system is usually fictitious and often greatly simplified; events may be slowed down. Fiction replaces reality and participants are held responsible for decisions" (p. 27). An excellent example of simulation is the animation on television that depicts what occurs during space shots. Role playing is another, more familiar example.

Megarry (1981) has also stated that even though the "notions of simulation and game are distinct, then, they are not incompatible; a *simulation game* is thus a learning experience in which participants recreate a competitive or cooperative reality by acting in some rule-bound way" (p. 27). Gordon (1970) stated this concept in a more concise manner: "Simulation is simply a more encompassing term and all games are simulations but not all simulations are games" (p. 12). Thus the term *simulation game* is born, a hybrid of two ideas with some similar components.

Simulation games may be played by one person or many; they may involve one small piece (or bit) or a larger amount of information or many facets; they may be played with the use of a game board, video, or a computer (bytes). The sophistication of a simulation or game is limited only by the creativity of the teacher or students involved.

History of Gaming

The quiet, sedate game of chess that is played on park benches and in exclusive clubs was developed as a representation of war more than 2,000 years ago (Gordon, 1970). Now, of course, we have simulation games for business, economics, politics, social systems, and education. It is important to note, however, that serious games and simulations originated in war.

According to Raser (1969), the "genesis and evolution of war games are obscure but they are closely related to and perhaps are a direct outgrowth of chess and similar board games played for pleasure" (p. 46). The Germans are on record as developing the first true war game called "Neue Kriegspiel" (Gordon, 1970, p. 46). Germany's neighbor, Prussia, used war games in its military academies, and consequently the popularity of war games spread to the United States and Great Britain (Raser, 1969).

The Germans, the first to exploit games for research and training, included such elements as logistics, time,

Sue Gavron, Bowling Green State University in Ohio, a teacher trainer of many interests who recently has spearheaded cinematographical research of disabled athletes.

money, relative strengths, chance elements, and tactics (Gordon, 1970). The idea of simulations was further developed and refined during World War II. Both sides used the game approach to find quick and effective solutions to urgent and complex problems.

After World War II, the gaming technique was applied to the high stakes area of business. These games included decisions on prices, labor, credit, and investments (Gordon, 1970). Parallel to this development, the Rand Corporation and Massachusetts Institute of Technology worked on game simulations for high military and government strategies. Some experts believe that the Russians utilized this approach for the analysis of the 1956 Hungarian uprising (Raser, 1969).

The use of simulation games involves not just the mechanism of the activity but also encompasses aspects of behavior theory and conflict resolution that contribute to the concept of game theory. Abt (1970) considered games as aids in problem solving and parallel process analyses. He believed that game theory is expressed in mathematical terms or conflict strategies and that these two components provide a scientific logical analysis of competitive processes.

Why Use Simulation Games?

The use of simulation games involves not just the mechanism of the activity but also encompasses aspects of behavior theory and conflict resolution that contribute to the concept of game theory. Abt (1970) considered games as aids in problem solving and parallel process analyses. He believed that game theory is expressed in mathematical terms or conflict strategies and that these two components provide a scientific logical analysis of competitive processes.

concerned about people making rational decisions in conflict situations. Gordon (1970) visualized games as models of processes meant to simulate and define structure and relationships between objects and events. Process is emphasized rather than the "winning concept" of the foregoing.

Thus in selecting an approach (i.e., simulation game), an instructor must be thoroughly familiar with the students who are to be involved, the nature of the game itself (i.e., rules, conflict, roles), and the objectives to be achieved as a result of utilizing this instructional approach. A simulation game should not be selected because it is cute or has a colorful board. The use of educational simulation games in teacher training and in the classroom should represent more than just a pleasant diversion from routine class procedures.

When using simulation games in an academic setting, certain outcomes, advantages, and game characteristics must be considered. Thiagarajan (1973) summarized some advantages of using simulation games.

1. Games help to bridge the gap between theory and practice.

2. Games help mix heterogeneous populations more efficiently.

3. Games force the learner to assume responsibility for learning.

4. Games have been used to encourage cooperation in learning.

5. Games permit the learner to receive a variety of experiences within a short time.

6. Games help learners master complex realities. (pp. vi-vii)

Abt (1970) stated other values and uses of simulation games.

1. Games are effective teaching and training devices.

2. Games motivate, communicate, and create dramatic representation.

3. Games give immediate feedback on consequences of one's actions.

4. Games enable the teacher to become a "coach" rather than a disciplinarian. (pp. 13, 21-22, 30)

Gordon (1970) found that simulation games allow students to reproduce chains of events that they could not do otherwise. Finally, Raser (1969) found that simulation games offer a safe way to try things without endangering human life.

From the foregoing information, it would seem as though simulation games represent an effective way to teach. However, there are some limitations to their use (Gordon, 1970).

1. Involvement can become too intense and cause students to lose sight of the objectives.

2. Some people question the wisdom of trying to produce anger or frustration in students.

3. Simulations/games may simplify too much.

4. Simulations/games may teach wrong values. (pp. 32-38)

Consequently, the use of simulation games does not by any means represent a panacea for teacher education. The current surge in computer literacy and computer use in education at all levels should be critically evaluated and used in balance with other approaches.

Effectiveness of Simulation Games in Education

Prior to 1970, research on the effectiveness of educational simulation games had been sparse (Raser, 1969). However, as more innovative instructional approaches developed, there was a demand for documentation of their effectiveness.

When evaluating the effectiveness of a particular simulation game, several aspects may be considered: the product itself, what is learned, and the length of retention of learning. In addition, Greenblat (1973) has developed an outline of six general categories to seek evidence of effectiveness of simulation games:

1. Motivation and interest

2. Cognitive learning

3. Changes in the character of later course work

4. Affective learning with respect to subject matter

5. General affective learning

6. Changes in classroom structure and relations

The research results so far are inconclusive. Shirts (1970) found that instructors' attitudes toward simulation gaming and students, as well as their knowledge and skill, may affect student experiences. Bredemier and Greenblat (1981) cite other procedural variables that may affect the experience of players such as introduction of game, explanation of game rules, and debriefing.

Seginer (1980) completed a study on game ability and academic ability as relates to social economic status (SES) and psychosocial mediators. She suggested that game ability and academic ability were two different variables in that the simulation game experience provided a meeting ground for low SES and middle-class students. Low SES students in public school were not hampered by inadequate vocabularies or discipline problems and played the game with appropriate strategies as did middle-class students.

Baker, Herman, and Yeh (1981) studied the effect of instructional adjuncts and their contributions to basic skills instruction in elementary schools in California. A summary of their findings includes the following:

1. Puzzles, games, and audiovisual activity were used in a significant proportion of elementary school classrooms in California.

2. A substantial number of teachers would spend funds on the purchase of such materials if offered a chance.

3. Teachers who report the availability of a large number of instructional options have classes that perform generally well.

4. The observed use of puzzles, games and, to a lesser extent, audiovisual devices appear negatively related to pupil performance. Additionally, the investigators concluded that instructional adjuncts may distract rather than provide incentive to learn. (pp. 88-89)

Although the foregoing studies were conducted on public school children, the results have inferences for teachers who plan to use simulation-type activities and for teacher trainers as well. This is one example in which the results of research with public school children have a direct need to be communicated to prospective teachers so that they may make informed and intelligent decisions in selecting simulation games.

Zuckerman (1975) developed the *Label Game* for special education majors. The process by which children are labeled was the game idea. The objective was for the trainees to experience this process via the simulation game. Results indicated positive attitude changes and knowledge gains.

Gavron (1976) developed the simulation game *Movement Mosaics* for use with undergraduate physical education majors taking a survey class in adapted physical education. The investigator made the following conclusions:

1. The use of a simulation game was accepted as an intervening teaching aid.

2. The simulation game was effective in teaching prospective teachers about needs, interests, and characteristics of moderately retarded children.

3. Knowledge learned from the simulation game remained relatively stable. (p. 69)

Although research on the effectiveness of simulation games has been highly suspect in the past, scholars such as Greenblat and Thiagarajan have been in the forefront in developing sound evaluation techniques. A need still exists for more quality research on the effects of various simulation gaming approaches (i.e., CAI, CMI, and video) on teacher trainees. Much of the available literature focuses on the impact of specific games on public school children and not enough on teacher preparation. For those so inclined, significant simulation gaming research is available on physiological responses (i.e., skin responses, heart rate, and pulse) and personality and gaming.

The Cutting Edge

As a teacher trainer, are you on the cutting edge? Are you willing to take the time and energy to use different teaching approaches with your future teachers so they in turn are competent enough to possibly incorporate them into their teaching situations? Are you ready to assist your future teachers in synthesizing theory and applying it to practice? Do you want to eliminate stories from *Time* magazine (June 16, 1980) that state that teachers cannot read or write or teach? Are you willing to try something more than the lecture approach to your classes? Are you willing to do more than just have your students sit in a wheelchair or wear blindfolds for 2 minutes of activity and call it role playing? Finally, can you competently use one or more of Megarry's common varieties of simulation games? If so, then you may be on the cutting edge.

With the explosion of personal computers, transference of simulation gaming techniques from pen and pencil and dice and board games can reach new heights. Increased use of interactive video/computer instruction characterizes this decade.

Teacher trainers should be on the cutting edge. By using simulation game activities, one may cover small or large bits of information via use of structured (or open-ended) games (boxes) with high tech components (bytes).

References

Abt, C. (1970). *Serious games*. New York: The Viking Press.

Baker, E., Herman, J.C., & Yeh, J. (1981). Fun and games: Their contribution to basic skills instruction in elementary school. *American Educational Research Journal, 18*(1), 83-92.

Bredemier, M.F., & Greenblat, C.S. (1981). The educational effectiveness of simulation games. *Simulation and Games, 12*(3), 307-322.

Gavron, S.J. (1976). *Movement mosaics: A simulation game for prospective adapted physical educators of retarded children*. Unpublished doctoral dissertation, Indiana University, Bloomington.

Gordon, A.K. (1970). *Games for growth: Education games in the classroom*. Palo Alto, CA: Science Research Associates.

Greenblat, C.S. (1973). Teaching with simulation games: A review of claims and evidence. *Teaching Sociology, 1*(1), 62-83.

Greenblat, C.S., & Duke, R.D. (1975). *Gaming-simulation: Rationale, design and applications*. New York: Sage.

Help! Teacher can't teach. (1980, June 16). *Time Magazine*, p. 16.

Konnan, A. (1972). *Thumbs up*. Palo Alto, CA: Peek.

Megarry, J. (1981). Simulations, games and the professional education of teachers. *Journal of Education for Teaching, 7*(1), 25-39.

Rapoport, A. (Ed.). (1974). *Game theory as a theory of conflict resolution*. Boston: D. Reidet.

Raser, J.R. (1969). *Simulation and society, an exploration of scientific gaming*. Boston: Allyn and Bacon.

Seginer, R. (1980). Game ability and academic ability. *Simulation and Games, 11*(4), 403-421.

Semmel, M.I. (1971). *Anticipation games*. Bloomington, IN: Center for Innovation in Teaching the Handicapped, Indiana University.

Shirts, R.G. (1970). Games students play. *Saturday Review, 53*, 81-82.

Thiagarajan, S. (Ed.). (1973). Current trends in simulation gaming. *Viewpoints* (Bulletin of the School of Education, Bloomington), Indiana University, **49**, vi-viii.

Toner, C.S. (1978). *Fun and Fitness, the Fun-Filled Physical Fitness Game*. Isle of Palms, SC: Cliff Toner Productions.

Twelker, P.A. (1967). Classroom simulation and teacher preparation. *The School Review, 75*, 197-204.

Tyler, J. L. (1973). Developing training packages. *Exceptional Children, 39*, 405-406.

Windell, I. (1975). *Development and evaluation of a module to train special education teacher trainees to determine a pupil's instructional reading level*. Unpublished doctoral dissertation, Indiana University, Bloomington.

Zuckerman, R. A. (1975). *Changes in knowledge and attitudes as a result of participation in a teacher education game on the labelling of handicapped children*. Unpublished doctoral dissertation, Indiana University, Bloomington.

Chapter 29

The Computer in Adapted Physical Education Professional Preparation

Tom Montelione and Ronald Davis

*T*he computer plays an ever-increasing role in today's society. Its effect has been such that it was chosen "Newsmaker of the Year" by *Time* Magazine in 1983 (Friedrich, 1983). The cost of owning a microcomputer has dropped dramatically, and its capabilities are now equal to those of the much larger computers of a few years ago.

Education has been greatly affected by this technological revolution. The number of computers in public schools grows by leaps and bounds each year. Colleges and universities are hard pressed to meet the computer usage demands of faculty and students. Indeed, the number of microcomputers available in some school districts surpasses those available on a typical college campus.

The importance of learning about and using the technology now available has never been more apparent. Several states (e.g., Utah, Texas) now require computer literacy as part of teacher certification. It is imperative that leaders in adapted physical education be aware of the trend and take full advantage of a computer's capabilities.

Computers should be conceptualized as tools that facilitate learning. According to Stein (1984a), "Computers will not and cannot replace teachers anymore than the advent of chalkboards, books, and audiovisual materials; some teacher roles and functions should be augmented by this new and powerful tool available for our use" (p. 41).

The purpose of this chapter is to examine the use of the computer in adapted physical education. Specifically, the types and amount of training necessary for teacher preparation at the graduate level are examined. Computer applications, including administrative use by the teacher and computer-assisted learning by the disabled student, are discussed.

Overview

Data processing, data storage, control of peripheral devices, and computer-assisted instruction are the most prominent applications of a computer in physical education (Cicciarella, 1981). The preparation of numerous form letters, each with a personalized name and address, or a "Top Ten" list or of an inventory are all examples of data storage and processing. Proctor (1980) advocates use of the computer in test and measurement courses and Stein (1984b) suggests its possibilities when used with severely handicapped children.

Programs created to meet the specific needs of the physical educator include exercise prescription (Brown, Gorman, & Daniel, 1983), body composition (Graham & Woolridge, 1983), student evaluation (Kramer, 1970), and exercise physiology (Stewart, 1977). These programs are examples of data processing and data storage previously mentioned.

One area in physical education in which the computer is fast becoming an indispensable tool is biomechanics. In biomechanics, as well as other areas of physical education,

> there is an increasing need for students of human performance . . . to deal with processes of quantification. Quantification is needed in order to find ways to achieve the higher levels of performance desired by such individuals as novices just learning skills, world-class athletes, and handicapped persons attempting to improve their skills. (Clark, Paul, & Davis, 1977, p. 628)

Quantified data entry need not take the form of numbers typed on a keyboard. When interfaced with a peripheral device, the digitizer, a computer can reduce digitized units on a screen to numerical quantities and aid in the analysis of human movement. Among other motor skills, digitized data have been used in the analysis of the hammer throw (Ariel, Walls, & Penny, 1980), the javelin throw (Ariel, Pettito, Penny, & Terauds, 1980; Kunz & Kaufman, 1980; Terauds, 1978), the shotput (Ariel, 1979), the handspring vault (Dainis, 1979), and sprint running (Mann & Sprague, 1980). Digitized data have also been used to analyze a novel motor skill (McGrain, 1980), compare canoe paddles (Nolan & Bates, 1982), establish validity for a mathematical model for the determination of total body mass centroid location in Down's Syndrome (Hall & DePauw, 1982) and compare racing wheelchairs (York & Kimura, 1987). In addition, the gaits of blind and cerebral palsied athletes have also been analyzed using digitized data reduced by a software program for the computer (Arnhold & McGrain, 1985; Beuter & Garfinkel, 1985; Pope, McGrain, & Arnhold, 1986).

Other areas in which the computer has been interfaced with existing physical education equipment to produce faster, more accurate results include dance (Sealy, 1983), exercise physiology (Beaver, Wasserman, & Whipp, 1973; Cordain, Johnson, & Ruhling, 1982; Donnelly, 1983; Pearce, Milhorn, Holloman, & Reynolds, 1977), and motor learning (Chasey, Barth, Martin, Cini, & Pupke, 1976; Engelhorn, 1983). The direct transfer of data to the computer rather than first recording scores on paper and then entering them into the computer eliminates one possible source of human error.

Computers in adapted physical education teacher training programs can supplement instruction, assist with service delivery planning, and contribute to research

Tom Montelione (left) of Queen's College, New York City, and Ron Davis (right) of Ball State University in Muncie, Indiana, both experts in the application of computer technology in adapted physical education and sports.

projects. Computer-assisted instruction (CAI) written for Public Law 94-142, assessment and evaluation, individualized educational programming, motor development, and other areas allow graduate students to supplement classroom instruction and learn at their individual pace.

Infusion into Normal Coursework

We live in a society that is increasingly information oriented. The physical educator of the future will be unable to function without basic awareness and knowledge of the computer. This competency can be attained, at least partially, through infusion of computer skills into normal course work.

No area of physical education is unaffected. A course in research and statistics is incomplete without at least mention of the computer's capabilities, if not actual hands-on use. Information gathering, whether for writing grants or reviewing research literature, is made immensely easier through a data base search (i.e., ERIC).

In the area of biomechanics a computer can be interfaced with a film analyzer and digitized coordinates (x, y) can be stored in the computer's memory for kinematic analysis. Programs are available to aid in areas of exercise

and diet prescription (Freifeld, 1983). These enrich an exercise science or physiology class (Donnelly, 1983).

CAI can be written for any subject area within physical education, including sport rules and strategies (Barlow & Bayalis, 1983). A word processing course aids in the preparation of reports, tests, and handouts. Record keeping for attendance, test scores, and fitness data can be incorporated into an administration class. The number of ways a computer can be infused into physical education is limited only by the scope of our imaginations.

Computer Training for Generalists

For adapted physical education purposes, a physical education generalist receives most of the necessary computer training from regular physical education courses. Within an adapted physical education survey course (or within other courses in which adapted physical education is infused), the generalist needs the following knowledge:

- Basic understanding of the microcomputer, including how to turn it on, insert a disk, and run a commercially available software program.

- State of the art as far as physical education software (programs) are concerned, where this software can be acquired, and on what microcomputers it may be run.

- Resource persons with computer expertise within a school district and ways district resources can best be used in adapted physical education.

Computer Training for Specialists

Specialists in adapted physical education at the public school level need to extend their expertise in computer usage beyond that of generalists. A microcomputer is more likely to be available than a mainframe model. Knowledge of the microcomputer and basic programming is thus essential.

A course on computers in education or more specifically computers in adapted physical education perhaps best fills the need for advanced training. Such a course should include an introduction to microcomputers, computer-assisted learning, knowledge of where to find appropriate software, programming skills in BASIC, alternative hardware use (the physical machine and its accessories), and how to best use the computer specialist who will probably be available in the school district. Research data analysis should be touched upon only briefly in the adapted physical education computer course because this topic is fully covered in the statistics class. Word processing should be examined only as it relates to the record-keeping potential of the computer.

Some common examples of CAI for disabled students include drill and practice, tutorials, games, problem solving, and guided discovery. The liberal use of graphics enlivens every learning experience. For the slow learner, the repetition of drill and practice allows for the overlearning necessary for information to be retained. Some computer-assisted instruction software is currently available for use in public school adapted physical education. Project REACT (Boettcher, 1980) from Minnesota is an example. It will probably be necessary, however, for practitioners to create their own software. If the specialist has been trained to develop computer programs that are "user friendly" (i.e., mistakes give rise to appropriate error messages that lead to easy correction), the disabled student will be more likely to learn from the computer experience.

CAI can be designed to help graduate adapted physical education students develop competencies in evaluation and assessment of handicapped students as well as placement and programming within the least restrictive environment. The graduate student must be able to establish long-range goals and short-term objectives, implement appropriate instructional strategies, and utilize efficient class organization skills. A computer-assisted instructional program written to capitalize on the computer's interactive and graphic capabilities makes the learning process from assessment to programming more manageable. A number of different assessment results, written into a program that randomly selects for these data and presents them in a computer readout, gives the future adapted physical education teacher a multitude of situations in which to practice previously learned skills.

In the future it is conceivable that other assessment tools such as the Bruininks Oseretsky Test of Motor Proficiency (Bruininks, 1978) or the Ohio State Scale of Intra Gross Motor Assessment (SIGMA) (cited in Loovis & Ersing, 1979) will be developed in computer software for use in writing Individualized Education Programs (IEPs). The specialist will enter a student's raw scores, and the computer will perform the analysis and suggest appropriate objectives and learning activities. It is important to realize, however, that the computer can only output whatever has been entered into it. According to Stein (1984a), it is highly doubtful that an appropriate IEP can be written on the basis of a computer program without additional input from the specialist.

While adapted physical education specialists need not be expert in systems analysis or hardware design, it is essential that they have at least an awareness in these areas as to the computer's capabilities. The computer specialist in a school district can assist in selection of appropriate technology if the adapted physical education specialist is able to make his or her wants known. This computer knowledge is especially important when a computer has to be adapted for use by a student who is physically disabled and unable to control a computer in the conventional manner.

Coaches of disabled athletes are beginning to develop computer software to assist with athletic training and record keeping. Illustrative of pioneers in this area are Dave Stephenson, coach of the Houston cerebral palsy team, and Glen Hebert, a computer specialist who is also a Class 2 cerebral palsied athlete. Further information about their work can be obtained from Glen Hebert, 3201 Drexell, Houston, TX 77027; telephone (713) 871-9640.

A data retrieval system has been developed for cerebral palsy sports in cooperation with Texas Woman's University (Adams, Wyeth, Rainbolt, & Montelione, 1984). The data bank contains demographic and sport socialization information regarding athletes who have cerebral palsy.

Programs can be written also to help coordinate the mailing of entry forms, their return, seeding and heating, and tournament scheduling at any sport meet for disabled persons. Record keeping is made easier and awards can be presented more quickly. The amount of repetitive paperwork necessary for even a small meet can be reduced. To achieve this, however, adapted physical educators need specific training in the application of computer technology to the administration of meets.

It is easy to envision a scenario for a local Special Olympics meet where initial letters are sent to coaches who are on a computerized mailing list, and their returned entries, including seeding information, are entered into the computer as they are received. Entries received just prior to the deadline are quickly assimilated and a workable schedule of events with the proper heating of all athletes is produced at the touch of a button. The results of each event are fed into the computer immediately after they occur, and meet results are available instantly for spectators, athletes, and the media.

The use of the computer enhances the adapted physical educator's ability to fulfill many roles. The computer is not a panacea but simply another tool. It should be neither feared nor idolized. "The new technology must be embedded in the curriculum, integrated with many other activities, and not isolated from the time-honored components of instruction" (Anandam & Kelly, 1982, p. 86).

An increasing number of computer-assisted instructional programs are being used in physical education. Hill (1975) described three computer-based resource units (CBRU) developed at the State University of New York, Buffalo. These units included physiology of exercise, sex education, and obesity and weight control. Hill stated in this regard,

> The CBRU allows instructors to select their own instructional objectives and students to select learning goals based on their own needs and interests.
>
> The objectives of a CBRU cover all possible study areas for a specific topic. The teacher and students study a list of these objectives to choose those fitting the particular needs and interests of their class. The computer . . . generates and prints a resource guide which contains content outlines, suggestions for large group activities, small group activities, instructional activities, and materials for each objective chosen. (p. 26)

Research on Computers in Physical Education

Among the first to develop microcomputer software specifically for use by adapted physical educators was Kelly (1981), whose doctoral dissertation was funded partly by Apple. Using the I CAN (Wessel, 1976) program, software was developed to enable teachers to write adapted physical education IEPs. Kelly's Prescribing Adapted Physical Education (PAPE) software was written for operation on a 48K Apple II with one disk drive and printer.

Use of PAPE begins with the teacher selecting from several computer options the motor skill level that best describes his or her handicapped student. The computer then presents a series of performance objectives from which the teacher chooses one. The computer then displays instructional activities and games specifically for implementing the objective.

Kelly field tested the PAPE software with 14 special education teachers in Plano, Texas, in an in-service training program of 5 weeks duration. The time required by these teachers to learn to use the PAPE program ranged from 20 to 120 minutes, with a mean of 60 minutes. At the end of the in-service, teachers could create and print a complete adapted physical education prescription in an average of 9.64 minutes. Further information about PAPE and other adapted physical education software can be obtained from Luke Kelly, who teaches at the University of Virginia at Charlottesville.

Williamson (1984), through the use of a computer, examined the possibility of integrating various disability groups for competition. In this study the times recorded for athletes who competed in the 1984 International Games for the Disabled were used as a basis for projecting the order of finish in integrated competition. The sorting ability of the computer was used to create simulated results of integrated competition on a "what if" basis. Williamson was able to demonstrate which events in swimming might be integrated, in whole or in part, and still provide equal opportunity for success for each of the disability groups involved.

Lease (1981) studied whether CAI can aid students in physical education by increasing their knowledge of kinesiology. The subjects were 11 students enrolled in a kinesiology course at Texas Woman's University.

Data were collected from 9 subjects on the first and second CAI programs and from subjects on the third and fourth CAI programs through the use of a pretest and a posttest comprised of 10 questions each. The first CAI program introduced computers in society and provided background information on the computer. The second through fourth CAIs were concerned with various topics in kinesiology.

Comparisons of pretest and posttest means on all four CAIs were made by t tests. The posttest means were significantly higher than the pretest means at the .05 level of significance. Lease pointed out, however, that the pretest and posttest of the fourth CAI program were determined not to be parallel forms of the same test. Lease concluded that "computer assisted instruction can aid students in physical education by increasing their knowledge of kinesiology" (p. 63).

Barlow, Markham, and Richards (1978) investigated the "feasibility of using PLATO in the precision motion analysis of high speed cinematographical data" (p. 62). The subjects in this study were 19 physical education majors at the University of Delaware.

Following photography of selected sport skill techniques and the development of cinematographic techniques to assess selected kinematic factors of these skills, 10 PLATO terminals were used in the determination of centers of gravity, joint angles, velocities, and accelerations. Among the benefits of PLATO CAI techniques listed by the investigators were "(a) accurate data reduction, (b) tremendous increase in quantity of quantified film data, and (c) considerable decrease in overall data reduction time" (p. 62).

Barlow and Bayalis (1983) described additional PLATO lessons available in physical education at the University of Delaware. A series of lessons have been developed in the areas of fitness, doubles racquetball strategy, mechanics of muscular contraction, basic mathematics skills, and film motion analysis.

All of the packages available are used to supplement class instruction, which is sometimes limited because of time constraints. The concepts and strategies learned through the PLATO lessons enable the students to better understand the required material and give them a knowledge base on which the instructor can build.

Boysen and Francis (1982) studied the use of the PLATO system to instruct a lesson in biomechanics. Both the control and experimental groups had 19 subjects. Subjects in each group were asked to analyze the same six free body diagrams.

The control group was given a worksheet and asked to specify significance, direction and location of each force, axis of rotation, and direction of angular acceleration. The worksheet was given as homework on a Monday, handed in on a Wednesday, and corrected and returned by Thursday.

Within the PLATO lesson, the experimental group completed the same assignment as the control group but received immediate feedback, both positive and negative. Both groups received instruction and evaluation in the same week.

Posttest data were used to compare the two groups. No significant difference was found between the groups ($t(34) = 1.897, p < .06$). A number of mitigating factors which may have affected the final results were noted by the investigators. These included the relative briefness of instruction on the topic (1 hour), the fact that the posttest results were not included in the course grade, and the fact that the students knew they were involved in an experiment designed to assess the instructional effectiveness of a computer lesson.

Despite the possible shortcomings in design, Boysen and Francis were encouraged by the fact that the results approached significance. They recommended a replication of the experiment using a larger sample size and better experimental controls. They concluded, "This study indicates that the PLATO lesson is a better instructional alternative than the worksheet, because more examples can be presented and evaluated than is possible using conventional instructor feedback" (p. 235).

Fry (1974/1975) used the PLATO authoring system to develop a computer-based simulation for teaching physical education curriculum planning, the Physical Education Curriculum Planning Program (PECPP). After two pilot testings the program underwent a final evaluative phase. The subjects in this final evaluative phase were five undergraduate women, four seniors and one junior, from the Department of Physical Education at the University of Illinois at Urbana-Champaign. They ranged in age from 20 to 21 years.

In order to accomplish the purpose of the study it was first necessary to instruct the subjects about the conceptual (theoretical) base from which to start and then proceed to practical applications. The subjects were required to design a physical education curriculum plan for grades 6, 7, and 8 based on a simulation of "a typical midwestern community. . . . Information was provided with regard to the community, school organization, resources available, and student and faculty characteristics" (p. 37). As is the case for most initial simulation experiences, the subjects were placed in an uncomplicated position in order to encourage greater focus on the specific problem to be solved.

Feedback was given at the end of each of the four proposed units of instruction and for each grade level regarding the subject's selection of purpose for a particular activity. This feedback took the form of "We agree," "OK," and "Questionable activity for this purpose" and was based on preselected criteria (p. 56). Additional feedback was given at the end of each grade and for the cumulative curriculum plan. This feedback was comparison of the subject's selection of purpose and the standards recommended.

After analyzing the data, Fry made the following conclusions:

1. Student participation in the program resulted in the development of acceptable physical education curriculum design for the school situation.

2. The Physical Education Curriculum Planning (PECP) program collected sufficient data to allow identification of many similarities and differences among students in the decision-making process.

3. The model represented by the PECP program was a feasible approach to teaching physical education curriculum planning. (p. 81)

Boyce and Wells (1983) designed procedures to develop and assess PLATO lessons in physical education. These procedures included (a) Phase One, initial design procedures, (b) Phase Two, actual programming of PLATO materials, and (c) Phase Three, formative evaluation of a lesson. Following the procedures outlined, a PLATO lesson was developed using Jewett and Mullan's Purpose Process Curriculum Framework (1977) as the subject matter.

During the formative evaluation phase the lesson was revised based on input received during an internal review with an expert in the subject area and a one-to-one evaluation with three students representative of the proposed target audience. A third type of formative evaluation was accomplished through the use of 10 volunteer graduate students (small group evaluation). Five of these students had received prior instruction in the subject area and five had not. In this stage the effectiveness of the lesson was evaluated.

A review of the results of the third stage indicated the average pretest score was 37.2% and the average posttest score was 81.7%. Average scores of those not receiving previous instruction were 21% lower on the pretest and 5% lower on the posttest.

These results may not have been entirely reliable because two out of the three students recording the lowest scores had their work on the lesson interrupted when the computer went "down" and was unavailable for a period of time. Based on the findings of the small group evaluation, a revision of the lesson was planned.

Montelione (1984) investigated the use of CAI on the learning of behavior management techniques for the physical education setting. The problem of this study was to compare the effectiveness of two instructional methods, CAI and lecture, in increasing knowledge of behavior management in undergraduate students enrolled in physical education major courses. All subjects were pre- and posttested using a 40-question, multiple choice test, the Montelione Behavior Management Test (MBMT). The MBMT had a test-retest reliability of .87 and an alpha coefficient of .76.

One experimental group received instruction in behavior management through lecture presentations, whereas the other received it through CAI. The control group received no instruction. The dependent variable was the posttest score on the MBMT. The experimental groups received 4 hours of instruction over a 2-week period.

A one-way ANCOVA was used to analyze the data. Significant differences were found among all three groups (F [2,36] = 15.57, $p < .01$). A Scheffé post hoc analysis revealed the CAI group to be superior to both the lecture and control groups, and the lecture group to be superior to the control group. The investigator concluded that CAI is more effective than the traditional lecture method of instruction.

Conclusion

Physical educators need to keep pace with the continuing advancement of technology. Those universities that do not do so will leave their graduates poorly equipped to match qualifications with graduates of schools that include computer training within their curriculum. Podemski (1981) states in this regard, "The future marketability of teacher training graduates may be directly related to the degree to which those graduates have an understanding of the uses of computer technology and a facility with specific instructional adaptations of computer" (p. 33).

References

Adams, C., Wyeth, D., Rainbolt, W., & Montelione, T. (1984). *Interagency cooperation in research: Partnership between an organization for disabled athletes and a university*. Paper presented at the American Alliance for Health, Physical Education, Recreation and Dance National Convention, Los Angeles, CA.

Anandam, K., & Kelly, J. (1982). Teaching and technology: Closing the gap. *Technical Horizons in Education Journal,* **10**(2), 84-90.

Ariel, G.B. (1979). Biomechanical analysis of shotputting. *Track and Field Quarterly Review,* **79**(4), 27-37.

Ariel, G.B., Pettito, R.C., Penny, M.A., & Terauds, J. (1980). Biomechanical analysis of the javelin throw. *Track and Field Quarterly Review,* **80**(1), 9-17.

Ariel, G.B., Walls, R.M., & Penny, M.A. (1980). Biomechanical analysis of the hammer throw. *Track and Field Quarterly Review,* **80**(1), 41-51.

Arnhold, R., & McGrain, P. (1985). *Selected kinematic patterns of visually impaired youth in sprint running*. *Adapted Physical Activity Quarterly,* **2**(3), 206-213.

Barlow, D.A., & Bayalis, P. (1983). Computer facilitated learning. *Journal of Physical Education, Recreation, and Dance,* **54**(9), 27-28.

Barlow, D.A., Markham, S., & Richards, J.G. (1978). PLATO facilitation of film analysis in biomechanics. *Track and Field Quarterly Review,* **78**(2), 62.

Beaver, W.L., Wasserman, K., & Whipp, B.J. (1973). On-line computer analysis and breath-by-breath graphical display of exercise function tests. *Journal of Applied Physiology,* **34**, 128-132.

Beuter, A., & Garfinkel, A. (1985). Phase plane analysis of limb trajectories in nonhandicapped and cerebral palsied subjects. *Adapted Physical Activity Quarterly,* **2**(3), 214-227.

Boettcher, J.A. (1980). *Project R.E.A.C.T.* (Information available from Project REACT, 66 Malcomb Ave., S.E., Minneapolis, MN 55414)

Boyce, B.A., & Wells, L.J. (1983). The development and assessment of a PLATO lesson on curriculum theory. *Journal of Teaching in Physical Education,* **3**(1), 58-66.

Boysen, J.P., & Francis, P.R. (1982). An evaluation of the instructional effectiveness of a computer lesson in biomechanics. *Research Quarterly for Exercise and Sport,* **53**, 232-235.

Brown, B.S., Gorman, D., & Daniel, M. (1983). Physical fitness evaluation and personalized exercise prescription (PEP) through microcomputers. *Collegiate Microcomputer,* **1**, 375-381.

Bruininks, R.H. (1978). *Bruininks Oseretsky Test of Motor Proficiency.* Circle Pines, MN: American Guidance Service.

Chasey, W.C., Jr., Barth, J., Martin, H., Cini, A., & Pupke, W. (1976). Stabilometer computerized analog recording system for studying gross motor skill learning. *Research Quarterly,* **47**, 524-525.

Cicciarella, C.F. (1981). Enter—The microcomputer. *Journal of Health, Physical Education, Recreation, and Dance,* **52**(6), 60-61.

Clark, F., Paul, T., & Davis, M. (1977). A convenient procedure and computer program for obtaining instantaneous velocities from stroboscopic photography. *Research Quarterly,* **48**, 628-631.

Cordain, L., Johnson, S.C., & Ruhling, R.O. (1982). Description of a low cost microcomputer system interfaced to exercise stress testing equipment. *Research Quarterly for Exercise and Sport,* **53**, 73-77.

Dainis, A. (1979). Cinematographic analysis of the handspring vault. *Research Quarterly,* **50**, 341-349.

Donnelly, J. (1983). Physiology and fitness testing. *Journal of Physical Education, Recreation, and Dance,* **54**(9), 24-26.

Engelhorn, R. (1983). Motor learning and control. *Journal of Physical Education, Recreation, and Dance,* **54**(9), 30-32.

Freifeld, K. (1983). Body management. *Personal Computing,* **1**(8), 60-61, 156.

Friedrich, O. (1983, January 3). Machine of the year. *Time,* pp. 14-24.

Fry, K.L. (1974/75). A computer-based simulation for physical education curriculum planning. *Dissertation Abstracts International,* **35**, 5901A. (University Microfilms No. 75-26, 492)

Graham, G.P., & Woolridge, W. (1983). Computer measurement of skinfolds. *Journal of Physical Education, Recreation, and Dance,* **54**(7), 68-69.

Hall, S., & DePauw, K. (1982). A photogrammetrically based model for predicting total body mass centroid location. *Research Quarterly for Exercise and Sport,* **53**, 37-45.

Hill, C.E. (1975). Computer-based resource units in health and physical education. *Journal of Physical Education and Recreation,* **46**(6), 26-27.

Jewett, A.E., & Mullan, M.R. (1977). *Curriculum design: Purposes and processes in physical education teaching-learning.* Washington, DC: AAHPERD.

Kelly, L.E. (1981). *Microcomputer assistance for educators in prescribing adapted physical education.* Unpublished doctoral dissertation, Texas Woman's University, Denton.

Kramer, W.D. (1970). A computerized system for analyzing and evaluating performance data in physical education. *Dissertation Abstracts International,* **31**, 2158A.

Kunz, H., & Kaufman, D.A. (1980). Essentials of the javelin throw: A biomechanical analysis. *Track and Field Quarterly Review,* **80**(1), 18-20.

Lease, B.J. (1981). *The development and implementation of a computer-assisted instruction series to be utilized as an aid to curriculum methodology in physical education.* Unpublished doctoral dissertation, Texas Woman's University, Denton.

Loovis, E.M., & Ersing, W.F. (1979). *Assessing and programming gross motor development for children.* Cleveland Heights, OH: Ohio Motor Assessment Associates.

Mann, R.V., & Sprague, P. (1980). A kinetic analysis of the ground leg during sprint running. *Research Quarterly for Exercise and Sport,* **51**, 334-348.

McGrain, P. (1980). Trends in selected kinematic and myoelectric variables associated with learning a novel motor task. *Research Quarterly for Exercise and Sport,* **51**, 509-520.

Montelione, T. (1984). *Computer assisted instruction in behavior management for the physical education setting.* Unpublished doctoral dissertation, Texas Woman's University, Denton.

Nolan, G., & Bates, B. (1982). A biomechanical analysis of the effects of two paddle types on performance in

North American canoe racing. *Research Quarterly for Exercise and Sport,* **53**, 50-57.

Pearce, D.H., Milhorn, H.T., Jr., Holloman, G.H., Jr., & Reynolds, W.J. (1977). Computer-based system for analysis of respiratory responses to exercise. *Journal of Applied Physiology: Respiratory, Environmental and Exercise Physiology,* **42**, 968-975.

Podemski, R.S. (1981). Computer technology and teacher education. *Journal of Teacher Education,* **32**(1), 29-33.

Pope, C.J., McGrain, P., & Arnhold, R. (1986). Running gait of the blind: A kinematic analysis. In C. Sherrill (Ed.), *Sport and disabled athletes* (pp. 173-177). Champaign, IL: Human Kinetics.

Proctor, A.J. (1980). Computers in tests and measurement courses. *Journal of Physical Education and Recreation,* **51**(8), 73-75.

Sealy, D. (1983). Computer programs for dance notation. *Journal of Physical Education, Recreation, and Dance,* **54**(9), 36-37.

Stein, J.U. (1984a). Microcomputer uses to promote physical proficiency and motor development of students with handicapped conditions. *The Physical Educator,* **41**, 21-29.

Stein, J.U. (1984b). Microcomputer uses to promote physical proficiency and motor development of students with handicapped conditions. *The Physical Educator,* **41**, 153-156.

Stewart, K.J. (1977). A FORTRAN program for reducing metabolic data when metering inspired air. *Research Quarterly,* **48**, 202-203.

Teacher training: Computers reach the lower grades. (1983). *Electronic Learning,* **3**(8), 44.

Terauds, J. (1978). Computerized biomechanical analysis of selected javelin throwers at the 1976 Montreal Olympiad. *Track and Field Quarterly Review,* **78**(1), 29-31.

Wessel, J.A. (1976). *I CAN.* Northbrook, IL: Hubbard Scientific.

Williamson, D.C. (1984). *An inquiry on the participation levels and comparative performances of competitors with particular focus on integrated competition.* Unpublished manuscript. (Available from Physical Education Division, Trent Polytechnic, Clifton, Nottingham, England NG11 8NS)

York, S., & Kimura, I. (1987). An analysis of basic construction variables of racing wheelchairs used in the 1984 International Games for the Disabled. *Research Quarterly for Exercise and Sport,* **58**(1), 16-20.

Editor's Note: See also

Brodie, D.A., & Thornhill, J. (1983). *Microcomputing in sport and physical education.* New York: Sterling.

Donnelly, J. (Ed.). (1987). *A practical guide to microcomputer use in physical education.* Champaign, IL: Human Kinetics.

Chapter 30

Personnel Preparation for Adapted Physical Education Administrative Roles

Kenneth W. Duke

*O*ne of the vital components of college and university professional preparation programs in adapted physical education has become the training of professionals equipped to fill emerging roles in public school program administration. The present discussion will proceed with the realization that such roles are many and varied, depending on factors such as size and level of sophistication of local education agencies. The discussion will center on an extensive (but not exhaustive) overview of public school administrative-management responsibilities related to adapted physical education programming. These functions are discussed under three arbitrary headings for convenience's sake. Included with these functions are possible suggestions to training institutions relating to opportunities for competency development as part of the ongoing educational process of the prospective administrator.

Academic Foundations

This section addresses those skill areas that should comprise a large portion of the graduate student's basic preparatory foundation. These skills and their development can be classified as primarily academic in nature.

Knowledge of Handicapping Conditions

A thorough knowledge of the major handicapping conditions is an essential part of the administrator's background. This knowledge includes the basic physical and behavioral characteristics of children and specific implications of these characteristics for exercise and physical activity. This basic knowledge of physiological and anatomical functioning should include variations in child development as affected by disease mechanisms. Preparation should also involve familiarity with adequate resource material for cases of lesser known or obscure syndromes. It is essential that such a fundamental background reflect sensitivity to the concept of holistic child education. The appropriateness of many future programming decisions will be dependent on this knowledge base.

Basic courses in adapted physical education and special education can help build this base. Practicum experiences that place the graduate student in settings with direct exposure to as many types of handicapped individuals as possible are invaluable.

Legal Awareness

The prospective administrator must know exactly what legislation stipulates concerning the education of handicapped individuals, specifically as the law relates to physical education. Stress should be placed on knowing what the law says, how it has been applied, legislative intent,

Ken Duke, former director of adapted physical education for the Dallas public schools.

and interpretation of legal implications applying to wide ranges of circumstances. Such awareness can be extremely beneficial for placement and instructional purposes, parent conferences, hearings, and legal proceedings. Application of legal information as it relates to physical education may be necessary because it involves parents, teachers, school administrators, multidisciplinary team members, and legal officials. The responsibility for program legality ultimately rests with the program administrator. Appropriate decisions can only be formulated, executed, justified, and upheld if the legal processes are assured to be correct.

Training programs can provide many materials related to special education law (PL 94-142, Sec. 504) and its application. The original document should be available, but various analyses, summaries, condensations, and interpretations are best for study purposes. It may also be valuable to arrange for attorneys who specialize in school law with experience in special education litigation to speak to classes. Directors of special education and adapted physical education can provide insight concerning legal applications in specific instances and effects of legal implications on programming in different school districts. (The graduate student will be interested in these variations in application, interpretation, and implementation.) Attending actual school placement meetings, hearings, and various meetings where the law is applied is recommended.

Motor Assessment

One of the most important concentrations in administrator training is proficiency development in motor assessment. Most pivotal decisions regarding placement and programming involve judgments based on some form of assessment results. Testing and the resulting interpretation of results are the basis for many critical child-related decisions. Therefore, the administrator must have a broad background relative to the testing process, due process steps in testing, assessment instruments and their application, and interpretation of testing data if sound educational decisions are to be made.

Adequate preparation will involve exposure to a wide variety of instruments to assess motor proficiency, skills, abilities, postures, and physical fitness. The graduate student should thoroughly review current assessment systems and instruments, giving consideration to application, feasibility, flexibility, versatility, and interpretation under varying circumstances and conditions that exist in school situations. After review, opportunities must be created to use tests in field settings. Field testing can be done in clinics, university classes where children are brought in, in special training sessions, or in schools themselves where cooperative arrangements are made. Experience can be gained while feedback is provided to school personnel, serving the needs of both groups. Role playing in classes during which class members must justify programming based on test results under various circumstances and involving many roles can also be valuable. Practical experience can also be gained by visiting teachers to discuss instruments used, observing testing environments, and attending actual meetings where program decisions are made. The graduate student can also gain and update knowledge through conferences, presentations, and publications. A sound background in measurement is obviously a vital element in preparation.

In-Service Training

Of prime consideration is advanced preparation in the area of in-service training. The future administrator will confront the problem of continuing education for large groups of working teachers who may have little exposure to adapted physical education. Veteran teachers may be intimidated or nonmotivated concerning an educational process that is new and different to them. In-service training needs must be analyzed, covering such factors as number of students to serve, available teachers, level of teacher knowledge, in-service time available, and current programming methods. Content of programs must be considered, especially if both physical education and special education teachers are involved. Content must be adjusted to meet the needs of these groups. Availability of trained specialists to assist with in-service will affect program coverage. Cooperative arrangements with other school district personnel and outside consultants may need to be established to meet in-service needs. Although this can be a complex area, the primary factors will always be content and time table. After the current ability status of the teachers is established, a systematic schedule of training sessions must be created. The content (what teachers need to know), sequence (prioritization of material), and spacing (when teachers are available) are the key administrative considerations.

The critical factor is preparation of knowledge of the many components that make up a sound adapted program (legal awareness, assessment, instructional techniques, etc.). With the knowledge of the many areas that must be considered in program planning, participation becomes the learning mode. The graduate student should attend and participate in as many training sessions as possible conducted by leading professionals. This participation will help with content selection, organizational techniques, materials, delivery styles, and adaptation to time frames, spaces, and participants. The next logical step is participation in an in-service delivery project. This project will probably be done through the university providing assistance to many school districts. Such an arrangement allows the novice to work with more experienced teacher trainers, beginning with small parts of programs and gradually assuming more responsibility. This process should progress until the novice can determine need, make preliminary arrangements, plan, organize, and carry out workshops, and conduct follow-up sessions with proficiency. Experience should be gained with widely differing types of teachers and school districts. Mastery of program content is always the secret to success.

Needs Assessment

The needs assessment process can be envisioned as the methodology that is enacted to determine programming needs. This definition is not to be interpreted as simplistic. The needs assessment process is considered a separate entity in the training program and is essential to the program manager in public schools. The results of needs analysis will determine short-term needs, long-range goals, and program direction. (The needs assessment relates to the entire program.) The complexity of this process will depend on the extent of the particular entity being assessed such as one class, one school, a cluster of schools, a small rural school district, or a large urban district. Basic organization can make this process systematic and manageable, considerably reducing frustration and inefficiency of time and effort expenditure. More importantly, proper analysis of a systematic needs assessment enables the administrator to initiate programming directed toward meeting the needs in a logical, progressive manner, while planning for both immediate objectives and long-range program goals.

Brief mention should be made of some of the key components in the needs assessment process. These components include an overview of types and numbers of handicapped students, a method to determine the extent of those needing services, a geographic location or cluster of patterns of students, a survey of instructional capabilities, the availability of support systems, in-service training needs, facilities and equipment, the current staff capacity for program delivery, personnel needs, a general administrative awareness of the role of the adapted physical education program, district compliance progression, and the current status of any litigation related to adapted physical education (proposed, ongoing, or settled). The analysis of data obtained through this process should result in proper prioritization and direction of effort toward identified needs, formalized in a systematic service delivery model. The administrator must give attention to and subsequently balance these components in some organized fashion, which is the central purpose of the needs assessment process.

The graduate trainee must have a solid preparatory background in program structure to know the various components necessary for a sound physical education program. A suggestion for preparation is extensive class projects involving the design of program models for hypothetical school systems, with numerous variables included, to be determined by needs analysis. This exercise should then extend to actual school districts, working with conditions as they really exist. An excellent target for such experience is small rural school districts. Projects may involve comparative arrangements with such districts whereby graduate personnel go into the district and plan, conduct, and analyze the needs assessment, culminating in appropriate program recommendations. Regional education agencies might also be sources for such cooperative efforts with varying types of school districts. This may include exploration of methods used by districts that have completed this process.

Placement Alternatives and Instructional Arrangements

Finding placement alternatives and making instructional arrangements are important administrative skills. Of concern are balancing physical skill, behavioral characteristics, and social maturity to create the proper instructional climate for physical education. This is the most child-related component mentioned because it is a learning process that necessitates involvement with many types of children directly in many different instructional environments. An often overlooked part of administrative background is experience with children (usually teaching). Called for are experiences with different children in differing instructional settings and groupings and experiences with different teaching techniques, structural approaches, and reinforcement tactics. Such experience will help when grouping or planning for effective instruction. Holistic need must again be balanced by constraints in the learning environment. The resulting administrative skill is awareness of different types of instructional arrangements that can be created and the accompanying ability to propose appropriate instructional alternatives. This skill can be valuable when attempting to balance established guidelines with realistic constraints and limitations in existing instructional environments. Flexibility and creativity will be needed as well as a clear delineation between least restrictive (mainstreaming, normalization) and most appropriate (individualized planning) education.

Such experience can best be obtained in two ways. One way is through university schools where school children are brought to classes taught and directed by graduate students. This arrangement allows the graduate student to freely manipulate, design, structure, and vary the instructional variables for experience in format, technique, and approach to instruction. Secondly, practicum experience should be arranged in which the trainees go into many types of schools and work with children under conditions applied externally (real world), where creativity may be taxed to create appropriate environments for motor education. These experiences should combine to provide those child-related experiences in learning (grouping, rates, styles, numbers, management) that will be valuable later to the administrator during decision making related to instruction.

Management-Oriented Skills

This section describes highly valued skills related to management that are more generalized and may be obtained partially through experience and on-the-job training as well as through formal preparation.

Awareness of the Public School Process

The potential administrator must have some grasp of how public schools function as systems. Too often educators are prepared for positions at specific levels in the system without accompanying awareness of the system as a whole. The administrator of a program must be able to function with an awareness of these various strata and their unique problems. The complexity of this task will, of course, vary with the size of the school district. Each district, regardless of size, will have established levels of administration, lines of authority, and channels of communication that must be understood (if one ever expects to manipulate the system to some degree). Roles of key personnel, specifically as related to the adapted physical education program, should be known as well as the functions that go with specific roles (it pays to know who really does what). Of particular importance in most school systems is the role of the school principal. Success or failure of many programs hinges on the approach and relationship of this key person.

An excellent familiarization method is to invite school administrators to speak to classes and outline structure, operations, and program interactions. These persons are usually eager for the opportunity to promote their district, and a wide variety of professionals can be approached. Another suggestion is field trips or visitations to school districts to spend time with personnel who can provide insight into program operations.

Organization

Although a bit intangible, a basic sense of organization can be acquired and is necessary for a program manager if progress in terms of attaining short-term objectives is consistent with long-range plans. Attention to detail is necessary in such tasks as scheduling, reporting, keeping records, and meeting deadlines. Day-to-day prioritization is important.

A thorough awareness of program functioning is the best organizational asset. This has been mentioned previously and can be supplemented by projects directed specifically toward organization. Time management seminars as well as identification and analysis of successful organizational structures may also be useful.

Program Implementation

Having been mentioned before in a broader sense, implementation here means getting the program in operation at the classroom level. This will make implementation meaningful to the teacher. Starting the program involves mainly interpreting needs, designing content of instructional programs for the teacher, structuring the learning environment, modifying and supplementing this environment, and helping initiate structured class sessions on a regular basis. Experience gained during the child-oriented (academic) phase will be invaluable here.

Evaluation

All too often programs are considered complete once in operation. The administrator must be constantly aware of need for evaluation, both of the overall program and its specific components. Evaluation is the only way in which progress can be realized, measured, and translated into relevant program goals. Virtually every stagnant educational effort lacks some evaluation mechanism. Evaluation must be considered an integral part of the program in the program structuring part of preparation. The evaluation portions of program models should be emphasized.

Team Functioning

The program administrator must learn to function as a team member in the multidisciplinary education format. Functioning as a team will involve integrating input with other areas and requires knowledge of the individualized education process, programming guidelines, and legal interpretations as they apply specifically to physical education. Some understanding of the roles of other team members is necessary. This can be accomplished by means of class lectures, interviews, and practicum experiences involving team operations.

Related Programs

The program director for adapted physical education must be able to interface with personnel from closely related programs. These may include persons from the therapies, health service, regular physical education, and athletics. Again, awareness of roles, overlap of services, and definition of function are necessary. The practicum and interview experiences in school districts are excellent training mediums.

Budgeting

Some experience with management and expenditure of funds may be necessary for the program manager. Basic budgetary techniques can be reviewed in courses related to administration. Budget managers make interesting speakers for classes. Wise expenditure of funds is a lesson learned from experience (often from unwise spending).

Personnel

Another area where experience is the training vehicle concerns matters related to personnel. Personnel is broad enough to include supervisory techniques, personal relations, and motivation. It also includes role and task assignment within the program, evaluation, determining the type of person needed to fill a particular position, and recruiting to find that specific person.

Proposal Development

An area that may be important is developing proposals to obtain funds. Program directors may need to write proposals to obtain supplementary funds to purchase equipment, funds for staff positions, and major funds for the program. Preparation for this function should include learning the basic mechanics of proposal development as well as becoming aware of sources of available funds. Such training is best obtained from proposal writing courses and seminars and by reviewing successful proposals.

Humanistically Related Skills

This section is concerned with those skills with an inner-directed base that are difficult to define and specify but are important to a successful program. The reader should keep in mind that these values originate in the inner self and are most influenced by personal relations.

Conceptualization is one of these skills and can be viewed in two distinct perspectives. Reality-based conceptualization involves being able to formulate a view of what the program should be and identifying the concrete steps necessary to reach that level given present developmental circumstances. Visionary conceptualization involves the ability to envision the program, sprinkle enough magic into it, and transform the present operational format into that vision. This is an inherent capability that training cannot develop.

Community awareness, which involves how parents feel about programs and children, is another area to consider. More specifically, it concerns how parents perceive the physical education program in the lives of their children and how the administrator may modify or accommodate these expectations. Work with community agencies and parent-related programs can help develop this awareness.

For school administrators with program responsibility, a useful skill to develop is that of productive compromise. This involves being able to balance reality with idealism, often accepting the less than ideal as a compromise in order to initiate an effort. Productive compromise should be seen as positive, however, in a developmental perspective. A productive compromise is seen as a temporary step in development toward the more ideal, never as a permanent condition or end point.

The program manager must realize that salesmanship is a professional quality that will always be a necessity. The administrator, particularly, is a salesperson as a representative of a program. Opportunities will always occur to sell physical education, and advantage should always be taken of such opportunities.

Lastly, and most importantly, a word must be said about philosophy. Every professional must have one. There must be allowance for patience, tolerance, and sensitivity to the values of others in the attainment of program goals. Standards must be upheld at a certain point. These things are all part of philosophy. Part of that philosophy should encompass the ideal that motor education is the single most important variable in programming for special children.

In conclusion, two points will be made: (a) Professional preparation directors should realize that public schools are training grounds, waiting to be used to the advantage of both schools (children) and preparation programs (students), and (b) the impact of the adapted area on the level of physical education programs in general can be profound. Quality administrators can play an important role in bringing these objectives to fulfillment.

Chapter 31

In-Service Teacher Education: A Review of General Practices and Suggested Guidelines for Adapted Physical Education Teacher Trainers

Garth Tymeson

*I*n-service education, as any other kind of education, has to do with helping people grow, learn, improve, enjoy, think, and do (Berman, 1977).

In-service teacher education (ISTE) is a complex phenomenon and has traditionally been a much studied aspect of school personnel training. Historical descriptions portray ISTE as a prominent focus of interest as early as the 1850s and 1860s (Tyler, 1971). The main intent of these past ISTE efforts was very comparable to present day thrusts. Original programs, usually in the form of 2- or 3-day institutes, were designed to reduce the discrepancy between what teachers were expected to know and what competencies they actually possessed (Tyler, 1971). This remedial purpose was quite similar to modern ISTE ventures, which are planned to improve and develop practicing teachers' skills in a variety of educational settings.

Contemporary ISTE literature is abundant with descriptive reports ranging from glowing praise for its contributions and effectiveness to accounts documenting the unplanned, deplorable, and irrelevant nature of most programs (Arends, Hersh, & Turner, 1978; Brimm & Tollett, 1974; Edelfelt, 1977; Hite & Howey, 1977). Research reports concerned with various elements of ISTE are also voluminous. Data related to complicated variables such as ownership, situational design, content, finance, collaboration, and evaluation have been studied and analyzed in several educational arenas (Baker, 1979; Bieber, 1978; Davies

& Armistead, 1975; Dunn & Harris, 1979; Houston & Frieberg, 1979; Howey, 1976; Howey & Joyce, 1978; Joyce & Showers, 1980).

The definition and practical interpretation of ISTE have been controversial issues warranting much debate. Among the synonyms commonly used in reference to ISTE are on-the-job training, renewal, staff development, continuing education, professional growth, and professional development. Authorities in the field have contributed extensively to the conceptualization of meaningful ISTE (Edelfelt & Johnson, 1975; Harris, 1980; Joyce, Howey, & Yarger, 1977; Lawrence, 1974; Nicholson, Joyce, Parker, & Waterman, 1976; Otto & Erickson, 1973; Rubin, 1971). According to the Texas Education Agency (1978), a functional definition of ISTE generally possesses interdependent subparts related to (a) planning, (b) situational design, (c) content, and (d) support. Refer to pages 405-406 for specific principles contained within each of these subparts.

The following definition proposed by Harris (1980) will be utilized in this report. He stated, "In-service teacher education is . . . any planned program of learning opportunities afforded staff members of schools, colleges, or other educational agencies already assigned positions" (p. 21).

The detail of this comprehensive definition necessitates a brief description of its components. First, *a planned program* is incorporated to purposely exclude accidental events that may create a need for or arise during ISTE. According to Harris, planned and systematic ISTE places

Garth Tymeson (center) of Northern Illinois University with Jennifer Wright (left), adapted physical education director of the Jefferson parish in Louisiana and Nancy Megginson (right) of Rouge River, Oregon. All are leaders in inservice training.

emphasis on designing learning experiences, assessing needs, projecting expectations, budgeting, assigning responsibilities, and evaluating. Second, *learning opportunities* separate ISTE from activities that are of educational value but do not relate directly to ISTE. Third, the specification of *staff members* and not teachers is made because educational personnel such as administrators, aides, supervisors, and board members should take part in ISTE. Fourth, *for the purpose of improving performance*, ISTE emphasizes further development, not maintenance, of knowledge, skills, and attitudes related to job practice. Fifth, *the individual* is the appropriate target of ISTE with the focus of needs assessment being directed toward specific staff members. Finally, *already assigned positions* center ISTE on augmenting competencies in present positions as opposed to new and possibly vague appointments. Adherence to this conceptual framework of components and subsequent principles should lead to relevant and effective ISTE programs in all fields.

In recent years, extensive emphasis has been placed on ISTE in the field of special education, including adapted physical education (Burrello & Sage, 1979; Cline & Fagen, 1979; Meyen, 1978; Schofer & McGough, 1977). This thrust has resulted from several stimuli. Notable among these was the passage of Public Law 94-142, The Education for All Handicapped Children Act of 1975. Regulations governing the implementation of this mandate require each state and local education agency to develop and put into operation a comprehensive system of personnel development (Department of Health, Education, and Welfare, 1977). An important function of these manpower planning procedures should be to guide the provision for preservice training and ISTE necessary to appropriately deliver guaranteed special education services to all handicapped children. Major priority thus far has been placed on ISTE efforts for regular educators who have been made to assume various service delivery roles with handicapped pupils (Siantz & Moore, 1977).

New direct service demands are not only facing regular classroom teachers. Least restrictive environment concepts and full educational opportunity benefits have rightfully been extended into physical education. The inclusion of physical education as part of the definition of special education in Public Law 94-142 is requiring physical educators to demonstrate new planning and instructional competencies in unfamiliar areas.

Several writers have cited an immediate and widespread need for ISTE in adapted physical education (Bird & Gansneder, 1979; Cowden, 1980; Harris, 1977; Jansma, 1977; Sherrill, 1986; Stokes, 1980). ISTE for adapted physical educators has continually been recognized as a priority by experts at the federal level in special education (Hillman, 1978).

Documented response to the adapted physical education ISTE deficiency has been encouraging. Systematic curriculum programs and accompanying ISTE management plans have had substantial national impact in the area of adapted physical education (Irmer, Odenkirk, & Glasenapp, 1979; Vodola, 1977; Wessel, Vogel, Knowles, & Green, 1976). Numerous state and local projects have additionally provided extensive exposure and training to school personnel (Bundschuh, Jackson, McLaughlin, & McLellan, 1980; Clelland, 1979; Cooper & Churton, 1979; DiRocco, 1979; Dunn & Harris, 1979; French, 1977; Hall, 1980; Horgan, 1979; Lange, 1979; Loovis & Taylor, 1979; Winnick & Jansma, 1978). Finally, several research studies have reported significant positive outcomes related to ISTE in adapted physical education (Cowden, 1980; Harris, 1977; Hurley, 1979; Knowles, 1981; Tymeson, 1981).

Despite these comprehensive efforts to provide ISTE in adapted physical education, a severe shortage of properly trained teachers still exists (Karper & Weiss, 1980). This deficiency of properly trained teachers may be the primary cause of recognized neglect in providing required adapted physical education to handicapped children throughout the United States (United States Department of Education, 1980). Until colleges and universities can produce sufficient numbers of adapted physical education specialists, public schools will have to train presently employed teachers for new roles, tasks, and competencies. It appears that ISTE is the most feasible way to meet these needs (Bird & Gansneder, 1979; Dunn & Harris, 1979; Karper & Weiss, 1980).

Adapted physical education ISTE presently relies heavily on 1- or 2-day workshops in an attempt to prepare personnel (Hurley, 1979; Spragens, 1979; Winnick & Jansma, 1978). Authorities in the area of ISTE question the impact and long-term benefit of such short programs (Hutson, 1979; Siantz & Moore, 1977). If ISTE is to be effective and result in lasting changes in teacher performance and program availability, it must be cooperatively planned and implemented by persons conducting the training and those responsible for direct service delivery (Baker, 1979; Burrello & Baker, 1979; Joyce & Showers, 1980). Guidelines are needed to facilitate such cooperative planning and immediate implementation of adapted physical education ISTE programs.

The remainder of this chapter will present a brief review of recommended ISTE standards that have evolved from general education. Guidelines for ISTE in adapted physical education based on this synthesis and current practices will then be presented.

Harris and Bessent (1969) presented an early text designed to assist supervisory practitioners in the development and implementation of ISTE programs. The need for such programs was based upon the following assumptions:

(a) Preservice preparation is rarely ideal and is primarily introductory in nature; (b) social and educational change render current practices obsolete or relatively ineffective in a short period of time; (c) coordination and articulation of instructional practices require changes in people; and (d) factors such as staff morale, stimulation, and motivation necessitate periodic ISTE efforts. Harris and Bessent accentuated the importance of stating goals and performance-based objectives related to desired outcomes of ISTE programs. A variety of delivery methods were recommended for ISTE programs, including lecture, illustrated lecture, demonstration, observation, role playing, and brainstorming. Each of these should be assessed in relation to whether they contribute to desired program outcomes on a continuum of objective levels including knowledge, comprehension, application, synthesis, values, attitudes, and adjustment.

Brimm and Tollett (1974) conducted a study in Tennessee to determine attitudes of teachers toward the types of ISTE they experienced. A sample of 646 teachers representing each of the 147 school districts in the state was used in the study. Results indicated the following weaknesses with ISTE: (a) lack of relevant programming; (b) inadequate planning; (c) need for clearly stated goals and objectives; and (d) insufficient planned follow-up. Recommendations for persons responsible for planning and implementing ISTE programs were (a) individual teachers' needs should be determined; (b) specific goals and objectives should be formulated and follow-up activities planned to ensure attainment of these objectives; (c) teachers should assist in planning ISTE; and (d) emphasis should be placed on improving teacher performance in the classroom.

Edelfelt and Johnson (1975) edited a text published by the National Education Association entitled *Rethinking Inservice Education*. The contributors included teacher organization staff members, university professors, state education department officials, superintendents of school districts, teachers, and staff development consultants. The following recommendations resulted from the publication: (a) ISTE programs should be collaborative efforts; (b) ISTE should be recognized as an essential element of the educational process; (c) ISTE should be based on personnel, school, and student needs; (d) ISTE should interface with curriculum development and instructional improvement; (e) ISTE should be planned locally by the people to be affected; (f) ISTE should be field based; (g) various incentives for participation should be explored; (h) ISTE should be individualized; and (i) a state support system should be developed to promote and facilitate ISTE.

A comprehensive series of nationwide studies investigating various issues related to ISTE were undertaken through a cooperative venture between the National Teacher Corps and the National Center for Educational Statistics

(Joyce et al., 1976). The authors indicated that despite great dissatisfaction with the present status of ISTE, as many as 250,000 persons may be engaged as instructors of ISTE in the United States. This figure represents an 8:1 ratio among teachers and ISTE providers. Two major concerns were reported: (a) The varieties of training options needed to be interfaced closely with needs of teachers and school districts, and (b) the problems related to optimal time and place of ISTE have not been solved.

Joyce et al. (1976) presented four dimensions on ISTE that must successfully interact to create one concrete guiding structure. These critical dimensions or systems were (a) governance—composed of the decision-making structures that legitimize activities and govern them; (b) substantive—composed of content and process of ISTE and concerns what is learned and how it is learned; (c) delivery—made up of incentives and involves motivation, access, and relevance to the role of the individual professional; and (d) modal—consisting of forms of ISTE, ranging from sabbaticals abroad to intensive on-site institutes.

Howey and Joyce (1978) presented an analysis of four basic problems associated with the multidimensional process of ISTE. These problem areas were labeled (a) conceptual, (b) legal-political-economical, (c) organizational-logistical, and (d) personal-psychological. Howey and Joyce indicated that the concept of ISTE was not well articulated. While affirming that its major objective was improved instruction for students, the authors suggested the following categories of ISTE: (a) job-embedded, (b) job-related, (c) general professional, (d) career credential, and (e) personal. It was found that this typology assisted in determining who should be ISTE instructors and who should finance various forms of ISTE.

In relation to the legal-political-economical issue, a general plea was for collaborative efforts among all potential contributors, including taxpayers. It was noted, however, that not all ISTE efforts required formal collaborative governance efforts. Critical conditions that Howey and Joyce considered detrimental to successful collaboration included (a) a lack of skill in cooperative decision making, (b) vested interests inhibiting open communication, (c) a lack of a conceptual framework to organize parties effectively, and (d) insufficient support for effective collaboration to develop. Legal issues, such as the implementation of least restrictive environment concepts in Public Law 94-142, were also mentioned as an example of the ever-increasing amount of legislative and judicial decisions that influence ISTE efforts. Structural-organizational modifications deemed necessary for contemporary ISTE programs included (a) strategies that periodically released the teacher during the course of the instructional day to engage in ISTE and (b) structural alterations in relationships between school and nonschool personnel in order to make on-site ISTE more of a reality.

Howey and Joyce estimated that 75% of teachers favored these strategies, but only 20% had opportunities to participate. Job-embedded forms of ISTE were judged to be highly desirable.

Finally, the importance of individual teachers in determining the outcomes of ISTE was noted. The personal-psychological dimension of ISTE was believed critical because of the deteriorating school conditions and diminishing esteem afforded the teaching profession. Teachers should be encouraged to continually upgrade their knowledge and skills and to participate actively in planning for such improvement.

Recommended Guidelines for ISTE in Adapted Physical Education

The following guidelines are presently in a format similar to one used in another publication (Texas Education Agency, 1978). Four critical components of an ISTE scheme are addressed, with several adapted physical education ISTE guidelines set forth in each.

Planning

School staff members are more likely to benefit from adapted physical education ISTE when

- teachers, administrators, regional consultants, and important others are directly involved with ISTE planning;
- interagency collaboration takes place in reference to resources, facilities, expertise, and manpower;
- ISTE efforts are formulated as a complete program, not a workshop;
- ISTE programs are directly linked to local, regional, state, and/or federal curriculum efforts, not fads;
- unique local, regional, and/or state circumstances are taken into consideration during ISTE planning and implementation (e.g., rural areas, lack of personnel, few substitute teachers, high turnover rates, etc.);
- ISTE program designs are in line with state department of education guidelines;
- ISTE programs are designed to allow for replication;
- administrators/supervisors of ISTE trainees document instructional schedules that allow sufficient time for program implementation (Vodola, 1977);
- individual teachers' needs assessment information is used as part of content planning phase;

- ISTE objectives and desired outcomes are specifically formulated in measurable terms;
- visitations are made to ISTE trainees' worksites to assess on-site circumstances prior to the program; and
- situational design and delivery, content and evaluation, and support components of the ISTE program are planned during this initial planning stage.

Situational Design and Delivery

Adapted physical education ISTE programs are more likely to accomplish their objectives when

- sessions are thoroughly planned prior to actual implementation;
- teachers are completely informed of objectives and planned outcomes prior to entrance into formal training;
- ISTE takes place during released time from the regular teaching schedule;
- ISTE takes place at the school site or a location very similar to it;
- teachers are relaxed and familiar with the presentors and other trainees;
- ISTE sessions are designed to incorporate a variety of delivery methods (lecture, demonstration, brainstorming, etc.);
- according to the scope and sequence of the ISTE content, sessions are of appropriate length and spaced so that trainees can successfully implement new information;
- demonstrations and guided experiences with handicapped students are provided for the ISTE trainees;
- appropriate resource and teaching material are compiled and distributed to ISTE trainees;
- individualized or small group (2-4) on-site ISTE sessions are used to supplement formal training;
- ISTE trainees independently apply turn-key training concepts after properly supervised experiences (Vodola, 1977); and
- if appropriate resources and manpower exist, college and university courses are designed and implemented to meet the specific needs of teachers and districts. Cooperative content planning then takes place.

Content and Evaluation

Adapted physical education ISTE programs are more likely to accomplish their objectives when

- content is specific to planned objectives and outcomes;

- content can be replicated;

- content is related to specific needs of the ISTE trainees and/or district;

- primary emphasis is placed on increasing knowledge, skills, and attitudes of teachers in their present positions;

- the effectiveness of the ISTE program is initially assessed by the performance of the teachers and gradually (after at least a year) by the performance of students receiving services from the teachers;

- content is derived from validated programs or other appropriate sources;

- at least the following adapted physical education content is thoroughly covered:

  — Role and scope of adapted physical education

  — Attitudinal and physical barriers to overcome

  — Handicapping conditions and their motor performance, with emotional, psychological, and social implications

  — Principles and practices of adapted physical education program development, implementation, and evaluation

  — Motor assessment

  — Individual education program planning

  — Diagnostic-prescriptive teaching

  — Least restrictive environment concepts and appropriate practices in physical education

  — Practical teaching activities

  — Resources for assistance in adapted physical education

  — Multidisciplinary aspects of special education service delivery;

- the total evaluation design is formulated prior to implementation of ISTE content;

- both formative and summative evaluation techniques are utilized;

- trainees are familiar with evaluation instruments prior to program implementation;

- evaluation is designed to measure individual progress and impact of the total program;

- evaluation is implemented in a nonthreatening way; and

- evaluation questions are formulated for each component and content phase of the program.

Support

Adapted physical education ISTE programs would be likely to benefit from

- recognition from state education department's special education officials;

- placement of adapted physical education projections in state and local comprehensive systems of personnel development reports;

- the opportunity to have input into the state education department's special education policies and procedures process, which should be done either by an appointed state level adapted physical education staff person or through experts in the field,

- sincere commitments by all agencies involved in the ISTE program;

- the availability of all necessary resources for proper implementation of ISTE programs;

- direct independent financial support as a recognized priority of the educational process; and

- the use of individual trainee incentive plans such as graduate credit, released time, or financial assistance.

References

Arends, R., Hersh, R., & Turner, J. (1978). Inservice education and the six o'clock news. *Theory Into Practice, 17*, 196-205.

Baker, K. (1979). *National inservice network: An emerging collaborative effort between general and special educators.* Bloomington, IN: Indiana University, National Inservice Network.

Berman, L. (1977). Curriculum leadership: That all may feel, value, and grow. In L. Berman and J. Roderick (Eds.), *Feeling, valuing, and the art of growing: Insights into the affective* (pp. 249-273). Washington, DC: Association for Supervision and Curriculum Development.

Bieber, R. (1978). A study of decision making for inservice education. *Dissertation Abstracts International, 39*, 4874A. (University Microfilms No. 7903555)

Bird, P., & Gansneder, B. (1979). Preparation of physical education teachers as required under Public Law 94-142. *Exceptional Children, 45*, 464-466.

Brimm, J., & Tollett, D. (1974). How do teachers feel about inservice education? *Educational Leadership,* **31,** 521-525.

Bundschuh, E., Jackson, T., McLaughlin, S., & McLellan, J. (1980). *Adapting physical education activities: Project dart inservice manual.* Athens, GA: University of Georgia.

Burrello, L., & Baker, K. (1979). *Developing a comprehensive system of personnel development through a peer planning and dissemination network.* Bloomington, IN: Indiana University, National Inservice Network.

Burrello, L., & Sage, D. (1979). *Leadership and change in special education.* Englewood Cliffs, NJ: Prentice-Hall.

Clelland, R. (1979). *A survey of personnel preparation in physical education and recreation for the handicapped: Vol. 6. The consumers guide series.* Albuquerque, NM: University of New Mexico, Teacher Education/Special Education.

Cline, D., & Fagen, S. (1979). *A list of alternative training outcomes for instructional personnel engaged in the education of the handicapped.* Bloomington, IN: Indiana University, National Inservice Network.

Cooper, W., & Churton, M. (1979). University of Southern Mississippi motor development inservice training project. In J. Dunn & J. Harris (Eds.), *Physical education for the handicapped: Meeting the need through inservice education* (pp. 103-106). Corvallis, OR: Oregon State University.

Cowden, J. (1980). *Administrator inservice training for program implementation in adapted and developmental physical education.* Unpublished doctoral dissertation, Texas Woman's University, Denton.

Davies, D., & Armistead, C. (1975). *Inservice education: Current trends in school policies and programs.* Washington, DC: National School Public Relations Association.

Department of Health, Education, and Welfare, Office of Education (1977, August 23). Education of handicapped children: Implementation of Part B of the education of the handicapped act. *Federal Register,* **42**(163), 42477-42491.

DiRocco, P. (1979). Inservice model to prepare physical education personnel to instruct the handicapped. In J. Dunn & J. Harris (Eds.), *Physical education for the handicapped: Meeting the need through inservice education* (pp. 72-80). Corvallis, OR: Oregon State University.

Dunn, J., & Harris, J. (Eds.). (1979). *Physical education for the handicapped: Meeting the need through inservice education.* Corvallis, OR: Oregon State University.

Edelfelt, R. (1977). The school of education and inservice education. *Journal of Teacher Education,* **30,** 39-41.

Edelfelt, R., & Johnson, M. (Eds.). (1975). *Rethinking inservice education.* Washington, DC: National Education Association.

French, R. (1977). *General considerations in physical education for pupils with special needs.* Paper presented as part of Project Outreach—Inservice Training in Physical Education for the Handicapped. Brockport, NY: State University College.

Hall, J. (1980). A working model for curricular modification. In D. Mood (Ed.), *Infuse workshop proceedings* (pp. 1-9). Boulder, CO: University of Colorado.

Harris, B. (1980). *Improving staff development through inservice education.* Boston: Allyn and Bacon.

Harris, B., & Bessent, W. (1969). *Inservice education: A guide to better practice.* Englewood Cliffs, NJ: Prentice-Hall.

Harris, J. (1977). *Compliance with Public Law 94-142 and its implications for physical education in Oregon.* Unpublished doctoral dissertation, University of Oregon, Eugene.

Hillman, W. (1978, January 11). *Personnel preparation needs in recreation and physical education for handicapped children, memorandum to Bureau of Education for the Handicapped staff and professional personnel.* Washington, DC: Bureau of Education for the Handicapped.

Hite, H., & Howey, K. (1977). *Planning inservice teacher education: Promising alternatives.* Washington, DC: American Association of Colleges for Teacher Education.

Horgan, J. (1979). Project stop-gap: A model staff development program for physical educators through inservice training. In J. Dunn & J. Harris (Eds.), *Physical education for the handicapped: Meeting the needs through inservice education* (pp. 81-86). Corvallis, OR: Oregon State University.

Houston, W., & Frieberg, H. (1979). Perceptual motion, blindman's bluff, and inservice education. *Journal of Teacher Education,* **30,** 7-9.

Howey, K. (1976). Putting inservice education into perspective. *Journal of Teacher Education,* **27,** 101-105.

Howey, K., & Joyce, B. (1978). A data base for future directions in inservice education. *Theory Into Practice,* **17,** 206-211.

Hurley, D. (1979). *Inservice training for diagnostic-prescriptive physical education: I CAN*. Unpublished doctoral dissertation, Texas Woman's University, Denton.

Hutson, H. (1979). *Inservice best practices: The learning of general education*. Bloomington, IN: Indiana University, National Inservice Network.

Irmer, L., Odenkirk, B., & Glasenapp, G. (1979). *PEOPEL (Physical Education Opportunity Program for Exceptional Learners): An administrators guide for secondary schools*. Phoenix, AZ: Union High School, District No. 210.

Jansma, P. (1977). Get ready for mainstreaming. *Journal of Physical Education and Recreation, 48*, 15-16.

Joyce, G., Howey, K., & Yarger, S. (1977). *Issues to face, ISTE report 1*. Syracuse: The National Dissemination Center.

Joyce, B., & Showers, B. (1980). Improving inservice training: The message of research. *Educational Leadership, 37*, 379-386.

Karper, W., & Weiss, R. (1980). The preparation of non-physical education teachers to teach physical education to handicapped students. *American Corrective Therapy Journal, 34*, 137-141.

Knowles, C. (1981). Concerns of teachers about implementing individualized instruction in the physical education setting. *Research Quarterly, 52*, 48-57.

Lange, E. (1979). Inservice for rural areas—Idaho. In J. Dunn & J. Harris (Eds.), *Physical education for the handicapped: Meeting the need through inservice education* (pp. 93-97). Corvallis, OR: Oregon State University.

Lawrence, G. (1974). *Patterns of effective inservice education: A state of the art summary of research on materials and procedures for changing teacher behaviors in inservice education*. Tallahasee, FL: State Department of Education.

Loovis, M., & Taylor, J. (1979). Physical education for the handicapped: A field-based model project for continuous professional development. In J. Dunn & J. Harris (Eds.), *Physical education for the handicapped: Meeting the need through inservice education* (pp. 63-71). Corvallis, OR: Oregon State University.

McCaffrey, M., Burrello, L., Strout, T., & Cline, D. (1979). *Toward a national inservice network: Training school personnel working with handicapped children*. Bloomington, IN: Indiana University, National Inservice Network.

Meyen, E. (1978). Inservice implications for implementing Public Law 94-142. *Journal of Special Education Technology, 2*, 4-10.

Nicholson, A., Joyce, B., Parker, D., & Waterman, F. (1976). *The literature on inservice teacher education: An analytic review* (ISTE report 3). Syracuse: The National Dissemination Center.

Otto, W., & Erickson, L. (1973). *Inservice education to improve reading instruction*. Newark, DE: International Reading Association.

Rubin, L. (Ed.). (1971). *Improving inservice education: Proposals and procedures for change*. Boston: Allyn and Bacon.

Schofer, R., & McGough, R. (1977). *Manpower planning for special educators: Planning a model and alternatives*. Columbia, MO: University of Missouri, Department of Special Education.

Sherrill, C. (1986). *Adapted physical education and recreation: A multidisciplinary approach* (3rd ed.). Dubuque, IA: Wm. C. Brown.

Siantz, J., & Moore, E. (1977). Inservice programming and preservice priorities. In J. Smith (Ed.), *Personnel preparation and Public Law 94-142: The map, the mission, and the mandate*. Albuquerque, NM: University of New Mexico, Special Education Department.

Spragens, J. (1979). *Inservice training of teachers to work in mainstreamed physical education*. Unpublished doctoral dissertation, Texas Woman's University, Denton.

Stokes, B. (1980). *The status of physical education in Louisiana as it relates to requirements of The Education for all Handicapped Children Act of 1975*. Unpublished doctoral dissertation, University of Southern Mississippi, Hattiesburg.

Texas Education Agency, State Board of Education. (1978). *A review of inservice education in Texas*. Austin: Author.

Tyler, R. (1971). Inservice education of teachers: A look at the past and future. In L. Rubin (Ed.), *Improving inservice education: Proposals and procedures for change* (pp. 5-17). Boston: Allyn and Bacon.

Tymeson, G. (1981). *An adapted physical education service delivery system utilizing an interagency inservice education model*. Unpublished doctoral dissertation, Texas Woman's University, Denton.

Vodola, T. (1977). *PROJECT ACTIVE administrative guide: Organizational and administrative strategies*. Oakhurst, NJ: Township of Ocean School District.

Wessel, J., Vogel, P., Knowles, C., & Green, G. (1976). *I CAN physical education curriculum materials.* Northbrook, IL: Hubbard Scientific.

Winnick, J., & Jansma, P. (Eds.). (1978). *Physical education inservice resource manual for implementation of The Education for all Handicapped Children Act (PL 94-142).* Brockport, NY: State University College.

Chapter 32

Personnel Training for Leadership in Sport for Athletes with Handicapping Conditions

Julian U. Stein

A natural outgrowth of physical activity programs involving participants with handicapping conditions has been the demand for more and better opportunities in sport. Over the years some opportunities in sport have been available for participants with handicapping conditions. For the most part, however, such opportunities have been in nonschool settings and have involved adults. Few opportunities have been available for students of school age. Enactment of The Education for All Handicapped Children Act (PL 94-142) and Section 504 of the Rehabilitation Act (PL 93-112) guaranteed free, appropriate education and equal opportunities in all activities to all individuals with handicapping conditions. No longer can individuals be denied opportunities to participate in sport activities at *any* level because of handicapping conditions.

Constitutionally guaranteed rights of individuals with handicapping conditions necessitate organizations supporting sport activities—public schools, local education agencies, colleges and universities, and community recreation agencies—to insure equal opportunities. Such insurance requires several considerations:

- Make necessary changes so that individuals with handicapping conditions participate in and are not discriminated against in regular competitive activities—interscholastic and intercollegiate competition as well as intramural, extramural, and club sport.

- Provide special activities where necessary so that individuals with handicapping conditions have equal opportunities to compete even though through specific segregated activities.

Sport Organizations for Athletes With Handicapping Conditions

Over the years various groups have sponsored competitive sport activities for athletes with specific handicapping conditions. Despite recent emphasis and entry onto the scene of a number of fledgling organizations, international competition goes back over 60 years! The first International Games for the Deaf were held in 1924, almost 30 years before teams from England and Denmark met in the first international wheelchair competition. Today organizations sponsor activities that provide highly competitive outlets for athletes with any conceivable handicapping condition, including those with the most severe and multiple conditions. A number of national organizations administer and support activities in the United States at national, regional, state, and local levels. Representative of such organizations are the following:

- United States Amputee Athletic Association (USAAA)
- United States Association for Blind Athletes (USABA)
- American Athletic Association for the Deaf (AAAD)
- Special Olympics

Julian Stein (left) of George Mason University in Virginia with James Mastro (right), Braille Sports Foundation, discussing research needed on blind athletes at the 1984 International Games for the Disabled.

- United States Cerebral Palsy Athletic Association (USCPAA)

- National Wheelchair Athletic Association (NWAA)

- National Handicapped Sports and Recreation Association (NHSRA)

For the most part each of these associations is affiliated with a companion international organization. International competition parallels opportunities involving able-bodied athletes. Olympic-type competition, world games, European games, Asian games, and Pan American games represent but a few of the international opportunities for athletes with handicapping conditions. Specialized opportunities such as Ski for Light, Gold Cup in wheelchair basketball, Goal Ball for individuals with visual impairments, and Stoke Mandeville (England) games in other wheelchair sports not only abound but are increasing.

Role of Sport Governance Bodies

Additional impetus to these efforts has been fostered through establishment of the Handicapped in Sports Committee of the United States Olympic Committee, now the Committee on Sports for the Disabled (COSD). This committee consists of 16 active members, two each from the National Wheelchair Athletic Association, the United States Cerebral Palsy Athletic Association, the United States Association for Blind Athletes, the American Athletic Association for the Deaf, the United States Amputee Athletic Assocation, the National Handicapped Sports and Recreation Association, and Special Olympics. One representative from each of these associations must be an athlete with a handicapping condition. The other six committee members are appointed at large by the United States Olympic Committee.

Among specific indications of progress have been (a) accepting this committee in the governance structure of the United States Olympic Committee, (b) opening Olympic Training Centers to athletes with handicapping conditions preparing for international competition, and (c) accepting the National Wheelchair Basketball Association as part of American Basketball U.S.A., the governing body for basketball in the United States.

The new Amateur Sports Act (PL 95-606) requires attention to sport for participants with handicapping conditions by the United States Olympic Committee, the organization charged through the Act with responsibility of coordinating all amateur sport involving international competition by United States teams. General directions and some specific approaches included in the Amateur Sports Act were gleaned from materials in and recommendations from the report of the President's Commission on Olympic Sports that dealt specifically with sport for the handicapped.

Despite the highly positive and successful model of the United States Olympic Committee integrating governance of and support for sport involving athletes with handicapping conditions with those for able-bodied athletes, too few sport governance bodies have become involved to the degree expected. The following actions reflect progress:

1. A Handicapped in Sports Committee has been established in the Pennsylvania Governor's Council on Physical Fitness and Sports, which sponsored the first All-Disabled Regatta in Philadelphia. Individuals with handicapping conditions are included on a full participation basis in the First Annual Keystone Games, also sponsored by the Pennsylvania Governor's Council on Physical Fitness and Sports.

2. The National Federation of State High School Associations has made changes in the rules of several sports so that they are not discriminatory and permit athletes with handicapping conditions to participate. Changes that have been made in playing rules include the following:

   - Prosthetic devices approved by state high school activity or athletic associations can be worn by athletes competing in interscholastic football and soccer, and wrestling requires that individuals competing with prosthetic devices weigh in with them.

   - Sighted partners or teammates can assist blind runners in distance events in track, cross country, and marathon running so long as they are identified to the management and other competitors and do not interfere with athletes. Various types of contact are permitted, including physical contact, verbal assistance, and use of short pieces of rope. Experiments are now being conducted with radio control through earphones to assist blind runners to compete more independently at higher levels of competition.

   - Deaf and hard-of-hearing runners and swimmers can gain equality in starts by increasing the caliber of starting pistols and putting the gun in a *down* rather than in the traditional *up* position.

Some state high school athletic or activities associations have also made special efforts to include individuals with handicapping conditions on equitable bases in activities they sponsor:

- During the 1980 outdoor track season, experiments were conducted in Illinois with light synchronized with the starter's gun to assist deaf sprinters and runners attain competitive starts with hearing athletes. Football teams from schools for the deaf compete against hearing opponents by keying offensive signals with a drum from the sidelines by special rulings in a number of states.

- Many states have changed academic eligibility rules so that mentally retarded and learning disabled students are not denied opportunities to take part in interscholastic sport because of an inability to pass a specific number of academic units or Carnegie Units. Some states have approached this by granting eligibility on the basis of appropriate progress in accredited special education programs (i.e., Missouri and Virginia). In other states these decisions are based on adequate progress toward attaining goals delineated in each student's individualized education programs (i.e., Louisiana).

The National Collegiate Athletic Association (NCAA) and the National Association for Intercollegiate Athletics (NAIA) have both given some recognition to individuals with handicapping conditions. In 1978 the NCAA authorized a special committee to study the situation and make recommendations for program implementation. Tim Nugent (Director of the Rehabilitation-Education Center, University of Illinois) and Stan Labanowich (Commissioner of the National Wheelchair Basketball Association) developed and submitted such a report. As of this date, however, no release of the report has been made and no apparent action has been taken. Discussions were initiated in 1978 with NAIA about changes in its bylaws and operating codes to make them non-discriminatory. Little if any definitive and assertive action has resulted.

Actions that have been taken at the collegiate level have been initiated and implemented by individual colleges and universities, along with efforts initiated by associations such as the National Wheelchair Basketball Association, which has for several years sponsored intercollegiate wheelchair basketball championships for both men and women.

Several states have organized special athletic associations for programs involving athletes with handicapping conditions. Representative of such groups is the *Minnesota Association for Adapted Athletics* (MAAA), established to promote competitive sport for students with physical disabilities within the state of Minnesota. The MAAA Board consists of parents, civic-minded professionals, adapted physical education teachers, and recreation professionals. The Minnesota State High School League has cited the MAAA for providing valuable physical and personal benefits to the young people in its adapted programs. Initial activity sponsored by MAAA was floor hockey, which has been followed with opportunities in soccer, track and field, and softball.

A 3-year plan was developed in Milwaukee, Wisconsin whereby programs for students with handicapping conditions in both regular and special schools were initiated on intramural and extramural bases. Club teams were organized during the second year, followed by fully recognized varsity teams during the third year. Both the Milwaukee and Wisconsin Athletic Leagues participated in, supported, and sanctioned these programs. Emanating from this effort has been *Mail-A-Graphic Track and Field Meets* for students in wheelchairs. Interest and participation in this annual competition are growing with teams from throughout the United States taking part. Athletes participate in designated activities, including those designed specifically for individuals in motorized wheelchairs, at their own schools after which times and distances for each event are submitted. Winners are determined on the basis of such performances; both individual and team awards are presented.

Despite individual efforts and progress, too little interaction has been noted among various governance bodies—those involved in sport for athletes with different handicapping conditions, those involved in sport for athletes with the same handicapping condition, and those involved in sport for able-bodied athletes and those involved in sport for athletes with handicapping conditions. If further growth and progress are to result, then interactions among *all* governance bodies responsible for sport are an absolute *must*. It can be done! For example, in Alberta (Canada) the South Alberta Games have been integrated for over 10 years; the Alberta Games for over 5 years. Events are included for individuals with handicapping conditions right along with events for able-bodied athletes. Sections and events for individuals in wheelchairs, the mentally retarded, and those with other handicapping conditions are included in these games. Only the Canadian National Games, the British Commonwealth Games, the Pan American Games, and the Olympic Games provide more prestigious competitions. In addition to integrating actual competition, these efforts in Alberta (as well as in other Canadian provinces) have resulted in close working relationships among regular sport governance bodies and those concerned with programs for athletes with handicapping conditions.

Many efforts related to training programs, introducing new activities, developing materials, and sponsoring competitions are coordinated by regular governance bodies, not special groups. As a result, athletes with handicapping conditions are increasingly becoming a part of regular sport programs and activities. As in a number of countries, able-bodied and disabled athletes train together for both regular and special competitions; such interactions have improved performances of many disabled athletes and brought about significant attitude changes in able-bodied athletes. Funds supporting sport activities, governance bodies, and competitions at all levels are more equitably divided under integrated conditions. Combining efforts, including solicitations of funds, results in a much more coordinated whole rather than having different groups always competing for support from the same populations and sources. Despite apparent consolidation through the Committee on Sports for the Disabled of the United States Olympic Committee, progress of the type described in Canada appears to be a long way off. As in most countries of the world, truly integrated sport programs for individuals with handicapping conditions do not appear on the horizon in the United States.

The Spirit of Competition

For some unknown reasons the general public, media, and even many professional providers of services still consider involving persons with handicapping conditions in sport as exclusively rehabilitation. These attitudes and perceptions must be eliminated so that recognition is given to the fact that individuals with handicapping conditions participate in sport activities for all the same reasons as able-bodied persons—competition at all levels, fitness, recreation, diversion, and fun. This is not to imply that sport activities have not and are not used as important parts of rehabilitation processes; this, however, is *not* the emphasis and focus of sport for the large majority of individuals with handicapping conditions.

The same goals, objectives, and motivations prevail among athletes competing in special segregated sport programs and activities as among able-bodied counterparts. Athletes taking part in the long and arduous season of the National Wheelchair Basketball Association have exactly the same goals, objectives, and motivations as college and university basketball players all over the country—to reach the final four and win the national championship!

Although certain adaptations and modifications are necessary to enable individuals with handicapping conditions to participate in certain sport activities, consumers (persons with handicapping conditions) themselves continue to emphasize that such changes should be minimal so that the integrity of the sport is neither compromised nor

lost. For example, in wheelchair basketball only minor modifications are made:

• Players are allowed 5, rather than 3, seconds in the lane.

• A physical advantage foul occurs when a player raises his or her buttocks off the chair. This is necessary to insure equitable competition among all players because individuals with different levels of spinal cord lesions, amputees, and postpolio athletes take part. Without such a rule, less-involved players could gain unfair advantages over more-involved individuals.

• When dribbling and holding the ball in the lap, a player can give impetus to the wheels only two times after which he or she must dribble, pass, or shoot; a player can glide as fast as opponents permit. When dribbling and wheeling simultaneously, there are no differences as to when an able-bodied basketball player moves and dribbles.

• Fouls in the back court by the defensive team result in two shots throughout the game.

International wheelchair basketball rules incorporate the basics of competition for able-bodied games; these include no front and back court divisions, a 30-second clock, and officials not having to handle the ball on violation turnovers in the back court. In some activities individuals with handicapping conditions and able-bodied athletes can compete against each other equitably. Such an approach has been instituted successfully in Canada, where different classes of athletes from wheelchair sport programs compete against each other. A pentathlon approach is used whereby every competitor participates in five events regularly contested in wheelchair games. Two of these must be track events, two field events, and the other is selected from weight lifting, slalom, and dartchery. Dartchery is a competitive sport combining elements of darts and archery; a dart target is shot at as in archery. Scoring scales, based on the world's record in each event for the specific class, are established. Times are converted to points, and points for each competitor in each event are then ranked from high to low. Event points are awarded from 21 to 1 so that 125 is the maximum that can be attained by any competitor. In one such competition, four different classes of competitors in wheelchairs and both males and females were represented in the first five finishers! This approach has applicability for crossing handicapping conditions as well as integrating able-bodied athletes and those with various handicapping conditions.

Medley relays in track, swimming, and special relay carnivals can include able-bodied and disabled athletes competing with and against one another. Relays consisting of legs contested by individuals with different handicapping conditions along with able-bodied teammates have many possibilities; nothing is fixed in concrete so that relay teams must always consist of four competitors.

Athletes With Handicapping Conditions as Consumers and Advocates

Athletes with handicapping conditions must be provided with more opportunities to serve as their own advocates. Often perceptions and approaches of able-bodied providers of services are *not* consistent with those of program participants. These differences were quite evident and accentuated during a Consumer Conference sponsored by the Unit on Programs for the Handicapped of the American Alliance for Health, Physical Education, Recreation and Dance in 1978. Representative of some of the recommended guidelines endorsed by participants representing four groups of handicapping conditions—blind and partially sighted; deaf and hard of hearing; cerebral palsied; ambulatory disabled including those with spinal cord injuries, amputees, postpolio, and other conditions resulting in the necessity to use wheelchairs while competing in sport activities—are the following:

- Categorical limitations imposed by the medical profession relative to physical education, recreation, and sport activities for individuals with handicapping conditions should be discouraged.

- Many activities suitable for able-bodied persons are suitable for individuals with disabilities.

- Disabled individuals should have foremost responsibility for their own advocacy and in implementing programs to ensure enforcement of existing laws as related and applied to physical education, recreation, and sport.

- Disabled persons must become aware of their legal and civil rights as related to physical education, recreation, and sport activities.

- Opportunities to participate in and contribute at decision- and policy-making levels must be provided for qualified disabled persons: Providers of services must seek out qualified disabled persons for these purposes.

- Disabled persons must be encouraged to enter the physical education, recreation, and coaching profes-

sions. An important part of this process is in educating disabled persons about these fields so they can make decisions regarding which of the professions to consider.

- Opportunities must be provided for qualified disabled persons to serve in teaching, leading, and coaching roles through physical education, recreation, and coaching professions.

- Much of the literature in the field is viewed with a jaundiced eye.

- Program organization and administrative flexibility are necessary so that individuals can be integrated into programs and activities where appropriate and separated if necessary. If separation is necessary, these activities should be designed with the specific needs of participants in mind and conducted in the least-restrictive environments. These programs should also be funded and provided with services on at least the same levels provided to able-bodied participants.

- Greater coordination is needed of efforts designed to communicate about and share the wealth of information, materials, and resources available throughout the field, both in the United States and in other countries.

- Existing conflicts among various groups of disabled persons must be resolved through regular communication and dialogue at local, state, regional, and national levels. This same type of communication and dialogue is also important among representatives from physical education and adapted physical education, recreation and therapeutic recreation, and sport fields.

- When establishing recreational or sport programs and activities involving disabled persons, consideration must be given to full involvement and utilization of the national organization responsible for the given activities or sports rather than comparable groups organized specifically for a given population of disabled persons. These national organizations must seek and accept input from qualified disabled persons *before* making decisions involving these populations. In some circumstances, special organizations may have to be created.

- People should work with and have appropriate practical experiences with disabled persons early in their undergraduate preservice professional education to determine whether they are suited to working with and leading these populations.

- Leaders of sport organizations for disabled persons should have full understanding of the sport as it is played by able-bodied participants.

- Public and private school, college and university, and community recreation departments are expected to meet their moral and legal responsibilities in providing appropriate physical education, recreational, and sport opportunities for persons with handicapping conditions.

- When modified activities are necessary, they should approximate original activities as closely as possible; basic and regular equipment should be adapted *only* to the degree necessary. The fewer the adaptations, the better.

- Courage and sympathy should be deemphasized because too much attention and overemphasis of these characteristics and traits can have adverse effects on an individual's self-concept.

- Limiting aspects of disabilities should be eliminated by adapting methods and activities according to *individual* needs.

- Emphasis should be placed on strengths and abilities of disabled individuals rather than their weaknesses and disabilities.

- An injury to a disabled individual is not in general any more serious than similar injuries to able-bodied persons.

- High levels of physical fitness are as important for disabled persons as for able-bodied persons.

- To accommodate individuals with disabilities, able-bodied participants should not be asked to change radically the rules of their games, activities, or sports.

- Disabled individuals capable of competing against able-bodied persons should be encouraged to do so rather than engage in special segregated programs and activities.

- Activities and efforts must be developed and implemented to bring about changes in attitudes of disabled persons toward physical activity, recreation, and sport as important contributors to high-quality lives and lifestyles that supplement and complement vocational endeavors and pursuits.

- Promoting disabled women as sport figures is important.

- In the same ways that federal financial support is given to teams participating in Olympic and other recognized international competitions, financial support must be given to disabled individuals in similar international competitions.

- Organizations that make rules for able-bodied individuals should be asked to alter these rules slightly when it means that disabled individuals could compete on a reasonably equal basis. Disabled athletes should be permitted to compete in Olympic trials in some events and in other similar sporting events.

- Whenever competition is reasonably equal, disabled individuals should be encouraged and permitted to compete against able-bodied opponents.

- Disabled groups deserve equal access to funding sources along with able-bodied groups.

- Recognition normally provided to able-bodied persons must also be provided to disabled persons at national and international levels.

- Programs and activities should be approached with no preconceived limitations or expectations of disabled participants.

- Keys to success are not found in special programs but rather in interpersonal relationships developed and maintained among all disabled and able-bodied participants and between participants and leaders.

- Disabled individuals of all ages need to be encouraged to participate actively in a variety of physical education, recreational, and sport activities.

- No requirements should be imposed on participation of disabled individuals above and beyond requirements for able-bodied participants in the same activity.

- Varying degrees of competition should be offered in sport and games to recognize the developmental aspects of competition itself and the differential interests and abilities of participants.

- Mixing disabled populations in activities is to be encouraged as in activities involving disabled and able-bodied participants.

- It is acceptable to have segregated programs consisting of separate disabled sport and recreational activities if desired.

- Disabled individuals need and are entitled to a variety of appropriate physical education, recreation, and sport programs including specialized programs based on disability groupings, mixed disability groups, and groups of individuals with and without disabilities. Selection of one or more of these approaches should be based on the purpose of the program and the nature of the populations served.

- Awards, rewards, and recognition provided in special physical education, recreation, sport, and competitive programs and activities should be the same as those provided in comparable programs and activities for able-bodied participants. Success, progress, and achievement should be realistically rewarded in these programs and activities.

Obviously, participants see the need for programs and activities to be as much as possible like those for able-bodied participants. It is vitally important to ensure maintenance of the integrity of these activities, especially when disabled and able-bodied people participate with and compete against each other. Too often games are modified to the extent that they lose their identity. Such an approach is not desired or healthy for any of the participants. Consider these examples:

- A single-arm amputee competing in butterfly and breaststroke events in swimming had to execute the stroke properly or be disqualified in the event. This is *not* discriminatory in that the individual could always compete in the free-style event and derive benefits from, not be excluded from, and not be discriminated against in the interscholastic swimming program.

- A paraplegic pitched for a softball team in the Lansing (Michigan) Parks and Recreation Department softball league with no restrictions on bunting imposed on opponents; to do so would have changed the nature of the game for all players. The team adjusted to the pitcher's inability to field bunts—he pitched from his knees—in that *it won the city championship!* When batting, he went four for four in the title game—a runner was permitted for the paraplegic player (this actually put his team at a greater disadvantage than when a player runs for himself).

- A double-arm amputee who competed in diving during her high school days had no special or different provisions when being judged; she was judged by the *same* criteria as all other competitors based on grace, effectiveness, and execution of dives. This same approach has been practiced for single-leg amputees who have competed in interscholastic and intercollegiate levels in gymnastics as well as athletes who have competed in gymnastics despite the aftereffects of polio.

- A boy placed second in his age class in Pass-Punt-Kick competition in Richmond, Virginia, despite having only one leg. Although he used a crutch for balance while competing, no special or different criteria were used in scoring his efforts.

Coaching Athletes With Handicapping Conditions

Throughout the years many athletes with handicapping conditions have had little professional coaching and guidance. As a result, many of these individuals have come nowhere near attaining their potentials in events and activities for which they were training so hard. In programs where individuals with background and experience in sport coached, training regimens were sound and resulted in performances more consistent with the athlete's true potential and intensity of training. In situations where properly trained coaches worked with these teams and their athletes, performances improved dramatically. For example, one individual who had little success in wheelchair track and field, despite regular and rigorous training, set four national track records and represented the United States in the Olympiad for the Physically Disabled in Arne, Holland in 1980 after only 3 years of assistance from an experienced and successful track coach. This is *not* an isolated incident.

Observations of athletes competing in various track events in wheelchairs have shown time splits to be exactly the same as for able-bodied runners in the same events. Competitors in field events apply the best and latest in form from able-bodied champions but adapt according to their conditions and functional abilities. For example, it is not uncommon to see Class IV and V athletes in wheelchairs using modified O'Brien turns in the shot put and as much of upper body portions of jump turns as possible in the discus.

Athletes with all types and levels of handicapping conditions use weight training to increase both muscular strength and endurance. It is interesting to note that George Murray, recognized wheelchair marathon champion of the world, during his first year of training for the Boston Marathon worked out on the track 3 days a week and lifted weights 3 other days of each week. Obviously many of the same traits and characteristics required for championship performances by able-bodied athletes are needed by individuals seeking comparable levels of performance in games specifically for athletes with handicapping conditions.

Potential of paraplegic athletes was shown dramatically in a study recently conducted in Canada. In this study myographic analyses were made of both fast- and slow-twitch muscle functions of Olympic and Olympiad athletes. Olympiad athletes scored in the same ranges as average Olympic athletes in terms of quality of function. In addition to the obvious application in emphasizing maximum development of intact muscles and muscle groups, results show that performances in power events such as sprints and weight lifting by paraplegic athletes are comparable with those of able-bodied athletes in the same events.

Although comparisons in weight lifting between able-bodied and disabled athletes are difficult at best for a variety of reasons—the bench press is *not* competitive but rather is a training lift for able-bodied athletes; body weight comparisons are deceiving because of different body proportions between able-bodied and disabled persons—performances of individuals with handicapping conditions are indeed impressive. For example, a 125-pound paraplegic from Sweden bench pressed 397-1/2 pounds, better than three times his body weight. On the other hand, Alexi, the Russian Olympic gold medal winner in both 1972 and 1976, has never achieved a bench press of even twice his body weight! Jon Robertson, postpolio lifter from California, has an unofficial bench press within 15 pounds of Alexi's best despite a difference in body weight of more than 120 pounds.

Leadership positions for individuals with handicapping conditions must be increased at all levels in sport programs, not just in special programs but in programs involving able-bodied participants as well. Many coaches working with deaf athletes are themselves deaf; increasing numbers of coaches in wheelchair sports are themselves former players or in roles of playing coaches. Legally blind coaches have long coached wrestling and other sports at state schools for the blind. Several individuals with cerebral palsy are actively involved in programs at all levels sponsored by the United States Cerebral Palsy Athletic Association. Under sponsorship of The Joseph P. Kennedy, Jr. Foundation, outstanding mentally retarded individuals assist with Special Olympics teams and serve as aides in recreation programs sponsored by community parks and recreation departments as well as in residential facilities for the mentally retarded.

Serving in leadership positions in regular programs needs greater attention at all levels. Numerous examples show that individuals with handicapping conditions can be successful coaches in regular programs. In Utah, a high school football coach with multiple sclerosis confined to a wheelchair led his team to the state championship, the first time a team from that school had won a state championship in any sport in more than 30 years. Several individuals in wheelchairs have coached high school, youth league, and community baseball and softball teams. At least two legally blind individuals have coached wrestling at regular senior high schools. Deaf and hard-of-hearing persons have coached various sports at both regular and special schools throughout the nation. Amputees have equally impressive records, including serving as fitness instructors at commercial health spas.

The approach of the Committee on Sports for the Disabled of the United States Olympic Committee, in which individuals with handicapping conditions *must* be active members of this Committee, needs to be emulated in other programs at all levels. *Representation at the important decision- and policy-making levels is a must*. For too long able-bodied providers of services have done what they felt groups being served wanted and needed. As a result many activities and approaches provided were neither needed nor wanted. Having disabled persons represented in such groups and heeding their words would alleviate such situations. These approaches will result in programs that are more consistent with interests and needs of populations being served; they will result also in methods, procedures, and techniques implemented in more economically feasible ways.

Role of the Media

When individuals are confronted with environments that are unfriendly despite accessibility laws and civil rights legislation, they learn easy, practical, and functional ways to attack such barriers. In this process many of the myths and exaggerations about program and facility accessibility will be reduced if not eliminated altogether. The media—all types at all levels—have contributed little in presenting the real picture of sport activities and programs involving athletes with handicapping conditions to the American public. Since its inception the *Sports Illustrated Annual* has included not one word about national and international performances and accomplishments of athletes with handicapping conditions. No mention has been made of outstanding records of individuals with handicapping conditions who take part in competitions with able-bodied athletes such as times of wheelchair marathoners, outstanding records and accomplishments of Harry Cordellos (totally blind) in the grueling triathlon, the maximarathon (50 miles), the Dipsea Race and Bay to Breakers swim in San Francisco, and water skiing at Cypress Gardens. Needless to say, there is little media coverage of individuals and teams in special competitions. Unfortunately, little time and space have been given to these and comparable achievements by national and local media.

It seems that only when sponsor support and/or political contacts can be obtained has coverage been attained. Then such programs have often focused on anything and everything but the competition itself and the athletes themselves. Political and social emphases along with personal stories have often left viewers or listeners with impressions and attitudes that reinforced attitudes that should be eradicated. Seldom in any media, printed, television, or radio, are these events and activities presented as what they truly are and in ways competitors want them to be viewed—as sport in the same ways as sport involving able-bodied athletes. Many times information and reports about these programs are found in the social sections of newspapers and in political and special feature sections in national magazines. For the most part television and radio present the few programs that reach the airwaves as special features, not competitive sport.

Competencies to be Developed in Personnel Training

Great strides continue to be made in providing more and better opportunities for individuals with all types and severities of handicapping conditions in and through competitive sport programs and activities. Obviously, much more needs to be done to make "a sport for every individual and an individual in every sport" reality for individuals with handicapping conditions. A number of cautions must be heeded, however, so that the same mistakes made in sport for able-bodied persons are not duplicated in these programs for athletes with handicapping conditions. Unfortunately, with the glitter and glamour of prestigious athletic competition, "the tail can start wagging the dog" very early. Many different competencies must be considered in both preservice and in-service programs for leadership personnel serving athletes with handicapping conditions, whether such service be in regular (integrated) or special (segregated) settings. The following skills are representative of such competencies:

• Demonstrate the ability to apply understanding of deviations from normal physical growth and development to analyses of sport skills

• Demonstrate proficiency in evaluating and analyzing sport performances in terms of motor deficits and deviations

• Demonstrate the ability to apply understanding of unique structures of individuals with disabilities to individualized coaching in both adapted and regular sport activities

• Demonstrate the ability to apply biomechanical principles that affect sport skill development to wheelchair, crutch, brace, and artificial limb use

• Demonstrate the ability to apply understanding of physiological and motor characteristics of athletes with physical, mental, sensory, neurological, and other specific health needs to sport programs designed for those with disabilities

• Demonstrate an understanding of roles and the significance of active participation in sport activities by individuals with disabilities

• Demonstrate the ability to apply understanding of the potential for human interaction and social behavior occurring in cooperative/competitive activities for individuals with disabilities

• Demonstrate the ability to work and cooperate with organizations that conduct regular or adapted sport programs and activities for individuals with disabilities

• Demonstrate the ability to apply understanding of the potential that sport provides for social interactions among individuals with and without disabilities

• Demonstrate the ability to apply understanding of atypical motor development to athletes with disabilities

• Demonstrate the ability to apply principles of motor learning to individuals with specific physical and motor needs as related to developing sport skills

• Demonstrate the ability to apply principles of motivation on the development of sport skills by athletes with disabilities

• Demonstrate an understanding of how participation in sport activities contributes to positive self-concepts of athletes with disabilities

• Demonstrate an understanding of the historical development of participation by athletes with disabilities in both regular and special sport programs

• Demonstrate an understanding of roles and the significance of professional and voluntary organizations on the development of professional standards, ethics, and programs related to sport programs involving athletes with disabilities

• Demonstrate an understanding of philosophies of participation in regular and special sport programs by athletes with disabilities

• Demonstrate the ability to apply a personal and a professional philosophy of sport programs activities for individuals with disabilities

• Demonstrate an understanding of ways individuals with disabilities realize and express their individualities and uniqueness through participation in sport programs and activities

• Demonstrate the ability to develop objectives that lead to fulfillment of sport goals in psychomotor, affective, and cognitive domains by athletes with disabilities

• Demonstrate the ability to assess sport skill needs of athletes with disabilities

• Demonstrate proficiency in planning instructional practices to meet the needs of athletes with disabilities

- Demonstrate an understanding of organizations that govern adapted and special sport and games involving participants with disabilities

- Demonstrate the ability to apply strategies for individualizing instruction and coaching techniques to athletes with disabilities in a variety of sport activities

- Demonstrate the ability to apply task analysis techniques in the process of individualizing instructional and coaching approaches

- Demonstrate the ability to function effectively as a member of a coaching staff

- Demonstrate the ability to apply principles of safety to wheelchair transfers, lifts, and assists needed when individuals with disabilities participate in sport activities

- Demonstrate an understanding of scientific bases of specifically contraindicated exercises and activities for athletes with disabilities

- Demonstrate the ability to apply principles of appropriate health practices to participation in sport activities by athletes with disabilities

- Demonstrate an understanding of effects of medication, fatigue, and illness on mental, physical, and motor performances of athletes with disabilities

- Demonstrate an understanding of implications of personal hygiene, posture, and nutrition for athletes with disabilities

Additional general and specific areas need to be considered for individuals serving in different capacities in sport programs involving athletes with disabilities. These include competencies in

- athletic training and sport medicine;

- one or more sports as a coach;

- preseason training activities including weight training;

- postseason training including preparation for regional, national, and international competitions;

- public relations and public information activities;

- technological areas including audiovisual equipment and materials and computerization;

- budgeting, finances, and fund raising;

- understanding and applying rules of specific sports;

- strategies of specific sports;

- planning and implementing individual and team transportation;

- handling equipment and supplies, including technological factors unique to specific devices necessary for sport programs involving athletes with disabilities (i.e., wheelchairs and field event tie downs); and

- rules and operations of governance bodies such as the National Federation of State High School Associations and its state affiliates, the National Collegiate Athletic Association, the National Association of Intercollegiate Athletics, the National Junior College Athletic Association, the Association of Intercollegiate Athletics for Women, and their conference affiliates.

Summary

Some individuals feel that the day in which events for athletes with handicapping conditions become part of regular Olympic Games is not in the too distant future. Some point to recent developments like the formation of the Committee on Sports for the Disabled of the United States Olympic Committee, the inclusion of the National Wheelchair Basketball Association in American Basketball U.S.A., and 800- and 1500-meter demonstration races in the 1984 Olympic Games as indicators of what is to come. Predictions have been made that wheelchair basketball could be included in the 1988 Olympic Games.

Highly competitive sport activities involving athletes with handicapping conditions represent competitive sport at their very best. Athletes train long and hard; competition is fierce with exceptions neither being expected nor given. Spectators unfamiliar with these activities often marvel at the skill, speed, agility, coordination, and endurance of these outstanding athletes. As with able-bodied sport at any level, this competition and preparation enable participants to draw upon every skill and ability they possess. They set goals and strive to attain each challenge, following through and working for success. Active participation in these activities help make Douglas MacArthur's prophetic words as true and applicable for disabled persons as for able-bodied persons: "On the fields of friendly strife are sown seeds that in other days and on other fields will bear fruits of victory" (Inscription on gymnasium wall, United States Military Academy at West Point, New York). From the perspective of the athlete

there is within us all some measure of competitive spirit, some little something that says, "Do it better!" This we try. Perhaps this is the only reason that we have become involved in sports.

Partly perhaps that we seek an outlet for nervous energy, which gathers during a day of study or a night of sleep. Perhaps we are lonely of spirit and seek a form of companionship and solace through struggle. We cannot say.

We only know this, that sports give to us a means by which we can express our true inner selves (a high school student).

These philosophies and principles are as true and applicable for disabled as able-bodied athletes.

Reference

American Alliance for Health, Physical Education, Recreation, and Dance. (1979, May). Cooperation unity prevails in consumer conference. *IRUC Briefings*, Section 4, p. 4.

Editor's Note

Sport socialization, training, and competition is increasingly viewed as a viable part of adapted physical education service delivery. Many graduate training programs include one or more theory courses, with practica, on sport and disabled students. Several of these programs require subscriptions to journals such as *Palaestra* and *Sports 'N Spokes* in lieu of or in addition to textbooks. *Palaestra* covers sports for all disabilities, while *Sports 'N Spokes* focuses on sports for individuals with spinal cord injuries, amputations, spina bifida, and postpolio. Addresses for ordering these journals are:

Palaestra, Challenge Publications Ltd., P.O. Box 508, Macomb, IL 61455.

Sports 'N Spokes, 5201 N. 19th Ave., Suite 111, Phoenix, AZ 85015.

For further insight into current status and research pertaining to sport and disabled individuals, see

Appenzeller, H. (1983). *The right to participate: The law and individuals with handicapping conditions in physical education and sports*. Charlottesville, VA: The Michie Co.

DePauw, K. (1986). Research on sport for athletes with disabilities. *Adapted Physical Activity Quarterly, 3*, 292-299.

Sherrill, C. (Ed.). (1986). *Sport and disabled athletes*. Champaign, IL: Human Kinetics.

Sherrill, C. (1986). *Adapted physical education and recreation: A multidisciplinary approach* (3rd ed.). Dubuque, IA: Wm. C. Brown.

Chapter 33

Teacher Training in Adapted Physical Education for Severely and Profoundly Handicapped Students

Paul Jansma

Law now mandates that all handicapped children, including those who are severely and profoundly handicapped (SPH), must receive free appropriate schooling. Educators and other service providers are also being increasingly challenged to provide educational, habilitation, and rehabilitation programs for SPH individuals of both pre- and postschool age. Among those who should provide such services are adapted physical education personnel.

This chapter begins with a rationale for an increased emphasis on specialized teacher training in adapted physical education for the SPH population. Specific related competencies to be addressed during this training and their manner of presentation are then discussed in separate sections. Last, numerous pedagogy models for use by adapted physical education professional preparation trainers are examined. These models come from varied sources and focus on divergent approaches to

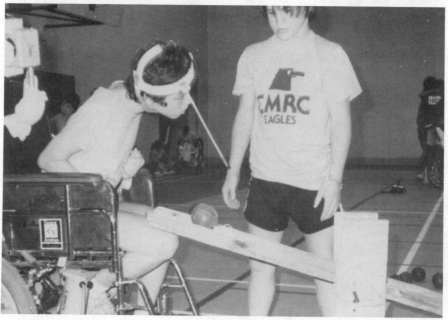

Severely disabled students typical of those Paul Jansma writes about in this chapter and in his book, *The Psychomotor Domain and the Seriously Handicapped.*

positively impact on the psychomotor domain of SPH individuals.

Rationale

All individuals have a developmental need to move. Learning to move efficiently, however, is usually a serious problem for the SPH because they typically lag so far behind the norm. In fact, nearly all the needs of the SPH are physical and motor in nature. Therefore the more serious a handicap, the more significant, generally, is training in the psychomotor domain.

Another guideline worth noting is that SPH individuals typically have more leisure time and, yet, most of them must be taught how to play and to appropriately engage in leisure time pursuits. Furthermore, we also know that the SPH population, particularly the seriously mentally retarded, generally learns by doing and is characterized as being more successful with concrete versus abstract challenges.

These guidelines, when taken together, provide a theoretical basis for the importance of physical training for the SPH. This training is not only an area of need for them but one in which they can develop and succeed. Add to this the mandates of law and a clear justification surfaces for the training and hiring of adapted physical education personnel.

The importance of attention to the psychomotor skill development of SPH individuals is also clearly recognized in special education (Bender & Valletutti, 1976; Bunker & Moon, 1983; Jansma, 1982; Mori & Masters, 1980; Van Etten, Arkell, & Van Etten, 1980) and physical education (French, 1979; Geddes, 1974; Jansma, 1984) literature. This literature further clarifies the need for systematic in-service and preservice training strategies to impact on the competence of SPH teachers, including adapted physical educators. With reference to the severely handicapped, Bunker and Moon state that "training specific motor skills is important since fine and gross movement is involved in accomplishing all other skills across all domains" (1983, p. 203).

Of particular significance to teacher trainers and trainees is empirical evidence that even the most seriously handicapped individual can be taught psychomotor skills. Stainback, Stainback, Wehman, and Spangiers (1983) demonstrated the acquisition, transfer, and generalization of physical fitness exercises in profoundly retarded adults. Cipani, Augustine, and Blomgren (1983) taught profoundly retarded adults to climb stairs safely. Hester (1981) reported positive effects of training on the standing and walking deficiencies of a profoundly retarded adolescent. Hopper and Wambold (1978) and Wehman and Marchant (1978) improved the independent play of severely mentally retarded children.

As more handicapped students are provided with appropriate physical education programs, more of those with mild and moderate handicaps are being directly served by regular physical educators and classroom teachers. This situation leaves the task of physically educating the SPH population of students to the adapted physical educator. Such education can be direct (teaching) or indirect (consulting with classroom teachers). The adapted physical education specialist is therefore a key to SPH programming.

Teacher Competencies

A specialization in adapted physical education for severely and profoundly handicapped students is justified by the many unique competencies needed to serve them. Even without such a subspecialization, adapted physical education trainees should at least be minimally competent to address the needs of their SPH charges. Below is an analysis of high priority competencies with rationales for their inclusion. They are grouped under headings that include awareness, knowledge and skills related to normal and abnormal development, medical knowledge, team functioning, knowledge of resources, testing and evaluation, prescribing, methodology, and practical experiences.

Normal and Abnormal Development

Competency #1: *Demonstrate a knowledge of normal and abnormal human growth and development.*

In essence this competency refers to familiarity with critical psychomotor developmental continua and their parts. These continua include, but are not limited to, the following: (a) apedal to quadrupedal to bipedal development, (b) primitive reflexes leading to righting reactions leading to equilibrium reactions, (c) proximo to distal development, (d) cephalo to caudal development, (e) random leads to purposeful movement, (f) development proceeds from bilateral to unilateral to homolateral to contralateral, (g) development proceeds from gross to fine motor, and (h) play develops from noninvolved to onlooker to isolate to parallel to associative to cooperative to competitive. The heterogeneity and/or low developmental level of the SPH population necessitates this knowledge of development.

Medical Knowledge

Competency #2: *Identify SPH conditions and syndromes and psychomotor characteristics of each.*

Some of the conditions and syndromes to be identified should include those associated with severe and profound mental retardation, cerebral palsy, behavior disorders, and multiple handicaps. Teachers (e.g., adapted physical educators) of the SPH will probably have students with these low incidence problems in their classes.

Competency #3: *Demonstrate knowledge of first aid and medication.*

The SPH population has a much higher incidence of seizures (and other conditions) and usage of medication. These have implications for movement.

Team Functioning

Competency #4: *Demonstrate knowledge of the importance of a team approach when providing services for the SPH.*

The more severe a handicapping condition, the more likely a team of specialists (including adapted physical educators) will be needed. The transdisciplinary team approach is claimed to be most effective with the SPH (McCormick & Goldman, 1979).

Knowledge of Resources

Competency #5: *Know written and organizational resources related to SPH and adapted physical education.*

Selected organizations like The Association for Persons with Severe Handicaps (TASH) presently focus on the SPH population. Specific curricula, pedagogical models, and current literature now exist in the area of adapted physical education for the SPH.

Competency #6: *List and describe legislation that impacts on the SPH and adapted physical education.*

Federal laws including PL 93-112 (The Rehabilitation Act of 1973), PL 94-142 (The Education for all Handicapped Children Act of 1975), PL 99-457 (The EHA Amendments of 1986), their amended acts, and sequel state legislation contain the mandates related to SPH that adapted physical educators are obligated to heed.

Testing and Evaluation

Competency #7: *Know psychomotor assessment tools for use with the SPH.*

Numerous tools with which to assess the present levels of psychomotor performance of the SPH are available for use by adapted physical educators (Jansma, 1980). Baseline information gleaned from such tools is required in order to write individualized educational programs and to teach the SPH.

Competency #8: *Discuss methods of collecting ongoing evaluation data, including the use of single subject time series techniques.*

Persons who teach SPH students need to collect data often in order to monitor small changes and to ensure accountability. Because the SPH population is so heterogeneous, ongoing data on individual students are needed.

Prescribing

Competency #9: *Demonstrate the ability to task analyze psychomotor skills.*

The breaking down of skills into their component parts, task analysis, is considered to be perhaps the most important competency area of all SPH teachers (Fredericks, Anderson, & Baldwin, 1979).

Competency #10: *Demonstrate knowledge of the importance of a functional skills curriculum.*

Many SPH individuals should not be taught fundamental low level developmental skills, particularly when they reach adolescence and beyond. Physical skills, adapted as necessary, which will permit them to function independently in school and nonschool environments, become a key to programming. Functional skills curricula and their importance for the SPH are well documented (Bricker & Filler, 1985; Brown et al., 1979, 1980).

Competency #11: *Demonstrate the ability to plan physical activities that are age-appropriate.*

SPH individuals may have a low developmental age while being significantly older chronologically. Physical activities presented should not insult a participant's age. Adapted physical educators need to learn and use activities that are age-sensitive and age-appropriate.

Methodology

Competency #12: *Discuss behavior management techniques for use with SPH individuals.*

Teaching cannot begin until behavior is under control. The SPH population is generally characterized as having more behavioral problems than other populations. Techniques such as self-defense (Garvey & Schepers, 1977), positive reinforcement, and stimulus control are key examples.

Competency #13: *List instructional techniques of importance to learning by SPH individuals.*

Adapted physical educators often need to employ techniques with SPH students that are rarely employed in regular physical education or with the mildly handicapped. These include, but are not limited to, awareness and arousal training, discrimination training, imitation training, multisensory training, haptic training, muscle education, passive and assistive levels of training, maintenance and generalization training, sensorimotor training, relaxation training, and proper lifting, carrying, and positioning of students.

Competency #14: *Discuss unique safety considerations relative to SPH students.*

Generally, SPH students have unique needs that must be met if safe activity participation can be expected. Examples include the use of appropriate helmets for those with frequent seizures and proper positioning for nonambulatory students with severe contractures.

Competency #15: *Demonstrate various modes of communication.*

Many SPH students are nonverbal. Adapted physical educators therefore need to learn alternative methods of communication such as communication boards and hand signing.

Competency #16: *Discuss how to make and utilize adaptive equipment.*

Often SPH students come to class in wheelchairs and/or need to function with the use of bolsters, wedges, prone boards, corner chairs, or standing platforms. Some of these adaptive devices can also be homemade. With this knowledge, and with the assistance of medical therapists, SPH students can have their physical activity needs more appropriately addressed.

Practical Experiences

Competency #17: *Positively affect the psychomotor behavior of SPH individuals in various settings.*

The real test of competence is success in the field. Success assumes the actualization of such competencies as testing, prescribing, utilizing methods, and evaluating.

Competency #18: *Function successfully on an educational team.*

Adapted physical educators should be given increasing responsibilities on an educational team during their preservice training. They should not be expected to assume major responsibilities without an appropriate internship.

Methods of Teacher Training

The priority competencies highlighted in the last section imply various adapted physical education teacher training methods. These primarily impact on the preservice training level, but also include such in-service recipients as grassroots adapted physical educators and college and university professors who need to keep abreast of developments in this subspecialty area.

Teacher training methods in adapted physical education for the SPH population do not differ radically from the standard. Lectures, demonstrations, audiovisual materials, guest speakers, readings, practicums in the field, conferences, workshops, seminars, and role playing all have their place.

Some variations within these teacher training methods are also being used. First, at the preservice level, a few of the recommended SPH-related courses are often taken outside of the department of physical education such as allied medicine, special education, and developmental psychology courses. Second, in the early 1980s the federal government started to fund in-service Leadership Training Grants. These permitted college and university professors to travel to model sites for specialized training and, in turn, their obligation typically was to disseminate their newly acquired knowledge back home. As an example in adapted physical education for the SPH, one such grant was funded at Oregon State University and involved the Data Based Gymnasium Approach (Dunn, 1983; Dunn, Morehouse, & Fredericks, 1985) in conjunction with Teaching Research, a division of the Oregon State system of higher education. The Data Based Gymnasium Approach is discussed later in this chapter.

These methods of SPH teacher training in adapted physical education are currently being used at various institutions of higher education around the country. Oregon State University has already been mentioned. Add to this list Texas Woman's University, The Ohio State University, and others.

Pedagogy Models for Adapted Physical Educators

At least 12 models of SPH-related pedagogy exist that adapted physical education teacher trainers can utilize *directly*. Some are more empirically based and some are more extensive than others. Some focus on behavior management, some on the development of psychomotor skills, and some on a combination of both.

These models are presented in no prioritized order and no judgement in this regard should be inferred. Also to be noted is that some of the authors or originators of these models are not adapted physical educators. This implies that a team approach should be used to address the numerous psychomotor problems of the SPH population.

Models of pedagogy having only indirect utility for adapted physical educators have been excluded. These include the controversial medically oriented Neurological Organization Model (Delacato, 1963, 1966), the occupational therapists' Sensory Integration Model (Ayres, 1972), and the physical therapists' Neurodevelopmental Model (Bobath, 1963, 1969, 1980; Bobath & Bobath, 1964, 1972), and Proprioceptive Neuromuscular Facilitation Model (Kabat & Knott, 1953).

Functional Skills Model

The most appropriate curriculum for severely and profoundly handicapped individuals is not necessarily one based on a traditional developmental model (Brown et al., 1979, 1980; White, 1980). The most seriously handicapped do not always follow the normal milestones that lead to the mature performance of a skill; this is certainly true for psychomotor tasks. Some of the reasons for this variation from the norm include sensory deficits (e.g., vision or hearing impairments), the presence of contractures, and/or the absence of limb function altogether.

With many seriously handicapped individuals, the expectation that certain mature skills will be efficiently and effectively learned (as the nonhandicapped learn them) is often quite unrealistic. A mature level of performance in numerous skill areas will, in fact, never be reached by many of them. The ultimate question then becomes, What skills will this special trainee need in order to function independently in the real world? Stated in other terms, Which critical functions or functional skills, adapted as necessary, can such a student learn that result in beneficial effects on his or her everyday environment?

In utilizing the functional skills model, the key to training is addressing that delicate balance between a student's specific skill competence and related demands of the environment. In this regard, the functional skills model permits specific skill competence to be displayed in different forms and recognizes that there are more than one means to an end. According to White (1980), the form of acceptable behavior and skill competence does not have to be specific and uniform for all individuals. "Any given sensory mode or motor movement might be used to achieve a virtually infinite range of critical effects" (p. 52). The major supposition is that all individuals have existing behaviors with which to work as a foundation for functional skill training.

In training, therefore, the teacher of a seriously handicapped student needs to consider the opposite of the developmental, "bottom to top" model of training that is typically used with the nonhandicapped and often with the mildly and moderately handicapped. Looking first toward end-point critical functions or functional skills is advocated instead in a "top to bottom" approach. Functional skills are targeted with an eye toward critical effects on the environment, taking all the potential of a student into account. After these functional skills or critical functions are determined, individualized training steps are formulated, adapted as necessary, and taught. For example, in order to be mobile (which has a critical

effect on the environment and can be the result of functional skill training), an individual could be programmed for any one of a variety of critical functions or functional skills that do not include walking. These could involve the motor-driven control of a wheelchair using a muscle twitch, rolling, scooter board mobility, standard wheelchair usage, use of crutches or a cane, cruising, or shuffling. Using the functional skills model, if a student's potential is motor-driven wheelchair usage, then that functional skill or critical function is taught using steps based on the characteristics of that student.

In using the functional skills model, trainers should be guided by additional principles. First, the visibility of a handicap should be minimized whenever possible. For example, using common movements whenever feasible is advised. Second, any action that accomplishes a critical effect on a student's environment should be acceptable. Refinements then occur. Third, any functional skill should be characterized, whenever possible, by efficiency and independence from other people and adaptive materials. Efficiency and independence also decrease visibility of a handicap. Fourth, all training of functional skills should address generalization and maintenance to the greatest degree possible. As examples, if mobility is being trained, maintenance of competent movement on not only smooth surfaces but also rough and more challenging surfaces in different environments is important. Instead of using the traditional balance beam to demonstrate balance (which has a potential critical effect on the environment), students can statically and/or dynamically balance within the limitations of their functional skill by "walking" on bleachers, "standing" on a curb, or "balancing" on a fallen tree trunk. Instead of lifting standard barbells to demonstrate strength (which has a potential critical effect on the environment), a student preparing for work at a sheltered workshop can be taught to correctly lift and transport blocks, tools, and other materials. Examples such as these involving functional skills can be given for any physical education area that has the potential for critical effects on a student's everyday environment (e.g., balance, strength, flexibility, cardiovascular endurance, etc.).

Those being trained at the preservice or in-service level for work with the seriously handicapped need to become acquainted with and be able to apply the concept of functional skill or critical function training toward the goal of critical environmental effects. Adapted physical education specialists will increasingly be charged with serving the seriously handicapped; therefore, their past reliance upon the developmental model needs to be reexamined in light of the characteristics of the SPH population and the real world environmental challenges that they must eventually face.

The Task Analysis Model

In contrast to teaching persons with mild or moderate handicapping conditions, the SPH population typically needs instruction in small steps that originate at a low developmental level. SPH students benefit most from what is referred to as the task analysis model of teaching. Task analysis can start at any level of development and with any skill, including those within the psychomotor domain.

In short, task analysis is the sequencing of any skill from its rudimentary to its advanced stage. This takes the form of a hierarchy of related subtasks, each subsequent one more challenging than the last in the chain. With regard to the seriously handicapped, "it . . . becomes necessary to perform task analysis to determine the prerequisite behaviors that lead to the attainment of higher-order objectives" (Crowe, Auxter, & Pyfer, 1981, p. 92).

In task analysis, specificity of skill substages is critical. To assure such specificity, all steps or building blocks in a task analysis need to be written in observable, measurable, and behavioral terms. Each subtask statement should include reference to the student, the target behavior, conditions of instruction, and the expected degree of success. The ultimate criterion for specificity in a task analysis is that another person can read and instruct using the analysis.

Task analysis can be viewed as a two-tiered system (French & Jansma, 1982). A general task analysis is a logical list of subtasks related to the development of a specific higher order skill. Task analyses are commonly listed for various skills in special education texts. However, some SPH learners cannot benefit fully from such a general format because of unique learner characteristics such as a specific sensory loss or maybe the absence of a limb. Special individualized steps may then need to be inserted and others deleted from the general task analysis chosen by a teacher. The second tier is individualized task analysis. "Individualized task analysis involves a sequencing of skills outside the repertoire of a specific learner, based on the person's developmental level, developmental needs and learning characteristics" (French & Jansma, 1982, p. 42). According to this definition, *developmental level* refers to the present level of a learner's functioning, *developmental need* refers to that level of a skill (or need) to which instruction is geared, and *learning characteristics* connote special traits of a particular learner that must be addressed in the teaching process (e.g., contractures). A related guideline here is that any task analysis process and the teacher involved should adapt to the student, not vice versa.

An example of a task analysis in the psychomotor domain might involve climbing stairs. A general and related individualized task analysis for this skill is contained in Table 33.1. The example provided in Table 33.1 can be modified as needed. Its purpose is to show how a task analysis is written progressively in behavioral terms and how needed adaptations can be made in order to individualize for a specific student.

Table 33.1 Task Analyses for Climbing Stairs

General	Individualized[a]
1. Walks up one stair with assistance, 2/2 trials.	1. Is transported from wheelchair to ground, with assistance, 1/1 trial.
2. Walks up one stair alone, 2/2 trials.	2. Transports self from wheelchair to ground, 1/1 trial.
3. Walks up three stairs alternating feet, down three stairs marking time, with assistance, 2/3 trials.	3. Slides up two stairs in reverse position on gluteals using arm action plus assistance, 2/2 trials.
4. Walks up and down three stairs alternating feet, no assistance, 3/3 trials.	4. Same as #3, no assistance.
5. Walks up staircase (10 stairs), alternating feet up and partially down, no assistance, 3/3 trials.	5. Slides up and down stairs in same position as #3, with assistance.
6. Walks up and down same staircase, alternating feet, no assistance, 3/3 trials.	6. Same as #5, no assistance.
7. Same as #6, blindfolded up.	7. Slides up eight stairs using same technique as #3, no assistance, in less than 3 minutes, 2/2 trials.
8. Same as #7, blindfolded up and down.	8. Transports self from wheelchair to stair lift, with assistance, 2/2 trials.
	9. Same as #8, no assistance.
	10. Operates button on stair lift with assistance, then alone, 3/3 trials.

[a]Student has no use of legs.

Behavioral Management Model

As a prerequisite to teaching any student, behavior management is logically required before any formal phase of the teaching process can begin (testing, instructing, evaluating, and following up). Behavior management is most dramatically needed with a seriously handicapped student who, for example, has an average attention span of less than 10 seconds. The SPH population, including the seriously emotionally disturbed and mentally retarded, therefore presents the greatest challenge relative to effective behavior management.

Not surprisingly, behavior management competencies are stressed in the preparation of adapted physical educators to work with the seriously handicapped (French, 1979). In this regard, the best physical educators are generally regarded as being the best behavior managers (Jansma, French, & Horvat, 1984).

The behavioral management model has come to be known as the most effective one for use with the seriously handicapped. It relies heavily on the principles of applied behavior analysis and operant conditioning. Some refer to it as behavior modification. Loovis (1980) summarizes the use of behavior modification in motor development and adapted physical education, including its use with the seriously handicapped. Empirical support of its effectiveness in this field and with this population also exists (Jansma, 1978). According to Dunn and French (1982), "operant conditioning should be one of the major focuses of special physical education teacher trainers in developing appropriate competencies in the area of behavior management" (p. 44).

The special education literature is still the primary source of information on the behavioral management model. Its numerous principles of behavior are capably summarized in three texts (Cooper, Heron, & Heward, 1987; Martin & Pear, 1983; Sulzer-Azaroff & Mayer, 1985). Some of the most common techniques and procedures that are associated with the behavioral management model include positive reinforcement, negative reinforcement, shaping, chaining, extinction, time out from reinforcement, response cost, overcorrection, counter control, token economy, behavioral contracting, contingency games, punishment, and stimulus control (including prompting and modeling). These are all applicable to the teaching of adapted physical education to the severely and profoundly handicapped. As examples, many are incorporated in the Data Based Gymnasium Model, the I CAN Adaptation Model, and the Game and Leisure Skill Model discussed later.

Sensorimotor Training Model

The most profoundly handicapped can benefit from specialized techniques that commonly employ a passive or assistive approach to the stimulation of senses and related basic movements. This is the key to the sensorimotor training model (Webb, 1969; Webb & Koller, 1979). All senses and associated movements are programmed

systematically. Senses, in this model, include those not usually attended to with nonhandicapped students like the gustatory, olfactory, tactile, and kinesthetic senses.

According to Webb (1969), four general areas or syndromes of deficiency must be addressed with the inert student. These are labeled level of awareness, movement, manipulation of the environment, and posture and locomotion.

Students requiring level of awareness training demonstrate gross problems relative to imposed stimuli. They need training in order to first become proficient in approach and avoidance and then discrimination reactions. Tactile and kinesthetic senses are stressed first in this area of training. These two sensory approaches are then combined into a haptic technique. Specific examples of raising levels of awareness might be the use of stroking to influence tactility, cuddling to enhance kinesthesis, or exposing a child to extreme odors to impact on the olfactory sense. Useful additional ideas related to the stimulation of each of the senses are expanded upon by Van Etten et al. (1980).

Movement training is an area emphasized by Webb as it relates to problems with the integration of primitive reflexes and the integration of motor effectors with multiple sensory receptors. Training activities in this area may include rolling, rocking, bouncing, and swinging, using such equipment as an air mattress, a beach ball, and a mat with different surfaces.

Manipulation of the environment training focuses on a student's deficits in manipulating objects, interacting with people, and intentionality of movement. Activities such as purposeful reaching, grasping, throwing, and holding are important in this phase of training.

Posture and locomotion training is the more advanced stage of sensorimotor training in this model. The primary objective here is to combat gravity-coping deficits. Developmentally low activities such as crawling, sitting, and even lifting the head while prone might be the training focus here. If enough progress is evident, training in standing, walking, and stair climbing might even be appropriate.

Webb, Schultz, and McMahill (1977) have combined their talents to develop a criterion-referenced test for use in sensorimotor training. Each of the four areas discussed above are addressed in the test. Subsequent programming, based on results using this AMP Index test, is geared toward the refinement of students' senses and their integration along with the integration of related basic motor movements.

I CAN Adaptation Model

The I CAN physical education curriculum was developed during the 1970s and early 1980s at Michigan State

University (Wessel, 1976-1980). It covers skills appropriate for preschool, kindergarten-12, and postschool students who have special needs. The I CAN Preprimary Motor and Play Skills Curriculum encompasses the areas of body control, locomotor activities, object control, health and physical fitness, play equipment usage, and play participation. The Primary Skills Curriculum covers fundamental motor skills, body management, health and physical fitness, and aquatics. The Sport-Leisure and Recreation Skills Curriculum includes backyard and neighborhood activities, outdoor activities, and dance and individual sport skills. Each skill area is addressed using a diagnostic-prescriptive, objective-based, instructional system that covers the gamut of planning, criterion-referenced assessing, prescribing, teaching, and evaluating. The use of field-tested performance objectives and related focal points, task analyses, ongoing assessment, individual and group score sheets, and common equipment and facilities are other aspects that characterize the I CAN materials. The federal government's National Diffusion Network has approved I CAN nationwide as a validated, exportable, and exemplary curriculum.

From 1976 to 1979 adaptations of the I CAN Curriculum were tested with severely and profoundly mentally retarded, severely emotionally disturbed, and autistic-like students. This work resulted in the I CAN Adaptation Model (Wessel, 1981). The adaptation manual associated with this model describes how to provide a quality physical education program for severely handicapped students of any chronological age. This manual is used in conjunction with the three basic I CAN curriculum packages, particularly the Preprimary Motor and Play Skills Curriculum because it is developmentally the lowest.

The adaptation manual specifically provides information on short- and long-term program planning in physical education using task analysis, operant conditioning strategies, and the ongoing documentation of student performance. Addendums to the manual include teaching suggestions, planning worksheets, and I CAN games for severely handicapped students. Key concepts that guide manual users center around the importance of an anti-label approach to teaching, programming for maintenance and generalization, stressing a functional skills approach, the need for a team approach, calendar year programming (not school year), and attention to the level of prompting required for skill performance. Many of these issues have been addressed directly through revisions in the I CAN Preprimary Curriculum.

The Data Based Gymnasium Model

The Data Based Gymnasium Model (Dunn, 1983; Dunn, Morehouse, & Fredericks, 1985) is intended for use with severely and profoundly handicapped students and emphasizes psychomotor skill development within a behavioral framework. This curriculum provides a bridge between therapeutically oriented motor programs and the more advanced physical education experiences, which include highly organized games, sport, and physical fitness skill.

This model originated at Oregon State University (OSU) and is largely based on completed and ongoing work at Teaching Research (a division of the Oregon State system of higher education), Monmouth, Oregon. The OSU/Teaching Research Physical Education Model has been successfully utilized with low-incidence handicapped students at Teaching Research's National Model Program for Severely Handicapped Children and elsewhere.

There are several keys to this model's utility: First, it addresses the physical education mandates of federal law including the issues of individualized instruction, physical education inclusion in individualized educational programs (IEPs), and physical education programming for all students including the nonambulatory and the most seriously handicapped. Second, the model curriculum incorporates task analysis of fundamental functional skills and ongoing data-based assessment of these psychomotor skills specifically in the areas of basic movement concepts, elementary games, physical fitness, and lifetime leisure. In this regard the data system presented in the model reflects a simplified system for use in training seriously handicapped students. For example, each student has a clipboard of programming information in an easy-to-follow format that can be transferred among staff and support personnel. Third, the Data Based Gymnasium Model recognizes the efficacy of behavioral procedures with the SPH population. Frequent and consistent attention is paid to the importance of verbally, visually, and physically cueing behaviors, making adjustments in behavior requirements, and reinforcing behavior (both social and psychomotor). Last, this model is based on the belief that instruction of the seriously handicapped child should be daily and involve multiple trials, should often require a one-to-one teacher to student ratio, should be milieu in nature, and should emphasize spot checks for retention of student skills. These requirements demand the creative use of personnel. As a solution, volunteers, parents, and paraprofessionals are considered to be absolutely essential and are therefore an integral component of the model. These additional support personnel are systematically trained and their skills are continually updated using another data-based system built into the model.

The Project MOBILITEE Model

The Project MOBILITEE Model (Hopewell Special Education Regional Resource Center, 1981) is the result of a multiyear federally funded project whose purpose was to disseminate information at the preservice and in-service levels related to *M*ovement *O*pportunities for *B*uilding *I*ndependence and *L*eisure *I*nterests through *T*raining *E*ducators and *E*xceptional Learners. This model specifically consists of a series of tests, a cross-indexed curriculum guide, and supplementary activities to implement the curriculum guide in adapted physical education for moderately and severely disabled students. The model was developed at the Hopewell Special Education Regional Resource Center in Hopewell, Ohio and was field tested throughout the state.

The tests in this model emphasize a qualitative approach to the measurement of adapted physical education-related skills. Each test item is broken down into three or four developmental levels, a system largely patterned after The Ohio State University Scale of Intra Gross Motor Assessment tool (Loovis & Ersing, 1979).

The model's physical and motor fitness items include a 20-foot dash, a 30-yard dash, a wheelchair push, push-ups, wheelchair push-ups, an agility run, a 5-minute walk/run, and posture screening. As one example, using the 20-foot dash, a score of 1 is awarded if the student takes more than 20 seconds to walk or propel a wheel-chair 20 feet; a score of 2 involves independently walk-ing or propelling a wheelchair 20 feet within a range of 14 to 20 seconds; a score of 3 is recorded if the stu-dent independently walks or propels a wheelchair 20 feet within a range of 10 to 14 seconds; and a score of 4 is given if the action occurs in 10 seconds or less.

The fundamental motor skill tests include throwing, throwing from a wheelchair, catching, striking, striking from a wheelchair, running, a wheelchair run, jumping, and kicking. For even lower functioning students, other fundamental motor skill tests include those that measure rolling, creeping and crawling, walking or wheelchair mobility, alternative mode(s) of movement (e.g., scoot-ing), maintenance of posture, prestriking, precatching, and prekicking. One other testing section is offered in the area of skills for games participation that emphasize social and emotional aspects. Such items that comply with rules and directions, teamwork, leadership/team member, and self-concept are measured.

These three broad areas of testing each have an accompanying cross-referenced curriculum guide and supplementary activities to use in programming. The project manual also includes appendices containing test-ing score sheets, further information on posture rating, and a bibliography. Free copies are available, while a supply lasts, by contacting the Ohio adapted physical education consultant within the Division of Elementary and Secondary Education, Ohio Department of Education, Columbus, OH.

The Project TRANSITION Model

Since 1979, adapted physical educators at The Ohio State University have attempted to address challenging questions related to psychomotor training and its poten-tial impact on the deinstitutionalization of seriously retarded adults. To assist in researching this area of inquiry, Project TRANSITION was funded from 1983 to 1986 by the U.S. Department of Education to specifi-cally investigate whether or not, and to what extent if any, training in selected physical fitness and hygiene activities enhance preparation for and success during the deinstitutionalization process.

Final results of this project's research indicate that both fitness and hygiene skills can be significantly im-proved in individuals targeted for deinstitutionalization. Both, therefore, are important "first impression" factors to be considered in America's overall deinstitutionaliza-tion thrust.

Adapted physical educators, health and hygiene person-nel, researchers, and personnel at developmental centers and group homes now have the following available to them (Jansma, Decker, McCubbin, Combs, & Ersing, 1986; Jansma, Ersing, & McCubbin, 1986; Jansma, McCubbin, Combs, Decker, & Ersing, 1987; McCubbin & Jansma, 1986):

- Functional, age-appropriate, valid, and reliable field-tested, task-analyzed training sequences and related training methods for the fitness areas of upper body strength, cardiovascular endurance, abdominal strength, trunk flexibility, and grip strength

- Functional, age-appropriate, valid, and reliable field-tested, task-analyzed training sequences and related training methods for the hygiene areas of face wash-ing, teeth brushing, hand washing, deodorant use, and overall appearance (hair, upper body, and lower body tidiness)

- Narratives and graphics that describe unique and cost-effective adapted equipment for fitness training with severely and profoundly mentally retarded adults

- A curriculum of supplementary activities to potentially improve the 10 fitness and hygiene skills that are the focus of Project TRANSITION

- A standardized scoring system in the area of fitness performance, and scoring systems in the areas of fitness and hygiene training that monitor both task comple-tion and degrees of prompt required (i.e., levels of independence)

- Research results on the effectiveness of Project TRANSITION's training with regard to fitness and hygiene pre- and poststudy measures and the effects of fitness and hygiene training on changes in pre- and poststudy adaptive behavior scores.

The Game and Leisure Skill Model

Wehman (1977a) has spearheaded the development of a Game and Leisure Skill Model for severely and profoundly developmentally disabled persons. An overview of the model for use by therapeutic recreation and adapted physical education personnel with the mildly, moderately, multiply, severely, and profoundly handicapped is provided in his text entitled: *Helping the mentally retarded acquire play skills: A behavioral approach* (1977). Wehman's rationale for this model is based largely on the suppositions that improved competence in this area will decrease the inappropriate behavior of these individuals, assist in their social development, help them behave in a more normalized fashion, and result in more constructive use of their leisure time.

Wehman's writings stress the use of behavior modification techniques as the most efficient and effective way to positively affect any observable psychomotor-related target behavior. Considerable empirical support exists for this hypothesis. Verbal prompting, modeling, physical guidance, and social praise have been used to increase the cooperative play and action on play materials by severely mentally retarded adults (Wehman, 1977a), to improve the independent and social play of severely and profoundly mentally retarded children (Wehman & Marchant, 1978), and to teach Frisbee and electronic bowling skills to severely mentally retarded adolescents (Horst, Wehman, Hill, & Bailey, 1981). These same behavioral strategies, coupled with backward chaining, were also used to increase competence in self-initiated table game behavior with severely and profoundly mentally retarded adolescents (Wehman, Renzaglia, Berry, Schutz, & Karen, 1978). Numerous proven behavioral strategies for increasing the toy play skills of SPH children have been succinctly summarized by Wehman (1979).

Related applications have been reported in the areas of physical fitness training and motor development. Situps, knee push-ups, and duck walking were taught to an SPH adolescent and adult using a tell-show-guide method, social praise, and forward chaining (Wehman et al., 1978). More significantly, Stainback et al. (1983) used the tell-show-guide method with tangible and social reinforcers in both an individual and group context to systematically train profoundly mentally retarded adults in leg stretching, hand-to-toe, and knee-bend exercises. Maintenance and generalization of these skills also occurred, along with the surprising acquisition of a few untrained skills (trunk bends and leg raises) in the group setting.

Almost all of the studies cited incorporate task analysis as an additional essential feature of training. Task analysis should therefore be included as a main ingredient, along with behavioral strategies, in the Game and Leisure Skill Model.

The Language, Arts, and Movement Programming (LAMP) Model

Sherrill (1979, 1983) espouses an integrated language-arts-movement education approach to promote psychomotor gains by SPH individuals. Three principles guide the implementation of the LAMP Model:

- Language, arts, and movement training should be integrated to help SPH students move from the sensorimotor to the preoperational stages of cognitive functioning and from the noninvolved to the cooperative stages of social play functioning (i.e., psychomotor, social, and cognitive learnings should be integrated).

- Movement, whether repetitious for range of motion outcomes or exploratory for sensorimotor learning, should always be integrated with language and, when possible, with rhythm. Language may be speaking, singing, chanting, or signing.

- Practice of basic motor skills should incorporate creative dance, rhythmic body action, and creative dramatics to promote education of the whole child, not just the physical (i.e., movement themes presented through language, explaining why a basic movement is important and how, when, and where it is used, contribute to functional skills learning).

The LAMP Model has been field tested extensively at Denton State School, a residential facility for SPH mentally retarded individuals in Texas, and through a nationwide project (five sites and 219 subjects) conducted by the National Committee • Arts for the Handicapped (NCAH), 1825 Connecticut Avenue, NW, Suite 418, Washington, DC 20009. The Texas Woman's University, in collaboration with Special Care School in Dallas, served as one of the five sites in the NCAH Study (Eddy, 1982; Sherrill & McBride, 1984), which specifically investigated the efficacy of an arts infusion intervention model to improve quality of life and functional skills of SPH students.

The arts infusion model, one example of the many forms of LAMP, is

> a multidisciplinary approach to individualized instructional intervention which is cooperatively planned and conducted by special educators and artists and/or arts educators. In this approach

dance, drama, music, and the visual arts are used to implement the long range goals and short term objectives of the individualized educational program of each child with severe handicaps. Puppetry is the central unifying art form through which the other arts are initially infused. Implementation of the model requires daily infusion of the arts within the school setting, periodic excursions to arts events in the community, and a Very Special Arts Festival conducted as the culminating activity for all project participants each year. Artists/arts educators not only provide direct service delivery but also conduct inservice training to assist school personnel and parents in learning how to incorporate arts into the functional skills training of children who are severely handicapped. (Sherrill & McBride, 1984, p. 316)

The empirical effectiveness of this Infusion Model is reported in the literature (Eddy, 1982; Sherrill & McBride, 1984). During a 5-month program, statistically significant gains were made in 7 of the 31 gross motor items on the Denver Developmental Screening Test. Analysis of photographs, videotapes, and interview data from parents and teachers revealed that

both arts personnel and special educators perceived positive change in the children, particularly in functional skills in the personal-social area (attention, responsiveness, spontaneity, initiative, self-expression, and social interaction). These, in turn, seemed to enhance quality of life in that the children appeared more "alive, active, and happier" than before the project began. Parents reported similar observations, typically that their children "laughed/smiled more, played/moved more, and talked/babbled more." Sherrill & McBride, 1984, p. 318)

Whereas the NCAH Arts Infusion Model used puppetry as the central unifying art, Sherrill recommends dance and rhythm-oriented movement education as the central unifying art in the LAMP model. This approach is depicted in a commercially available film, *A Very Special Dance*, which features Anne Riordan with SPH mentally retarded adults and states the psychomotor values derived. According to Sherrill, the arts can and should be used to implement the long-range goals and short-term objectives of each SPH student's physical education and/or special education IEP. The key to such educationally relevant progress is task analysis; examples of evaluation approaches that use task analysis appear in *Creative Arts for the Severely Handicapped* (Sherrill, 1979, pp. 199-213).

Let's Play to Grow Model

The Let's Play to Grow Model (Joseph P. Kennedy, Jr. Foundation, 1977) was developed by Eunice Kennedy Shriver, the executive vice president of the Joseph P. Kennedy, Jr. Foundation. This model is strictly practical in nature, in contrast to theoretical models of pedagogy. According to literature from the Foundation, the Let's Play to Grow concept consists of a program of play, games, and activities for people with special needs, including the severely handicapped and their families. It is unique in its focus on the involvement of parents, siblings, grandparents, professionals, and volunteers in an ongoing program of shared play and recreation. This program was originally referred to as Families Play to Grow (1970s) and was extensively field-tested around the United States. The result of this preliminary work was the Let's Play to Grow Model.

The model specifically consists of 17 Play Guides, four of which have particular applicability with the SPH population. These include guides on sensory stimulation; rhythm, movement, and dance; waterplay; and basic ball skills. These guides describe to family members and professionals how to adapt movement activities for various handicapping conditions. Even though the primary intent of the program is not direct service by professionals, this resource is one with which adapted physical educators should be familiar so that they can introduce it to and use it with the families of handicapped children.

Adapted physical educators can also be instrumental by initiating Let's Play to Grow Clubs, which usually consist of 5 to 15 families. The professional's involvement moves to a resource status once leadership is taken over by parents. More than 200 of these clubs currently form an international network.

Let's Play to Grow kits are available in both English and Spanish. In addition to the guides, the kit includes a clearly written manual for use by parents and teachers with an accompanying award system, which involves the delivery of colorful iron-on patches and certificates of achievement signed by noted celebrities. Each award is contingent upon 30 hours of active play by any handicapped participant. The kit also includes a Club Leader's Manual with ideas on how to start and run a club.

This model program is endorsed by the Academy of Family Physicians; the President's Council on Physical Fitness; the President's Committee on Mental Retardation; the American Alliance for Health, Physical Education, Recreation and Dance; the National Association for Retarded Citizens; the National Recreation and Park Association; and other related groups.

The Orff-Schulwerk Model

This model of training originated in the 1920s by a German composer named Carl Orff. The model focuses on movement, music, and language. In essence, Orff believed that music can be learned by anyone on a physical level and then on a cognitive level (e.g., reading notes), if intellectual ability permits. This unique educational model uses rhythm instruments and the body parts (e.g., hands, feet) of participants. Verse can be adapted to the developmental level of learners, even the most seriously handicapped. Bitcon (1976) and Bitcon and Ball (1974) describe the Orff-Schulwerk Model, including use by those at the preintellectual and nonverbal level.

Orff-Schulwerk sessions can be geared toward a large or small group and one-to-one instruction. Simple rhythms, chants, and verses are intended to initiate participant movement. Such movements may include tapping feet, clapping hands, nodding the head, or striking a rhythm instrument. If more intrusive prompts are required, a haptic approach to instruction is advised and the inclusion of teacher assistants, aides, or volunteers is suggested.

Imitation of models and sensorimotor development activities are two potential areas of impact on SPH students when using the Orff-Schulwerk technique. Endless examples can be cited. Students can be prompted with tell, show, or physical guidance techniques to imitate a leader who may be (a) tapping a certain body part to music or verse, (b) shaking a rhythm instrument slowly, (c) pointing to any given object in response to a musical or verbal cue, and (d) reaching in certain directions as occasioned by beats of music. Sensorimotor activities may include passive lifting of a participant's body parts to a certain musical beat, active assistive bumping of body parts in response to a leader's verbal chant, and active responding by walking to or away from rhythmical or musical sound sources. In the Orff-Schulwerk technique, simple rhythms, music, and verse may all be potential keys to one or more aspects of the psychomotor development of developmentally low individuals.

Conclusion

Attention to the needs of seriously handicapped students has only recently surfaced. The conduct of research and its dissemination, advocacy by experts in the field, and changes in public law have been significant catalysts in this regard. Consistently highlighted among the needs of this population are psychomotor domain deficits.

This chapter presents state of the art information related to the area of SPH professional preparation within adapted physical education. At least 12 relevant models of pedagogy presently exist for direct use by adapted physical education teacher trainers and their trainees. In addition, the specification of numerous related competencies, along with a greater number of SPH individuals needing psychomotor training, may justify the development of a specialized professional preparation tract that focuses exclusively on adapted physical education for seriously handicapped students. Such a tract has already been developed at a number of institutions of higher education in the field of special education. Such a movement in adapted physical education may be near.

References

Ayres, J. (1972). *Sensory integration and learning disorders*. Los Angeles: Western Psychological Services.

Bender, M., & Valletutti, P. (1976). *Teaching the moderately and severely handicapped: Curriculum objectives, strategies, and activities* (Vol. I). Baltimore: University Park Press.

Bitcon, C. (1976). *Alike and different, the clinical and educational use of Orff-Schulwerk*. Santa Ana, CA: Rosha Press.

Bitcon, C., & Ball, T. (1974). Generalized imitation and Orff-Schulwerk. *Mental Retardation, 12*, 36.

Bobath, B. (1963). Treatment, principles and planning in cerebral palsy. *Physiotherapy, 49*, 122-124.

Bobath, B. (1969). The treatment of neuromuscular disorders by improving patterns of coordination. *Physiotherapy, 55*, 18-22.

Bobath, K. (1980). *A neurophysiological basis for the treatment of cerebral palsy*. Philadelphia: J.B. Lippincott.

Bobath, K., & Bobath, B. (1964). The facilitation of normal postural reactions and movements in the treatment of cerebral palsy. *Physiotherapy, 50*, 246-262.

Bobath, K., & Bobath, B. (1972). Cerebral palsy diagnosis and assessment and neurodevelopmental approach to treatment. In P.H. Pearson & C.E. Williams (Eds.), *Physical therapy services in the developmental disabilities* (pp. 31-185). Springfield, IL: Charles C. Thomas.

Bricker, D., & Filler, J. (Eds.). (1985). *Severe mental retardation: From theory to practice.* Reston, VA: Council for Exceptional Children.

Brown, L., Banston, M.B., Hamre-Nietupski, S., Pumpian, I., Certo, N., & Gruenewald, L. (1979). A strategy for developing chronological age appropriate and functional curricular content for severely handicapped adolescents and young adults. *Journal of Special Education, 13*(1), 81-90.

Brown, L., Falvey, M., Pumpian, I., Baumgart, D., Nisbet, J., Ford, A., Schroeder, J., & Loomis, R. (1980). *Curricular strategies for teaching severely handicapped students functional skills in school and nonschool environments* (Vol. X). Madison, WI: Madison Metropolitan School District.

Bunker, L.K., & Moon, S. (1983). Motor skills. In M. Snell (Ed.), *Systematic instruction of the moderately and severely handicapped* (2nd ed., pp. 203-226). Columbus, OH: Charles E. Merrill.

Cipani, E., Augustine, A., & Blomgren, E. (1983). Teaching profoundly retarded adults to ascend stairs safely. *Education and Training of the Mentally Retarded, 17*(1), 51-54.

Cooper, J.O., Heron, T., & Heward, W.L. (1987). *Applied behavior analysis.* Columbus, OH: Charles E. Merrill.

Crowe, W., Auxter, D., & Pyfer, J. (1981). *Principles and methods of adapted physical education and recreation* (4th ed.). St. Louis: C.V. Mosby.

Delacato, C. (1963). *The diagnosis and treatment of speech and reading problems.* Springfield, IL: Charles C. Thomas.

Delacato, C. (1966). *Neurological organization and reading.* Springfield, IL: Charles C. Thomas.

Dunn, J. (1983). Physical activity for the severely handicapped: Theoretical and practical considerations. In R. Eason, T. Smith, & F. Caron (Eds.), *Adapted physical activity: From theory to application* (pp. 63-73). Champaign, IL: Human Kinetics.

Dunn, J., & French, R. (1982). Operant conditioning: A tool for special physical educators in the 1980s. *Exceptional Education Quarterly, 3*(1), 42-53.

Dunn, J., Morehouse, J., & Fredericks, H.D.B. (1985). *Physical education for the severely handicapped: A systematic approach to a data based gymnasium.* Austin: Pro-Ed Publishers.

Eddy, J. (1982). *The music came from deep inside: Professional artists and severely handicapped children.* New York: McGraw-Hill.

Fredericks, H., Anderson, R., & Baldwin, V. (1979). Identifying competency indicators of teachers of the severely handicapped. *AAESPH REVIEW, 4*(1), 81-95.

French, R. (1979). Direction or misdirection in physical education for mentally retarded students. *Journal of Physical Education and Recreation, 50*(7), 22-23.

French, R., & Jansma, P. (1982). *Special physical education.* Columbus, OH: Charles E. Merrill.

Garvey, E., & Schepers, J. (1977). Physical control techniques and defense holds for use with aggressive retarded adults. *Mental Retardation, 15*, 29-31.

Geddes, D. (1974). Physical activity: A necessity for severely and profoundly mentally retarded individuals. *Journal of Health, Physical Education and Recreation, 45*(3), 73-74 & 76.

Hester, S. (1981). Effects of behavioral modification on the standing and walking deficiencies of a profoundly retarded child: A case report. *Physical Therapy, 61*(6), 907-911.

Hopewell Special Education Regional Resource Center. (1981). *Project MOBILITEE.* Columbus, OH: Ohio Department of Education.

Hopper, C., & Wambold, C. (1978). Improving the independent play of severely mentally retarded children. *Education and Training of the Mentally Retarded, 13*(1), 42-46.

Horst, G., Wehman, P., Hill, J., & Bailey, C. (1981). Developing age-appropriate leisure skills in severely handicapped adolescents. *Teaching Exceptional Children, 14*(1), 11-15.

Jansma, P. (1978). Operant conditioning principles applied to disturbed male adolescents by a physical educator. *American Corrective Therapy Journal, 32*(3), 71-78.

Jansma, P. (1980). Psychomotor domain tests for the severely and profoundly handicapped. *The Association for the Severely Handicapped Journal, 5*(4), 368-381.

Jansma, P. (1982). Physical education for the severely and profoundly handicapped. *Exceptional Education Quarterly, 3*(1), 35-41.

Jansma, P. (Ed.). (1984). *The psychomotor domain and the seriously handicapped* (2nd ed.). Lanham, MD: University Press of America.

Jansma, P., Decker, J., McCubbin, J., Combs, C., & Ersing, W. (1986). Adapted equipment for improving the fitness of severely retarded adults. *American Corrective Therapy Journal, 40*, 136-141.

Jansma, P., Ersing, W., & McCubbin, J. (1986). *The effects of physical fitness and personal hygiene training on the preparation for community placement of institutionalized mentally retarded adults* (Final Report, Grant No. G008300001). Washington, DC: U.S. Department of Education, Office of Special Education and Rehabilitative Services.

Jansma, P., French, R., & Horvat, M. (1984). Behavioral engineering in physical education. *Journal of Physical Education, Recreation and Dance,* **55**(6), 80-81.

Jansma, P., McCubbin, J., Combs, C., Decker, J., & Ersing, W. (1987). *Fitness and hygiene programming for the severely handicapped: A curriculum-embedded assessment guide.* Columbus, OH: Moody's.

Joseph P. Kennedy, Jr. Foundation. (1977). *Let's play-to-grow: For families, for schools, for communities.* Washington, DC: Author.

Kabat, H., & Knott, M. (1953). Proprioceptive facilitation techniques for treatment of paralysis. *Physical Therapy Review,* **33**, 53-64.

Loovis, E. (1980). Behavior modification: Its application in physical education/motor development for children with special needs. *American Corrective Therapy Journal,* **34**(1), 19-24.

Loovis, E., & Ersing, W. (1979). *Assessing and programming gross motor development for children.* Cleveland Heights, OH: Ohio Motor Assessment Associates.

Martin, G., & Pear, J. (1983). *Behavior modification: What it is and how to do it* (2nd ed.). Englewood Cliffs, NJ: Prentice-Hall.

McCormick, L., & Goldman, R. (1979). The transdisciplinary model: Implications for service delivery and personnel preparation for the severely and profoundly handicapped. *AAESPH Review,* **4**(2), 152-161.

McCubbin, J., & Jansma, P. (1987). The effects of training selected psychomotor skills and the relationship to adaptive behavior. In M. Berridge & G. Ward (Eds.), *International perspectives on adapted physical activity* (pp. 119-125). Champaign, IL: Human Kinetics.

Mori, A., & Masters, L. (1980). *Teaching the severely mentally retarded: Adaptive skills training.* Germantown, MD: Aspen Systems.

Sherrill, C. (Ed.). (1979). *Creative arts for the severely handicapped* (2nd ed.). Springfield, IL: Charles C. Thomas.

Sherrill, C. (1983). Pedagogy in the psychomotor domain for the severely handicapped. In R. Eason, T. Smith, & F. Caron (Eds.), *Adapted physical activity: From theory to application* (pp. 74-88). Champaign, IL: Human Kinetics.

Sherrill, C., & McBride, H. (1984). An arts infusion intervention model for severely handicapped children. *Mental Retardation,* **22**(6), 316-320.

Stainback, S., Stainback, W., Wehman, P., & Spangiers, L. (1983). Acquisition and generalization of physical fitness exercises in three profoundly retarded adults. *The Journal of the Association for the Severely Handicapped,* **8**(2), 47-55.

Sulzer-Azaroff, B., & Mayer, G. (1985). *Applying behavior analysis procedures with children and youth* (2nd ed.). New York: Holt, Rinehart & Winston.

Van Etten, G., Arkell, C., & Van Etten, C. (1980). *The severely and profoundly handicapped: Programs, methods, and materials.* St. Louis: The C.V. Mosby Company.

Webb, R. (1969). Sensory-motor training of the profoundly retarded. *American Journal of Mental Deficiency,* **74**, 283-295.

Webb, R., & Koller, J. (1979). Effects of sensorimotor training on intellectual and adaptive skills of profoundly retarded adults. *American Journal of Mental Deficiency,* **83**, 490-496.

Webb, R., Schultz, B., & McMahill, J. (1977). *AMP Index #1* (9th revision). Glenwood, IA: Glenwood State Hospital School.

Wehman, P. (1977a). *Helping the mentally retarded acquire play skills: A behavioral approach.* Springfield, IL: Charles C. Thomas.

Wehman, P. (1977b). Research on leisure time and the severely developmentally disabled. *Rehabilitation Literature,* **38**(4), 98-105.

Wehman, P. (1979). Instructional strategies for improving toy play skills of severely handicapped children. *AAESPH Review,* **4**(2), 125-135.

Wehman, P., & Marchant, J. (1978). Improving free play skills of severely retarded children. *The American Journal of Occupational Therapy,* **32**(2), 100-104.

Wehman, P., Renzaglia, A., Berry, G., Schutz, R., & Karen, O. (1978). Developing a leisure skill repertoire in severely and profoundly handicapped persons. *AAESPH Review,* **3**(3), 162-171.

Wessel, J. (1976-1980). *I CAN: Individualized physical education curriculum materials.* Northbrook, IL: Hubbard Scientific.

Wessel, J. (Ed.). (1981). *I CAN adaptation manual: Teaching physical education to severely handicapped students*. East Lansing, MI: Michigan State University.

White, O. (1980). Adaptive performance objectives: Form versus function. In W. Sailor, B. Wilcox, & L. Brown (Eds.), *Methods of instruction for severely handicapped students* (pp. 47-69). Baltimore: Paul H. Brookes.

Chapter 34

The Use of Efficiency Systems in Adapted Physical Education Professional Preparation at the College Level

Ronald French and Paul Jansma

College faculty who are training students in the area of adapted physical education, in addition to their teaching responsibilities, must publish and generate intramural and extramural funds. In order to devote more time to scholarly pursuits without decreasing the quality of learning that is occurring in the classroom, efficiency systems must be developed and implemented. The following are our guidelines to assist in the development of efficiency systems to allow more time for scholarly pursuits or infuse scholarly pursuits into classroom instruction:

1. Do not teach the same class marking period after marking period. Could the course be taught in mass lecture or could two sections of the course be taught in back-to-back hours?

2. Do not teach a course daily. Arrange the course hours to allow at least 1 day per week for scholarly pursuits.

3. Prepare lectures with more than one purpose. Could a lecture be polished and then submitted to a journal or to a regional or national conference for presentation? Maybe the material could be used in the preparation of a grant proposal.

4. Do not continually lecture on a topic that another professional could who possesses equal or superior competencies. Allowing others to lecture will reduce class preparation time. These professionals could be from a public or private agency such as United Cerebral Palsy, Special Olympics, or the Easter Seal Society, whose responsibilities include public speaking. Another source of speakers is faculty members in special education. In addition, graduate students may be appropriate. Many times these students are in training to become college professors and need the opportunity to prepare and present lectures under the guidance of a faculty member.

5. Do not lecture on a topic when audiovisual material can be used to provide an equal or better explanation. Catalogs are available that provide information on audiovisual materials in adapted physical education. Two of these are the following:

   • Publications and Audiovisual Catalog
     American Alliance for Health, Physical Education, Recreation and Dance
     Reston, Virginia

   • Film Catalog
     The Athletic Institute
     North Palm Beach, Florida

Two visual tape packets have been developed especially for use in adapted physical education courses:

• I'm Special
  Division of Education
  University of South Florida
  Tampa, Florida 33620

• This packet is a series of physical education video tapes on such topics as PL 94-142, individualized educational programs, and selecting and modifying appropriate activities.

• Physical Education Programs for Handicapped Students in Iowa (PEPHSI)
  Special Education Division
  Iowa State Department of Public Instruction
  Des Moines, Iowa 50319

  This is a manual with accompanying video tapes. The topics discussed are legislation and physical education, medication and physical activity, assessment and evaluation, program/placement alternatives, modification and adaptation of activities, rhythms, equipment, and aquatics.

6. Do not assign graduate students projects that are time fillers. Projects should serve as the basis for a presentation, grant proposal, or publication, such as the following:

Ron French, Texas Woman's University, senior author of *Special Physical Education* with Paul Jansma. French and Jansma taught together at Brockport State University in New York and continue many projects together.

- Conduct a needs assessment for in-service training in special physical education that may lead to a grant or part of a grant proposal.

- Develop and conduct a workshop on instructional techniques used in sport for the disabled as the culminating course experience. Include a proceedings with abstracts of all presentations that can be disseminated.

- Investigate, as a class project, specific topics such as perceptual learning styles of learning disabled students.

7. Do not view audiovisual material over and over again in class. Many times audiovisual material can be viewed by students at the college media center during their study time. Learning packets should be developed to guide students to the pertinent information that will be discussed in class and/or may appear on an examination. These packets will decrease the amount of traditional class time.

8. Do not continually commit the same information to memory and then write it on the chalkboard year after year. A lecture outline can be placed on transparencies, as can charts and graphs. The outline will provide the key words for your lecture and reduce preparation time.

9. Do not hand score written examinations that can be scanned and evaluated at the college computer center. A professor can develop a pool of questions on a specific topic that can be categorized on the basis of the level of difficulty. Each time questions are needed, the number of questions and the number from each category of difficulty are determined. The questions are then automatically randomized, and the test is developed through the use of the computer. Questions can also be easily added or deleted.

10. Combine scholarly grantsmanship endeavors with instructional improvement. In many cases intramural grants funding is available to develop modules of course materials, audiovisual aids, or a lecture series. Examples of extramural grant funding could involve projects through a school district and the federal government in the area of professional preparation to develop audiovisual material or conduct special projects.

11. Establish a reasonable number of strictly enforced office hours similar to that of a dentist, physician, or lawyer. This will curtail or eliminate unscheduled interruptions.

12. Create an efficient filing and information retrieval system. A system of this type can take a considerable time to establish, but it will pay off down the road for the conscientious professional.

13. Have students place some information on audio tapes that can be listened to while you are driving. Student journals and daily logs of teaching experiences can easily be modified and placed on tape.

14. Have student teachers in adapted physical education videotape some of their classes. Then have the student come to your office and discuss the class with you. This technique should not replace all visitations but could replace some.

In summary, a faculty member in the area of adapted physical education, responsible for dissemination as well as pursuing knowledge, can no longer continually spend hour after hour in class preparation each week. This is particularly true if no released time is given for scholarly pursuits. Scholarly efforts can be incorporated into class instruction. The quantity of time of student instruction and student interaction can be reduced to work on scholarly projects. Hopefully, some of these guidelines for developing efficiency systems will increase the effectiveness of your scholarly efforts without decreasing the quality of instruction.

Appendix A
National Awards and Recipients

Recipients of awards sponsored by the American Alliance for Health, Physical Education, Recreation and Dance and for the National Consortium on Physical Education and Recreation for the Handicapped are listed in this appendix. A brief description of the criteria for each award precedes the recipient list.

National Consortium on Physical Education and Recreation for the Handicapped (NCPERH) Awards

Established 1982, the purpose of the NCPERH Awards is to recognize outstanding contributions in designated areas of leadership by Congressmen, Senators, and specialists in adapted physical education and therapeutic recreation.

Recipients of the NCPERH Awards are the following:

Scholarship Contribution Award (instituted 1982)

Hollis Fait	1982
John Nesbitt	1983
David Auxter	1984
Claudine Sherrill	1985
Joseph Winnick	1986

Distinguished Service Award (instituted 1981)

William Hillman	1981
Leon Johnson	1982
Grace Reynolds	1983
Ernest Bundschuh	1984
John Dunn	1985
Louis Bowers	1986

Congressional Award (instituted 1981)

Congressman Carl Perkins (KY)	1981
Senator Lowell Weicker (CT)	1981
Dennis Vinton	1981
Billy Ray Stokes	1982
Max Forman	1983
Lane Goodwin	1984
Michael Churton	1985
No award given	1986

Research Award (instituted 1982)

James Horgan	1982
Lawrence Rarick	1983
Dennis Vinton	1984
No award given	1985, 1986

Note. In 1981, Mel Appell was given a Special Award for his contributions to physical education and recreation for the handicapped.

Mabel Lee Award

Established 1976, this award shall be bestowed on young members of the Alliance who have demonstrated outstanding potential for scholarship, teaching, and/or professional leadership. The award shall be presented at the national AAHPERD convention. Not more than two Mabel Lee Awards may be given each year. The recipients shall have demonstrated a quality of performance that, if continued, indicates they will develop into distinguished members of the profession.

The recipient shall:

1. Be an active member of the Alliance.

2. Be less than 36 years of age.

3. Have demonstrated outstanding potential in scholarship, teaching, and/or professional leadership as reflected by (a) publications; (b) citations, awards, or other recognition for outstanding teaching, coaching, administration, or performing; *or* (c) active leadership roles in District and/or National Associations of the Alliance.

Recipients of the Mabel Lee Award who have an asterisk (*) next to their names are leaders in adapted physical education.

Brown, P. Timothy	1980
Bunker, Linda	1979
Cureton, Kirk J.	1983
*DePauw, Karen	1983
East, Whitfield	1986
Geadelmann, Patricia Lou	1981
*Gorman, Dean R.	1985
*Grosse, Susan J.	1982
Haywood, Kathleen M.	1984
Howell, Reet	1979
Lumpkin, Angela	1984
O'Brien, Dianne E.	1980
Owens, JoAnne L.	1978
Pate, Russell Robert	1981
Perry, Jean L.	1985
Plowman, Sharon A.	1976
Pruett, Diane M.	1982
Sholtis, Mary G.	1976
Teeple, Janet B.	1978
Weiss, Maureen	1986

Honor Fellow Award

Established 1931, this award recognizes meritorious service on the part of members of the American Alliance for Health, Physical Education, Recreation and Dance and is in the form of a certificate to be presented with ceremony to the recipient at the time of the national convention. If the recipient is unable to attend the national convention, arrangements may be made for the presentation at the state or district convention. No more than seven Honor Awards may be given in one year. The Honor Awards have been divided into two categories, "college and university" and "non-college and university."

The recipient shall:

1. Have served professionally in school (preschool, elementary, secondary), college, or community programs for a period of at least ten years prior to nomination.

2. Be a member of this Alliance. Former members who have retired from professional work may be exempt from this requirement.

3. Be a person of high moral character and personal integrity who exemplifies the spirit of devoted service to the professions and who has by his or her leadership and industry made an outstanding and noteworthy contribution to the advancement of health, physical education, recreation, or dance.

4. Be at least 35 years of age and shall have preparation in one or more areas of professional concern of the Alliance.

5. Present evidence of leadership or meritorious contribution in any five or more categories of service from the following:

Leadership

- A member of the Board of Directors of American Alliance.

- President of a district HPERD Association.

- President of a state HPERD Association.

- Chairman of a section or council in American Alliance, a district of the Alliance or outstanding long term service in state associations of HPERD.

- President of an affiliated organization of American Alliance for Health, Physical Education, Recreation and Dance or one closely allied to the Alliance, such as the National College Physical Education Association for Men, the National Association of Physical Education for College

Women, the American School Health Association, or the American College of Sports Medicine.

Committee Work

- Chair of a committee of American Alliance.

- Committee work over a period of three years or more with local, state, district, or the national organization either in the Alliance or with an organization promoting the same general objectives as the Alliance or an organization affiliated with it.

Writing/Research

- Systematic research which has helped advance the profession.

- Author or coauthor of one or more books on health, physical education, recreation, or dance.

- Author of five or more articles accepted and published by magazines of national scope or brought out in monograph form.

- Author of articles for handbooks, newspapers, magazines not covered above.

Speaking/Teaching/Coaching/Performing/Supervising and Directing

- Significant addresses before educational groups, conventions, assemblies, luncheon meetings, radio presentations, and other such meetings held in the interest and promotion of health, physical education, recreation, and dance.

- Recognized outstanding school or college teaching or coaching performance and/or administrative leadership ability and success.

- Outstanding contributions to HPERD through success in the medium of performing arts.

- Outstanding achievements in HPERD through program supervision or directing in school systems or community departments or agencies.

- An outstanding, original contribution to the profession which has affected its philosophy or practices, not included in the above.

Hundreds of persons have received this award because several are given each year. Consequently, only recipients who have made contributions to adapted physical education are listed.

Bancroft, Jessie	1931
Brace, David K.	1933
Clarke, David H.	1977

Clarke, H. Harrison	1955
Daniels, Arthur	1957
Davis, Ernest P.	1971
Fait, Hollis	1969
Giauque, C.D.	1939
Holland, Robert	1982
Homans, Amy	1931
Johnson, Warren	1971
Leighton, Jack	1979
McCraw, Lynn	1974
McCristal, King	1966
McKenzie, R. Tait	1931
Morgan, Cecil	1977
Pomeroy, Janet	1972
Rarick, G. Lawrence	1964
Rathbone, Josephine	1938
Scott, Harry	1935
Sherrill, Claudine	1979
Sinclair, Caroline	1966
Stafford, George T.	1944
Stein, Julian	1983
Vodola, Thomas	1980
Walker, Leroy T.	1972
Weiss, Raymond	1962
Wessel, Janet	1978
Worthingham, Catherine	1945

R. Tait McKenzie Award

Established 1968, this award provides the means through which the American Alliance for Health, Physical Education, Recreation and Dance recognizes significant contributions of its members who, through distinguished service outside the Alliance (or its component Associations), reflect prestige, honor, and dignity to the Alliance. The awards shall be presented at the national convention. Not more than two McKenzie Awards may be given each year.

The recipient shall:

1. Be an active member of the Alliance.

2. Have made significant contributions through work outside the normal work of the Alliance (e.g., government, general education, public health, international affairs, etc.) which reflect favorably on the Alliance.

3. Be highly regarded by his or her professional peers.

Recipients of the R. Tait McKenzie Award who have an asterisk (*) next to their names are leaders in adapted physical education as well as other areas.

Allen, Catherine L.	1980
Biles, Fay	1986
Blaufarb, Celia Marjorie	1985
Friermood, Harold T.	1983
Fritz, Harry	1984
Hall, J. Tillman	1978
Hein, Fred V.	1973
Hepworth, Connie Jo Matthews	1985
Holbrook, Leona	1969
*Humphrey, James H.	1976
*Johnson, Warren R.	1981
Lee, Mabel	1968
Lockman, Evelyn E.	1982
Manley, Helen M.	1970
Nixon, John E.	1978
*Sills, Frank D.	1969
Vendien, Lynn	1986
*Wessel, Janet A.	1983

Luther Halsey Gulick Medal

Established 1923, this award shall be regarded as the highest award that the American Alliance for Health, Physical Education, Recreation and Dance can bestow on its members in recognition of long and distinguished service to one or more of the professions represented in the Alliance. It shall be in the form of a medal, presented annually (unless the Committee agrees that no worthy candidate has been nominated for any given year) at the national convention. Not more than one Gulick Award shall be given each year.

The recipient shall:

1. Be clearly outstanding in his or her profession.

2. Exemplify the best in service, research, teaching, and/or administration.

3. Be recognized by the membership of the Alliance as a noteworthy leader.

4. Be the type of person whose life and contributions could inspire youth to live vigorously, courageously, and freely as citizens in a free society.

5. Currently be a member of the Alliance and shall have held such membership for at least 10 years.

6. Have been formally recognized by his or her peers by some form of national award for outstanding professional contributions, for example, a National Honor Award.

Recipients of the Luther Halsey Gulick Award who have an asterisk (*) next to their names are leaders in adapted physical education as well as other areas.

Abernathy, Ruth	1965
Ainsworth, Dorothy S.	1960
Allen, Catherine L.	1970
Alley, Louis A.	1985
Anderson, William G.	1945
*Bancroft, Jessie H.	1924
*Brace, David K.	1963
Brownell, Clifford L.	1962
Burchenal, Elizabeth	1950
Cassidy, Rosalind	1956
*Clarke, H. Harrison	1978
Cozens, Frederick W.	1953
Cureton, Thomas K., Jr.	1975
Davis, Elwood Craig	1965
Esslinger, Arthur	1967
Fisher, George J.	1929
Forker, Barbara	1984
Glassow, Ruth B.	1964
Gulick, Luther Halsey	1923
H'Doubler, Margaret	1971
Hetherington, Clark W.	1928
Holbrook, Leona	1974
Huelster, Laura	1986
Hughes, William L.	1954
Langton, Clair V.	1957
La Porte, William Ralph	1951
Lee, Mabel	1948
Lockhart, Aileene	1980
Lynn, Minni L.	1968
Manley, Helen	1958
McCloy, Charles H.	1944
Methany, Eleanor	1977
Miller, Ben W.	1976
Mitchell, Elmer Dayton	1949

Murray, Ruth Lovell	1979
Nash, Jay Bryan	1940
Neilson, Neils P.	1961
Nordly, Carl L.	1955
Oberteuffer, Delbert	1959
Perrin, Ethel	1946
Savage, Charles W.	1952
Scott, M. Gladys	1981
Sliepcevich, Elena	1979
Smith, Julian W.	1972
Steinhaus, Arthur H.	1969
Storey, Thomas A.	1926
Trilling, Blanche M.	1947
Ulrich, Celeste	1983
*Walker, Leroy T.	1982
Williams, Jesse Feiring	1939
Wood, Thomas D.	1925

William G. Anderson Award

Established 1949, this award shall be bestowed on persons who are *not* members of the Alliance, but who have contributed significantly to health education, physical education, sports, recreation, dance, and/or safety education through their efforts in allied or auxiliary fields, such as medicine, public health, education, government, and so forth. The awards shall be presented at the national convention. Not more than three Anderson awards may be given each year.

The recipient shall:

1. Not be a member of the Alliance.

2. Be at least 40 years of age.

3. Be of high moral character.

4. Have made important contributions to health education, physical education, sports, recreation, dance, and/or safety education from the vantage point of his or her profession (medicine, public health, general education, government, etc.).

Recipients of the William G. Anderson Award who have an asterisk (*) next to their names are leaders primarily in physical education and recreation for the handicapped.

Allman, Fred L., Jr.	1976
Bauer, William Waldo	1955

Beiswanger, George W.	1984	*Rusk, Howard A.	1960
Brown, Ethel G.	1965	Sabin, Albert B.	1963
Brown, Margaret C.	1953	Salk, Jonas E.	1956
Brundage, Avery	1956	Scanlan, Mazie V.	1949
Bryant, Carroll L.	1962	Schmidt, William S.	1970
*Buell, Charles E.	1974	Shaffer, T.E.	1964
Burney, Leroy E.	1958	*Shriver, Eunice Kennedy	1977
Conner, Forrest E.	1963	Staley, Seward Charles	1951
Cooper, Kenneth H.	1978	Steinhaus, Arthur H.	1951
*Cordellos, Harry C.	1980	Terry, Walter	1980
Crampton, C. Ward	1959	Waksman, Selman A.	1962
Davis, Elwood Craig	1954	Wayman, Agnes R.	1952
Dill, David	1979	White, Paul Dudley	1959
Eisenhower, Dwight D.	1961	Wolffe, Joseph B.	1961
Fleming, Robert S.	1982		
Fowler, Charles B.	1985		
Fox, James Rogers	1966		
Fox, Samuel M.	1976		
Gary, Charles	1986		
Goldberger, I.H.	1963		
Hellebrandt, Frances A.	1960		
Jacobson, Edmund	1974		
Kelly, John B., Jr.	1984		
Kessler, Henry Howard	1956		
Langton, Clair V.	1954		
Larimore, G.W.	1964		
Leon, Arthur S.	1981		
*Lipton, Benjamin H.	1975		
*Lowman, Charles L.	1959		
Mahlmann, John J.	1982		
Manley, Helen	1951		
Masters, Hugh	1950		
McDonough, Thomas E.	1953		
Menninger, Karl A.	1956		
Meyerding, Edward A.	1956		
Morrison, Robert Hugh	1955		
Moss, Bernice R.	1952		
Neal, Josiah G.	1972		
Nissen, George	1979		
*Nugent, Timothy J.	1976		
Olds, Glenn	1986		
Randall, Harriett Bulpitt	1971		
Rockefeller, David, Jr.	1983		
Rogers, James E.	1954		

Alliance Scholar Award

Established 1976, this award is to encourage and facilitate research which will enrich the depth and scope of health, leisure, and movement-related activities; and to disseminate the findings to individuals in the profession and other interested and concerned populations.

Recipients of the Alliance Scholar Award who have an asterisk (*) next to their names are leaders in adapted physical education as well as other areas.

Beyrer, Mary K.	1978
*Clarke, H. Harrison	1981
Costill, David L.	1980
Lockhart, Aileene	1985
Montoye, Henry J.	1976
Morgan, William	1983
Nelson, Richard C.	1982
*Rarick, G. Lawrence	1979
Safrit, Margaret	1986
Van Huss, Wayne	1984
Zeigler, Earle F.	1977

Fellow of the American Academy of Physical Education

Founded in 1926, election as a fellow (i.e., member) of the American Academy of Physical Education is one of the highest honors a physical educator can receive. Membership in the Academy is limited to 100-150 active fellows; there are also fellows emereti, associate fellows, and corresponding fellows.

The Statement of Purpose of the Academy, revised and approved in 1977, is as follows.

> The dual purpose of the American Academy of Physical Education shall be to encourage and promote the study and educational applications of the art and science of human movement and physical activity and to honor by election to its membership persons who have directly or indirectly contributed significantly to the study of and/or application of the art and science of human movement and physical activity.
>
> The Academy shall promote its dual purpose by means of recognizing and encouraging the continued exemplary, scholarly, and professional productivity of its individual members; synthesizing and transmitting knowledge about human movement and physical activity at annual scholarly meetings and via publications of Academy Proceedings; fostering philosophic considerations regarding purposes of and issues and values related to human movement and physical activity; annually bestowing honors for outstanding contributions to the field of physical education.

Active Fellows (1987) who are recognized leaders in adapted physical education are:

Clarke, David H.

Clarke, H. Harrison

Drowatzky, John J.

Gruber, Joseph

Sherrill, Claudine

Stein, Julian

Wade, Michael

Fellows Emereti (1987) who made substantial contributions to adapted, developmental, and corrective physical education are:

Humphrey, James

Rarick, G. Lawrence

Rathbone-Karpovich, Josephine

Sills, Frank

Vannier, Maryhelen

Weiss, Raymond A.

Deceased Fellows who made substantial contributions to adapted, developmental, corrective, or special physical education are:

Bancroft, Jessie J.	(1867-1952)
Brace, David K.	(1891-1971)
Daniels, Arthur S.	(1906-1966)
Fait, Hollis	(1918-1984)
Homans, Amy Morris	(1858-1933)
Johnson, Warren	(1921-1982)
Ling, Per Henrick	(1776-1839)
Lowman, Charles Leroy	(1879-1977)
McKenzie, R. Tait	(1867-1938)
Scott, Harry A.	(1894-1972)
Stafford, George	(1894-1968)

Therapeutics Council, AAHPERD Special Recognition Award

Established 1983, this award recognizes an individual or group that has made a unique or significant contribution to the promotion of health, physical education, recreation or dance for individuals with disabilities.

Recipients of Special Recognition Award of The Therapeutics Council of AAHPERD are:

1983	Riordan, Anne
	Hermann, Jane
1984	Fait, Hollis
	Mocha, Sue
1985	Sherrill, Claudine
	Mastro, James
1986	Broadhead, Geoffrey
	Reams, David

Appendix B
Adapted Physical Education—Functions and Competencies

1971-72 AAHPERD Functions and Competencies[1]

1. *Function*—Assess and evaluate the physical and motor status of individuals with a variety of handicapping conditions.

   Competencies

   - Identify physical and motor tolerance limits for participation in various exercises and physical activity (movement oriented) programs.

   - Analyze specific movement and exercise problems/capacities.

   - Determine physical and motor (movement) needs of individuals.

2. *Function*—Develop (design, plan), implement (conduct), and evaluate diversified programs of physical education for individuals and groups with a variety of handicapping conditions.

   Competencies

   - Understand the general nature of specific types of handicaps and their potential effects on both learning and participating in a variety of physical activities.

   - Interpret and apply assessments of individuals to develop appropriate programs of exercise and physical activity on both an individual and group basis.

   - Evaluate individual progress and program effectiveness.

3. *Function*—Participate in interprofessional situations providing special programs or services for individuals or groups, including coordination of such services for a program.

   Competencies

   - Identify and utilize resources of professionals in other related disciplines.

   - Integrate programs of individuals and/or groups with other instructional, treatment, and rehabilitation programs.

   - Interpret evaluations and programs of individuals to other professionals, laypersons, and families.

The competencies listed in Table B.1 are needed by physical education generalists and adapted physical education specialists. They are approved by the American Alliance for Health, Physical Education, Recreation and Dance.

_____

[1]*From* American Association for Health, Physical Education, and Recreation (1973). *Professional preparation in adapted physical education, therapeutic recreation, and corrective therapy.* Washington, DC: Author.

Table B.1   1981 AAHPERD Competencies for Adapted Physical Education Service Delivery

Physical education generalist	Adapted physical education specialist
Biological Foundations *Kinesiology*	
- Demonstrate understanding of functional anatomy as it applies to analyses of motor skills.	- Demonstrate ability to apply understanding of motor dysfunctions and their implications to adapted physical education programs.
- Demonstrate understanding of the organization and function of the nervous system including implications of neuromuscular relationships and functioning.	- Demonstrate ability to apply understanding of neurological disorders and their implications to motor functioning.
- Demonstrate understanding of deviations from normal physical growth and development, including musculoskeletal deviations, neurological disorders, and neuromuscular deficiencies.	- Demonstrate ability to apply understanding of deviations from normal physical growth and development to analyses of motor skills.
- Demonstrate understanding of influences which the human structure exerts on motor capabilities of individuals with or without disabilities.	- Demonstrate proficiency in evaluating and analyzing motor performances in terms of motor dysfunctions.
- Demonstrate proficiency in evaluating and analyzing motor performances and motor dysfunctions in terms of biomechanical principles and laws.	- Demonstrate ability to apply understanding of unique structures of individuals with disabilities to individualized instruction in adapted physical education.
	- Demonstrate ability to apply biomechanical principles which affect motor functioning to wheelchair, crutch, braces, and artificial limb use.
	- Demonstrate ability to apply biomechanical principles which affect motor functioning to posture, and neurological, muscular, and other specific physical health needs.

Continued

Continued   *Physiology of Exercise*

- Demonstrate understanding of immediate as well as long term physiological response of the human body to exercise.

- Demonstrate ability to design instructional physical education programs in accordance with essential physiological considerations and principles.

- Demonstrate proficiency in conducting instructional physical education programs in accordance with essential physiological considerations and principles.

- Demonstrate proficiency in communicating physiological benefits of regular physical activity for program participants.

- Demonstrate ability to apply research findings from exercise physiology to instructional physical education programs.

- Demonstrate knowledge of how dysfunctions affect physiological responses to exercise.

- Demonstrate ability to design instructional physical education programs in accordance with essential physiological considerations and principles specific to individuals with disabilities.

- Demonstrate proficiency in conducting instructional physical education programs in accordance with essential physiological considerations and principles specific to individuals with disabilities.

- Demonstrate ability to apply research findings in the area of exercise physiology specific to individuals with disabilities.

Physiological and Motor Functioning

- Demonstrate understanding of the components of physiological and motor functioning

- Demonstrate understanding of functional capacity, complexity, and adaptability of the human organism as bases for skillful motor performances.

- Demonstrate understanding of anatomical and physiological deviations in the human organism and effect such deviations have on motor performances.

- Demonstrate understanding of specific basis for preventing and caring for injuries common to physical education, sport, dance, and play activities.

- Demonstrate ability to apply an understanding of physiological functioning of individuals with physical, mental, sensory, neurological and other specific health needs to programs designed to improve motor performances of these individuals with disabilities.

- Demonstrate ability to apply an understanding of physiological motor characteristics for individuals with physical, mental, sensory, neurological and other specific health needs to programs designed to improve motor performances of these individuals with disabilities.

- Demonstrate ability to apply techniques for the prevention and care of injuries specific to individuals with specific disabilities.

Sociological Foundations
Sport, Dance, and Play

- Demonstrate understanding of roles and importance of sports, dance, and play activities to individuals living in contemporary American society, including their significance for individuals with disabilities.

- Demonstrate understanding of ethnic, social, and cultural aspects of sports, dance, and play.

- Demonstrate knowledge of roles and importance of sports, dance, and play for individuals in the community, including such opportunities for individuals with disabilities.

- Demonstrate awareness of community opportunities in sports, dance, and play for individuals with disabilities.

- Demonstrate understanding of values of lifetime physical activities to all individuals, including those with disabilities.

- Demonstrate ability to analyze the role and significance of sport, dance, and play in the lives of individuals with disabilities.

- Demonstrate understanding of roles and significance of lifetime physical activities for individuals with disabilities.

- Demonstrate understanding of influences of community social agencies on sport, dance, and play in lives of individuals with disabilities.

Cooperative/Competitive Activities

- Demonstrate understanding of the potential of cooperative/ competitive activities for human interaction and social behavior.

- Demonstrate knowledge of organizations which conduct adapted sport, dance and play programs and activities for individuals with disabilities.

- Demonstrate ability to apply understanding of the potential for human interactions and social behavior occurring in cooperative/ competitive activities for individuals with disabilities.

- Demonstrate ability to work and cooperate with organizations which conduct adapted sport, dance, and play programs and activities for individuals with disabilities.

Social Development

- Demonstrate understanding of social learnings involved in experiencing human movement and its effects on perception, motivation, and personality.

- Demonstrate understanding of the potential that sport, dance, and play provides for social interactions among individuals with and without disabilities.

- Demonstrate ability to apply understanding of the potential that sport, dance, and play provides for social interaction among individuals with and without disabilities.

Psychological Foundations
Human Growth and Development

- Demonstrate understanding of human growth and development.
- Demonstrate understanding of how deviations in normal human growth and development can result in disabilities.
- Demonstrate knowledge of normal and atypical motor development.

- Demonstrate ability to apply understanding of deviations in normal human growth and development of individuals with physical, mental, sensory, neurological, and other specific health needs.
- Demonstrate ability to apply understanding of atypical motor development to individuals with disabilities.

Motor Learning

- Demonstrate proficiency in applying principles of motor learning to teaching and learning of motor skills.
- Demonstrate ability to apply principles of motivation, including to individuals with disabilities, on learning of motor skills.

- Demonstrate ability to apply principles of motor learning to individuals with specific physical and motor needs.
- Demonstrate ability to apply principles of motivation on development of motor skills by individuals with disabilities.

Self-Concept and Personality Development

- Demonstrate understanding of relationships among positive and negative movement experiences and self-concept.
- Demonstrate ability to help students with and without disabilities develop positive self-concepts.
- Demonstrate ability to apply skills and techniques to assist individuals with and without disabilities overcome attitudinal barriers which can affect interpersonal relationships and development of positive self-concepts.
- Demonstrate understanding of relationships between an individual's personality development and participation in physical education, sport, dance, and play programs.

- Demonstrate understanding of how participating in physical and motor activities contributes to positive self-concepts of individuals with disabilities.
- Demonstrate ability to apply understanding of how interpersonal relationships are affected by participation in physical and motor activities.
- Demonstrate ability to apply skills and techniques to assist individuals with disabilities overcome additional barriers which can affect interpersonal relationships and development of positive self-concept.

Management of Behavior

- Demonstrate ability to apply various methods for developing appropriate student behavior.
- Demonstrate an understanding of principles of motivation as they affect human behavior and promote motor performance.

- Demonstrate ability to apply appropriate techniques for managing behavior (i.e., Behaviorism, Existentialism, Humanism).
- Demonstrate ability to apply techniques of motivation to enhance acceptable behavior and promote motor performance.

Historical–Philosophical Foundations
Historical Development

- Demonstrate understanding of the historical development of physical education.
- Demonstrate understanding of roles and significance of physical education professional organizations on development of professional standards, ethics, and programs related to physical education.

- Demonstrate understanding of the historical development of adapted physical education.
- Demonstrate understanding of roles and significance of professional and voluntary organizations on development of professional standards, ethics, and programs related to adapted physical education.

Philosophical Development

- Demonstrate understanding of the philosophies of physical education.
- Demonstrate ability to apply a personal/professional philosophy of physical education.
- Demonstrate understanding of current issues and emerging trends in physical education and their philosophical significances.
- Demonstrate ability to identify ways that individuals realize and express their individualities and uniquenesses through physical education, sport, dance, and play programs.

- Demonstrate understanding of the philosophies of adapted physical education.
- Demonstrate ability to apply a personal/professional philosophy of adapted physical education.
- Demonstrate understanding of current issues and emerging trends in adapted physical education and their philosophical significances.
- Demonstrate understanding of ways individuals with disabilities realize and express their individualities and uniquenesses through physical education, sport, dance, and play programs.

Continued

Continued

Assessment and Evaluation
Program Goals and Objectives

- Demonstrate understanding of goals and objectives of physical education, including programs and activities for individuals with disabilities.

- Demonstrate ability to identify performance or instructional objectives leading to fulfillment of physical education goals in psychomotor, affective, and cognitive domains.

- Demonstrate ability to apply goals and objectives of adapted physical education.

- Demonstrate ability to develop instructional objectives which lead to fulfillment of physical education goals in psychomotor, affective, and cognitive domains by individuals with disabilities.

Screening and Assessment

- Demonstrate proficiency in using appropriate instruments—i.e., screening devices through standardized test—and procedures to measure physiological, biomechanical, and psychomotor functions.

- Demonstrate ability to select various assessment instruments for measuring physical and motor performance.

- Demonstrate ability to construct various assessment instruments for measuring physical and motor performance.

- Demonstrate proficiency in applying appropriate instruments and procedures for measuring levels of physiological, biomechanical, and psychomotor functioning of individuals with disabilities.

- Demonstrate proficiency in applying appropriate criteria in constructing assessment instruments for measuring physical and motor performances of students with disabilities.

Evaluation

- Demonstrate proficiency in using appropriate instruments to evaluate physical and motor needs of individual students.

- Demonstrate ability to apply basic evaluation principles in determining student progress in physical education.

- Demonstrate ability to interpret evaluation results as they apply to physical education goals, objectives, and activities.

- Demonstrate proficiency in applying evaluation results to appropriate physical education goals, objectives, and activities.

- Demonstrate proficiency in applying appropriate instruments in determining physical and motor needs of individuals with disabilities.

- Demonstrate proficiency in applying principles of evaluation in determining student progress in adapted physical education.

Curriculum Planning, Organization, and Implementation
Program Planning

- Demonstrate ability to plan instructional programs emphasizing the following areas
  - physical and motor fitness
  - fundamental motor skills and patterns
  - skills in aquatics, dance, individual and group games and sports, including lifetime sports and leisure skills.

- Demonstrate proficiency in planning instructional programs to meet needs of students with disabilities emphasizing the following areas
  - physical and motor fitness
  - fundamental motor skills and patterns
  - skills in aquatics, dance, individual and group games and sports, including lifetime sports and leisure skills.

- Demonstrate ability to plan individual physical education programs based on goals and objectives established by an interdisciplinary team.

- Demonstrate ability to adapt physical and motor fitness activities, fundamental motor skills and patterns, aquatics and dance, and individual and group games and sports, including lifetime sports and leisure skills, to accommodate needs of individuals with disabilities.

- Demonstrate understanding of organizations that govern adapted sports and games.

Individual Instruction

- Demonstrate understanding of the principles of individualized instruction.

- Demonstrate ability to plan physical education programs based on student's current levels of performance.

- Demonstrate ability to apply strategies for individualizing instruction for students with disabilities in a variety of instructional settings.

- Demonstrate ability to apply task analysis techniques in the process of individualizing instruction.

Continued

Continued

- Develop ability to apply strategies for individualizing instruction in regular physical education settings.

- Demonstrate ability to implement appropriate physical education programs for individuals with disabilities based on each student's current level of performance.

Program Implementation

- Demonstrate understanding of relationships among supportive factors (i.e., administrative policies, facilities, equipment, faculty, community) and effective implementation of physical education curricula.

- Demonstrate understanding of role and significance of physical educators as members of interdisciplinary teams.

- Demonstrate ability to implement appropriate physical education curricula for individuals with disabilities based on adequate supportive factors (i.e., administrative policies, facilities, equipment, faculty, and community).

- Demonstrate ability to function effectively as a member of an interdisciplinary team.

- Demonstrate ability to apply appropriate techniques for facilitating interdisciplinary communication among all persons working with individuals with disabilities.

Safety Considerations

- Demonstrate understanding of safety principles related to physical and motor activities.

- Demonstrate knowledge of specific safety considerations for individuals with disabilities when they participate in physical education, sport, dance, and play program activities.

- Demonstrate ability to apply principles of safety to wheelchair transfers, lifts, and assists needed when individuals with disabilities participate in physical activities.

- Demonstrate understanding of scientific bases for specifically contraindicated exercises and activities for individuals with disabilities.

Health Considerations

- Demonstrate understanding of appropriate health principles and practices related to physical and motor activities.

- Demonstrate knowledge of special health considerations when individuals with disabilities participate in physical education, sport, dance, and play programs.

- Demonstrate ability to apply principles of appropriate health practices to participation in physical and motor activities by individuals with disabilities.

- Demonstrate understanding of effects of medication, fatigue, and illness on mental, physical, and motor performances of individuals with disabilities.

- Demonstrate understanding of implications of personal hygiene, posture, and nutrition for individuals with disabilities.

Appendix C

Glossary of Contemporary Adapted Physical Education Leaders in the United States

This glossary is limited to national leaders who have made major contributions to adapted physical education since 1975. With the exception of Hollis Fait and Warren Johnson, all individuals are still living and still contributing.

Criteria for inclusion in this glossary were that an individual be (a) an author or coauthor of two or more commercially published adapted physical education textbooks, videotapes, or assessment instruments; or (b) an editor of an adapted physical education/sports for disabled journal or newsletter; or (c) *two* or more of the following:

- Author, coauthor, or editor of commercially published adapted physical education textbook, videotape, or assessment instrument. *Note dates of books in descriptions of leaders are for first editions to show approximately when leadership began.*

- Published over 10 articles in refereed journals and/or chapters in books and/or on Editorial Board of *Adapted Physical Activity Quarterly.*

- Chair of AAHPERD national structure pertaining to therapeutics or adapted physical education.

- President of National Consortium on Physical Education and Recreation for the Handicapped (NCPERH).

- Recipient of AAHPERD national level award.

- Recipient of NCPERH award.

- Election as Fellow of American Academy of Physical Education.

- Over 10 years of experience in grant writing/management.

- Major shaper of federal legislation and/or politician or government employee who has advocated strongly for adapted physical education.

- Founder of a sports for disabled organization or first director of an organization/agency with national impact on adapted physical education.

---

[1]*Note.* Anyone who meets these criteria and who has been omitted from this list should contact the editor to be included in future listings.

Adams, Ronald.—University of Virginia Hospital at Charlottesville. Director of Therapeutic Recreation and Adapted Physical Education at Children's Rehabilitation Center since 1972. Senior author of *Games, Sports, and Exercise for the Physically Handicapped,* 1972.

Appell, Mel.—Division of Innovation and Development, Office of Special Education Programs, Washington, DC. Project officer for most research in physical education and recreation for handicapped funded by federal government from 1968 to 1981.

Arnheim, Daniel.—San Diego State University since 1984, but best known for many years of leadership at California State College at Long Beach. Author of *Physical Education for Special Populations* (1985), *The Clumsy Child* (1979), *Modern Principles of Athletic Training* (1977), and first three editions of *Principles and Methods of Adapted Physical Education* (senior author).

Auxter, David.—Slippery Rock State College, Pennsylvania. One of the authors of *Principles and Methods of Adapted Physical Education* (1973). One of the first grant directors (1970-71). Expert in legislation and litigation related to physical education for handicapped individuals.

Beaver, David.—Western Illinois University in Macomb. One of the founders of the U.S. Association for Blind Athletes and past chairman of its Sports Committee. Member of first USOC Handicapped in Sports Committee. Founder and editor of journal, *Palaestra.*

Bowers, Louis.—University of South Florida at Tampa. One of the first grant directors (1969-70) and cofounder of the National Consortium on Physical Education and Recreation for Handicapped. Director of Play Learning Center and Demonstration Project for Handicapped Children, 1974-1977, and of I'M SPECIAL research/demonstration project, 1979 through the present.

Broadhead, Geoffrey.—Louisiana State University at Baton Rouge. Editor of *Adapted Physical Activity Quarterly.* Major researcher in adapted physical education, assessment, and motor development.

Buell, Charles.—San Juan Capistrano, California. Legally blind, foremost consumer-leader in physical education for disabled. Author of *Physical Education for Blind Children* (1966) and *Physical Education and Recreation for the Visually Handicapped* (1973). One of the organizers of U.S. Association for Blind Athletes. Recipient of William G. Anderson Award.

Bundschuh, Ernest.—University of Georgia. President of National Consortium on Physical Education and

Recreation for Handicapped, known for innovation in teacher training. Director of Special Project entitled Comprehensive System of Personnel Development Physical Education (CSPD PE), a computer-based needs assessment management system.

Clarke, David.—University of Maryland. President of the American Academy of Physical Education (1984-85) and recipient of AAHPERD Honor Award for service in many areas, including adapted physical education.

Churton, Michael.—Appalachian State University in North Carolina. Editor of NCPERH Newsletter, 1981-1986. President of NCPERH and chair of AAHPERD Therapeutic Council. Expert on advocacy, legislation, and ecological approach.

Clarke, David.—University of Maryland. President of the American Academy of Physical Education (1984-85) and recipient of AAHPERD Honor Award for service in many areas, including adapted physical education.

Clarke, H. Harrison.—Retired after many years at the University of Oregon. Senior author with son David of *Developmental and Adapted Physical Education* (1963) and of research methods text. President of the American Academy of Physical Education (1969-70) and recipient of AAHPERD Honor Award, Luther Halsey Gulick Medal, and Alliance Scholar Award.

Cordellos, Harry.—San Francisco. Author of book on teaching aquatics to blind persons and known internationally as a blind athlete and marathon runner, speaker, and consultant. Recipient of William G. Anderson Award.

Cratty, Bryant.—University of California at Los Angeles. Author of numerous books on perceptual motor learning in 1960s and 1970s and of *Adapted Physical Education for Children and Youth*, 1980.

Davies, Evelyn.—Retired after many years at Indiana University. Author with Arthur Daniels of *Adapted Physical Education* (responsible for complete revisions, 1975 and thereafter). Initiated masters and doctoral training programs in adapted physical education at IU (1971-72) which produced such leaders as Jean Pyfer, Janet Seaman, Marti Puthoff, and Sue Gavron.

DePauw, Karen.—Washington State University at Pullman. Coauthor with Janet Seaman of *The New Adapted Physical Education*, 1982. Chair of sub-

committee on research for the Committee on Sports for the Disabled (COSD) of the U.S. Olympic Committee. Recipient of Mabel Lee Award for young AAHPERD Leaders. Active in many organizations.

Drowatsky, John.—University of Toledo in Ohio. Researcher in motor learning and author of *Physical Education for the Mentally Retarded* (1971). Fellow of American Academy of Physical Education.

Dunn, John.—Oregon State University. Coauthor with Hollis Fait of *Special Physical Education* (1984 edition) and *A Data Based Gymnasium* (1980). President of National Consortium on Physical Education and Recreation for Handicapped (1981) and chair of both Therapeutic Council and Adapted Physical Education Academy. Authority on severely handicapped and behavior management.

Eason, Robert.—University of New Orleans. Senior editor of *Proceedings of Third Symposium of the International Federation of Adapted Physical Activity*. Major research in areas of learning disabilities, motor learning, and relaxation.

Eichstaedt, Carl.—Illinois State University at Normal. Coauthor with L. Kalakian of *Developmental/Adapted Physical Education: Making Ability Count*, 1982.

Ersing, Walter.—Ohio State University. One of the first grant directors (1969-70). Coauthor with Ruth Wheeler on one of the first status studies in adapted physical education professional preparation and writer/speaker/leader in professional preparation history, trends, and issues. Coauthor of assessment instrument, OHIO SIGMA.

Fait, Hollis.—Deceased, 1984. University of Connecticut. Authored or coauthored 23 books, including *Adapted Physical Education*, 1960; title changed to *Special Physical Education*, 1966. Innovator of term/concept of special physical education. One of first grant writers (1970-71). Fellow of American Academy of Physical Education and recipient of many awards.

Folio, Rhonda.—Tennessee Technological University in Cookeville. Author of *Physical Education Programming for Exceptional Learners* (1985) and senior author of the *Peabody Developmental Motor Scales* (1983).

French, Ronald.—Texas Woman's University. Previously at University of Utah (directed grant program) and

SUNY at Brockport with Winnick and Jansma. Coauthor with Paul Jansma of *Special Physical Education*, 1982. Extremely versatile researcher and writer, with numerous published articles. Expert on behavior management and pedagogy.

Gallahue, David.—Indiana University. Author of many texts on motor development of children, including *Fundamental Movement: A Developmental and Remedial Approach* (1978) with Bruce McClenaghan. Former editor of *The Physical Educator*.

Geddes, Dolores.—Retired from University of Southern California. One of first grant directors (1969-70) at Indiana State University at Terre Haute. Author/editor of numerous books for AAHPERD while employed by Unit on Programs for Handicapped, 1973-1975. Author of *Physical Activities for Individuals With Handicapping Conditions* (1978) and *Psychomotor Individualized Educational Programs for Intellectual, Learning, and Behavioral Disabilities* (1981).

Goodwin, Lane.—University of Wisconsin at LaCrosse. Writer of first training grant for University of Utah (1971-72) and grant director at LaCrosse thereafter. Director of series of Midwestern Conferences on Adapted Physical Education.

Grosse, Susan.—F.J. Gaenslen School, Milwaukee. Author of *Physical Education Activities for the Uncoordinated Student* and public school leader in adapted physical education. Frequent contributor to AAHPERD publications. Recipient of Mabel Lee Award for young leaders. Expert on aquatics.

Hayden, Frank.—International Special Olympics, Inc. Also physical education professor at McMaster University, Hamilton, Canada. First Director of Special Olympics, Inc. in 1968. Author of *Physical Fitness for Mentally Retarded* (1964).

Hillman, William.—Division of Assistance to States, Office of Special Education Programs (OSEP), Washington, DC, from 1981 to 1987. Advocate, consultant, and friend to physical education and recreation grant writers. Staff member, 1968-1981, of Division of Training programs of OSEP (then Bureau of Education for Handicapped, BEH). Played major role in physical education and recreation funding. Past president of National Therapeutic Recreation Society. Cofounder of National Consortium on Physical Education and Recreation for the Handicapped.

Holland, Robert.—Retired after many years as Physical Education Consultant, Ohio Department of Education. Helped draft PL 90-170 legislation for Senator Edward Kennedy in early 1960s. Served as first director of AAHPER Project on Recreation and Fitness for the Mentally Retarded (1965), later named AAHPERD Unit on Programs for the Handicapped.

Horgan, James.—University of Illinois at Chicago Circle. Previously at Temple University. Major researcher in adapted physical education and motor learning of disabled.

Horvat, Michael.—University of Georgia. Previously at University of Nevada. Editor of *Nevada Physical Education for the Handicapped Resource Manual* (1983) and *Fitness, Games, Sports, and Activities for the Handicapped Guide* (n.d.). Chair of Adapted Physical Activity Council and active in research, especially in parent training and fitness.

Jansma, Paul.—Ohio State University. Previously at SUNY at Brockport with J. Winnick and R. French. Coauthor with R. French of *Special Physical Education* (1982) and editor of *The Psychomotor Domain and the Seriously Handicapped* (1984).

Johnson, Leon.—University of Missouri. One of the first grant directors (1969-70). First president of National Consortium on Physical Education and Recreation for Handicapped, 1975.

Johnson, Warren.—Deceased. University of Maryland. Developed concept of undergraduate practica and/or clinical experiences via Children's Developmental Clinic in early 1950s. Author of *Science and Medicine in Exercise and Sports* (1974) and *Sex Education and Counseling of Special Groups* (1975). Influenced such leaders as Louis Bowers, Ernie Bundschuh, and Glenn Roswal.

Kalakian, Leonard.—Mankato State University in Minnesota. Author with Carl Eichstadt of *Developmental/Adapted Physical Education: Making Ability Count* (1982), with Joan Moran of *Movement Experiences for the Mentally Retarded or Emotionally Disturbed Child* (1974), and with Judy Werder of *Assessment in Adapted Physical Education* (1985).

Keogh, Jack.—University of California at Los Angeles. One of the first grant directors (1971-72). Leader in research and training relating movement development to movement problems and self-concept of children. Author with David Sugden of *Movement Skill Development* (1985).

Klesius, Stephen.—University of South Florida, Tampa. Coworker with Louis Bowers on I'M SPECIAL project and leader in perceptual motor development teacher training. Coauthor of *Meaningful Movement for Developing Children* (1985).

Knowles, Claudia.—Special Education Department, Texas Education Agency. One of the leading adapted physical education specialists within state educational agencies (SEAs). Previously grant director at University of Texas at Austin and Materials Development Coordinator for I CAN Curriculum Project at Michigan State University. Several published articles on in-service training.

Lange, Ernie.—University of New Mexico. Previously grant director at Appalachian State University and University of Idaho. Author with Lowell Masters and Allen Mori of *Adapted Physical Education: A Practitioner's Guide*, 1983.

Lipton, Benjamin.—New York. Founder of National Wheelchair Athletic Association (1958) and chairman of its executive committee until 1981. Also founder of National Wheelchair Games (NWG) and U.S. Wheelchair Sports Fund (USWSF). Member of first USOC Handicapped in Sports Committee.

Loovis, Michael.—Cleveland State University in Ohio. Chair of Therapeutics Section and coauthor with Walter Ersing of assessment instrument, OHIO SIGMA.

Lundegren, Herberta.—Pennsylvania State University. Professional preparation expertise in both adapted physical education and therapeutic recreation. Associate editor of *Adapted Physical Activity Quarterly* and author with Patricia Farrell of *Evaluation for Leisure Service Managers: A Dynamic Approach* (1985).

McClenaghan, Bruce.—University of South Carolina. Theme editor of special populations issue of *The Physical Educator*, 1981-1984; associate editor of *The Physical Educator*, 1985 to present. Coauthor with David Gallahue of *Fundamental Movement: A Developmental and Remedial Approach* (1978).

McCubbin, Jeffrey.—Texas Christian University at Fort Worth. Previously at Ohio State University.

Editor of *NCPERH Newsletter* from 1986 to present. Author with Ron Adams and others of *Games, Sports, and Physical Exercises for the Physically Disabled* (1982).

Moran, Joan.—Private business in Denton, TX. Previously at Texas Woman's University. Author with Leonard Kalakian of *Movement Experiences for the Mentally Retarded or Emotionally Disturbed Child*, 1974. Director of first funded training program at University of Utah (1971-72).

Morris, G.S. Don.—California State Polytechnic University at Pomona. Author of *How to Change the Games Children Play* (1976) on which games analysis intervention research is based, *Elementary Physical Education: Toward Inclusion* (1980), and *Physical Education from Intent to Action* (1985).

Pyfer, Jean.—Texas Woman's University. Author with D. Auxter of *Principles and Methods of Adapted Physical Education* (1981). Previously grant director at University of Kansas. Primary expertise in assessment and neurological problems.

Rarick, G. Lawrence.—Retired after many years at University of California at Berkeley. Previously at University of Wisconsin. One of the first grant directors (1969-70). Pioneer in research concerning motor characteristics and fitness of mentally retarded and Special Olympics. Editor of *Physical Activity: Human Growth and Development* (1973). Fellow of American Academy of Physical Education and recipient of many honors, including the AAHPERD Scholar Award.

Reams, David.—City of Miami, Florida, Adapted Physical Education, Program Director. Editor of AAHPERD Newsletter, *ABLE BODIES*. Promoter of annual Junior Orange Bowl Sports Ability Games in Florida and of youth sports for disabled.

Reynolds, Grace.—YMCA, Longview, Washington. Grant director for many special projects pertaining to aquatics for handicapped and mainstreaming. Author of *A Swimming Program for the Handicapped*, (1973) and a series of YMCA books on mainstreaming in agency settings.

Roice, Robert.—Los Angeles County Public Schools. Public school leader in adapted physical education. Served as conference director for first and subsequent National Conference on Physical Activity for the Exceptional Individual, 1973-1979.

Schofer, Richard.—University of Missouri. Leading advocate of physical education and recreation for handicapped with the special education profession. Only special education member of National Consortium on Physical Education and Recreation for Handicapped. Director of Manpower Planning Project in Special Education which promoted cooperative planning between physical educators and special educators. Published numerous monographs.

Seaman, Janet.—California State University at Los Angeles. Director of adapted physical education training program. Leader in adapted physical education credential movement in California. Author with K. DePauw of *The New Adapted Physical Education*, 1982. Author of the *Los Angeles Unified School District Adapted Physical Education Assessment Scale* (1982) and several other instruments.

Sherrill, Claudine.—Texas Woman's University. Initiated masters and doctoral training programs in adapted physical education at TWU (1972-73). President of National Consortium on Physical Education and Recreation for Handicapped (1977). Author of *Adapted Physical Education and Recreation: A Multidisciplinary Approach* (1976) and editor of *Creative Arts for the Severely Handicapped* (1979) and *Sport and Disabled Athletes* (1986). Primary expertise in social/psychological foundations and self-actualization through humanistic teaching. Fellow of the American Academy of Physical Education. Recipient of AAHPERD Honor Award.

Shriver, Eunice Kennedy.—Founder (1968) and president of Special Olympics, Inc. Recipient of William G. Anderson Award.

Songster, Thomas.—Joseph P. Kennedy, Jr. Foundation. Director of Sports for Special Olympics, Inc. Developed sports training programs for certification of Special Olympics coaches and edited several training manuals.

Stein, Julian.—George Mason University in Virginia since fall 1981. Previously Director of AAHPERD Unit on Programs for the Handicapped from 1966 to 1981, also Director of AAHPERD membership and computer services. Author/editor of numerous books published by AAHPERD and of articles in all major journals. Largely responsible for such adapted physical education professional preparation trends as generic or noncategorical approach, competency based training, consumer (i.e., disabled person) involvement, and mainstreaming emphasis

through direction of BEH/OSE/OSEP funded special projects in personnel training. Fellow of the American Academy of Physical Education and recipient of the AAHPERD Honor Award.

Stokes, Billy Ray.—State education agency in Louisiana. Previously with Louisiana Department of Mental Retardation. Largely responsible for Louisiana's model public school programming in adapted physical education, its leadership in Special Olympics, and its teacher certification in adapted physical education.

Strauss, Robert.—Trinity University, San Antonio, TX. Author with Karen De Oreo of *Assessment of Individual Motor Skills* (AIMS) *Assessment Manual* (1979) and *Activities Manual*. Chair of AAHPERD Therapeutic Section.

Surburg, Paul.—Indiana University. Prolific writer-researcher in motor learning and sport medicine.

Ulrich, Dale.—Indiana University. Previously at Southern Illinois University. Author of *Test of Gross Motor Development* (TGMD). Expertise in research, statistics, and assessment.

Vodola, Thomas.—VEE, Inc., New Jersey. Many years as Director of PROJECT ACTIVE, a National Diffusion Network (NDN) developer/demonstrator project with a strong teacher training component from 1974 until June 1983. Also administrator in Township of Ocean School District, Oakhurst, New Jersey. Project impacted training of over 2,000 practitioners in at least 25 states. Author of *Individualized Physical Education Program for the Handicapped Child* (1973) and the *PROJECT ACTIVE Teacher Training Model Kit*, which contains 12 manuals for implementation of programs for handicapped students. Recipient of AAHPERD Honor Award.

Wade, Michael.—University of Minnesota. Previously at Southern Illinois University. Section editor on Activities for Special Populations for *Research Quarterly for Exercise and Sport* from 1984-1986. Expertise in motor learning, especially in relation to mental retardation. Fellow of the American Academy of Physical Education.

Walker, Leroy.—North Carolina Central University in Durham. One of first grant directors (1971-72). Conducted institute on physical education and recreation for handicapped training for Black colleges and universities in early 1970s. Past president of AAHPERD. Member of first USOC Handicapped in Sport Committee. Recipient of AAHPERD Honor Award and of Luther Halsey Gulick Medal.

Weiss, Raymond.—Retired after many years at New York University. Innovator in doctoral level teacher training. Fellow of the American Academy of Physical Education. Recipient of AAHPERD Honor Award.

Wessel, Janet.—Retired after many years at Michigan State University. One of the first grant directors but early emphasis was on research and demonstration rather than training. Developer of PROJECT I CAN which was field tested and validated through research demonstration funding. Only physical educator to serve as a member of National Advisory Committee on the Handicapped, 1973-1977. Chairperson of State of Michigan System of Personnel Development for Handicapped, 1977-79. Author of *Planning Individualized Educational Programs in Special Education* (1978), *I CAN System and Instructional Resource Materials* (1977), and of *Achievement-Based Curriculum Development in Physical Education* (1986). Recipient of AAHPERD Honor Award and of R. Tait McKenzie Award.

Winnick, Joseph.—State University College (SUNY) at Brockport. President of National Consortium on Physical Education and Recreation for Handicapped, 1979. Author of *Early Movement Experiences and Development: Habilitation and Remediation* (1979), publicized as the first graduate level textbook in adapted physical education. Editor also of several monographs resulting from conferences at SUNY such as *Piaget for Regular and Special Physical Educators and Recreators* (1975), *Physical Education Inservice Resource Manual for Implementation of PL 94-142* (1978), *The Preparation of Regular Physical Educators for Mainstreaming* (1979), and *Special Athletic Opportunities for Individuals with Handicapping Conditions* (1981). Author with Francis Short of *Physical Fitness Testing of the Disabled: Project UNIQUE* (1985).

Wisher, Peter.—Retired from Gallaudet College, Washington, DC. Foremost spokesperson/leader in physical education and dance for deaf students. Founder of first performing modern dance group of deaf students. Active in National Dance Association.

Table C.1 Summary of National Leaders in Adapted Physical Education

Leaders	Author or editor of book, video-tape, or test	Editor of journal or newsletter	10 published articles or APAQ Editorial Board	Chair of AAHPERD national structure	President of NCPERH	Recipient of national AAHPERD award	Recipient of NCPERH award	Fellow of American Academy of Physical Education	10 years of grant writing	Shaper of legislation	First director or founder of organization or journal
Adams, Ronald	X								X		
Appell, Mel						X				X	
Arnheim, Daniel	X								X		
Auxter, David	X		X	X				X	X	X	
Beaver, David		X									X
Bowers, Louis	X				X			X	X		X
Broadhead, Geoffrey	X	X	X								
Buell, Charles	X	X	X				X				X
Bundschuh, Ernest				X	X			X	X		
Carlson, Robert B.		X		X							
Churton, Michael				X	X			X	X	X	
Clarke, David	X		X	X		X		X			
Clarke, H. Harrison	X		X	X		X		X			
Cordellos, Harry	X					X					
Cratty, Bryant	X					X					
Davies, Evelyn	X			X					X		
DePauw, Karen	X		X	X		X			X		
Drowatsky, John	X							X			

Continued

Continued

Name											
Dunn, John	X	X	X	X	X				X		
Eason, Robert	X		X								
Eichstaedt, Carl									X		
Ersing, Walter	X								X		
Fait, Hollis	X		X			X			X		
Folio, Rhonda	X						X				
French, Ronald	X		X								
Gallahue, David	X	X							X		
Geddes, Dolores	X		X						X		
Goodwin, Lane	X			X			X				
Grosse, Susan	X					X					
Hayden, Frank	X										
Hillman, William						X				X	X
Holland, Robert						X				X	X
Horgan, James			X				X		X		
Horvat, Michael			X	X					X		
Jansma, Paul	X		X						X		
Johnson, Leon				X	X		X				
Johnson, Warren	X		X			X		X			
Kalakian, Leonard	X								X		
Keogh, Jack	X		X						X		
Klesius, Stephen	X								X		
Knowles, Claudia	X								X		
Lange, Ernie	X								X		
Lipton, Benjamin						X					X
Loovis, Michael	X		X	X					X		
Lundegren, Herberta	X	X	X								
McClenaghan, Bruce	X	X									
McCubbin, Jeffrey	X	X									
Moran, Joan	X								X		
Morris, G.S. Don	X										
Pyfer, Jean	X			X					X		
Rarick, G. Lawrence	X		X			X	X	X	X		
Reams, David		X				X					
Reynolds, Grace	X						X		X		
Roice, Robert				X							X
Schofer, Richard	X								X	X	
Seaman, Janet	X			X							
Sherrill, Claudine	X		X	X	X	X	X	X	X		
Shriver, Eunice Kennedy						X				X	X
Songster, Thomas	X								X		
Stein, Julian	X	X	X	X		X		X	X	X	
Stokes, Billy Ray							X		X		
Strauss, Robert	X			X							
Surburg, Paul			X						X		
Ulrich, Dale	X		X								
Vodola, Thomas	X	X				X			X		
Wade, Michael			X						X		
Walker, Leroy							X			X	
Weiss, Raymond			X			X		X	X		
Wessel, Janet	X			X		X			X		
Winnick, Joseph	X		X		X		X		X		
Wisher, Peter			X	X							X

Appendix D
Outline for Writing a Résumé

RÉSUMÉ

Name and Current Position
Social Security Number
Professional Address and Telephone
Home Address and Telephone
Birth Date

ACADEMIC PREPARATION

Educational Background
Teaching Certificates
Specialized Nondegree Training or Inservice
Areas of Expertise

SALARIED EMPLOYMENT

Teaching Experience
Nonteaching Experience

SERVICE

Offices Held

Editorial and/or Review Work
Committee and/or Board of Directors Work
Volunteer Work (Teaching, coaching, officiating, etc.)
Workshops and Speeches

RESEARCH AND SCHOLARSHIP

Books and Chapters in Books (Published)
Thesis, Dissertation, Papers (Unpublished Works)
Articles in Nonrefereed Journals,
ERIC Publications, Proceedings
Articles in Refereed Journals
Research and/or Papers in Progress

PROFESSIONAL MEMBERSHIPS

CONFERENCES OR MAJOR SPORTS EVENTS ATTENDED

HONORS/SCHOLARSHIPS

TRAVEL

Appendix E

Adapted Physical Education Books (published since 1975)

General Textbooks Used in Adapted Physical Education Courses

Arnheim, D.D., & Sinclair, W.A. (1975). *The clumsy child* (2nd ed.). St. Louis: C.V. Mosby.

Arnheim, D.D., & Sinclair, W.A. (1985). *Physical education for special populations: A developmental, adapted, and remedial approach*. Englewood Cliffs, NJ: Prentice-Hall.

Auxter, D., & Pyfer, J. (1985). *Principles and methods of adapted physical education and recreation* (5th ed.). St. Louis: C.V. Mosby. Fourth edition (1981) was by Crowe, Auxter, and Pyfer. Senior author on other editions was Arnheim.

Clarke, H.H., & Clarke, D.H. (1978). *Developmental and adapted physical education* (2nd ed.). Englewood Cliffs, NJ: Prentice-Hall.

Cratty, B.J. (1975). *Remedial motor activity for children*. Philadelphia: Lea & Febiger.

Cratty, B.J. (1980). *Adapted physical education for children and youth*. Denver: Love.

Daniels, A.S., & Davies, E.A. (1975). *Adapted physical education* (3rd ed.). New York: Harper and Row.

Eichstaedt, C.B., & Kalakian, L.H. (1987). *Developmental/adapted physical education: Making ability count* (2nd ed.). Minneapolis, MN: Burgess.

Fait, H.F., & Dunn, J.M. (1982). *Special physical education: Adapted, corrective, developmental* (5th ed.). Philadelphia: W.B. Saunders.

Folio, M.R. (1985). *Physical education programming for exceptional learners*. Rockville, MD: Aspen Systems Corporation.

French, R.W., & Jansma, P. (1982). *Special physical education*. Columbus, OH: Charles E. Merrill.

Geddes, D. (1978). *Physical activities for individuals with handicapping conditions* (2nd ed.). St. Louis: C.V. Mosby.

Geddes, D. (1981). *Psychomotor individualized education programs for intellectual, learning, and behavioral disabilities*. Boston: Allyn and Bacon.

Groves, L. (Ed.). (1979). *Physical education for special needs*. Cambridge, England: Cambridge University Press.

Gubbay, S. (1975). *The clumsy child*. Philadelphia: W.B. Saunders.

Masters, L.F., Mori, A.A., & Lange, E.K. (1983). *Adapted physical education: A practitioner's guide*. Gaithersburg, MD: Aspen Systems Corporation.

Miller, A.G., & Sullivan, J.V. (1982). *Teaching physical activities to impaired youth*. New York: John Wiley & Sons.

Seaman, J., & DePauw, K. (1982). *The new adapted physical education: A developmental approach*. Palo Alto, CA: Mayfield.

Sherrill, C. (1986). *Adapted physical education and recreation: A multidisciplinary approach* (3rd ed.). Dubuque, IA: Wm. C. Brown.

Vannier, M. (1977). *Physical activities for the handicapped*. Englewood Cliffs, NJ: Prentice-Hall.

Vodola, T. (1976). *Project ACTIVE Maxi-Mini Kit*. Oakhurst, NJ: Township of Ocean School District. Includes nine adapted physical education manuals. Based on Vodola, T. (1973). *Individualized physical education program for the handicapped child*. Englewood Cliffs, NJ: Prentice-Hall.

Wessel, J. (1977). *Planning individualized education programs in special education: With examples from I CAN physical education*. Northbrook, IL: Hubbard.

Wessel, J., & Kelly, L. (1986). *Achievement-based curriculum development in physical education*. Philadelphia: Lea & Febiger.

Wheeler, R.H., & Hooley, A.M. (1976). *Physical education for the handicapped* (2nd ed.). Philadelphia: Lea & Febiger.

Winnick, J.P. (1979). *Early movement experiences and development: Habilitation and remediation*. Philadelphia: W.B. Saunders.

Wiseman, D.C. (1982). *A practical approach to adapted physical education*. Reading, MA: Addison-Wesley.

Specialized Textbooks Used in Specific Adapted Physical Education Courses

Assessment

American Alliance for Health, Physical Education, and Recreation. (no date, circa 1976). *Testing for impaired, disabled, and handicapped individuals*. Washington, DC: Author.

McClenaghan, B., & Gallahue, D. (1978). *Fundamental movement: A developmental and remedial approach*. Philadelphia: W.B. Saunders.

Werder, J., & Kalakian, L. (1985). *Assessment in adapted physical education*. Minneapolis, MN: Burgess.

Winnick, J., & Short, F. (1985). *Physical fitness testing of the disabled: Project UNIQUE*. Champaign, IL: Human Kinetics.

Curriculum and Instruction

Morris, G.S.D. (1980). *Elementary physical education: Toward inclusion.* Salt Lake City: Brighton.

Morris, G.S.D. (1980). *How to change the games children play* (2nd ed.). Minneapolis, MN: Burgess.

Mosston, M. (1981). *Teaching physical education* (2nd ed.). Columbus, OH: Charles E. Merrill. (1st ed., 1966)

Wessel, J., & Kelly, L. (1986). *Achievement-based curriculum development in physical education.* Philadelphia: Lea & Febiger.

Physical Education for Severely Handicapped Students

Dunn, J., Morehouse, J., & Fredericks, H.D.B. (1985). *Physical education for the severely handicapped: A systematic approach to a data based gymnasium* (2nd ed.). Austin: Pro-Ed. (1st ed. Dunn, J., et al. 1980) *A data based gymnasium.* Monmouth, OR: Instructional Development Corporation.

Jansma, P. (Ed.). (1984). *The psychomotor domain and the seriously handicapped* (2nd ed.). Lanham, MD: University Press of America.

Wessel, J. (1981). *I CAN adaptation manual: Teaching physical education to severely handicapped students.* East Lansing, MI: Michigan State University.

Legal, Historical, and Philosophical Foundations, Teacher Training Methodology, and Administration

Appenzeller, H. (1983). *The right to participate: The law and individuals with handicapping conditions in physical education and sports.* Charlottesville, VA: Michie.

Sherrill, C. (Ed.). (1987). *Leadership training in adapted physical education.* Champaign, IL: Human Kinetics.

Research Collections and Readings in Adapted Physical Education and Sport

Berridge, M., & Ward, G. (Eds.). (1986). *International perspectives on adapted physical activity.* Champaign, IL: Human Kinetics.

Eason, R., Smith, T., & Caron, F. (Eds.). (1983). *Adapted physical activity: Proceedings of the Third Symposium of the International Federation of Adapted Physical Activity.* Champaign, IL: Human Kinetics.

McLeish, E. (Ed.). (1985). *Adapted physical activities: Proceedings of the Fourth Symposium of the International Federation of Adapted Physical Activity.* London: Author.

Sherrill, C. (Ed.). (1986). *Sport and disabled athletes.* Champaign, IL: Human Kinetics.

Sports for Disabled Individuals

Adams, R.C., Daniel, A.N., McCubbin, J.A., & Rullman, L. (1982). *Games, sports, and exercises for the physically handicapped* (3rd ed.). Philadelphia: Lea & Febiger.

Guttmann, L. (1976). *Textbook of sport for the disabled.* Aylesbury, England: HM & M.

Sherrill, C. (Ed.). (1986). *Sport and disabled athletes: Proceedings of the International Scientific Congress.* Champaign, IL: Human Kinetics.

Special Olympics, Inc. (1981 on). *Sports skills instructional manuals.* Washington, DC: Author.

Van Hal, L., Rarick, G.L., & Vermeer, A. (1984). *Sport for mentally handicapped: Mentally handicapped sport symposium of The Netherlands—USA Bicentennial.* Haarlem, The Netherlands: Vitgeverij de Vrieseborch. (U.S. distributor is Human Kinetics)

Early Childhood Adapted Physical Education

American Alliance for Health, Physical Education, and Recreation. (1976). *Early intervention for handicapped children through programs of physical education and recreation.* Washington, DC: Author.

Evans, J. (1980). *They have to be carefully taught.* Reston, VA: American Alliance for Health, Physical Education, Recreation, and Dance.

McClenaghan, B., & Gallahue, D. (1978). *Fundamental movement: A developmental and remedial approach.* Philadelphia: W.B. Saunders.

Adapted Physical Education Focusing on One Disability

Adams, R.C., Daniel, A.N., McCubbin, J.A., & Rullman, L. (1982). *Games, sports, and physical exercises for the physically disabled* (3rd ed.). Philadelphia: Lea & Febiger.

Buell, C.E. (1983). *Physical education for blind children* (2nd ed.). Springfield, IL: Charles C. Thomas.

Colvin, N.R., & Finholt, J.M. (1981). *Guidelines for physical educators of mentally handicapped youth: Curriculum, assessment, IEPs.* Springfield, IL: Charles C. Thomas.

Hackett, L. (1975). *Movement exploration and games for the mentally retarded* (5th printing). Palo Alto, CA: Peek.

Moran, J.M., & Kalakian, I.H. (1977). *Movement experiences for the retarded or emotionally disturbed child* (2nd ed.). Minneapolis, MN: Burgess.

Rarick, G.L., Dobbins, D.A., & Broadhead, G.D. (1976). *The motor domain and its correlates in educationally handicapped children*. Englewood Cliffs, NJ: Prentice-Hall.

Appendix F

AAHPERD Publications in Adapted Physical Education (1968-1981)

These primary sources can be found in many university libraries under the Alliance/Association name rather than that of the author or editor, which (in many instances) is not mentioned. With a few exceptions, the author or editor was Dr. Julian Stein, Director of the AAHPER(D) Unit on Programs for the Handicapped, during these years.

Books

1968   Special Fitness Test Manual for Mildly Mentally Retarded Persons

1968   Physical Activities for the Mentally Retarded

1968   Programming for the Mentally Retarded in Physical Education and Recreation

1969   Practical Guide for Teaching the Mentally Retarded to Swim

1971   Best of Challenge, Vol. I

1971   Resource Guide in Sex Education for the Mentally Retarded

1972   Special Olympics Instructional Manual—From Beginners to Champions

1973   Physical Education and Recreation for the Visually Handicapped

1974   Best of Challenge, Vol. II

1974   Challenging Opportunities for Special Populations in Aquatic, Outdoor, and Winter Activities

1975   Annotated Research Bibliography in Physical Education, Recreation, & Psychomotor Function of Mentally Retarded Persons

1975   Motor Fitness Testing Manual for the Moderately Mentally Retarded

1975   Physical Education and Recreation for Impaired, Disabled, and Handicapped Individuals: Past, Present, Future

1975   Physical Education and Recreation for Individuals with Multiple Handicapping Conditions (rev, 1978)

1975   Testing for Impaired, Disabled, and Handicapped Individuals

1976   Aquatic Recreation for the Blind

1976   Adapted Physical Education Guidelines: Theory and Practices for the 70's & 80's

1976   Annotated Listing of Films: Physical Education and Recreation for Impaired, Disabled, and Handicapped Persons, 2nd ed.

1976   Careers in Activity and Therapy Fields

1976   Dance for Physically Disabled Persons: A Manual for Teaching Ballroom, Square and Folk Dances to Users of Wheelchairs and Crutches

1976   Early Intervention for Handicapped Children Through Programs of Physical Education and Recreation

1976   Guide to Information Systems in Physical Education and Recreation for Impaired, Disabled, & Handicapped Persons

1976   Involving Impaired, Disabled, and Handicapped Persons in Regular Camp Programs

1976   Making Workshops Work in Physical Education and Recreation for Special Populations

1976   Physical Activities for Impaired, Disabled, and Handicapped Individuals

1976   Physical Education, Recreation, and Related Programs for Autistic and Emotionally Disturbed Children

1976   Physical Education, Recreation, and Sports for Individuals with Hearing Impairments

1976   Physical Education and Recreation for Cerebral Palsied Individuals

1976   Professional Preparation in Adapted Physical Education, Therapeutic Recreation, and Corrective Therapy

1976   Values of Physical Education, Recreation, and Sports for All

1977   Best of Challenge, Vol. III

1977   Choosing and Using Phonograph Records for Physical Education, Recreation, and Related Activities

1977   Making Physical Education and Recreation Facilities Accessible to All

1977   Materials on Creative Arts for Persons with Handicapping Conditions

1978   Get a Wiggle On: A Booklet to Assist With Blind or Visually Impaired Infants

1978   Move It: A Guide for Helping Visually Handicapped Children Grow

1978   Physical Education and Recreation for Individuals With Multiple Handicapping Conditions: References and Resources

1980   Strokes and Strokes: An Instructor's Manual for Developing Swim Programs for Stroke Victims

1980   Dance for the Handicapped

1980   Individualized Leisure Programs for Disabled Individuals

Periodicals

1965-1970 *Challenge*, a newsletter on physical education and recreation for the handicapped

1968-1970 *Outlook*, a newsletter about physical education and recreation for individuals with all conditions except mental retardation

1970-1982 *IRUC Briefings*, a newsletter resulting from the merger of *Challenge* and *Outlook*

1978-1982 *Practical Pointers*, approximately 60 issues of practical How-To-Do-It publications ranging 10 to 50 pages each

1978	Volume I	14 issues
1979	Volume II	10 issues
1980	Volume III	12 issues
1981	Volume IV	12 issues
1982	Volume V	9 issues

1982-   *Able Bodies*, a newsletter published quarterly. Continued after the closing of the AAHPER(D) Unit on Programs for the Handicapped

Appendix G

Voluntary and Professional Organizations

The following chronology lists events that have influenced the development of voluntary and professional organizations related to adapted physical education.

1847—American Medical Association formed. Shortly thereafter (1849), Elizabeth Blackwell (the first woman doctor in the United States) obtained a medical degree.

1870—National Education Association (NEA) formed by the amalgamation of several education groups.

1876—American Association on Mental Deficiency (AAMD). First president was Edouard Seguin. For detailed history, see Sloan, W., & Stevens, H. (1976). *A century of concern: A history of the American Association on Mental Deficiency.* Washington, DC: AAMD.

1885—Association for the Advancement of Physical Education, the forerunner of AAHPERD, organized. First president was Edward Hitchcock, MD. Many of the early members were physicians. Name changes include American Physical Education Association, 1903; American Association for Health and Physical Education, 1937; American Association for Health, Physical Education, and Recreation, 1938; American Alliance for Health, Physical Education, and Recreation, 1974; American Alliance for Health, Physical Education, Recreation and Dance, 1979. For detailed history, see April 1985 issue of *Journal of Physical Education, Recreation, and Dance.*

1892—American Psychological Association founded.

1896—Revival of Olympic Games from ancient Greek times by Baron Pierre de Coubertin.

1906—Playground Association of America founded. This was the forerunner of the National Recreation and Park Association.

1917—National Society for the Promotion of Occupational Therapy, the forerunner of the American Occupational Therapy Association (1921), formed. Membership included physicians, nurses, social workers, teachers, artists, and a few individuals already employed as occupational therapists. George Edward Barton and William Rush Dunton, respectively, were the first two presidents. Dunton is considered the "father of the profession." For detailed history, see Hopkins, H., & Smith, H. (Eds.). (1983). *Willard and Spackman's Occupational Therapy* (6th ed.). Philadelphia: J.B. Lippincott.

1919—National Easter Seals Society for Crippled Children and Adults founded.

1921—The American Women's Physical Therapeutic Assocation formed, with Mary McMillan as its first president. In 1922, the name was changed to The American Physiotherapy Association. For detailed history of this organization, see January-February 1946 issue of *The Physiotherapy Review.*

1922—The International Council for the Education of Exceptional Children formed, with Elizabeth Farrell as its first president. In 1958 name was changed to The Council for Exceptional Children (CEC). For detailed history of this organization, see November 1976 issue of *Exceptional Children.*

1926—American Academy of Physical Education founded. Founding fathers were Clarke W. Hetherington, R. Tait McKenzie, Thomas A. Story, William H. Burdick, and Jay B. Nash. Election to this prestigious body is one of the highest honors a physical educator may receive.

1938—National Association of State Directors of Special Education (NASDSE) formed.

1938—National Association of Guidance Supervisors (NAGS) formed. In 1960, name was changed to Association for Counselor Education and Supervision (ACES).

1945—American Athletic Association for the Deaf (AAAD). This was the first special population in the United States to form its own sports organization.

1946—Association for Physical and Mental Rehabilitation (APMR) established, the forerunner of American Corrective Therapy Association (ACTA). Name changed to ACTA in 1967. For history, see Davis, J.E. (1967). The historic promise of corrective therapy in American culture. *Journal of the Association for Physical and Mental Rehabilitation,* **21**(2), 48-53. Name of this journal changed in 1967 to *American Corrective Therapy Journal.*

1948—National Foundation for Infantile Paralysis formed by Franklin D. Roosevelt. In 1958, this Foundation became the National Foundation-March of Dimes and turned attention to birth defects and genetic counseling.

1949—National Wheelchair Basketball Association (NWBA) founded. For detailed history, see dissertation by Stan Labanowich, 1975, University of Illinois.

1950—The National Association for Music Therapy, Inc. (NAMT) was formed.

1950—The National Association for Retarded Citizens (NARC) founded. Name changed in 1979 to Association for Retarded Citizens (ARC).

1954—National Council for Accreditation of Teacher Education (NCATE) assumed responsibility for accreditation of physical education training. Previously this had been done by the American Association of Colleges for Teacher Education (AACTE).

1956—National Wheelchair Athletic Association (NWAA) organized. Founder was Ben Lipton.

1964—Association for Children with Learning Disabilities (ACLD) formed. Name changed in 1980 to ACALD, Inc. (An Association for Children and Adults with Learning Disabilities).

1966—American Dance Therapy Association, Inc. (ADTA) founded in New York City. First president was Marian Chace.

1967—National Handicapped Sports and Recreation Association (NHSRA), which governs winter sports, was organized.

1967—National Therapeutic Recreation Society (NTRS) created as a branch of the National Recreation and Park Association.

1968—Special Olympics, Inc., founded.

1968—AAHPER Unit on Programs for the Handicapped replaced the Project on Recreation and Fitness for the Mentally Retarded, which began in 1965.

1973—National Ad Hoc Committee on Physical Education and Recreation for the Handicapped formed by BEH project directors at Minneapolis (AAHPER) conference.

1974—AAHPER was reorganized as the American Alliance for Health, Physical Education, and Recreation with seven independent associations. Three of these included programs for the handicapped: ARAPCS (Association for Research, Administration, Professional Councils and Societies): NASPE (National Association for Sport and Physical Education): and AALR (American Association for Leisure and Recreation).

1974—American Association for the Education of the Severely/Profoundly Handicapped (AAESPH) formed. In 1980 the name of this organization changed to the Association for the Severely Handicapped (TASH) and the title of its journal became *JASH, Journal of Association for Severely Handicapped.*

1975—National Consortium on Physical Education and Recreation for the Handicapped (NCPERH) evolved from National Ad Hoc Committee. First president was Leon Johnson, University of Missouri. For additional information, see April 1986 issue of *Adapted Physical Activity Quarterly.*

1976—United States Association for Blind Athletes (USABA) formed.

1977—International Federation of Adapted Physical Activity founded. First symposium held in Montreal.

1978—National Association of Sports for Cerebral Palsy (NASCP) founded. Name changed in 1987 to United States Cerebral Palsy Athletic Association (UCPAA).

1979—AAHPER's name was officially changed to AAHPERD (American Alliance for Health, Physical Education, Recreation and Dance), thereby giving recognition to dance as a discipline separate from physical education.

1979—The United States Olympic Committee (USOC) organized a Committee for the Handicapped in Sports, with Kathryn Sallade Barclift elected as its first chairperson. This committee brought representatives from the five major sports organizations for handicapped athletes together for the first time. This structure is now called the Committee on Sports for the Disabled (COSD).

1979—National Association for Physical Education in Higher Education (NAPEHE) formed by the merger of the National Association for Physical Education of College Women (founded 1924) and The National College Physical Education Association for Men (founded 1897). Its official publication is *Quest.*

1981—United States Amputee Athletic Association (USAAA) formed.

1984—American Therapeutic Recreation Association, Inc. (ATRA) formed. Prime movers in this split from NTRS were Ira Hutchison and David Park, past executive directors of NTRS. First president was Peg Connolly.

1986—Adapted Physical Activity Council of AAHPERD formed by the merger of NASPE's Adapted Physical Education Academy and ARAPCS's Therapeutic Council. The new structure is housed within ARAPCS. For additional information, see April 1986 issue of *Adapted Physical Activity Quarterly.*

Appendix H

Federal Legislation Impacting on Education, Training, and Research in Adapted Physical Education

Federal legislation affecting adapted physical education is listed in the following chronology. Note that laws derive their numbers from the Congress which passes them. For example, PL 85-926 was the 926th law passed by the 85th Congress.

1958—PL 85-926 was passed, authorizing grants to universities and colleges and to state education agencies for training personnel in mental retardation. This legislation represents the beginning of the federal government's commitment to the rights of handicapped persons.

1963—PL 88-164 amended 1958 legislation to encompass all handicapped groups that require special education.

1964—Civil rights legislation (PL 88-352) passed.

1965—PL 89-10, the Elementary and Secondary Education Act (ESEA), was passed. Included Titles I to IV. Many innovative public school physical education programs, now nationally well known, were funded under Title III (later IVC). Among these programs were Vodola's Project ACTIVE in New Jersey and Long's Project PEOPEL in Arizona.

1965—PL 89-313, Federal Assistance to State Operated and Supported Schools for the Handicapped. This law was cited as the source of statistics and services for persons in state-supported schools and residential centers until 1982, when the Education Consolidation and Improvement Act (ECIA) was implemented.

1966—PL 89-750 created the Bureau of Education for the Handicapped (BEH) within the Office of Education of HEW. BEH, which became the Office of Special Education (OSE) in 1980, has been the agency that funds university training programs in physical education and recreation for the handicapped.

1967—PL 90-170, Title V, Section 502, amended ESEA to support training, research, and demonstration projects specifically in physical education and recreation for the handicapped. This was part of the Mental Retardation Amendments originally supported by Senator Edward Kennedy and signed by President Lyndon B. Johnson.

1968—PL 90-480, Elimination of Architectural Barriers to Physically Handicapped, passed. This was the first federal legislation pertaining to architectural barriers.

1970—PL 91-230, Title VI, Education of the Handicapped Act (EHA), passed. This was the first major legislation leading to the subsequent passage of PL 94-142 in 1975.

1972—Title IX legislation (PL 92-318) passed.

1973—PL 93-112, the Rehabilitation Amendments, completely recodified the old Vocational Rehabilitation Act and placed emphasis upon expanding services to more severely handicapped clients. Section 504, the "nondiscrimination clause," which specified that no qualified handicapped person shall be excluded from federally assisted programs or activities, is the best known part of the law. PL 93-112 was not implemented, however, until 1977, when its rules and regulations were agreed upon and published in the May 4, 1977, issue of the *Federal Register*.

1975—PL 94-142 enacted. This is now considered Part B of EHA legislation. Called the "Education for All Handicapped Children Act," it stated specifically that *instruction in physical education* shall be provided for all handicapped children. PL 94-142 was not implemented until 1977 when its rules and regulations were published in the August 23 issue of the *Federal Register*.

1977—PL 95-49 enacted. This was a reauthorization of PL 91-230 (EHA) and provided for the continued funding of special education training, including physical education and recreation.

1978—PL 95-602, the Developmentally Disabled (DD) Assistance and Bill of Rights Act was passed, updating DD legislation of 1970 and 1975.

1978—PL 95-606, the Amateur Sports Act, recognized the sports organizations of disabled athletes as part of the United States Olympic Committee structure.

1979—PL 96-88 changed the status of the old United States Office of Education within HEW to a Department of Education. Shirley M. Hufstedler was appointed its first Secretary. HEW was disbanded.

1980—Reorganization was completed for the two new departments replacing HEW. These new structures are the Department of Education (ED) and the Department of Health and Human Services (HHS). Within ED's seven principal program offices, the Office of Special Education and Rehabilitative Services (OSERS) relates to the handicapped. Principal components of OSERS are Office of Special Education (OSE), which replaces BEH; Rehabilitation Services Administration (RSA); and National Institute of Handicapped Research.

1981—PL 97-35, The Education Consolidation and Improvement Act. This law affected ESEA grants like Project ACTIVE. It represented a major shift in education policy from categorical to block funding.

1983—PL 98-199, The Education of the Handicapped Act (EHA) Amendments of 1983. This law extended the authorizations of appropriations for all of the EHA discretionary programs through 1986. Whereas previous laws had listed physical education and recreation as independent discretionary programs, PL 98-199 did not.

1985—PL 99-177, the Gramm-Rudman-Hollings Deficit Control Amendment signed to end the federal budget deficit by providing automatic across-the-board cuts in federal programs over a 5-yr period.

1986—PL 99-457, The Education of the Handicapped Act (EHA) Amendments of 1986. This law extended the authorizations of EHA appropriations for the next 3 years.

1986—PL 99-372, Handicapped Children's Protection Act, passed.

Appendix I
Example of a Written Committee Report

The committee report listed in this appendix is provided for two purposes: (a) to serve as a model for other committee chairpersons to follow when writing a report, and (b) to provide the text of an important action by AAHPERD regarding therapeutics/adapted physical education.

Complete Text of the Report[1]

Based upon the charge given by Alliance President, Wayne Osness, in a letter dated June 22, 1983, the Coordinating Committee for Programs on Special Populations met at Oregon State University, Corvallis, on September 23-25, 1983. All members of the Committee were present.

During the three day meeting, the Committee reviewed the charge and held open and indepth discussions. This report addresses each of the four charges as listed below:

1. Review current activities of the Alliance relating to professionals working with special populations.

2. Study possible duplication of services and unmet needs as presently experienced within the Alliance for this group of professionals.

3. Recommend the most effective structure/governance within the Alliance that will meet the needs of these professionals. Consider the overall structure and mission of the Alliance, and remain consistent with the resources available to other similar structures.

4. The Committee is to select its own Chair and report to the Executive Committee prior to February 1, 1984. The report will then be presented to the Board in Anaheim with Executive Committee recommendations.

Recognizing the sensitivity and complexity of the issues facing the Committee, the following guiding principles served as the basis for discussion and recommendations:

1. That the best interests of the members of the Alliance are paramount.

2. That the best interests of the structure and mission of the Alliance are important.

3. That a posture of professional advocacy for programs for special populations is essential.

4. That the Unit on Programs for the Handicapped has provided outstanding leadership and vital service to

our membership and profession, and that selected services be retained.

As a basis for our recommendations, the Committee undertook a close and extensive review of existing Alliance structures, the charge of each, and their corresponding programs and activities: Alliance documents including a historical report on the Unit on Programs for the Handicapped, reports from the Adapted Physical Education Academy and Therapeutics Council, letters and correspondence; and a discussion of the impact that the Unit on Programs for the Handicapped has had upon the significant leadership role that the Alliance has achieved over the past 17 years.

In a period of acute economic shortfalls, it is encumbent upon the Alliance and strongly felt by this Committee that efficiency in providing services for special populations can only be affected by a thorough review of services. The programs, projects, and activities currently conducted for professionals serving special populations include, but are not limited to, the following:

1. Disseminate information about and for disabled populations.

2. Sponsor conferences, meetings, symposia, workshops, and demonstrations on physical education, recreation, and dance for the handicapped.

3. Propose guidelines on the professional preparation of specialists.

4. Plan and implement meetings and activities related to the national convention (program sessions, indepth workshops, drop-in centers, demonstrations, socials, etc.).

5. Coordinate with other professionals, associations, and societies which serve special populations.

6. Recognize and promote leaders who have served populations with special needs.

7. Promote programs and services through state and district associations.

8. Solicit and review articles submitted to *JOPERD* and other Alliance periodicals.

9. Establish advisory boards.

10. Solicit and review manuscripts for publication by the Alliance.

The Committee reviewed the tasks fulfilled by the Unit on Programs for the Handicapped. The Unit is to be recognized for the unique and meritorious services that it has contributed to the profession and the prominence

---

[1]From J. Dunn (1984, May) Merger. *Able Bodies,* **3**(2), 1, 7.

that it has brought to the Alliance, both nationally and internationally. Listed below are those activities which the Unit has fulfilled:

1. Solicit, edit, and author manuscripts specific to programs and activities for the handicapped.

2. Solicit a regular column for publication in *JOPERD* and *UPDATE*.

3. Enhance the visibility of the Alliance through its services and commitment to the disabled.

4. Serve as a clearinghouse on information about programs and activities for the disabled.

5. Submit grants and contracts for external funds.

6. Provide direct services on the special needs of handicapped persons to professionals throughout the United States.

7. Solicit nominations for the Alliance Chavin Memorial Award.

8. Serve as a consultant to professionals and organizations nationally and internationally.

9. Promote cooperation and leadership with other Alliance structures.

10. Solicit and review articles submitted to Alliance publications.

11. Monitor legislation concerning programs for special populations.

12. Present information on Alliance concerns at hearings, conventions, and workshops about special populations.

13. Plan programs for presentation at the national convention.

The primary unmet need at this time as identified by the Committee is the coordination and communication among those structures providing services/sponsoring activities for those working with special populations.

Our review suggests that duplication is evident in the type of programs/activities offered by the four associations (ARAPCS, AALR, NASPE, NDA). This problem can be remedied by closer coordination in program planning. A solution for this problem is suggested in the recommendations. A more serious problem exists, however, in the duplication of activities sponsored by the Therapeutics Council and the Adapted Physical Education Academy. It is evident to the Committee that a clear distinction between the missions of these two organizations is difficult to discern.

Given the Alliance Board's action relative to the Unit on Programs for the Handicapped, it is apparent to the Committee that the activities sponsored by the Unit must be assumed by those currently involved in providing services for the handicapped. Since some of the activities are unique and broad-based, they can best be accommodated by a structure which incorporates the needs of various associations. This is essential to eliminate creating a void which would lead to further unmet needs.

Keeping in mind the guiding principles, the extensive/exhaustive review, and Committee deliberations, the following recommendations are presented as unanimously agreed upon by the Committee.

Recommendations:

1. A Commission on "Service for the Disabled" be established.

2. The Therapeutics Council and Adapted Physical Education Academy be merged into one structure.

Rationale for First Recommendation

The Committee believes that it is essential that selected activities which are shared among the associations be managed through the Commission. The Committee believes that the Commission is essential to ensure that services for the disabled will be efficiently and effectively provided. Furthermore, the Commission will assist the Alliance maintain its visibility as an organization which has and will continue to serve the disabled. The Commission will assume some responsibilities which have been provided by the Unit on Programs for the Handicapped. These initially will include: publication of a newsletter, i.e., *ABLE BODIES*, and the coordination of convention program planning. Other activities as assigned by the associations will be considered and pursued, where appropriate. Acceptance of this responsibility will be shared by the associations through the Commission. A budget of $6,500 per year is necessary to assist the Commission provide services related to disabled populations which historically have been encouraged and fostered by AAHPERD. These funds will be used to procure secretarial assistance, purchase supplies, cover mailing and duplication costs, and publish *ABLE BODIES*. The Committee recommeds that AAHPERD funds be allocated for a period of three to five years after which time the Commission's activities would be expected to be self-supporting. *ABLE BODIES* is now disseminated to approximately 4,000 members. Reports indicate that the newsletter is well received and viewed as a significant instrument for informing members of Alliance activities and current professional programs, events, trends, and developments. Associated benefits of the publication include enhancing the image of the Alliance and serving to maintain and encourage membership.

The Commission will be composed of representatives selected by the substructures of the respective associations involved and other structures who may wish to be included. Operating guidelines will be developed by the Commission. The Committee recommends that the Commission be reviewed by the board of Governors during its third year of operation.

Rationale for Second Recommendation

The merger of the Adapted Physical Education Academy and the Therapeutics Council is seen as a positive step toward the elimination of duplication of services. The Committee was impressed with the extensive list of the services provided by the Therapeutics Council and the Adapted Physical Education Academy, but found it difficult to separate out unique function and responsibility of the two structures. Duplications of services and professional efforts cannot be justified in light of the need for comprehensive and coordinated service for disabled populations. The merger of these two structures is justified for the following reasons:

1. The merger of the two structures will more clearly communicate to the membership the close and interrelated relationship between adapted physical education and therapeutic services. Furthermore, a combined structure will allow for the coordination of activities and services, and at the same time. The two structures have maintained an informal relationship in which leaders and members have been commonly shared.

2. Convention program planning would be coordinated to ensure efficient use of program slots and to avoid duplication and overlap. Although good relationships exist now between the structures, a merger would minimize confusion on the part of AAHPERD or program providers.

3. Eliminate confusion on the part of AAHPERD members as to perceived and real differences between the structures. The Committee was unable to discern "real" differences between the intent and primary purpose of the two.

4. Promote coordinated services and leadership to members who are interested in providing quality human movement experiences for disabled individuals. The present system does not allow for the efficient use of the intent and strength of AAHPERD members in addressing the needs of disabled persons.

The Committee recognized that a merger of the Adapted Physical Education Academy and the Therapeutics Council will be accepted by the 4,000 Alliance members who have identified with the two structures only if assurance is made that the quality and level of service which have historically been provided do not decrease. For this reason, the Committee recommends the following:

1. All services previously performed by the two separate groups be offered through the merged organization. This would involve sponsorship of 6-8 programs at the annual convention.

2. The merged structure should utilize a leadership structure with elected officials, similar to that now employed by the Adapted Physical Education Academy and Therapeutics Council.

3. The merged structure should be housed in the association which provides evidence to the Board of Governors that it can best respond to the needs of the members of the structure. Consideration should be given to the association's commitment, financial support, and proposed organization for the merged structure. It is essential that a financial basis be proposed which recognizes the large numbers of members who identify with special populations and that consideration be given to an organizational plan which allows for visibility within and outside of AAHPERD.

4. The decision as to which association the merged structure should be housed in is to be determined by the Board of Governors after reviewing the proposed plans submitted by the associations and seeking input from the affected membership.

The Committee recognizes that the recommendations offered in this report will be justified only if the Committee, the Executive Committee, and the Board of Governors work together to ensure Alliance members that the services and activities provided by AAHPERD will be enhanced and not eroded through the implementation of these recommendations. Without an appropriate structure with sufficient visibility and resources to assist members to provide needed services, we fear that an erosion in membership is probable. We believe that AAHPERD has a record of service to the disabled of which it can justifiably be proud. We believe that if our recommendations are reviewed carefully and discussed from the perspective of the members and the disabled persons they wish to serve, the AAHPERD's commitment to the disabled will be ensured for many years to come.

Future Directions

The report and subsequent actions taken by the Board requires that two major issues be resolved prior to the 1985 Convention in Atlanta. First, in what AAHPERD structure should the substructure created by the merger of the Adapted Academy and the Therapeutics Council be placed? The Committee report identifies criteria by which this decision should be made. The underlying premise is that the decision should be consistent with the approximately 4,000 affected members' needs and perceptions as to which structure offers the most desirable plan. Second, how will the Committee on Programs for the Disabled function? A committee composed of representatives of the various structures will be appointed soon by President Bea Orr to undertake the task of developing operating procedures and guidelines for the Committee.

In reading the report and reviewing the action of the Board of Governors, it is clear that the future direction of programs for the handicapped rests with the AAHPERD members who are committed to special populations. The opportunity now exists for the affected members to be united in their efforts to coordinate services, develop programs, and communicate with AAHPERD leaders the importance of programs which respond to all segments of society, including the disabled. In essence, the quality of programs and services provided for special populations through AAHPERD will be dependent upon the talent, energy, and commitment of adapted physical education professionals. We have the opportunity to determine our future as a professional society. The Committee for Programs on Special Populations and others have indicated their confidence in our ability to accept this responsibility. As concerned professionals, we must unite in our effort to ensure that AAHPERD's commitment to programs for the disabled continues to grow and flourish within this new organizational realignment.

Comments on the report should be forwarded to:

John M. Dunn, Chair,
Coordinating Committee for Programs on Special
  Populations
Langton Hall 214
Oregon State University
Corvallis, OR 97331.

Appendix J
Sample Letter
to Congressperson

THE UNIVERSITY OF IOWA

IOWA CITY, IOWA 52242

Recreation Education Program
Area 319: 353-4989

November 20, 1974

Congressman Ed Mezvinsky
1404 LHOB
Washington, D.C.

Dear Congressman Mezvinsky:

Enclosed is an announcement which describes the Bureau of Education for the handicapped <u>Physical Education and Recreation Program.</u>

We now have seven years experience with this program. The Program has been the only means of stimulating and supporting development in recreation for handicapped children. Through this program some 300 graduate students are currently in training at some 40 universities in 20 states. Over 100 graduate each year and with few exceptions they take positions in schools, agencies, community programs and institutions where they open up new programs and services.

This program has provided the only Federal support for research and demonstration that we have in physical education and recreation for handicapped children. This research is currently contributing significantly to our ability to educate and rehabilitate for total living.

However, the fact is that nationally no more than 10 per cent of school age handicapped children are receiving physical education and recreation services. Our national priorities <u>must include</u> letting handicapped children have a chance to live full and complete lives including play (just for the fun of it like other kids), <u>must include</u> providing physical education and recreation as a means to achieve cognitive, physical and affective growth and development, and <u>must include</u> providing opportunity for the ill and handicapped to participate in the nation's recreational, cultural, park and leisure opportunities.

Part of the price that Mr. Average American pays in his-and-her consumption of $250 billion annually in recreation and leisure goods and services is the denial of even one penny a year to give the ill and handicapped a chance to participate in recreation the way the able-bodied do.

As this nation prepares to celebrate its 200th anniversary spending $200 million many times over for the celebration, be assured that not even 10 percent of these Bicentennial events will include the ill and handicapped. We know the reasons that the public rejects involvement of the ill and handicapped - ignorance, prejudice, fear. Thus, it is incumbent on our humanitarian leaders to provide for these children and youth.

-2-

The BEH Physical Education and Recreation Program now receives $1.5 million a year for training and $350,000 a year for research. This designated $1.85 million amount is approximately .5 percent of the Bureau's budget of $295 million.

Although the PER Program was authorized to receive $10 million for the first three years, it received only $2 million, or about one-fifth of what was needed. It has continued to operate at a one-fifth level. As a result, the existing projects are underfunded and in dire need of increased support. Further, only 23 states are receiving any assistance. States with great need are not funded and thus are falling farther behind each year in meeting the physical education and recreation needs of their handicapped children.

I appeal to you for your intervention and support of the following:

The authorization and appropriation of $10 million for FY 1975-76 to be added to the Bureau of Education for the Handicapped budget; these funds to be expended for training, $5 million; research and demonstration, $5 million. And, that guidelines for the administration of these funds for both training and research/demonstration be developed through the assistance of the Congressionally authorized National Advisory Committee on Physical Education and Recreation for Handicapped Children. This must not decrease the overall funding for the Bureau's other programs which are now quite underfunded.

Handicapped children and youth, their parents and friends, and the professional rehabilitation community in Iowa and throughout the nation shall deeply appreciate every assistance that you can provide. I know that without your help now that literally millions of handicapped children will be denied the human and social and civil and educational right to physical education and recreation.

Yours, in service to the handicapped.

Sincerely,

John A. Nesbitt, Chairman
Recreation Education Program

JAN/ls

Appendix K
The Golden Rule and Eleven Cardinal Principles of Grant Application Writing

John Nesbitt

University teachers in adapted physical education and therapeutic recreation are often expected to possess competencies in grant writing and management. Since 1967, grant money to fund personnel preparation programs in physical education and recreation for the handicapped has been available through the Bureau of Education for the Handicapped (now called Special Education Programs) in Washington, DC. The general principles to follow in preparing a grant proposal are similar for federal agencies, state programs, and private organizations or foundations. A general rule for grant writing and eleven principles that are important for successful grant writing are discussed in the following sections.

"Golden Rule" of Grant Application Writing

The key to successful grant application writing, whether initiated by an academic department, recreation department, or service agency, is to have a sound program planned for which the grant is written. This "Golden Rule" of program soundness may be stated as follows:

> The substantive planning, research, assessment, and creative conceptualization of a new or better way to deliver service and the actual writing of the proposal should be so sound from professional, scientific, and scholarly points of view that when the process is completed, the external support desired will be secondary to the actual programmatic progress that has already been made. *The agency, institution, or community should be ready to go ahead with or without external support.* If this is not the case, then the grant application preparation has not been done adequately.

Cardinal Principle No. 1: Read the Instructions

One of the first failings in writing grant applications is the penchant that writers have for not reading the instructions, guidelines, agency policies, *Federal Register* statements, legislative reports, and other paraphernalia that come with the packet from the grant agency. Writers can save themselves work, frustration, and money by reading as thoroughly as possible all the information that is provided.

Cardinal Principle No. 2: Consult Others Who Have Received Grants

In general, grant writers can expect to receive assistance from other grant writers who have preceded them in the process. Some will be generous with time and materials; others will be stingy. That is simply the way things are. However, if the grant writer perseveres, he or she probably will be able to obtain assistance from colleagues and associates.

Cardinal Principle No. 3: Get Acquainted With Agency and Project Staff

Whether making application to a federal or state agency, an association or organization, or an educational institution or foundation, the grant writer will be well advised to seek out opportunities to meet staff who are charged with the responsibility of administering the grant program. The aim of getting acquainted is not to seek favors. (Anyone who approaches the granting agency with favor seeking in mind can anticipate disappointment.) The aim is to humanize the process, to improve communication, and to increase understanding.

Cardinal Principle No. 4: Use or Develop Grant Writing Competencies

The fourth principle is to develop grant writing competencies. Ultimately, grant management competencies will be needed, but to start, one needs skill in grant writing.

What are the competencies needed to write grant applications for submission to federal agencies, foundations, private associations, or university committees? Where are these competencies learned and practiced? Too often, detractors of the grant system and grant writing talk about proposals using terms such as "grantsmanship." This term misleads people and potential application writers.

Many writers of grant applications learned their skills by conducting research and writing reports for their master's theses and doctoral dissertations. To these competencies were added competencies in program and curriculum design and evaluation.

Lacking this type of learning experience, writers may take advantage of special courses and seminars where the competencies are taught. In addition, more than 100 books and booklets on the subject of program development and application writing may be consulted. No one of these books has all the answers, but a visit to a well-stocked development office will give any prospective writer access to half a dozen different volumes that will answer most of the general questions. Many universities and cities have development offices. Of course, the on-the-job experience of learning while doing is possible but is not without its pitfalls and frustrations. Competencies that are used in research provide excellent learning for planning and writing grant applications. However, competition for support funds is always intense. The application is the means of competing with other individuals and disciplines for some portion of funds. Whenever one receives funds, at least nine others have been denied funds. To win over nine other applicants, an application must be highly competitive. The application must demonstrate that the writer can do the best job in solving the most important problem.

Cardinal Principle No. 5: Write Competent Statements of Need and Secure Supportive Letters

Most applications contain general statements about the field, the problems or needs being addressed, and reviews of the literature. In providing these, the writer should present an authoritative discourse. This discourse would be similar in form to an intensive review of the literature. The discourse should reflect the status (state of the art) of the problem or need at the national, regional, state, and local levels. Obviously, it should demonstrate a keen awareness of historical background as well as current trends and patterns, anticipated trends and patterns, controversies or conflicting schools of thought. The reader of applications will be particularly interested in the insights (conventional or innovative) and the general and specific strategies to meet needs and solve problems proposed by the writer.

When general statements (e.g., reviews of the literature) are written with such poor quality that they would not be approved in a master's thesis level review of the literature, the lack of knowledge suggested by the statements is apparent to the nonspecialization reader as well as the specialization reader. For example, an entire departmental faculty submitted a research proposal in which the hypothesis/problem was buried at the end of the proposal in a paragraph entitled, "General Background." A panel of five evaluators spent 45 minutes dissecting the proposal looking for the problem. Foremost, basic

scholarly and scientific processes and competencies should be demonstrated.

The application for support should demonstrate professional knowledge of the field in terms of professional literature, status of research, status of program and service delivery, status of professional standards for personnel, service and training, and status of legislation and public programs. To nonspecialization and specialization readers, many of the applications for grants betray various gaps in professional knowledge of the writers. What is desired is a comprehensive, insightful, illuminating review that inspires the evaluators' confidence that the proposer is going to attack problems and needs in a forceful manner which will solve quandaries and meet people's needs. Too often the submitted proposal suggests that the proposer has written an incomplete and inconclusive annotated bibliography that was obtained by rummaging through a pile of miscellaneous articles and reports at the bottom of the bookshelf.

Grant application writers should anticipate that readers will not be misled by the illusion of support. The letter that contains a concrete offer of time, money, personnel, facilities, equipment, materials, and services will result in positive ratings of institutional support. By contrast, letters that suggest support but provide only vague reference to what will actually be provided will result in skepticism.

Letters of support should not be confused with letters indicating endorsement and assurance of cooperation. Letters of endorsement from appropriate officials tell readers that the necessary support has been obtained. Further, letters assuring cooperation tell readers that broader community involvement in the project will be provided and that a larger community will, in turn, benefit from the project.

Cardinal Principle No. 6: Use Competency-Based and Discrepancy Evaluation Methods

In terms of general curriculum competence, every teacher-educator reader will have extensive training and experience in curriculum development, evaluation of curriculum, and research on curriculum. Thus these teacher-educator readers have a keen awareness of structure, processes, resources, and procedures that compose strong curricula. Special education delivers some of the best teacher preparation provided in the United States. Any application, particularly a recreation or physical education application, that does not meet high standards of design will be rated poorly. Because there is always a shortage of funds, only those applications with high ratings can expect funding.

A perfect system of education may never exist. However, for professional disciplines such as special education, adapted physical education, therapeutic recreation service, and the helping disciplines, competency-based instruction comes as close to achieving organized education's potential as any system devised. The discrepancy evaluation system that has been encouraged by the U.S. Department of Education is one of the best systems for evaluation being used in the United States today. The writer who demonstrates strong capability in competency-based instruction and in discrepancy evaluation can anticipate high ratings on those components of the proposal.

Cardinal Principle No. 7: Secure Real Support

Many federal grant applications include the requirement of evidence of real and substantive support from a parent institution, community, or state that will receive the grant. Often the grant requirements are for increasing levels of support from the parent institution or state or community. Generally, this support is demonstrated through letters of support that are included with the grant application.

The problem with this aspect of grant application preparation is that may institutions are reluctant to provide the basic, continuing, or increasing support that is required by the grant agency. Thus, in lieu of actual support, institutions and agencies write letters that intimate or suggest support and assistance. The techniques used in some of these letters are skillful. Reading the letter, one can almost "feel" the support. But, in fact, the support is not there nor will it be there in the future. The final resolution of the problem is that when the federal funding terminates, so does the program or service.

Individuals and panels who review proposals for funding agencies quickly gain skill in discerning between writers who promise program support from their institution and those who can deliver it. To ascertain that colleges, universities, and agencies fulfill their promises, federal agencies call for quarterly reports on program delivery, strong evaluation designs, and proposals that clearly state expected outcomes, anticipated results, and methods of disseminating results.

Cardinal Principle No. 8: Report Fully and Widely

When projects involving research, program development, curriculum development, and so forth take place at public expense, the persons and agencies receiving funds for these various projects should make every possible effort to disseminate the new findings and insights as widely as possible. The benefits of widely disseminating new information are obvious: Institutions and agencies will be better able to serve more people more effectively.

The federal agency requirement of reporting is fully justified. If anything, more frequent reporting should be called for and reports should be disseminated more widely. Thus the proposal writer should anticipate providing wide dissemination of clear, concise, substantive reports.

Cardinal Principle No. 9: Write for Evaluators Outside Area of Specialization

Application writers should be alerted to the fact that their proposal will be evaluated by professional personnel outside their areas of specialization. Thus the proposal must be written in a manner that will communicate effectively to scholars, researchers, curriculum specialists, disability specialists, and academic administrators from other disciplines and professions. Writers must recognize that physical education and recreation service has a low priority in any agency devoted solely to education. They must design their program plan with this in mind and write the application accordingly.

Nonspecialization readers will be aware that they do not have background on the specifics in physical education and recreation service. Thus they will be reserved in judging certain aspects of an application. However, nonspecialization readers will be particularly alert to anything contained in the application that relates to their area of specialization. For example, specialists in mental retardation will evaluate critically anything that relates directly or indirectly to mental retardation. The evaluation that the reader makes on one section can influence his or her evaluation of an entire application.

When a proposal indicates that university students will be prepared to serve all disease and disability groups, then the specialist in mental retardation will be very interested in exactly the means that will be used to provide training that will ultimately benefit the student who is retarded. Grant writers should anticipate that they may be writing for readers who are not entirely favorable to their disciplines or who may be more favorable to other services and other disciplines.

Cardinal Principle No. 10: Plan and Work Well in Advance of Deadlines

Generally, the novice grant application writer fails to plan far enough ahead and fails to work on particular tasks far enough in advance of the deadline for submission of a given application. A grant application writer should anticipate submission of an application 1 to 2 years in advance of the deadline. This will allow for the orderly planning and completion of tasks within a reasonable time frame. Like any long-range project, the completion of a reasonable number of tasks each week over an extended period of time will ultimately result in a completed project.

Many aspects of grant application preparation cannot be rushed. Internally, other individuals or units must be informed, and advice as well as concurrence must be obtained; this takes time. Externally, agencies and organizations need time to consider whether they wish to cooperate with a project and how they might cooperate. Time is required for library research, to request information and materials, to obtain advice either through personal consultation or correspondence. In general, the grant writer who undertakes preparation of an application in a limited amount of time before the deadline will find the experience so demanding and frustrating that he or she will be disinclined ever to be involved in grant writing again.

Cardinal Principle No. 11: Present a Sound Budget

The interests of the project will be best served if a sound, realistic, complete, tight, and substantiated budget is presented with the grant application. Proposers should be alerted to the pitfalls of ''proposal budget padding.'' The proposal evaluation is carried on by people who are trained and experienced in curriculum and program development and delivery. They have reviewed 100 to 250 proposals ranging from 25 pages for $5,000 to 500 pages for $5 million. Readers have a thorough awareness of the costs of curriculum development and delivery. ''Haggling'' (i.e., asking for $500 in supplies in the hope of negotiating $250) undermines the credibility of the proposal. The writer should know precisely how much it costs to do the job and propose exactly that, no more and no less. Evaluators want to believe every word of a proposal because the approved, negotiated proposal becomes a contract of authorization (i.e., money awarded for services to be provided and ''products'' that will be delivered).

Another undesirable feature in a budget is travel that is not justified (e.g., the proposer writes simply, ''Travel—$500''). If travel is needed, explain why. What work will be done? What report will result? What benefit to the program will result? What clearly defined objectives or goals will be achieved and what ''product'' will result?

In general, a budget built from the bottom up in which every known cost is related to achievement of specific project or program objectives is most desirable. Generalizations about supplies, travel, support personnel, and so on are not helpful to evaluators who are acutely aware of the limited funds available.

Conclusion

The ''Golden Rule'' and eleven principles of grant application writing are obviously only a few features for consideration. Grant planning, writing, and management involve a complex series of processes and functions. However, the novice grant writer may find some of the previous discussions to be helpful in the initial stages of his or her grant writing career.

Many aspects of grant writing and management discourage persons from becoming involved. Grant writers automatically add a number of deadlines to their work agendas. Grant writers present themselves to be judged by a panel of specialists. Very few people seek opportunities to take tests, to have their work evaluated, and to be criticized. Additionally, the grant writer, who becomes grant manager, is confronted with a number of management tasks (e.g., personnel, finances, and scheduling in the day-to-day job). Ultimately, the success of the project may rest on the managerial skills of the grant writer.

Why, then, would one want to undertake the grant writing job? Grants for training, special projects, research, demonstration, and other types of innovation are among the foremost means that we have to solve some of the problems that confront people who are disabled. It may be possible through grants of various kinds to make life better for more people.

The grant application writing process may couple one's personal sense of responsibility with one's best professional, scientific, or scholarly skills to the goal of solving the attitudinal, architectural, and aspirational barriers confronting people who are disabled. Achieving these goals is worth the effort.

Editor's Note

For further assistance with grant writing, consult *How to Write and Process a Competitive Grant Proposal* by Thomas Vodola, published by VEE, Inc., P.O. Box 2093, Neptune City, New Jersey 07753. It may also be helpful to associate yourself with other grant writers by joining the National Consortium on Physical Education and Recreation for the Handicapped (see chapter 4). Individuals in the Office of Special Education Programs, U.S. Department of Education, Washington, DC (area code 202-732-1037) are also good resources. When telephoning, ask for the physical education/recreation advocate or consultant.

Author Index

Abelson, A., 87
Abt, C., 380, 381, 382
Adams, K.O., 277–278
Adams, R.C., 305
Adamson, G., 53
Ajzen, I., 232
Alkin, M., 136
Allen, J., 279
Aloia, G., 278
Ames, L.B., 273
Anderson, D.W., 290
Anderson, H.H., 374
Anderson, J., 68
Anderson, W., 26, 65
Anooshian, V.B., 44
Appel, M., 75, 77
Appenzeller, H., 55, 182, 183
Arnheim, D., 47, 51, 55, 97, 305
Aufsesser, P., 70
Austin, D., 71, 274
Auxter, D., 10, 39, 46, 47, 51, 55, 70,
    75, 77, 97, 100, 136, 196, 212, 266,
    271
Baber, D.J., 114
Bailey, W., 271
Baker, E., 130, 383
Baker, J., 342
Bales, C.F., 374
Ball, E., 73
Ball, T.S., 271
Balow, B., 89
Bancroft, J., 30, 65
Barker, R., 200, 218, 219, 334
Barlow, D.A., 390
Barr, M.W., 29
Barrow, H., 170
Barsch, R., 48, 212, 215
Bascom, F., 68
Bass, B., 165
Baumeister, A., 351, 352
Beaver, D., 56, 82, 121
Bechtold, W., 376
Belknap, H., 68
Bellamy, T., 367
Bell, T., 89
Belmont, J.M., 353
Berkson, G., 355
Berridge, M.E., 83
Berrol, C., 271
Berryman, D., 73
Beuter, A., 271
Bird, P., 51, 53, 403
Bitcon, C., 435
Bloom, B., 11–16, 125–126, 128, 129,
    130
Bobbitt, F., 128
Bollesen, C., 18, 295
Bonatis, G., 57
Borkowski, J.G., 353

Boswell, B., 57
Bowers, L., 37, 46, 48, 51, 58, 73, 74,
    77, 90, 91, 97, 276, 277
Boyce, B.A., 391
Boynton, B., 66
Boysen, J.P., 390
Brace, D., 34, 39, 44, 46, 48
Brackett, E.G., 30
Bredemier, M.F., 383
Brigance, A., 175, 176
Brimm, J., 404
Broadhead, G.D., 9, 52, 56, 86, 120,
    121
Brown, A.L., 353
Brown, C., 128
Brown, J., 269
Brown, L.M., 68
Brown, V., 18
Browning, R., 11
Broxterman, J., 209
Bruininks, R., 56, 172, 175, 176
Bruner, J., 208
Bruton, G., 18
Buell, C., 29, 34, 51, 97, 221, 305
Bullock, C., 77
Bundschuh, E., 3, 37, 38, 51, 56, 70,
    77, 78, 293, 294, 303
Bunker, L.K., 425
Burnette, W., 96
Burns, R.W., 130
Burrello, L., 403
Butterfield, E.C., 353
Campbell, J., 281
Carlson, R.B., 48, 70, 121
Carmichael, L., 155
Caron, F., 83
Carter, J.L., 269
Carter, K., 274
Cassidy, R., 128
Caswell, R., 82
Centers, L., 271
Chasey, W., 51, 70, 77, 78, 153, 228,
    230, 235, 269, 271, 353, 354
Chavez, R., 37
Cheffers, J.T.F., 374
Churton, M., 57, 70, 77, 79, 91, 100,
    200, 203
Cipani, E., 425
Cizek, R., 71
Clarke, D., 24, 26, 36, 39, 305
Clarke, H.H., 24, 26, 33–36, 38–40, 66,
    68, 305
Clausen, J., 355
Clelland, R., 53, 291
Clemmons, A., 157
Cohn, E., 142–144
Colestock, C., 30–31, 65
Colvin, N.R., 305
Compton, D., 77, 100

Conant, J.B., 67
Connor, H., 70
Cooper, H., 30–31
Cooper, P., 294
Cooper, W., 51
Copeland, A., 82
Cordellos, H., 51, 221, 419
Corder, W., 38, 269, 277
Coscarelli, M., 95
Cowden, J., 59, 70, 71, 228, 229, 231,
    238, 403
Cratty, B.J., 7, 49, 55, 213, 271, 272,
    274, 305
Cristaldi, J., 36
Crowe, W., 47, 136
Cruickshank, W., 48, 49, 212, 215
Crumbliss, K., 274
Cyphers, V., 44
DaBramo, E., 293
Daniel, A., 97
Daniels, A., 24, 26, 33, 34, 35, 38–40,
    66, 67, 305
Darling, R., 221
Darst, P.W., 375, 377
Davies, E., 24, 26, 32, 33, 34, 40, 47,
    51, 55, 67, 291
Davis, E., 69
Davis, R., 56, 387
Davis, W., 213
DeBonis, E., 46, 73, 75, 90
Delacato, C., 212, 215
DeOreo, K., 196, 213
DePauw, K., 2, 3, 7, 9, 52, 55, 57, 70,
    71, 136, 180, 212, 292, 293
deVarona, D., 82
Dewey, J., 27, 128
Deyton, J., 32
Dolphin, J., 215
Drew, L.C., 28, 30
Drowatzky, J., 52
Duehl, A.N., 271
Duke, K., 18
Dummer, G., 350, 353
Dunn, J., 44, 54, 55, 70, 71, 74, 78, 79,
    93, 100, 102, 175, 193–194, 204,
    293, 305, 430, 431
Eason, R., 83
Edelfelt, R., 404
Edgar, C., 273
Eichstaedt, C., 55, 59, 305
Eisenhower, D., 67
Elkins, E.C., 66
Ersing, W., 46, 49, 50, 51, 56, 73, 78,
    90, 129, 192, 195, 266, 432
Ervin, S., 275
Evans, J., 55–57
Evans, M., 75
Fait, H., 35, 36, 39, 40, 46, 51, 52, 55
    68, 97, 305

Fewell, R., 56, 175
Fischer, J., 69
Fishbein, M., 232
Flanagan, M.E., 44, 70
Flanders, N.A., 374
Flavell, J., 276
Flexner, A., 64
Folio, R., 55, 56, 175, 279
Forman, M., 77
Fornas, V., 31
Foss, P., 275
Frankenburg, W., 175, 176
Franklin, S.B., 271
French, R., 40, 55, 58, 279, 303, 305,
    306
Fretz, B.R., 272, 273
Frith, G., 221
Frost, L., 66
Frost, R., 343
Frostig, M., 48, 209, 212, 215, 273
Fruge, J., 148, 293
Fry, K.L., 390
Funk, D.C., 269
Gagne, R.M., 208
Gallagher, J., 89, 367
Gallanter, L., 363
Galloway, C.M., 374
Galloway, H.F., 271
Gansneder, B., 53
Gart, W., 70
Gavron, S., 380, 381, 383
Geddes, D., 44, 46, 48, 51, 52, 69, 73,
    90, 95, 97, 189, 305
Gephart, W., 135
Getman, G., 48, 208, 212, 215, 273
Giauque, C.D., 66
Gillanders, D., 68
Gilliam, J., 181
Glidden, L.M., 354
Godfrey, B., 73, 90
Gold, M.W., 352, 366
Goldberg, I., 367
Goldthwait, J., 30, 31
Goodlad, J.L., 219
Goodman, L., 49, 184
Goodwin, L., 44, 45, 47, 51, 70, 75
Gordon, A.K., 381, 382
Gorman, D., 2
Gour, A., 25, 30
Granger, F., 30, 32
Greenblat, C.S., 380, 382, 383
Gregg, L., 66
Griffin, N.S., 70
Gronlund, N.E., 130
Grosse, S., 2, 69, 293
Grover, G., 68
Guard, P., 79
Guldager, V., 271
Gulick, L.H., 26, 65

Guthrie, J., 142
Guts-Muth, J.F., 25
Halgren, A., 273
Hall, G.E., 290, 291
Hall, G.S., 27
Hall, J., 312, 313
Hallahan, D., 48, 49, 213
Hambrick, W., 46, 73, 90
Hammill, D.D., 18, 49, 209, 215
Hanna, D., 26, 27, 65
Haring, N.G., 273
Harper, W., 345
Harris, B., 403, 404
Harris, J., 114, 402
Harrow, A., 125
Harter, S., 272
Hartwell, E., 27, 65
Harvey, J., 89
Hasazi, J.E., 352
Hawkins, D., 74, 75
Hayden, F., 39, 40, 47, 80
Hebert, G., 388
Heilbuth, L., 18, 20, 181, 187
Heitman, R.J., 355
Heller, M., 89
Hemenway, M., 27
Henry, F.M., 10–11
Hepworth, C., 71
Hester, S., 425
Hetherington, C.W., 26
Hill, C.E., 389
Hill, S.D., 271, 273
Hillman, W., 44, 46, 51, 52, 53, 73, 74,
    75, 90, 91, 100, 155, 403
Hilsendager, D., 44
Hirst, C., 52
Hitchcock, E., 26, 65
Hobbs, N., 200, 219
Hodges, A., 79
Holland, J.M., 355
Holland, R., 39, 40, 47, 68, 89, 97, 99,
    293
Holm, B.M., 68
Homans, A.M., 27, 65
Hooley, A., 24, 26, 37, 47, 70
Hopper, C., 425
Horgan, J., 354, 407
Horvat, M., 71, 79
Hough, J.E., 374
Howe, C., 39, 79
Howley, K., 404, 405
Huber, C., 82
Huber, J., 175, 176, 293
Hughes, J., 175, 176
Humphrey, F., 77, 99, 100
Hungerfield, C., 71
Hunt, V., 66
Hunter, A., 29, 48
Hurley, D., 70, 293, 303

Inman, C., 79
Irmer, L., 293
Itard, J., 208, 213
Jack, H., 44
Jackson-Glass, K., 274
Jahn, F.L., 25
James, W., 27
Jansma, P., 40, 55, 228, 232, 242, 279,
    306, 402, 433
Jay, D., 57
Jenkins, J.R., 18
Jewett, A., 127, 128, 129, 391
Johnson, D., 271
Johnson, L., 44, 46, 51, 70, 74, 75, 77,
    98, 100, 175, 176
Johnson, R., 58, 99
Johnson, W., 37, 38, 40, 55, 314
Jones, P., 153
Jones, S.A., 114
Joyce, G., 404
Kalakian, L., 52, 55, 59, 172, 175
Kane, R., 82
Karp, J., 92, 192
Karper, W., 271
Karpovich, P., 36
Karrer, R., 355
Kavale, K., 49
Kelly, J., 100
Kelly, L., 55, 193, 389
Kelso, J.A., 353
Kennedy, E., 46, 72, 74, 77, 81, 89, 99
Kennedy, J., 39, 79, 80, 94, 419, 432
Keogh, J., 48, 51, 56, 73, 75, 213
Kephart, N., 48, 73, 175, 176, 208, 209,
    212, 214, 271, 272, 273
Kilpatrick, W.H., 27
Klein, K., 68, 70
Klesius, S., 44, 58
Knapczyk, D., 276
Knowles, C., 148
Koegal, R., 276
Konnan, A., 380
Kovacic, C., 68
Kowalski, E., 57
Krathwohl, D., 11-16, 125, 335, 344
Kroll, W., 64, 343
Krupski, A., 351
Kruse, R., 36
Kupferer, H., 39
Kurtz, R., 220
La Vor, M., 87
Labanowich, S., 75, 82, 414
Lamarre, J., 82
Landreth, G., 162, 163
Lane, E., 70
Lange, E., 45, 51, 55, 186
Laski, F., 364, 370
Lawrence, E., 271
Lease, B., 389

Lessinger, L., 135, 136
Levy, J., 354, 355
Lewin, K., 219
Lewis, D., 26, 65
Lewis, W.W., 202
Liemohn, W., 57, 70
Likert, R., 228
Lillie, D., 271
Ling, H., 65
Ling, P.H., 25–27, 65
Lippitt, L., 28–30
Lipton, B., 82
Little, J., 51
Lockhart, A., 125
Logan, G., 36
Londe, C., 27
Loovis, E.M., 56, 70, 279, 388, 430
Lowman, C., 30–31, 33, 34, 65, 66
Loy, J., 343
Lubin, E., 274, 293
Lucito, L., 89
Lundegren, H., 120
Luria, A.R., 353
MacArthur, D., 421
MacKinnon, D.W., 16
Mager, R., 129-130
Mahoney, M., 271
Mancini, V., 272, 374
Mann, L., 44, 213
Marlow, M., 278
Martin, E., 74, 78, 89, 107, 151
Martin, M.M., 49, 273
Martino, L., 278
Maslow, P., 209
Massengale, J., 342, 345
Masters, L., 55, 186, 305
Mastro, J., 124, 221
Matthews, D.K., 36
Matthews, P., 275
Mattson, P.D., 49
Maurer, A., 276
Mawdsley, R.H., 376
Mayhall, W.F., 18
McClenaghan, B., 121
McCloy, C.H., 35, 300
McCraw, L., 46, 73, 77, 90, 97
McCristal, K., 66
McCubbin, J., 79, 269, 433
McDaniel, C., 278
McDaniels, G., 89
McGee, R., 170
McGinn, J., 68
McIntyre, M., 345
McKenzie, R.T., 29, 30, 35, 65
McMillan, M., 30, 32
Megarry, J., 380, 381
Megginson, N., 124, 188, 228, 229, 232, 233, 250, 402
Mello, J., 68

Mercer, C.D., 351, 352
Merrick, R., 70, 71
Merrifield, H.H., 68
Metcalf, H., 66
Metheney, E., 128
Metteer, R., 196
Michaelis, E., 52
Miller, A., 55, 305
Minner, S., 219
Mintzberg, H., 345
Montague, R., 82
Montelione, T., 56, 124, 233, 266, 387, 391
Montessori, M., 208, 212, 214
Moran, J., 48, 51, 52, 74, 75, 93, 305
Morgan, C., 38, 44, 48, 51, 66, 68
Morgan, D., 184
Mori, A., 55, 186, 305
Morris, G.S.D., 8, 175, 278
Morris, R., 276
Morrison, T., 273
Mosely, M.L., 69
Mosher, E., 65
Mosston, M., 8, 128
Mueller, G., 36
Mueller, M., 79
Mullan, M.R., 128
Murray, G., 418
Myklebust, H.R., 271
Naisbitt, J., 143, 146
Naor, M., 312
Nashman, H., 46, 73, 90, 97
Neal, L., 71
Nesbitt, J., 72, 74, 75, 77, 86, 98, 99
Neumann, M.E., 312
Newsom, M.M., 82
Nezol, A.J., 278
Nichols, W., 68
Nideffer, F.D., 354
Nissen, H., 25, 27, 30
Nixon, J., 10, 24, 128, 174
Nixon, R., 88
Nugent, T., 33, 414
Oakley, T., 58, 114, 124, 131, 203, 230, 231, 233
Oliver, J., 39, 40, 269, 271, 272
Orff, C., 435
Orr, B., 71
Ottenbacher, K., 273
Owen, E., 82
Owens, M., 195
Pace, C.R., 129
Palk, B., 94
Paloutzian, R., 276
Park, D., 77, 100
Patton, M.Q., 133–134
Payscy, F., 70
Peterson, C., 75
Peterson, P., 92

Phillips, W., 44
Piaget, J., 208, 212, 214, 274, 275
Pierce, E.C., 79
Pino, E., 136
Podemski, R.S., 391
Poley, M., 68
Pomeroy, J., 68
Popham, W.J., 130
Poretta, D., 353
Posse, N., 27, 30, 65
Price, M., 184
Proctor, A.J., 386
Provus, M., 132–133
Pyfer, J., 10, 47, 55, 70, 136, 187, 208, 212, 272, 273
Rabe, B., 92
Rapoport, A., 382
Rarick, G.L., 7, 10, 37, 39, 46, 47, 51, 52, 55, 56, 68, 73, 90, 97, 269, 275
Raser, J.R., 380, 381
Rathbone, J., 31, 33–37, 66
Reagan, R., 88, 91, 92, 107
Reams, D., 196
Reber, R., 271, 274
Reger, G., 140, 143
Reid, G., 213, 274, 353
Reynolds, B.J., 312
Reynolds, M., 369
Rhodes, W.C., 202
Rich, S., 374, 376
Richardson, D., 82
Richer, J., 276
Rider, B., 209
Riechle, J., 368
Ringo, M., 68
Riordan, A., 56, 71, 434
Rizzo, T., 228, 232, 245
Roach, E., 175, 176
Robertson, J., 419
Rogers, C., 259
Rogers, F.R., 36
Roice, R., 18, 70, 293
Romanczyk, R., 276
Ross, S., 271
Rossmiller, R., 140
Roswal, G., 37, 38, 72, 297
Roswal, P., 57, 312
Rotundo, N., 353
Rowe, J., 274
Ryan, B., 68
Sadlo, L., 68
Saettler, H., 89
Safrit, M., 170, 171, 342
Sallade, K., 82
Sapora, A., 73
Santomier, J., 6, 279
Sargent, D.A., 26, 27, 28
Saunders, M., 183
Schipper, W., 228

Schofer, R., 89, 151, 403
Scott, H.A., 33–35, 128–129, 130, 291
Scott, T., 67
Scriven, M., 130
Seaman, J., 7, 9, 44, 48, 55, 71, 136, 170, 172, 180, 212, 266, 305
Seginer, R., 383
Seguin, E., 208, 214
Semmel, M.I., 380
Sengstock, W., 39
Sessoms, H.D., 73
Shaw, V., 36, 66
Shearer, L., 70
Shelton, R., 68, 70
Sherrill, C., 4, 6, 7, 10, 24, 32, 33, 48, 51, 52, 56, 58, 68, 77, 78, 87, 97, 100, 120, 121, 124, 128, 136, 152, 187, 188, 200, 212, 213, 221, 225, 228, 232, 233, 250, 260, 266, 274, 306, 402, 433, 434
Shirts, R.G., 383
Shotick, S., 276
Shriver, E.K., 45, 67, 77, 80, 81
Siedentop, D., 128
Sills, F., 68, 97
Simpson, F., 68, 97
Simpson, J.M., 272
Sims, R., 70
Sinclair, C., 66
Sinclair, W., 55
Sloan, M., 71
Smith, T., 83
Snyder, R., 129, 130, 291
Solomon, A., 269
Songster, T., 80, 100
Sontag, E., 79, 89, 100
Spande, M., 67
Spitz, R.Z., 34
Stafford, G., 30, 31, 33, 66
Stafford, R., 362
Stainback, S., 425, 433
Stake, R., 130–131
Stanfield, J., 275
Steadman, D., 367
Stedman, D., 223
Stein, J., 10, 37–40, 44, 45, 47, 48, 51, 57, 68–71, 73, 75, 77, 82, 83, 95–98, 129, 155, 221, 266, 277, 293, 386, 388
Stein, T., 68
Steinhaus, A., 64
Stephenson, D., 388
Stevens, T., 78
Stoedefalke, K., 70
Stokes, B.R., 114, 131, 153, 402
Stone, E., 32
Strauss, A.A., 212, 214
Strauss, R., 70, 196, 266, 293, 331
Strichart, S., 220

Stufflebeam, D.L., 131–132
Suchman, E.A., 130
Sugden, D., 353
Sullivan, J., 55
Surburg, P., 352
Szymanski, D., 75
Taylor, G.H., 26
Tead, O., 343
Temerson, L., 68
Thaigarajan, S., 382, 383
Thorndike, E., 27
Tomporowski, P., 269
Toner, C.S., 380
Troester, C., 67
Troyer, M., 129
Tufts, J., 107
Turnbull, H.R., 136
Tyler, R.W., 128, 402
Tymeson, G., 54, 59, 70, 71, 212, 402
Ulrich, C., 128
Valletutti, P., 162, 163
Valos, G., 99
Van Andel, G., 274
Van Dalen, D., 124, 125
Van der Mars, H., 376
Van Etten, G., 430
Van Huss, W., 68
Vannier, M., 52, 305
Verhoven, P., 73, 100
Vinton, D., 75, 77, 100
Vodola, T., 51, 55, 88, 89, 97, 106,
    136, 175, 176, 178, 192, 269, 405
Wacker, D.P., 353
Wade, M., 56
Walker, L., 48, 51, 82
Watson, P.C., 232
Webb, R., 273, 430
Webster, G., 203
Wehman, P., 276, 425, 433
Weininger, O., 271
Weintraub, F., 87
Weiss, R., 51, 55

Wells, K., 68
Werder, J., 172, 175
Werner, H., 212, 214
Wessel, J., 51, 52, 55, 67, 73, 97, 99,
    100, 128, 155, 175, 176, 178, 181,
    189, 193, 296, 389, 431
Weston, A., 26, 27
Wheeler, R., 24, 26, 47, 49, 305
Whelan, R., 89
White, O., 428
Wide, A., 26, 27, 56
Wiederholt, J.L., 18
Will, M., 78, 79, 107
Williams, H., 213
Williamson, D.C., 389
Wilson, G., 69
Wilson, W., 186, 228
Windell, I., 380
Winnick, J., 48–52, 55, 57, 74, 75, 97,
    175, 176, 305
Wiseman, D., 55, 305
Wisher, P., 56, 70
Withall, J., 374
Witt, P., 121
Wolfe, W., 99
Wolfensberger, W., 220
Womer, F., 172
Wood, T.D., 26
Wooten-Kolan, E., 70, 95
Worthington, C., 65, 66
Wright, B., 272
Wright, H.F., 200, 218, 219
Wright, J., 272, 402
Wuest, D.A., 376
Wyeth, D., 221, 223
Wysocki, B.A., 271
Yates, J.R., 312
Yavorsky, D.K., 133
York, R., 368
Zeaman, D., 351, 352
Zuckerman, R.A., 380, 383

Subject Index

AAHPER(D) guidelines, 50, 53, 98, 293, 303, 350, 355
AAHPERD Unit on Programs for Handicapped, 68–71, 94–96, 99
Accountability, 58, 135–137, 181–182, 266, 268, 280
Accreditation, 58–59, 148
ACTIVE, 192
Adapted Physical Activity Council, 3, 9
Adapted Physical Activity Quarterly, 9, 24, 56
Adapted physical education
  competencies, 3, 6, 33, 50, 53, 97–98, 151, 162–167, 291–299
  definitions, 4, 6, 35, 149
  goals, 4, 6, 7, 8
  history, 10, 23–103
  issues, 98, 99, 101
  journals, 9, 56, 95, 120–121
  legal bases, 178, 186
  organizations, 3, 24, 51, 54, 71–77
  philosophy, 4–5, 7, 8–11, 362–364, 400
  purpose, 7
  roles/jobs, 16–18, 40, 50, 98, 126, 221, 336
  scope, 4, 5, 28, 37
  services, 6
  tasks, 98, 218
  terminology, 4, 10, 29, 33, 35, 40
  theory, 5, 6
Administration, 2, 18, 181–183, 202, 204, 230–231, 238–241, 313, 336, 338–339, 396–400
Advisory groups, 99–100
Advocacy, 6, 13, 20, 57, 75, 78–79, 87, 95, 101, 151, 152, 155–157, 181, 205, 218–224, 308, 416–417
Affective. *See* Domains
Aides, 101, 203, 261–262
AIMS, 196
Alumnae, 334
American Educational Research Association, 130
Annual report to Congress, 79, 113–114, 140, 154–155, 183
Assessment, 6, 19, 55, 156, 170–176, 197, 209, 318, 321, 336, 365–366, 397
Assessment instruments, 55, 119–120, 175–176, 426
Attitude, 6, 12, 57, 94, 101, 147, 148, 166, 175, 184, 218, 221, 224, 228–255, 262, 274, 303, 305–306, 312, 362, 383, 404
Attitude assessment, 228–255
Average per pupil expenditure, 140–145
Awards, 2, 29, 52, 417
Battle of the Systems, 25, 28
Behavior management, 279, 426
Bellwether states, 143, 146
Block grants, 91-92
Bureau of Education for the Handicapped, 73, 88–89, 94, 96–98, 106
CAFIAS, 373–377
Case history, 320
Case studies, 380
Categorical grants, 91–92, 93
Certification, 20–21, 37, 58–59, 292–299
  endorsement, 20–21, 58–59, 292–299
  licensure, 20–21, 292–299
  registration, 20–21, 58–59, 292–299

Civil War, 26, 27
Client-centered theory, 259, 314
Coaching disabled athletes, 418–419
Cognitive. *See* Domains
Communication, 7, 93, 101, 120, 162–167, 181, 186, 188, 259, 262–263
Competencies, 3, 6, 33, 50, 53, 97–98, 151, 162–167, 290–293, 303, 420
Competency-based education, 290–291
Comprehensive System of Personnel Development, 56, 113, 140, 151–152, 364
Computer-assisted instruction, 387, 388
Computers, 56, 233, 342, 380, 386–391
Consumers, 221, 416–417
Context, Input, Process, and Product Model, 131–132
Contract teaching, 224
Coordination of Related Services, 20, 49, 50, 156, 162, 165, 261, 338
Corrective
  exercise, 26, 29, 31
  gymnastics, 28
  physical education, 31, 32
  therapy, 32, 68
Counseling, 6, 19, 162, 257–263, 274, 337
Countenance Model, 130–131
Course approaches
  categorical, 48, 302, 305, 308
  combined, 5, 57, 303, 305
  generic, 50, 97, 205, 302, 305, 308, 313, 336
  noncategorical. *See* generic
Course competencies, 303, 307, 425–427
Course development, 11, 47, 49–50, 57, 101, 175, 302–308, 336–338
Course grading, 303, 307–308, 316
Course models, 306–308
Course objectives, 306
Courses
  adapted physical education survey, 37, 47, 57, 221, 295, 302–308, 336–338
  assessment, 175, 336–337, 365
  camping, 317–318
  correctives, 28, 37
  counseling, 165, 337
  dance for handicapped, 56
  developmental teaching, 337–338
  grantsmanship, 114
  IEP, 337
  interpersonal communication, 165
  medical gymnastics, 28
  motor learning, 349–356
  physical education for mentally retarded, 47
  physical education for severely handicapped, 55, 422–435
  practicum, 37, 47, 303, 305, 312–331, 398
  sport for disabled, 79, 82, 317, 412–422
Creative activity, 3, 16, 118, 380
Creative behaviors, 11, 57, 162, 166, 267, 274–275
Creativity, 9, 16
Criteria for
  placement, 186–187
  speaking/writing, 222

Criteria for evaluating
  CSPD, 151–152
  faculty performance, 3
  grants, 111–112
  letters, 225
  programs, 174
  seminars, 347
  state plans, 149–151
Crossdisciplinary approach, 101, 126, 219
CSPD. *See* Comprehensive System of Personnel Development
Curricular approaches, 192–197
Curriculum theory, 125–129
Daily log, 323
Data-based gymnasium, 193–194, 431
Deadtime, 368
Dean's Grants, 93
Depression, Great, 32
Direct service delivery models
  AIMS, 196
  behavior management, 429
  data-based gymnasium, 193–194, 431
  developmental, 210–213, 315
  ecological, 200–205
  Every Child A Winner, 195
  functional skills, 365, 368–369, 428
  game and leisure skill model, 275, 433
  I CAN, 193, 430–431
  Language, Arts, and Movement Programming, 433–434
  Let's Play to Grow, 196, 434
  Orff-Schulwerk, 435
  Project ACTIVE, 192
  Project COMPAC, 196
  Project MOBILITEE, 195, 431–432
  Project PEOPEL, 193, 262, 276, 279
  Project Success, 196
  Project TRANSITION, 432–433
  sensorimotor training, 430
  SIGMA, Performance-Based, 195
  Special Olympics sport instruction, 196, 275
  task analysis, 196, 429
Discipline/subdiscipline, 5, 9, 10, 11, 24, 94, 173, 174
Discrepancy Evaluation Model, 132–133
Discretionary legislation, 87, 92, 144, 145
Dissertation research, 114, 119
Domains
  affective, 6, 8, 11, 12, 13, 125, 228, 261, 266, 278, 335, 344, 382
  cognitive, 8, 11, 14–16, 125, 228, 266
  psychomotor, 6, 7, 8, 125, 226
Due process, 181, 182–183
Ecological approach, 57, 128, 200–205, 213, 218–219, 334
Ecosystem, 200, 219
Efficiency systems, 440–441
EHA legislation, 87–88, 101, 106, 112
Employment of handicapped, 275
Employment of teachers, 16–19, 59, 154–155
Entitlement funds, 144–145
Epistemology, 4, 5, 6
Evaluation forms, 325–327, 346–347
Evaluation models, 130–135

Evaluation principles, 129, 133
Evaluation theory, 125–135, 163, 171–172, 399
Evaluation trends, 129, 152
Evaluating faculty performance, 2–3
Exercise
  corrective, 29, 31
  individual, 28, 29
Federal aid, 86, 92, 101, 144–145
Federal funding agency, 106–107
Federal Register, 87, 339
Finance, 86, 108–109, 140–147
Fitness, 268–269, 274
Flanders' Interaction Analysis System, 374–375
Functional skills curriculum, 365–366, 368, 426, 428
Funding, 86, 90–91, 106–114, 173–174, 314, 441
Funding impact, 94–98
Funding priorities, 93, 98–101, 107, 112, 113
Future, 20–21, 59, 101, 299
Games analysis intervention, 278
Games, simulation, 380–383, 388
GAPES, 266
Generalization training, 368
Goals, 7–8, 20–21, 137, 171, 266–269, 279, 280, 291
Graduate degrees
  creation of, 28
  adapted physical education specialization, 48
Graduate training programs in adapted physical education, creation of, 46, 97
Grant application package, 110–112
Grant review process, 109–110
Grant writing, 17, 46, 51, 56, 106–114, 342–343, 440–441
GRAPES, Project, 57
Group dynamics, 162–167, 262–263, 338
Gymnastics
  aesthetical, 25
  corrective, 28
  curative, 27
  educational, 25, 27
  German, 25–26
  hygienic, 25, 28
  medical, 25, 26, 27, 28, 30
  military, 25
  remedial, 27–28
  Swedish, 25–26
  therapeutic, 28
Handicapping conditions, high incidence, 302
Handicapping conditions, official
  deaf, 271, 274, 277, 412, 416
  deaf-blind, 271
  hard of hearing, 271, 274, 277, 416
  mentally retarded, 44, 46, 52, 79–81, 89, 196, 219, 220, 269, 271, 272, 273, 274, 275, 276, 277, 278, 279, 302, 413, 419
  multihandicapped, 317
  orthopedically impaired, 81, 196, 219, 222–223, 233, 269–271, 272, 273, 275, 277, 302, 413, 415, 416, 418
  other health impaired, 269, 274
  seriously emotionally disturbed, 200, 269, 271, 276, 277, 278, 302

specific learning disability, 208, 233, 269, 271, 273, 274, 278, 302
speech impaired, 276, 277
visually handicapped, 81, 196, 221, 275, 278, 413, 416, 419
Handicapping conditions, severe, 18, 193, 267, 268, 269, 272, 275, 276, 286, 336, 425–435
History, 10, 23–103, 212, 213–215, 219–221
Holistic/whole child, 167
Honor award, 2
Humanism, 64, 128, 165, 222, 259, 260
Humanistic skills, 400
Hydrotherapy, 31
I CAN, 389, 430–431
IEP, 178–189, 268, 363
IEP form, 156, 322
IEP position paper, 156, 184
I'M SPECIAL Project, 58
Individual differences theory, 6–7, 201
Information processing, 351–355
Infusion, 5, 20, 33, 57, 96, 101, 303, 313, 387
Inservice training, 6, 17, 18, 44, 51, 54, 58, 97, 100, 101, 151, 157, 174, 200, 202, 232, 336, 338, 339, 340, 397, 402–406
Instructional technology, 362–370
Integration of curriculum, 33
Integration of students, 7, 94, 97, 120, 149, 156, 184–185, 231–232, 277, 370
Interaction analysis system, 373–377
Interaction patterns, 376
Interdisciplinary arena, 162–167
IRUC, 94, 95
Issues/concerns, 20, 49–50, 58–59, 98, 149, 155–157, 363
Job functions, 19–20, 98, 126, 187–188, 218, 224
Joint Dissemination Review Panel, 192, 195, 196
Journals, 31, 56, 79, 120–121
Kinesics, 164, 259
Knowledge base, 6–7, 124–125
Laws
    PL 89-10, 87, 88
    PL 89-750, 88–89
    PL 90-170, 44, 46–47, 72, 73, 89–90, 97, 99
    PL 91-230, 46, 51, 75, 106
    PL 93-112, 365, 412, 426
    PL 93-380, 75, 87
    PL 94-142, 3, 10, 15–16, 18–20, 44, 46, 51, 54, 57, 59, 75–77, 86–87, 94, 113, 119, 162, 170–171, 172, 178, 200, 293, 362, 403, 412, 426
    PL 95-49, 75, 87
    PL 95-606, 56, 81, 82, 270, 413
    PL 96-88, 86, 106
    PL 97-35, 88, 92
    PL 98-199, 75, 87, 103
    PL 99-457, 75, 87, 426
Leadership, 2, 3, 16, 24, 203, 334, 343, 344
Leadership qualities, 2, 54, 64, 344–345
Leadership training, 2, 334–345
Legal awareness, 396
Legislation, 75, 86–90, 94, 170
Legislative process, 150, 223–224
Leisure counseling, 260–261, 275

Lesson plan, 323
Letter writing, 95, 223–225, 313
Listening, 107, 163–165, 259
Litigation, 101, 142, 181, 362–370
Local education agency, 101, 145, 146, 156, 172, 178, 179, 186, 187, 232–233
Luther Halsey Gulick Medal, 2

Mabel Lee Award, 2
Magic circle technique, 262–263
Management skills, 399–400
Measurement, 171
Media, 419–420
Megatrends, 146
Membership, 4, 335
Mental health, 274
Mentors, 24, 107, 120, 334, 338, 345
MOBILITEE, 195, 431–432
Models
    Achievement Based Curriculum, 129, 315
    assessment, 172
    communication, 163–164
    curriculum, 126–129
    diagnostic-prescriptive, 192–193
    ecological, 200–205, 213, 218, 219, 234
    educational, 30, 49, 50, 56
    evaluation, 130–135
    legislative statute, 75
    medical, 27, 30, 49, 50, 56
    perceptual-motor, 210, 272–273
    service delivery/programs, 192–197, 428–435
    Significant Experience, 312, 313
    teacher training, 101, 125–129, 312, 313, 315
Monitoring, 150, 155, 156, 179, 200
Motor learning, 329–332, 350–356
Multidisciplinary approach, 5, 7, 10, 25, 50, 64, 163–167, 173, 188, 219, 330–332, 396, 433
National Diffusion Network, 192–197, 279
Needs assessment, 56, 113, 114, 137, 151, 153, 228, 235–255, 339–340, 397–399, 403, 441
Neurodevelopmental Model, 427
Neurological Organization Model, 427
Noncompliance issues, 363
Normal schools, 26, 27
Objectives, 7, 129–130, 137, 171, 184, 291
Observation tools, 373–377
Opinions, 229
Organizations
    Adapted Physical Activity Council, 3, 9, 67, 70, 95
    American Alliance for Health, Physical Education, Recreation, and Dance, 2, 3, 9, 24, 25, 31, 50–51, 56, 64–72, 74, 268
    American Corrective Therapy Association, 32, 68
    American Physiotherapy Association, 30–33, 68
    American Psychology Association, 11
    Association for Research, Administration, Professional Councils and Societies (ARAPCS), 3
    Council for Exceptional Children, 3, 36, 113
    International Federation of Adapted Physical Activity, 9, 82–83
    National Association for Intercollegiate Athletics, 414

National Association for Physical Education in Higher Education (NAPEHE), 4

National Association of State Directors of Special Education, 147

National Collegiate Athletic Assocation, 414

National Consortium on Physical Education and Recreation for the Handicapped, 3, 24, 51, 54, 72–77, 87, 94, 98–101, 112, 155–157, 231, 235–237

National Dance Association, 56

National Federation of State High School Associations, 413

National Therapeutic Recreation Society, 58, 74

Special Olympics, Inc., 79–81, 196, 223, 255, 273, 275, 413

Sport Organizations, 3, 18–19, 56, 79–82, 155, 219, 255, 270, 413, 421

United States Department of Education, 2, 35, 86, 87, 89, 106, 110

United States Olympic Committee, 56, 82, 271, 413, 421

Palaestra, 56, 79

Panels/panelists, 109–110

Parent training, 18, 33, 58, 204

Parents, 101, 120, 180, 182, 183, 196, 200, 205, 206, 223, 228, 315, 317, 362, 400

PEATH, 232, 245–249

Pedagogy, 7, 57, 127

  service delivery, 7–8, 364, 366, 376

  leadership training, 2, 345

  teacher training, 56–57, 363, 369–370

Peer counseling, 262–263

Peer teaching, 173, 261–262, 376

PEOPEL, 193, 262, 279

Perceptual motor training, 48–49, 207–215, 272–273

Personnel roles, 16–18, 40, 50, 98, 126, 336

Personnel training

  parents, 18, 33, 58, 204

  related services, 203–204

  researchers, 336

  teachers, 28, 32–33, 202–203

Philosophical issues, 4, 5, 45, 49, 89, 98, 101

Philosophy, 4, 7, 12, 20–21, 26, 57, 131, 134, 142, 176, 178, 200, 221, 258, 336, 400

  of adapted physical education service delivery, 4–5, 201, 362–364, 400

  of adapted physical education discipline, 6–7, 8–9, 10–11

  of funding, 101

  of IEP, 178, 362–364

  of mainstreaming, 4, 178, 200, 370, 398

  of sport for disabled, 412, 416–417, 421

  of teacher training, 5–6, 7, 57, 266, 335, 336

Physical therapy, 7, 30, 31, 32

Pioneer teacher training programs, 26, 27, 28

Placement, 156, 186–187, 201, 369

Playground design, 277

Politics, 92, 106, 107

Posture correction, 26, 31, 34

Practica, 53, 312–332

  competencies, 303

  environment, 314

  experiences, 304, 317, 330, 341

  first, 37, 97

  grant requirement, 111

prerequisites, 312

  recommended, 47, 50, 303–304, 336

  research, 312

Preservice training, 17, 18, 57, 151, 200, 305, 336, 340–341, 376, 427

Profession, 6, 64, 124

Profession organizations. *See* organizations

Professional preparation

  conferences, 4–5

  First National, 97, 98

  Jackson's Mill, 33

  national, on competencies, 293

  perceptual motor, 48

  Pere Marquette, 33

  Regional, on competencies, 97

  trends, 97, 126

Programmed instruction, 367

Promotion, 2

Proprioceptive Neuromuscular Facilitation Model, 427

Proximics, 164

Publishing, 3, 51, 55, 118–121, 335

Pupil/counselor ratios, 258

Pupil/teacher ratios, 141–142, 162, 178, 186, 272

Quality control, 58–59, 290, 293

R. Tait McKenzie Award, 29

Reauthorization legislation, 87, 94, 112

Reconstruction aides, 30, 32

Reflective listening, 163, 164, 165, 259–260

Rehabilitation, 27, 30

Related services, 97, 141, 156, 203–204, 261

Related services delivery models, 427

Relaxation training, 273–274

Research

  competencies, 2–3

  history, 31, 34, 52, 54

  integration, 44

  needed studies, 7, 11, 20, 53, 54, 97, 114, 118–121, 128, 141, 145, 155, 173, 181, 184, 186, 187, 209–210, 213, 219, 220, 224, 269, 271, 275, 277, 350–351, 356, 377

  professional preparation, 34, 37–39, 118–121

  responsibilities, 118–121

  survey studies, 33, 35, 37, 44–47, 52, 53, 57, 153, 184

  values of physical education, 266–283

Research Quarterly, 31, 56

Resource persons, 261

Resource room, 18

Résumé, 2, 58

Role model, 334, 336, 338, 342

Role playing, 380

Roles, 16–18, 40, 50, 126, 336

Roots, historical

  in European gymnastics, 25

  in medicine, 24, 25, 26

  in special education, 24, 29, 30, 33, 47, 48

SAPEN, 233, 250–255

Scanner process, 202

School attendance, 26

School districts, 6, 86, 118, 136, 137, 156–157, 232–233, 398–399

School finance, 140–147

Schools
  private, 181, 182, 184
  public, 26, 29, 31, 33, 35, 40, 44
  residential, 18, 29, 33, 35, 40, 148
Self-actualization, 6–8, 64, 262, 266–267
Self-concept, 6, 218, 262, 266, 271–272, 315
Seminars, 346–347
Sensory Integration Model, 427
Sensory integration theory, 213–215, 272
Service, 2, 3, 64, 79, 119, 223–224
Service delivery. *See* direct, related
Severely handicapped, 267, 276, 336, 425–435
Simulation, 380–383
Special education, 24, 29, 30, 33, 47, 50, 97, 203, 363
Specialization, 9–11, 32, 44, 48–49, 53, 288, 425
Sport adaptations, 415
Sport governance bodies, 413–414
Sports
  handicapped, 31, 33, 56, 263, 269
  Kennedy family, 39, 419
  origin of, 26, 412
Sports for disabled training, 317, 334, 412–421
State aid, 101, 144–145
State board of education, 86, 147, 302
State certification requirements
  Alabama, 297–299
  Georgia, 294–295
  Louisiana, 294
  Michigan, 296–297
  Minnesota, 295–296
State education agency, 101, 110, 113, 114, 146, 147–148, 153, 156, 172, 179, 230–231, 293
State plan, 113, 145, 146, 148–151, 155, 156, 178, 187
Statutory legislation, 87
Support, 313, 406
Systematic observation, 373–377
Task analysis, 7, 15, 194, 197, 363, 426, 428, 429, 434
Taxonomy, 11–16, 125–126, 129, 335
Teacher training approaches
  generalist, 32, 57, 387
  inclusion of units, 5
  infusion, 5, 20, 33, 57, 303, 313, 387
  separate, 5, 37, 44, 313
  specialist, 9–11, 32, 44, 48–49, 53, 288, 425
Teacher training concerns, 20, 49
Teacher training focus
  crossdisciplinary, 101, 126, 129
  interdisciplinary, 50, 162–167, 219

  multidisciplinary, 5, 7, 10, 24, 40, 64, 162, 163–167, 173, 188, 219, 330–332
  unidisciplinary, 5
Teacher training levels
  graduate, 5, 9, 11, 44, 48, 94, 126–127, 140
  undergraduate, 5, 6, 44, 48, 56
Teacher training types
  inservice, 6, 17, 18, 44, 51, 54, 58, 97, 151, 157, 174, 200, 232, 336, 338, 339–340, 397, 402–406
  leadership, 342–347
  preservice, 17, 18, 57, 151, 200, 305, 336, 340–341, 376, 427
Teaching, 7–9, 19, 23, 302–308, 337
Teaching models. *See* Direct service
Team approach, 162–167, 258, 330–332, 399, 404, 406, 426
Team teaching, 18, 399
Telethons, 222, 223
Tenure, 56, 119
Textbooks
  contemporary, 47, 48, 52, 55, 305
  earliest, 27, 30–32, 34–36, 39
  adapted physical education title, 9, 35
  special physical education title, 36
  Sports for the Handicapped, 33, 422
Theory, 6–7, 55, 124–130, 218, 228, 259, 312
United States Code, 87
United States Constitution, 86, 142, 146, 182, 362–363
United States Department of Education, 106, 110, 148, 184, 220
Utilization-focused model, 2, 35, 86, 87, 89, 133–134
Validated teaching practices, 197–362
Values of adapted physical education, 266–283
  creative expression, 274–275
  fun/tension release, 273–274
  leisure skills, 275, 425
  motor skills and patterns, 269–271, 425
  perceptual motor, 272–273
  physical fitness, 268–269
  play/game skills, 275–277, 425
  positive self-concept, 271–272
  social competency, 277–279
Values clarification, 4, 12–13, 20, 344–345
Values training, 335, 344–345
Videotapes, 58, 374, 376, 441
Vocalics, 164
Volunteers, 4, 194, 204, 220–221, 313
Wars, 30–33
Wheelchair sports training, 269